Algorithms and Architectures

Neural Network Systems Techniques and Applications

Edited by **Cornelius T. Leondes**

VOLUME 1. Algorithms and Architectures

VOLUME 2. Optimization Techniques

VOLUME 3. Implementation Techniques

VOLUME 4. Industrial and Manufacturing Systems

VOLUME 5. Image Processing and Pattern Recognition

VOLUME 6. Fuzzy Logic and Expert Systems Applications

VOLUME 7. Control and Dynamic Systems

Algorithms and Architectures

Edited by

Cornelius T. Leondes
Professor Emeritus
University of California
Los Angeles, California

VOLUME **1** OF

Neural Network Systems Techniques and Applications

ACADEMIC PRESS
San Diego London Boston New York Sydney Tokyo Toronto

This book is printed on acid-free paper. ♾

Academic Press
a division of Harcourt Brace & Company
525 B Street, Suite 1900, San Diego, California 92101-4495, USA
http://www.apnet.com

Academic Press Limited
24-28 Oval Road, London NW1 7DX, UK
http://www.hbuk.co.uk/ap/

Library of Congress Card Catalog Number: 97-80441

International Standard Book Number: 0-12-443861-X

Printed and bound in the United Kingdom
Transferred to Digital Printing, 2011

Contents

Statistical Theories of Learning in Radial Basis Function Networks

Jason A. S. Freeman, Mark J. L. Orr, and David Saad

Synthesis of Three-Layer Threshold Networks

Jung Hwan Kim, Sung-Kwon Park, Hyunseo Oh, and Youngnam Han

Weight Initialization Techniques

Mikko Lehtokangas, Petri Salmela, Jukka Saarinen, and Kimmo Kaski

Fast Computation in Hamming and Hopfield Networks

Isaac Meilijson, Eytan Ruppin, and Moshe Sipper

Multilevel Neurons

J. Si and A. N. Michel

Probabilistic Design

Sumio Watanabe and Kenji Fukumizu

Short Time Memory Problems

M. Daniel Tom and Manoel Fernando Tenorio

Reliability Issue and Quantization Effects in Optical and Electronic Network Implementations of Hebbian-Type Associative Memories

Pau-Choo Chung and Ching-Tsorng Tsai

Finite Constraint Satisfaction

Angelo Monfroglio

Parallel, Self-Organizing, Hierarchical Neural Network Systems

O. K. Ersoy

Dynamics of Networks of Biological Neurons: Simulation and Experimental Tools

M. Bove, M. Giugliano, M. Grattarola, S. Martinoia, and G. Massobrio

Contributors

Numbers in parentheses indicate the pages on which the authors' contributions begin.

M. Bove (401), Department of Biophysical and Electronic Engineering, Bioelectronics Laboratory and Bioelectronic Technologies Laboratory, University of Genoa, Genoa, Italy

Yun-Chung Chu (425), Department of Mechanical and Automation Engineering, The Chinese University of Hong Kong, Shatin, New Territories, Hong Kong, China

Pau-Choo Chung (261), Department of Electrical Engineering, National Cheng-Kung University, Tainan 70101, Taiwan, Republic of China

O. K. Ersoy (363), School of Electrical and Computer Engineering, Purdue University, West Lafayette, Indiana 47907

Jason A. S. Freeman (1), Centre for Cognitive Science, University of Edinburgh, Edinburgh EH8 9LW, United Kingdom

Kenji Fukumizu (181), Information and Communication R & D Center, Ricoh Co., Ltd., Kohoku-ku, Yokohama, 222 Japan

M. Giugliano (401), Department of Biophysical and Electronic Engineering, Bioelectronics Laboratory and Bioelectronic Technologies Laboratory, University of Genoa, Genoa, Italy

M. Grattarola (401), Department of Biophysical and Electronic Engineering, Bioelectronics Laboratory and Bioelectronic Technologies Laboratory, University of Genoa, Genoa, Italy

Youngnam Han (61), Mobile Telecommunication Division, Electronics and Telecommunication Research Institute, Taejon, Korea 305-350

Kimmo Kaski (87), Laboratory of Computational Engineering, Helsinki University of Technology, FIN-02150 Espoo, Finland

Jung Hwan Kim (61), Center for Advanced Computer Studies, University of Southwestern Louisiana, Lafayette, Louisiana 70504

Mikko Lehtokangas (87), Signal Processing Laboratory, Tempere University of Technology, FIN-33101 Tampere, Finland

S. Martinoia (401), Department of Biophysical and Electronic Engineering, Bioelectronics Laboratory and Bioelectronic Technologies Laboratory, University of Genoa, Genoa, Italy

G. Massobrio (401), Department of Biophysical and Electronic Engineering, Bioelectronics Laboratory and Bioelectronic Technologies Laboratory, University of Genoa, Genoa, Italy

Isaac Meilijson (123), Raymond and Beverly Sackler Faculty of Exact Sciences, School of Mathematical Sciences, Tel-Aviv University, 69978 Tel-Aviv, Israel

A. N. Michel (155), Department of Electrical Engineering, University of Notre Dame, Notre Dame, Indiana 46556

Angelo Monfroglio (293), Omar Institute of Technology, 28068 Romentino, Italy

Hyunseo Oh (61), Mobile Telecommunication Division, Electronics and Telecommunication Research Institute, Taejon, Korea 305-350

Mark J. L. Orr (1), Centre for Cognitive Science, University of Edinburgh, Edinburgh EG8 9LW, United Kingdom

Sung-Kwon Park (61), Department of Electronic Communication Engineering, Hanyang University, Seoul, Korea 133-791

Eytan Ruppin (123), Raymond and Beverly Sackler Faculty of Exact Sciences, School of Mathematical Sciences, Tel-Aviv University, 69978 Tel-Aviv, Israel

David Saad (1), Department of Computer Science and Applied Mathematics, University of Aston, Birmingham B4 7ET, United Kingdom

Jukka Saarinen (87), Signal Processing Laboratory, Tampere University of Technology, FIN-33101 Tampere, Finland

Petri Salmela (87), Signal Processing Laboratory, Tampere University of Technology, FIN-33101 Tampere, Finland

J. Si (155), Department of Electrical Engineering, Arizona State University, Tempe, Arizona 85287-7606

Moshe Sipper (123), Logic Systems Laboratory, Swiss Federal Institute of Technology, In-Ecublens, CH-1015 Lausanne, Switzerland

Manoel Fernando Tenorio (231), Purdue University, Austin, Texas 78746

M. Daniel Tom (231), GE Corporate Research and Development, General Electric Company, Niskayuna, New York 12309

Ching-Tsorng Tsai (261), Department of Computer and Information Sciences, Tunghai University, Taichung 70407, Taiwan, Republic of China

Sumio Watanabe (181), Advanced Information Processing Division, Precision and Intelligence Laboratory, Tokyo Institute of Technology, 4259 Nagatuda, Midori-ku, Yokohama, 226 Japan

Preface

Inspired by the structure of the human brain, artificial neural networks have been widely applied to fields such as pattern recognition, optimization, coding, control, etc., because of their ability to solve cumbersome or intractable problems by learning directly from data. An artificial neural network usually consists of a large number of simple processing units, i.e., neurons, via mutual interconnection. It learns to solve problems by adequately adjusting the strength of the interconnections according to input data. Moreover, the neural network adapts easily to new environments by learning, and it can deal with information that is noisy, inconsistent, vague, or probabilistic. These features have motivated extensive research and developments in artificial neural networks. This volume is probably the first rather diversely comprehensive treatment devoted to the broad areas of algorithms and architectures for the realization of neural network systems. Techniques and diverse methods in numerous areas of this broad subject are presented. In addition, various major neural network structures for achieving effective systems are presented and illustrated by examples in all cases. Numerous other techniques and subjects related to this broadly significant area are treated.

The remarkable breadth and depth of the advances in neural network systems with their many substantive applications, both realized and yet to be realized, make it quite evident that adequate treatment of this broad area requires a number of distinctly titled but well integrated volumes. This is the first of seven volumes on the subject of neural network systems and it is entitled *Algorithms and Architectures*. The entire set of seven volumes contains

Volume 1: *Algorithms and Architectures*

Volume 2: *Optimization Techniques*

Volume 3: *Implementation Techniques*

Volume 4: *Industrial and Manufacturing Systems*
Volume 5: *Image Processing and Pattern Recognition*
Volume 6: *Fuzzy Logic and Expert Systems Applications*
Volume 7: *Control and Dynamic Systems*

The first contribution to Volume 1 is "Statistical Theories of Learning in Radial Basis Function Networks," by Jason A. S. Freeman, Mark J. L. Orr, and David Saad. There are many heuristic techniques described in the neural network literature to perform various tasks within the supervised learning paradigm, such as optimizing training, selecting an appropriately sized network, and predicting how much data will be required to achieve a particular generalization performance. This contribution explores these issues in a theoretically based, well-founded manner for the radial basis function network. It treats issues such as using cross-validation to select network size, growing networks, regularization, and the determination of the average and worst-case generalization performance. Numerous illustrative examples are included which clearly manifest the substantive effectiveness of the techniques presented here.

The next contribution is "The Synthesis of Three-Layer Threshold Networks," by Jung Hwan Kim, Sung-Kwon Park, Hyunseo Oh, and Youngnam Han. In 1969, Minsky and Papert (reference listed in the contribution) demonstrated that two-layer perception networks were inadequate for many real world problems such as the exclusive-OR function and the parity functions which are basically linearly inseparable functions. Although Minsky and Papert recognized that three-layer threshold networks can possibly solve many real world problems, they felt it unlikely that a training method could be developed to find three-layer threshold networks to solve these problems. This contribution presents a learning algorithm called expand-and-truncate learning to synthesize a three-layer threshold network with guaranteed convergence for an arbitrary switching function. Evidently, to date, there has not been found an algorithm to synthesize a threshold network for an arbitrary switching function. The most significant such contribution is the development for a three-layer threshold network, of a synthesis algorithm which guarantees the convergence for any switching function including linearly inseparable functions, and automatically determines the required number of threshold elements in the hidden layer. A number of illustrative examples are presented to demonstrate the effectiveness of the techniques.

The next contribution is "Weight Initialization Techniques," by Mikko Lehtokangas, Petri Salmela, Jukka Saarinen, and Kimmo Kaski. Neural networks such as multilayer perceptron networks (MLP) are powerful models for solving nonlinear mapping problems. Their weight parameters are usually trained by using an iterative gradient descent-based optimization routine called the backpropagation algorithm. The training of neural networks can be viewed as a nonlinear optimization problem in which the goal is to find a set of network weights that minimize the cost function. The cost function, which is usually a function of the network mapping errors, describes a surface in the weight space, which is often referred to as the error surface. Training algorithms can be viewed as methods for searching the minimum of this surface. The complexity of the search is governed by the nature of the surface. For example, error surfaces for MLPs can have many flat regions, where learning is slow, and long narrow "canyons" that are flat in one direction and steep in the other directions. However, for reasons noted in this contribution, the BP algorithm can be very slow to converge in realistic cases. This contribution is a rather comprehensive treatment of efficient methods for the training of multilayer perceptron networks and radial basis function networks. A number of illustrative examples are presented which clearly manifest the effectiveness of the techniques.

The next contribution is "Fast Computation in Hamming and Hopfield Networks," by Isaac Meilijson, Eytan Ruppin, and Moshe Sipper. The performance of Hamming networks is analyzed in detail. This is the most basic and fundamental neural network classification paradigm. Following this, a methodological framework is presented for the two iteration performance of Hopfieldlike attractor neural networks. Both are illustrated through several examples. Finally, it is noted that the development of Hamming–Hopfield "hybrid" networks may allow the achievement of the merits of both paradigms.

The next contribution is "Multilevel Neurons," by J. Si and A. N. Michel. This contribution treats discrete time synchronous multilevel nonlinear dynamic neural network systems. It presents qualitative analysis of the properties of this important class of neural network systems, as well as synthesis techniques for this system in associative memory applications. Compared to the usual neural networks with two state neurons, neural networks that utilize multilevel neurons will, in general, and for a given application, require fewer neurons and thus fewer interconnections. This results in simpler neural network system implementations by means of VLSI technology. This contribution includes simulations that verify the effectiveness of the techniques presented.

The next contribution is "Probabilistic Design," by Sumio Watanabe and Kenji Fukumizu. This chapter presents probabilistic design techniques for neural network systems and their applications. It shows that neural networks can be viewed as parametric models, and that their training algorithms can then be treated as an iterative search for the maximum likelihood estimator. Based on this framework, the author then presents the design of three models. The first model has enhanced capability to reject unknown inputs, the second model is capable of expressing the reliability of its own inferences, and the third has the capability to illustrate input patterns for a given category. This contribution then considers what is referred to as a probability competition neural network, and its performance is experimentally determined with three-layer perceptron neural networks. Statistical asymptotic techniques for such neural network systems are also treated with illustrative examples in the various areas. The authors of this contribution express the thought that advances in neural network systems research based on their probabilistic framework will build a bridge between biological information theory and practical engineering applications in the real world.

The next contribution is "Short Time Memory Problems," by M. Daniel Tom and Manoel Fernando Tenorio. This contribution treats the hysteresis model of short term memory, that is, a neuron architecture with built-in memory characteristics as well as a nonlinear response. These short term memory characteristics are present in the nerve cell, but they have not as yet been well addressed in the literature on computational methods for neural network systems. Proofs are presented in the Appendix of the chapter to demonstrate that the hysteresis model's response converges under repetitive stimulus, thereby facilitating the transformation of short term memory into long term synaptic memory. The conjecture is offered that the hysteresis model retains a full history of its stimuli, and this, of course, has significant implications in the implementation of neural network systems. This contribution considers and illustrates a number of other important aspects of memory problems in the implementation of neural network systems.

The next contribution is "Reliability Issues and Quantization Effects in Optical and Electronic Network Implementations of Hebbian-Type Associative Memories," by Pau-Choo Chung and Ching-Tsorng Tsai. Hebbian-type associative memory (HAM) has been utilized in various neural network system applications due to its simple architecture and well-defined time domain behavior. As such, a great deal of research has been devoted to analyzing its dynamic behavior and estimating its memory storage capacity requirements. The real promise for the practical application of HAMs depends on their physical realization by means of specialized hardware. VLSI and optoelectronics are the two most prominent techniques being investigated for physical realization. A further issue is techniques in complexity reduction in the physical realization of HAMs. These include trade-off studies between system complexity and performance, pruning techniques to reduce the number of required interconnections and, hence, system complexity, and other techniques in system complexity reduction such as threshold cutoff adjustments. This contribution is a rather comprehensive treatment of practical techniques for the realization of Hebbian-type associative memory neural network systems, and it includes a number of illustrative examples which clearly manifest the substantive effectiveness of the techniques presented.

The next contribution is "Finite Constraint Satisfaction," by Angelo Monfroglio. Constraint satisfaction plays a crucial role in the real world and in the field of artificial intelligence and automated reasoning. Several discrete optimization problems, planning problems (scheduling, engineering, timetabling, robotics), operations research problems (project management, decision support systems, advisory systems), database management problems, pattern recognition problems, and multitasking problems can be reconstructed as finite constraint satisfaction problems. This contribution is a rather comprehensive treatment of the significant utilization of neural network systems in the treatment of such problems, which by their nature, are of very substantial applied significance in diverse problem areas. Numerous illustrative examples are included which clearly manifest the substantive effectiveness of the techniques presented.

The next contribution is "Parallel, Self-Organizing, Hierarchical Neural Network Systems," by O. K. Ersoy. Parallel self-organizing hierarchical neural network systems (PSHNN) have many attractive properties, such as fast learning time, parallel operation of self-organizing neural networks (SNNs) during testing, and high performance in applications. Real time adaptation to nonoptimal connection weights by adjusting the error detection bounds and thereby achieving very high fault tolerance and robustness is also possible with these systems. The number of stages (SNNs) needed with PSHNN depends on the application. In most applications, two or three stages are sufficient, and further increases in number may actually lead to worse testing performance. In very difficult classification problems, the number of stages increases and the overall training time increases. However, the successive stages use less training time due to the decrease in the number of training patterns. This contribution is a rather comprehensive treatment of PSHNNs, and their significant effectiveness is manifest by a number of illustrations.

The next contribution to this volume is "Dynamics of Networks of Biological Neurons: Simulation and Experimental Tools," by M. Bove, M. Giugliano, M. Grattarola, S. Martinoia, and G. Massobrio. This contribution presents methods to obtain a model appropriate for a detailed description of simple networks developing *in vitro* under controlled experimental conditions. This aim is motivated by the availability of new experimental tools which allow the experimenter to track the electrophysiological behavior of such networks with an accuracy never reached before. The "mixed" approach here, based on the use of both modeling and experimental tools, becomes of great relevance in explaining complex collective behaviors emerging from networks of neurons, thus providing new analysis tools to the field of computational neuroscience.

The final contribution to this volume is "Estimating the Dimensions of Manifolds Using Delaunay Diagrams," by Yun-Chung Chu. An "n" dimensional Euclidean space R^n can be divided into nonoverlapping regions, which have come to be known as Voronoi regions. The neighborhood connections defining the relationships between the various Voronoi regions has induced a graph structure that has come to be known as a Delaunay diagram. The Voronoi partitioning recently has become a more active topic in the neural network community, as explained in detail in this contribution. Because of the rather formal structural content of this contribution, it will be of interest to a wide range of readers. With the passage of time, as the formal structure presented in this contribution is developed and exploited from an applied point of view, its value as a fundamentally useful reference source will undoubtedly grow.

This volume on algorithms and architectures in neural network systems clearly reveals the effectiveness and essential significance of the techniques and, with further development, the essential role they will play in the future. The authors are all to be highly commended for their splendid contributions to this volume, which will provide a significant and unique reference source for students, research workers, practitioners, computer scientists, and others on the international scene for years to come.

Cornelius T. Leondes

Statistical Theories of Learning in Radial Basis Function Networks

Jason A. S. Freeman
Centre for Cognitive Science
University of Edinburgh
Edinburgh EH8 9LW
United Kingdom

Mark J. L. Orr
Centre for Cognitive Science
University of Edinburgh
Edinburgh EG8 9LW
United Kingdom

David Saad
Department of Computer Science and Applied Mathematics
University of Aston
Birmingham B4 7ET
United Kingdom

I. INTRODUCTION

There are many heuristic techniques described in the neural network literature to perform various tasks within the supervised learning paradigm, such as optimizing training, selecting an appropriately sized network, and predicting how much data will be required to achieve a particular generalization performance. The aim of this chapter is to explore these issues in a theoretically based, well-founded manner for the radial basis function (RBF) network. We will be concerned with issues such as using cross-validation to select network size, growing networks, regularization, and calculating the average- and worst-case generalization performance. Two RBF training paradigms will be considered: one in which the hidden units are fixed on the basis of statistical properties of the data, and one with hidden units which adapt continuously throughout the training period. We also probe the evolution of the learning process over time to examine, for instance, the specialization of the hidden units.

Algorithms and Architectures

A. Radial Basis Function Network

RBF networks have been successfully employed in many real world tasks in which they have proved to be a valuable alternative to multilayer perceptrons (MLPs). These tasks include chaotic time-series prediction [1], speech recognition [2], and data classification [3]. Furthermore, the RBF network is a universal approximator for continuous functions given a sufficient number of hidden units [4]. The RBF architecture consists of a two-layer fully connected network (see Fig. 1), with an input layer which performs no computation. For simplicity, we use a single output node throughout the chapter that computes a linear combination of the outputs of the hidden units, parametrized by the weights $\mathbf{w}$ between hidden and output layers. The defining feature of an RBF as opposed to other neural networks is that the basis functions (the transfer functions of the hidden units) are radially symmetric.

The function computed by a general RBF network is therefore of the form

$$f(\boldsymbol{\xi}, \mathbf{w}) = \sum_{b=1}^{K} w_b s_b(\boldsymbol{\xi}), \tag{1}$$

where $\boldsymbol{\xi}$ is the vector applied to the input units and s_b denotes basis function b.

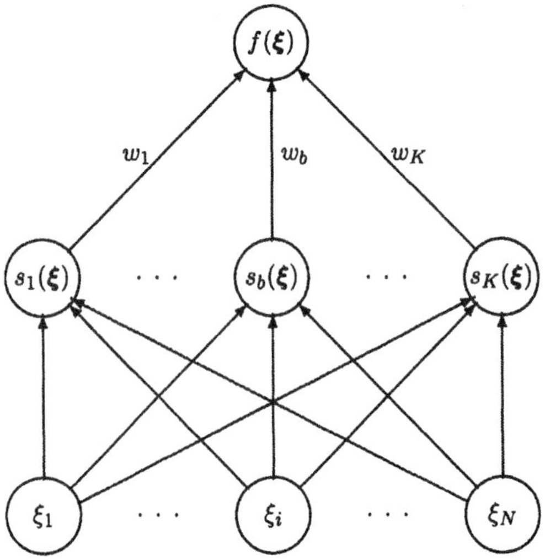

Figure 1 The radial basis function network. Each of N components of the input vector $\boldsymbol{\xi}$ feeds forward to K basis functions whose outputs are linearly combined with weights $\{w_b\}_{b=1}^{K}$ into the network output $f(\boldsymbol{\xi})$.

The most common choice for the basis functions is the Gaussian, in which case the function computed becomes

$$f(\boldsymbol{\xi}, \mathbf{w}) = \sum_{b=1}^{K} w_b \left(\frac{-\|\boldsymbol{\xi} - \mathbf{m}_b\|^2}{2\sigma_B^2} \right), \tag{2}$$

where each hidden node is parametrized by two quantities: a center $\mathbf{m}$ in input space, corresponding to the vector defined by the weights between the node and the input nodes, and a width σ_B.

Other possibilities include using Cauchy functions and multiquadrics. Functions that *decrease* in value as one moves toward the periphery are most frequently utilized; this issue is discussed in Section II.

There are two commonly employed methods for training RBFs. One approach involves fixing the parameters of the hidden layer (both the basis function centers and widths) using an unsupervised technique such as clustering, setting a center on each data point of the training set, or even picking random values (for a review, see [5]). Only the hidden-to-output weights are adaptable, which makes the problem linear in those weights. Although fast to train, this approach often results in suboptimal networks because the basis function centers are set to fixed values. This method is explored in Section II, in which methods of selecting and training optimally sized networks using techniques such as cross-validation and ridge regression are discussed. Forward selection, an advanced method of selecting the centers from a large fixed pool, is also explored. The performance that can be expected from fixed-hidden-layer networks is calculated in Section III, using both Bayesian and probably approximately correct (PAC) frameworks.

The alternative is to adapt the hidden-layer parameters, either just the center positions or both center positions and widths. This renders the problem nonlinear in the adaptable parameters, and hence requires an optimization technique, such as gradient descent, to estimate these parameters. The second approach is computationally more expensive, but usually leads to greater accuracy of approximation. The generalization error that can be expected from this approach can be calculated from a worst-case perspective, under the assumption that the algorithm finds the best solution given the available data (see Section III). It is perhaps more useful to know the *average* performance, rather than the worst-case result, and this is explored in Section IV. This average-case approach provides a complete description of the learning process, formulated in terms of the overlaps between vectors in the system, and so can be used to study the phenomenology of the learning process, such as the specialization of the hidden units.

II. LEARNING IN RADIAL BASIS FUNCTION NETWORKS

A. Supervised Learning

In supervised learning problems we try to fit a model of the unknown target function to a training set D consisting of noisy sampled input–output pairs:

$$D = \left\{(\boldsymbol{\xi}_p, \hat{y}_p)\right\}_{p=1}^{P}. \tag{3}$$

The caret (hat) in $\hat{y}_p$ indicates that this value is a sample of a stochastic variable, y_p, which has a mean, $\bar{y}_p$, and a variance, σ_p^2. If we generated a new training set with the same input points, $\{\boldsymbol{\xi}_p\}_{p=1}^{P}$, we would get a new set of output values, $\{\hat{y}_p\}_{p=1}^{P}$, because of the random sampling. The outputs are not completely random and in fact it is their deterministic part, as a function of the input, which we seek to estimate in supervised learning.

If the weights, $\{w_b\}_{b=1}^{K}$, which appear in the model provided by an RBF network [defined by Eq. (1)] were the only part of the network to adapt during training, then this model would be linear. That would imply a unique minimum of the usual sum-squared-error cost function,

$$C(\mathbf{w}, D) = \sum_{p=1}^{P} \left(f(\boldsymbol{\xi}_p, \mathbf{w}) - \hat{y}_p\right)^2, \tag{4}$$

which can be found by a straightforward computation (the bulk of which is the inversion of a square matrix of size K). There would be no confusion caused by local minima and no need for computationally expensive gradient descent algorithms. Of course, the difficulty is in determining the right set of basis functions, $\{s_b\}_{b=1}^{K}$, to use in the model (1). More likely than not, if the training set is ignored when choosing the basis functions we will end up having too many or too few of them, putting them in the wrong places, or giving them the wrong sizes. For this reason we have to allow other model parameters (as well as the weights) to adapt in learning, and this inevitably leads to some kind of nonlinear algorithm involving something more complicated than just a matrix inverse.

However, as we shall see, even though we cannot get away from nonlinearity in the learning problem, we are not thereby restricted to algorithms which construct a vector space of dimension equal to the number of adaptable parameters and search it for a good local minimum of the cost function—the usual approach with neural networks. This section investigates alternative approaches where the linear character of the underlying model is to the foremost in both the analysis (using linear algebra) and implementation (using matrix computations).

The section is divided as follows. It begins with some review material before describing the main learning algorithms. First, Section II.B reminds us why, if the model were linear, the cost function would have a single minimum and how it could be found with a single matrix inversion. Section II.C describes bias and variance, the two main sources of error in supervised learning, and the trade-off which occurs between them. Section II.D describes some cost functions, such as generalized cross-validation (GCV), which are better than sum-squared-error for effective generalization. This completes the review material and the next two subsections describe two learning algorithms, both modern refinements of techniques from linear regression theory. The first is ridge regression (Section II.E), a crude type of regularization, which balances bias and variance by varying the amount of smoothing until GCV is minimized. The second is forward selection (Section II.F), which balances bias and variance by adding new units to the network until GCV reaches a minimum value. Section II.G concludes this section and includes a discussion of the importance of local basis functions.

B. Linear Models

The two features of RBF networks which give them their linear character are the single hidden layer (see Fig. 1) and the weighted sum at the output node [see Eq. (1)]. Suppose that the transfer functions in the hidden layer, $\{s_b\}_{b=1}^{K}$, were fixed in the sense that they contained no free (adaptable) parameters and that their number (K) was also fixed. What effect does that have if we want to train the network on the training set (3) by minimizing the sum-squared-error (4)?

As is well known in statistics, *least squares* applied to linear models leads to linear equations. This is so because when the model (1) is substituted into the cost (4), the resulting expression is quadratic in the weight vector and, when differentiated and set equal to zero, results in a linear equation. It is a bit like differentiating $ax^2 - 2bx + b$ and setting the result to zero to obtain $x = b/a$ except it involves vectors and matrices instead of scalars. We can best show this by first introducing the *design matrix*

$$\mathbf{H} = \begin{bmatrix} s_1(\xi_1) & s_2(\xi_1) & \cdots & s_K(\xi_1) \\ s_1(\xi_2) & s_2(\xi_2) & \cdots & s_K(\xi_2) \\ \vdots & \vdots & \ddots & \vdots \\ s_1(\xi_P) & s_2(\xi_P) & \cdots & s_K(\xi_P) \end{bmatrix}, \tag{5}$$

a matrix of P rows and K columns containing all the possible responses of hidden units to training set input points. Using this matrix we can write the response of the network to the inputs as the P-dimensional vector

$$[f(\xi_1, \mathbf{w}) \quad f(\xi_2, \mathbf{w}) \quad \cdots \quad f(\xi_P, \mathbf{w})]^\top = \mathbf{H}\mathbf{w},$$

where each row of this matrix equation contains an instance of (1), one for each input value. To obtain a vector of errors we subtract this from

$$\hat{\mathbf{y}} = [\hat{y}_1 \quad \hat{y}_2 \quad \cdots \quad \hat{y}_P]^\top,$$

the vector of actual observed responses, and multiply the result with its own transpose to get the sum-squared-error, the cost function (4),

$$\begin{aligned} C(\mathbf{w}, D) &= (\mathbf{H}\mathbf{w} - \hat{\mathbf{y}})^\top (\mathbf{H}\mathbf{w} - \hat{\mathbf{y}}) \\ &= \mathbf{w}^\top \mathbf{H}^\top \mathbf{H}\,\mathbf{w} - 2\hat{\mathbf{y}}^\top \mathbf{H}\,\mathbf{w} + \hat{\mathbf{y}}^\top \hat{\mathbf{y}}, \end{aligned}$$

which is analogous to $ax^2 - 2bx + c$. Differentiating this cost with respect to $\mathbf{w}$ and equating the result to zero then leads to

$$\mathbf{H}^\top \mathbf{H}\widehat{\mathbf{w}} = \mathbf{H}\hat{\mathbf{y}},$$

which is analogous to $ax = b$. This equation is linear in $\widehat{\mathbf{w}}$, the value of the weight vector at the minimum cost. The solution is

$$\widehat{\mathbf{w}} = (\mathbf{H}^\top \mathbf{H})^{-1} \mathbf{H}^\top \hat{\mathbf{y}}, \tag{6}$$

which in statistics is called the *normal equation*. The computation of $\widehat{\mathbf{w}}$ thus requires nothing much more than multiplying the design matrix by its own transpose and computing the inverse.

Note that the weight vector which satisfies the normal equation has acquired the caret notation. This is to signify that this solution is conditioned on the particular output values, $\hat{\mathbf{y}}$, realized in the training set. The statistics in the output values induces a statistics in the weights so that we can regard $\widehat{\mathbf{w}}$ as a sample of a stochastic variable $\mathbf{w}$. If we used a different training set we would not arrive at the same solution $\widehat{\mathbf{w}}$; rather, we would obtain a different sample from an underlying distribution of weight vectors.

After learning, the predicted output, $\hat{y}$, from a given input $\boldsymbol{\xi}$ is

$$\begin{aligned} \hat{y} &= \sum_{b=1}^{K} \widehat{w}_b\, s_b(\boldsymbol{\xi}) \\ &= \mathbf{s}^\top \widehat{\mathbf{w}}, \end{aligned} \tag{7}$$

where $\mathbf{s} = [s_1(\boldsymbol{\xi}) \quad s_2(\boldsymbol{\xi}) \quad \cdots \quad s_K(\boldsymbol{\xi})]^\top$ is the vector of hidden unit responses to the input. Again, $\hat{y}$ can be regarded as a sample whose underlying statistics depends on the output values sampled in the training set. Also the dependencies of $\hat{y}$ on $\widehat{\mathbf{w}}$ (7) and of $\widehat{\mathbf{w}}$ on $\hat{\mathbf{y}}$ (6) are linear so we can easily estimate a variance for the prediction from knowledge of the variance of the outputs,

$$\begin{aligned}\sigma_y^2 &= \langle (y-\bar{y})^2 \rangle = \mathbf{s}^\top \langle (\mathbf{w}-\overline{\mathbf{w}})(\mathbf{w}-\overline{\mathbf{w}})^\top \rangle \mathbf{s} \\ &= \mathbf{s}^\top (\mathbf{H}^\top\mathbf{H})^{-1}\mathbf{H}^\top \langle (\mathbf{y}-\bar{\mathbf{y}})(\mathbf{y}-\bar{\mathbf{y}})^\top \rangle \mathbf{H}(\mathbf{H}^\top\mathbf{H})^{-1}\mathbf{s},\end{aligned}$$

where $\bar{y}$, $\overline{\mathbf{w}}$, and $\bar{\mathbf{y}}$ are the mean values of the stochastic variables y, $\mathbf{w}$, and $\mathbf{y}$. For example, in the case of independently identically distributed (IID) noise,

$$\langle (\mathbf{y}-\bar{\mathbf{y}})(\mathbf{y}-\bar{\mathbf{y}})^\top \rangle = \sigma^2 \mathbf{I}_P, \tag{8}$$

in which case

$$\langle (\mathbf{w}-\overline{\mathbf{w}})(\mathbf{w}-\overline{\mathbf{w}})^\top \rangle = \sigma^2 (\mathbf{H}^\top\mathbf{H})^{-1}$$

and also

$$\sigma_y^2 = \sigma^2 \mathbf{s}^\top (\mathbf{H}^\top\mathbf{H})^{-1}\mathbf{s}.$$

We will often refer to the matrix

$$\mathbf{A}^{-1} = (\mathbf{H}^\top\mathbf{H})^{-1} \tag{9}$$

as the *variance matrix* because of its appearance in the equation for the variance of the weight vector.

Several remarks about the foregoing analysis of strictly linear models are worth noting. First, (6) is valid no matter what type of function the $\{s_b\}_{b=1}^K$ represent. For example, they could be polynomial, trigonometric, logistic, or radial, as long as they are fixed and the only adaptable parameters are the network weights. Second, the least squares principle which led to (6) can be justified by maximum likelihood arguments, as covered in most statistics texts on estimation [6] or regression [7]. In this context (6) is strictly only true under the assumption of independent, identically distributed noise (8). The more general case of independent but non-identically distributed noise, where

$$\langle (\mathbf{y}-\bar{\mathbf{y}})(\mathbf{y}-\bar{\mathbf{y}})^\top \rangle = \mathbf{\Sigma} = \begin{bmatrix} \sigma_1^2 & 0 & \cdots & 0 \\ 0 & \sigma_2^2 & \cdots & 0 \\ \vdots & \vdots & \ddots & \vdots \\ 0 & 0 & \cdots & \sigma_P^2 \end{bmatrix},$$

leads to a *weighted least squares* principle and the normal equation becomes

$$\hat{\mathbf{w}} = \left(\mathbf{H}^\top \mathbf{\Sigma}^{-1}\mathbf{H}\right)^{-1}\mathbf{H}^\top \mathbf{\Sigma}^{-1}\hat{\mathbf{y}}.$$

For simplicity we will assume independent, identically distributed noise in what follows. However, it is easy to modify the analysis for the more general case.

Third, a useful matrix, one which will appear frequently in what follows, is the *projection matrix*

$$\mathbf{J} = \mathbf{I}_P - \mathbf{H}\mathbf{A}^{-1}\mathbf{H}^{\top}. \tag{10}$$

When the weight vector is at its optimal value, $\widehat{\mathbf{w}}$ (6), then the sum-squared-error is

$$\begin{aligned} C(\widehat{\mathbf{w}}, D) &= (\mathbf{H}\widehat{\mathbf{w}} - \hat{\mathbf{y}})^{\top}(\mathbf{H}\widehat{\mathbf{w}} - \hat{\mathbf{y}}) \\ &= \hat{\mathbf{y}}^{\top}\hat{\mathbf{y}}^{\top} - \hat{\mathbf{y}}^{\top}\mathbf{H}\mathbf{A}^{-1}\mathbf{H}^{\top}\hat{\mathbf{y}} \\ &= \hat{\mathbf{y}}^{\top}\mathbf{J}\hat{\mathbf{y}}. \end{aligned} \tag{11}$$

$\mathbf{J}$ projects $\hat{\mathbf{y}}$ perpendicular to the subspace (of P-dimensional space) spanned by linear combinations of the columns of $\mathbf{H}$.

A simple one-dimensional supervised learning problem, which we will use for demonstration throughout this section, is the following. The training set consists of $P = 50$ input–output pairs sampled from the target function

$$y = \frac{1 - e^{-\xi}}{1 + e^{-\xi}}. \tag{12}$$

The inputs are randomly sampled from the range $-10 \leqslant \xi \leqslant 10$ and Gaussian noise of standard deviation $\sigma = 0.1$ is added to the outputs. A radial basis function

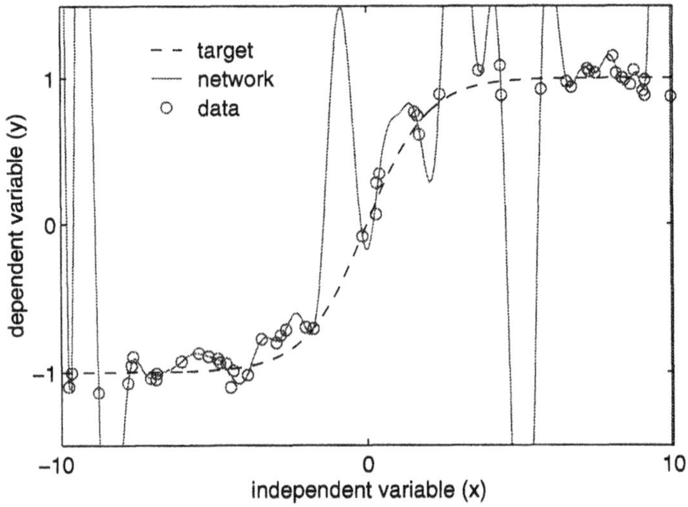

Figure 2 The target function (dashed curve), the sampled data (circles), and the output of an RBF network trained on this data (solid curve). The network does not generalize well on this example because it has too many hidden units.

network with $K = 50$ hidden units and Gaussian transfer functions

$$s_b(\xi) = \exp\left(\frac{-(\xi - \xi_b)^2}{\sigma_B^2}\right)$$

is constructed by placing the centers of the basis functions on the input training points, $\{\xi_p\}_{p=1}^{P}$, and setting their radii to the constant value $\sigma_B = 2$. The data, the target function, and the predicted output of the trained network are shown in Fig. 2.

Clearly, the network has not generalized well from the training set in this example. The problem here is that the relatively large number of hidden units (equal in number to the number of patterns in the training set) has made the network too flexible and the least squares training has used this flexibility to fit the noise (as can be seen in the figure). As we discuss in the next section, the cure for this problem is to control the flexibility of the network by finding the right balance between bias and variance.

C. Bias and Variance

If the generalization error of a neural network when averaged over an infinite number of training sets is zero, then that network is said to have zero bias. However, such a property, while obviously desirable, is of dubious comfort when dealing, as one does in practice, with just a single training set. Indeed, there is a second more pernicious source of generalization error which can often be abated by the deliberate introduction of a small amount of bias, leading to a reduction in the total error.

The generalization error at a particular input $\boldsymbol{\xi}$ is

$$E = \langle\langle [y(\boldsymbol{\xi}) - f(\boldsymbol{\xi})]^2 \rangle\rangle,$$

where $y(\boldsymbol{\xi})$ is the target function, $f(\boldsymbol{\xi})$ is a fit (the output of a trained network), and the averaging is taken over training sets; this average is denoted by $\langle\langle \cdots \rangle\rangle$.

A little manipulation [8] of this equation leads to

$$E = E_S + E_V,$$

where

$$E_S = [y(\boldsymbol{\xi}) - \langle\langle f(\boldsymbol{\xi}) \rangle\rangle]^2$$

is the bias (the squared error between the target and the average fit) and

$$E_V = \langle\langle [f(\boldsymbol{\xi}) - \langle\langle f(\boldsymbol{\xi}) \rangle\rangle]^2 \rangle\rangle,$$

is the variance (the average squared difference between the fits and the average fit).

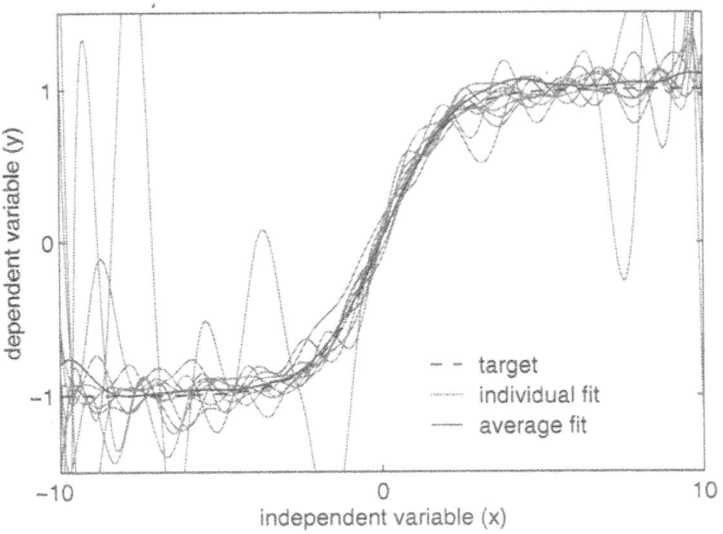

Figure 3 Examples of individual fits and the average fit to 1000 replications of the supervised learning problem of Section II.B (see Fig. 2) with a very mildly regularized RBF network ($\gamma = 10^{-13}$).

Bias and variance are illustrated in the following example where we use ridge regression to control their trade-off. Ridge regression is dealt with in more detail in Section II.E, but basically it involves adding an extra term to the sum-squared-error which has the effect of penalizing high weight values. The penalty is controlled by the value of a single parameter γ and affects the balance between bias and variance. Setting $\gamma = 0$ eliminates the penalty and any consequences ridge regression might have.

Figure 3 shows a number of fits to training sets similar to the one used in the previous subsection (see Fig. 2). The plotted curves are a small selection from a set of 1000 fits to 1000 training sets differing only in the choice of input points and the noise added to the output values. The radial basis function network which is performing the learning is also similar to that used previously except that a small amount of ridge regression, with a regularization parameter of $\gamma = 10^{-13}$, has been incorporated. In this case, with such a low value for γ, ridge regression has little effect except to alleviate numerical difficulties in performing the inverse in (6).

Note that although the average fit in Fig. 3 is close to the target (low bias), the individual fits each have large errors (high variance). The network has too many free parameters making it oversensitive to the noise in individual training sets. The fact that it performs well on average is of little practical benefit.

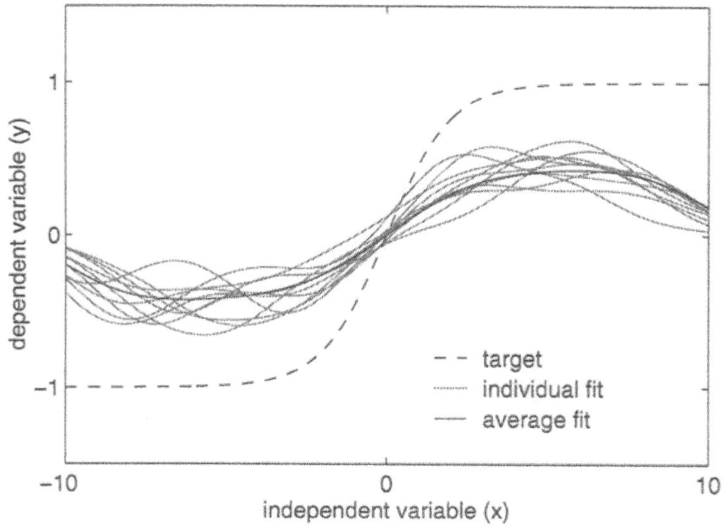

Figure 4 The same as Fig. 3 except the RBF network is strongly regularized ($\gamma = 100$).

In contrast, Fig. 4 shows the performance of the same network on the same training sets except the regularization parameter has been set to the high value of $\gamma = 100$. This has the effect of increasing the bias and reducing the variance. The individual fits are all quite similar (low variance), but the average fit is no longer close to the target (high bias). The two figures illustrate opposite extremes in the trade-off between bias and variance. Although the total error is about the same in both cases, it is dominated by variance in Fig. 3 and by bias in Fig. 4.

In Section II.E we will discuss ways to balance this trade-off by choosing a value for the regularization parameter which tries to minimize the total error. Regularization is one way to control the flexibility of a network and its sensitivity to noise; subset selection is another (see Section II.F). First we discuss alternative cost functions to the sum-squared-error.

D. Cross-Validation

Cross-validation is a type of model selection criterion designed to estimate the error of predictions on future unseen data, that is, the generalization error. It can be used as a criterion for deciding between competing networks by selecting the one with the lowest prediction error. Cross-validation, variants of which we describe in subsequent text, is very common, but there are other approaches (see [9] and references therein). Most involve an upward adjustment to the sum-squared-error (11) to compensate for the flexibility of the model [10].

Cross-validation generally involves splitting the training set into two or more parts, training with one part, testing on another, and averaging the errors over the different ways of swapping the parts. Leave-one-out cross-validation is an extreme case where the test sets always contain just one example. The averaging is done over the P ways of leaving out one from a set of P patterns.

Let $f_p(\boldsymbol{\xi}_p)$ be the prediction of the network for the pth pattern in the training set after it has been trained on the $P-1$ other patterns. Then the leave-one-out cross-validation error is [11]

$$\hat{\sigma}^2_{\mathrm{CV}} = \frac{1}{P}\sum_{p=1}^{P}\left(\hat{y}_p - f_p(\boldsymbol{\xi}_p)\right)^2.$$

It can be shown [10] that the pth error in this sum is

$$\hat{y}_p - f_p(\boldsymbol{\xi}_p) = \frac{\hat{y}_p - \hat{\mathbf{y}}^\top \mathbf{H}\mathbf{A}^{-1}\mathbf{s}_p}{1 - \mathbf{s}_p^\top \mathbf{A}^{-1}\mathbf{s}_p},$$

where $\mathbf{A}^{-1}$ is the variance matrix (9) and $\mathbf{s}_p$ is the transpose of the pth row of the design matrix (5). The numerator of this ratio is the pth component of the vector $\mathbf{J}\hat{\mathbf{y}}$, where $\mathbf{J}$ is the projection matrix (10) and the denominator is the pth component of the diagonal of $\mathbf{J}$. Therefore, the vector of errors is

$$\begin{bmatrix} \hat{y}_1 - f_1(\boldsymbol{\xi}_1) \\ \hat{y}_2 - f_2(\boldsymbol{\xi}_2) \\ \vdots \\ \hat{y}_P - f_P(\boldsymbol{\xi}_P) \end{bmatrix} = \left(\mathrm{diag}(\mathbf{J})\right)^{-1}\mathbf{J}\hat{\mathbf{y}},$$

where $\mathrm{diag}(\mathbf{J})$ is the same as $\mathbf{J}$ along the diagonal, but is zero elsewhere. The predicted error is the mean of the squares of these errors and so

$$\hat{\sigma}^2_{\mathrm{CV}} = \frac{1}{P}\hat{\mathbf{y}}^\top \mathbf{J}\left(\mathrm{diag}(\mathbf{J})\right)^{-2}\mathbf{J}\hat{\mathbf{y}}. \tag{13}$$

The term $\mathrm{diag}(\mathbf{J})$ is rather awkward to deal with mathematically and an alternative but related criterion, known as *generalized cross-validation* (GCV) [12], where the diagonal is replaced by a kind of average value, is often used instead:

$$\hat{\sigma}^2_{\mathrm{GCV}} = \frac{P\hat{\mathbf{y}}^\top \mathbf{J}^2\hat{\mathbf{y}}}{(\mathrm{tr}(\mathbf{J}))^2}. \tag{14}$$

We again demonstrate with the example of Section II.B (see Fig. 2) using ridge regression. Section II.E covers ridge regression in more detail but the essential point is that a single parameter γ controls the trade-off between bias and variance.

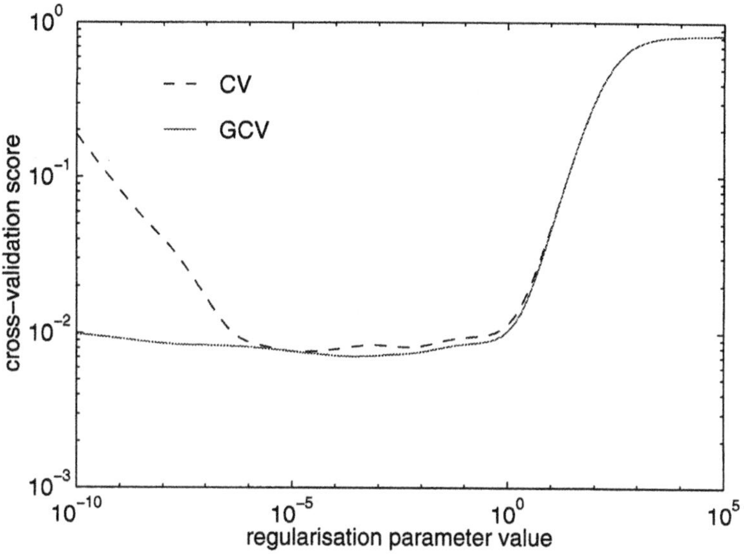

Figure 5 The CV and GCV scores for different values of the regularization parameter γ with the data and network of the example in Section II.B (Fig. 2). The network with the lowest predicted error, according to these criteria, has $\gamma \approx 10^{-4}$.

Networks with different values for this parameter are competing models which can be differentiated by their predicted error. In this case, networks with values for γ which are too low or too high will both have large predicted errors because of, respectively, high variance or high bias. The network with the lowest predicted error is likely to have some intermediate value of γ, as shown in Fig. 5.

E. Ridge Regression

If a network learns by minimizing sum-squared-error (4) and if it has too many free parameters (weights) it will soak up too much of the noise in the training set and fail to generalize well. One way to reduce the sensitivity of a network without altering the number of weights is to inhibit large weight values by adding a penalty term to the cost function:

$$C(\mathbf{w}, D, \gamma) = \sum_{p=1}^{P} \left(f(\boldsymbol{\xi}_p, \mathbf{w}) - \hat{y}_p \right)^2 + \gamma \sum_{b=1}^{K} w_b^2. \tag{15}$$

In general, the addition of such penalty terms is a type of *regularization* [13] and this particular form is known variously as *zero-order regularization* [14], *weight decay* [15], and *ridge regression* [16].

In maximum likelihood terms, ridge regression is equivalent to imposing a Gaussian prior distribution on the weights centered on zero with a spread inversely proportional to the size of the regularization parameter γ. This encapsulates our prior belief that the target function is smooth because the neural network requires improbably high weight values to produce a rough function.

Penalizing the sum of squared weights is rather crude and arbitrary, but ridge regression has proved popular because the cost function is still quadratic in the weight vector and its minimization still leads to a linear system of equations. More sophisticated priors [17] need nonlinear techniques. Differentiating the cost (15) and equating the result with zero, just as we did with sum-squared-error in Section II.B, leads to a change in the variance matrix which becomes

$$\mathbf{A}^{-1} = \left(\mathbf{H}^\top \mathbf{H} + \gamma \mathbf{I}_K\right)^{-1}.$$

The optimal weight

$$\widehat{\mathbf{w}} = \mathbf{A}^{-1}\mathbf{H}^\top \hat{\mathbf{y}} \tag{16}$$

and the projection matrix

$$\mathbf{J} = \mathbf{I}_P - \mathbf{H}\mathbf{A}^{-1}\mathbf{H}^\top \tag{17}$$

both retain the same algebraic form as before but are, of course, affected by the change in $\mathbf{A}^{-1}$. The sum-squared-error at the weight vector which minimizes the cost function (15) is

$$\sum_{p=1}^{P} \left(f(\xi_p, \widehat{\mathbf{w}}) - \hat{y}_p\right)^2 = \hat{\mathbf{y}}^\top \mathbf{J}^2 \hat{\mathbf{y}},$$

whereas the minimum value of the cost function itself is

$$C(\widehat{\mathbf{w}}, D, \gamma) = \hat{\mathbf{y}}^\top \mathbf{J} \hat{\mathbf{y}},$$

and the variance of the weight vector (assuming IID noise of size σ^2 on the training set outputs) is

$$\left\langle (\mathbf{w} - \overline{\mathbf{w}})(\mathbf{w} - \overline{\mathbf{w}})^\top \right\rangle = \sigma^2\left(\mathbf{A}^{-1} - \gamma, \mathbf{A}^{-2}\right).$$

Although the actual number of weights, K, is not changed by ridge regression, the *effective number of parameters* [18, 19] is less and given by

$$\begin{aligned} \lambda &= p - \mathrm{tr}(\mathbf{J}) \\ &= m - \gamma\, \mathrm{tr}(\mathbf{A}^{-1}). \end{aligned} \tag{18}$$

Note that $\mathbf{J}$ is no longer a projection matrix when $\gamma > 0$, in particular $\mathbf{J} \neq \mathbf{J}^2$. However, for convenience we will continue to refer to it by this name. Similarly the variance matrix is not as simply related to the variance of the weight vector as when there is no regularization, but we will, nevertheless, persist with the name.

The example shown in Fig. 5 of Section II.D illustrates the effect of different values of the regularization parameter on the error prediction made by leave-one-out and generalized cross-validation. We can use the location of the minimum value of such model selection criteria to choose an optimal value for γ. Leave-one-out cross-validation is mathematically awkward because of the diagonal term, but generalized cross-validation, though nonlinear in its dependence on γ, can be minimized through a reestimation formula. Differentiating GCV and equating the result to zero yields a constraint on $\hat{\gamma}$, the value of γ at any minimum of GCV [10]:

$$\hat{\gamma} = \frac{\hat{\mathbf{y}}^\top \mathbf{J}^2 \hat{\mathbf{y}}\, \mathrm{tr}(\mathbf{A}^{-1} - \hat{\gamma}\mathbf{A}^{-2})}{\widehat{\mathbf{w}}^\top \mathbf{A}^{-1} \widehat{\mathbf{w}}\, \mathrm{tr}(\mathbf{J})}. \tag{19}$$

This is not a solution because the right hand side also depends on $\hat{\gamma}$. However, a series of values which converge on a solution can be generated by repeated evaluations of the right hand side starting from an initial guess. Figure 6 demonstrates this on the same training set and network used for Figs. 2 and 5. The solid curve shows GCV as a function of γ (the same as in Fig. 5). Two series of reestimated values for $\hat{\gamma}$ generated by (19) are shown: one starting from a high value and one starting from a low value. Both series converge toward the minimum at $\gamma \approx 3 \times 10^{-4}$.

A refinement of the basic ridge regression method is to allow each basis function to have its own regularization parameter and to use the cost function

$$C(\mathbf{w}, D, \gamma) = \sum_{p=1}^{P} \left(f(\xi_p, \mathbf{w}) - \hat{y}_p\right)^2 + \sum_{b=1}^{K} \gamma_b w_b^2.$$

We call this variant of the standard method *local ridge regression* [20] because the effect of each regularization parameter is confined to the the area of influence of the corresponding localized RBF. In the case of nonlocal types of basis functions (e.g., polynomial or logistic) the name would not be so apt. The prior belief which this penalty encapsulates is that the target function is smooth but not necessarily equally smooth in all parts of the input space.

The variance matrix for local ridge regression is

$$\mathbf{A} = \left(\mathbf{H}^\top \mathbf{H} + \boldsymbol{\Gamma}\right)^{-1},$$

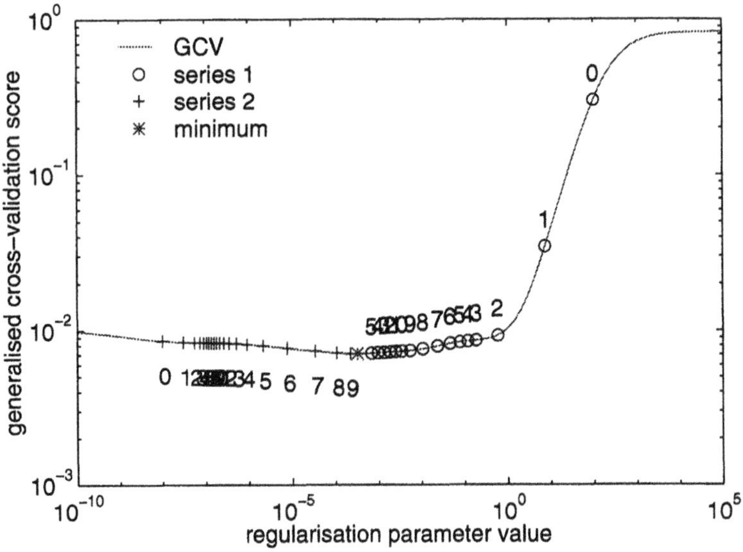

Figure 6 Two series generated by (19) converge toward the minimum GCV. The first series (marked with small circles) starts from a high value ($\hat{\gamma} = 100$) and moves to the left. The second series (marked with small crosses) starts from a low value ($\hat{\gamma} = 10^{-8}$) and moves to the right. The last digit of the iteration number (which starts at 0) is plotted above (series 1) or below (series 2) the curve.

where

$$\mathbf{\Gamma} = \begin{bmatrix} \gamma_1 & 0 & \cdots & 0 \\ 0 & \gamma_2 & \cdots & 0 \\ \vdots & \vdots & \ddots & \vdots \\ 0 & 0 & \cdots & \gamma_K \end{bmatrix}.$$

The optimal weight $\widehat{\mathbf{w}}$ (16) and the projection matrix $\mathbf{J}$ (17) are given by the usual formulae.

Optimizing these multiple regularization parameters with respect to a model selection criterion is more of a challenge than the single parameter of standard ridge regression. However, if the criterion used is generalized cross-validation (Section II.D), then another reestimation scheme, though of a different kind than (19), is possible. It turns out [20, 10] that if all the regularization parameters are held fixed bar one, then the value of the free parameter which minimizes GCV can be calculated deterministically (it may possibly be infinite). Thus GCV can be minimized by optimizing each parameter in turn, perhaps more than once, until no further significant reduction can be achieved. This is equivalent to a series of one-dimensional minimizations along the coordinate axis to find a minimum of

GCV in the K-dimensional space to which γ belongs and is the closest we get in this section to the type of nonlinear gradient descent algorithms commonly used in fully adaptive networks.

A hidden unit with $\gamma_b = 0$ adds exactly one unit to the effective number of parameters (18) and its weight is not constrained at all by the regularization. A hidden unit with $\gamma_b = \infty$ adds nothing to the effective number of parameters and its weight is constrained to be zero. At the end of the optimization process hidden units with infinite regularization parameters can be removed from the network, and in this sense local ridge regression can be regarded as another kind of subset selection algorithm (Section II.F).

Optimization of γ is such a highly nonlinear problem that we recommend paying special attention to the choice of initial values: It appears that random values tend to lead to bad local minima. A sensible method is to apply a different RBF algorithm as a first step to produce the initial values, and then apply local ridge regression to further reduce GCV. For example, the subset of hidden units chosen by forward selection (Section II.F) can be started with $\gamma_b = 0$, whereas those not selected can be started with $\gamma_b = \infty$.

Alternatively, if an optimal value is first calculated for the single regularization parameter of standard ridge regression, then the multiple parameters of local ridge regression can all start off at this value. To demonstrate, we did this for the example problem described before and illustrated in Figs. 2, 5, and 6. At the optimal value of the single regularization parameter, $\hat{\gamma} = 3 \times 10^{-4}$, which applies to all $K = 50$ hidden units, the GCV score is $\hat{\sigma}^2_{\mathrm{GCV}} \approx 7.0 \times 10^{-3}$. When local ridge regression is applied using these values as the initial guesses, GCV is further reduced to approximately 6.2×10^{-3} and 32 of the original 50 hidden units can be removed from the network, their regularization parameters having been optimized to a value of ∞.

F. Forward Selection

In the previous subsection we looked at ridge regression as a means of controlling the balance between bias and variance by varying the effective number of parameters in a network of fixed size. An alternative strategy is to compare networks made up of different subsets of basis functions drawn from the same fixed set of candidates. This is called *subset selection* in statistics [21]. To find the best subset is usually intractable, as there are too many possibilities to check, so heuristics must be used to limit the search to a small but hopefully interesting fraction of the space of all subsets. One such algorithm, called *forward selection*, starts with an empty subset to which is added one basis function at a time—the one which most reduces the sum-squared-error—until some chosen criterion, such as GCV (Section II.D), stops decreasing. Another algorithm is *backward elimina-*

tion, which starts with the full subset from which is removed one basis function at a time—the one which least increases the sum-squared-error—until, once again, the selection criterion stops decreasing.

In forward selection each step involves growing the network by one basis function. Adding a new function causes an extra column, consisting of its responses to the P inputs in the training set, to be appended to the design matrix (5). Using standard formulae from linear algebra concerning the inverse of partitioned matrices [22], it is possible to derive the formula [10] to update the projection matrix (9) from its old value to its new value after the addition of an extra column,

$$\mathbf{J}_{K+1} = \mathbf{J}_K - \frac{\mathbf{J}_K \mathbf{s}\mathbf{s}^\top \mathbf{J}_K}{\mathbf{s}^\top \mathbf{J}_K \mathbf{s}}, \tag{20}$$

where $\mathbf{J}_K$ is the old value (for K basis functions), $\mathbf{J}_{K+1}$ is the new value (including the extra one), and $\mathbf{s}$ is the column being added to $\mathbf{H}$.

The decrease in sum-squared-error due to the addition of the extra basis function is then, from (11) and (20), given by

$$C(\widehat{\mathbf{w}}_K, D) - C(\widehat{\mathbf{w}}_{K+1}, D) = \frac{(\hat{\mathbf{y}}^\top \mathbf{J}_K \mathbf{s})^2}{\mathbf{s}^\top \mathbf{J}_K \mathbf{s}}. \tag{21}$$

If basis functions are being picked one at a time from a set and added to a growing network, the criterion for selection can be based on finding the basis function which maximally decreases the sum-squared-error. Therefore (21) needs to be calculated for each potential addition to the network and when the choice is made the projection matrix needs updating by (20) ready for the next selection. Of course the sum-squared-error could be reduced further and further toward zero by the addition of more basis functions. However, at some stage the generalization error of the network, which started as all bias error (when $K = 0$), will become dominated by variance as the increased flexibility provided by the extra hidden units is used to fit noise in the training set. A model selection criterion such as cross-validation (Section II.D) can be used to detect the transition point and halt the subset selection process. $\mathbf{J}_K$ is all that is needed to keep track of CV (13) or GCV (14).

Figure 7 demonstrates forward selection on our usual example (see Figs. 2, 5, and 6). Instead of imposing a hidden layer of $K = 50$ units, we allow the algorithm to choose a subset from among the same 50 radial basis functions. In the event shown, the algorithm chose 16 radial basis functions, and GCV reached a minimum of approximately 7×10^{-3} before the 17th and subsequent selections caused it to increase.

A method called *orthogonal least squares* (OLS) [23, 24] can be used to reduce the number of computations required to perform forward selection by a factor equal to the number of patterns in the training set (P). It is based on making each new column in the design matrix orthogonal to the space spanned by the existing

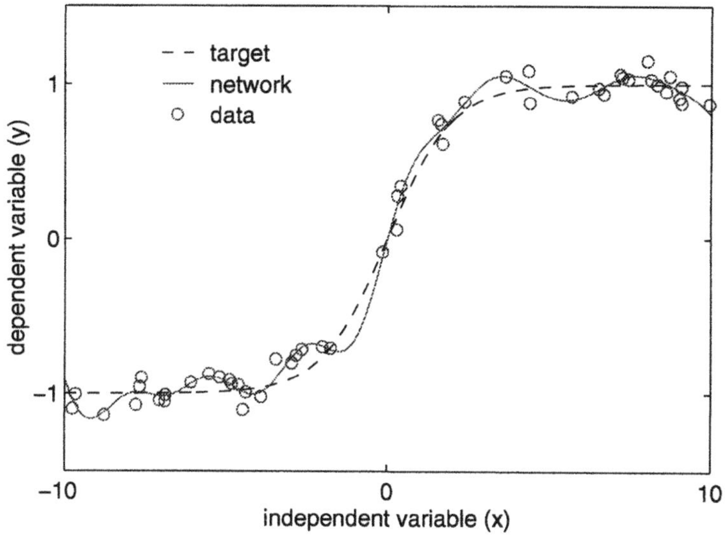

Figure 7 The usual data set (see Section II.B and Fig. 2) interpolated by a network of 16 radial basis functions selected from a set of 50 by forward selection.

columns. This has the computationally convenient effect of making the variance matrix diagonal while not affecting the calculations dependent on it because the parallel components have no effect. Forward selection can be combined with ridge regression into *regularized forward selection* and can result in a modest decrease in average generalization error [24]. OLS is less straightforward in this context but still possible.

G. Conclusion

In multilayer networks, where the function modeled by the network cannot be expressed as a sum of products of weights and basis functions, supervised learning is implemented by minimizing a nonlinear cost function in multidimensional parameter space. However, the single hidden layer of radial basis function networks creates the opportunity to treat the hidden-output weights and the input-hidden weights (the centers and radii) in different ways, as envisaged in the original RBF network paper [25]. In particular, the basis functions can be generated automatically from the training set and then individually regularized (as in local ridge regression) or distilled into an essential subset (as in forward selection).

Combinations of the basic algorithms are possible. Forward selection and ridge regression can be combined into regularized forward selection, as previously men-

Table I

The Mean Value, Standard Deviation, Minimum Value, and Maximum Value of the Mean-Squared-Error (MSE) of Four Different Algorithms Applied to 1000 Replications of the Learning Problem Described in Section II.B

	MSE $\times 10^{-3}$			
Algorithm[a]	Mean	Std	Min	Max
RR	5.7	5.3	0.9	64.6
FS	7.6	19.2	1.0	472.5
RFS	5.3	4.4	0.9	55.1
RFS + LRR	5.4	4.8	0.8	67.9

[a] The first three algorithms are ridge regression (RR), forward selection (FS), and regularized forward selection (RFS). The fourth (RFS + LRR) is local ridge regression (LRR) where the output from regularized forward selection (RFS) has been used to initialize the regularization parameters.

tioned. Ridge regression, forward selection, and regularized forward selection can each be used to initialize the regularization parameters before applying local ridge regression, creating a further three algorithms. We tested four algorithms on 1000 replications of the learning problem described in Section II.B, varying only the input points and the output noise in the training set. In each case generalized cross-validation was used as the model selection criterion. Their performance was measured by the average value (over the 1000 training sets) of the mean (over a set of test points) of the squared error between the network output and the true target function. Table I summarizes the results. It also gives the standard deviation, minimum value and maximum value, of the mean-squared-errors for each algorithm.

The results confirm what was seen before with other examples [24, 20], namely, that regularized forward selection performs better on average than either ridge regression or forward selection alone and that local ridge regression does not make much difference when the target function is very simple (as it is in this example).

What, if anything, is special about radial functions as opposed to, say, polynomials or logistic functions? Radial functions such as the Gaussian, $\exp[-(\xi - m)^2/\sigma_B^2]$, or the Cauchy, $\sigma_B^2/[(\xi - m)^2 + \sigma_B^2]$, which monotonically decrease away from the center, rather than the multiquadric type, $\sqrt{(\xi - m)^2 + \sigma_B^2}/\sigma_B$, which monotonically increases, are more commonly used in practice, and their distinguishing feature is that they are localized. We can think of at least two key questions about this feature.

The first concerns whether localization can be exploited to speed up the learning process. Whereas centers and data which are well separated in the input space can have little interaction, it may be possible to break down the learning problem into a set of smaller local problems whose combined solution requires less computation than a single large global solution. The second question is whether localized basis functions offer any advantage in generalization performance and whether this advantage is general or restricted to certain types of applications. These are research topics which presently concern us and with which we are actively engaged.

III. THEORETICAL EVALUATIONS OF NETWORK PERFORMANCE

Empirical investigations generally address the performance of one network of one architecture applied to one problem. A good theoretical evaluation can answer questions about the performance of a class of networks applied to a range of problems. In addition, such an evaluation may provide insights into principled methods for optimizing training, selecting a good architecture for a problem, and the effects of noise. With an empirical investigation, there are often many implementational issues that are glossed over, yet which may significantly influence the results; a theoretical evaluation will make assumptions explicit.

Several theoretical frameworks have been employed to analyze the RBF with fixed basis functions. We will focus on those we feel to be most important: the statistical mechanics and Bayesian statistics approaches (see [26] for an overview; [27–29] for RBF-specific formulations), which are so similar that they will be treated together; the PAC framework [30, 31], and the approximation error/estimation error framework [32, 33]. Aside from their considerable technical differences, the frameworks differ in both the scope of their results and their precision. For instance, the Bayesian approach requires knowledge of the input distribution, but gives average-case results, whereas the PAC framework is essentially distribution-free, but gives only weak bounds on the generalization error. The basic aim of all the approaches is the same, however: to make well-founded statements about the generalization error; once this is calculated or bounded, one can then begin to examine questions that are relevant to practical use, such as how best to optimize training, how an architecture copes with noise, and so forth.

A. Bayesian and Statistical Mechanics Approaches

The key step in both the Bayesian and statistical mechanics approaches is to construct a distribution over weight space (the space of all possible weight vectors), conditioned on the training data and on particular parameters of the learning process. To do this, the training algorithm for the weights that impinge on the student output node is considered to be stochastic in nature; modeling the noise process as zero-mean additive Gaussian noise leads to the following form for the probability of the data set given the weights and training algorithm parameters (the likelihood):[1]

$$\mathcal{P}(D|\mathbf{w},\beta) = \frac{\exp(-\beta E_D)}{Z_D}, \tag{22}$$

where E_D is the training error on the data and Z_D is a normalization constant. This form resembles a Gibbs distribution over weight space. It also corresponds to imposing the constraint that minimization of the training error is equivalent to maximizing the likelihood of the data [34]. The quantity β is a *hyperparameter,* controlling the importance of minimizing the error on the training set. This distribution can be realized practically by employing the Langevin training algorithm, which is simply the gradient descent algorithm with an appropriate noise term added to the weights at each update [35]. Furthermore, it has been shown that the gradient descent learning algorithm, considered as a stochastic process due to random order of presentation of the training data, solves a Fokker–Planck equation for which the stationary distribution can be approximated by a Gibbs distribution [36].

To prevent overdependence of the distribution of student weight vectors on the details of the noise, one can introduce a regularizing factor, which can be viewed as a prior distribution over weight space. Such a prior is *required* by the Bayesian approach, but it is not necessary to introduce a prior in this explicit way in the statistical mechanics formulation. Conditioning the prior on the hyperparameter γ which controls the strength of regularization,

$$\mathcal{P}(\mathbf{w}|\gamma) = \frac{\exp(-\gamma E_W)}{Z_W}, \tag{23}$$

where E_W is a penalty term based, for instance, on the magnitude of the student weight vector, and $Z_W = \int_W d\mathbf{w} \exp(-\gamma E_W)$ is the normalizing constant. See Section II.E for a discussion of regularization.

The Bayesian formulation proceeds by employing Bayes' theorem to derive an expression for the probability of a student weight vector given the training data and training algorithm parameters

$$\begin{aligned} \mathcal{P}(\mathbf{w}|D,\gamma,\beta) &= \frac{\mathcal{P}(D|\mathbf{w},\beta)\mathcal{P}(\mathbf{w}|\gamma)}{\mathcal{P}(D|\gamma,\beta)} \\ &= \frac{\exp(-\beta E_D - \gamma E_W)}{Z}, \end{aligned} \tag{24}$$

[1]Note that, strictly, $\mathcal{P}(D|\mathbf{w},\gamma,\beta)$ should be written $\mathcal{P}((\hat{y}_1,\ldots,\hat{y}_P)|(\xi_1,\ldots,\xi_P),\mathbf{w},\gamma,\beta)$ because it is desired to predict the output terms from the input terms, rather than predict both jointly.

where $Z = \int d\mathbf{w} \exp(-\beta E_D - \gamma E_W)$ is the partition function over student space. The relative settings of the two hyperparameters mediate between minimizing the training error and regularization.

The statistical mechanics method focuses on the partition function. Because an explicit prior is not introduced, the appropriate partition function is Z_D rather than Z. We wish to examine generic architecture performance independently of the particular data set employed, so we want to perform an average over data sets, denoted by $\langle\langle \cdots \rangle\rangle$. This average takes into account both the position of the data in input space and the noise. By calculating the average free energy, $F \equiv -1/\beta \langle\langle \log Z_D \rangle\rangle$, which is usually a difficult task involving complicated techniques such as the replica method (see [26]), one can find quantities such as the average generalization error. The difficulty is caused by the need to find the average free energy over all possible data sets. Results are exact in the thermodynamic limit,[2] which is not appropriate for localized RBFs due to the infinite system size ($N \rightarrow \infty$) requirement. The thermodynamic limit can be a good approximation for even quite small system size (i.e., $N = 10$), however. In the rest of this section we will follow the Bayesian path, which directly employs the posterior distribution $\mathcal{P}(\mathbf{w}|D, \gamma, \beta)$ rather than the free energy; the statistical mechanics method is reviewed in detail in [26].

1. Generalization Error: Gibbs Sampling versus the Bayes-Optimal Approach

It is *impossible* to examine generalization without having some *a priori* idea of the target function. Accordingly, we utilize a student–teacher framework, in which a teacher network produces the training data which are then learned by the student. This has the advantage that we can control the learning scenario precisely, facilitating the investigation of cases such as the exactly realizable case, in which the student architecture matches that of the teacher, the overrealizable case, in which the student can represent functions that cannot be achieved by the teacher, and the unrealizable case, in which the student has insufficient representational power to emulate the teacher.

As discussed in [27], there are several approaches one can take in defining generalization error. The most common definition is the expectation over the input distribution of the squared difference between the target function and the estimating function. Denoting an average with respect to the input distribution as $\langle \cdots \rangle$,

$$E = \left\langle (f(\boldsymbol{\xi}, \mathbf{w}^0) - f(\boldsymbol{\xi}, \mathbf{w}))^2 \right\rangle. \tag{25}$$

[2] $N \rightarrow \infty,\ P \rightarrow \infty,\ \alpha = P/N$ finite.

From a practical viewpoint, one only has access to the empirical risk, or test error, $C(f, D) = 1/P_T \sum_{p=1}^{P_T} (y_p - f(\boldsymbol{\xi}_p, \mathbf{w}))^2$, where P_T is the number of data points in the test set. This quantity is an approximation to the expected risk, defined as the expectation of $(y - f(\boldsymbol{\xi}, \mathbf{w}))^2$ with respect to the joint distribution $\mathcal{P}(\mathbf{x}, y)$. With an additive noise model, the expected risk simply decomposes to $E + \sigma_\eta^2$, where σ_η^2 is the variance of the noise. Some authors equate the expected risk with generalization error by considering the squared difference between the *noisy* teacher and the student. A more detailed discussion of these quantities can be found in [33].

When employing a stochastic training algorithm, such as the Langevin variant of gradient descent, two possibilities for average generalization error arise. If a single weight vector is selected from the ensemble, as in usually the case in practice, Eq. (25) becomes

$$E_G = \left\langle \int_W d\mathbf{w}\, \mathcal{P}(\mathbf{w}|D, \gamma, \beta)\big(f(\boldsymbol{\xi}, \mathbf{w}^0) - f(\boldsymbol{\xi}, \mathbf{w})\big)^2 \right\rangle. \tag{26}$$

If, on the other hand, a Bayes-optimal approach is pursued, which, when considering squared error, requires one to take the expectation of the estimate of the network, generalization error takes the form[3]

$$E_B = \left\langle \left(f(\boldsymbol{\xi}, \mathbf{w}^0) - \int_W d\mathbf{w}\, \mathcal{P}(\mathbf{w}|D, \gamma, \beta) f(\boldsymbol{\xi}, \mathbf{w}) \right)^2 \right\rangle. \tag{27}$$

It is impractical from a computational perspective to find the expectation of the estimate of the network, but the quantity E_B is interesting because it represents the best guess, in an average sense.

2. Calculating Generalization Error

The calculation of generalization error involves evaluating the averages in Eqs. (26) and (27), and then, because we want to examine performance independently of the particular data set employed, performing the average over data sets.

We will focus on the most commonly employed RBF network, which comprises a hidden layer of Gaussian response functions. The overall functions com-

[3]Note that the difference between E_G and E_B is simply the average variance of the student output over the ensemble, so $E_G = E_B + \langle \mathrm{Var}(f(\boldsymbol{\xi}, \mathbf{w})) \rangle$. This is *not* the same as the decomposition of generalization error into bias and variance, as discussed in Section II.C, which deals with averages over all possible data sets. The decomposition used here applies to an ensemble of weight vectors generated in response to a single data set.

puted by the student and teacher networks, respectively, are therefore

$$f_S(\boldsymbol{\xi}, \mathbf{w}) = \sum_{b=1}^{K} w_b \exp\left(-\frac{\|\boldsymbol{\xi} - \mathbf{m}_b\|^2}{2\sigma_B^2}\right) = \mathbf{w} \cdot \mathbf{s}(\boldsymbol{\xi}), \tag{28}$$

$$f_T(\boldsymbol{\xi}, \mathbf{w}^0) = \sum_{u=1}^{M} w_u^0 \exp\left(-\frac{\|\boldsymbol{\xi} - \mathbf{n}_u\|^2}{2\sigma_B^2}\right) = \mathbf{w}^0 \cdot \mathbf{t}(\boldsymbol{\xi}). \tag{29}$$

Note that the centers of the teacher need not correspond in number or position (or even in width) to those of the student, allowing the investigation of overrealizable and unrealizable cases. IID Gaussian noise of variance σ^2 is added to the teacher output in the construction of the data set.

Defining E_D as the sum of squared errors over the training set and defining the regularization term $E_W = 1/2\|\mathbf{w}\|^2$, E_G and E_B can be found from Eqs. (24), (26), and (27). The details of the calculations are too involved to enter into here; full details can be found in [27, 28]. Instead, we will focus on the results of the calculations and the insights that can be gained from them. To understand the results, it is necessary to introduce some quantities. We define the matrix $\mathbf{G}$ as the set of pairwise averages of student basis functions with respect to the input distribution, such that $\mathbf{G}_{ij} = \langle s_i s_j \rangle$, and define the matrices $\mathbf{L}_{ij} = \langle s_i t_j \rangle$ and $\mathbf{K}_{ij} = \langle t_i t_j \rangle$ as the equivalents for student–teacher and teacher–teacher pairs, respectively; these matrices represent the positions of the centers via the average pairwise responses of the hidden units to an input. The four-dimensional tensor $\mathbf{J}_{ijkl} = \langle s_i s_j t_k t_m \rangle$ represents an average over two student basis functions (SBFs) and two teacher basis functions (TBFs)[4]

$$\begin{aligned}\langle\langle E_G \rangle\rangle = {} & \frac{1}{P}\left\{\operatorname{tr}\mathbf{G}\Lambda + \sigma^2\beta^2 \operatorname{tr}\left[(\mathbf{G}\Lambda)^2\right]\right\} \\ & + \mathbf{w}^{0\top}\left\{\beta^2\left[\frac{1}{P}\operatorname{tr}\Lambda\mathbf{G}\Lambda\mathbf{J} + \left(1 - \frac{1}{P}\right)\mathbf{L}^\top\Lambda\mathbf{G}\Lambda\mathbf{L}\right]\right. \\ & \left. - 2\beta\Lambda^\top L + K\right\}\mathbf{w}^0,\end{aligned} \tag{30}$$

where Λ is defined by

$$\Lambda^{-1} = \frac{\gamma}{P} I + \beta\mathbf{G}. \tag{31}$$

From $\langle\langle E_G \rangle\rangle$, one can readily calculate

$$\langle\langle E_B \rangle\rangle = \langle\langle E_G \rangle\rangle - \frac{\operatorname{tr}\mathbf{G}\Lambda}{P}. \tag{32}$$

[4]The trace over $\Lambda G \Lambda J$ is over the first two indices, resulting in an $M \times M$ matrix.

These results look complicated, but can be understood through a schematic decomposition:

$$E_G = \text{student output variance} + \text{noise error} + \text{student–teacher mismatch}, \tag{33}$$

$$E_B = \text{noise error} + \text{student–teacher mismatch}. \tag{34}$$

Explicit expressions for all the relevant quantities appear in [27, 28].

3. Results

We examine three classes of results: the exactly realizable case, where the student architecture exactly matches that of the teacher; the overrealizable case, where the student is more representationally powerful than the teacher, and the unrealizable case, in which the student cannot emulate the teacher even in the limit of infinite training data.

a. Exactly Realizable Case

The realizable case is characterized by $E_G, E_B \to 0$ as $P \to \infty$, such that the student can exactly learn the teacher. In the exactly realizable case studied here, the student RBF has the same number of basis functions as the teacher RBF.

By making some simplifying assumptions it becomes possible to derive expressions for optimal parameter settings. Specifically, it is assumed that each SBF receives the same activation during training and that each pair of basis functions receives similar amounts of pairwise activation. Many of the common methods of selecting the basis function positions will encourage this property of equal activation to be satisfied, such as maximizing the likelihood of the inputs of the training data under a mixture model given by a linear combination of the basis functions, with the priors constrained to be equal. Simulations showing that the assumptions are reasonable can be found in [27].

We use G_D to represent the diagonals of $\mathbf{G}$, while G_O represents the remaining entries of $\mathbf{G}$. First, taking G_O to be 0, so that the basis functions are completely localized, simple expressions can be derived for the optimal hyperparameters. For E_B, the ratio of γ_{opt} to β_{opt} is independent of P:

$$\frac{\gamma_{\text{opt}}}{\beta_{\text{opt}}} = \frac{M\sigma^2}{\|\mathbf{w}^0\|^2}. \tag{35}$$

For E_G, the quantities are P dependent:

$$\beta_{\text{opt}} = \frac{\gamma(2\gamma\|\mathbf{w}^0\|^2 + M)}{M(2\gamma\sigma^2 - G_D P)}, \tag{36}$$

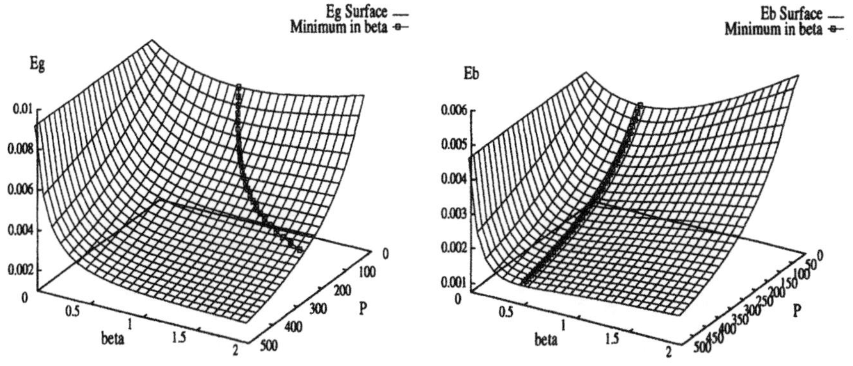

(a) (b)

Figure 8 Generalization error (a) E_G and (b) E_B as a function of number of examples P and error sensitivity β. At the minimum in E_G with respect to β, $\beta \to \infty$ as $P \to \infty$; the minimum in E_B with respect to β is independent of P.

$$\gamma_{\text{opt}} = \frac{G_D M P \beta (2\beta\sigma^2 + 1)}{2\|\mathbf{w}^0\|^2 \beta G_D P - M}. \tag{37}$$

Allowing terms linear in the interaction parameter, G_O, leads to optimal parameters which have an additional dependence on the cross-correlation of the teacher weight vector. For instance, to minimize E_B, the optimal ratio of γ_{opt} to β_{opt} is

$$\frac{\gamma_{\text{opt}}}{\beta_{\text{opt}}} = \frac{G_D M \sigma^2}{G_D \|\mathbf{w}^0\|^2 + G_O \sum_{b,c:\, b \neq c} w_b^0 w_c^0}. \tag{38}$$

The optimization of training with respect to the full expression for E_B can only be examined empirically. Once again only the *ratio* of γ_{opt} to β_{opt} is important, and this ratio is proportional to σ^2. E_G, on the other hand, always requires joint optimization of γ and β. The discrepancy in optimization requirements is due to the variance term in E_G, which is minimized by taking $\beta \to \infty$. The error surfaces for E_G and E_B as a function of P and β are plotted in Fig. 8a and b. The fact that E_G depends on P, whereas E_B is independent of P, can be seen clearly.

b. Effects of Regularization

The effects of regularization are very similar for E_G and E_B. These effects are shown in Fig. 9a, in which E_B is plotted versus P for optimal regularization, overregularization (in which the prior is dominant over the likelihood), and underregularization. The solid curve results from optimal regularization and demonstrates the lowest value of generalization error that can be achieved on average.

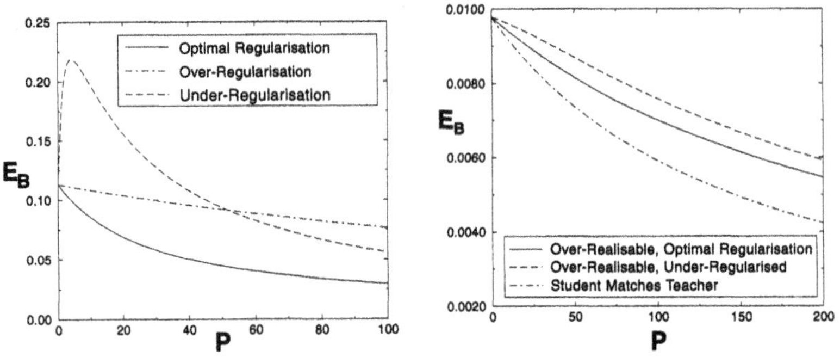

(a) (b)

Figure 9 (a) The effects of regularization. The solid curve represents optimal regularization ($\gamma = 2.7,\ \beta = 1.6$), the dot–dash curve illustrates the overregularized case ($\gamma = 2.7,\ \beta = 0.16$), and the dashed curve shows the highly underregularized case ($\gamma = 2.7,\ \beta = 16$). The student and teacher were matched, each consisting of three centers at $(1, 0)$, $(-0.5, 0.866)$, and $(-0.5, -0.866)$. Noise with variance 1 was employed. (b) The overrealizable case. The dashed curve shows the overrealizable case with training optimized as if the student matches the teacher ($\gamma = 3.59,\ \beta = 2.56$), the solid curve illustrates the overrealizable case with training optimized with respect to the true teacher ($\gamma = 3.59,\ \beta = 1.44$), whereas the dot–dash curve is for the student matching the teacher ($\gamma = 6.52,\ \beta = 4.39$). All the curves were generated with one teacher center at $(1, 0)$; the overrealizable curves had two student centers at $(1, 0)$ and $(-1, 0)$. Noise with variance 1 was employed.

The dot–dash curve represents the overregularized case, showing how reduction in generalization error is substantially slowed. The dashed curve is for the highly underregularized case, which in the $\gamma/\beta \to 0$ case gives a divergence in both E_G and E_B. The initial increase in error is due to the student learning details of the noise, rather than of the underlying teacher.

In general, given sufficient data, it is preferable to underregularize rather than overregularize. The deleterious effects of underregularization are recovered from much more rapidly during the training process than the effects of overregularization.

It is important to note that in the $P \to \infty$ limit (with N fixed), the settings of γ and β are irrelevant as long as $\beta \neq 0$. Intuitively, an infinite amount of data overwhelms any prior distribution.

c. *Overrealizable Scenario*

Operationally, selecting a form for the student implies that one is prepared to believe that the teacher has an identical form. Therefore optimization of training parameters must be performed on the basis of this belief. When the student is overly powerful, this leads to underregularization, because the magnitude of the teacher weight vector is believed to be larger than the true case. This is illustrated in Fig. 9b; the dashed curve represents generalization error for the underregularized case in which the training parameters have been optimized as if the teacher has the same form as the student, whereas the solid curve represents the same student, but with training optimized with respect to the true teacher.

Employing an overly powerful student can drastically slow the reduction of generalization error as compared to the case where the student matches the teacher. Even with training optimized with respect to the true teacher form, the matching student greatly outperforms the overly powerful version due to the necessity to suppress the redundant parameters during the training process. This requirement for parameter suppression becomes stronger as the student becomes more powerful. The effect is shown in Fig. 9b; generalization error for the matching student is given by the dot–dash curve, whereas that of the overly powerful but correctly optimized student is given by the solid curve.

d. Unrealizable Scenario

An analogous result to that of the overrealizable scenario is found when the teacher is more powerful than the student. Optimization of training parameters under the belief that the teacher has the same form as the student leads to overregularization, due to the assumed magnitude of the teacher weight vector being greater than the actual magnitude. This effect is shown in Fig. 10, in which the solid curve denotes generalization error for the overregularized case based on the belief that the teacher matches the student, whereas the dashed curve shows the

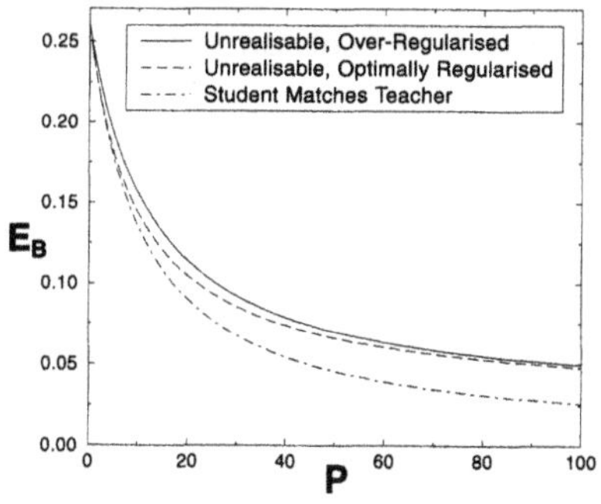

Figure 10 The unrealizable case. The solid curve denotes the case where the student is optimized as if the teacher is identical to it ($\gamma = 2.22$, $\beta = 1.55$); the dashed curve demonstrates the student optimized with knowledge of the true teacher ($\gamma = 2.22$, $\beta = 3.05$), whereas, for comparison, the dot–dash curve shows a student which matches the teacher ($\gamma = 2.22$, $\beta = 1.05$). The curves were generated with two teacher centers at $(1, 0)$ and $(-1, 0)$; the unrealizable curves employed a single student at $(1, 0)$. Noise with variance 1 was utilized.

error for an identical student when the parameters of the true teacher are known; this knowledge permits optimal regularization.

The most significant effect of the teacher being more powerful than the student is the fact that the approximation error is no longer zero, because the teacher can never be exactly emulated by the student. This is illustrated in Fig. 10, where the dot–dash curve represents the learning curve when the student matches the teacher (and has a zero asymptote), whereas the two upper curves show an underpowerful student and have nonzero asymptotes.

To consider the effect of a mismatch between student and teacher, the infinite example limit was calculated. In this limit, the variance of the student output and error due to noise on the training data both disappear, as do transient errors due to the relation between student and teacher, leaving only the error that cannot be overcome within the training process. Note that since the variance of the student output vanishes, $\langle\langle E_G\rangle\rangle = \langle\langle E_B\rangle\rangle$:

$$\langle\langle E_G\rangle\rangle \stackrel{P\to\infty}{=} \mathbf{w}^{0\top}\{\mathbf{K} - \mathbf{L}^\top\mathbf{G}^{-1}\mathbf{L}\}\mathbf{w}^0. \tag{39}$$

Recalling that $\mathbf{G}$, $\mathbf{L}$, and $\mathbf{K}$ represent the average correlations between pairs of student–student, student–teacher, and teacher–teacher basis functions, respectively, the asymptotic generalization error is essentially a function of the correlations between hidden unit responses. There is also a dependence on input-space dimension, basis function width, and input distribution variance via the normalization constants, and on the hidden-to-output weights of the teacher. In the realizable case $\mathbf{G} = \mathbf{L} = \mathbf{K}$, and it can be seen that the asymptotic error disappears. Note that this result is independent of the assumption of diagonal–off-diagonal form for $\mathbf{G}$.

e. Dependence of Estimation Error on Training Set Size

In the limit of no weight decay, it is simple to show that the portion of the generalization error that can be eliminated through training (i.e., that not due to mismatch between student and teacher) is inversely proportional to the number of training examples. For this case the general expression of Eq. (33) reduces to

$$\langle\langle E_G\rangle\rangle = \frac{K}{P}\left\{\frac{1}{\beta} + \sigma^2\right\} + \frac{1}{P}\mathbf{w}^{0\top}\{\operatorname{tr}\mathbf{G}^{-1}\mathbf{J} - \mathbf{L}^\top\mathbf{G}^{-1}\mathbf{L}\}\mathbf{w}^0. \tag{40}$$

Taking $\gamma \to 0$, the only P dependencies are in the $1/P$ prefactors. This result has been confirmed by simulations. Plotting the log of the averaged empirical generalization error versus log P gives a gradient of -1. It is also apparent that, with no weight decay, the best policy is to set $\beta \to \infty$, to eliminate the variance of the student output. This corresponds to selecting the student weight vector most consistent with the data, regardless of the noise level. This result is also independent of the form of $\mathbf{G}$.

B. Probably Approximately Correct Framework

The probably approximately correct (PAC) framework, introduced by Valiant [37], derives from a combination of statistical pattern recognition, decision theory, and computational complexity. The basic position of PAC learning is that to successfully learn an unknown target function, an estimator should be devised which, with high probability, produces a good approximation of it, with a time complexity which is at most a polynomial function of the input dimensionality of the target function, the inverse of the accuracy required, and the inverse of the probability with which the accuracy is required. In its basic form, PAC learning deals only with two-way classification, but extensions to multiple classes and real-valued functions do exist (e.g., [30]). PAC learning is *distribution-free*; it does not require knowledge of the input distribution, as does the Bayesian framework. The price paid for this freedom is much weaker results—the PAC framework produces worst-case results in the form of upper bounds on the generalization error, and these bounds are usually weak. It gives no insight into average-case performance of an architecture.

In the context of neural networks, the basic PAC learning framework is defined as follows. We have a *concept class* C, which is a set of subsets of input space X. For two-way classification, we define the output space $Y = \{-1, +1\}$. Each concept $c \in C$ represents a task to be learned. We also have a *hypothesis space* H, also a set of subsets of X, which need not equal C. For a network which performs a mapping $f\colon X \mapsto Y$, a hypothesis $h \in H$ is simply the subset of X for which $f(\xi) = +1$. Each setting of the weights of the network corresponds to a function f; hence, by examining all possible weight settings, we can associate a class of functions F with a particular network and, through this, we can associate a hypothesis space with the network.

In the learning process, we are provided with a data set D of P training examples, drawn independently from $\mathcal{P}_X$ and labeled $+1$, if the input pattern ξ is an element of concept c, and -1, otherwise. The network, during training, forms a hypothesis h via weight adjustment, and we quantify the error of h w.r.t. c as the probability of the symmetric difference Δ between c and h:

$$\mathrm{error}(h, c) = \sum_{\xi \in h \Delta c} \mathcal{P}_X(\xi). \tag{41}$$

We can now define PAC learnability: the concept class C is PAC learnable by a network if, for all concepts $c \in C$ and for all distributions $\mathcal{P}_X$, it is true that when the network is given at least $p(N, 1/\epsilon, 1/\delta)$ training examples, where p is a polynomial, then the network can form a hypothesis h such that

$$\Pr\left[\mathrm{error}(h, c) > \epsilon\right] \leqslant \delta. \tag{42}$$

Think of δ as a measure of confidence and of ϵ as an error tolerance. This is a worst-case definition, because it requires that the number of training examples must be bounded by a single fixed polynomial for all concepts $c \in C$ and all distributions $\mathcal{P}_X$. Thus, for fixed N and δ, plotting ϵ as a function of training set size gives an upper bound on *all* learning curves for the network. This bound may be very weak compared to an average case.

1. Dimension

To use the PAC framework, it is necessary to understand the concept of Vapnik–Chervonenkis (VC) dimension. VC dimension [38] is related to the notion of *capacity* introduced by Cover [39]. Let F be a class of functions on X, with range $\{-1, +1\}$, and let D_i be a set of i points drawn from X. A *dichotomy* on D induced by a function $f \in F$ is defined as a partition of D into the disjoint subsets D^+ and D^-, such that $\xi \in D^+$, if $f(\xi) = +1$, and $\xi \in D^-$, otherwise. We denote the number of distinct dichotomies of D_i induced by all $f \in F$ by $\Delta_F(D_i)$. D_i is *shattered* by F if $\Delta_F(D_i) = 2^{|D_i|}$. Putting this more intuitively, D_i is shattered by F if every possible dichotomy of D_i can be induced by F. Finally, for given i, defining $\Delta_F(i)$ as the maximum of $\Delta_F(D_i)$ over all D_i, we can define the VC dimension of F as the largest integer i such that $\Delta_F(i) = 2^i$. Stating this more plainly, the VC dimension of F is the cardinality of the largest subset of X that is shattered by F.

The derivation of VC dimension for RBFs that perform two-way classification is beyond the scope of this chapter (see [40]), but for fixed Gaussian basis functions, the VC dimension is simply equal to the number of basis functions.

2. Probably Approximately Correct Learning for Radial Basis Functions

Combining the PAC definition with the VC dimension result allows the derivation of both necessary and sufficient conditions on the number of training examples required to reach a particular level of error with known confidence. The necessary conditions state that if we *do not* have a minimum number of examples, then there is a known finite probability that the resulting generalization error will be greater than the tolerance ϵ. The sufficient conditions tell us that if we *do* have a certain number of examples, then we can be sure (with known confidence) that the error will always be less than ϵ.

Let us examine the sufficient conditions first. Again the proof is beyond the scope of this chapter (see [40]). We start with a RBF with K fixed basis functions and a bias, a sequence of P training points drawn from $\mathcal{P}_X$, and a fixed error tolerance $\epsilon \in (0, 0.25]$. If it is possible to train the net to find a weight vector $\mathbf{w}$ such that the net correctly classifies at least the fraction $1 - \epsilon/2$ of the *training* set, then we can make the following statements about the generalization performance:

$$\text{if} \quad P \geqslant \frac{32(K+1)}{\epsilon} \ln \frac{32}{\epsilon}, \quad \text{then} \quad \delta < 8 \exp(-1.5(K+1)); \tag{43}$$

$$\text{if} \quad P \geqslant \frac{64(K+1)}{\epsilon} \ln \frac{64}{\epsilon}, \quad \text{then} \quad \delta < 8 \exp\left(\frac{-\epsilon P}{32}\right). \tag{44}$$

Thus we know that given a certain number of training pairs P and a desired error level ϵ, we can put an upper bound on the probability that the actual error will exceed our tolerance.

The necessary conditions are derived from a PAC learning result from [41]. Starting with any $\delta \in (0, 1/100]$ and any $\epsilon \in (0, 1/8]$, if we take a class of functions F for which the VC dimension $\mathcal{V}(F) \geqslant 2$ and if we have a number of examples P such that

$$P < \max\left[\frac{1-\epsilon}{\epsilon} \ln \frac{1}{\delta}, \frac{\mathcal{V}(F)-1}{32\epsilon}\right], \tag{45}$$

then we know that there exists a function $f \in F$ and also a distribution $\mathcal{P}_{X \times Y}$ for which all training examples are classified correctly, but for which the probability of obtaining an error rate greater than ϵ is at least δ. This tells us that if we do not have at least the number of training examples required by Eq. (45), then we can be sure that we can find a function and distribution such that our error and confidence requirements are violated.

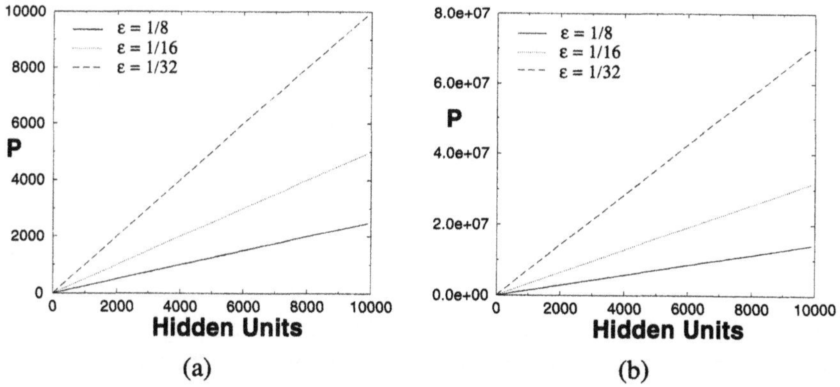

Figure 11 (a) Necessary conditions. The number of examples required is plotted against the number of hidden units. With less than this many examples, one can be sure that there is a distribution and function for which the error exceeds tolerance. (b) Sufficient conditions. The number of examples is again plotted against the number of hidden units. With at least this many examples, one can be sure (with known high confidence) that for all distributions and functions, the error will be within tolerance.

For Gaussian RBFs, Eq. (45) simplifies to

$$P < \frac{K-1}{32\epsilon}. \tag{46}$$

Plotting the necessary and sufficient conditions against number of hidden units (Fig. 11a and b) from Eqs. (43) and (46) reveals that there is a large gap between the upper and lower bounds on the number of examples required. For instance, for 100 hidden units, the upper bound is 142,000 examples, whereas the lower bound is a mere 25 examples! This indicates that these bounds are not tight enough to be of practical use.

3. Haussler's Extended Probably Approximately Correct Framework

Haussler generalized the standard PAC learning model to deal with RBFs with a single real-valued output and adjustable centers [30]. This new framework is now presented, along with the results, restrictions, and implications of the work, but the details of the derivations are beyond the scope of this chapter.

The previously described model, which deals only with classification, is extended under the new framework. As before, our task is to adjust the weights of the student RBF to find an estimating function f_S that minimizes the average generalization error $E(f_S)$. The notion of a teacher network is not used; the task is described by a distribution $\mathcal{P}_{X\times Y}$ over input space and output space, which defines the probability of the examples. We do require that E is bounded, so that the expectation always exists.

Denoting the space of functions that can be represented by the student as F_S, we define $\text{opt}(F_S)$ as the infimum of $E(f_S)$ over F_S, so that the aim of learning is to find a function $f_S \in F_S$ such that $E(f_S)$ is as near to $\text{opt}(F_S)$ as possible.

To quantify this concept of nearness, we define a distance metric d_v for $r, s \geqslant 0,\ v > 0$:

$$d_v(r, s) = \frac{|r-s|}{v+r+s}. \tag{47}$$

The quantity v scales the distance measure (although not in a proportional sense). This measure can be motivated by noting that it is similar to the function used in combinatorial optimization to measure the quality of a solution with respect to the optimal. Letting $s = \text{opt}(F_S)$ and $r = E(f_S)$, then this distance measure gives

$$d_v(E(f_S), \text{opt}) = \frac{|E(f_S) - \text{opt}(F_S)|}{v + E(f_S) + \text{opt}(F_S)}, \tag{48}$$

whereas the corresponding combinatorial optimization function is

$$\frac{|E(f_S) - \text{opt}(F_S)|}{\text{opt}(F_S)}. \tag{49}$$

The new measure has the advantages that it is well behaved when either argument is zero and is symmetric (so that it is a metric).

The framework can now be defined, within which the quantity ϵ can again be thought of as an error tolerance (this time expressed as a distance between actual and optimal error), whereas δ is a confidence parameter. A network architecture can solve a learning problem if $\forall v > 0,\ \epsilon \in (0, 1),\ \delta \in (0, 1)$, there exists a finite sample size $P = P(v, \epsilon, \delta)$ such that for any distribution[5] $\mathcal{P}_{X\times Y}$ over the examples, given a sample of P training points drawn independently from $\mathcal{P}_{X\times Y}$, then with probability at least $1 - \delta$, the network adjusts its parameters to perform function f such that

$$d_v\big(E(f_S), \text{opt}(F_S)\big) \leqslant \epsilon, \tag{50}$$

i.e., the distance between the error of the selected estimator and that of the best estimator is no greater than ϵ.

To derive a bound for RBFs, Haussler employs the following restrictions. First, generalization error $E(f_S)$ is calculated as the expectation of the absolute difference between the network prediction and the target; squared difference is more common in actual usage. Absolute difference is also assumed for the training algorithm. Second, all the weights must be bounded by a constant β. The result takes the form of bounding the distance between the error on the training set, denoted by $E_T(f_S)$, and the generalization error.

For an RBF which maps $\Re^N$ to the interval [0, 1], with $v \in (0, 8/(\max(N, K)+1)]$, $\epsilon, \delta \in (0, 1)$, and given that we have a sample size of

$$\mathcal{O}\left(\frac{1}{\epsilon^2 v}\left(W\left(\log\frac{1}{\epsilon v} + \log \beta K\right) + \log\frac{1}{\delta}\right)\right), \tag{51}$$

then we can be sure up to a known confidence that there are no functions for which the distance between training error and generalization error exceeds our tolerance. Specifically, we know that

$$\Pr\big[\exists f_S \in F_S\colon d_v\big(E_T(f), E(f_S)\big) > \epsilon\big] \leqslant \delta. \tag{52}$$

Fixing the weight bound β simplifies the sample size expression to

$$\mathcal{O}\left(\frac{1}{\epsilon^2 v}\left(W \log\frac{K}{\epsilon v} + \log\frac{1}{\delta}\right)\right). \tag{53}$$

[5] Subject to some measure-theoretic restrictions; see [30].

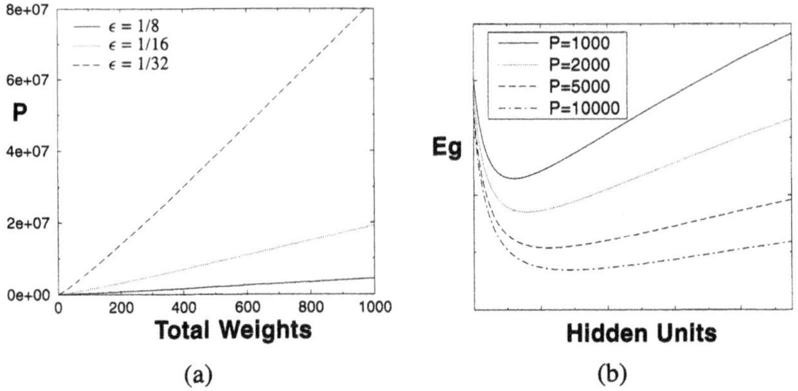

Figure 12 (a) Sample size bound for the extended PAC framework, illustrated for three values of the error tolerance ϵ. The dependence of sample size on the total number of weights in the network is nearly linear. (b) Generalization error versus number of hidden units for the Niyogi and Girosi framework, for fixed numbers of examples. The trade-off between minimizing approximation error and minimizing estimation error results in an optimal network size.

As with the basic PAC framework, this result describes the worst case scenario—it tells us the probability that there exists a distribution $\mathcal{P}_{X \times Y}$ and a function f_S for which the distance between training error and generalization error will exceed our tolerance. Thus, for a particular distribution, the result is likely to be very weak. However, it can be used to discern more general features of the learning scenario. In particular, by fixing the error tolerance ϵ, distance parameter υ, and confidence δ, the sample size needed is related in a near-linear fashion to the number of parameters in the network. This is illustrated, along with the dependence on the error tolerance ϵ, in Fig. 12a, which shows the sample size needed to be sure that the difference between training and generalization error is no more than the tolerance for $\epsilon = 1/8,\ 1/16$, and $1/32$.

4. Weaknesses of the Probably Approximately Correct Approach

The primary weakness of the PAC approach is that it gives worst-case bounds—it does not predict learning curves well. Whereas the sample complexity is defined in PAC learning as the worst-case number of random examples required over *all* possible target concepts and *all* distributions, it is likely to overestimate the sample complexity for any particular learning problem. This is not the end of it; as in most cases, the worst-case sample complexity can only be bounded, not calculated exactly. This is the price one has to pay to obtain distribution-free results.

The basic PAC model requires the notion of a target concept and deals only with the noise-free case. However, these restrictions are overcome in the extended framework of Haussler [30], in which the task is defined simply by a distribution $X \times Y$ over the examples.

C. Approximation Error/Estimation Error

Although Haussler's extended PAC model allows for cases in which the problem cannot be solved exactly by the network, it does not explicitly address this scenario. Niyogi and Girosi [33] construct a framework which divides the problem of bounding generalization error into two parts: the first deals with *approximation error*, which is the error due to a lack of representational capacity of the network. Approximation error is defined as the error made by the best possible student; it is the minimum of $E(f_S)$ over F_S. If the task is realizable, the approximation error is zero. The second part examines *estimation error*, which takes account of the fact that we only have finite data, and so the student selected by training the network may be far from optimal. The framework pays no attention to concepts such as local minima; it is assumed that given infinite data, the best hypothesis will always be found.

Again, we take the approach of introducing the framework and then focusing on the results and their applicability, rather than delving into the technicalities of their derivation (see [33]).

The task addressed is that of regression—estimating real-valued targets. The task is defined by the distribution $\mathcal{P}_{X\times Y}$. One measure of performance of the network is the average squared error between prediction and target (the *expected risk*):

$$C(f_S) = \left\langle \left(y - f_S(\xi)\right)^2 \right\rangle = \int_{X\times Y} \delta\xi\, \delta y\, \mathcal{P}(\xi, y)\left(y - f_S(\xi)\right)^2. \tag{54}$$

The expected risk decomposes to

$$C(f_S) = \left\langle \left(f_0(\xi) - f_S(\xi)\right)^2 \right\rangle + \left\langle \left(y - f_0(\xi)\right)^2 \right\rangle, \tag{55}$$

where $f_0(\xi)$, the regression function, is the conditional mean of the output given a particular input. Setting $f_S = f_0$ minimizes the expected risk, so the task can now be considered one of reconstructing the regression function with the estimator. If we consider the regression function to be produced by a teacher network, the first term of Eq. (55) becomes equal to the definition of generalization error employed in the Bayesian framework, Eq. (25), and the second term is the error due to noise on the teacher output. If this noise is additive and independent of ξ, Eq. (55) can simply be written as $C(f_S) = E(f_S) + \sigma^2$.

Of course, in practice the expected risk $C(f_S)$ is unavailable to us, as $\mathcal{P}_{X\times Y}$ is unknown, and so it is estimated by the empirical risk $C(f_S, D)$ (discussed in Section III.A.1), which converges in probability to $C(f_S)$ for each f_S [although not necessarily for all f_S simultaneously, which means the function that minimizes $C(f_S)$ does not necessarily minimize $C(f_S, D)$]. As in the extended PAC framework, the question becomes: How good a solution is the function that minimizes $C(f_S, D)$?

The approach taken by Niyogi and Girosi is to bound the average squared difference between the regression function and the estimating function produced by the network. They term this quantity *generalization error*; it is the same definition as employed in the Bayesian framework.

Following the decomposition of the expected risk [Eq. (55)], the generalization error can be bounded in the manner

$$E \leqslant \left|C(f_S^{\mathrm{opt}}) - C(f_0)\right| + \left|C(f_S^{\mathrm{opt}}) - C(f_S)\right|, \tag{56}$$

where f_S^{opt} is the optimal solution in the class of possible estimators, that is, the best possible weight setting for the network. Thus we see that the generalization error is bounded by the sum of the approximation error (the difference between the error of the best estimator and that of the regression function) and the estimation error (the difference between the error of the best estimator and the actual estimator). By evaluating the two types of error, generalization error can be bounded.

Applying this general framework to RBFs, we address the task of bounding generalization error in RBFs with Gaussian basis functions with fixed widths and adjustable centers. Further, the weightings of the basis functions are bounded in absolute value. We present the main result: the full derivation can be found in [33].

For any $\delta \in (0, 1)$, for K nodes, P training points, and input dimension N, with probability greater than $1 - \delta$,

$$E \leqslant \mathcal{O}\left(\frac{1}{K}\right) + \mathcal{O}\left(\left[\frac{KN\log(KP) - \log\delta}{P}\right]^{1/2}\right). \tag{57}$$

The first term is approximation error, which decreases as $\mathcal{O}(1/K)$, so it is clear that given sufficient basis functions, any regression function can be approximated to arbitrary accuracy; this agrees with the results of Hartman *et al.* [4]. For a fixed network, the estimation error is governed by the number of patterns—ignoring constant terms, it decreases as $\mathcal{O}([\log P/P]^{1/2})$. Note that this is considerably slower than the result for the average case analysis with known Gaussian input distribution, for which the estimation error (with no weight decay) scales as $1/P$. Again, this is the price paid for obtaining (almost) distribution-free bounds. Note that the bound is worst case; it obtains for almost all distributions and almost all learning tasks.[6]

The first thing to notice about the bound is that the estimation error will converge to zero only if the number of data points P goes to infinity more quickly than the number of basis functions K. In fact there exists an optimal rate of growth such that given a fixed amount of data, there is an optimal number of basis functions so that generalization error is minimized. This phenomenon is simply caused by the two components of generalization error, as approximation error is reduced by increasing the network size, while, for a fixed number of examples, estimation error is reduced by decreasing network size. To illustrate this, generalization error is plotted against network size for several values of P in Fig. 12b.

The optimal network size can be calculated, for large K. The number of hidden units required is found to scale in the manner

$$K \propto \left(\frac{P}{N \log P}\right)^{1/3}. \tag{58}$$

It must again be emphasized that these results depend on finding the best possible estimator for a given size data set, and are based on worst-case bounds which require almost no knowledge of the input distribution.

D. Conclusion

It is clear that there is a trade-off across the frameworks between specificity of the task and precision of the results. The Bayesian framework requires knowledge of the input distribution and of the concept class; it provides average-case results which correspond excellently with empirical data. The statistical mechanics framework is very similar to this in construction, but proceeds by working with the average free energy rather than directly with the posterior distribution over weight space. These methods are perhaps most useful as tools with which to probe and analyze learning scenarios, such as the overrealizable case and the effects of regularization. The PAC framework is very rigorous and gives distribution-free results, so very little knowledge of the task is required, but it provides only loose worst-case bounds on generalization error, which are of limited practical use. The framework of Niyogi and Girosi combines PAC-like results with those from approximation theory, so again it suffers from the problem of giving only loose bounds. It is not suitable for predicting how many training examples you will need for a given performance on a task, but it can be employed to study generic features of learning tasks, such as the appropriate setting of network complexity to optimize the balance between reducing approximation error and estimation error.

[6]See [33] for technical conditions for the bound to hold. Essentially the regression function must obey some functional constraints.

IV. FULLY ADAPTIVE TRAINING—AN EXACT ANALYSIS

The training paradigms reviewed in the previous sections are based on algorithms for fixing the parameters of the hidden layer, including both the basis function centers and widths, using various techniques (for a review, see [5]). Only the hidden-to-output weights are then adaptable, making the problem linear and easy to solve.

As stated previously, although the linear approach is very fast computationally, it generally gives suboptimal networks since basis function centers are set to fixed, suboptimal values. The alternative is to adapt and optimize some or all of the hidden-layer parameters. This renders the problem nonlinear in the adaptable parameters, and hence requires the employment of an optimization technique, such as gradient descent, for adapting these parameters. This approach is computationally more expensive, but usually leads to greater accuracy of approximation. This section investigates analytically the dynamical approach in which nonlinear basis function centers are continuously modified to allow convergence to optimal models.

A large number of optimization techniques have been employed for adapting network parameters (some of the leading techniques are mentioned in [5, 15]). In this section we concentrate on one of the simplest methods—gradient descent—which is amenable to analysis. There are two methods in use for gradient descent. In *batch learning*, one attempts to minimize the additive training error over the entire data set; adjustments to parameters are performed only once the full training set has been presented. The alternative approach, examined in this paper, is *on-line learning*, in which the adaptive parameters of the network are adjusted after each presentation of a new data point. There has been a resurgence of interest analytically in the on-line method, because certain technical difficulties caused by the variety of ways in which a training set of given size can be selected are avoided, so complicated techniques commonly used in statistical mechanical analysis of neural networks, such as the replica method [15], are unnecessary.

The dynamics of the training process is stochastic, governed by the stream of random training examples presented to the network sequentially. Network parameters are modified dynamically with respect to their performance on the examples presented. One approach to understanding the learning process is to directly model the evolution of the probability distribution for the parameters; this has been investigated by several authors (e.g., [42–44]) primarily in the asymptotic regime.

An alternative analytical method, which relies on statistical mechanics techniques for identifying characteristic macroscopic variables that capture the main features of the dynamics, can be employed to avoid the need for a detailed study of the microscopic dynamics. This approach recently was used by several authors to investigate the learning dynamics in "soft committee machines" (SCM) and in general to study two-layer networks [45–48]; it provides a complete description of the learning process, formulated in terms of the overlaps between vectors in the system. Similar techniques have been used to study the learning dynamics in discrete machines and to devise optimal training algorithms (e.g., [49]).

In this section we present a method for analyzing the behavior of an RBF, in an *on-line* learning scenario whereby network parameters are modified after each presentation of a training example. This allows the calculation of generalization error as a function of a set of macroscopic variables which characterize the main properties of the adaptive parameters of the network. The dynamical evolution of the mean and variance of these variables can be found, allowing not only the investigation of generalization capabilities, but also allowing the internal dynamics of the network, such as specialization of hidden units, to be analyzed.

A. On-Line Learning in Radial Basis Function Networks

We examine a gradient descent on-line training scenario on a continuous error measure, using a Gaussian student RBF, as described in Section III.A.2. Because we again desire to examine generalization error in a variety of controlled scenarios, we employ a Gaussian teacher RBF to generate the examples; the training data generated by the teacher, for simplicity, are not corrupted with noise (see [50]). As before, the number M and position of the hidden units need not correspond to that of the student RBF, which allows investigation of overrealizable and unrealizable cases. This represents a *general* training scenario because, being universal approximators, RBF networks can approximate any continuous mapping to a desired degree.

Training examples will consist of input–output pairs $(\boldsymbol{\xi}, y)$, where the components of $\boldsymbol{\xi}$ are uncorrelated Gaussian random variables of mean 0 and variance σ_x^2, whereas y is generated by applying $\boldsymbol{\xi}$ to the teacher RBF.

We will consider the centers of the basis functions (input-to-hidden weights) and the hidden-to-output weights to be adjustable; for simplicity, the widths of the basis functions are taken as fixed to a common value σ_B. The evolution of the centers of the basis functions are described in terms of the overlaps between center vectors $Q_{bc} \equiv \mathbf{m}_b \cdot \mathbf{m}_c$, $R_{bu} \equiv \mathbf{m}_b \cdot \mathbf{n}_u$, and $T_{uv} \equiv \mathbf{n}_u \cdot \mathbf{n}_v$, where T_{uv} is constant and describes characteristics of the task to be learnt.

The full dynamics for finite systems is described by monitoring the evolution of the probability distributions for the microscopic or macroscopic variables.[7] In

[7]For very large systems one may consider only the averages and neglect higher-order terms. This has been exploited for studying multilayer perceptrons [45–48], but is irrelevant for investigating RBF networks.

this analysis, we have examined both the means and the variances of the adaptive parameters, showing analytically and via computer simulations that the fluctuations are practically negligible.

B. Generalization Error and System Dynamics

We will define generalization error as quadratic deviation, which matches the definition employed previously [Eq. (25)],

$$E = \left\langle \tfrac{1}{2}[f_S - f_T]^2 \right\rangle, \tag{59}$$

where $\langle \cdots \rangle$ denotes an average over input space with respect to the measure $\mathcal{P}_X$.

Substituting the definitions of of student and teacher in Eqs. (28) and (29) leads to

$$E = \tfrac{1}{2}\left\{ \sum_{bc} w_b w_c \langle s_b s_c \rangle + \sum_{uv} w_u^0 w_v^0 \langle t_u t_v \rangle - 2 \sum_{bu} w_b w_u^0 \langle s_b t_u \rangle \right\}. \tag{60}$$

Whereas the input distribution is Gaussian, the averages are Gaussian integrals and so can be performed analytically; the resulting expression for generalization error is given in the Appendix. Each one of the averages, as well as the generalization error itself, depends only on some combination of Q, R, and T. It is therefore sufficient to monitor the evolution of the parameters Q and R (T is fixed and defined by the task) to evaluate the performance of the network.

Expressions for the time evolution of the overlaps Q and R can be derived by employing the gradient descent rule, $\mathbf{m}_b^{p+1} = \mathbf{m}^p + \eta/(N\sigma_B^2)\delta_b(\boldsymbol{\xi} - \mathbf{m}_b)$, where $\delta_b = (f_T - f_S)w_b s_b$ and η is the learning rate which is explicitly scaled with $1/N$. Taking products of the learning rule with the various student and teacher vectors one can easily derive a set of rules for describing the evolution of the overlaps means:

$$\begin{aligned} \langle \Delta Q_{bc} \rangle &= \frac{\eta}{N\sigma_{B2}} \left\langle \left[\delta_b(\boldsymbol{\xi} - \mathbf{m}_b^p) \cdot \mathbf{m}_c^p + \delta_c(\boldsymbol{\xi} - \mathbf{m}_c^p) \cdot \mathbf{m}_b^p\right] \right\rangle \\ &\quad + \left(\frac{\eta}{N\sigma_B^2}\right)^2 \left\langle \delta_b \delta_c (\boldsymbol{\xi} - \mathbf{m}_b^p) \cdot (\boldsymbol{\xi} - \mathbf{m}_c^p) \right\rangle, \end{aligned} \tag{61}$$

$$\langle \Delta R_{bu} \rangle = \frac{\eta}{N\sigma_B^2} \left\langle \delta_b(\boldsymbol{\xi} - \mathbf{m}_b^p) \cdot \mathbf{n}_u \right\rangle. \tag{62}$$

The evolution of the hidden-to-output weight vector can be similarly derived via the learning rule, although one should note that, being a finite-dimensional vector, there is no natural macroscopic property related to it. Because the hidden-to-output weights play a significantly different role than the input-to-hidden weights, it may be sensible to use different learning rates in the respective update equations.

Here, for simplicity, we will use the same learning rate for both the centers and the hidden-to-output weights, although with different scaling, $1/K$, yielding

$$\langle \Delta w_b \rangle = \frac{\eta}{K}\big\langle (f_T - f_S) s_b \big\rangle. \tag{63}$$

These averages can be carried out analytically in a direct manner. The full averaged expressions for ΔQ, ΔR, and $\Delta \mathbf{w}$ are given in the Appendix.

Solving the set of difference equation analytically is difficult. However, by iterating Eqs. (61), (62), and (63) from certain initial conditions, one may obtain a complete description of the learning process evolution. This allows one to examine facets of learning such as specialization of the hidden units and the evolution of generalization error.

C. Numerical Solutions

To demonstrate the evolution of the learning process, we iteratively solved Eqs. (62), (61), and (63) for a particular training scenario. The task consists of three SBFs learning a *graded* teacher of three TBFs, where *graded* implies that the square norms of the TBFs (diagonals of T) differ from one another. For this task, $T_{00} = 0.5$, $T_{11} = 1.0$, and $T_{22} = 1.5$. The teacher in this example is uncorrelated, so that the off-diagonals of T are 0, and the teacher hidden-to-output weights w^0 are set to 1. The learning process is illustrated in Fig. 13. Figure 13a (solid curve) shows the evolution of generalization error, calculated from Eq. (60), while Fig. 13b–d shows the evolution of the equations for the means of R, Q, and $\mathbf{w}$, respectively, calculated by numerically iterating Eqs. (62), (61), and (63) from random initial conditions found by sampling from the following uniform distributions: Q_{bb} and w_b are sampled from $U[0, 0.1]$, while $Q_{bc,\, b \neq c}$ and R_{bc} from $U[0, 10^{-6}]$. These initial conditions will be used for most of the examples given throughout the paper and reflect random correlations expected by arbitrary initialization of large systems. Input dimensionality $N = 8$, learning rate $\eta = 0.9$, input variance $\sigma_\xi^2 = 1$, and basis function width $\sigma_B^2 = 1$ will be used for most of the examples and will be assumed unless stated otherwise.

The evolution presented in Fig. 13a–d is typical, consisting of four main phases. Initially, there is a short *transient* phase in which the overlaps and hidden-to-output weights evolve from their initial conditions to reach an approximately steady value ($P = 0$ to 1000). Then a *symmetric* phase, characterized by a plateau in the evolution of the generalization error, occurs (Fig. 13a, solid curve; $P = 1000$ to 7000), corresponding to a lack of differentiation among the hidden units; they are unspecialized and learn an average of the hidden units of the teacher, so that the student center vectors and hidden-to-output weights are similar

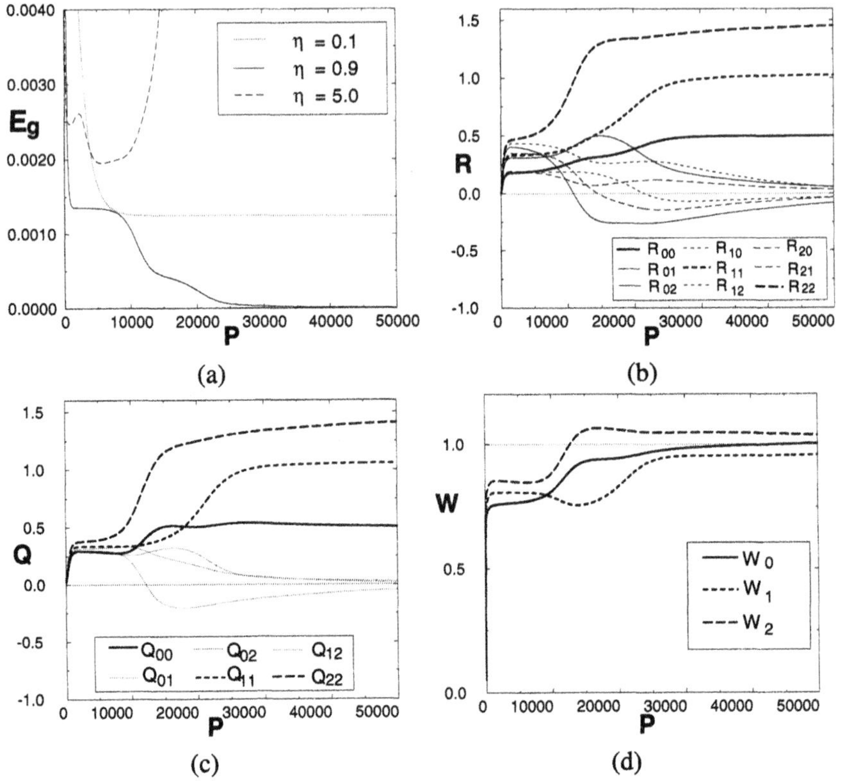

Figure 13 The exactly realizable scenario with positive TBFs. Three SBFs learn a graded, uncorrelated teacher of three TBFs with $T_{00} = 0.5,\ T_{11} = 1.0$, and $T_{22} = 1.5$. All teacher hidden-to-output weights are set to 1. (a) The evolution of the generalization error as a function of the number of examples for several different learning rates $\eta = 0.1,\ 0.9,\ 5$. (b), (c) The evolution of overlaps between student and teacher center vectors and among student center vectors, respectively. (d) The evolution of the mean hidden-to-output weights.

(Fig. 13b–d).[8] The symmetric phase is followed by a *symmetry-breaking* phase in which the student hidden units learn to specialize and become differentiated from one another ($P = 7000$ to 20,000). Finally there is a long *convergence* phase as the overlaps and hidden-to-output weights reach their asymptotic values. Because the task is realizable, this phase is characterized by $E \to 0$ (Fig. 13a, solid curve) and by the student center vectors and hidden-to-output weights asymptotically approaching those of the teacher (i.e., $Q_{00} = R_{00} = 0.5,\ Q_{11} = R_{11} =$

[8] The differences between the overlaps R in Fig. 13b result from differences in the teacher vector lengths and would vanish if the overlaps were normalized.

1.0, $Q_{22} = R_{22} = 1.5$, with the off-diagonal elements of both Q and R being zero; $\forall b,\ w_b = 1$).[9]

These phases are generic in that they are observed—sometimes with some variation such as a series of symmetric and symmetry-breaking phases rather than just one—in every on-line learning scenario for RBFs so far examined. They also correspond to the phases found for multilayer perceptrons [47, 48]. In the current analysis we will concentrate on realizable cases ($M = K$) and on analyzing the symmetric phase and the asymptotic convergence. A more detailed study of the various phases and of other training scenarios, such as overrealizable ($K > M$) and unrealizable ($M > K$) cases, will appear elsewhere [51, 52].

D. Phenomenological Observations

Examining the numerical solutions for various training scenarios leads to some interesting observations. We will first examine the effect of the learning rate on the evolution of the training process using a similar task and training conditions as before. If η is chosen to be too small (here, $\eta = 0.1$), there is a long period in which there is no specialization of the student basis functions (SBFs) and no improvement in generalization ability: the process becomes trapped in a symmetric subspace of solutions; this is the symmetric phase. Given asymmetry in the initial conditions of the students (i.e., in R, Q, or $\mathbf{w}$) or of the task itself, this subspace will always be escaped, but the time period required may be prohibitively large (Fig. 13a, dotted curve). The length of the symmetric phase increases with the symmetry of the initial conditions . At the other extreme, if η is set too large, an initial transient takes place quickly, but there comes a point from which the student vector norms grow extremely rapidly, until the point where, due to the finite variance of the input distribution and local nature of the basis functions, the student hidden units are no longer activated during training (Fig. 13a, dashed curve, with $\eta = 5.0$). In this case, the generalization error approaches a finite value as $P \to \infty$ and the task is not solved. Between these extremes lies a region in which the symmetric subspace is escaped reasonably quickly and $E \to 0$ as $P \to \infty$ for the realizable case (Fig. 13a, solid curve, with $\eta = 0.9$). The SBFs become specialized and, asymptotically, the teacher is emulated exactly. These results for the learning rate are qualitatively similar to those found for soft committee machines and multilayer perceptrons [45–48].

Another observation is related to the dependence of the training dynamics, especially that of the symmetric phase, on the training task. The symmetric phase is a phenomenon which depends on the symmetry of the task as well as that of the initial conditions. Therefore, one would expect a shorter symmetric phase in inherently asymmetric tasks.

[9]The arbitrary labels of the SBFs were permuted to match those of the teacher.

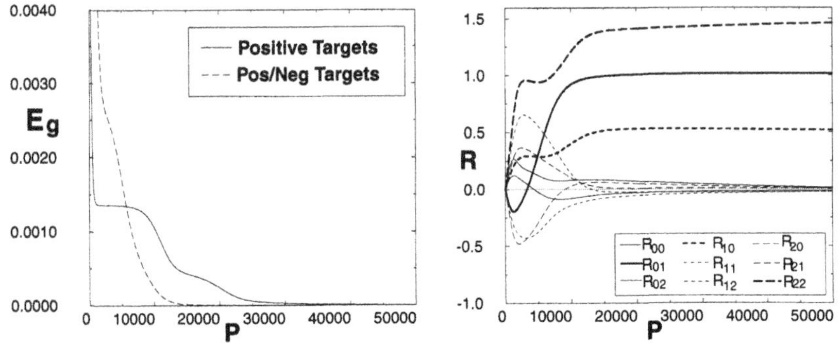

(a) (b)

Figure 14 The exactly realizable scenario defined by a teacher network with a mixture of positive and negative TBFs. Three SBFs learn a graded, uncorrelated teacher of three TBFs with $T_{00} = 0.5$, $T_{11} = 1.0$, and $T_{22} = 1.5$; $w_0^0 = 1$, $w_1^0 = -1$, $w_2^0 = 1$. (a) The evolution of the generalization error for this case and, for comparison, the evolution in the case of all positive TBFs. (b) The evolution of the overlaps between student and teacher centers R.

To examine this expectation, the task employed had the single change that the sign of one of the teacher hidden-to-output weights was flipped, thus providing two categories of targets: positive and negative. The initial conditions of the student remained the same as in the previous task, with the same input dimensionality $N = 8$ and learning rate $\eta = 0.9$.

The evolution of generalization error and the overlaps for this task are shown in Fig. 14a and b, respectively. Dividing the targets into two categories effectively eliminates the symmetric phase; this can be seen by comparing the evolution of the generalization error for this task (Fig. 14a, dashed curve) with that for the previous task (Fig. 14a, solid curve). It can be seen that there is no longer a plateau in the generalization error. Correspondingly, the symmetries between SBFs break immediately, as can be seen by examining the overlaps between student and teacher center vectors (Fig. 14b); this should be compared with Fig. 13b, which denotes the evolution of the overlaps in the previous task. Note that the plateaus in the overlaps (Fig. 13b, $P = 1000$ to 7000) are not found for the antisymmetric task.

The elimination of the symmetric phase is an extreme result caused by the small size of the student network (three hidden units). For networks with many hidden units, one finds instead parallel symmetric phases, each shorter than the single symmetric phase in the corresponding task with only positive targets, in which there is one symmetry between the hidden units seeking positive targets and another between those seeking negative targets. This suggests a simple and easily implemented strategy for increasing the speed of learning when targets are predominantly positive (negative): Eliminate the bias of the training set by subtracting (adding) the mean target from each target point. This corresponds to an old heuristic among RBF practitioners. It follows that the hidden-to-output weights should be initialized evenly between $+1$ and -1, to reflect this elimination of bias.

E. Symmetric Phase

To obtain generic characteristics of the symmetric phase it would be useful to simplify the equations as well as the task examined. We adopt the following assumptions: The symmetric phase is a phenomenon that is predominantly associated with small η, so terms of η^2 may be neglected. The hidden-to-output weights are clamped to $+1$. The teacher is taken to be *isotropic*; that is, teacher hidden unit weight vectors are taken to have *identical norms* of 1, each having no overlap with the others; therefore $T_{uv} = \delta_{uv}$. This has the result that the student norms Q_{bb} are very similar in this phase, as are the student–student correlations, so $Q_{bb} \equiv Q$ and $Q_{bc,\, b \neq c} \equiv C$, where Q becomes the square norms of the SBFs and C is the overlap between any two different SBFs.

To simplify the picture further one may consider the set of orthogonal unit vectors constituting the task as basis vectors to the subspace spanned by the teacher vectors [47]. Any student vector may be represented by its projections on the basis vectors and an additional vector orthogonal to the teacher vectors subspace; the latter, depending on the learning rate η, is negligible in the symmetric phase. Whereas in the symmetric phase student weight vector projections on the teacher vectors are identical, R, one can represent any student vectors quite accurately as $\mathbf{m}_b = \sum_{u=1}^{M} R_{bu}\mathbf{n}_u = R\sum_{u=1}^{M}\mathbf{n}_u$. Furthermore, this reduction to a single overlap parameter leads to $Q = C = MR^2$, so the evolution of the overlaps can be described as a single difference equation for R. The analytic solution of Eqs. (61), (62), and (63) under these restrictions is still rather complicated. However, because we are primarily interested in large systems, that is, large K, we will examine the most dominant terms in the solution. Expanding in $1/K$ and discarding higher-order terms, at the fixed point one obtains

$$R = 1\Big/\left(K\left(1 + \sigma_B^2 - \sigma_B^2 \exp\left[\left(\frac{1}{2\sigma_B^2}\right)\frac{\sigma_B^2 + 1}{\sigma_B^2 + 2}\right]\right)\right). \tag{64}$$

Substituting these expressions into the general equation for the generalization error [Eq. (60)] shows that generalization error at the symmetric fixed point increases monotonically with K (Fig. 15a), in good agreement with the value obtained from the numerical solution for the system even for modest values of K.

Figure 15b compares these quantities for $K = 8$: the solid line shows the analytic value of generalization error at the fixed point ($E = 0.0242$), while the

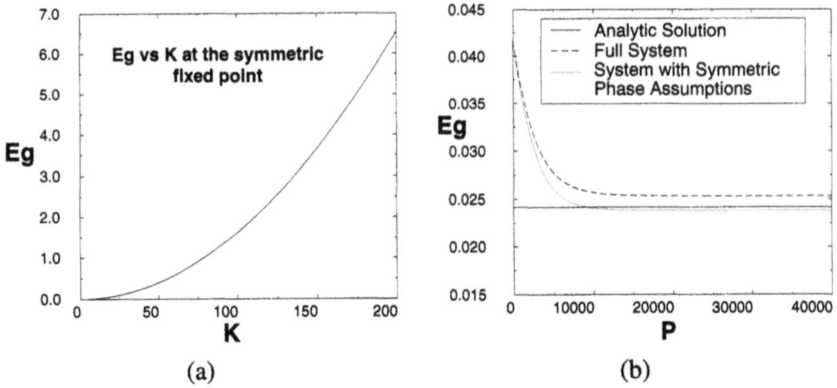

Figure 15 (a) Generalization error versus K at the symmetric fixed point. The generalization error is found by substituting the values of the overlaps at the symmetric fixed point into the general equation for generalization error [Eq. (60)]. It can be seen that generalization error monotonically increases with K. (b) Comparison of the analytic solution for the symmetric fixed point (solid line) to that of the iterated system under the symmetric phase assumptions (dotted line) and to that of the full iterated system without the assumptions (dashed line) for $K = 8$.

dotted line represents the iterated system under the symmetric phase assumptions detailed in the foregoing text ($E = 0.0238$ at the symmetric plateau). For comparison, the dashed curve shows the evolution of E for the full system learning an isotropic teacher, with $\eta = 0.1$. The value of E at the symmetric plateau is 0.0251, which is close to the value for the system under the symmetric assumptions: the slight difference is caused by the truncation of the equation for the evolution of Q [Eq. (61)] to first order in η under the symmetric assumptions; this difference disappears as η approaches zero.

The symmetric phase represents an unstable fixed point of the dynamics. The stability of the fixed point, and thus the breaking of the symmetric phase, can be examined via an eigenvalue analysis of the dynamics of the system near the fixed point. The method employed is similar to that detailed in [47] and will be presented in full elsewhere [52]. We use a set of four equations (permuting SBF labels to match those of the teacher) for $R_{bb} \equiv R$, $R_{bu,\, b \neq u} \equiv S$, $Q_{bb} \equiv Q$, and $Q_{bc,\, b \neq c} \equiv C$. Linearizing the dynamical equations around the fixed point results in a matrix which dominates the dynamics; this matrix has three attractive (negative) eigenvalues and one positive eigenvalue ($\lambda_1 > 0$) which dominates the escape from the symmetric subspace. The positive eigenvalue scales with K and represents a perturbation which breaks the symmetries between the hidden units. This result is in contrast to that for the SCM [47], in which the dominant eigenvalue scales with $1/K$. This implies that for RBFs the more hidden units in the network, the *faster* the symmetric phase is escaped, resulting in negligible symmetric phases for large systems, whereas in SCMs the opposite is true. This difference is caused by the contrast between the localized nature of the basis function in the RBF network and the global nature of sigmoidal hidden nodes in SCM. In the SCM case, small perturbations around the symmetric fixed point result in relatively small changes in error because the sigmoidal response changes very slowly as one modifies the weight vectors. On the other hand, the Gaussian response decays exponentially as one moves away from the center, so small perturbations around the symmetric fixed point result in massive changes that drive the symmetry-breaking. When K increases, the error surface looks very rugged, emphasizing the peaks and increasing this effect, in contrast to the SCM case, where more sigmoids means a smoother error surface.

F. Convergence Phase

To gain insight into the convergence of the on-line gradient descent process in a realizable scenario, a simplified learning scenario similar to that utilized in the symmetric phase analysis was employed. The hidden-to-output weights are again fixed to $+1$, and the teacher is taken to be defined by $T_{uv} = \delta_{uv}$. The scenario can be extended to adaptable hidden-to-output weights, and this will be presented in [52]. The symmetric phase restrictions do not apply here, and the overlaps between a particular SBF and the TBF that it is emulating are not similar to the overlaps between that SBF and the other TBFs, so the system reduces to four different adaptive quantities: $Q \equiv Q_{bb}$, $C \equiv Q_{bc,\, b \neq c}$, $R \equiv R_{bb}$, and $S \equiv R_{bc,\, b \neq c}$. Linearizing this system about the known fixed point of the solution $(Q = 1,\ C = 0,\ R = 1,\ S = 0)$, yields a linear differential equation with a four-dimensional matrix governing the dynamics. The eigenvalues of the matrix control the dynamics of the converging system: these are demonstrated in Fig. 16a for $K = 10$. In every case examined, there is a single critical eigenvalue λ_c that controls the stability and convergence rate of the system (shown in boldface type on the figure), a nonlinear subcritical eigenvalue, and two subcritical linear eigenvalues. The value of η at $\lambda_c = 0$ determines the maximum learning rate for convergence to occur; for $\lambda_c > 0$ the fixed point is unstable. Note that this applies only to the convergence phase, and may differ during earlier stages of learning. The convergence of the overlaps is controlled by the critical eigenvalue; therefore, the value of η at the single minimum of λ_c determines the optimal learning rate (η_{opt}) in terms of the fastest convergence of the generalization error to the fixed point.

Examining η_c and η_{opt} as a function of K (Fig. 16b), one finds that both quantities scale as $1/K$. The maximum and optimal learning rates are inversely proportional to the number of hidden units of the student. Obtained numerically, the ratio of η_{opt} to η_c is approximately $2/3$.

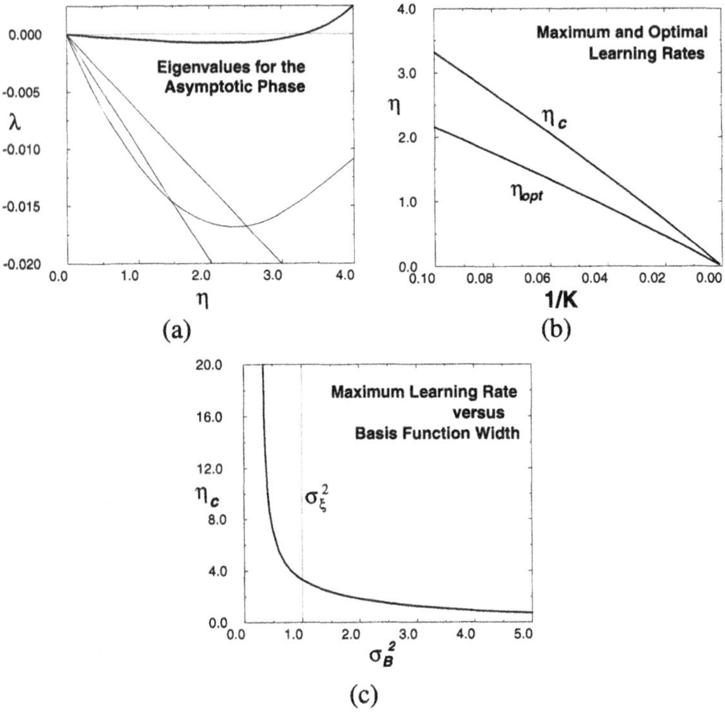

Figure 16 Convergence phase. (a) The eigenvalues of the four-dimensional matrix controlling the dynamics of the system linearized about the asymptotic fixed point, as a function of η. The critical eigenvalue is shown in boldface type. (b) The maximum and optimal learning rates found from the critical eigenvalue. These quantities scale as $1/K$. (c) The maximum learning rate as a function of basis function width.

Finally, the relationship between basis function width and η_c is plotted in Fig. 16c. When the widths are small, η_c is very large because it becomes unlikely that a training point will activate any of the basis functions. For $\sigma_B^2 > \sigma_\xi^2$, $\eta_c \sim 1/\sigma_B^2$.

G. Quantifying the Variances

Whereas we have examined so far only the dynamics of the means, it is necessary to quantify the variances in the adaptive parameters to justify considering only the mean updates.[10] By making assumptions as to the form of these vari-

[10]When employing the thermodynamic limit one may consider the overlaps as well as the hidden-to-output weights, if their update is properly scaled [48], as self-averaging. In that case it is sufficient to consider only the means, neglecting higher-order moments.

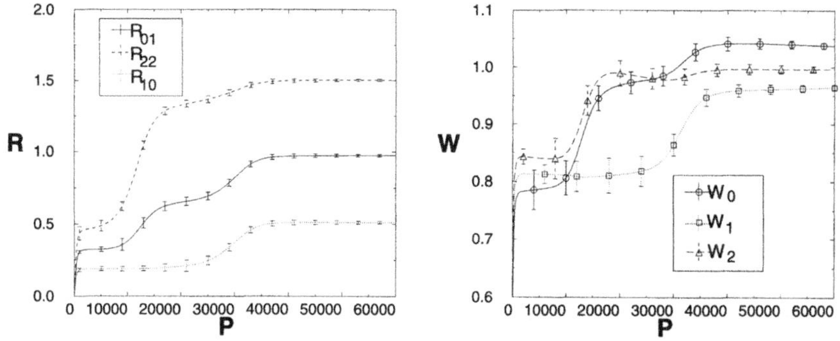

(a) (b)

Figure 17 Evolution of the variances of the (a) overlaps R and (b) hidden-to-output weights $\mathbf{w}$. The curves denote the evolution of the means, while the error bars show the evolution of the fluctuations about the mean. Input dimensionality $N = 10$, learning rate $\eta = 0.9$, input variance $\sigma_\xi^2 = 1$, and basis function width $\sigma_B^2 = 1.0$.

ances, it is possible to derive equations describing their evolution. Specifically, it is assumed that the means of the overlaps can be written as the sum of the average value (calculated as in Section IV.B), a *dynamic* correction due to the randomness of the training example, and a *static* correction, which vanishes as system size becomes infinite. The update rules are treated similarly in terms of a mean, dynamic correction, and static correction; the method is detailed in [42] and, for the soft committee machine, in[53]. It has been shown that the variances must vanish in the thermodynamic limit for realizable cases [42]. This method results in a set of difference equations describing the evolution of the variances of the overlaps and hidden-to-output weights (similar to [48]) as training proceeds. A detailed description of the calculation of the variances as applied to RBFs will appear in [52]. Figure 17a and b shows the evolution of the variances, plotted as error bars on the mean, for the dominant overlaps and the hidden-to-output weights using $\eta = 0.9$, $N = 10$ on a task identical to that described in Section IV.C. Examining the dominant overlaps R first (Fig. 17a), the variances follow the same pattern for each overlap, but at different values of P. The variances begin at 0, then increase, peaking at the symmetry-breaking point at which the SBF begins to specialize on a particular TBF, and then decrease to 0 again as convergence occurs. Looking at each SBF in turn, for SBF 2 (dashed curve), the overlap begins to specialize at approximately $P = 2000$, where the variance peak occurs; for SBF 0 (solid curve), the symmetry lasts until $P = 10{,}000$, again where the variance peak occurs; and for SBF 1 (dotted curve), the symmetry breaks later at approximately $P = 20{,}000$, again where the peak of the variance occurs. The variances then dwindle to 0 for each SBF in the convergence phase.

Essentially the same pattern occurs for the hidden-to-output weights (Fig. 17b). The variances increase rapidly until the hidden units begin to specialize, at which point the variances peak; this is followed by the variances decreasing to 0 as convergence occurs. For SBFs 0 (solid curve) and 2 (dashed curve), the peaks occur in the $P = 5000$ to 10,000 region, whereas for SBF 1 (dotted curve), the last to specialize, the peak is seen at $P = 20{,}000$. For both overlaps and hidden-to-output weights, the mean is an order of magnitude larger than the standard deviation at the variance peak, and much more dominant elsewhere; the ratio becomes greater as N is increased.

The magnitude of the variances is influenced by the degree of symmetry of the initial conditions of the student and of the task in that the greater this symmetry, the larger the variances. Discussion of this phenomenon can be found in [53]; it will be explored at greater length for RBFs in a future publication.

H. Simulations

To confirm the validity of the analytic results, simulations were performed in which RBFs were trained using on-line gradient descent. The trajectories of the overlaps were calculated from the trajectories of the weight vectors of the network, whereas generalization error was estimated by finding the average error on a 1000 point test set. The procedure was performed 50 times and the results were averaged, subject to permutation of the labels of the student hidden units to ensure the average was meaningful.

Typical results are shown in Fig. 18. The particular example shown is for an exactly realizable system of three student hidden units and three teacher hidden units at $N = 5, \eta = 0.9$. Figure 18a shows the close correspondence between empirical test error and theoretical generalization error: at all times, the theoretical result is within one standard deviation of the empirical result. Figure 18b, c, and d shows the excellent correspondence between the trajectories of the theoretical overlaps and hidden-to-output weights and their empirical counterparts; the error bars on the simulation distributions are not shown as they are approximately as small as or smaller than the symbols. The simulations demonstrate the validity of the theoretical results.

I. Conclusion

In this section we analyzed on-line learning in RBF networks using the gradient descent learning rule. The analysis is based on calculating the evolution of the means of a set of characteristic macroscopic variables representing overlaps

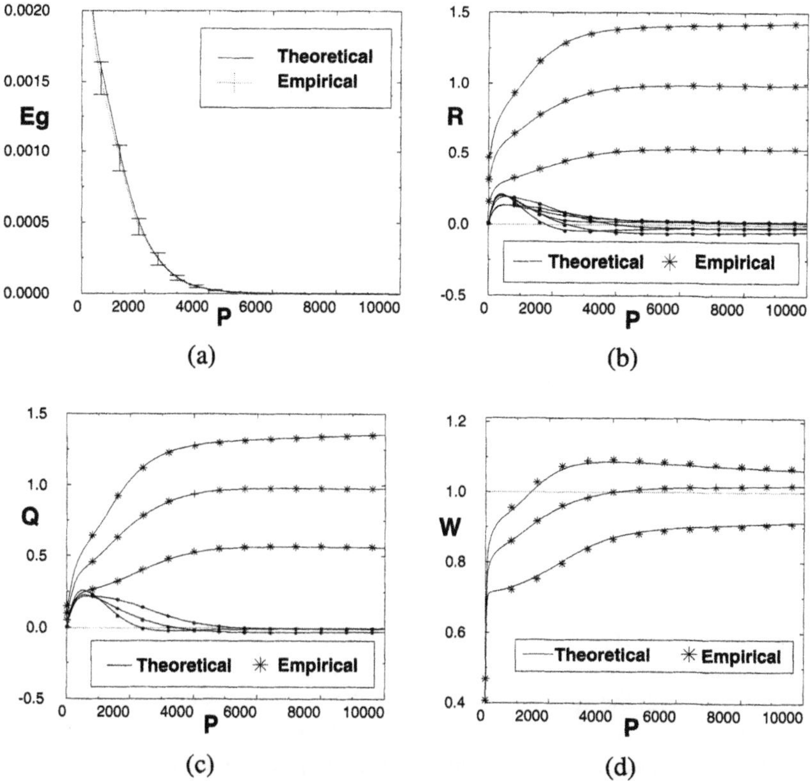

Figure 18 Comparison of theoretical results with simulations. The simulation results are averaged over 50 trials. The labels of the student hidden units have been permuted where necessary to make the averages meaningful. Empirical generalization error was approximated with the test error on a 1000 point test set. Error bars on the simulations are at most the size of the larger asterisks for the overlaps (b) and (c) and at most twice this size for the hidden-to-output weights (d). Input dimensionality $N = 5$, learning rate $\eta = 0.9$, input variance $\sigma_\xi^2 = 1$, and basis function width $\sigma_B^2 = 1$.

between parameter vectors of the system, the hidden-to-output weights, and the generalization error.

This method was used to explore the various stages of the training process comprising a short transitory phase in which the adaptive parameters move from the initial conditions to the symmetric phase; the symmetric phase itself, characterized by lack of differentiation between the hidden units; a symmetry-breaking phase in which the hidden units become specialized; and a convergence phase in which the adaptive parameters reach their final values asymptotically. The theoretical framework was used to make some observations on training conditions which affect the evolution of the training process, concentrating on realizable training scenarios where the number of student hidden nodes equals that of the teacher. Three regimes were found for the learning rate: too small, leading to unnecessarily long trapping times in the symmetric phase; intermediate, leading to fast escape from the symmetric phase and convergence to the correct target; and too large, which results in a divergence of student basis function norms and failure to converge to the correct target. Additionally, it was shown that employing both positive and negative targets leads to much faster symmetry-breaking; this appears to be the underlying reason behind the neural network folklore that targets should be given zero mean.

Whereas the analysis focused on the evolution of the macroscopic parameters means, it was necessary to quantify the variance in the overlaps and hidden-to-output weights; this was shown to be initially small, to peak at the symmetry-breaking point, and then to converge to zero as the overlaps and hidden-to-output weights converge. The more symmetric the initial conditions, the more fluctuation is obtained at the symmetry-breaking. In general, the fluctuations were not significantly large to question the method.

Further analysis was carried out for the two most dominant phases of the learning process: the symmetric phase and the asymptotic convergence. The symmetric phase, under simplifying conditions, was analyzed and the values of generalization error and the overlaps at the symmetric fixed point were found, which are in agreement with the values obtained from the numerical solutions. The convergence phase was also studied by linearizing the dynamical equations around the asymptotic fixed point; both the maximum and optimal learning rates were calculated for the exponential convergence of the generalization error to the asymptotic fixed point and were shown to scale as $1/K$. The dependence of the maximum learning rate on the width of the basis functions was also examined and, for $\sigma_B^2 > \sigma_\xi^2$, the maximum learning rate scales approximately as $1/\sigma_B^2$.

To validate the theoretical results we carried out extensive simulations on training scenarios which strongly confirmed the theoretical results.

Other aspects of on-line learning in RBF networks, including unrealizable cases, the effects of noise and regularizers, and the extension of the analysis of the convergence phase to fully adaptable hidden-to-output weights, will appear in future publications.

V. SUMMARY

We have presented a wide range of viewpoints on the statistical analysis of the RBF network. In the first section, we concentrated on the traditional variant of the RBF, in which the center parameters are fixed before training, and discussed the theory of linear models, the bias–variance dilemma, theory and practice of cross-validation, regularization, and center selection, as well as the advantages of employing localized basis functions. The second section described analytical methods that can be utilized to calculate generalization error in traditional RBF networks and the insights that can be gained from analysis, such as the rate of decay of generalization error, the effects of over- and underregularizing, and finding optimal parameters. The frameworks presented in this section range from those dealing with average-case analysis, which give precise predictions under tightly specified conditions, to those which deal with more general conditions but provide worst-case bounds on performance which are not of great practical use. Finally we moved on to the more general RBF in which the center parameters are allowed to adapt during training, which requires a more computationally expensive training method but can give more accurate representations of the training data. For this model, we calculated average-case generalization error in terms of a set of macroscopic parameters, the evolution of which gave insight into the stages associated with training a network, such as the specialization of the hidden units.

APPENDIX

Generalization Error:

$$E = \frac{1}{2}\left\{ \sum_{bc} w_b w_c I_2(b,c) + \sum_{uv} w_u^0 w_v^0 I_2(u,v) - 2\sum_{bu} w_b w_u^0 I_2(b,u) \right\}. \tag{65}$$

ΔQ, ΔR, and Δw:

$$\begin{aligned} \langle \Delta Q_{bc} \rangle &= \frac{\eta}{N\sigma_B^2}\{w_b[\overline{J}_2(b;c) - Q_{bc}\overline{I}_2(b)] + w_c[\overline{J}_2(c;b) - Q_{bc}\overline{I}_2(c)]\} \\ &\quad + \left(\frac{\eta}{N\sigma_B^2}\right)^2 w_b w_c \{\overline{K}_4(b,c) + Q_{bc}\overline{I}_4(b,c) \\ &\quad - \overline{J}_4(b,c;b) - \overline{J}_4(b,c;c)\}, \end{aligned} \tag{66}$$

$$\langle \Delta R_{bu} \rangle = \frac{\eta}{N\sigma_B^2} w_b \{\overline{J}_2(b;u) - R_{bu}\overline{I}_2(b)\}, \tag{67}$$

$$\langle \Delta w_b \rangle = \frac{\eta}{K}\overline{I}_2(b). \tag{68}$$

$\overline{I}$, $\overline{J}$, and $\overline{K}$:

$$\overline{I}_2(b) = \sum_u w_u^0 I_2(b,u) - \sum_d w_d I_2(b,d), \tag{69}$$

$$\overline{J}_2(b;c) = \sum_u w_u^0 J_2(b,u;c) - \sum_d w_d J_2(b,d;c), \tag{70}$$

$$\begin{aligned}\overline{I}_4(b,c) &= \sum_{de} w_d w_e I_4(b,c,d,e) + \sum_{uv} w_u^0 w_v^0 I_4(b,c,u,v)\\ &\quad -2\sum_{du} w_d w_u^0 I_4(b,c,d,u).\end{aligned} \tag{71}$$

$$\begin{aligned}\overline{J}_4(b,c;f) &= \sum_{de} w_d w_e J_4(b,c,d,e;f) + \sum_{uv} w_u^0 w_v^0 J_4(b,c,u,v;f)\\ &\quad -2\sum_{du} w_d w_u^0 J_4(b,c,d,u;f),\end{aligned} \tag{72}$$

$$\begin{aligned}\overline{K}_4(b,c) &= \sum_{de} w_d w_e K_4(b,c,d,e) + \sum_{uv} w_u^0 w_v^0 K_4(b,c,u,v)\\ &\quad -2\sum_{du} w_d w_u^0 K_4(b,c,d,u).\end{aligned} \tag{73}$$

***I*, *J* and *K*:** In each case, only the quantity corresponding to averaging over student basis functions is presented. Each quantity has very similar counterparts in which teacher basis functions are substituted for student basis functions. For instance, $I_2(b,c) = \langle s_b s_c \rangle$ is presented, whereas $I_2(u,v) = \langle t_u t_v \rangle$ and $I_2(b,u) = \langle s_b t_u \rangle$ are omitted:

$$\begin{aligned}I_2(b,c) &= (2l_2\sigma_\xi^2)^{-N/2}\\ &\quad \times \exp\left[\frac{-Q_{bb} - Q_{cc} + (Q_{bb} + Q_{cc} + 2Q_{bc})/2\sigma_B^2 l_2}{2\sigma_B^2}\right],\end{aligned} \tag{74}$$

$$J_2(b,c;d) = \left(\frac{Q_{bd} + Q_{cd}}{2l_2\sigma_B^2}\right) I_2(b,c), \tag{75}$$

$$\begin{aligned}I_4(b,c,d,e) &= (2l_4\sigma_\xi^2)^{-N/2}\exp\left[\frac{-Q_{bb} - Q_{cc} - Q_{dd} - Q_{ee}}{2\sigma_B^2}\right]\\ &\quad \times \exp\big[\big(Q_{bb} + Q_{cc} + Q_{dd} + Q_{ee} + 2(Q_{bc} + Q_{bd} + Q_{be}\\ &\quad + Q_{cd} + Q_{ce} + Q_{de})\big)(4l_4\sigma_B^4)^{-1}\big],\end{aligned} \tag{76}$$

$$J_4(b,c,d,e;f) = \left(\frac{Q_{bf} + Q_{cf} + Q_{df} + Q_{ef}}{2l_4\sigma_B^2}\right) I_4(b,c,d,e), \tag{77}$$

$$K_4(b,c,d,e) = \left(\frac{2Nl_4\sigma_B^4 + Q_{bb} + Q_{cc} + Q_{dd} + Q_{ee}}{4l_4\sigma_B^4} + \frac{2(Q_{bc} + Q_{bd} + Q_{be} + Q_{bf} + Q_{cd} + Q_{ce} + Q_{de})}{4l_4^2\sigma_B^4}\right) \times I_4(b,c,d,e). \tag{78}$$

Other Quantities:

$$l_2 = \frac{2\sigma_\xi^2 + \sigma_B^2}{2\sigma_B^2\sigma_\xi^2}, \tag{79}$$

$$l_4 = \frac{4\sigma_\xi^2 + \sigma_B^2}{2\sigma_B^2\sigma_\xi^2}. \tag{80}$$

ACKNOWLEDGMENTS

J.A.S.F and D.S. would like to thank Ansgar West and David Barber for useful discussions. D.S. would like to thank the Leverhulme Trust for their support (F/250/K).

REFERENCES

[1] M. Casdagli. Nonlinear prediction of chaotic time series. *Physica D* 35:335–356, 1989.
[2] M. Niranjan and F. Fallside. Neural networks and radial basis functions in classifying static speech patterns. *Computer Speech Language* 4:275–289, 1990.
[3] M. K. Musavi, K. H. Chan, D. M. Hummels, K. Kalantri, and W. Ahmed. On the training of radial basis function classifiers. *Neural Networks* 5:595–603, 1992.
[4] E. J. Hartman, J. D. Keeler, and J. M. Kowalski. Layered neural networks with gaussian hidden units as universal approximators. *Neural Comput.* 2:210–215, 1990.
[5] C. M. Bishop. *Neural Networks for Pattern Recognition*. Oxford Univ. Press, Oxford, 1995.
[6] Y. Bar-Shalom and T. E. Fortmann. *Tracking and Data Association*. Academic Press, London, 1988.
[7] J. O. Rawlings. *Applied Regression Analysis*. Wadsworth & Brooks/Cole, Pacific Grove, CA, 1988.
[8] S. Geman, E. Bienenstock, and R. Doursat. Neural networks and the bias/variance dilemma. *Neural Comput.* 4:1–58, 1992.
[9] B. Efron and R. J. Tibshirani. *An Introduction to the Bootstrap*. Chapman and Hall, London, 1993.
[10] M. J. L. Orr. Introduction to radial basis function networks, 1996. Available at http://www.cns.ed.ac.uk/people/mark.html.
[11] D. M. Allen. The relationship between variable selection and data augmentation and a method for prediction. *Technometrics* 16:125–127, 1974.
[12] G. H. Golub, M. Heath, and G. Wahba. Generalised cross-validation as a method for choosing a good ridge parameter. *Technometrics* 21:215–223, 1979.

[13] A. N. Tikhonov and V. Y. Arsenin. *Solutions of Ill-Posed Problems.* Winston, Washington, DC, 1977.

[14] W. H. Press, S. A. Teukolsky, W. T. Vetterling, and B. P. Flannery. *Numerical Recipes in C*, 2nd ed. Cambridge Univ. Press, Cambridge, UK, 1992.

[15] J. Hertz, A. Krogh, and R. G. Palmer. *Introduction to the Theory of Neural Computation. Santa Fe Institute Lecture Notes*, Vol. I. Addison-Wesley, Reading, MA, 1989.

[16] A. E. Hoerl and R. W. Kennard. Ridge regression: Biased estimation for nonorthogonal problems. *Technometrics* 12:55–67, 1970.

[17] C. Bishop. Improving the generalisation properties of radial basis function neural networks. *Neural Comput.* 3:579–588, 1991.

[18] D. J. C. MacKay. Bayesian interpolation. *Neural Comput.* 4:415–447, 1992.

[19] J. E. Moody. The effective number of parameters: An analysis of generalisation and regularisation in nonlinear learning systems. In *Neural Information Processing Systems 4*, (J. E. Moody, S. J. Hanson, and R. P. Lippmann, Eds.), pp. 847–854. Morgan Kaufmann, San Mateo, CA, 1992.

[20] M. J. L. Orr. Local smoothing of radial basis function networks. In *International Symposium on Artificial Neural Networks*, Hsinchu, Taiwan, 1995. Available at http://www.cns.ed.ac.uk/people/mark.html.

[21] A. J. Miller. *Subset Selection in Regression.* Chapman and Hall, London, 1990.

[22] R. A. Horn and C. R. Johnson. *Matrix Analysis.* Cambridge Univ. Press, Cambridge, UK, 1985.

[23] S. Chen, C. F. N. Cowan, and P. M. Grant. Orthogonal least squares learning for radial basis function networks. *IEEE Trans. Neural Networks* 2:302–309, 1991.

[24] M. J. L. Orr. Regularisation in the selection of radial basis function centres. *Neural Comput.* 7:606–623, 1995.

[25] D. S. Broomhead and D. Lowe. Multivariate functional interpolation and adaptive networks. *Complex Systems* 2:321–355, 1988.

[26] T. L. H. Watkin, A. Rau, and M. Biehl. The statistical mechanics of learning a rule. *Rev. Mod. Phys.* 65:499–556, 1993.

[27] J. A. S. Freeman and D. Saad. Learning and generalisation in radial basis function networks. *Neural Comput.* 7:1000–1020, 1995.

[28] J. A. S. Freeman and D. Saad. Radial basis function networks: Generalization in overrealizable and unrealizable scenarios. *Neural Networks* 9:1521–1529, 1996.

[29] S. Holden and M. Niranjan. Average-case learning curves for radial basis function networks. Technical Report CUED/F-INFENG/TR.212, Department of Engineering, University of Cambridge, 1995.

[30] D. Haussler. Generalizing the pac model for neural net and other learning applications. Technical Report UCSC-CRL-89-30, University of California, Santa Cruz, 1989.

[31] S. Holden and P. Rayner. Generalization and PAC learning: some new results for the class of generalized single-layer networks. *IEEE Trans. Neural Networks* 6:368–380, 1995.

[32] F. Girosi and T. Poggio. Networks and the best approximation theory. Technical Report, A.I. Memo 1164, Massachusetts Institute of Technology, 1989.

[33] P. Niyogi and F. Girosi. On the relationship between generalization error, hypothesis complexity and sample complexity for radial basis functions. Technical Report, AI Laboratory, Massachusetts Institute of Technology, 1994.

[34] E. Levin, N. Tishby, and S. A. Solla. A statistical approach to learning and generalisation in layered neural networks. In *Colt '89: 2nd Workshop on Computational Learning Theory*, pp. 245–260, 1989.

[35] T. Rögnvaldsson. On Langevin updating in multilayer perceptrons. *Neural Comput.* 6:916–926, 1994.

[36] G. Radons, H. G. Schuster, and D. Werner. Drift and diffusion in backpropagation learning. In *Parallel Processing in Neural Systems and Computers* (R. Eckmiller *et al.*, Eds.). Elsevier, Amsterdam, 1990.

[37] L. G. Valiant. A theory of the learnable. *Comm. ACM* 27:1134–1142, 1984.

[38] V. N. Vapnik and A. Y. Chervonenkis. On the uniform convergence of relative frequencies of events to their probabilities. *Theory Probab. Appl.* 17:264–280, 1971.

[39] T. Cover. Geometrical and statistical properties of systems of linear inequalities with application to pattern recognition. *IEEE Trans. Electromagnetic Compatibility* 14:326–334, 1965.

[40] S. Holden. On the theory of generalization and self-structuring in linearly weighted connectionist networks. Ph.D. Thesis, University of Cambridge, 1994.

[41] E. Baum and D. Haussler. What size net gives valid generalization? *Neural Comput.* 1:151–160, 1989.

[42] T. Heskes and B. Kappen. Learning processes in neural networks. *Phys. Rev. A* 44:2718–2726, 1991.

[43] T. K. Leen and G. B. Orr. Optimal stochastic search and adaptive momentum. In *Advances in Neural Information Processing Systems* (J. D. Cowan, G. Tesauro, and J. Alspector, Eds.), Vol. 6, pp. 477–484. Morgan Kaufmann, San Mateo, CA, 1994.

[44] S. Amari. Backpropagation and stochastic gradient descent learning. *Neurocomputing* 5:185–196, 1993.

[45] M. Biehl and H. Schwarze. Learning by online gradient descent. *J. Phys. A: Math. Gen.* 28:643, 1995.

[46] D. Saad and S. Solla. Exact solution for on-line learning in multilayer neural networks. *Phys. Rev. Lett.* 74:4337–4340, 1995.

[47] D. Saad and S. Solla. On-line learning in soft committee machines. *Phys. Rev. E* 52:4225–4243, 1995.

[48] P. Riegler and M. Biehl. On-line backpropagation in two-layered neural networks. *J. Phys. A: Math. Gen.* 28:L507–L513, 1995.

[49] M. Copelli and N. Caticha. On-line learning in the committee machine. *J. Phys. A: Math. Gen.* 28:1615–1625, 1995.

[50] J. A. S. Freeman and D. Saad. RBF networks: Noise and regularization in online learning. Unpublished.

[51] J. A. S. Freeman and D. Saad. On-line learning in radial basis function networks. *Neural Computation*, to appear.

[52] J. A. S. Freeman and D. Saad. Dynamics of on-line learning in radial basis function networks. *Phys. Rev. E*, to appear.

[53] D. Barber, D. Saad, and P. Sollich. Finite-size effects in on-line learning of multilayer neural networks. *Europhys. Lett.* 34:151–156, 1996.

Synthesis of Three-Layer Threshold Networks*

Jung Hwan Kim
Center for Advanced Computer Studies
University of Southwestern Louisiana
Lafayette, Louisiana 70504

Sung-Kwon Park
Department of Electronic
Communication Engineering
Hanyang University
Seoul, Korea 133-791

Hyunseo Oh
Mobile Telecommunication Division
Electronics and Telecommunication
Research Institute
Taejon, Korea 305-350

Youngnam Han
Mobile Telecommunication Division
Electronics and Telecommunication
Research Institute
Taejon, Korea 305-350

In this chapter, we propose a learning algorithm, called expand-and-truncate learning (ETL), to synthesize a three-layer threshold network (TLTN) with guaranteed convergence for an arbitrary switching function. To the best of our knowledge, an algorithm to synthesize a threshold network for an arbitrary switching function has not been found yet. The most significant contribution of this chapter is the development of a synthesis algorithm for a three-layer threshold network that guarantees convergence for any switching function, including linearly inseparable functions, and automatically determines a required number of threshold elements in the hidden layer. For example, it turns out that the required number of threshold elements in the hidden layer of a TLTN for an n-bit parity function is equal to n. The threshold element in the proposed TLTN employs only integer weights and integer thresholds. Therefore, this will greatly facilitate the actual hardware implementation of the proposed TLTN through the currently available digital very large scale integration (VLSI) technology. Furthermore, the learning

*This research was partly supported by an Electronics and Telecommunication Research Institute grant and a System Engineering Research Institute grant.

speed of the proposed ETL algorithm is much faster than the backpropagation learning algorithm in a binary field.

I. INTRODUCTION

In 1969, Minsky and Papert [1] demonstrated that two-layer perceptron networks were inadequate for many real-world problems such as the exclusive-OR (XOR) function and parity functions that are basically linearly inseparable functions. Although Minsky and Papert recognized that three-layer threshold networks can possibly solve many real-world problems, they felt it unlikely that a training method could be developed to find three-layer threshold networks that could solve these problems [2]. A learning algorithm *has not been found yet* which can synthesize a three-layer threshold network (TLTN) for any arbitrary switching function, including linearly inseparable functions.

Recently, the backpropagation learning (BPL) algorithm was applied to many binary-to-binary mapping problems. Because the BPL algorithm requires the activation function of a neuron to be differentiable and the activation function of a threshold element is not differentiable, the BPL algorithm can not be used to synthesize a TLTN for an arbitrary switching function. Moreover, because the BPL algorithm searches the solution in continuous space, the BPL algorithm applied to binary-to-binary mapping problems results in long training time and inefficient performance. Typically, the BPL algorithm requires an extremely high number of iterations to obtain even a simple binary-to-binary mapping [3]. Also, in the BPL algorithm, the number of neurons in the hidden layer required to solve a given problem is not known *a priori*. Whereas the number of threshold elements in the input and the output layers is determined by the dimensions of the input and output vectors, respectively, the abilities of three-layer threshold networks depend on the number of threshold elements in the hidden layer. Therefore, one of the most important problems in application of three-layer threshold networks is to determine the necessary number of elements in the hidden layer. It has been widely recognized that the Stone–Weierstrass theorem does not give a practical guideline in determining the required number of neurons [4].

In this chapter, we propose a geometrical learning algorithm, called expand-and-truncate learning (ETL), to synthesize TLTN with guaranteed convergence for any generation of binary-to-binary mapping, including any arbitrary switching function. The threshold element in the proposed TLTN employs only integer weights and integer thresholds. This will greatly facilitate hardware implementation of the proposed TLTN using currently available VLSI technology.

One of significant differences between BPL and the proposed ETL is that ETL finds a set of required separating hyperplanes and determines the integer weights and integer thresholds of threshold elements based on a geometrical analysis of given training inputs. These hyperplanes separate the inputs that have the same desired output from the other input. Hence, training inputs located between two neighboring hyperplanes have the same desired output. BPL, however, indirectly finds the hyperplanes by minimizing the error between the actual output and the desired output with a gradient descent method. ETL always guarantees convergence for any binary-to-binary mapping and automatically determines the required number of threshold elements in the hidden layer, whereas BPL cannot guarantee convergence and cannot determine the required number of hidden neurons. Also, the learning speed of ETL is much faster than BPL for the generation of binary-to-binary mapping.

This chapter is organized as follows. Section II describes the preliminary concepts including the definition of a threshold element. Section III discusses how to find the hidden layer and determine the required number of threshold elements in the hidden layer. Section IV discusses how an output threshold element learns to combine the outputs of hidden threshold elements to produce the desired output. In Section IV, we prove that the output of an output threshold element is a linearly separable function of the outputs of the hidden threshold elements. In Section V, the proposed ETL algorithm is applied to three examples and the results are compared with those of other approaches. Discussion is given in Section VI. Finally, concluding remarks are given in Section VII.

II. PRELIMINARIES

DEFINITION. A threshold element (TE) has k two-valued inputs, $x_1, x_2, \ldots, x_k$, and a single two-valued output, y. Its internal parameters are a threshold T and weights $w_1, w_2, \ldots, w_k$, where each weight w_i is associated with a particular input variable x_i. The values of the threshold T and the weights w_i may be any real number. The input–output relation of the TE is defined as

$$y = \begin{cases} 1, & \text{if } \sum_{i=1}^{n} w_i x_i - T \geqslant 0, \\ 0, & \text{otherwise.} \end{cases}$$

Suppose that a set of n-bit training input vectors is given and a binary desired output is assigned to each training input vector. By considering an n-bit input vector as a vertex of an n-dimensional hypercube, we can analyze the given problem geometrically. Assume that these two classes of training input vectors (i.e., vertices) can be separated by an $(n-1)$-dimensional hyperplane which is expressed as a net function

$$\text{net}(X, T) = w_1x_1 + w_2x_2 + \cdots + w_nx_n - T = 0, \tag{1}$$

where w_is and T are constant. In this case, the set of training inputs is said to be linearly separable (LS), and the $(n-1)$-dimensional hyperplane is the separating hyperplane. The $(n-1)$-dimensional separating hyperplanes can be established by an n-input TE. Notice that the input–output relation of the TE can be related with the corresponding hyperplane of Eq. (1). Actually the TE bears more information than a hyperplane. The TE assigns either 1 or 0 to each side of a hyperplane, whereas a hyperplane merely defines a border between two groups of vertices. To match a separating hyperplane with a TE, we need to properly assign either 1 or 0 to each side of the separating hyperplane.

If a given binary-to-binary mapping function has the property of linear separability, then the function can be realized by only one TE. However, if the given function is not a LS function, then more than one TE is required to realize the function. The main problem is how to decompose the linearly inseparable function into two or more LS functions and how to combine these LS functions [5]. We propose a method to decompose any linearly inseparable function into multiple LS functions based on a geometrical approach and to combine these LS functions to produce desired outputs. Our proposed method demonstrates that any binary-to-binary mapping function can be realized by a three-layer threshold network (TLTN) with one hidden layer.

III. FINDING THE HIDDEN LAYER

In this section, the geometrical learning algorithm called expand-and-truncate learning (ETL) is proposed to decompose any linearly inseparable function into multiple LS functions. For any binary-to-binary mapping, the ETL will determine the required LS functions, each of which is realized by one TE in the hidden layer.

ETL finds a set of separating hyperplanes based on a geometrical analysis of the training inputs, so that inputs located between two neighboring hyperplanes have the same desired outputs. Whereas one separating hyperplane can be established by one TE, the number of required TEs in the hidden layer is equal to the number of required hyperplanes.

We would like to describe the fundamental ideas behind the proposed ETL algorithm by using a simple example. Let us consider, for instance, a function of three input variables $f(x_1, x_2, x_3)$. If inputs are $\{000, 010, 011, 111\}$, then $f(x_1, x_2, x_3)$ produces 1; if inputs are $\{001, 100, 110\}$, then $f(x_1, x_2, x_3)$ produces 0; if input vertices are $\{101\}$, then we do not care what $f(x_1, x_2, x_3)$ produces. In other words, the given example can be considered as having seven training inputs. By considering an n-bit input as a vertex in an n-dimensional hypercube, we can visualize the given problem and thus analyze it easily. A 3-bit input can be considered as a vertex of a unit cube. The vertices whose desired outputs are 1 and 0 are called a *true vertex* and a *false vertex*, respectively.

DEFINITION. A *set of included true vertices* (SITV) is a set of true vertices which can be separated from the rest vertices by a specified hyperplane.

We begin the ETL algorithm by selecting one true vertex. The first selected true vertex is called a core vertex. The first vertex will be selected based on the clustering center found by the modified k-nearest neighboring algorithm [6]. In this example, the first true vertex selected is {000}.

LEMMA 1. *Let a set of n-bit vertices consist of a core true vertex v_c and the vertices v_i for $i = 1, \ldots, n$, whose ith bit is different from that of v_c (i.e., whose Hamming distance from the core vertex is 1). There always exists a hyperplane which separates the true vertices in this set from other training vertices (i.e., false vertices in this set as well as false and true vertices whose Hamming distance from the core vertex is more than 1), and the separating hyperplane is*

$$w_1x_1 + w_2x_2 + \cdots + w_nx_n - T = 0,$$

where

$$w_i = \begin{cases} 1, & \text{if } f(v_i) = 1 \text{ and } v_c^i = 1, \\ -1, & \text{if } f(v_i) = 1 \text{ and } v_c^i = 0, \\ 2, & \text{if } f(v_i) = 0 \text{ and } v_c^i = 1, \\ -2, & \text{if } f(v_i) = 0 \text{ and } v_c^i = 0, \end{cases}$$

$$T = \sum_{k=1}^{n} w_k v_c^k - 1.$$

v_c^i indicates the ith bit of the vertex v_c. The weights (w_is) are assigned such that if $v_c^i = 1$, then $w_i > 0$; else $w_i < 0$.

Proof. The proof can be done by showing that with the weights (w_is) and threshold (T) which are defined in Lemma 1,

$$\sum_{k=1}^{n} w_k v_t^k - T \geqslant 0 \quad \text{for any true vertex } v_t \text{ in the given set,}$$

$$\sum_{k=1}^{n} w_k v_r^k - T < 0 \quad \text{for any other training vertex } v_r.$$

Case 1. The core true vertex v_c:

$$\sum_{k=1}^{n} w_k v_c^k - T \geqslant \sum_{k=1}^{n} w_k v_c^k - \left(\sum_{k=1}^{n} w_k v_c^k - 1\right) \geqslant 0.$$

Case 2. $f(v_i) = 1$ and $v_c^i = 1$ (i.e., $v_i^i = 0$):

$$\sum_{k=1}^{n} w_k v_i^k - T = \sum_{k=1}^{n} w_k v_c^k - w_i v_c^i - T = \sum_{k=1}^{n} w_k v_c^k - 1 - \left(\sum_{k=1}^{n} w_k v_c^k - 1\right) \geqslant 0.$$

Case 3. $f(v_i) = 1$ and $v_c^i = 0$ (i.e., $v_i^i = 1$):

$$\sum_{k=1}^{n} w_k v_i^k - T = \sum_{k=1}^{n} w_k v_c^k + w_i v_i^i - T = \sum_{k=1}^{n} w_k v_c^k - 1 - \left(\sum_{k=1}^{n} w_k v_c^k - 1\right) \geqslant 0.$$

Case 4. $f(v_i) = 0$ and $v_c^i = 1$ (i.e., $v_i^i = 0$):

$$\sum_{k=1}^{n} w_k v_i^k - T = \sum_{k=1}^{n} w_k v_c^k - w_i v_c^i - T = \sum_{k=1}^{n} w_k v_c^k - 2 - \left(\sum_{k=1}^{n} w_k v_c^k - 1\right) < 0.$$

Case 5. $f(v_i) = 0$ and $v_c^i = 0$ (i.e., $v_i^i = 1$):

$$\sum_{k=1}^{n} w_k v_i^k - T = \sum_{k=1}^{n} w_k v_c^k + w_i v_i^i - T = \sum_{k=1}^{n} w_k v_c^k - 2 - \left(\sum_{k=1}^{n} w_k v_c^k - 1\right) < 0.$$

Case 6. Let v_d be a vertex whose Hamming distance from the core vertex is more than 1. The weights are assigned such that if $v_c^i = 1$, then $w_i > 0$; else $w_i < 0$. Therefore,

$$\sum_{k=1}^{n} w_k v_d^k - T \leqslant \sum_{k=1}^{n} w_k v_c^k - 2 - \left(\sum_{k=1}^{n} w_k v_c^k - 1\right) < 0. \qquad \blacksquare$$

COROLLARY 1. *Let n-bit vertices whose Hamming distance from the core true vertex v_c is less than d be true vertices. The following hyperplane always separates the true vertices, whose Hamming distance from the core true vertex v_c is less than d, from the rest vertices,*

$$w_1 x_1 + w_2 x_2 + \cdots + w_n x_n - T = 0,$$

where

$$w_i = \begin{cases} 1, & \text{if } v_c^i = 1, \\ -1, & \text{if } v_c^i = 0, \end{cases}$$

$$T = \sum_{k=1}^{n} w_k v_c^k - (d - 1).$$

Proof. Let v_t be a true vertex whose Hamming distance from the core true vertex v_c is less than d and let v_r be a vertex whose Hamming distance from the core true vertex v_c is equal to or greater than d. The proof can be done by showing that with the given weights (w_is) and threshold (T),

$$\sum_{k=1}^{n} w_k p_t^k - T \geqslant 0 \quad \text{for a vertex } v_t,$$

$$\sum_{k=1}^{n} w_k p_r^k - T < 0 \quad \text{for a vertex } v_r.$$

Let v_z be a vertex whose Hamming distance from the core true vertex v_c is less than z. Whereas the weights are assigned such that if $v_c^i = 1$, then $w_i = 1$, else $w_i = -1$,

$$\sum_{k=1}^{n} w_k v_z^k = \sum_{k=1}^{n} w_k v_c^k - z.$$

The Hamming distance between the vertex v_t and the core vertex v_c is less than d; hence,

$$\sum_{k=1}^{n} w_k v_d^k \geqslant \sum_{k=1}^{n} w_k v_c^k - (d-1) - T = 0.$$

Whereas the Hamming distance between the vertex v_r and the core vertex v_c is equal to or greater than d,

$$\sum_{k=1}^{n} w_k v_d^k < \sum_{k=1}^{n} w_k v_c^k - (d-1) - T = 0. \qquad \blacksquare$$

According to the Lemma 1, the hyperplane $-2x_1 - x_2 - 2x_3 + 1 = 0$ will separate the SITV $\{000, 010\}$ from the other training vertices $\{001, 100, 011, 110, 111\}$. This hyperplane is geometrically expanded to add to the SITV possibly more input vertices which produce the same output, while keeping linear separability. By trying to separate more vertices with one hyperplane, this step may reduce the total number of required hyperplanes, that is, the number of required TEs. To choose an input vertex to be included in the SITV, it is logical to choose the true vertex nearest to the vertices in the SITV in the Euclidean distance sense; there could be more than one. The reason to choose the nearest vertex first is that as the chosen vertex gets closer to the vertices in the SITV, the probability that the vertices in the SITV are separated from the rest vertices becomes higher. The nearest true vertex can be found by considering the Hamming distance (HD) from the vertices in the SITV. In the given example, the nearest true vertex is $\{011\}$. Let us call this vertex a trial vertex. We try to expand the hyperplane to include a trial vertex $\{011\}$ such that the hyperplane separates the true vertices $\{000, 010, 011\}$

from the other training vertices {001, 100, 111}. To determine whether such a hyperplane exists and find the hyperplane, a geometrical approach is proposed next.

LEMMA 2. *Consider a function f: $\{0, 1\}^n \to \{0, 1\}$. The value of f divides the 2^n points of n-tuples (i.e., 2^n vertices of the n-cube) into two classes: those for which the function is 0 and those for which it is 1. A function f is linearly separable if and only if there exists a hypersphere such that all true vertices lie inside or on the hypersphere and, vice versa, all false vertices lie outside.*

Proof. Consider the reference hypersphere (RHS)

$$\left(x_1 - \tfrac{1}{2}\right)^2 + \left(x_2 - \tfrac{1}{2}\right)^2 + \cdots + \left(x_n - \tfrac{1}{2}\right)^2 = n/4. \tag{2}$$

Notice that the center of the RHS is the center of the n-dimensional hyperunit cube and all the 2^n vertices are on the RHS.

Necessity: Suppose that only k vertices lie inside or on the hypersphere,

$$\sum_{i=1}^{n}(x_i - c_i)^2 = r^2,$$

and the other vertices lie outside the hypersphere. This implies that for the k vertices,

$$\sum_{i=1}^{n}(x_i - c_i)^2 \leqslant r^2, \tag{3}$$

and for the other vertices lying outside,

$$\sum_{i=1}^{n}(x_i - c_i)^2 > r^2. \tag{4}$$

Unless $k = 2^n$ or 0, the hypersphere must intersect the RHS. If $k = 2^n$ (or 0), all (or none) are true vertices. In these cases, the function f becomes trivial. For the nontrivial function f, we always find the intersection of the two hyperspheres. Subtracting Eq. (1) from Eq. (2), we obtain

$$\sum_{i=1}^{n}(1 - 2c_i)x_i \leqslant r^2 - \sum_{i=1}^{n} c_i^2. \tag{5}$$

Equation (5) indicates that the k vertices lie on a side of the hyperplane or on the hyperplane,

$$\sum_{i=1}^{n}(1 - 2c_i)x_i = r^i - \sum_{i=1}^{n} c_i^2.$$

Also by substracting Eq. (2) from Eq. (4), we can show that the other vertices lie on the other side of the same hyperplane. Therefore, the necessity of the theorem has been proved.

Sufficiency: Suppose that k true vertices lie on one side of the hyperplane or on the hyperplane,

$$\sum_{i=1}^{n} a_i x_i = T, \tag{6}$$

where a_is and T are arbitrary constants, and the false vertices lie on the other side.

First, suppose that

$$\begin{aligned} \sum_{i=1}^{n} a_i x_i &\leqslant T, \quad \text{for the } k \text{ true vertices,} \\ &> T, \quad \text{for the false vertices.} \end{aligned} \tag{7}$$

Whereas Eq. (2) is true for any vertex, by adding Eq. (2) to Eq. (7) we obtain

$$\sum_{i=1}^{n} \left(a_i x_i + x_i^2 - x_i\right) \leqslant T. \tag{8}$$

Notice that Eq. (8) is true only for the k true vertices. Equation (8) is modified to obtain

$$\sum_{i=1}^{n} \left(x_i - \tfrac{1}{2}(1 - a_i)\right)^2 \leqslant T + \tfrac{1}{4}(1 - a_i)^2. \tag{9}$$

This indicates that these k true vertices are located inside the hyperplane or on the hypersphere. Similarly, it can be shown that the false vertices lie outside this hypersphere.

Second, consider when

$$\sum_{i=1}^{n} a_i x_i > T \tag{10}$$

for the k true vertices. Adding Eq. (2) to Eq. (10), we obtain

$$\sum_{i=1}^{n} \left(x_i - \tfrac{1}{2}(1 - a_i)\right)^2 > T + \tfrac{1}{4}(1 - a_i)^2.$$

This indicates that the k true vertices lie outside the hypersphere and the false vertices lie inside the hyperplane or on the hypersphere. ■

Consider the RHS and an n-dimensional hypersphere which has its center at $(C_1/C_0, C_2/C_0, \ldots, C_n/C_0)$ and its radius r. C_0 is the number of elements in the SITV including the trial vertex. C_i is calculated as

$$C_i = \sum_{k=1}^{C_0} v_k^i,$$

where v_k is an element in the SITV and v_k^i is the ith bit of v_k. Notice that the point $(C_1/C_0, C_2/C_0, \ldots, C_n/C_0)$ in the n-dimensional space represents the center of gravity of all elements in the SITV.

If the SITV can be linearly separated from the other training vertices, there must exist a hypersphere which includes the SITV and excludes the other training vertices, as shown in Lemma 2. To find such a hypersphere, consider the hypersphere whose center is located at the center of gravity of all vertices in the SITV. If this hypersphere separates, this one can do with the minimum radius. On the other hand, a hypersphere with its center away from the center of gravity must have a longer radius to allow inclusion of all the elements in the SITV. This will obviously increase the chance of including the vertex which is not a SITV element. Hence, the hypersphere with its center at the center of gravity is selected and called a separating hypersphere, which is

$$\left(x_1 - \frac{C_1}{C_0}\right)^2 + \left(x_2 - \frac{C_2}{C_0}\right)^2 + \cdots + \left(x_n - \frac{C_n}{C_0}\right)^2 = r^2. \tag{11}$$

When this separating hypersphere intersects the RHS, an $(n-1)$-dimensional hyperplane is found as shown in Lemma 2. By subtracting Eq. (11) from Eq. (2) and multiplying by C_0, the separating hyperplane is

$$(2C_1 - C_0)x_1 + (2C_2 - C_0)x_2 + \cdots + (2C_n - C_0)x_n - T = 0,$$

where T is a constant; that is, if there exists a separating hyperplane, the following should be met:

$$\sum_{i=1}^{n}(2C_i - C_0)v_t^i - T \geqslant 0, \quad \text{for each vertex } v_t \text{ in the SITV,}$$

$$\sum_{i=1}^{n}(2C_i - C_0)v_r^i - T < 0, \quad \text{for each vertex } v_r \text{ from the rest vertices.}$$

Therefore, each vertex v_t in the SITV and each vertex v_r satisfies

$$\sum_{i=1}^{n}(2C_i - C_0)v_t^i > \sum_{i=1}^{n}(2C_i - C_0)v_r^i.$$

Let $t_{\min}$ be the minimum value of $\sum_{i=1}^{n}(2C_i - C_0)v_t^i$ among all vertices in the SITV and let $f_{\max}$ be the maximum of $\sum_{i=1}^{n}(2C_i - C_0)v_r^i$ among the rest vertices.

If $t_{\min} > f_{\max}$, then there exists a separating hyperplane which is

$$(2C_1 - C_0)x_1 + (2C_2 - C_0)x_2 + \cdots + (2C_n - C_0)x_n - T = 0,$$

where $T = \lceil (t_{\min} + f_{\max})/2 \rceil$ and $\lceil x \rceil$ is the smallest integer greater than or equal to x.

If $t_{\min} \leqslant f_{\max}$, then a hyperplane which separates the SITP from the rest vertices does not exist; thus the trial vertex is removed from the SITV. For the given example, $t_{\min} = \text{Minimum}[-3x_1 + x_2 - x_3]$ for the SITV $\{000, 010, 011\}$; thus $t_{\min} = 0$. In addition, $f_{\max} = \text{Maximum}[-3x_1 + x_2 - x_3]$ for vertices $\{001, 100, 110, 111\}$; thus $f_{\max} = -1$. Whereas $t_{\min} > f_{\max}$ and $T = 0$, the hyperplane $-3x_1 + x_2 - x_3 = 0$ separates the vertices in the SITV $\{000, 010, 011\}$ from the rest vertices.

To separate more true vertices with one hyperplane, another true vertex is chosen using the same criteria as earlier and tested to see if the new trial vertex can be added to the SITV. This procedure continues until no more true vertices can be added to the SITV. For the given example, it turns out that the SITV includes only $\{000, 010, 011\}$. If all true vertices of the given problem are included in the SITV, the given problem is a LS function and only one TE is required for the given problem. However, if all true vertices cannot be included in the SITV, more than one TE is required for the given problem. The method to find the other required hyperplanes, that is, the other TEs, is described next.

The first hyperplane could not expand to add more true vertices to the SITV because of the existence of false vertices around the hypersphere; that is, these false vertices block the expansion of the first hypersphere. To train more vertices, the expanded hypersphere must include the false vertices in addition to the true vertices in the SITV of the first hypersphere. For this reason, *false vertices are converted into true vertices, and true vertices which are not in the SITV are converted into false vertices.* Note that the desired output for each vertex is only temporarily converted; that is, the conversion is needed only to obtain the separating hyperplane. Now, expand the first hypersphere to add more true vertices to the SITV until no more true vertices can be added to the SITV. When the expanded hypersphere meets the RHS, the second hyperplane (i.e., TE) is found.

If the SITV includes all true vertices (i.e., the remaining vertices are all false vertices), then the learning is converged; otherwise, the training vertices which are not in the SITV are converted again and the same procedure is repeated. The foregoing procedure can get stuck even when there are more true vertices still left to be included. Consider the case that when ETL tries to add any true vertex to the SITV, no true vertex can be included. Then ETL converts the not-included true vertices and false vertices into the false vertices and true vertices, respectively. When ETL tries to include any true vertex, no true vertex can be included even after conversion. Hence, the procedure is trapped and it cannot proceed further. This situation is due to the limited degrees of freedom in separating hyperplanes using only integer coefficients (i.e., weights). If this situation does not occur until the SITV includes all true vertices, the proposed ETL algorithm is converged by finding all required TEs in the hidden layer.

If the foregoing situation (i.e., no true vertex can be included even after conversion) occurs, ETL declares the vertices in the SITV as "don't care" vertices so that these vertices no longer will be considered in the search for other required TEs. Then ETL continues by selecting a new core vertex based on the clustering center among the remaining true vertices. Until all true vertices are included, ETL proceeds in the same way as explained earlier. Therefore, ETL eventually will be converged, and the convergence of the proposed ETL algorithm is always guaranteed. The selection of the core vertex is not unique in the process of finding separating hyperplanes. Accordingly, the number of separating hyperplanes for a given problem can vary depending upon the selection of the core vertex and the selection of trial vertices. By trying all possible selections, the minimal number of separating hyperplanes can always be found.

Let us discuss the three-bit function example given earlier. Because the SITV of the first TE includes only {000, 010, 011}, the remaining vertices are converted to expand the first hypersphere; that is, the false vertices {001, 100, 110} are converted into true vertices and the remaining true vertex {111} is converted into a false vertex. Choose one true vertex, say {001}, and test if the new vertex can be added to the SITV. It turns out that the SITV includes all currently declared true vertices {000, 010, 011, 001, 100, 110}. Therefore, the algorithm is converged by finding two separating hyperplanes; that is, two required TEs, in the hidden layer.

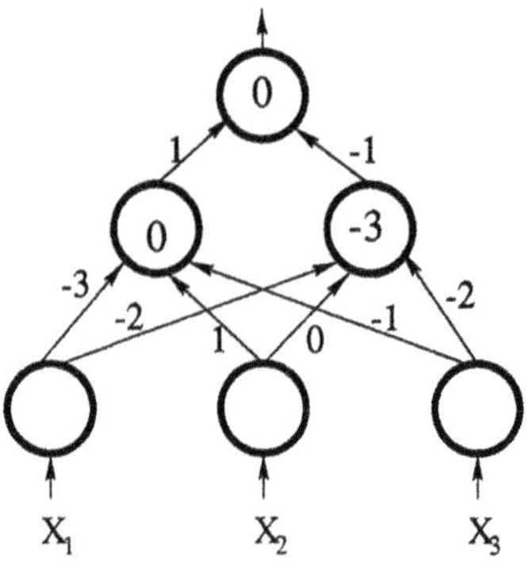

Figure 1 The structure of a three-layer threshold network for the given example. The numbers inside the circles indicate theshold. Reprinted with permission from J. H. Kim and S. K. Park, *IEEE Trans. Neural Networks* 6:237–247, 1995 (©1995 IEEE).

Table I

The Analysis of the Hidden Layer for the Given Example

Input	Desired output	Hidden layer 1st TE	Hidden layer 2nd TE	Output TE
000, 010, 011	1	1	1	1
001, 100, 110	0	0	1	0
111	1	0	0	1

The second required hyperplane is

$$(2C_1 - C_0)x_1 + (2C_2 - C_0)x_2 + \cdots + (2C_n - C_0)x_n - T = 0,$$

where $C_0 = 6$, $C_1 = 2$, $C_2 = 3$, and $C_3 = 2$; that is, $-2x_1 - 2x_3 - T = 0$. Hence, $t_{\min} = -2$ and $f_{\max} = -4$. Whereas $t_{\min} > f_{\max}$ and $T = -3$, the required hyperplane is $-2x_1 - 2x_3 + 3 = 0$. Figure 1 shows the structure of a TLTN for the given example. Table I analyzes the outputs of TEs in the hidden layer for input vertices. In Table I, note that linearly inseparable input vertices are transformed into a linearly separable function at the output of the hidden layer.

IV. LEARNING AN OUTPUT LAYER

After all required hyperplanes (i.e., all required TEs on the hidden layer) are found, one output TE is needed in the output layer to combine the outputs of the TEs in the hidden layer. In this section, we will discuss how to combine the outputs of hidden TEs to produce the desired output.

DEFINITION. A hidden TE is defined as *a converted hidden TE* if the TE was determined based on converted true vertices which were originally given as false vertices and converted false vertices which were originally given as true vertices. If all required hidden TEs are found using only one core vertex, then every even-numbered hidden TE is a converted hidden TE, such as the second TE in Fig. 1.

If ETL finds all required separating hyperplanes using only one core vertex, the weights and threshold of one output TE are set as follows. The weight of the link from the odd-numbered hidden TE to the output TE is set to 1. The weight of the link from the even-numbered TE to the output TE is set to -1, because each even-numbered TE is a converted hidden TE. By setting the threshold of the output TE to 0 (1) if the hidden layer has an even (odd) number of TEs, the three-layer threshold network always produces the correct output to each training input. Figure 1 shows the weights and the threshold of the output TE for the given example, because for the given example ETL finds all required hyperplanes using only one core vertex {000}.

If ETL uses more than one core vertex to find all required hyperplanes, the weights and threshold of the output TE cannot be determined straightforwardly as before. For further discussion, we need the following definition.

DEFINITION. A positive successive product (PSP) function is defined as a Boolean function which is expressed as

$$B(h_1, h_2, \ldots, h_n) = h_1 \circ \big(h_2 \circ \big(\cdots \circ (h_{n-1} \circ h_n)\big) \cdots\big),$$

where the operator $\circ$ is either a logical AND or a logical OR. A PSP function can also be expressed as

$$B(h_1, h_2, \ldots, h_n) = h_1 \circ (B(h_2, h_3, \ldots, h_n)) \quad \text{and} \quad B(h_{n-1}, h_n) = h_{n-1} \circ h_n.$$

An example of a PSP function is

$$B(h_1, h_2, \ldots, h_7) = h_1 + h_2(h_3 + h_4(h_5 + h_6 h_7)).$$

From the definition of a PSP function, it can be easily shown that a PSP function is always a positive unate function [7]. It should be noted that a LS function is always a unate function, but a unate function is not always a LS function.

LEMMA 3. *A PSP function is a LS function.*

Proof. Express a PSP function as

$$B(h_1, h_2, \ldots, h_n) = h_1 \circ (B(h_2, h_3, \ldots, h_n)).$$

Then the function in the innermost nest is

$$B(h_{n-1}, h_n) = h_n - 1 \circ h_n.$$

First, consider the case that the operator $\circ$ is a logical OR. In this case $B(h_{n-1}, h_n) = h_{n-1} + h_n$. Hence, $B(h_{n-1}, h_n)$ is clearly a LS function. Second, consider the case that the operator $\circ$ is a logical AND. Then $B(h_{n-1}, h_n) = h_{n-1} h_n$. Thus, $B(h_{n-1}, h_n)$ is also a LS function. Therefore, the function in the innermost nest, $B(h_{n-1}, h_n)$, is always a LS function. Whereas the function in the innermost nest can be considered as a binary variable to the function in the next nest, the function in the next nest is also a LS function. Continuing this process, a PSP function can be expressed as $B(h_1, h_2, \ldots, h_n) = h_1 \circ z$, where z is a binary variable corresponding to $B(h_2, h_3, \ldots, h_n)$. Therefore, a PSP function is a LS function. ■

Lemma 3 means that a TE can map any PSP function because a PSP function is a LS function. Using a PSP function, an output TE function can be expressed as the function of the outputs of the hidden TEs.

A TE has to assign 1 to the side of a hyperplane having true vertices and 0 to the other side. However, in ETL a converted hidden TE assigns 1 to the side of a hyperplane having original false vertices and 0 to the other side having original true vertices. Therefore, without transforming the outputs of converted hidden TEs, an output TE function cannot be a PSP function of the outputs of hidden TEs. To make a PSP function, the output of each converted hidden TE is complemented and fed into the output TE. Complementing the output of a converted hidden TE is identical to multiplying by (-1) the weight from this TE to the output TE and subtracting this weight from the threshold of the output TE; that is, if the output TE is realized by the weight threshold $\{w_1, w_2, \ldots, w_j, \ldots, w_n; T\}$ whose inputs are $h_1, h_2, \ldots, h'_j, \ldots, h_n$, then the output TE is also realized by weightthreshold $\{w_1, w_2, \ldots, -w_j, \ldots, w_n; T - w_j\}$ whose inputs are $h_1, h_2, \ldots, h_j, \ldots, h_n$.

LEMMA 4. *After the hidden TEs are determined by ETL, an output TE function can always be expressed as a PSP function of the outputs of hidden TEs if the output of each converted hidden TE is complemented.*

Proof. Without loss of generality, let us assume that ETL finds i_1 hidden TEs $\{n_{11}, n_{12}, \ldots, n_{1i_1}\}$ from the first core vertex, i_2 hidden TEs $\{n_{21}, n_{22}, \ldots, n_{2i_2}\}$ from the second core vertex, and i_k hidden TEs $\{n_{k1}, n_{k2}, \ldots, n_{ki_k}\}$ from the kth core vertex. Let h_{ij} be either the output of the n_{ij} TE, if j is an odd number, or the complemented output of the n_{ij} TE, if j is an even number (i.e., n_{ij} is a converted hidden TE). The first TE n_{11} separates only true vertices. Hence, if $h_{11} = 1$, then the output of the output TE should be 1 regardless of the outputs of other hidden TEs. Therefore, the output TE function can be expressed as

$$B(h_{11}, h_{12}, \ldots, h_{ki_k}) = h_{11} + (B(h_{12}, \ldots, h_{ki_k})),$$

which represents a logical OR operation.

The second TE n_{12} separates only false vertices. Thus, the $h_{12} = 1$ side of the hyperplane h_{12} includes true vertices as well as false vertices, and true vertices will be separated by the rest hidden TEs. Note that the true vertices which are not separated by n_{11} are located only in the $h_{12} = 1$ side of the hyperplane h_{12}. Therefore, the output TE function can be expressed as

$$\begin{aligned} B\big(h_{11}, h_{12}, \ldots, h_{ki_k}\big) &= h_{11} + \big(B(h_{12}, \ldots, h_{ki_k})\big) \\ &= h_{11} + h_{12}\big(B(h_{13}, \ldots, h_{ki_k})\big), \end{aligned}$$

which represents a logical AND operation.

Now, we can generalize for a TE n_{ij} as follows. If j is an odd number, then

$$B\big(h_{ij}, h_{ij+1}, \ldots, h_{ki_k}\big) = h_{ij} + B\big(h_{ij+1}, \ldots, h_{ki_k}\big),$$

which represents a logical OR operation. If j is an even number, then

$$B(h_{ij}, h_{ij+1}, \ldots, h_{ki_k}) = h_{ij}\big(B(h_{ij+1}, \ldots, h_{ki_k})\big),$$

which represents a logical AND operation. Therefore, the output TE function can always be expressed as a PSP function

$$B(h_{11}, h_{12}, \ldots, h_{ki_k}) = h_{11} \circ (h_{12} \circ (\cdots \circ (h_{nk_k-1} \circ h_{ki_k})) \cdots),$$

where the operator $\circ$ following h_{ij} indicates a logical OR, if j is an odd number, or indicates a logical AND, if j is an even number. ■

As an example, consider Fig. 2 where only the dashed region requires the desired output as 1. In Fig. 2, h_1 separates 1s; thus the logical OR operation follows. The same thing is true for h_4. Because h_2 separates 0 in Fig. 2, the logical AND operation follows. The same things are true for h_3. Therefore, we can easily express the output as

$$B(h_1, h_2, h_3, h_4, h_5) = h_1 + h_2\big(h_3(h_4 + h_5)\big). \quad (12)$$

Note that Eq. (12) is a PSP function as we proved.

Lemma 4 shows that an output TE function is a LS function of the outputs of hidden TEs. The way to determine the weights of the output TE is to find a PSP function of the outputs of hidden TEs and then transform the PSP function into the net function. For a given PSP function $f(h_1, h_2, \ldots, h_n)$, there exists a systematic method to generate a net function net(H, T). The systematic method is given next.

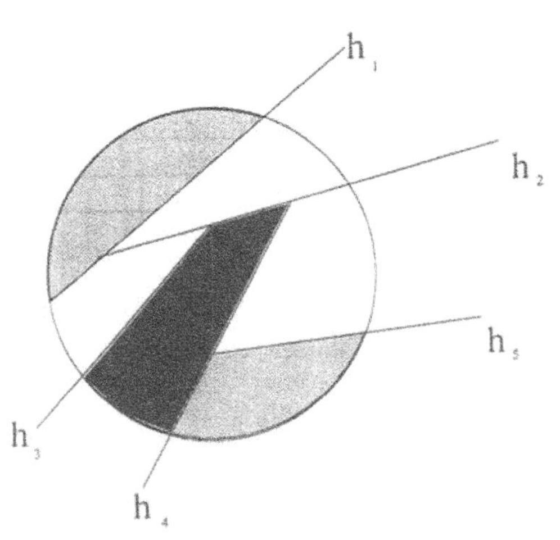

Figure 2 Input vectors are partitioned by ETL. Reprinted with permission from J. H. Kim and S. K. Park, *IEEE Trans. Neural Networks* 6:237–247, 1995 (©1995 IEEE).

The method starts from the innermost net function net_n. The net_n is set to $h_n - 1$ because $\text{net}_n \geqslant 0$ if $h_n = 1$ and $\text{net}_n < 0$ if $h_n = 0$. Let us find the next net function net_{n-1}. If the operation between h_n and h_{n-1} is a logical OR, then $\text{net}_{n-1} = (-\text{Min}[\text{net}_n])h_{n-1} + \text{net}_n$, where $\text{Min}[\text{net}_n]$ is the minimum value of net_n. Because $\text{Min}[\text{net}_n] = \text{Min}[h_n - 1] = -1$, $\text{net}_{n-1} = h_{n-1} + h_n - 1$.

If the operation between h_n and h_{n-1} is a logical AND, then $\text{net}_{n-1} = (\text{Max}[\text{net}_n] + 1)h_{n-1} + \text{net}_n - (\text{Max}[\text{net}_n] + 1)$, where $\text{Max}[\text{net}_n]$ is the maximum value of net_n. Because $\text{Max}[\text{net}_n] = \text{Max}[h_n - 1] = 0$, $\text{net}_{n-1} = h_{n-1} + h_n - 2$.

Continuing this process, the net function $\text{net}(H, T)$ is determined. The weight from the ith hidden TE to the output TE is the coefficient of h_i in the net function, and the threshold of the output TE is the constant in the net function.

As an example, let us consider Eq. (12) to generate a net function from a PSP function:

$$\begin{aligned}
\text{net}_5 &= h_5 - 1, \\
\text{net}_4 &= (-\text{Min}[\text{net}_5])h_4 + \text{net}_5 = h_4 + h_5 - 1, \\
\text{net}_3 &= (\text{Max}[\text{net}_4] + 1)h_3 + \text{net}_4 - (\text{Max}[\text{net}_4] + 1) = 2h_3 + h_4 + h_5 - 3, \\
\text{net}_2 &= (\text{Max}[\text{net}_3] + 1)h_2 + \text{net}_3 - (\text{Max}[\text{net}_3] + 1) \\
&= 2h_2 + 2h_3 + h_4 + h_5 - 5, \\
\text{net}_1 &= (-\text{Min}[\text{net}_2])h_1 + \text{net}_2 = 5h_1 + 2h_2 + 2h_3 + h_4 + h_5 - 5.
\end{aligned}$$

Therefore, the net function for Eq. (12) is expressed as

$$\text{net}(H, T) = 5h_1 + 2h_2 + 2h_3 + h_4 + h_5 - 5.$$

Notice that if $B(x_1, x_2, \ldots, x_n) = 1$, then $\text{net}(X, T) \geqslant 0$; else $\text{net}(X, T) < 0$.

The foregoing discussions are summarized in the following lemma.

LEMMA 5. *For any generation of binary-to-binary mapping, the proposed ETL algorithm always converges, finding the three-layer threshold network whose hidden layer has as many TEs as separating hyperplanes.*

V. EXAMPLES

In this section, we apply the proposed ETL to three kinds of problems and compare the results with other approaches.

A. APPROXIMATION OF A CIRCULAR REGION

Consider the same example problem as considered in [3]. The given problem is to separate a certain circular region in the two-dimensional space which is a square with sides of length 8 with the coordinate origin in the lower left corner,

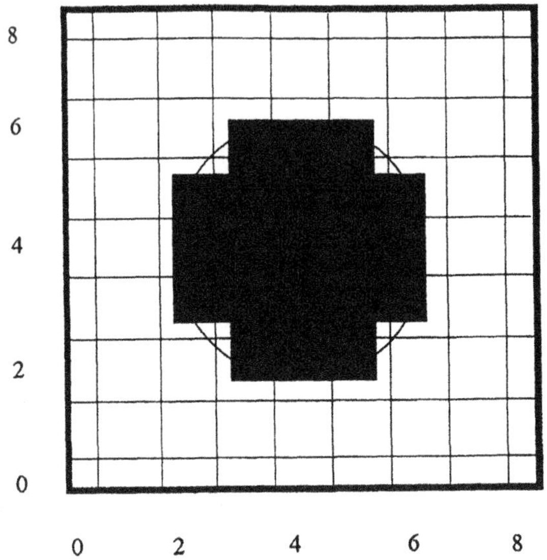

Figure 3 Circular region obtained by 6-bit quantization. Reprinted with permission from J. H. Kim and S. K. Park, *IEEE Trans. Neural Networks* 6:237–247, 1995 (©1995 IEEE).

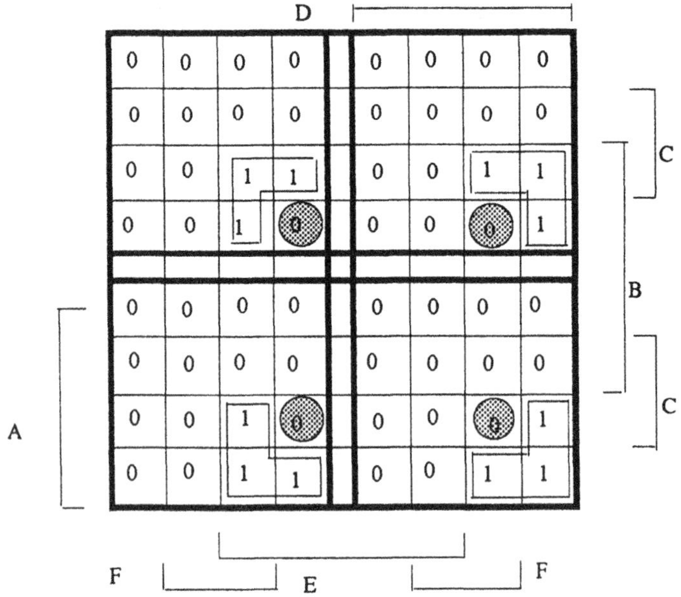

Figure 4 Karnaugh map of the circular region obatined by 6-bit quantization. Reprinted with permission from J. H. Kim and S. K. Park, *IEEE Trans. Neural Networks* 6:237–247, 1995 (©1995 IEEE).

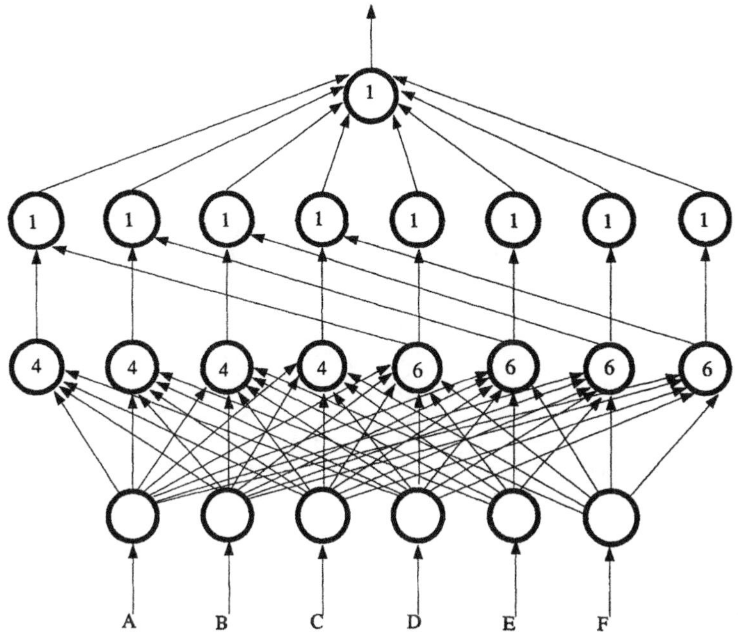

Figure 5 The BLTA solution for the approximation of a circular region using 6-bit quantization. Reprinted with permission from J. H. Kim and S. K. Park, *IEEE Trans. Neural Networks* 6:237–247, 1995 (©1995 IEEE).

as shown in Fig. 3. A circle of diameter 4 is placed within the square, locating the center at (4, 4), and then the space is sampled with 64 grid points located at the center of 64 identical squares covering the large square. Of these points, 42 fall outside of the circle (the desired output 0) and 12 fall within the circle (the desired output 1), as shown in Fig. 3. Figure 4 shows the Karnaugh map of the corresponding function. As shown in Fig. 5, the Booleanlike training algorithm (BLTA) solution to the given problem requires 17 neurons [3]. Our proposed ETL trains the given problem by decomposing into six LS functions with five hidden TEs and combining the outputs of five hidden TEs with one output TE. The structure of a three-layer threshold network is shown in Fig. 6.

High resolution approximation to the circular region can be obtained by increasing the input bit length. We resampled the space containing the circular region, resulting in a 64×64 grid (6 bits $\times$ 6 bits of quantization). The BLTA solution to this problem requires 501 TEs [3]. The proposed ETL algorithm solves the problem, requiring seven hidden TEs and one output TE—far less than the BLTA solution. Table II shows the weights and threshold of seven hidden TEs. Whereas

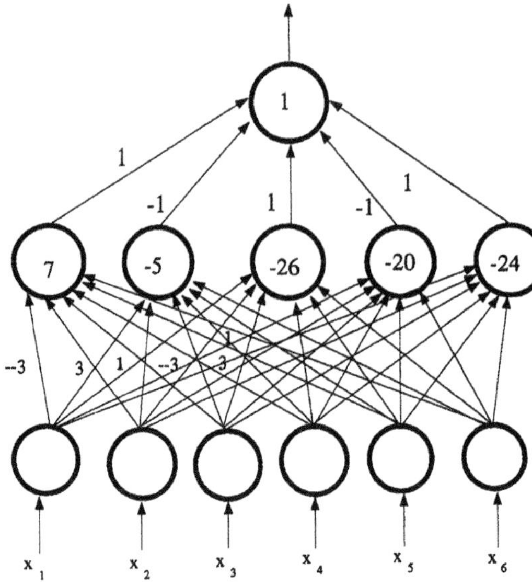

Neuron	Input						
	w_{i1}	w_{i2}	w_{i3}	w_{i4}	w_{i5}	w_{i6}	T_i
1	-3	3	1	-3	3	1	7
2	-29	-3	-1	-3	3	1	-5
3	-29	-3	-1	-3	3	1	-26
4	-19	-13	1	-3	3	1	-20
5	-16	-16	0	0	0	0	-24

Figure 6 The three-layer threshold network for the approximation of a circular region using 6-bit quantization. Reprinted with permission from J. H. Kim and S. K. Park, *IEEE Trans. Neural Networks* 6:237–247, 1995 (©1995 IEEE).

ETL used only one core vertex, the weights and threshold of the output TE are set straightforwardly as discussed earlier.

B. Parity Function

A parity function is an error detection code which is widely used in computers and communications. As an example, consider a 4-bit odd-parity function. The input vertex {1111} is selected as a core true vertex. According to Lemma 3, the

Table II
The Three-Layer Threshold Network for the Approximation of a Circular Region Using 12-Bit Quantization

Hidden TE	Weights and threshold of the hidden TE												
	w_{i1}	w_{i2}	w_{i3}	w_{i4}	w_{i5}	w_{i6}	w_{i7}	w_{i8}	w_{i9}	w_{i10}	w_{i11}	w_{i12}	T_i
1	−13	13	13	13	3	1	−13	13	13	13	3	1	79
2	−14	12	12	12	2	0	−14	14	14	14	2	0	42
3	−13	13	13	13	3	1	13	−13	−13	−13	−3	−1	49
4	−14	12	12	12	2	0	14	−14	−14	−14	−4	−2	14
5	13	−13	−13	−13	−3	−1	−13	13	13	13	3	1	49
6	10	−16	−16	−16	−6	−4	−16	10	10	10	2	0	0
7	13	−13	−13	−13	−3	−1	13	−13	−13	−13	−3	−1	19

hyperplane $x_1+x_2+x_3+x_4 = 4$ separates the core true vertex {1111} from the rest of the vertices. Whereas all neighboring vertices whose Hamming distance (HD) from the core vertex is 1 are false vertices, the hyperplane cannot be expanded to include more vertices. Hence, false vertices and the rest of the true vertices (all true vertices except 1111) are converted into true vertices and false vertices, respectively. According to Corollary 1, the second hyperplane $x_1 + x_2 + x_3 + x_4 = 3$ separates the true vertices whose HD from the core vertex is less than 2, from the rest vertices whose HD from the core vertex is equal to or greater than 2. Repeating the foregoing procedure, the proposed ETL synthesizes a 4-bit odd-parity function, requiring four hidden TEs and one output TE as shown in Fig. 7. The weights of the output TE connecting the odd-numbered TE and even-numbered TE in the hidden layer are set to 1 and −1, respectively, because the even-numbered hidden TEs are the converted hidden TEs. By setting the threshold of the output TE to 0, the three-layer threshold network shown in Fig. 7 always produces the desired output. Table III analyzes the output of TEs for each input. In Table III, note that the linearly inseparable parity function is transformed into four LS functions in the hidden layer.

In general, the three-layer threshold network for an n-bit parity function can be synthesized as follows. The number of required hidden TEs is n, and the threshold of the ith hidden TE is set to $n - (i - 1)$, given that the input vertex {1111} is selected as a core vertex; that is, the ith hyperplane (i.e., the ith TE),

$$x_1 + x_2 + \cdots + x_n = n - (i - 1),$$

separates the vertices whose HD from the core vertex {1111} is less than i from the vertices whose HD from the core vertex is equal to or greater than i. For an n-bit odd-parity function, the weights of the output TE are set such that the

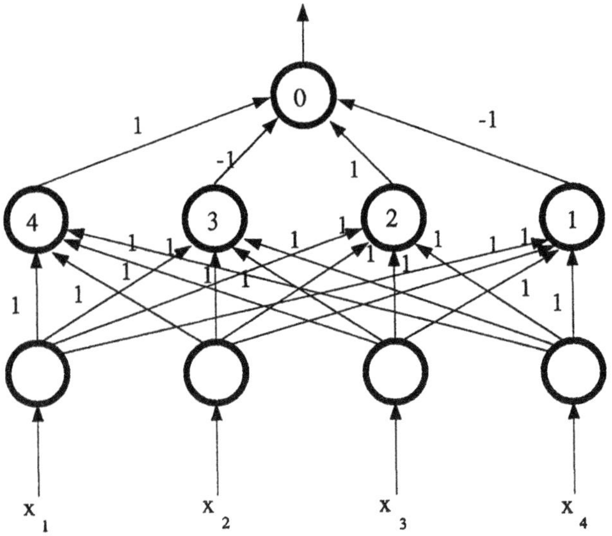

Figure 7 The structure of a three-layer threshold network for a 4-bit odd-parity function. The numbers inside the circles indicate thresholds. Reprinted with permission from J. H. Kim and S. K. Park, *IEEE Trans. Neural Networks* 6:237–247, 1995 (©1995 IEEE).

weight from the ith hidden TE is set to $(-1)^n$ if i is an odd number and are set to $(-1)^{n+1}$ if i is an even number, and the threshold of the output TE is set to 0. For an n-bit even-parity function, the weights of the output TE are set such that the weight from the ith hidden TE is set to $(-1)^n$ if i is an odd number and are set to $(-1)^{n+1}$ if i is an even number, and the threshold is set to 1.

Table III

The Analysis of the Hidden Layer for 4-Bit Odd-Parity Function

Input pattern	Desired output	Hidden layer TE_1	TE_2	TE_3	TE_4	Output TE
1111	1	1	1	1	1	1
0111, 1011, 1101, 1110	0	0	1	1	1	0
0010, 0101, 0110						
0010, 0101, 0110	1	0	0	1	1	1
0001, 0010, 0100, 1000	0	0	0	0	1	0
0000	0	0	0	0	0	0

C. 7-Bit Function

A 7-bit function is randomly generated such that the function produces output 1 for 35 input vertices, and produces output 0 for 35 input vertices. The other input vertices are "don't care" vertices. The proposed ETL is applied to synthesize the 7-bit function whose true and false vertices are given in Table IV. The ETL algorithm synthesizes the function by first selecting the true input vertex {0000000} as a core vertex. As shown in Table IV, the first hyperplane separates 24 true vertices from the rest vertices. To find the second hyperplane, the ETL algorithm converts the remaining 11 true vertices and 35 false vertices into 11 false vertices and 35 true vertices, respectively. After ETL trains 16 converted true vertices which the second hyperplane separates from the remaining vertices, ETL again converts the remaining 19 converted true vertices and 11 converted false vertices into false vertices and true vertices, respectively. Because ETL could not train any true vertex even after conversion, ETL declares the vertices in the SITV (in this case, 40 vertices) as "don't care" vertices and selects another core vertex {1000100} among the remaining 11 true vertices and continues the learning process. It turns out that the given function requires seven hidden TEs. Because the ETL used more than one core vertex, the weights and the threshold of the output TE are determined by using the concept of the PSP function.

Table IV

The Weights and Thresholds of the Hidden Threshold Elements and the Corresponding Input Vertices for the Given 7-Bit Function

Hidden threshold element: Corresponding input vertices	Weights and threshold of the hidden TE							
	w_{i1}	w_{i2}	w_{i3}	w_{i4}	w_{i5}	w_{i6}	w_{i7}	T_i
1st_TE: 0,1,2,4,8,16,32,64, 3,5,9,17,33,65,21,34,36, 40,48,69,81,96,101,66.(true)	−18	6	−24	−24	−24	−6	24	−27
2nd_TE: 6,10,15,18,23,27, 12,14,20,22,24,26,29, 31,44,46.(false)	−34	−6	−22	−18	−18	0	18	−45
3rd_TE: 68,84,100,102,108,116.(true)	10	2	−4	−4	10	−2	−10	15
4th_TE: 78,86,92,94,124,126, 28,30,60,52,62,54,90.(false)	17	3	13	3	15	1	−29	31
5th_TE: 80,72.(true)	24	4	12	8	12	0	−32	26
6th_TE: 56,58,95.(false)	23	5	15	11	11	1	−33	28
7th_TE: 93,117,85,87.(true)	33	5	23	13	13	−1	−23	40

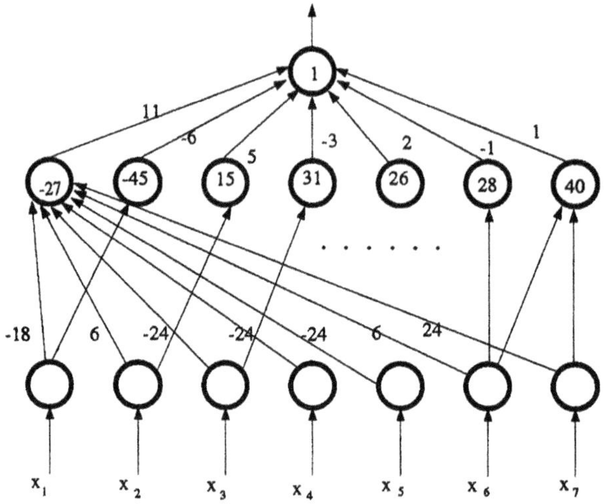

Figure 8 The three-layer threshold network for the given 7-bit function. The weights and thresholds of the hidden threshold elements are given in Table IV. Reprinted with permission from J. H. Kim and S. K. Park, *IEEE Trans. Neural Networks* 6:237–247, 1995 (©1995 IEEE).

Table IV shows the partitioning of input vertices by seven hyperplanes. The final of output TE can be systematically expressed as a PSP function of outputs of seven hidden TEs which is

$$B(h_1, h_2, \ldots, h_7) = h_1 + h_2(h_3 + h_4(h_5 + h_6\, h_7)).$$

Following the systematic method of Section IV, a net function $\text{net}(H, T)$ is

$$\text{net}(H, T) = 11h_1 + 6h_2 + 5h_3 + 3h_4 + 2h_5 + h_6 + h_7 - 11.$$

Because the second, fourth, and sixth hidden TEs are converted hidden TEs, the outputs of these TEs were complemented and fed into the output TE. The structure of the three-layer threshold network for the given example is shown in Fig. 8.

VI. DISCUSSION

The proposed ETL algorithm may serve as a missing link between multilayer perceptrons and backpropagation networks (BPNs). When the perceptron was abandoned, the multilayer perceptron was also abandoned. When BPN later was found to be powerful, its theoretical root was found in the multilayer perceptron. Unfortunately, however, BPN cannot be used for training the multilayer perceptrons with hard-limiter activation functions. Moreover, BPN is not efficient at all for training binary-to-binary mappings. The proposed ETL algorithm is basically for multilayer perceptrons with the geometrical approach.

ETL has another advantage over other learning algorithms. Because ETL uses TEs which employ only integer weights and an integer threshold, the hardware implementation of the proposed three-layer threshold network will be greatly facilitated through currently available digital VLSI technology. Also, the TE employing a hard-limiter activation function is much less costly to simulate in software than the neuron employing a sigmoid activation function [8].

The three-layer threshold network having multiple outputs can be synthesized by applying the proposed ETL to each output independently. Although this approach yields fast execution time by synthesizing multiple outputs in parallel, it does not seem to be a good solution in terms of a required number of TEs. Another approach is to partition the input vertices into groups corresponding to their outputs such as $\{G_1, G_2, \ldots, G_n\}$, because only one output TE will be fired (i.e., 1) for each input vertex. The input vertex in G_1 will be trained in the same manner as the function of single output, regarding the true vertices in the rest groups $\{G_1, G_2, \ldots, G_n\}$ as false vertices. After training G_1, the input vertices in G_1 will be regarded as "don't care" vertices for the training of the rest groups. The training of G_2 will require more separating hyperplanes, in addition to the hyperplanes of G_1 which always separate the input vertices of G_2. The training of G_2 will regard the vertices in the rest groups $\{G_3, G_4, \ldots, G_n\}$ as false vertices. Following this procedure up to the last group G_n, all the required hidden TEs will be found. The ith output TE is connected to the hidden TEs only up to G_i; that is, the ith output TE is connected to the hidden TE of G_k, for $k > i$. Once all the required hidden TEs are found, the weights between the hidden TEs and the output TEs and thresholds of the output TEs will be determined using the concept of the PSP function.

VII. CONCLUSION

In this chapter, the synthesis algorithm called expand-and-truncate learning (ETL) is proposed to synthesize a three-layer threshold network for any binary-to-binary mapping problem. We have shown that for any generation of binary-to-binary mapping, the proposed ETL algorithm always converges and finds the three-layer threshold network by automatically determining a required number of TEs in the hidden layer. The TE employs only integer weights and an integer threshold. Therefore, this will greatly facilitate actual hardware implementation of the proposed three-layer threshold network through available digital VLSI technology.

REFERENCES

[1] M. Minsky and S. Papert. *An Introduction to Computational Geometry*. MIT Press, Cambridge, MA, 1969.
[2] M. Caudill and C. Butler. *Naturally Intelligent Systems*. MIT Press, Cambridge, MA, 1990.
[3] D. L. Gray and A. N. Michel. A training algorithm for binary feedforward neural network. *IEEE Trans. Neural Networks* 3:176–194, 1992.
[4] N. E. Cotter. The Stone–Weierstrass lemma and its application to neural networks. *IEEE Trans. Neural Network* 1:290–295, 1990.
[5] S. Park, J. H. Kim, and H. Chung. A learning algorithm for discrete multilayer perceptron. In *Proceedings of the International Symposium on Circuits and Systems*, Singapore, June 1991.
[6] R. O. Duda and P. E. Hart. *Pattern Classification and Scene Analysis*. Wiley, New York, 1973.
[7] S. Muroga. *Threshold Logic and Its Applications*. Wiley, New York, 1971.
[8] P. L. Bartlett and T. Downs. Using random weights to train multilayer networks of hard-limiting units. *IEEE Trans. Neural Networks* 3:202–210, 1992.

Weight Initialization Techniques

Mikko Lehtokangas
Signal Processing Laboratory
Tempere University of Technology
FIN-33101 Tampere, Finland

Petri Salmela
Signal Processing Laboratory
Tampere University of Technology
FIN-33101 Tampere, Finland

Jukka Saarinen
Signal Processing Laboratory
Tampere University of Technology
FIN-33101 Tampere, Finland

Kimmo Kaski
Laboratory of Computational Engineering
Helsinki University of Technology
FIN-02150 Espoo, Finland

I. INTRODUCTION

Neural networks such as multilayer perceptron network (MLP) are powerful models for solving nonlinear mapping problems. Their weight parameters are usually trained by using an iterative gradient descent-based optimization routine called the backpropagation (BP) algorithm [1]. The training of neural networks can be viewed as a nonlinear optimization problem in which the goal is to find a set of network weights that minimize the cost function. The cost function, which is usually a function of the network mapping errors, describes a surface in the weight space, often referred to as the error surface. Training algorithms can be viewed as methods for searching the minimum of this surface. The complexity of the search is governed by the nature of the surface. For example, error surfaces for MLPs can have many flat regions where learning is slow and long narrow "canyons" that are flat in one direction and steep in the other directions. It has been shown [2, 3] that the problem of mapping a set of training examples onto a neural network is NP-complete. Further, it has been shown [4] that the asymptotic rate of convergence of the BP algorithm is very slow, at best on the order of $1/t$. Thus, in realistic cases, the large number of very flat and very steep parts of the surface makes it difficult to search the surface efficiently using the BP algorithm. In addition, the cost function is characterized by a large number of local minima with values in the vicinity of the best or global minimum.

Because of the complexity of search space, the main drawbacks of backpropagation training are that it is slow and is unreliable in convergence. The major reasons for this poor training performance are *the problem of determining optimal steps*, that is, size and direction in the weight space in consecutive iterations, and *the problem of network size* and *weight initialization*. It is apparent that the training speed and convergence can be improved by solving any of these problems.

To tackle the slowness of the learning process, most research has focused on improving the optimization procedure. That is, many studies have concentrated on optimizing the step size. This has resulted in many improved variations of the standard BP. The proposed methods include for instance the addition of a momentum term [1], an adaptive learning rate [5], and second-order algorithms [6–8]. As a consequence some of these BP variations have been shown to give quite impressive results in terms of the rate of convergence [8].

To solve the problem of network size, various strategies have been used. One of the first approaches was to start with a large initial network configuration, and then either prune the network once it has been trained [9, 10] or include complexity terms in the objective function to force as many weights as possible to zero [11–13]. Although pruning does not always improve the generalization capability of a network [14] and the addition of terms to the error function sometimes hinders the learning process [13], these techniques usually give satisfactory results. Alternatively, another strategy for minimal network construction has been to add/remove units sequentially during training [15–17].

However, the improved training algorithms and optimal network size do not guarantee adequate convergence because of the initialization problem. When the initial weight values are poor the training speed is bound to get slower even if improved algorithms are used. In the worst case the network may converge to a poor local optimum. Therefore, it is also important to improve the weight initialization strategy as well as the training algorithms and network size optimization. Very good and fast results can obviously be obtained when a starting point of the optimization process is very close to an optimal solution.

The initialization of the network with small random weights is a commonly employed rule. The motivation for this is that large absolute values of weights cause hidden nodes to be highly active or inactive for all training samples, and thus insensitive to the training process. Randomness is introduced to prevent nodes from adopting similar functions. A common way to handle the initialization problem is to restart the training with new random initial values if the previous ones did not lead to adequate convergence [18]. In many problems this approach can be too extensive to be an adequate strategy for practical usage because the time required for training can increase to an unacceptable length.

A simple and obvious nonrandom initialization strategy is to linearize the network and then calculate the initial weights by using linear regression. For example, in the case of MLP the network can be linearized by replacing the sigmoidal activation functions with their first-order Taylor approximations [19]. The advantage of this approach is that if the problem is more or less linear then most of the training is done before the iterative weight adjusting is even started. However, if the problem is highly nonlinear this method does not perform any better than random initialization. A wide variety of other kinds of initialization procedures have been studied [20–30].

In the following sections we will illustrate the usage of stepwise regression for weight initialization purposes. This is an attractive approach because it is a very general scheme and can be used for initialization of different network architectures. Here we shall consider initialization of multilayer perceptron networks and radial basis function networks.

II. FEEDFORWARD NEURAL NETWORK MODELS

In this section the specific network structures we use are briefly explained so that the usage of the initialization methods can be clearly understood.

A. Multilayer Perceptron Networks

In general MLPs can have several hidden layers. However, for the sake of simplicity we will consider here MLPs with one hidden layer. The activation function in the hidden layer units was chosen to be the tanh function, and the output units were taken to be linear. The equation for this kind of a network structure can be written as

$$o_k = v_{0k} + \sum_{j=1}^{q} v_{jk} \tanh\left(w_{0j} + \sum_{i=1}^{p} w_{ij} x_i \right), \tag{1}$$

in which o_k is the output of the kth output unit, v_{jk} and w_{ij} are the network weights, p is the number of network inputs, and q is the number of hidden units. The training of the network is done in a supervised manner such that for inputs x_i the network outputs o_k are forced to approach the desired outputs d_k. Hence, in training the weights are adjusted in such a way that the difference between the obtained outputs o_k and the desired outputs d_k is minimized. Usually this is done by minimizing the cost function

$$E = \sum_{k=1}^{r} \sum_{e=1}^{n} (d_{e,k} - o_{e,k})^2, \tag{2}$$

in which the parameter r is the number of network outputs and n is the number of training examples. The minimization of the cost function is usually done by gradient descent methods, which have been extensively studied in the field of optimization theory [31]. In the experiments presented in the following sections we used the Rprop training routine [32, 33].

B. Radial Basis Function Networks

The structure of radial basis function networks (RBFNs) is similar to the one hidden layer MLP discussed in preceding text. The main difference is that the units in the hidden layer have a different kind of activation function. For this some radially symmetric functions, such as the Gaussian function, are used. Here we will use the Gaussian functions in which case the formula for the RBFN can be written as

$$o_k = v_{0k} + \sum_{j=1}^{q} v_{jk} \exp\left(- \sum_{i=1}^{p} (x_i - c_{ij})^2 / w_j^2 \right), \tag{3}$$

in which o_k is the output of the kth output unit, v_{jk} are the network weights, w_j are parameters for adjusting the width of the Gaussians, c_j define the location of the Gaussians in the input space, p is the number of network inputs, and q is the number of hidden units. As in the case of MLP the training of RBFNs can be done in a fully supervised manner. Thus Eq. (2) can be used as a cost function and its minimization can be done with gradient descent-based optimization routines. However, it has been suggested that some partially heuristic methods may be more efficient in practice [34, 35]. Because the training of RBFNs seem to be still quite problematic, we will concentrate here solely on estimating initial values for the parameters. We will call this initial training because the network performance after the initialization procedures is already quite good.

III. STEPWISE REGRESSION FOR WEIGHT INITIALIZATION

To begin with we discuss the basics of linear regression. In that a certain response Y is expressed in terms of available explanatory variables $X_1, X_2, \ldots, X_Q$, these variables form a complete set from which the regression equation is chosen.

Usually there are two opposing criteria in the selection of a resultant equation. First, to make the equation useful we would like our model to include as many Xs as possible so that reliable fitted values can be determined. Second, because of the costs involved in obtaining information on a large number of Xs and subsequently monitoring them, we would like the equation to include as few Xs as possible. The compromise between these two criteria is what is usually called selecting the best regression equation [36, 37]. To do this there are at least two basic approaches, namely, the *backward elimination* and the *forward selection* methods.

In backward elimination a regression equation containing all variables is computed. Then the partial F-test value is calculated for every variable, each treated as though it were the last variable to enter the regression equation. The lowest partial F-test value is compared with a preselected significance level and if it is below the significance level, then the corresponding variable is removed from consideration. Then the regression equation is recomputed, partial F-test values are calculated for the remaining variables as previously, and elimination is continued. If at some point the lowest F value is above the significance level, then the current regression equation is adopted. To summarize, in backward elimination the variables are pruned out of the initial regression equation one by one until a certain criterion is met.

The forward selection method takes a completely opposite approach. There the starting point is the minimal regression equation to which new variables are inserted one at a time until the regression equation is satisfactory. The order of insertion can be determined, for example, by using correlation coefficients as a measure of the importance for variables not yet in the equation. There are several different procedures for forward selection. The one utilized here is roughly as follows. First we select the X most correlated with Y and then calculate the relevant regression equation. Then the residuals from the regression are considered as response values, and the next selection (of the remaining Xs) is the X most correlated with the residuals. This process is continued to any desired stage.

It is apparent that the foregoing regressor selection methods cannot be used for training neural networks. However, as will be shown later they may be useful in weight initialization. To understand how this can be done we must first acknowledge that neural networks are also regression equations in which the hidden units are the regressors. Further, the weight initialization can be interpreted as hidden unit initialization. Thus in practice we can initialize Q hidden units with random values and then select the q most promising ones with some selection procedure. Now the problem is how to select the well initialized hidden units. One solution is to use the regressor selection procedures which are directly applicable to this problem. Whereas none of the regressor selection procedures is fully optimal and whereas the actual training will be performed after initialization, it is recommended to use the simplest selection procedures to minimize the computational load. This means that in practice we can restrict ourselves to use of forward selection methods. In the following sections several practical regressor selection methods are presented for neural networks initialization.

IV. INITIALIZATION OF MULTILAYER PERCEPTRON NETWORKS

The training of a multilayer perceptron network starts by giving initial values to the weights. Commonly small random values are used for initialization. Then weight adjustment is carried out with some gradient descent-based optimization routine. Regardless of the many sophisticated training algorithms the initial values given to the weights can dramatically affect the learning behavior. If the initial weight values happen to be poor, it may take a long time to obtain adequate convergence; in the worst case the network may get stuck to a poor local minimum. For this reason, several initialization methods have been proposed and studied [21, 22, 24–26, 29, 38, 39]. In the following the *orthogonal least squares* (OLS) and *maximum covariance* (MC) initialization methods are presented. The idea in both of these methods is to use candidate initial values for the hidden units and then use some criterion to select the most promising initial values.

A. Orthogonal Least Squares Method

Originally the OLS method was used for regressor selection in training RBFNs [40]. However, if one examines Eqs. (1) and (3), it is apparent that both MLP and RBFN can be regarded as regression models where each of the hidden units represents one regressor. Therefore, in the MLP weight initialization the problem is to choose those regressors that have the best initial values. Naturally, the selection of the best regressors for an MLP can also be done by applying the OLS procedure. A practical OLS initialization algorithm can be described as follows:

1. Create Q candidate hidden units ($Q \gg q$, with q describing the desired number of hidden units) by initializing the weights feeding them with random values. In this study the relation $Q = 10q$ was used. In addition uniformly distributed random numbers from the interval $[-4; 4]$ were used to initialize candidate units.
2. Select the q best initialized hidden units by using the OLS procedure. The procedure for the single-output case is presented in [38, 40] and for the multi-output case in [41].
3. Optimize the weights feeding the output unit(s) with linear regression. Let the obtained least squares optimal regression coefficients be the initial values for the weights feeding the output unit(s).

B. Maximum Covariance Method

The MC initialization scheme [39] is based on an approach similar to the OLS initialization scheme. First a large number of candidate hidden units are created by initializing their weights with random values. Then the desired number of hidden units is selected among the candidates by using the MC criterion which is significantly simpler than the OLS criterion. Finally, weights feeding the output units are calculated with linear regression. A practical MC initialization algorithm can be described as follows:

1. This step is identical with the first step of the OLS initialization.
2. Do not connect the candidate units to the output units yet. At this time the only parameters feeding the output units are the bias weights. Set the values of the bias weights to be such that the network outputs are the means of the desired output sequences.
3. Calculate the sum of absolute covariances for each of the candidate units from the equation

$$C_j = \frac{1}{n} \sum_{k=1}^{r} \left| \sum_{e=1}^{n} (y_{j,e} - \bar{y}_j)(\varepsilon_{k,e} - \bar{\varepsilon}_k) \right|, \quad j = 1, \ldots, Q, \tag{4}$$

in which $y_{j,e}$ is the output of the jth hidden unit for the eth example. The parameter $\bar{y}_j$ is the mean of the jth hidden unit outputs, $\varepsilon_{k,e}$ is the output error, and $\bar{\varepsilon}_k$ is the mean of the output errors at the kth output unit.

4. Find the maximum covariance C_j and connect the corresponding hidden unit to the output units. Decrement the number of candidate hidden units Q by 1.
5. Optimize the currently existing weights that feed the output units with linear regression. Note that the number of these weights is increased by 1 for each output every time a new candidate unit is connected to the output units, and because of the optimization the output errors change each time.
6. If q candidate units have been connected to the output units, then quit the initialization phase. Otherwise repeat steps 3–5 for the remaining candidate units.

C. Benchmark Experiments

Next a comparison between the orthogonal least squares, maximum covariance, and random initialization methods is presented. In random initialization the q hidden units were initialized with uniformly distributed random numbers in the interval $[-0.5; 0.5]$. The training was done in two phases. In the first phase the network weights were initialized; in the second phase weight adjustments were done with the Rprop algorithm [32]. Two benchmark problems are considered, namely, the 4 × 4 chessboard problem explained in Appendix I and the two-spiral problem explained in Appendix II.

The effect of the initialization methods was studied in terms of visually representative training curves. In other words the misclassification percentage error metric was plotted as a function of the training epochs. After an epoch each of the training patterns was applied once to the network. The misclassification percentage error metric indicates the proportion of incorrectly classified output items. The 40-20-40 scheme is used which means that if the total range of the desired outputs is 0.0–1.0, then any value below 0.4 is considered to be 0 ("off") and any value above 0.6 is considered to be 1 ("on"). Values between 0.4 and 0.6 are automatically classified as incorrect.

Because all the tested methods have randomness, the training procedures were repeated 100 times by using a different set of random numbers each time. The plotted training curves are the averages of these 100 repetitions. With the average curve the upper and lower deviation curves also were plotted in the same picture to indicate the variations between the worst and the best training runs. These deviation curves were calculated as averages of deviations from the average curve.

The training curves for the 4 × 4 chessboard problem are depicted in Figs. 1–3, and the computational costs of the initialization methods are shown in Table I. In this problem the MC and OLS initializations lead to significantly better convergence than the random initialization. For given training epochs the average training curves of the MC and OLS methods reach about an 80% lower error level

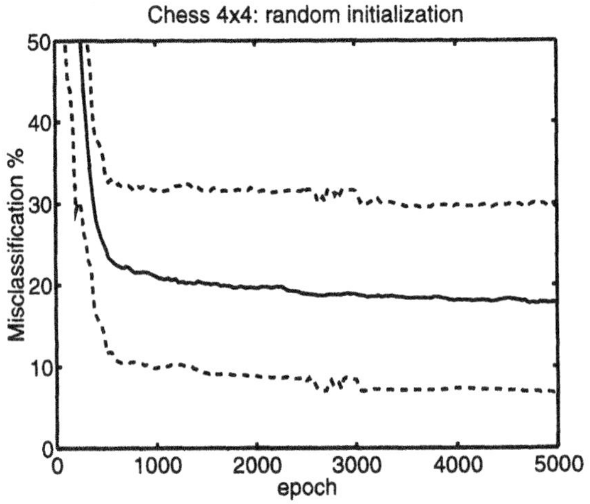

Figure 1 Training curves for the chess 4 × 4 problem with random initialization. The solid line is the average curve and the dashed lines are upper and lower deviations, respectively.

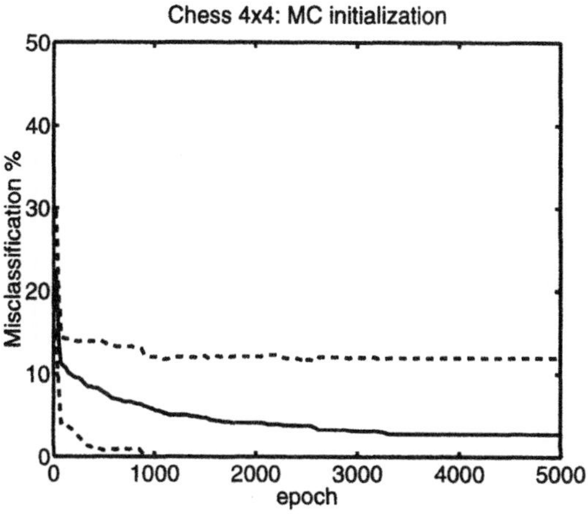

Figure 2 Training curves for the chess 4 × 4 problem with MC initialization. The solid line is the average curve and the dashed lines are upper and lower deviations, respectively.

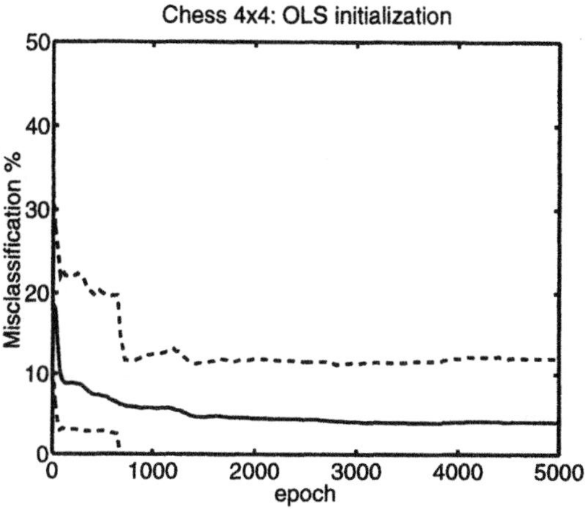

Figure 3 Training curves for the chess 4 × 4 problem with OLS initialization. The solid line is the average curve and the dashed lines are upper and lower deviations, respectively.

Table I

Computational Costs of the Initialization Methods for the 4 × 4 Chessboard Problem

Method	n	Q	q	Cost (epochs)
Random	16	—	6	~0
MC	16	60	6	20
OLS	16	60	6	70

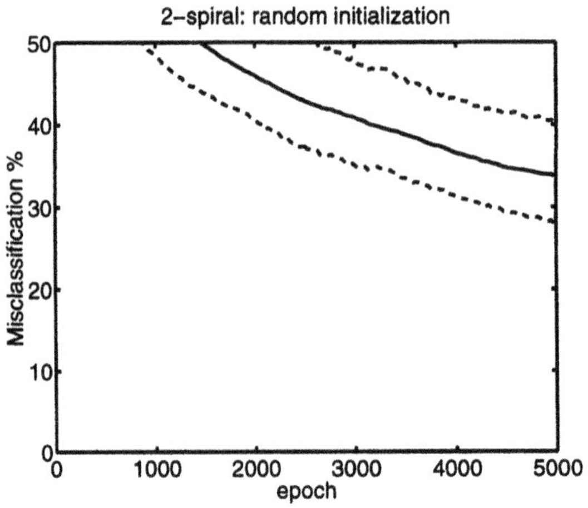

Figure 4 Training curves for the two-spiral problem with random initialization. The solid line is the average curve and the dashed lines are upper and lower deviations, respectively.

than with random initialization. Also the lower deviation curves of the MC and OLS methods show that the all-correct classification result can be obtained with these initialization methods. The training curves obtained with the MC initialization method are slightly better than those obtained with the OLS method. When

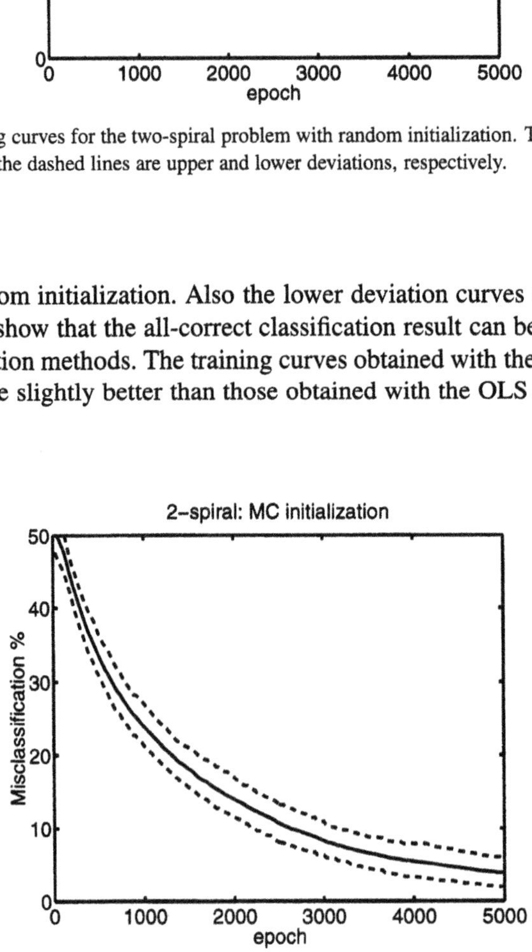

Figure 5 Training curves for the two-spiral problem with MC initialization. The solid line is the average curve and the dashed lines are upper and lower deviations, respectively.

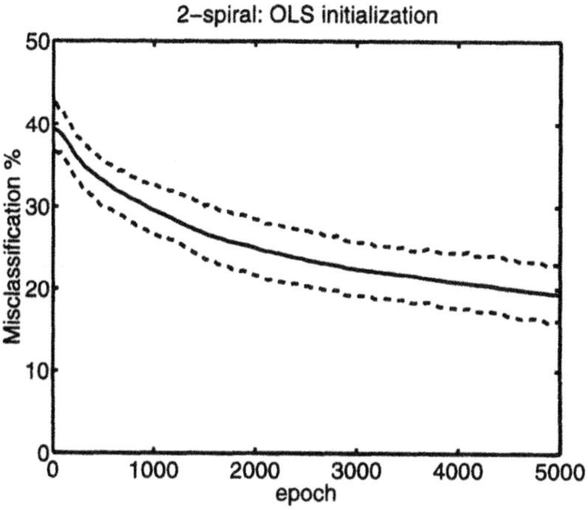

Figure 6 Training curves for the two-spiral problem with OLS initialization. The solid line is the average curve and the dashed lines are upper and lower deviations, respectively.

comparing in terms of computational costs, it is apparent that the MC and OLS methods both have acceptable low costs. Whereas the MC initialization corresponds only to 20 epochs of training with Rprop, it seems to be a better method than the OLS method in this problem.

The training curves for the two-spiral problem are depicted in Figs. 4–6, and the computational costs of the initialization methods are shown in Table II. Also in this problem both the MC and OLS methods improve the convergence significantly compared with the random initialization. However, now the MC method is superior to the OLS method when both the convergence and computational costs are compared. The large computational cost of the OLS method is due to the orthogonal decomposition, which becomes more and more costly as the size of the modeled problem increases.

Table II

Computational Costs of the Initialization Methods for the Two-Spiral Problem

Method	n	Q	q	Cost (epochs)
Random	194	—	42	~ 0
MC	194	420	42	180
OLS	194	420	42	2100

V. INITIAL TRAINING FOR RADIAL BASIS FUNCTION NETWORKS

A. STEPWISE HIDDEN NODE SELECTION

One approach to train the RBFNs is to add hidden units to the network one at a time during the training process. A well known example of such an algorithm is the OLS procedure [40], which is in fact one way to do stepwise regression. Even though the OLS procedure has been found to be an efficient method, its main drawback is the relatively large computational cost. Here two fast stepwise regression methods are applied for hidden unit selection as initial training for RBFNs, namely, the *maximum correlation* (MCR) method and *local error maximization* (LEM) method [42]. In both methods the practical algorithms are the same except for the criterion function used for the selection of the hidden units. The MCR algorithm can be described by the following steps:

1. Create Q candidate hidden units ($Q \gg q$, where the q is the desired number of hidden units). In this study Gaussian activation functions were used in the hidden units. Therefore, candidate creation means that values for the reference vectors and width parameters of the Gaussian hidden units must be determined with some algorithm. Here the K-means clustering algorithm [35] was used to calculate the reference vectors. In the K-means algorithm the input space is divided into K clusters, and the centers of these clusters are set to be the reference vectors of the candidate units. The width parameters were all set to be equal according to the heuristic equation

$$w_j^2 = D^2/(q+1), \qquad j = 1, \ldots, Q, \tag{5}$$

in which D is the maximum Euclidean distance between any two input patterns (in the training set) of the given problem.

2. Do not connect the candidate units to the output unit yet. The only parameter feeding the output unit at this time is the bias weight. Set the bias weight value to be such that the network output is the mean of the desired output sequence.

3. Calculate the correlation for each of the candidate units from the equation

$$C_j = \frac{\operatorname{cov}(y_{j,e}, \varepsilon_e)}{\sigma(y_{j,e})\sigma(\varepsilon_e)}, \qquad j = 1, \ldots, Q, \tag{6}$$

in which $\operatorname{cov}(y_{j,e}, \varepsilon_e)$ is the covariance between the jth hidden unit outputs and the network output error, $\sigma(y_{j,e})$ is the standard deviation of the jth hidden unit outputs, and $\sigma(\varepsilon_e)$ is the standard deviation of the network output errors.

4. Find the maximum absolute correlation $|C_j|$ and connect the corresponding hidden unit to the output unit. Decrement the number of candidate hidden units Q by 1.

5. Optimize with linear regression the currently existing weights that feed the output unit. Note that the number of these weights is increased by 1 every time a new candidate unit is connected to the output unit, and because of the optimization the output error changes each time.

6. If q candidate units have been connected to the output unit, then quit the hidden unit selection procedure. Otherwise repeat steps 3–5 for the remaining candidate units.

In the foregoing MCR method the aim is to maximize the correlation cost function. The LEM method has exactly the same steps as the MCR except that the cost function now is

$$E_j = \left(\sum_{e=1}^{n} y_{j,e}|\varepsilon_e|\right) \Big/ \left(\sum_{e=1}^{n} y_{j,e}\right), \tag{7}$$

in which n is the number of training samples. Thus in the LEM method the new hidden unit is selected from the input space area whose weighted average absolute error is the largest. Although the presented criteria Eqs. (6) and (7) are for initial training of single-output RBFNs, they can be directly expanded to the multi-output case.

B. Benchmark Experiments

Next the performances of the OLS, MCR, and LEM methods are tested with two benchmark problems. In the first problem the task is to train the RBFN with GaAs metal-semiconductor field-effect transistor (MESFET) characteristics. More details about this problem are described in Appendix III. In the second problem the network is trained to classify credit card data; see Appendix IV for details. In the MESFET problem the training performance is studied in terms of the normalized mean square error (NMSE)

$$\text{NMSE} = \frac{1}{n\sigma_d^2} \sum_{e=1}^{n} \varepsilon_e^2, \tag{8}$$

in which σ_d is the standard deviation of the desired output sequence. In the credit card problem the misclassification percentage metric is used in which the 40-20-40 scheme is utilized to classify the outputs. In the candidate hidden units creation heuristic K-means clustering was used. Therefore the training was repeated 50 times for each scheme and the presented training curves are the averages of

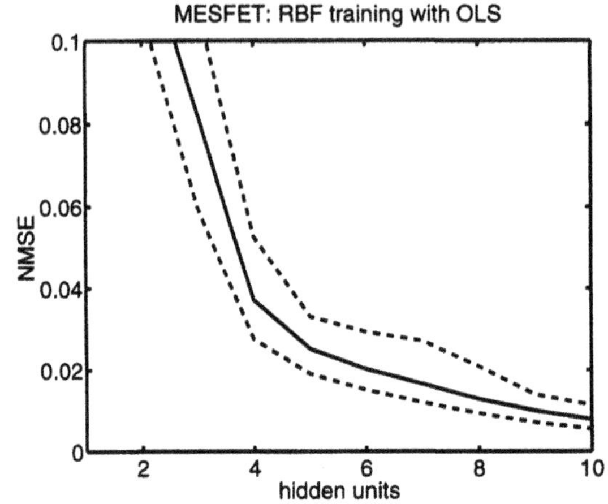

Figure 7 Training curves for the MESFET problem with OLS training. The solid line is the average curve and the dashed lines are upper and lower deviations, respectively.

50 repetitions. As in Section IV we have calculated the upper and lower deviation curves and present them accordingly.

The training curves for the MESFET problem are depicted in Figs. 7–9. In this problem the MCR method gives the worst results, and the results given by

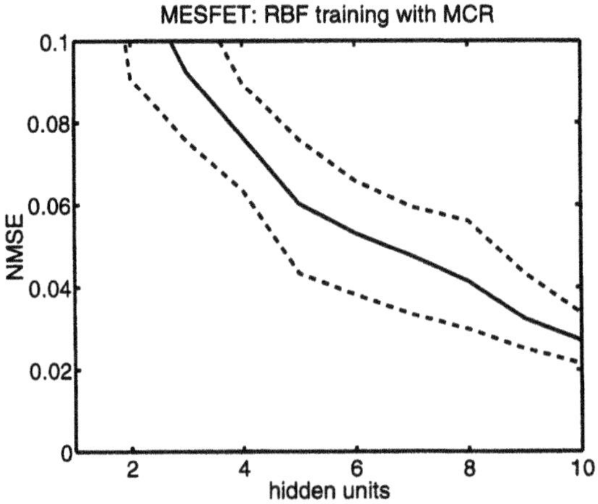

Figure 8 Training curves for the MESFET problem with MCR training. The solid line is the average curve and the dashed lines are upper and lower deviations, respectively.

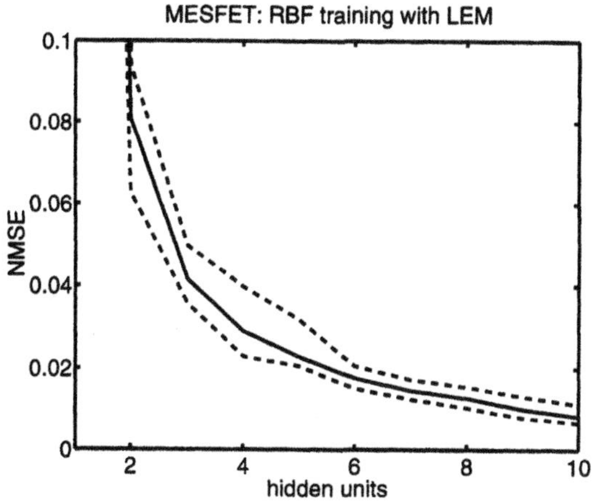

Figure 9 Training curves for the MESFET problem with LEM training. The solid line is the average curve and the dashed lines are upper and lower deviations, respectively.

the LEM and OLS methods are virtually the same. For the credit card problem the training curves are depicted in Figs. 10–12. In this case the LEM method gives slightly worse results than the MCR and OLS methods. The MCR and OLS methods give practically the same performance.

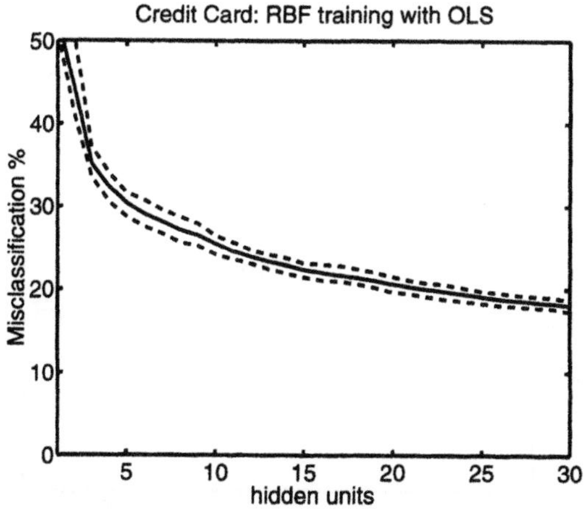

Figure 10 Training curves for the credit card problem with OLS training. The solid line is the average curve and the dashed lines are upper and lower deviations, respectively.

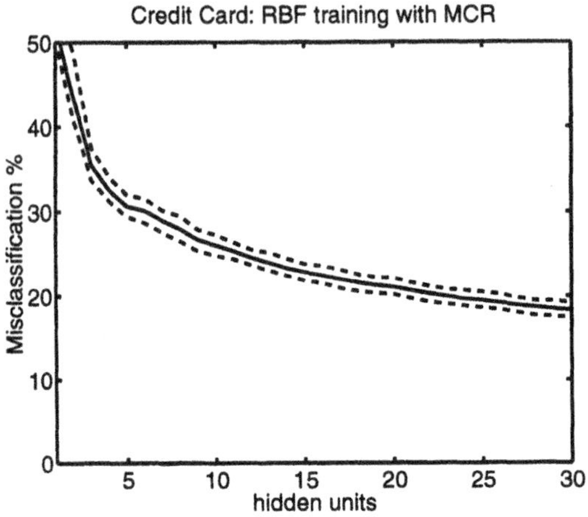

Figure 11 Training curves for the credit card problem with MCR training. The solid line is the average curve and the dashed lines are upper and lower deviations, respectively.

The foregoing training results show that the proposed methods can reach the same level of training performance as the OLS method. However in terms of computation speed of training it can be seen in Table III that the MCR and LEM methods are significantly faster. The speed-up values were calculated from the floating point operations needed for the hidden unit selection procedures.

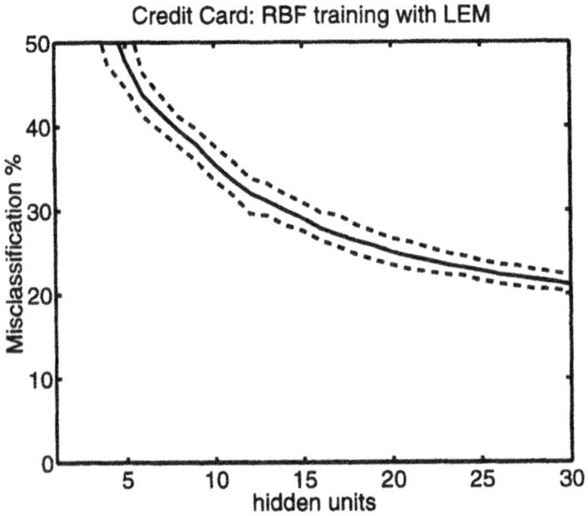

Figure 12 Training curves for the credit card problem with LEM training. The solid line is the average curve and the dashed lines are upper and lower deviations, respectively.

Table III

Speed-up Values for the MCR and LEM Methods Compared with the OLS Method

Problem	Method	Q	q	Speed-up
MESFET	OLS	44	10	Reference
	MCR	44	10	3.5
	LEM	44	10	3.9
Credit card	OLS	150	30	Reference
	MCR	150	30	4.4
	LEM	150	30	4.5

VI. WEIGHT INITIALIZATION IN SPEECH RECOGNITION APPLICATION

In previous sections the benchmarks demonstrated that the weight initialization methods can play a very significant role. In this section we want to investigate how weight initialization methods function in the very challenging application of isolated spoken digit recognition. Specifically we study the performances of two initialization methods in a hybrid of a self-organizing map (SOM) and a multilayer perceptron (MLP) network that operates as part of a recognition system; see Fig. 13. However, before entering the problem of initialization we briefly discuss general features of speech recognition and the principle of the SOM classifier.

A. Speech Signals and Recognition

Acoustic speech signals contain a lot of redundant information. Moreover, these signals are influenced by the environment and equipment, more specifically by distorted acoustics, telephone bandwidth, microphone, background noise, etc. As a result received signal is always corrupted with additive and/or convolutional noise. In addition the pronunciation of the phonemes and words, that is, the speech

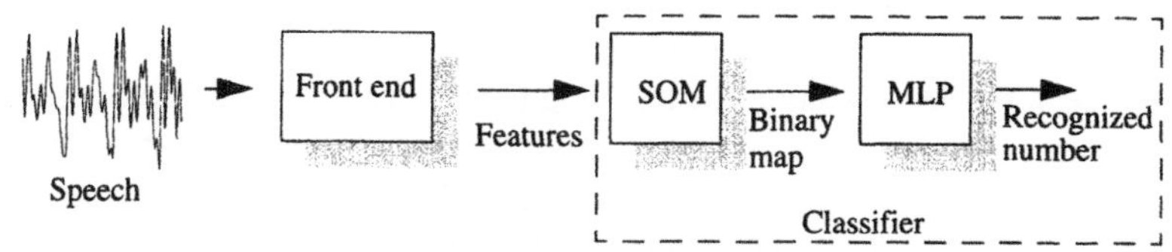

Figure 13 Block diagram of the recognition system.

units, varies greatly between speakers owing to, for example, speaking rate, mood, gender, dialects, and context. As a consequence, there are temporal and frequency variations. Further difficulties arise when the speaker is not cooperative or uses synonyms or a word not included in the vocabulary. For example "yes" might be pronounced "yeah" or "yep." Despite these difficulties, the fundamental idea of speech recognition is to provide enhanced access to machines by using voice commands [43].

In the case of isolated word recognition, the recognition system is usually based on pattern recognition technology. This kind of system can roughly be divided into the front end and the classifier as depicted Fig. 13. The purpose of the front end is to reduce the effects of the environment, equipment, and speaker characteristics on speech. It also transforms acoustic speech signals into sequences of speech frames, that is, feature vectors, thus reducing the redundancy of speech. The speech signal fed to the front end is sampled at 8–16 kHz, whereas the feature vectors representing the time varying spectra of sampled speech are calculated approximately at 100 Hz frequency. Commonly a feature vector consists of mel scaled cepstral coefficients [44]. These coefficients might be accompanied by zero-crossing rate, power ratio, and derivatives of all the coefficients [44, 45]. The sequence of feature vectors of a spoken word forms a speech pattern, whose size depends mainly on the speaking rate and the pronunciation of a speaker.

According to a set of measurements the recognizers often classify speech partially or completely into categories. In the following tests we use a neural classifier which is a hybrid of a self-organized map [46] and a multilayer perceptron; see Fig. 13. The SOM performs the time normalization for speech patterns and the MLP performs the pattern classification. Such hybrids have been used successfully in isolated digit recognition [47, 48].

B. Principle of the Classifier

The detailed structure of the hybrid classifier can be seen in Fig. 14, where the SOM is trained to classify single speech frames, that is, feature vectors. Each feature vector activates one neuron which is called a winner. All the winner neurons of the SOM are stored in a binary matrix of the same dimension as the SOM. If a neuron has been a winner, the corresponding matrix element is unity. Therefore the SOM serves as a sequential mapping function that transforms feature vector sequences of speech signal into a two dimensional binary image. After mapping all the speech frames of a digit, the resulting binary image is a pattern of the pronounced digit as seen in Figs. 14 and 15. A vector made by cascading the columns of this binary pattern is used to excite the MLP. The output neuron of the MLP that has the highest activation indicates the recognized digit as shown in Fig. 15.

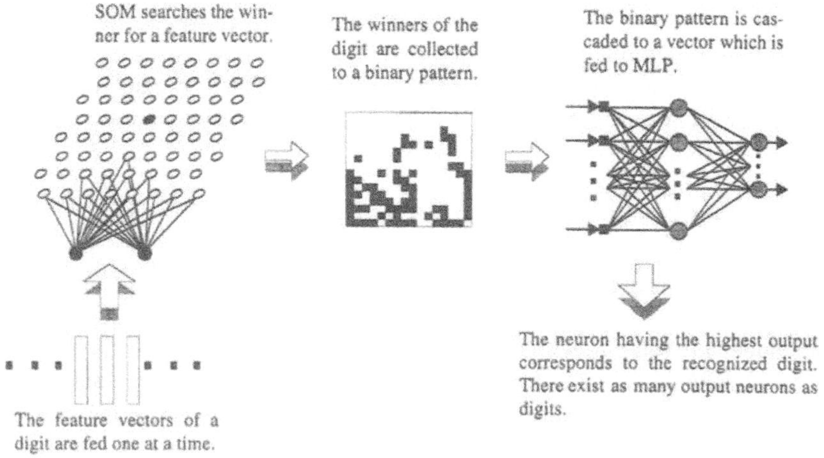

Figure 14 The structure of the hybrid neural network classifier.

The digit samples in isolated word recognition applications usually contain noise for some length of time before and after the sample. If these parts are also mapped into binary patterns, the word boundaries do not have to be determined for the classifier. Thus some of the code vectors of SOM are activated to noise, as seen in the lower left corners of the binary images in Fig. 15, whereas the rest of

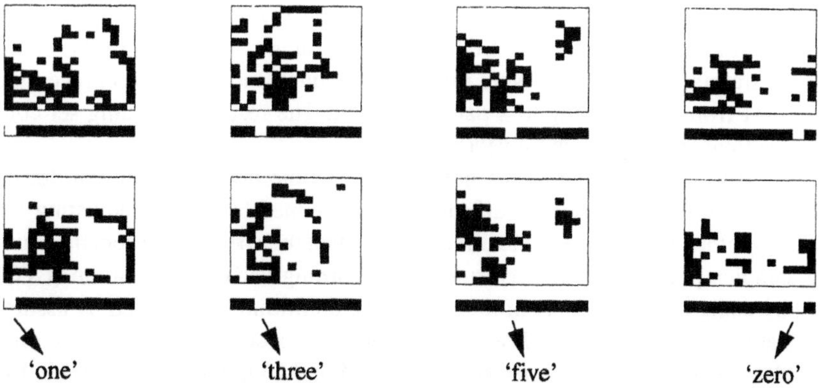

Figure 15 The binary patterns that represent the winner neurons of SOM for a digit. The bars below the binary patterns show the activation levels of the outputs of MLP for the digit. Light colors represent higher activation; dark colors represent lower activation.

the SOM is activated by phonemes and their transitions. However, the temporal information of the input acoustic vector sequence is lost in binary patterns and only information about the acoustic content is retained. This may cause confusion among words that have similar acoustic content but differing phoneme order [48].

C. Training the Hybrid Classifier

Both the training and test data sets consist of 11 male pronounced TIDIGITS [49], namely, "1," "2," ..., "9," "zero," and "oh." Every digit of the training set includes 110 samples with known starting and ending points. The test set contains 112 samples of each digit in arbitrary order without known starting and ending points. Thus there are a total of 1210 and 1232 samples in the training and test sets, respectively. The signal to noise ratios of both these sets were set to 15 dB by adding noise recorded in a moving car. The resulting samples were transformed to feature vectors consisting of 12 cepstral, 12 delta cepstral, energy, and delta energy coefficients. Each element of the feature vectors was scaled with the standard deviation of the element, which emphasized mainly the delta and energy coefficients. The test set was not used in training the SOM or the MLP.

The simulations were done with SOM_PAK [50], LVQ_PAK [50], and MATLAB [51] software packages. The SOM had 16×16 neurons forming a hexagonal structure, having a Gaussian neighborhood function and an adaptation gain decreasing linearly to 1. Each code vector of the SOM was initialized with uniformly distributed random values. In addition, each code vector component had approximately the same range of variation as the corresponding data component. Because the digits contained arbitrary time of noise before and after them, the training set contained a large amount, in fact one third, of pure noise. Therefore two thirds of the samples of the training set of the SOM were cut using known word boundaries to prevent the SOM from becoming overtrained by the noise. During training the 11 digits were presented at equal frequency, thus preventing the SOM from overtraining to a particular digit. The resulting training set contained a total of 72,229 feature vectors.

The self-organizing map does not always become organized enough during training. Therefore a better classification was obtained by slightly adjusting the weight vectors of the SOM to the direction in which they better represent the training samples [52]. This was performed with learning vector quantization (LVQ) [46] by using the training set of the SOM. The algorithm was applied by assuming that there exist as many classes as neurons, and each neuron belongs to only one class. The training parameters of the SOM and LVQ are listed in Table IV. The resulting feature map constructed the binary patterns for all the MLPs used in following simulations. However, at that time the training set samples were not cut using the known word boundaries.

Table IV

The SOM and LVQ Training Parameters

	Number of steps	Alpha	Radius
SOM rough training	72,229	0.7	15
SOM fine tuning	7,222,900	0.02	3
LVQ tuning	722,290	0.005	—

The structures of all MLPs were fixed to 256 inputs, a hidden layer of 64 neurons, and the output layer of 11 neurons, each representing a spoken digit. The hyperbolic tangent was used as an activation function in both of the layers. The MLP was initialized with a maximum covariance method [39] or with a Nquyen–Widrow (NW) random generator [26]. The latter method initializes the neurons of the MLP so that their linear region occurs within the region of input space where the input patterns are likely to occur. This initialization is very fast and close to random initialization. The deviation for hidden layer neurons given by the NW method, approximately ± 0.009, was also used as the deviation of candidate neurons in the MC method. The initializations of every MLP using the MC method were performed with same parameter values. The number of candidates Q and training set samples[1] n were set to 640 and 561, respectively. The off-line training was done with the modified momentum backpropagation (MBP) [53], the simple backpropagation (BP) [54], or the Rprop algorithm [32] using mean square error (MSE) as the cost function. The same training set was used for all the algorithms. For each of these algorithms the average flops required per epoch is shown in Table V. During the first epoch of each algorithm the number of the flops is bigger than presented in Table V, but it did not have an effect on results

Table V

The Average Flops Required for an Iteration (One Epoch)

Algorithm	Flops
Rprop	85,297,256
MBP	85,026,473
BP	84,875,102

[1] The training set samples were same the for each MC initialization.

Table VI
The Costs (in Flops and Epochs) of Initialization Methods with 256 x 64 x 11 Sized MLP

	Q	n	Flops	Cost (epochs)
MC	320	561	597,420,644	~ 7
	640	561	944,626,762	~ 11
	1280	561	1,639,036,725	~ 19
NW	—	—	240,829	~ 0

to be presented in the following section. The flops required in the MC and NW initializations are shown in Table VI.

For each algorithm, regardless of which initialization method was used, there were 20 training sessions. The length of training for the algorithms and the frequency at which the performance of the MLPs was checked with both training and test sets are shown in Table VII. The length of trainings with the NW initialized MLPs trained with BP were longer due to slower convergence as expected. The momentum value α was 0.9 for the MBP algorithm and the learning rate μ was 0.0001 for both the BP and the MBP algorithms. The other training parameters for MBP where chosen according to [53]. The learning rate increase factor ϕ and decrease factor β were set to 1.05 and 0.7, respectively, and the maximum error ratio was 1.04. Guidance for the training parameters of the Rprop algorithm was presented in [32, 33]. The values for the decrease and increase factors were set to $\eta^- = 0.5$ and $\eta^+ = 1.2$, respectively. The minimum and maximum update values were restricted to $\Delta_{\max} = 1$ and $\Delta_{\min} = 10^{-8}$. All the update values Δ_{ij} of both layers were set to an initial value $\Delta_0 = 0.0001$.

Table VII
The Length of MLP Training, and Performance Testing Frequency

	MC initialization		NW initialization	
Algorithm	Epochs	Test freq. (epochs)	Epochs	Test freq. (epochs)
Rprop	100	2	300	2
MBP	1500	10	1500	10
BP	1000	10	2000	10

D. Results

The training behavior of the MLPs after using either the NW or the MC initialization method are shown in Figs. 16–19. The performance of the MLP was measured with both the test and training sets. The upper line in the figures represents the largest recognition error per epoch; the lower line shows the smallest recognition error per epoch that occurred among the 20 training sessions; the line in the middle is the average performance per epoch.

The MC initialized MLPs trained with the MBP or the Rprop algorithm seem to reach the local minimum early and then start slightly overfitting the training data as seen in Figs. 16 and 17. The "bump" in the figures, which seems to be formed by the MBP algorithm, is probably due to increasing learning rate because the same effect did not appear in the case of the simple BP algorithm with MC initialized weight matrices. The BP trained MLPs had quite similar but slower convergence behavior compared with the MBP trained MLP. Thus pictures of BP trained MLPs are not included. It can also be seen that when using any of the training algorithms for MC initialized networks, the convergence of the training set is faster and stops at a higher level of error than with NW initialized networks.

The mean recognition rates of the test set for NW initializations are approximately 10% in each of the three cases as seen in Table VIII. However, in the case of MC initialization the performance is already about 96% without any training. Therefore the speed-up S_1 representing the gain achieved by using only the MC initialization can be calculated with the equation

$$S_1 = \frac{a - c}{a} \cdot 100\%, \tag{9}$$

where a is the number of epochs required for the NW initialized MLP to reach 96% recognition level of the test set and c is the cost of the MC initialization. These figures are given in Tables VI and IX, respectively, and the speed-ups due to MC initialization are shown in Table X. Note that the cost of NW initialization was neglected in S_1. The other speed-up values S_2 represent the gain of the MC initialization method when using the previously mentioned MLP training algorithms. These figures are obtained with the equation

$$S_2 = \frac{b - d - c}{b} \cdot 100\%, \tag{10}$$

in which b is the number of epoch when the NW initialized MLP has reached a performance level that is comparable to the minimum of the mean error percentage that occurred at epoch d in MC initialized MLPs[2] (compare Tables VIII

[2]Using Rprop training and MC initialization the minimum of mean error percentage was better than when using NW initialization. Therefore S_2 was calculated for the case of Rprop in Table X by using b having the number of the epoch corresponding to the minimum of the mean error percentage in Table VIII (in the third column from the left).

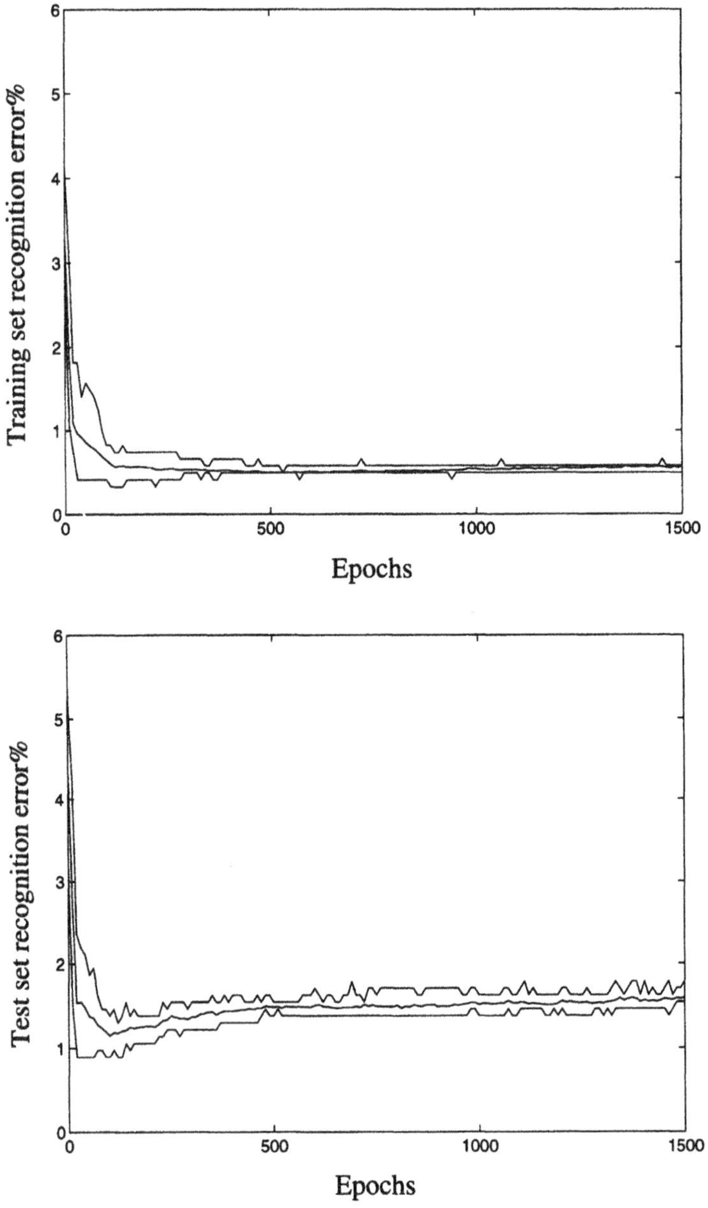

Figure 16 Convergence of the MC initialized MLP when trained with the modified MBP algorithm. The upper and lower figures represent the training and test set convergences, respectively. The upper line in the figures is the largest recognition error per epoch; the lower line is the smallest recognition error per epoch that occurred among the 20 training sessions; the line in the middle is the average of the performance per epoch.

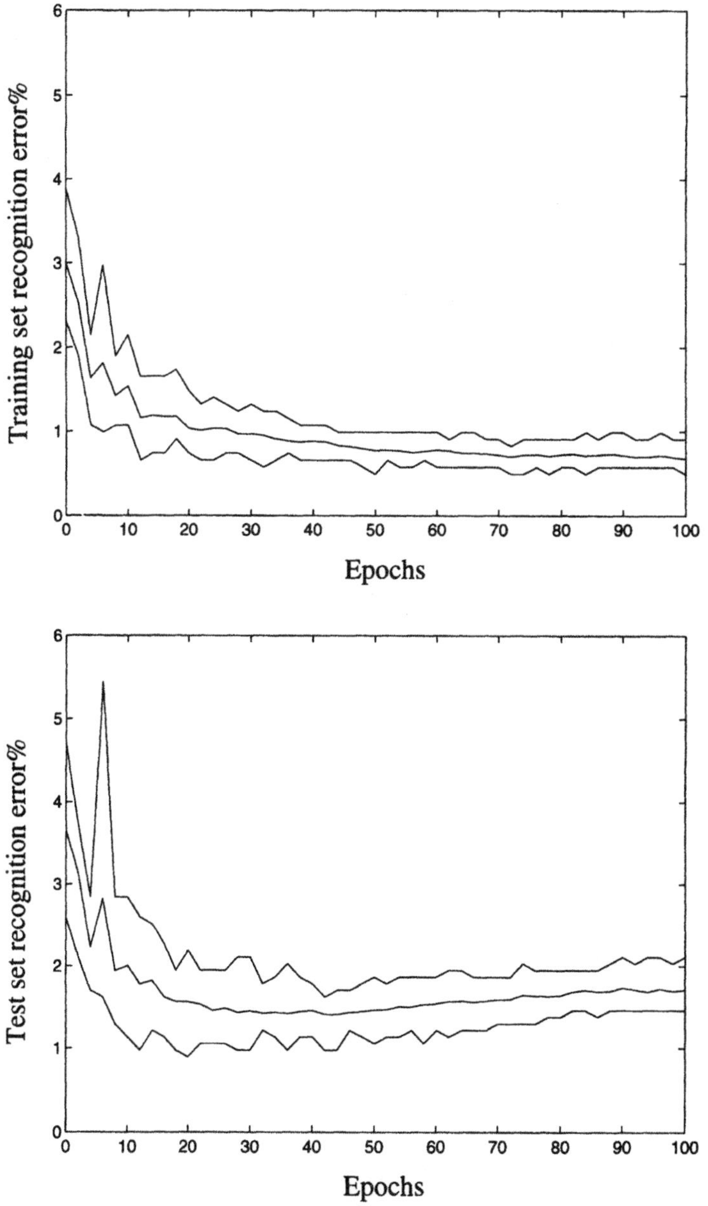

Figure 17 Convergence of the MC initialized MLP when trained with the Rprop algorithm. The upper and lower figures represent the training and test set convergences, respectively. The upper line in the figures is the largest recognition error per epoch; the lower line is the smallest recognition error per epoch that occurred among the 20 training sessions; the line in the middle is the average of the performance per epoch.

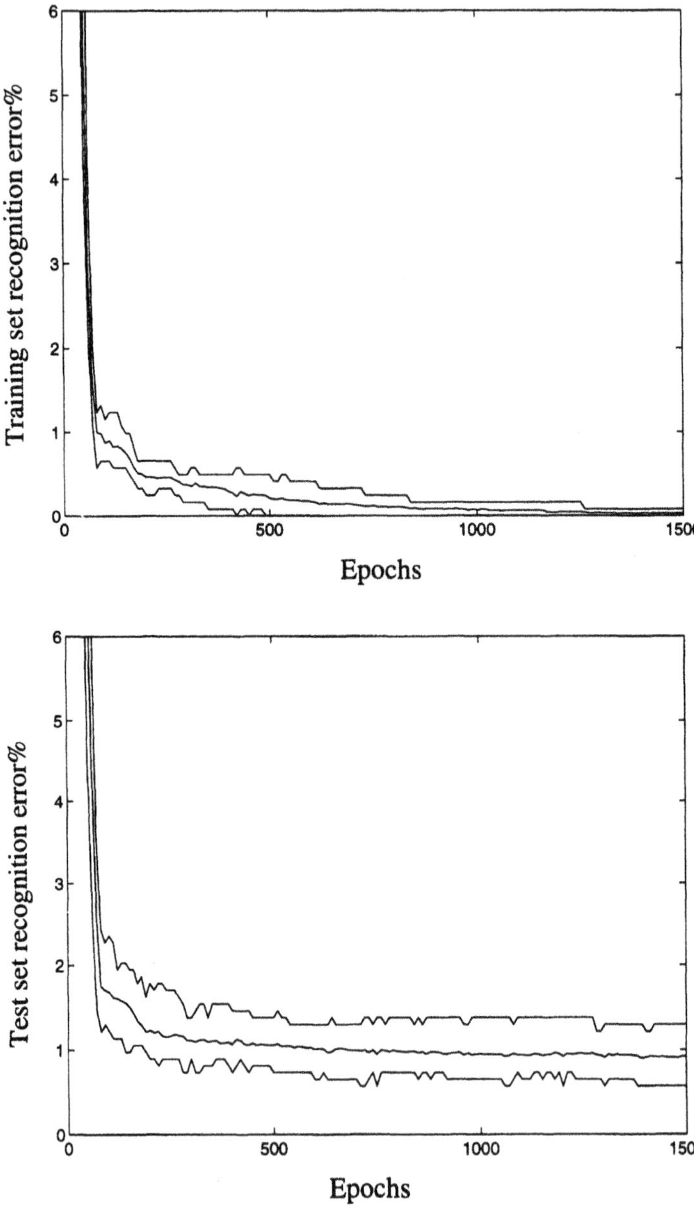

Figure 18 Convergence of the NW initialized MLP when trained with the modified MBP algorithm. The upper and lower figures represent the training and test set convergences, respectively. The upper line in the figures is the largest recognition error per epoch; the lower line is the smallest recognition error per epoch that occurred among the 20 training sessions; the line in the middle is the average of the performance per epoch.

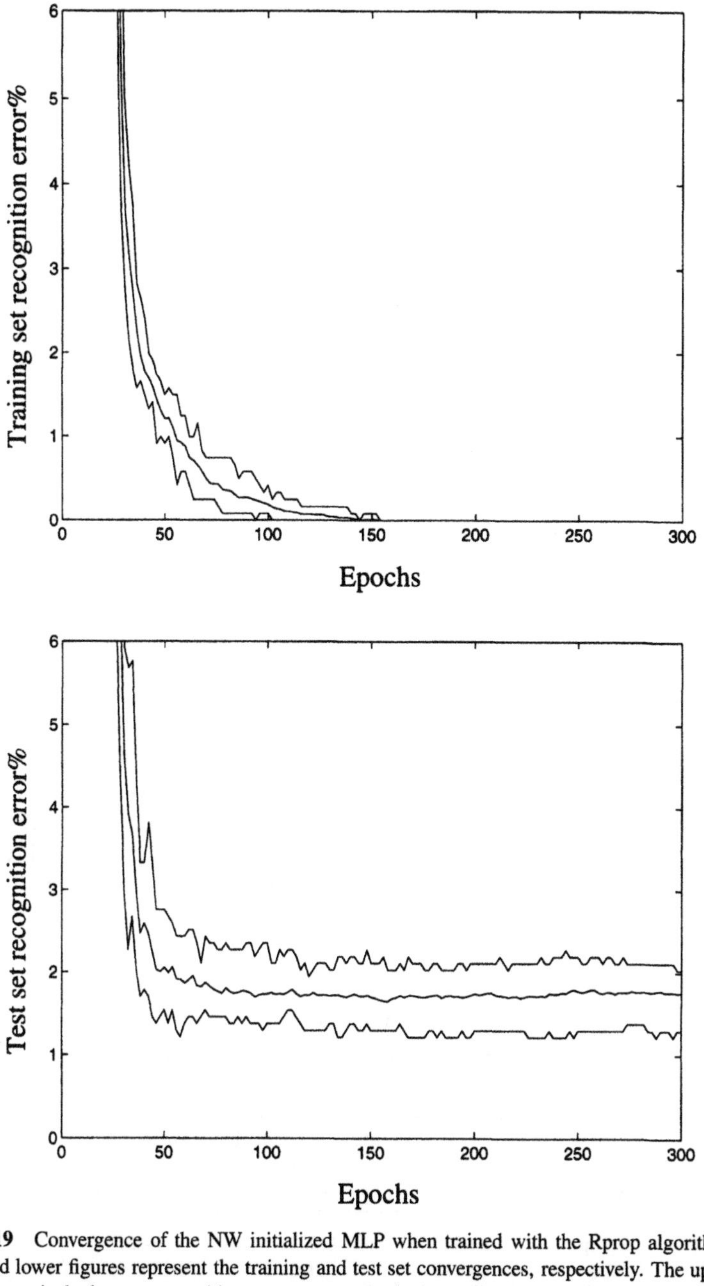

Figure 19 Convergence of the NW initialized MLP when trained with the Rprop algorithm. The upper and lower figures represent the training and test set convergences, respectively. The upper line in the figures is the largest recognition error per epoch; the lower line is the smallest recognition error per epoch that occurred among the 20 training sessions; the line in the middle is the average of the performance per epoch.

Table VIII

The Effects of NW Initialization on the Test Set Recognition Errors[a]

Algorithm	Initial mean of error%	Mean of standard deviation of error%	Minimum of mean of error% and the epoch	The epoch, when mean error% has reached level of minimum of mean error% of MC initialized MLP	Mean of errors $\leq 4\%$ after (epochs)
Rprop	89.8701	0.0030	1.6477/158	—	32
MBP	89.8377	0.0019	0.8994/1390	290	70
BP	90.0771	0.0022	1.1039/1790	1110	150

[a] There were 20 training sessions for each algorithm.

and IX). The cost of MC initialization c was also taken into account when calculating the values of S_2. These speed-up values show that despite the cost of MC initialization, the training speed of MLP is increased significantly.

The differences were small in the average performances of trained networks. The MC initialized networks seemed to end up with a slightly better local minimum when the Rprop training algorithm was used. On the other hand, when backpropagation algorithms were used, the NW initialized networks generalized slightly better. Despite the fact that a slightly better recognition performance was achieved by using the NW initialization and backpropagation algorithms, the cost of the NW initialization is that considerably longer training times are needed. For example, when the MBP training algorithm was used, on average only three more digits were classified correctly, but it took several hundreds of epochs longer to

Table IX

The Effects of MC Initialization on the Test Set Recognition Errors[a]

Algorithm	Initial mean of error%	Mean of standard deviation of error%	Minimum of mean of error% and the epoch
Rprop	3.6688	0.0024	1.4083/44
MBP	4.4278	0.0009	1.1445/100
BP	3.9286	0.0017	1.1567/280

[a] There were 20 training sessions for each algorithm.

Table X
The Speed-up Values of the MC Initialization

Algorithm	S_1 (epochs)	S_1 (%)	S_2 (epochs)	S_2 (%)
Rprop	21	65.6	103	65.2
MBP	59	84.3	179	61.7
BP	139	92.7	819	73.8

reach that level. The deviation of the recognition errors for the algorithms (see Tables VIII and IX) were calculated using only those epochs for which the mean error level was smaller than 4% in the case of NW initialization. When the MC initialization was used, all the error values were used. Comparing the deviations shows that for MC initialized networks the deviations of the recognition errors are smaller than with NW initialized networks.

The deviation of the initial weight values and the number of candidates were constant in all the previous MC initializations. It was set according to deviation given by the NW algorithm. To study the effect of deviation and the number of candidates in the MC initialization, some additional tests were made. Each test was repeated 11 times with different MC initialized weights for the $256 \times 64 \times 11$ sized MLP. In the initializations the number of training samples was 561. The training was performed with the MBP algorithm having the same parameter values as in the foregoing simulations. The results in Table XI suggest that the change

Table XI
The Effect of the Parameter Values of MC Initialization on Test Set Convergence[a]

Q, deviation of candidates	n	Initial mean of error%	Mean of standard deviation of error%	Minimum of mean of error% and the epoch
320, ± 0.007	561	3.90	0.0009	1.08/120
320, ± 0.011	561	4.57	0.0010	1.15/150
640, ± 0.006	561	3.95	0.0010	1.17/130
640, ± 0.011	561	4.14	0.0010	1.12/130
1280, ± 0.020	561	3.25	0.0009	1.15/100

[a] In each case, the results are calculated from 11 sessions. The MBP was used for training.

in deviation and number of candidates did not have a significant effect on the final performance level. However, the number of epochs, when the minimum of the mean of errors occurred, was increased a bit in all of the cases except when using 1280 candidates. Moreover, in this case the initial mean error was smaller than in any of the cases in Table IX.

VII. CONCLUSION

Weight initialization of multilayer perceptron networks and radial basis function networks have been discussed. In particular, stepwise regression methods were suggested for the initialization. This approach is very attractive because it is very general and is a simple way to provide some intelligence for initial weight selection. Several practical modeling experiments were also presented. They clearly showed that proper initialization can improve the learning behavior significantly.

APPENDIX I: CHESSBOARD 4 × 4

The $m \times m$ chessboard problem is one generalization for the well known and widely used exclusive-OR (XOR) problem. There are two inputs, namely, the X-Y coordinates on the $m \times m$ sized chessboard. For white squares the output is "off" (or 0) and for the black squares the output is "on" (or 1). Thus, the XOR problem is equivalent to the chessboard 2×2 problem. The chessboard 4×4 problem is depicted in Fig. 20. For this problem the number of training examples is $n = 16$.

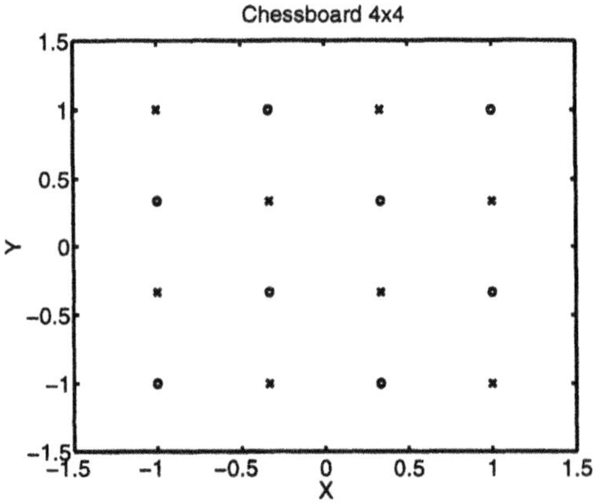

Figure 20 The chessboard 4 × 4 problem. Circles represent the "off" and crosses represent the "on" values.

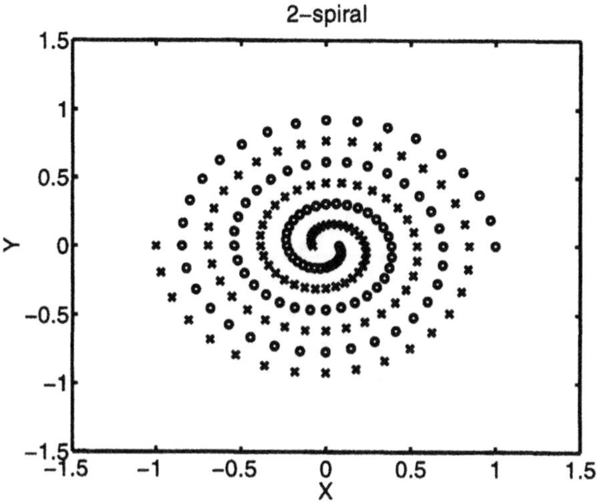

Figure 21 The two-spiral problem. Circles represent the "off" and crosses represent the "on" values.

APPENDIX II: TWO SPIRALS

In the two-spirals problem there are two inputs which correspond to the X-Y coordinates. Half of the input patterns produce "on" (or 1) and another half produce "off" (or 0) to the output. The training points are arranged in two interlocking spirals as depicted in Fig. 21. The total number of training examples is $n = 194$.

APPENDIX III: GaAs MESFET

In this modeling problem the task is to train a model with measured GaAs MESFET characteristic as depicted in Fig. 22. These data was obtained from [55] in which the electrical device modeling problem was considered. There are two inputs: the gate voltage and the drain voltage of a GaAs MESFET. The output is the drain current of the MESFET. The number of training examples is $n = 176$.

APPENDIX IV: CREDIT CARD

The task in this modeling problem is to predict the approval or nonapproval of a credit card for a customer. The training set consists of $n = 690$ examples, and each one of them represents a real credit card application. The output describes whether the bank (or similar institution) granted the credit card or not. There are

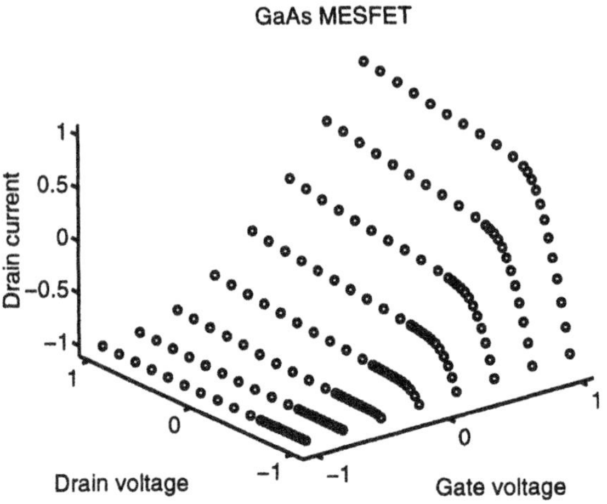

Figure 22 The GaAs MESFET modeling problem. The measurement data have been scaled to the interval [−1; 1].

51 input attributes, whose meaning is unexplained for confidentiality reasons. In 307 cases (44.5% of 690) the credit card was granted and in 383 cases (55.5% of 690) the credit card was denied. More details of this data set can be found in [56].

REFERENCES

[1] D. Rumelhart, G. Hinton, and R. Williams. Learning internal representations by error propagation. In *Parallel Distributed Processing: Explorations in the Microstructure of Cognition* (D. Rumelhart, J. McClelland, and the PDP Research Group, Eds.), Chap. 8, pp. 318–362. MIT Press, Cambridge, MA, 1986.

[2] A. Blum and R. Rivest. Training a 3-node neural network is NP-complete. In *Proceedings of Computational Learning Theory, COLT'88*, pp. 9–18, 1988.

[3] S. Judd. On the complexity of loading shallow neural networks. *J. Complexity* 4:177–192, 1988.

[4] G. Tesauro and Y. Ahmad. Asymptotic convergence of backpropagation. *Neural Comput.* 1:382–391, 1989.

[5] R. Jacobs. Increased rates of convergence through learning rate adaptation. *Neural Networks* 1:295–307, 1988.

[6] S. Fahlman. An empirical study of learning speed in backpropagation networks. Technical Report CMU-CS-88–162, Carnegie Mellon University, 1988.

[7] M. Pfister and R. Rojas. Speeding-up backpropagation — a comparison of orthogonal techniques. *Proceedings of the International Joint Conference on Neural Networks, IJCNN'93*, Vol. 1, pp. 517–523, 1993.

[8] W. Schiffmann, M. Joost, and R. Werner. Optimization of the backpropagation algorithm for training multilayer perceptrons. Technical Report, Institute of Physics, University of Koblenz, 1992.

[9] M. Mozer and P. Smolensky. Skeletonization: A technique for trimming tha fat from a network via relevance assessment. In *Advances in Neural Information Processing Systems 1* (D. Touretzky, Ed.), pp. 107–115, Morgan Kaufman, San Mateo, CA. 1989.

[10] J. Sietsma and R. Dow. Neural net pruning — why and how. *Proceedings of the IEEE 2nd International Conference on Neural Networks*, Vol. I, pp. 326–333, IEEE Press, New York, 1988.

[11] C. Bishop. Curvature-driven smoothing in backpropagation neural networks. *Proceedings of INNC'90*, Vol. II, pp. 749–752. Kluwer Academic Publishers, Norwell, MA, 1990.

[12] Y. Chauvin. Dynamic behavior of constrained backpropagation networks. In *Advances in Neural Information Processing Systems 2*, (D. Touretzky, Ed.), pp. 643–649. Morgan Kaufmann, San Mateo, CA, 1990.

[13] S. Hanson and L. Pratt. Comparing biases for minimal network construction with backpropagation. In *Advances in Neural Information Processing Systems 1*, (D. Touretzky, Ed.), pp. 177–185. Morgan Kaufmann, San Mateo, CA, 1989.

[14] J. Sietsma and R. Dow. Creating artificial neural networks that generalize. *Neural Networks* 4:67–79, 1991.

[15] T. Ash. Dynamic node creation in backpropagation networks. *Connection Sci.* 1:365–375, 1989.

[16] S. Fahlman and C. Lebiere. The cascade-correlation learning architecture. In *Advances in Neural Information Processing Systems 2* (D. Touretzky, Ed.), pp. 524–532. Morgan Kaufman, San Mateo, CA, 1990.

[17] Y. Hirose, K. Yamashita, and S. Hijiya. Backpropagation algorithm which varies the number of hidden units. *Neural Networks* 4:61–66, 1991.

[18] W. Schmidt, S. Raudys, M. Kraaijveld, M. Skurikhina, and R. Duin. Initializations, backpropagations and generalizations of feedforward classifiers. *Proceedings of the 1993 IEEE International Conference on Neural Networks*, Vol. 1, pp. 598–604. IEEE Press, New York, 1993.

[19] T. Burrows and M. Niranjan. The use of feed-forward and recurrent neural networks for system identification. Technical Report 158, Engineering Department, Cambridge University, 1993.

[20] Y. Chen and F. Bastani. Optimal initialization for multilayer perceptrons. *Proceedings of the 1990 IEEE International Conference on Systems, Man and Cybernetics*, pp. 370–372. IEEE Press, New York, 1990.

[21] T. Denoeux and R. Lengelle. Initializing back propagation networks with prototypes. *Neural Networks* 6:351–363, 1993.

[22] G. Drago and S. Ridella. Statistically controlled activation weight initialization (SCAWI). *IEEE Trans. Neural Networks* 3:627–631, 1992.

[23] T. Kaylani and S. Dasgupta. Weight initialization of MLP classifiers using boundary-preserving patterns. *Proceedings of the 1994 IEEE International Conference on Neural Networks*, pp. 113–118. IEEE Press, New York, 1994.

[24] L. Kim. Initializing weights to a hidden layer of a multilayer neural network by linear programming. *Proceedings of the International Joint Conference on Neural Networks*, Vol. 2, pp. 1701–1704, 1993.

[25] G. Li, H. Alnuweiri, and Y. Wu. Acceleration of back propagations through initial weight pretraining with delta rule. *Proceedings of the IEEE International Conference on Neural Networks*, Vol. 1, pp. 580–585. IEEE Press, New York, 1993.

[26] D. Nquyen and B. Widrow. Improving the learning speed of 2-layer neural networks by choosing initial values of the adaptive weights. *Proceedings of the International Joint Conference of Neural Networks, ICNN'90*, Vol. 3, pp. 21–26, 1990.

[27] R. Rojas. Optimal weight initialization for neural networks. *Proceedings of the International Conference on Artificial Neural Networks, ICANN'94*, pp. 577–580, 1994.

[28] H. Shimodaira. A weight value initialization method for improving learning performance of the backpropagation algorithm in neural networks. *Proceedings of the 6th International Conference on Tools with Artificial Intelligence, TAI'94*, pp. 672–675, 1994.

[29] L. Wessels and E. Barnard. Avoiding false local minima by proper initialization of connections. *IEEE Trans. Neural Networks* 3:899–905, 1992.
[30] N. Weymaere and J-P. Martens. Design and initialization of two-layer perceptrons using standard pattern recognition techniques. *Proceedings of the 1993 International Conference on Systems, Man and Cybernetics*, pp. 584–589, 1993.
[31] R. Fletcher. *Practical Methods of Optimization*, 2nd ed. Wiley, Chichester, 1990.
[32] M. Riedmiller and H. Braun. A direct adaptive method for faster backpropagation learning: the Rprop algorithm. *Proceedings of the IEEE International Conference on Neural Networks*. IEEE Press, New York, 1993.
[33] M. Riedmiller. Advanced supervised learning in multilayer perceptrons — from backpropagation to adaptive learning algorithms. Special Issue on Neural Networks. *Int. J. Comput. Standards Interfaces* 5, 1994.
[34] J. Moody and C. Darken. Learning with localized receptive fields. *Proceedings of the 1988 Connectionist Models Summer School* (D. Touretzky, G. Hinton, and T. Sejnowski, Eds.), pp. 133–143, 1988.
[35] J. Moody and C. Darken. Fast learning in networks of locally-tuned processing units. *Neural Comput.* 1:281–294, 1989.
[36] N. Draper and H. Smith. *Applied Regression Analysis*, 1st ed. Wiley, New York, 1966 (2nd ed., 1981).
[37] G. Seber. *Linear Regression Analysis*. Wiley, New York, 1977.
[38] M. Lehtokangas, J. Saarinen, P. Huuhtanen, and K. Kaski. Initializing weights of a multilayer perceptron network by using the orthogonal least squares algorithm. *Neural Comput.* 7:982–999, 1995.
[39] M. Lehtokangas, P. Korpisaari, and K. Kaski. Maximum covariance method for weight initialization of multilayer perceptron network. *Proceedings of the European Symposium on Artificial Neural Networks, ESANN'96*, pp. 243–248, 1996.
[40] S. Chen, C. Cowan, and P. Grant. Orthogonal least squares learning algorithm for radial basis function networks. *IEEE Trans. Neural Networks* 2:302–309, 1991.
[41] S. Chen, P. Grant, and C. Cowan. Orthogonal least-squares algorithm for training multioutput radial basis function networks. *IEE Proc. F* 139:378–384, 1992.
[42] M. Lehtokangas, S. Kuusisto, and K. Kaski. Fast hidden node selection methods for training radial basis function networks. Plenary, panel and special sessions. *Proceedings of the International Conference on Neural Networks, ICNN'96*, pp. 176–180, 1996.
[43] L. R. Rabiner. Applications of voice processing to telecommunications. *Proc. IEEE* 82:199–230, 1994.
[44] J. W. Picone. Signal modeling techniques in speech recognition. *Proc. IEEE* 81:1214–1247, 1993.
[45] S. Furui. Speaker independent isolated word recognition using dynamic features of speech spectrum. *IEEE Trans. Acoustic Speech Signal Processing* 34:52–59, 1986.
[46] T. Kohonen. *Self-Organizing Maps*. Springer-Verlag, New York, 1995.
[47] M. Kokkonen and K. Torkkola. Using self-organizing maps and multi-layered feed-forward nets to obtain phonemic transcription of spoken utterances. *Speech Commun.* 9:541–549, 1990.
[48] H. Zezhen and K. Anthony. A combined self-organizing feature map and multilayer perceptron for isolated word recognition. *IEEE Trans. Signal Processing* 40:2651–2657, 1992.
[49] R. G. Leonard. A database of speaker-independent digit recognition. *Proceedings of the International Conference on Acoustics, Speech, and Signal Processing, ICASSP-84*, Vol. 3, p. 42.11, 1984.
[50] T. Kohonen, J. Hynninen, J. Kangas, and J. Laaksonen. Self-Organizing Map Program Package version 3.1 and Learning Vector Quantization Program Package version 3.1. Helsinki University of Technology, 1995. Available at ftp://cochlea.hut.fi/pub/.

[51] MathWorks Inc., MATLAB for Windows version 4.2c.1, 1994.

[52] P. Salmela, S. Kuusisto, J. Saarinen, K. Laurila, and P. Haavisto. Isolated spoken number recognition with hybrid of self-organizing map and multilayer perceptron. *Proceedings of the International Conference on Neural Networks, ICNN'96*, Vol. 4, pp. 1912–1917, 1996.

[53] T. Vogl, J. Mangis, A. Rigler, W. Zink, and D. Alkon. Accelerating the convergence of the back-propagation method. *Biological Cybernetics* 59:257–263, 1988.

[54] S. Haykin. *Neural Networks, A Comprehensive Foundation*. Macmillan, New York, 1994.

[55] P. Ojala, J. Saarinen, P. Elo, and K. Kaski. A novel technology independent neural network approach on device modelling interface. *IEEE Proc. G, Circuits, Devices and Systems* 142:74–82, 1995.

[56] L. Prechelt. Proben 1—a set of neural network benchmark problems and benchmarking rules, Technical Report, University of Karlsruhe, 1994. Available by anonymous FTP from ftp.ira.uka.de in directory /pub/papers/techreports/1994 in file 1994–21.ps.Z. The data set is also available from ftp.ira.uka.de in directory /pub/neuron in file proben1.tar.gz.

Fast Computation in Hamming and Hopfield Networks

Isaac Meilijson
Raymond and Beverly Sackler Faculty of Exact Sciences
School of Mathematical Sciences
Tel-Aviv University
69978 Tel-Aviv, Israel

Eytan Ruppin
Raymond and Beverly Sackler Faculty of Exact Sciences
School of Mathematical Sciences
Tel-Aviv University
69978 Tel Aviv, Israel

Moshe Sipper
Logic Systems Laboratory
Swiss Federal Institute of Technology
In-Ecublens
CH-1015 Lausanne
Switzerland

I. GENERAL INTRODUCTION

This chapter reviews the work presented in [1, 2], concerned with the development of fast and efficient variants of the Hamming and Hopfield networks. In the first part, we analyze in detail the performance of a Hamming network—the most basic and fundamental neural network classification paradigm. We show that if the activation function of the memory neurons in the original Hamming network is replaced by an appropriately chosen simple threshold function, the "winner-take-all" subnet of the Hamming network (known to be the essential factor determining the time complexity of the network's computation) may be altogether discarded. Under some conditions, the resulting threshold Hamming network correctly classifies the input patterns in a *single iteration*, with probability approaching 1.

In the second part of this chapter, we present a methodological framework describing the two-iteration performance of Hopfieldlike attractor neural networks with history-dependent, Bayesian dynamics. We show that the optimal signal (activation) function has a *slanted sigmoidal* shape, and provide an intuitive account of activation functions with a nonmonotone shape. We show that even in situations where the input patterns are applied to only a small subset of the network

Algorithms and Architectures

neurons (and little information is hence conveyed to the network), optimal signaling allows for fast convergence of the Hopfield network to the correct memory states, getting close to them in just two iterations.

II. THRESHOLD HAMMING NETWORKS

A. Introduction

Neural networks are frequently employed as associative memories for pattern classification. The network typically classifies input patterns into one of several memory patterns it has stored, representing the various classes. A conventional measure used in the context of binary vectors is the Hamming distance, defined as the number of bits by which the pattern vectors differ. The Hamming network (HN) calculates the Hamming distance between the input pattern and each memory pattern, and selects the memory with the smallest Hamming distance, which is declared "the winner." This network is the most straightforward associative memory. Originally presented in [3–5], it has received renewed attention in recent years [6, 7].

The framework we analyze is a HN storing $m+1$ memory patterns $\xi^1, \xi^2, \ldots, \xi^{m+1}$, each being an n-dimensional binary vector with entries ± 1. The $(m+1)n$ memory entries are independent with equally likely ± 1 values. The input pattern x is an n-dimensional vector of ± 1s, randomly generated as a distorted version of one of the memory patterns (say ξ^{m+1}), such that $P(x_i = \xi_i^{m+1}) = \alpha$, $\alpha > 0.5$, where α is the initial similarity between the input pattern and the *correct* memory pattern ξ^{m+1}.

A typical HN, sketched in Fig. 1, is composed of two subnets:

1. The *similarity* subnet, consisting of an n-neuron input layer and an m-neuron memory layer. Each memory-layer neuron i is connected to all n input-layer neurons.
2. The *winner-take-all* (WTA) subnet, consisting of a fully connected m-neuron topology.

A memory pattern ξ^i is stored in the network by letting the values of the connections between memory neuron i and the input-layer neurons j ($j = 1, \ldots, n$) be

$$a_{ij} = \xi_j^i. \tag{1}$$

The values of the weights W_{ij} in the WTA subnet are chosen so that for each $i, j = 1, 2, \ldots, m+1$,

$$W_{ii} = 1, \qquad -1/m < W_{ij} < 0 \text{ for } i \neq j. \tag{2}$$

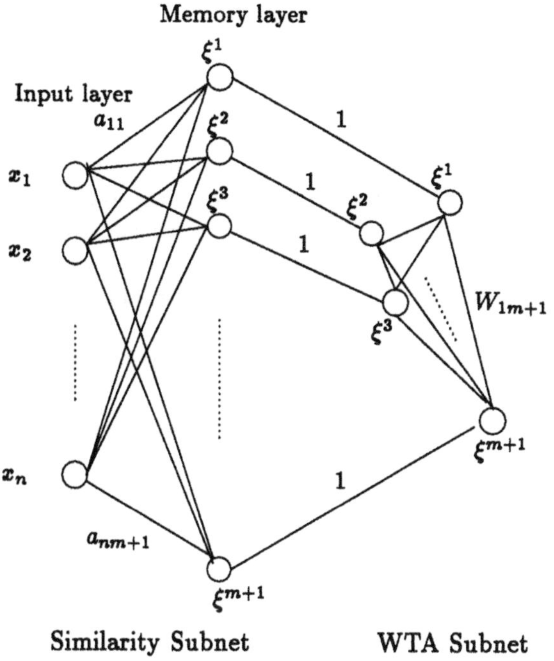

Figure 1 A Hamming net.

After an input pattern x is presented on the input layer, the HN computation proceeds in two steps, each performed in a different subnet:

1. Each memory neuron i $(1 \leqslant i \leqslant m+1)$ in the similarity subnet computes its *similarity* Z_i with the input pattern

$$Z_i = \frac{1}{2}\left(\sum_{j=1}^{n} a_{ij}x_j + n\right) = \frac{1}{2}\left(\sum_{j=1}^{n} \xi_j^i x_j + n\right). \tag{3}$$

2. Each memory neuron i in the similarity subnet transfers its Z_i value to its duplicate in the WTA network (via a single "identity" connection of magnitude 1). The WTA network then finds the pattern j with the maximal similarity: each neuron i in the WTA subnet sets its initial value $y_i(0) = Z_i/n$ and then computes $y_i(t)$ iteratively $(t = 1, 2, \ldots)$ by

$$y_i(t) = \Theta_0\left(\sum_j W_{ij}y_j(t-1)\right), \tag{4}$$

where Θ_T is the threshold logic function

$$\Theta_T(u) = \begin{cases} u, & \text{if } u \geqslant T, \\ 0, & \text{otherwise.} \end{cases} \tag{5}$$

These iterations are repeated until the activity levels of the WTA neurons no longer change and the only memory neuron remaining active (i.e., with a positive y_i) is declared the winner. It is straightforward to see that given a winner memory neuron i, its corresponding memory pattern ξ^i can be retrieved on the input layer using the weights a_{ij}. The network's *performance* level is the probability that the winning memory will be the correct one, $m+1$.

Whereas the computation of the similarity subnet is performed in a single iteration, the time complexity of the network is primarily due to the time required for the convergence of the WTA subnet. In a recent paper [8], the worst-case convergence time of the standard WTA network described in the preceding text was shown to be on the order of $\Theta(m \ln(mn))$ iterations. This time complexity can be very large, as simple entropy considerations show that the capacity of HNs is approximately given by

$$m \approx \sqrt{2\pi n\alpha(1-\alpha)}e^{nG(\alpha)}, \tag{6}$$

where

$$G(\alpha) = \ln 2 + \alpha \ln \alpha + (1-\alpha)\ln(1-\alpha). \tag{7}$$

As an example, if $\alpha = 0.7$ (70% correct entries) and $n = 400$, the memory capacity is $m \approx 10^7$, resulting in a large overall running time of the corresponding HN.

We present in this chapter a detailed analysis of the performance of a HN classifying distorted memory patterns. Based on our analysis, we show that it is possible to completely discard the WTA subnet by letting each memory neuron i in the similarity subnet operate the threshold logic function Θ_T on its calculated similarity Z_i. If the value of the threshold T is properly tuned, only the neuron standing for the "correct" memory class will be activated. The resulting threshold Hamming network (THN) will perform correctly (with probability approaching 1) in a single iteration. Thereafter, we develop a close approximation to the error probabilities of the HN and the THN. We find the optimal threshold of the THN and compare its performance with that of the original HN.

B. Threshold Hamming Network

We first present some sharp approximations to the binomial distribution (proofs of these lemmas are given in [1]).

LEMMA 1. *Let* $X \sim \text{Bin}(n, p)$. *If* x_n *are integers such that* $\lim_{n\to\infty}(x_n/n) = \beta \in (p, 1)$, *then*

$$P(X = x_n) \approx \frac{1}{\sqrt{2\pi n\beta(1-\beta)}} \exp\left\{ -n\left[\beta \ln\frac{\beta}{p} + (1-\beta)\ln\frac{1-\beta}{1-p}\right]\right\} \tag{8}$$

and

$$P(X \geqslant x_n) \approx \frac{1-p}{(1-\frac{p}{\beta})\sqrt{2\pi n\beta(1-\beta)}} \times \exp\left\{ -n\left[\beta \ln\frac{\beta}{p} + (1-\beta)\ln\frac{1-\beta}{1-p}\right]\right\} \tag{9}$$

in the sense that the ratio between the LHS and RHS converges to 1 *as* $n \to \infty$. *For the special case* $p = \frac{1}{2}$, *let* $G(\beta) = \ln 2 + \beta\ln\beta + (1-\beta)\ln(1-\beta)$. *Then*

$$P(X = x_n) \approx \frac{\exp\{-nG(\beta)\}}{\sqrt{2\pi n\beta(1-\beta)}}, \tag{10}$$

$$P(X \geq x_n) \approx \frac{\exp\{-nG(\beta)\}}{(2-\frac{1}{\beta})\sqrt{2\pi n\beta(1-\beta)}}. \tag{11}$$

The rationale for the next two lemmas will be intuitively clear by interpreting X_i $(1 \leqslant i \leqslant m)$ as the similarity between the initial pattern and (wrong) memory i, and Y as the similarity with the correct memory $m + 1$. If we use x_n as the threshold, the decision will be correct if all X_i are below x_n and Y is above x_n. We will expand on this point later.

LEMMA 2. *Let* $X_i \sim \text{Bin}(n, \frac{1}{2})$ *be independent,* $\gamma \in (0, 1)$, *and let* x_n *be as in Lemma 1. If (up to a nearest integer)*

$$m = \left(2 - \frac{1}{\beta}\right)\sqrt{2\pi n\beta(1-\beta)}\left(\ln\frac{1}{\gamma}\right)e^{nG(\beta)}, \tag{12}$$

then

$$P(\max(X_1, X_2, \ldots, X_m) < x_n) \approx \gamma. \tag{13}$$

LEMMA 3. *Let* $Y \sim \text{Bin}(n, \alpha)$ *with* $\alpha > \frac{1}{2}$, *let* (X_i) *and* γ *be as in Lemma 2, and let* $\eta \in (0, 1)$. *Let* x_n *be the integer closest to* $n\beta$, *where*

$$\beta = \alpha - \sqrt{\frac{\alpha(1-\alpha)}{n}}z_\eta - \frac{1}{2n} \tag{14}$$

and z_η *is the* η *quantile of the standard normal distribution, that is,*

$$\eta = \frac{1}{\sqrt{2\pi}}\int_{-\infty}^{z_\eta} e^{-x^2/2}\,dx. \tag{15}$$

Then, if Y and (X_i) are independent,

$$P(\max(X_1, X_2, \ldots, X_m) < Y) \geqslant P(\max(X_1, X_2, \ldots, X_m) < x_n \leqslant Y) \quad (16)$$

and the RHS of (16) converges to $\gamma\eta$ for m as in (12) and $n \to \infty$.

Bearing in mind these three lemmas, recall that the similarities $(Z_1, Z_2, \ldots, Z_m, Z_{m+1})$ are independent. If $\mathrm{Max}(Z_1, Z_2, \ldots, Z_m, Z_{m+1}) = Z_j$ for a single memory neuron j, the conventional HN declares ξ^j the "winning pattern." Thus, the probability of error is the probability of a tie or of getting $j \neq m+1$. Let X_j be the similarity between the input vector and the jth memory pattern ($1 \leqslant j \leqslant m$) and let Y be the similarity with the correct memory pattern ξ^{m+1}. Clearly, X_j is $\mathrm{Bin}(n, \frac{1}{2})$-distributed and Y is $\mathrm{Bin}(n, \alpha)$-distributed. We now propose a THN having a threshold value x_n: As in the HN, each memory neuron in the similarity subnet computes its similarity with the input pattern, but now, each memory neuron i whose similarity X_i is at least x_n declares itself the winner. There is no WTA subnet. An error may arise if there is a multiplicity of memory neurons declaring themselves the winner, there is no winning pattern, or a wrong single winner. The threshold x_n is chosen so as to minimize the error probability.

To build a THN with probability of error not exceeding ϵ, observe that expression (13) gives the probability γ that no wrong pattern declares itself the winner, whereas expression (15) gives the probability η that the correct pattern $m+1$ declares itself the winner. The product of these two terms is the probability of correct decision (i.e., the performance level) of the THN, which should be at least $1-\epsilon$. Given n, ϵ, and α, a THN may be constructed by simply choosing even error probabilities, that is, $\gamma = \eta = \sqrt{1-\epsilon}$. Then we determine β by (14), let x_n be the integer closest to $n\beta$, and determine the memory capacity m using (12). If m, ϵ, and α are given, a THN may be constructed in a similar manner, because it is easy to determine n from m and ϵ by iterative procedures. Undoubtedly, the HN is superior to the THN, as explicitly shown by inequality (16). However, as we shall see, the performance loss using the THN can be recovered by a moderate increase in the network size n, whereas time complexity is drastically reduced by the abolition of the WTA subnet. In the next subsection we derive a more efficient choice of x_n (with uneven error probabilities), which yields a THN with optimal performance.

C. Hamming Network and an Optimal Threshold Hamming Network

To find an optimal THN, we replace the ad hoc choice of $\gamma = \eta = \sqrt{1-\epsilon}$ [among all pairs (γ, η) for which $\gamma\eta = 1-\epsilon$] by the choice of the threshold x_n that maximizes the storage capacity $m = m(n, \epsilon, \alpha)$. We also compute the error probability $\epsilon(m, n, \alpha)$ of the HN for arbitrary m, n, and α, and compare it with ϵ, the error probability of the THN.

Let ϕ (Φ) denote the standard normal density (cumulative distribution function) and let $r = \phi/(1-\Phi)$ denote the corresponding failure rate function. Then,

LEMMA 4. *The optimal proportion δ between the two error probabilities satisfies*

$$\delta = \frac{1-\gamma}{1-\eta} \approx \frac{r(z_\eta)}{\sqrt{n\alpha(1-\alpha)}\ln(\beta/(1-\beta))}. \tag{17}$$

Proof. Let $M = \max(X_1, X_2, \ldots, X_m)$ and let Y denote the similarity with the correct memory pattern, as before. We have seen that

$$P(M < x) \approx \exp\left\{-m\frac{\exp\{-nG(\beta)\}}{\sqrt{2\pi n\beta(1-\beta)}(2-1/\beta)}\right\}.$$

Whereas $G'(\beta) = \ln(\beta/(1-\beta))$, then by Taylor expansion,

$$\begin{aligned} P(M < x) &= P(M < x_0 + x - x_0) \\ &\approx \exp\left\{-m\frac{\exp\{-n[G(\beta + (x-x_0)/n)]\}}{\sqrt{2\pi n\beta(1-\beta)}(2-1/\beta)}\right\} \\ &\approx \exp\left\{-m\frac{\exp\{-nG(\beta) - (x-x_0)\ln(\beta/(1-\beta))\}}{\sqrt{2\pi n\beta(1-\beta)}(2-1/\beta)}\right\} \\ &= (P(M < x_0))^{(\beta/(1-\beta))^{x_0-x}} = \gamma^{(\beta/(1-\beta))^{x_0-x}} \end{aligned} \tag{18}$$

(in accordance with Gnedenko extreme-value distribution of type 1 [9]). Similarly,

$$\begin{aligned} P(Y < x) &= \exp\{\ln P(Y < x_0 + x - x_0)\} \\ &= \exp\left\{\ln P\left(Z < \frac{x_0 - n\alpha}{\sqrt{n\alpha(1-\alpha)}} + \frac{x - x_0}{\sqrt{n\alpha(1-\alpha)}}\right)\right\} \\ &\approx P(Y < x_0)\exp\left\{\frac{\phi(z)}{\Phi^*(z)}\frac{x-x_0}{\sqrt{n\alpha(1-\alpha)}}\right\} \\ &= (1-\eta)\exp\left\{r(z)\frac{x-x_0}{\sqrt{n\alpha(1-\alpha)}}\right\}, \end{aligned} \tag{19}$$

where $\Phi^* = 1 - \Phi$. The probability of correct recognition using a threshold x can now be expressed as

$$\begin{aligned} &P(M < x)P(Y \geqslant x) \\ &\quad\approx \gamma^{(\beta/(1-\beta))^{x_0-x}}\left(1 - (1-\eta)\exp\left\{r(z)\frac{x-x_0}{\sqrt{n\alpha(1-\alpha)}}\right\}\right). \end{aligned} \tag{20}$$

We differentiate expression (20) with respect to $x_0 - x$, and equate the derivative at $x = x_0$ to zero, to obtain the relation between γ and η that yields the optimal threshold, that is, that which maximizes the probability of correct recognition. This yields

$$\gamma = \exp\left\{ - \frac{r(z)}{\sqrt{n\alpha(1-\alpha)}\ln(\beta/(1-\beta))} \frac{1-\eta}{\eta} \right\}. \tag{21}$$

We now approximate

$$1-\gamma \approx -\ln\gamma \approx \frac{r(z)}{\sqrt{n\alpha(1-\alpha)}\ln(\beta/(1-\beta))}(1-\eta), \tag{22}$$

and thus the optimal proportion between the two error probabilities is

$$\delta = \frac{1-\gamma}{1-\eta} \approx \frac{r(z)}{\sqrt{n\alpha(1-\alpha)}\ln(\beta/(1-\beta))}. \quad \blacksquare \tag{23}$$

Based on Lemma 4, if the desired probability of error is ϵ, we choose

$$\gamma = 1 - \frac{\delta\epsilon}{1+\delta}, \qquad \eta = 1 - \frac{\epsilon}{(1+\delta)}. \tag{24}$$

We start with $\gamma = \eta = \sqrt{1-\epsilon}$, obtain β from (14) and δ from (17), recompute η and γ from (24), and iterate. The limiting values of β and γ in this iterative process give the maximal capacity m (by 12) and threshold x_n (as the integer closest to $n\beta$).

We now compute the error probability $\epsilon(m, n, \alpha)$ of the original HN (with the WTA subnet) for arbitrary m, n, and α, and compare it with ϵ.

LEMMA 5. *For arbitrary n, α, and ϵ, let m, β, γ, η, and δ be as calculated before. Then the probability of error $\epsilon(m, n, \alpha)$ of the HN satisfies*

$$\epsilon(m, n, \alpha) \approx \Gamma(1-\delta) \frac{1 - e^{-\delta \ln(\beta/(1-\beta))}}{\delta \ln(\beta/(1-\beta))} \frac{(\epsilon\delta)^{\delta}}{(1+\delta)^{1+\delta}} \epsilon, \tag{25}$$

where

$$\Gamma(t) = \int_0^\infty x^{t-1} e^{-x}\, dx \tag{26}$$

is the Gamma function.

Proof.

$$\begin{aligned} P(Y \leqslant M) &= \sum_x P(Y \leqslant x) P(M = x) \\ &= \sum_x P(Y \leqslant x)[P(M < x+1) - P(M < x)] \end{aligned}$$

$$\approx \sum_x P(Y \leqslant x_0) e^{-\delta(x_0 - x)\ln(\beta/(1-\beta))} \Big[\big(P(M < x_0)\big)^{(\beta/(1-\beta))^{x_0-x-1}} - \big(P(M < x_0)\big)^{(\beta/(1-\beta))^{x_0-x}} \Big]. \tag{27}$$

We now approximate this sum by the integral of the summand: Let $b = \beta/(1-\beta)$ and $c = \delta \ln(\beta/(1-\beta))$. We have seen that the probability of incorrect performance of the WTA subnet is equal to

$$P(Y \leqslant M) \approx \sum_x P(Y \leqslant x_0) e^{-c(x_0-x)} \Big[(P(M < x_0))^{b^{(x_0-x-1)}} - \big(P(M < x_0)\big)^{b^{(x_0-x)}} \Big]$$
$$\approx (1-\eta) \int_{-\infty}^{\infty} \big(\gamma^{b^{y-1}} - \gamma^{b^y}\big) e^{-cy}\, dy. \tag{28}$$

Now we transform variables $t = b^y \ln 1/\gamma$ to get the integral in the form

$$e^{-c}(1-\eta) \int_0^{\infty} \big(e^{-t} - e^{-bt}\big) \left(\frac{t}{\ln 1/\gamma}\right)^{-c/\ln b} \frac{dt}{t \ln b}$$
$$= K_1 \int_0^{\infty} \big(e^{-t} - e^{-bt}\big) t^{-(1+K_2)}\, dt. \tag{29}$$

This is the convergent difference between two divergent Gamma function integrals. We perform integration by parts to obtain a representation as an integral with t^{-K_2} instead of $t^{-(1+K_2)}$ in the integrand. For $0 \leq K_2 < 1$, the corresponding integral converges. The final result is then

$$(1-\eta) \frac{1 - e^{-c}}{c} \Gamma\left(1 - \frac{c}{\ln b}\right) \left(\ln \frac{1}{\gamma}\right)^{c/\ln b}. \tag{30}$$

Hence, we have

$$P(Y \leqslant M) \approx (1-\eta) \frac{1 - e^{-\delta \ln(\beta/(1-\beta))}}{\delta \ln(\beta/(1-\beta))} \Gamma(1-\delta) \left(\ln \frac{1}{\gamma}\right)^{\delta}$$
$$\approx \Gamma(1-\delta) \frac{1 - e^{-\delta \ln(\beta/(1-\beta))}}{\delta \ln(\beta/(1-\beta))} \frac{(\epsilon\delta)^{\delta}}{(1+\delta)^{1+\delta}} \epsilon \tag{31}$$

as claimed. Expression (25) is presented as $K(\epsilon, \delta, \beta) \cdot \epsilon$, where $K(\epsilon, \delta, \beta)$ is the factor (≤ 1) by which the probability of error ϵ of the THN should be multiplied in order to get the probability of error of the original HN with the WTA subnet. For small δ, K is close to 1. However, as will be seen in the next subsection, K is typically smaller. ■

Table I
Percentage of Error ($n = 150$, $\alpha = 0.75$)

m	100	200	400	800	1600	3200
(threshold)	(99)	(100)	(100)	(101)	(102)	(102)
HN						
Predicted	0.031	0.05	0.1	0.15	0.25	0.41
Experimental	0.02	0.04	0.15	0.10	0.19	0.47
THN						
Predicted	1.1	1.47	1.96	2.57	3.33	4.27
Experimental	1.24	1.46	2.27	2.31	3.08	4.25

D. Numerical Results

We examined the performance of the HN and the THN via simulations (of 10,000 runs each) and compared their error rates with those expected in accordance with our calculations. Due to its probabilistic characterization, the THN may perform reasonably only above some minimal size of n (depending on α and m). The results for such a "minimal" network, indicating the percent of errors at various m values, are presented in Table I. As evident, the experimental results corroborate the accuracy of the THN and HN calculations already at this relatively small network storing a very small number of memories in relation to its capacity. The performance of the THN is considerably worse than that of the corresponding HN. However, as shown in Table II, an increase of 50% in the input-layer size n yields a THN which performs about as well as the previous HN.

Figure 2 presents the results of theoretical calculations of the HN and THN error probabilities for various values of α and m as a function of n. Note the large

Table II
Percentage of Error ($n = 225$, $\alpha = 0.75$)

m	100	200	400	800	1600	3200
(threshold)	(147)	(147)	(148)	(149)	(149)	(150)
HN						
Predicted	0.0002	0.0003	0.0006	0.001	0.002	0.0036
Experimental	0	0	0	0	0	0.01
THN						
Predicted	0.06	0.09	0.12	0.17	0.22	0.3
Experimental	0.09	0.09	0.14	0.17	0.13	0.29

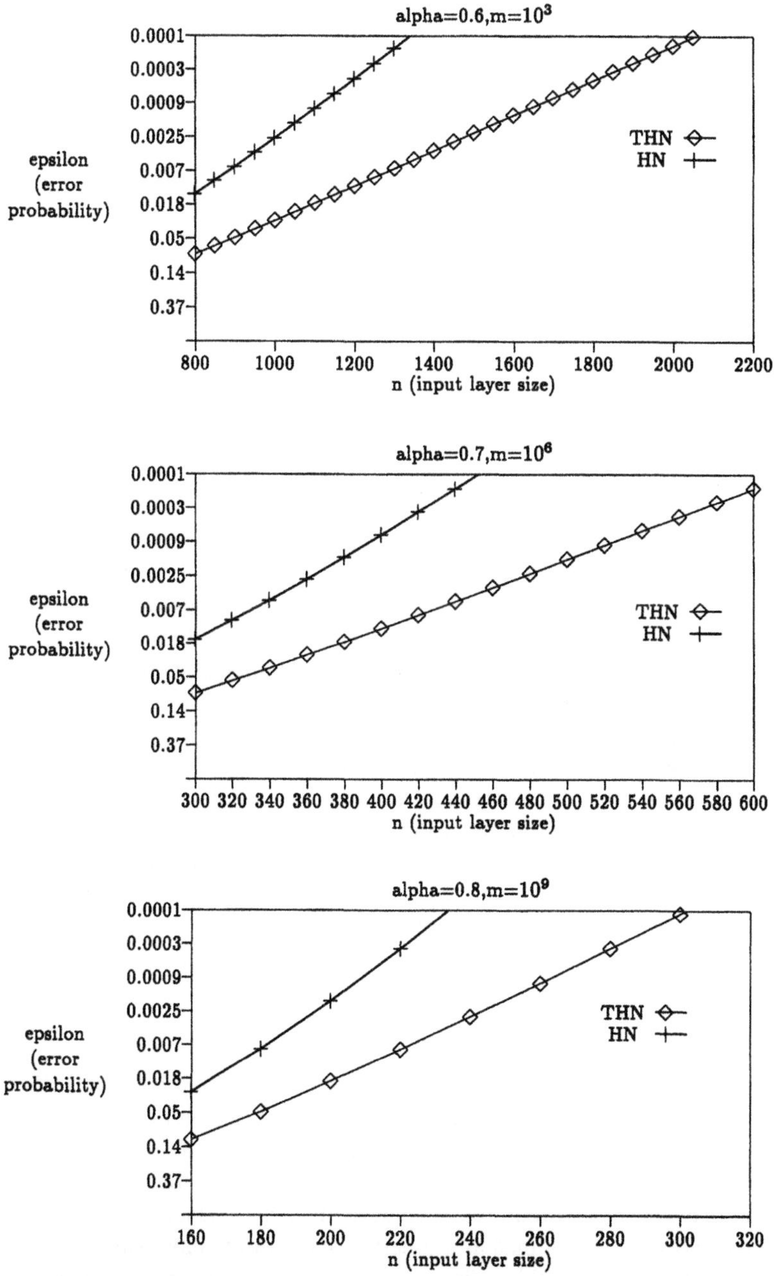

Figure 2 Probability of error as a function of network size. Three networks are depicted, displaying the performance at various values of α and m.

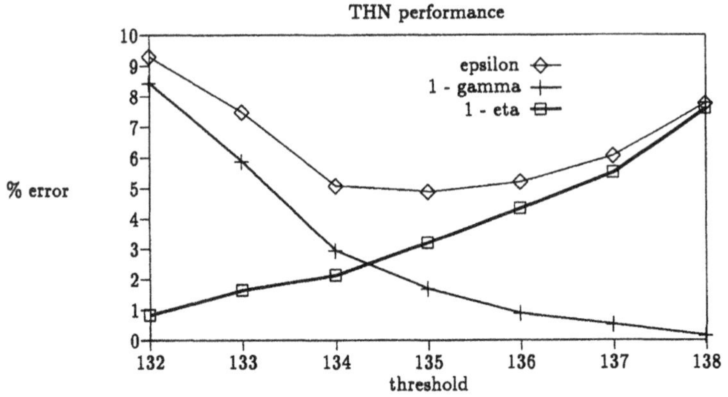

Figure 3 Threshold sensitivity of the THN ($\alpha = 0.7$, $n = 210$, $m = 825$).

difference in the memory capacity as α varies. For graphical convenience, we have plotted $\log 1/\epsilon$ versus n. As seen previously, a fair rule of thumb is that a THN with $n' \approx 1.5n$ neurons in the input layer performs as well as a HN with n such neurons. To see this, simply pass a horizontal line through any error rate value ϵ and observe the ratio between n and n' obtained at its intersections with the corresponding ϵ vs n plots.

To examine the sensitivity of the THN network to threshold variation, we fix $\alpha = 0.7$, $n = 210$, $m = 825$, and let the threshold vary between 132 and 138. As we can see in Fig. 3, the threshold value 135 is optimal, but the performance with threshold values of 134 and 136 is practically identical. The magnitude of the two error types varies considerably with the threshold value, but this variation has no effect on the overall performance near the optimum, and these two error probabilities might as well be taken equal to each other.

E. Final Remarks

In this section we analyzed in detail the performance of a HN and THN classifying inputs that are distorted versions of the stored memory patterns (in contrast to randomly selected patterns). Given an initial input similarity α, a desired storage capacity m, and performance level $1 - \epsilon$, we described how to compute the minimal THN size n required to achieve this performance. As we have seen, the threshold x_n is determined as a function of the initial input similarity α. Obviously, however, the THN it defines will achieve even higher performance when presented with input patterns having initial similarity greater than α. It was shown that although the THN performs worse than its counterpart HN, an approximately

50% increase in the THN input-layer size is sufficient to fully compensate for that. Whereas the WTA network of the HN may be implemented with only $O(3m)$ connections [8], both the THN and the HN require $O(mn)$ connections. Hence, to perform as well as a given HN, the corresponding THN requires $\approx$ 50% more connections, but the $O(m\ln(mn))$ time complexity of the HN is drastically reduced to the $O(1)$ time complexity of the THN.

III. TWO-ITERATION OPTIMAL SIGNALING IN HOPFIELD NETWORKS

A. INTRODUCTION

It is well known that a given cortical neuron can respond with a different firing pattern for the same synaptic input, depending on its firing history and on the effects of modulatory transmitters (see [10, 11] for a review). Working within the convenient framework of Hopfieldlike attractor neural networks (ANN) [12, 13], but motivated by the history-dependent nature of neuronal firing, we now extend the investigation of the two-iteration performance of feedback neural networks given in [14]. We now study continuous input/output signal functions which govern the firing rate of the neuron (such as the conventional sigmoidal function [15, 16]). The notion of a synchronous instantaneous "iteration" is now viewed as an abstraction of the overall dynamics for some short length of time during which the firing rate does not change significantly. We analyze the performance of the network after two such iterations, or intermediate times spans, a period sufficiently long for some significant neural information to be fed back within the network, but shorter than those the network may require for falling into an attractor. However, as demonstrated in Section III.F, the performance of history-dependent ANNs after two iterations is sufficiently high compared with that of memoryless (history-independent) models that the analysis of two iterations becomes a viable end in its own right.

Examining this general family of signal functions, we now search for the computationally most efficient history-dependent neuronal signal (firing) function and study its performance. We derive the optimal analog signal function, having the *slanted sigmoidal* form illustrated in Fig. 4a, and show that it significantly improves performance, both in relation to memoryless dynamics and versus the performance obtained with the previous dichotomous signaling. The optimal signal function is obtained by subtracting from the conventional sigmoid signal function some multiple of the current input field. As shown in Fig. 4a (or in Fig. 4b, plotting the discretized version of the optimal signal function), the neuron's signal may have a sign opposite to the one it "believes" in. In [17–19] it was also observed that the capacity of ANNs is significantly improved by using nonmonotone analog

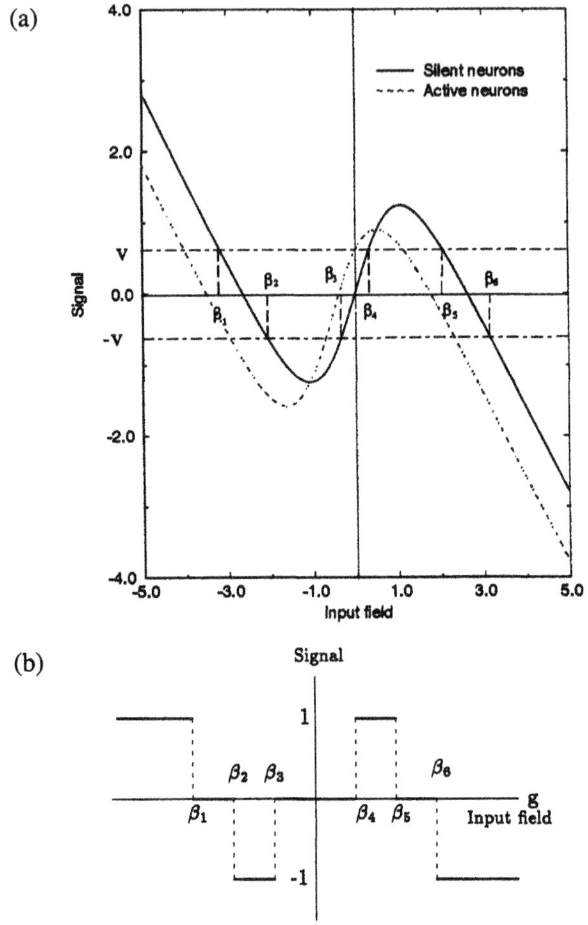

Figure 4 (a) A typical plot of the slanted sigmoid. Network parameters are $N = 5000$, $K = 3000$, $n_1 = 200$, and $m = 50$. (b) A sketch of its discretized version.

signal functions. The limit (after infinitely many iterations) under dynamics using a nonmonotone function of the current input field, similar in form to the slanted sigmoid, was studied. The Bayesian framework we work in provides a clear intuitive account of the nonmonotone form and the seemingly bizarre sign reversal behavior. As we shall see, the slanted sigmoidal form of the optimal signal function is mainly a result of collective cooperation between neurons, whose "common goal" is to maximize the network's performance. It is rather striking that the resulting slanted sigmoid endows the analytical model with some properties characteristic of the firing of cortical neurons; this collectively optimal function may be hard-wired into the cellular biophysical mechanisms determining each neuron's firing function.

B. Model

Our framework is an ANN storing $m + 1$ memory patterns $\xi^1, \xi^2, \ldots, \xi^{m+1}$, each an N-dimensional vector. The network is composed of N neurons, each of which is randomly connected to K other neurons. The $(m + 1)N$ memory entries are independent with equally likely ± 1 values. The initial pattern X, synchronously signaled by L ($\leqslant N$) *initially active* neurons, is a vector of ± 1s, randomly generated from one of the memory patterns (say $\xi = \xi^{m+1}$) such that $P(X_i = \xi_i) = (1 + \epsilon)/2$ for each of the L initially active neurons and $P(X_i = \xi_i) = (1 + \delta)/2$ for each *initially quiescent* (nonactive) neuron. Although $\epsilon, \delta \in [0, 1)$ are arbitrary, it is useful to think of ϵ as being 0.5 (corresponding to an initial similarity of 75%) and of δ as being 0 — a quiescent neuron has no prior preference for any given sign. Let $\alpha_1 = m/n_1$ denote the initial memory load, where $n_1 = LK/N$ is the average number of signals received by each neuron.

We follow a Bayesian approach under which the neuron's signaling and activation decisions are based on the *a posteriori* probabilities assigned to its two possible true memory states, ± 1. We distinguish between *input fields* that model incoming spikes and *generalized fields* that model history-dependent, adaptive postsynaptic potentials. Clearly, the *prior probability* that neuron i has memory state $+1$ is

$$\lambda_i^{(0)} = P(\xi_i = 1 | X_i, I_i) = \begin{cases} \dfrac{1+\epsilon}{2}, & \text{if } X_i = 1,\ I_i = 1, \\ \dfrac{1-\epsilon}{2}, & \text{if } X_i = -1,\ I_i = 1, \\ \dfrac{1+\delta}{2}, & \text{if } X_i = 1,\ I_i = 0, \\ \dfrac{1-\delta}{2}, & \text{if } X_i = -1,\ I_i = 0, \end{cases}$$

$$= \frac{1 + (\epsilon I_i + \delta(1 - I_i))X_i}{2} = \frac{1}{1 + e^{-2g_i^{(0)}}}, \tag{32}$$

where $I_i = 0, 1$ indicates whether neuron i has been active (i.e., transmitted a signal) in the first iteration, and the *generalized field* $g_i^{(0)}$ is given by

$$g_i^{(0)} = \begin{cases} g(\epsilon)X_i, & \text{if } i \text{ is active,} \\ g(\delta)X_i, & \text{if } i \text{ is quiescent,} \end{cases} \tag{33}$$

where

$$g(t) = \operatorname{arctanh}(t) = \frac{1}{2}\log\frac{1+t}{1-t}, \qquad 0 \leqslant t < 1. \tag{34}$$

We also define the *prior belief* that neuron i has memory state $+1$,

$$O_i^{(0)} = \lambda_i^{(0)} - (1 - \lambda_i^{(0)}) = 2\lambda_i^{(0)} - 1 = \tanh(g_i^{(0)}), \tag{35}$$

whose possible values are $\pm\epsilon$ and $\pm\delta$ (the belief is simply a rescaling of the probability from the $[0, 1]$ interval to $[-1, +1]$).

The input field observed by neuron i as a result of the initial activity is

$$f_i^{(1)} = \frac{1}{n_1}\sum_{j=1}^{N} W_{ij} I_{ij} I_j X_j, \tag{36}$$

where $I_{ij} = 0, 1$ indicates whether a connection exists from neuron j to neuron i and W_{ij} denotes its magnitude, given by the Hopfield prescription

$$W_{ij} = \sum_{\mu=1}^{m+1} \xi_i^{\mu}\xi_j^{\mu}, \qquad W_{ii} = 0. \tag{37}$$

As a result of observing the input field $f_i^{(1)}$, which is approximately normally distributed (given ξ_i, X_i, and I_i) with mean and variance

$$E\big(f_i^{(1)}|\xi_i, X_i, I_i\big) = \epsilon\xi_i, \tag{38}$$

$$\operatorname{Var}\big(f_i^{(1)}|\xi_i, X_i, I_i\big) = \alpha_1, \tag{39}$$

neuron i changes its opinion about $\{\xi_i = 1\}$ from $\lambda_i^{(0)}$ to the *posterior probability*

$$\lambda_i^{(1)} = \big(P\xi_i = 1|X_i, I_i, f_i^{(1)}\big) = \frac{1}{1 + e^{-2g_i^{(1)}}}, \tag{40}$$

with a corresponding *posterior belief* $O_i^{(1)} = \tanh(g_i^{(1)})$, where $g_i^{(1)}$ is conveniently expressed as an additive generalized field [see Lemma 1(II) in [14]]

$$g_i^{(1)} = g_i^{(0)} + \frac{\epsilon}{\alpha_1} f_i^{(1)}. \tag{41}$$

We now get to the second iteration, in which, as in the first iteration, some of the neurons become active and signal to the network. Unlike the first iteration, in which initially active neurons had independent beliefs of equal strength and simply signaled their states in the initial pattern, the preamble to the second iteration finds neuron i in possession of a personal history $(X_i, I_i, f_i^{(1)})$, as a function of which the neuron has to determine the signal to transmit to the network. Although the history-independent Hopfield dynamics choose $\text{sign}(f_i^{(1)})$ as this signal, we model the signal function as $h(g_i^{(1)}, X_i, I_i)$. This seems like four different functions of $g_i^{(1)}$. However, by symmetry, $h(g_i^{(1)}, +1, I_i)$ should be equal to $-h(-g_i^{(1)}, -1, I_i)$. Hence, we only have two functions of $g_i^{(1)}$ to define: $h_1(\cdot)$ for the signals of the initially active neurons and $h_0(\cdot)$ for the quiescent ones. For mathematical convenience we would like to insert into these functions random variables with unit variance. By (39) and (41), the conditional variance $\text{Var}(g_i^{(1)}|\xi_i, X_i, I_i)$ is $(\epsilon/\alpha_1)^2\alpha_1 = (\epsilon/\sqrt{\alpha_1})^2$. We thus define $\omega = \epsilon/\sqrt{\alpha_1}$ and let

$$h\big(g_i^{(1)}, X_i, I_i\big) = X_i h_{I_i}\big(X_i g_i^{(1)}/\omega\big). \tag{42}$$

The field observed by neuron i following the second iteration (with n_2 updating neurons per neuron) is

$$f_i^{(2)} = \frac{1}{n_2}\sum_{j=1}^{N} W_{ij} I_{ij} h\big(g_j^{(1)}, X_j, I_j\big), \tag{43}$$

on the basis of which neuron i computes its posterior probability

$$\lambda_i^{(2)} = P\big(\xi_i = 1 | X_i, I_i, f_i^{(1)}, f_i^{(2)}\big) \tag{44}$$

and corresponding posterior belief $O_i^{(2)} = 2\lambda_i^{(2)} - 1$, which will be expressed in Section IV.C as $\tanh(g_i^{(2)})$.

As announced earlier, we stop at the preceding two information-exchange iterations and let each neuron express its final choice of sign as

$$X_i^{(2)} = \text{sign}\big(O_i^{(2)}\big). \tag{45}$$

The performance of the network is measured by the final similarity

$$S_f = P\big(X_i^{(2)} = \xi_i\big) = \frac{(1 + (1/N)\sum_{j=1}^{N} X_j^{(2)}\xi_j)}{2} \tag{46}$$

(where the last equality holds asymptotically).

Our first task is to present (as simply as possible) an expression for the performance under arbitrary architecture and activity parameters, for general signal functions h_0 and h_1. Then, using this expression, our main goal is to find the best choice of signal functions which maximize the performance attained. We find these functions when there are either no restrictions on their range set or they are restricted to the values $\{-1, 0, 1\}$, and calculate the performance achieved in Gaussian, random, and multilayer patterns of connectivity. The optimal choice will be shown to be the *slanted sigmoid*

$$h(g_i^{(1)}, X_i, I_i) = O_i^{(1)} - cf_i^{(1)} \tag{47}$$

for some c in $(0, 1)$. We present explicitly all formulas. Their derivation is provided in [2].

C. Rationale for Nonmonotone Bayesian Signaling

1. Nonmonotonicity

The common Hopfield convention is to have neuron i signal sign($f_i^{(1)}$). Another possibility, studied in [14], is to signal the preferred sign only if this preference is strong enough; otherwise, to remain silent. However, an even better performance was achieved by counterintuitive signals which are not monotone in $g_i^{(1)}$ [14, 17, 19]. In fact, precisely those neurons that are *most* convinced of their signs should signal the sign *opposite* to the one they so strongly believe in! We would like to offer now an intuitive explanation for this seeming pathology, and proceed later to the mathematics leading to it.

In the initial pattern, the different entries X_i and X_j are conditionally independent given ξ_i and ξ_j. This is not the case for the input fields $f_i^{(1)}$ and $f_j^{(1)}$, whose correlation is proportional to the synaptic weight W_{ij} [14]. For concreteness, let $\epsilon = 0.5$ and $\alpha_1 = 0.25$ and suppose that neuron i has observed an input field $f_i^{(1)} = 3$. Neuron i now knows that either its true memory state is $\xi_i = +1$, in which case the "noise" in the input field is $3 - \epsilon = 2.5$ (i.e., 5 standard deviations above the mean), or its true memory state is $\xi_i = -1$ and the noise is $3 + \epsilon = 3.5$ (or 7 standard deviations above the mean). In a Gaussian distribution, deviations of 5 or 7 standard deviations are very unusual, but 7 is so much more unusual than 5, that neuron i is practically convinced that its true state is $+1$. However, neuron i knows that its input field $f_i^{(1)}$ is grossly inflicted with noise and because the input field $f_j^{(1)}$ of neuron j is correlated with its own, neuron i would want to warn neuron j that its input field has unusual noise too and should not be believed at face value. Neuron i, a good student of regression analysis, wants to tell neuron j, without knowing the weight W_{ij}, to subtract from its field a multiple of $W_{ij} f_i^{(1)}$. This is accomplished, to the simultaneous benefit of all neurons j, by signaling a multiple of $-f_i^{(1)}$. We see that neuron i, out of "purely altruistic traits," has a conflict between the positive act of signaling its assessed true sign and the negative act of signaling the opposite as a means of correcting the fields of its peers. It is not surprising that this inhibitory behavior is dominant only when field values are strong enough.

2. Potential of Bayesian Updating

Neuron i starts with a prior probability $\lambda_i^{(0)} = P(\xi_i = +1)$ and after observing input fields $f_i^{(1)}, f_i^{(2)}, \ldots, f_i^{(t)}$ computes the posterior probability

$$\lambda_i^{(t)} = P\big(\xi_i = +1 | f_i^{(1)}, f_i^{(2)}, \ldots, f_i^{(t)}\big). \tag{48}$$

It now signals

$$h_i^{(t)} = h^{(t)}\big(\lambda_i{}^{(0)}, f_i^{(1)}, f_i^{(2)}, \ldots, f_i^{(t)}\big) \tag{49}$$

and computes the new input field

$$f_i^{(t+1)} = \sum_j W_{ij} I_{ij} h_j^{(t)}. \tag{50}$$

This description proceeds inductively.

The stochastic process $\lambda_i^{(0)}, \lambda_i^{(1)}, \lambda_i^{(2)}, \ldots$ is of the form

$$X_t = E(Z | Y_1, Y_2, \ldots, Y_t),$$

where $Z = I_{\{\xi_i = +1\}}$ is a (bounded) random variable and the Y process adds in every stage some more information to the data available earlier. Such a process is termed a *Martingale* in probability theory. The following facts are well known, the first being actually the usual definition

1. For all t,

$$E(X_{t+1} | Y_1, Y_2, \ldots, Y_t) = X_t \quad \text{a.s.}$$

(where a.s. means almost surely or except for an event with probability 0).

2. In particular, $E(X_t)$ is the same for all t.

3. If the finite interval $[a, b]$ is such that $P(a \leqslant X_t \leqslant b) = 1$ for all t and Ψ is a convex function on $[a, b]$, then for all t,

$$E\big(\Psi(X_{t+1}) | Y_1, Y_2, \ldots, Y_t\big) \geqslant \Psi(X_t) \quad \text{a.s.}$$

4. In particular, for all t,

$$E\big(\Psi(X_t)\big) \leqslant E\big(\Psi(X_{t+1})\big).$$

5. (A special case of Doob's Martingale convergence theorem.) For every bounded Martingale (X_t) there is a random variable X such that

$$X_t \to X \quad \text{as } t \to \infty, \text{ a.s.}$$

and in fact the Martingale is the sequence of "opinions" about X: For all t,

$$X_t = E(X | Y_1, Y_2, \ldots, Y_t) \quad \text{a.s.}$$

6. In particular, $E(X) = E(X_t)$ and $E(\Psi(X)) \geqslant E(\Psi(X_t))$ for all t, for any convex function Ψ defined on $[a, b]$.

A neuron with posterior probability $\lambda_i^{(t)}$ as in (48) decides momentarily that its true state is $+1$ if $\lambda_i^{(t)} > 1/2$ and -1 if $\lambda_i^{(t)} < 1/2$. The strength of belief, or confidence in the preferred state, is given by the *convex* function $\Psi(x) = \mathrm{Max}(x, 1-x)$ applied to the $[0, 1]$-bounded martingale $(\lambda_i^{(t)})$. For large N, the current *similarity* of the network, or proportion of neurons whose preferred state is the correct one, is mathematically characterized as $E(\Psi(\lambda_i^{(t)}))$. By the preceding statements, Bayesian updatings are always such that every neuron has a well defined final decision about its state (we may call this a fixed point) and the network's similarity increases with every iteration, being at the fixed point even higher. This holds true for arbitrary signal functions h, and not only for those that are in some sense optimal. By the preceding statements, whatever similarity we achieve after two Bayesian iterations is a lower bound for what can be achieved by more iterations, unlike memoryless Hopfield dynamics which are known to do reasonably well at the beginning even below capacity, in which case they converge eventually to random fixed points [20].

D. PERFORMANCE

1. Architecture Parameters

This subsection introduces and illustrates certain parameters whose relevance will become apparent in Section III.D.3. There are N neurons in the network and K incoming synapses projecting on every neuron. If there is a synapse from neuron i to neuron j, the probability is r_2 that there is a synapse from neuron j to neuron i. If there are synapses from i to j and from j to k, the probability is r_3 that there is a synapse from i to k. If there are synapses from i to each of j and k, and from j to l, the probability is r_4 that there is a synapse from k to l.

We saw in [14] that Bayesian neurons are adaptive enough to make r_2 irrelevant for performance, but that r_3 and r_4, which we took simply to be K/N assuming *fully random connectivity*, are of relevance. It is clear that if each neuron is connected to its K closest neighbors, then r_2 is 1 and r_3 and r_4 are large. For *fully connected* networks all three are equal to 1.

For *Gaussian connectivity*, if neurons i and j are at a distance x from each other, then the probability that there is a synapse from j to i is

$$P(\text{synapse}) = pe^{-x^2/2s^2}, \tag{51}$$

where $p \in (0, 1]$ and $s^2 > 0$ are parameters. Whereas the sum of n independent and identically distributed Gaussian random vectors is Gaussian with variance n

times as large as that of the summands, we get that in d-dimensional space

$$\begin{aligned} r_k &= \int p \exp\left(-\frac{1}{2s^2}\sum_{i=1}^{d} x_i^2\right) \frac{\exp(-(1/2s^2(k-1))\sum_{i=1}^{d} x_i{}^2)}{(2\pi(k-1)s^2)^{d/2}}\, dx_1\, dx_2 \cdots dx_d \\ &= \frac{p}{k^{d/2}} \int \frac{(\exp(-1/2s^2)((k-1)/k))\sum_{i=1}^{d} x_i^2}{(2\pi s^2((k-1)/k))^{d/2}}\, dx_1\, dx_2 \cdots dx_d \\ &= \frac{p}{k^{d/2}}. \end{aligned} \tag{52}$$

Thus, in three-dimensional space, $r_2 = p/(2\sqrt{2})$, $r_3 = p/(3\sqrt{3})$, and $r_4 = p/8$, depending on the parameter p but not on s.

For *multilayered networks* in which there is full connectivity between consecutive layers but no other connections, r_2 and r_4 are equal to 1 and r_3 is 0 (unless there are three layers cyclically connected, in which case $r_3 = 1$ as well).

2. One-Iteration Performance

Clearly, if neuron i had to choose for itself a sign on the basis of one iteration, this sign would have been

$$X_i^{(1)} = \operatorname{sign}(O_i{}^{(1)}). \tag{53}$$

Hence, letting $\omega = \epsilon/\sqrt{\alpha_1}$, if $P(X_i = \xi_i) = (1+t)/2$ (where t is either ϵ or δ), then after one iteration (similar to [21]),

$$\begin{aligned} P(X_i^{(1)} = \xi_i) &= P(\lambda_i^{(1)} > 0.5|\xi_i = 1) = P\left(g(t)X_i + \frac{\epsilon}{\alpha_1} f_i{}^{(1)} > 0 \mid \xi_i = 1\right) \\ &= \frac{1+t}{2} P\left(g(t) + \frac{\epsilon}{\alpha_1}(\epsilon + \sqrt{\alpha_1}Z) > 0\right) \\ &\quad + \frac{1-t}{2} P\left(-g(t) + \frac{\epsilon}{\alpha_1}(\epsilon + \sqrt{\alpha_1}Z) > 0\right) \\ &= \frac{1+t}{2}\Phi\left(\omega + \frac{g(t)}{\omega}\right) + \frac{1-t}{2}\Phi\left(\omega - \frac{g(t)}{\omega}\right), \end{aligned} \tag{54}$$

where Z is a standard normal random variable and Φ is its distribution function. Letting

$$Q^*(x,t) = \frac{1+t}{2}\Phi\left(x + \frac{g(t)}{x}\right) + \frac{1-t}{2}\Phi\left(x - \frac{g(t)}{x}\right), \qquad 0 \leqslant t < 1,\ x > 0, \tag{55}$$

we see that (54) is expressible as $Q^*(\omega, t)$. Whereas the proportion of initially active neurons is n_1/K, the similarity after one iteration is

$$S_1 = \frac{n_1}{K} Q^*(\omega, \epsilon) + \left(1 - \frac{n_1}{K}\right) Q^*(\omega, \delta). \tag{56}$$

As for the relation between the current similarity S_1 and the initial similarity, observe that $Q^*(x, t)$ is strictly increasing in x and converges to $(1 + t)/2$ as $x \downarrow 0$. Hence, S_1 strictly exceeds the initial similarity $(n_1/K)(1 + \epsilon)/2 + (1 - n_1/K)(1 + \delta)/2$. Furthermore, S_1 is a strictly increasing function of n_1 $(= m/\alpha_1)$.

3. Second Iteration

To analyze the effect of a second iteration, it is necessary to identify the (asymptotic) conditional distribution of the new input field $f_i^{(2)}$, defined by (43), given $(\xi_i, X_i, I_i, f_i^{(1)})$. Under a working paradigm that, given ξ_i, X_i, and I_i, the input fields $(f_i^{(1)}, f_i^{(2)})$ are jointly normally distributed, the conditional distribution of $f_i^{(2)}$ given $(\xi_i, X_i, I_i, f_i^{(1)})$ should be normal with mean depending linearly on $f_i{}^{(1)}$ and variance independent of $f_i{}^{(1)}$. More explicitly, if (U, V) are jointly normally distributed with correlation coefficient $\rho = \mathrm{Cov}(U, V)/(\sigma_U \sigma_V)$, then

$$E(V|U) = E(V) + \rho(\sigma_V/\sigma_U)\big(U - E(U)\big) \tag{57}$$

and

$$\mathrm{Var}(V|U) = \mathrm{Var}(V)\big(1 - \rho^2\big). \tag{58}$$

Thus, the only parameters needed to define dynamics and evaluate performance are $E(f_i^{(2)}|\xi_i, X_i, I_i)$, $\mathrm{Cov}(f_i^{(1)}, f_i^{(2)}|\xi_i, X_i, I_i)$, and $\mathrm{Var}(f_i^{(2)}|\xi_i, X_i, I_i)$. In terms of these, the conditional distribution of $f_i^{(2)}$ given $(\xi_i, X_i, I_i, f_i{}^{(1)})$ is normal with

$$\begin{aligned} E\big(f_i^{(2)}&|\xi_i, X_i, I_i, f_i{}^{(1)}\big) \\ &= E\big(f_i{}^{(2)}|\xi_i, X_i, I_i\big) \\ &\quad + \frac{\mathrm{Cov}(f_i{}^{(1)}, f_i{}^{(2)}|\xi_i, X_i, I_i)}{\mathrm{Var}(f_i{}^{(1)}|\xi_i, X_i, I_i)}\big(f_i{}^{(1)} - E\big(f_i{}^{(1)}|\xi_i, X_i, I_i\big)\big) \end{aligned} \tag{59}$$

and

$$\mathrm{Var}(f_i{}^{(2)}|\xi_i, X_i, I_i, f_i{}^{(1)}) = \mathrm{Var}(f_i{}^{(2)}|\xi_i, X_i, I_i) - \frac{\mathrm{Cov}^2(f_i{}^{(1)}, f_i{}^{(2)}|\xi_i, X_i, I_i)}{\mathrm{Var}(f_i{}^{(1)}|\xi_i, X_i, I_i)}. \tag{60}$$

Assuming a model of joint normality, as in [14], we rigorously identify limiting expressions for the three parameters of the model. Although we do not have as yet sufficient formal evidence pointing to the correctness of the joint normality assumption, the simulation results presented in Section III.F fully support the adequacy of this common model.

In [14] we proved that $E(f_i^{(2)} \mid \xi_i, X_i, I_i)$ is a linear combination of ξ_i and $X_i I_i$, which we denote by

$$E\big(f_i^{(2)} | \xi_i, X_i, I_i\big) = \epsilon^* \xi_i + b X_i I_i. \tag{61}$$

We also proved that $\mathrm{Cov}(f_i^{(1)}, f_i^{(2)} \mid \xi_i, X_i, I_i)$ and $\mathrm{Var}(f_i^{(2)} \mid \xi_i, X_i, I_i)$ are independent of (ξ_i, X_i, I_i). These parameters determine the *regression coefficient*

$$a = \frac{\mathrm{Cov}(f_i^{(1)}, f_i^{(2)} | \xi_i, X_i, I_i)}{\mathrm{Var}(f_i^{(1)} \mid \xi_i, X_i, I_i)} \tag{62}$$

and the *residual variance*

$$\tau^2 = \mathrm{Var}(f_i^{(2)} | \xi_i, X_i, I_i, f_i^{(1)}). \tag{63}$$

These facts remain true in the current more general framework. We presented in [2] formulas for a, b, ϵ^* and τ^2, whose derivation is cumbersome. The posterior probability that neuron i has memory state $+1$ is [see (40) and Lemma 1(II) in [14]]

$$\begin{aligned} \lambda_i^{(2)} &= P(\xi_i = 1 | X_i, I_i, f_i^{(1)}, f_i^{(2)}) \\ &= \frac{1}{1 + \exp\{-2[g_i^{(1)} + ((\epsilon^* - a\epsilon)/\tau^2)(f_i^{(2)} - a f_i^{(1)} - b X_i I_i)]\}}, \end{aligned} \tag{64}$$

from which we obtain the final belief $O_i^{(2)} = 2\lambda_i^{(2)} - 1 = \tanh(g_i^{(2)})$, where $g_i^{(2)}$ should be defined as

$$\begin{aligned} g_i^{(2)} = {} & \left(\frac{\epsilon}{\alpha_1} - \frac{(\epsilon^* - a\epsilon)a}{\tau^2}\right) f_i^{(1)} + \left(\frac{\epsilon^* - a\epsilon}{\tau^2}\right) f_i^{(2)} \\ & + \begin{cases} g(\delta) X_i, & \text{if } I_i = 0, \\ \left(g(\epsilon) - \dfrac{b(\epsilon^* - a\epsilon)}{\tau^2}\right) X_i, & \text{otherwise,} \end{cases} \end{aligned} \tag{65}$$

to yield the final decision $X_i^{(2)} = \mathrm{sign}(g_i^{(2)})$. Since $(f_i^{(1)}, f_i^{(2)})$ are jointly normally distributed given (ξ_i, X_i, I_i), any linear combination of the two, such as the one in expression (65), is normally distributed. After identifying its mean and variance, a standard computation reveals that the final similarity $S_2 = P(X_i^{(2)} = \xi_i)$—our global measure of performance—is given by a formula similar to expression (56) for S_1, with heavier activity n^* than n_1,

$$S_2 = \frac{n_1}{K} Q^*\left(\frac{\epsilon}{\sqrt{\alpha^*}}, \epsilon\right) + \left(1 - \frac{n_1}{K}\right) Q^*\left(\frac{\epsilon}{\sqrt{\alpha^*}}, \delta\right), \tag{66}$$

where

$$\alpha^* = \frac{m}{n^*} = \frac{m}{n_1 + m((\epsilon^*/\epsilon - a)/\tau)^2}. \tag{67}$$

In agreement with the ever-improving nature of Bayesian updatings, S_2 exceeds S_1 just as S_1 exceeds the initial similarity. Furthermore, S_2 is an increasing function of $|(\epsilon^*/\epsilon - a)/\tau|$.

E. Optimal Signaling and Performance

By optimizing over the factor $|(\epsilon^*/\epsilon - a)/\tau|$ determining performance, we showed in [2] that the optimal signal functions are

$$h_1(y) = R^*(y, \epsilon) - 1, \qquad h_0(y) = R^*(y, \delta), \tag{68}$$

where R^* is

$$R^*(y, t) = \frac{1}{\epsilon}\left(1 + r_3\omega^2\right)\left[\tanh(\omega y) - c\left(\omega y - g(t)\right)\right] \tag{69}$$

and c is a constant in (0, 1).

The nonmonotone form of these functions, illustrated in Fig. 4, is clear. Neurons that have already signaled +1 in the first iteration have a lesser tendency to send positive signals than quiescent neurons. The signaling of quiescent neurons which receive no prior information ($\delta = 0$) has a symmetric form.

The signal function of the initially active neurons may be shifted without affecting performance: If instead of taking $h_1(y)$ to be $R^*(y, \epsilon) - 1$, we take it to be $R^*(y, \epsilon) - 1 + \Delta$ for some arbitrary Δ, we will get the same performance because the effect of such Δ on the second iteration input field $f_i^{(2)}$ would be [see (43)] the addition of

$$\frac{1}{n_2} \sum_{j=1}^{N} W_{ij} I_{ij} \Delta X_j I_j = \Delta \frac{n_1}{n_2} f_i^{(1)}, \tag{70}$$

which history-based Bayesian updating rules can adapt to fully. As shown in [2], Δ appears nowhere in $(\epsilon^*/\epsilon - a)$ or in τ, but it affects a. Hence, Δ may be given several roles:

- Setting the ratio of the coefficients of $f_i^{(1)}$ and $f_i^{(2)}$ in (65) to a desired value, mimicking the passive decay of the membrane potential.

• Making the final decision $X_i{}^{(2)}$ [see (65)] free of $f_i{}^{(1)}$, by letting the coefficient of the latter vanish. A judicious choice of the value of the reflexivity parameter r_2 (which, just as Δ, does not affect performance) can make the final decision $X_i^{(2)}$ free of whether the neuron was initially quiescent or active. For the natural choice $\delta = 0$ this will make the final decision free of the initial state as well and become simply the usual history-independent Hopfield rule $X_i{}^{(2)} = \text{sign}(f_i^{(2)})$, except that $f_i^{(2)}$ is the result of carefully tuned slanted sigmoidal signaling.

• We may take $\Delta = 1$, in which case both functions h_0 and h_1 are given simply by $R^*(y, t)$, where $t = \epsilon$ or δ depending on whether the neuron is initially active or quiescent. Let us express this signal explicitly in terms of history. By Table I and expression (42), the signal emitted by neuron i (whether it is active or quiescent) is

$$\begin{aligned} h(g_i{}^{(1)}, X_i, I_i) &= X_i h_{I_i}\left(\frac{X_i g_i{}^{(1)}}{\omega}\right) \\ &= \frac{1 + r_3\omega^2}{\epsilon} X_i\Big[\tanh\big(X_i g_i{}^{(1)}\big) - c\big(X_i g_i{}^{(1)} - g(t)\big)\Big] \\ &= \frac{1 + r_3\omega^2}{\epsilon}\Big[\tanh\big(g_i{}^{(1)}\big) - c\big(g_i{}^{(1)} - X_i g(t)\big)\Big] \\ &= \frac{1 + r_3\omega^2}{\epsilon}\Big[\tanh\big(g_i^{(1)} - c f_i^{(1)}\big)\Big]. \end{aligned} \tag{71}$$

We see that the signal is essentially equal to the sigmoid [see expression (41)] $\tanh(g_i^{(1)}) = 2\lambda_i^{(1)} - 1$, modified by a correction term depending only on the current input field, in full agreement with the intuitive explanations of Section III.C. This correction is never too strong; note that c is always less than 1. In a fully connected network c is simply

$$c = \frac{1}{1 + \omega^2},$$

that is, in the limit of low memory load ($\omega \to \infty$), the best signal is simply a sigmoidal function of the generalized input field.

To obtain a discretized version of the slanted sigmoid, we let the signal be $\text{sign}(h(y))$ as long as $|h(y)|$ is large enough, where h is the slanted sigmoid. The resulting signal, as a function of the generalized field, is (see Fig. 4a and b)

$$h_j(y) = \begin{cases} +1, & y < \beta_1{}^{(j)} \text{ or } \beta_4{}^{(j)} < y < \beta_5{}^{(j)}, \\ -1, & y > \beta_6{}^{(j)} \text{ or } \beta_2{}^{(j)} < y < \beta_3{}^{(j)}, \\ 0, & \text{otherwise}, \end{cases} \tag{72}$$

where $-\infty < \beta_1{}^{(0)} < \beta_2{}^{(0)} \leqslant \beta_3{}^{(0)} < \beta_4{}^{(0)} \leqslant \beta_5{}^{(0)} < \beta_6{}^{(0)} < \infty$ and $-\infty < \beta_1{}^{(1)} < \beta_2{}^{(1)} \leqslant \beta_3{}^{(1)} < \beta_4{}^{(1)} \leqslant \beta_5{}^{(1)} < \beta_6{}^{(1)} < \infty$ define, respectively, the firing pattern of the neurons that were silent and active in the first iteration. To find the best such discretized version of the optimal signal, we search numerically for the activity level v which maximizes performance. Every activity level v, used as a threshold on $|h(y)|$, defines the (at most) 12 parameters $\beta_i^{(j)}$ (which are identified numerically via the Newton–Raphson method) as illustrated in Fig. 4b.

F. Results

Using the formulation presented in the previous subsection, we investigate numerically the two-iteration performance achieved in several network architectures with optimal analog and discretized signaling.

Figure 5 displays the performance achieved in the network, when the input signal is applied only to the small fraction (4%) of neurons which are active in

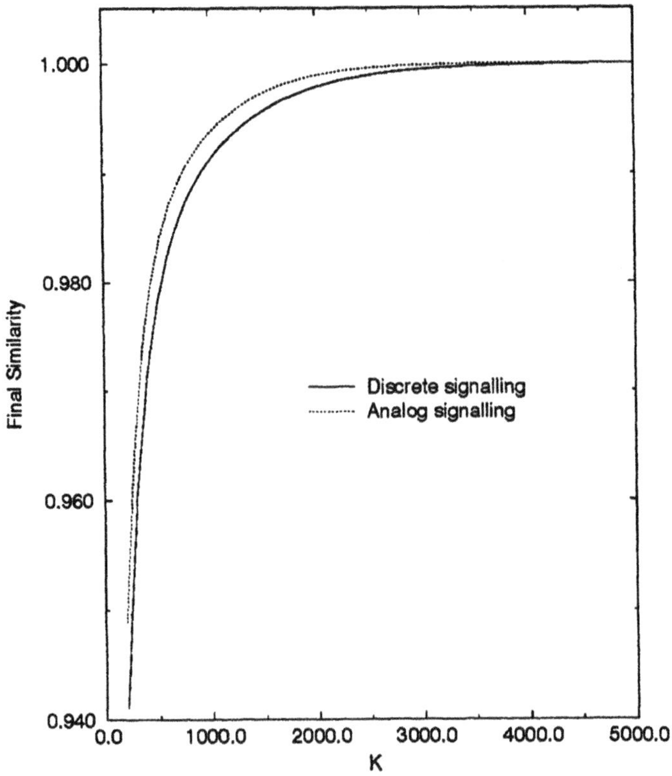

Figure 5 Two-iteration performance in a low-activity network as a function of connectivity K. Network parameters are $N = 5000$, $m = 50$, $n_1 = 200$, $\epsilon = 0.5$, and $\delta = 0$.

the first iteration (expressing possible limited resources of input information). Although low activity is enforced in the first iteration, the number of neurons allowed to become active in the second iteration is not restricted, and the best performance is typically achieved when about 70% of the neurons in the network are active (both with optimal signaling and with the previous, heuristic signaling). We see that (for $K > 1000$) near perfect final similarity is achieved, even when the 96% initially quiescent neurons get no initial clue as to their true memory state, if no restrictions are placed on the second iteration activity level. The performance loss due to discretization is not considerable.

Figure 6 illustrates the performance when connectivity and the number of signals received by each neuron are held fixed, but the network size is increased. A region of decreased performance is evident at mid-connectivity ($K \approx N/2$) values, due to the increased residual variance. Hence, for neurons capable of form-

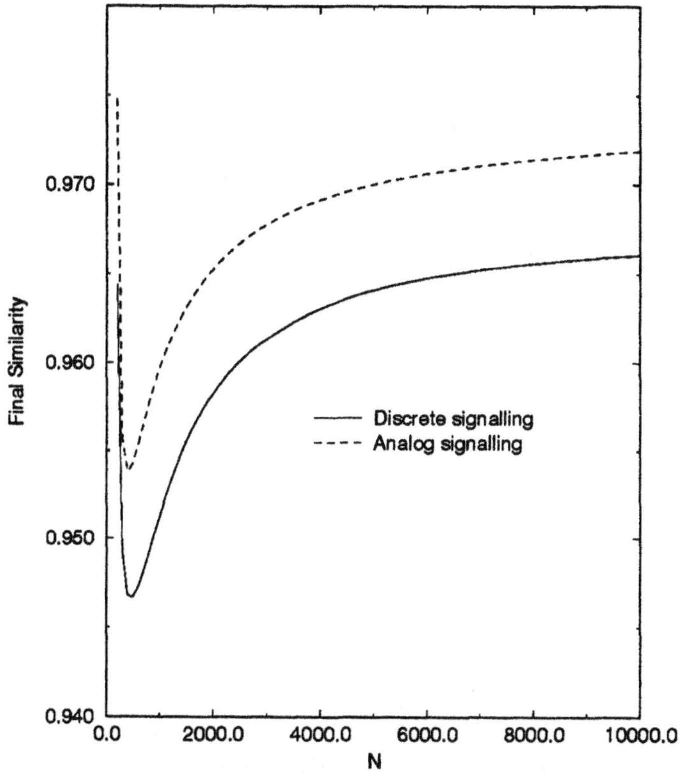

Figure 6 Two-iteration performance in a full-activity network as a function of network size N. Network parameters are $n_1 = K = 200$, $m = 40$, and $\epsilon = 0.5$.

ing K connections on the average, the network should be either fully connected or have a size N much larger than K. Because (unavoidable eventually) synaptic deletion would sharply worsen the performance of fully connected networks, cortical ANNs should indeed be sparsely connected. As evident, performance approaches an upper limit (the performance achieved with $r_3 = 0$ and $r_4 = 0$) as the network size is increased, and any further increase in the network size is unrewarding. The final similarity achieved in the fully connected network (with $N = K = 200$) should be noted. In this case, the memory load (0.2) is significantly above the critical capacity of the Hopfield network [22], but optimal history-dependent dynamics still manage to achieve a rather high two-iteration similarity (0.975) from initial similarity 0.75. This is in agreement with the findings of [17, 18], that showed that nonmonotone dynamics increase capacity.

Our theoretical predictions have been extensively examined by network simulations, and already in relatively small-scale networks, close correspondence is achieved. For example, simulating a fully connected network storing 100 memories with 500 neurons, the performance achieved with discretized dynamics under initial full activity (averaged over 100 trials, with $\epsilon = 0.5$ and $\delta = 0$) was 0.969 versus the 0.964 predicted theoretically. When m, n_1, and K were reduced by half (i.e., $N = 500$, $K = 250$, $m = 50$, and $n_1 = 250$) the predicted performance was 0.947 and that achieved in simulation was 0.946. When m, n_1, and K were further reduced by half (into $K = 125$, $m = 25$, and $n_1 = 125$) the predicted performance was 0.949 and that actually achieved was 0.953. In a larger network, with $N = 1500$, $K = 500$, $m = 50$, $n_1 = 250$, $\epsilon = 0.5$, and $\delta = 0$, the predicted performance is 0.977 and that obtained numerically was 0.973.

Figure 7 illustrates the performance achieved with various network architectures, all sharing the same network parameters N, K, m and input similarity parameters n_1, ϵ, δ, but differing in the spatial organization of the neurons' synapses. Five different configurations are examined, characterized by different values of the architecture parameters r_3 and r_4, as described in Section III.D.1. The upper bound on the final similarity that can be achieved in ANNs in two iterations is demonstrated by letting $r_3 = 0$ and $r_4 = 0$. A lower bound (i.e., the worst possible architecture) on the performance gained with optimal signaling has been calculated by letting $r_4 = 1$ and searching for r_3 values that yielded the worst performance (such values began around 0.6 and increased to ≈ 0.8 as K was increased). The performance of the multilayered architecture was calculated by letting $r_4 = 1$ and $r_3 = 0$. Finally, the worst performance achievable with two- and three-dimensional Gaussian connectivity [corresponding to $p = 1$ in (51)] has been demonstrated by letting $r_3 = 1/3$, $r_4 = 1/4$ and $r_3 = 1/(3\sqrt{3})$, $r_4 = 1/8$, respectively. As evident, even in low-activity sparse-connectivity conditions, the decrease in performance with Gaussian connectivity (in relation, say, to the upper bound) does not seem considerable. Hence, history-dependent ANNs can work well in a corticallike architecture. It is interesting but not surprising to

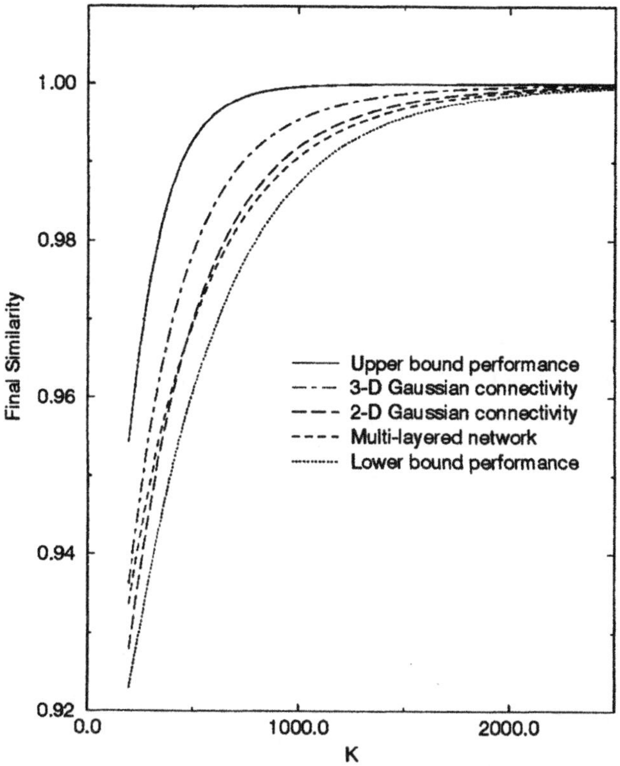

Figure 7 Two-iteration performance achieved with various network architectures, as a function of the network connectivity K. Network parameters are $N = 5000$, $n_1 = 200$, $m = 50$, $\epsilon = 0.5$, and $\delta = 0$.

see that three-dimensional Gaussian-connectivity architecture is superior to the two-dimensional one along the whole connectivity range. Random connectivity, with $r_3 = r_4 = K/N$, is not displayed, but is slightly above the performance achieved with three-dimensional Gaussian connectivity.

G. Discussion

We have shown that Bayesian history-dependent dynamics make performance increase with every iteration, and that two iterations already achieve high similarity. The Bayesian framework gives rise to the slanted sigmoid as the optimal signal function, displaying the nonmonotone shape proposed by [18]. The two-iteration performance has been analyzed in terms of general connectivity architectures, initial similarity, and activity level.

The optimal signal function has some interesting biological perspectives. The possibly asymmetric form of the function, where neurons that have been silent in the previous iteration have an increased tendency to fire in the next iteration versus previously active neurons, is reminiscent of the bithreshold phenomenon observed in biological neurons (see [23] for a review), where the threshold of neurons held at a hyperpolarized potential for a prolonged period of time is significantly lowered. As we have shown in Section III.E, the precise value of the parameter Δ leads to different biological interpretations of the slanted sigmoid signal function. The most obvious interpretation is letting Δ set the ratio of the coefficients of $f_i^{(1)}$ and $f_i^{(2)}$ so as to mimic the decay of the membrane voltage. Perhaps more important, the finding that history-dependent neurons can maintain optimal performance in the face of a broad range of Δ values points out that neuromodulators may change the form of the signal function without changing the performance of the network. Obviously, the history-free variant of the optimal final decision is not resilient to such modulatory changes.

The performance of ANN models can be heavily affected by dynamics, as exhibited by the sharp improvements obtained by fine tuning the neuron's signal function. When there is a sizable evolutionary advantage to fine tuning, theoretical optimization becomes an important research tool: the solutions it provides and the qualitative features it deems critical may have their parallels in reality. In addition to the computational efficiency of nonmonotone signaling, the numerical investigations presented in the previous subsection point to a few more features with possible biological relevance:

- In an efficient associative network, input patterns should be applied with high fidelity on a small subset of neurons, rather than spreading a given level of initial similarity as a low fidelity stimulus applied to a large subset of neurons.
- If neurons have some restriction on the number of connections they may form, such that each neuron forms some K connections on the average, then efficient ANNs, converging to high final similarity within few iterations, should be sparsely connected.
- With a properly tuned signal function, corticallike Gaussian-connectivity ANNs perform nearly as well as randomly connected ones.

IV. CONCLUDING REMARKS

This chapter has presented efficient dynamics for fast memory retrieval in both Hamming and Hopfield networks. However, as shown, the linear (in network size) capacity of the Hopfield network is no match for the exponential capacity of the

Hamming network, even with efficient dynamics. However, it is tempting to believe that the more biologically plausible distributed encoding manifested in the Hopfield network may have its own computational advantages. In our minds, a promising future challenge might be the development of Hamming–Hopfield hybrid networks which may allow the merits of both paradigms to be enjoyed. A possible step toward this goal may involve the incorporation of the activation dynamics presented in this chapter, in a unified manner.

The feasibility of designing a hybrid Hamming–Hopfield network stems from the straightforward observation that the single-layer Hopfield network dynamics can be mapped in a one-to-one manner onto a bilayered Hamming network architecture. This is easy to see by noting that each Hopfield iteration calculating the input field f_i of neuron i may be represented as

$$f_i = \sum_j W_{ij} X_j = \sum_j \sum_\mu \xi_i^\mu \xi_j^\mu X_j = \sum_\mu \xi_i^\mu \sum_j \xi_j^\mu X_j = \sum_\mu \xi_i^\mu Ov_\mu, \quad (73)$$

where, in the terminology of the HN, $Ov_\mu = (Z_\mu - n)/2$. Hence, each iteration in the original single-layered Hopfield network may be carried out by performing two subiterations in the bilayered Hamming architecture: In the first, the input pattern is applied to the input layer and the resulting overlaps Ov_μ are calculated on the memory layer. Thereafter, in the second subiteration, these overlaps are used following Eq. (73) to calculate the new input fields of the next Hopfield iteration for the neurons of the input layer. This hybrid network architecture hence raises the possibility of finding efficient signaling functions which may enhance its performance and lead to highly efficient memory systems.

As evident, there is much to gain in terms of space and time complexity by using efficient dynamics in both feedforward and feedback networks. One may wonder if such efficient signaling functions have biological counterparts in the brain.

REFERENCES

[1] I. Meilijson, E. Ruppin, and M. Sipper. A single iteration threshold Hamming network. *IEEE Trans. Neural Networks* 6:261–266, 1995.

[2] I. Meilijson and E. Ruppin. Optimal signaling in attractor neural networks. *Network* 5:277–298, 1994.

[3] K. Steinbuch. Die lernmatrix. *Kybernetic* 1:36–45, 1961.

[4] K. Steinbuch and U. A. W. Piske. Learning matrices and their applications. *IEEE Trans. Electron. Computers* 846–862, 1963.

[5] W. K. Taylor. Cortico-thalamic organization and memory. *Proc. Roy. Soc. London Ser. B* 159:466–478, 1964.

[6] R. P. Lippman, B. Gold, and M. L. Malpass. A comparison of Hamming and Hopfield beural nets for pattern classification. Technical Report TR-769, Lincoln Laboratory, MIT, Cambridge, MA, 1987.

[7] E. E. Baum, J. Moody, and F. Wilczek. Internal representations for associative memory. *Biol. Cybernetics* 59:217–228, 1987.

[8] P. Floreen. The convergence of Hamming memory networks. *IEEE Trans. Neural Networks* 2:449–457, 1991.

[9] M. R. Leadbetter, G. Lindgren, and H. Rootzen. *Extremes and Related Properties of Random Sequences and Processes*. Springer-Verlag, Berlin, 1983.

[10] B. W. Connors and M. J. Gutnick. Intrinsic firing patterns of diverse neocortical neurons. *Trends in Neuroscience* 13:99–104, 1990.

[11] P. C. Schwidt. Ionic currents governing input-output relations of betz cells. In *Single Neuron Computation* (T. McKenna, J. Davis, and S. F. Zornetzer, eds.), pp. 235–258. Academic Press, San Diego, 1992.

[12] J. J. Hopfield. Neural networks and physical systems with emergent collective abilities. *Proc. Nat. Acad. Sci. U.S.A.* 79:2554, 1982.

[13] J. J. Hopfield. Neurons with graded response have collective computational properties like those of two-state neurons. *Proc. Nat. Acad. Sci. U.S.A.* 81:3088, 1984.

[14] I. Meilijson and E. Ruppin. History-dependent attractor neural networks. *Network* 4:195–221, 1993.

[15] H. R. Wilson and J. D. Cowan. Excitatory and inhibitory interactions in localized populations of model neurons. *Biophys. J.* 12:1–24, 1972.

[16] J. C. Pearson, L. H. Finkel, and G. M. Edelman. Plasticity in the organization of adult cerebral cortical maps: A computer simulation based on neuronal group selection. *J. Neurosci.* 7:4209–4223, 1987.

[17] S. Yoshizawa, M. Morita, and S.-I. Amari. Capacity of associative memory using a nonmonotonic neuron model. *Neural Networks* 6:167–176, 1993.

[18] M. Morita. Associative memory with nonmonotone dynamics. *Neural Networks* 6:115–126, 1993.

[19] P. De Felice, C. Marangi, G. Narduli, G. Pasquariello, and L. Tedesco. Dynamics of neural networks with non-monotone activation function. *Network* 4:1–9, 1993.

[20] S. I. Amari and K. Maginu. Statistical neurodynamics of associative memmory. *Neural Networks* 1:67–73, 1988.

[21] H. English, A. Engel, A. Schutte, and M. Stcherbina. Improved retrieval in nets of formal neurons with thresholds and non-linear synapses. *Studia Biophys.* 137:37–54, 1990.

[22] D. J. Amit, H. Gutfreund, and H. Sompolinsky. Storing infinite numbers of patterns in a spin-glass model of neural networks. *Phys. Rev. Lett.* 55:1530–1533, 1985.

[23] D. C. Tam. Signal processing in multi-threshold neurons. In *Single Neuron Computation* (T. McKenna, J. Davis, and S. F. Zornetzer, eds.), pp. 481–501. Academic Press, San Diego, 1992.

Multilevel Neurons*

J. Si
Department of Electrical Engineering
Arizona State University
Tempe, Arizona 85287-7606

A. N. Michel
Department of Electrical Engineering
University of Notre Dame
Notre Dame, Indiana 46556

This chapter is concerned with a class of nonlinear dynamic systems: discrete-time synchronous multilevel neural systems. The major results presented in this chapter include a qualitative analysis of properties of this type of neural systems and also a synthesis procedure of these systems in associative memory applications. When compared to the usual neural networks with two-state neurons, networks which are endowed with multilevel neurons will in general, for a given application, require fewer neurons and thus fewer interconnections. This is an important consideration in very large scale integration (VLSI) implementation. VLSI implementation of such systems has been accomplished with a specific application to analog-to-digital (A/D) conversion.

I. INTRODUCTION

The neural networks proposed by Cohen and Grossberg [1], Grossberg [2], Hopfield [3], Hopfield and Tank [4, 5], and others (see, e.g., [6–13]) constitute important models for associative memories. (For additional references on this

*This research was supported in part by the National Science Foundation under grants ECS 9107728 and ECS 9553202. Most of the material presented here is adapted with permission from *IEEE Trans. Neural Networks* 6:105–116, 1995 (©1995 IEEE).

subject, consult the literature cited in books, e.g., [14–18] and in the survey paper [19].)

In VLSI implementations and even in optical implementations of artificial feedback neural networks, reductions in the number of neurons and in the number of interconnections (for a given application) are highly desirable. To address these issues, we propose herein artificial neural network models which are endowed with multilevel threshold nonlinearities for the neuron models. Specifically, we consider a class of synchronous, discrete-time neural networks which are described by a system of first order linear difference equations, given by

$$x_i(k+1) = \sum_{j=1}^{n} T_{ij} s_j(x_j(k)) + I_i, \qquad i = 1, \ldots, n, \ k = 0, 1, 2, \ldots, \tag{1}$$

where $s_j(\cdot)$ are multilevel threshold functions representing the neurons, I_i are external bias terms, T_{ij} denote interconnection coefficients, and the variables $x_i(k)$ represent the inputs to the neurons. Recent progress in nanostructure electronics suggests that multilevel threshold characteristics can be implemented by means of quantum devices [20, 21].

If an n-dimensional vector with each component of b-bit length is to be stored in a neural network with binary state neurons, then an $n \times b$ order system may be used. Alternatively, an n-dimensional neural network may be employed for this purpose, provided that each neuron can represent a b-bit word. In the former case, the number of interconnections will be of order $(n \times b)^2$, whereas in the latter case, the number of interconnections will only be of order n^2.

Existing work which makes use of quantizer-type multilevel, discrete-time neural networks and which employes the outer product method as a synthesis tool was reported by Banzhaf [22], who demonstrated the effectiveness of the studied neural networks only for the restrictive case of orthogonal input patterns.

A generalized outer product method was also used by Fleisher [23] as a synthesis tool for artificial neural networks (with multilevel neuron models) operating in an asynchronous mode. Convergence properties were established in [23] under the assumption that the interconnection matrix is symmetric and has zero diagonal elements. The outer product method used in [23], as in other references (see e.g., [3, 19]), suffers from the fact that the desired memories are not guaranteed to be stored as asymptotically stable equilibria.

Guez *et al.* [24] made use of an eigenvalue localization theorem by Gersgorin to derive a set of sufficient conditions for the asymptotic stability of each desired equilibrium to be stored in a neural network endowed with multilevel threshold functions. The stability conditions are phrased in terms of linear equations and piecewise linear inequality relations. Guez *et al.* [24] suggested a linear programming method for the design of neural networks which can be solved by another neural network; however, they provide no specific information for this procedure.

Using energy function arguments, Marcus *et al.*. [8, 9] developed a global stability criterion which guarantees that the neural network will converge to fixed-point attractors. This stability criterion places a limit on the maximum gain of the nonlinear threshold functions (including multilevel threshold functions), and when this limit is exceeded, the system may develop oscillations. Marcus *et al.* [8, 9] showed that when the matrix $T + (RB)^{-1}$ (R and B are matrices containing information of parallel resistance and maximum slope of the sigmoid function, respectively) is positive definite, then the network is globally stable. Although this condition is less conservative than the one derived herein, there are no indications in [8, 9] of how to incorporate this global stability condition into a synthesis procedure. Furthermore, because [8, 9] do not provide a stability analysis for a given equilibrium of the network, no considerations for asymptotic stability constraints for the learning rules (the Hebb rule and the pseudo-inverse rule) are made.

Other studies involving multistate networks include [25–27]. In Meunier *et al.* [25], an extensive simulation study has been carried out for a Hopfieldlike network consisting of three-state $(-1, 0, +1)$ neurons, whereas Rieger [26] studied three different neuron models and developed some interesting results concerning the storage capacity of the network. Jankowski *et al.* [27] studied complex-valued associative memory by multistate networks. It is worth noting that hardware implementations of the multistate networks have been accomplished with an application in A/D conversion [28].

In this chapter we first conduct a local qualitative analysis of neural networks (1), independent of the number of levels employed in the threshold nonlinearities. In doing so, we perform a stability analysis of the equilibrium points of (1), using the large scale systems methodology advocated in [29, 30]. In arriving at these results, we make use of several of the ideas employed in [13]. Next, by using energy function arguments [1–5, 8, 9], we establish conditions for the global stability of the neural network (1) when the interconnecting structure is symmetric. Finally, by modifying the approach advanced in [12], we develop a synthesis procedure for neural networks (1) which guarantees the asymptotic stability of each memory to be stored as an asymptotically stable equilibrium point and which results in a globally stable neural network. This synthesis procedure is based on the local and global qualitative results discussed in the preceding text. A simulation study of a 13 neuron system is carried out to obtain an indication of the storage capacity of system (1).

II. NEURAL SYSTEM ANALYSIS

This section consists of four parts: In the first subsection we discuss the neuron models considered herein; in the second subsection we describe the class of neural networks treated; in the third subsection we establish local qualitative properties for the neural networks considered; and in the final subsection we address global qualitative aspects of the present neural networks. In the interests of readability, all proofs are presented in the Appendix.

A. NEURON MODELS

We concern ourselves with neural networks which are endowed with multilevel neurons. *Idealized* models for these neurons may be represented, for example, by bounded quantization nonlinearities of the type shown in Fig. 1. Without loss of generality, we will assume that the threshold values of the quantizers are integer-valued. For purposes of discussion, we will identify for these quantizers a finite set of points p_i^*, $i = 1, \ldots, m$, determined by the intersections of the graph of the quantizer and the line $v = \sigma$, that is,

$$v_i^* = \tilde{s}(x_i^*) = x_i^*, \qquad i = 1, \ldots, m.$$

For the neural networks under consideration we will consider approximations $s(\cdot)$ of the foregoing idealized neuron model $\tilde{s}(\cdot)$ that have the following properties: $s(\cdot)$ is continuously differentiable, $s''(\cdot)$ exists, $s(\sigma) = 0$ if and only if $\sigma = 0$, $s(\sigma) = -s(-\sigma)$, $s(\cdot)$ is monotonically increasing, and $s(\cdot)$ is bounded,

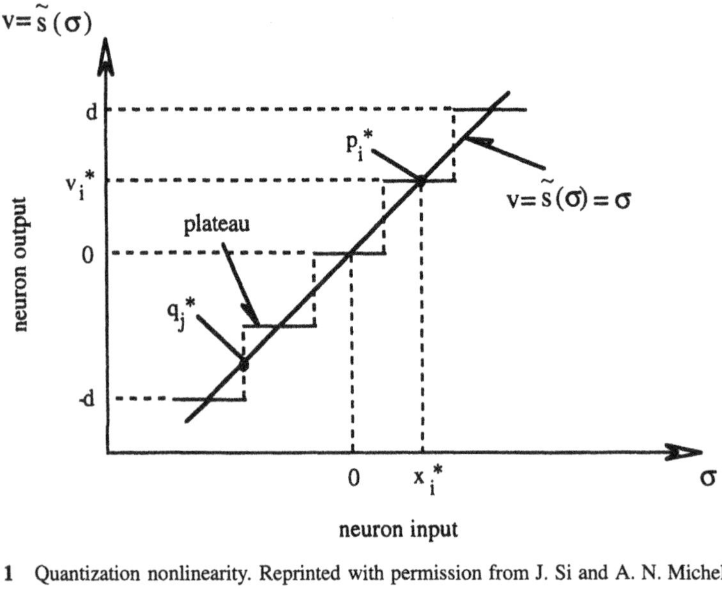

Figure 1 Quantization nonlinearity. Reprinted with permission from J. Si and A. N. Michel, *IEEE Trans. Neural Networks* 6:105–116, 1995 (©1995 IEEE).

that is, there exist constants d such that $-d < s(\sigma) < d$ for all $\sigma \in R$, and $\lim_{\sigma\to d} s^{-1}(\sigma) = +\infty$, $\lim_{\sigma\to -d} s^{-1}(\sigma) = -\infty$, $\int_0^x s^{-1}(\sigma)\,d\sigma = \infty$, $x \to \pm d$. We will assume that $s(\cdot)$ approximates $\tilde{s}(\cdot)$ as closely as desired. Referring to Fig. 2, this means that at the finite set of points $p_i^* = (x_i^*, s(x_i^*))$ located on the plateaus which determine the *integer-valued thresholds*

$$v_i^* = s(x_i^*), \qquad i = 1, \ldots, m,$$

we have

$$\frac{d}{d\sigma}s(\sigma)\bigg|_{\sigma=x_i^*} = m_i^* \leqslant m^*, \qquad i = 1, \ldots, m, \tag{2}$$

where $m^* > 0$ can be chosen to be arbitrarily small, but *fixed*. Also, still referring to Fig. 2, at the finite set of points $q_j^* = (x_j^*, s(x_j^*))$ we have

$$\frac{d}{d\sigma}s(\sigma)\bigg|_{\sigma=x_j^*} = M_j \geqslant M, \qquad j = 1, \ldots, m-1,$$

where $M < \infty$ is arbitrarily large, but *fixed*. Note that for such approximations we will have

$$s(x_i^*) = x_i^*, \qquad i = 2, \ldots, m-1,$$

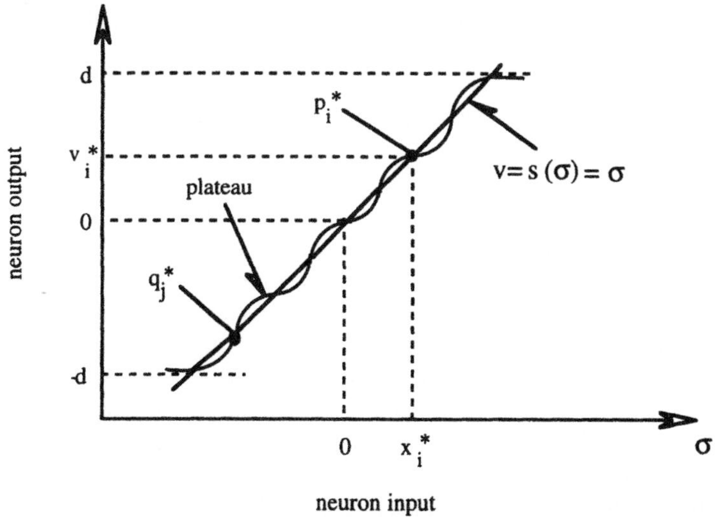

Figure 2 Multilevel sigmoidal function: an approximation of the quantization nonlinearity. Reprinted with permission from J. Si and A. N. Michel, *IEEE Trans. Neural Networks* 6:105–116, 1995 (©1995 IEEE).

and

$$\left| -d - s(x_1^*) \right| < k, \quad \text{and} \quad \left| d - s(x_m^*) \right| < k,$$

where $k > 0$ is arbitrarily small, but *fixed*. For practical purposes then, we will assume that for $i = 1, \ldots, m,\ s(x_i^*)$ are integer-valued.

Henceforth, we will say that functions $s(\cdot)$ of the type described in the foregoing text (which approximate quantization nonlinearities $\tilde{s}(\cdot)$ of the type considered in the foregoing text) belong to class A.

B. Neural Networks

We consider discrete-time neural networks described by a system of equations of the form of Eq. (1),

$$x_i(k+1) = \sum_{j=1}^{n} T_{ij} s_j(x_j(k)) + I_i, \qquad i = 1, \ldots, n,\ k = 0, 1, 2, \ldots,$$

where $x = (x_1, \ldots, x_n)^T \in R^n,\ T_{ij} \in R,\ I_i \in R$, and $s_j\colon R \to R$ is assumed to be in class A. The functions $s_j(\cdot),\ j = 1, \ldots, n$, represent neurons, the constants $T_{ij},\ i, j = 1, \ldots, n$, make up the system interconnections, the $I_i,\ i = 1, \ldots, n$, represent external bias terms, and $x_i(k)$ denotes the input to neuron i at time k, whereas $v_i(k) = s_i(x_i(k))$ represents the output of the ith neuron at time k. We assume that neural network (1) operates synchronously, that is, all neurons are updated simultaneously at each time step.

Letting $T = [T_{ij}] \in R^{n\times n},\ I = (I_1, \ldots, I_n)^T \in R^n$, and $s(\cdot) = (s_1(\cdot), \ldots, s_n(\cdot))^T$, we can represent the neural network (1) equivalently by

$$x(k+1) = Ts\big(x(k)\big) + I, \qquad k = 0, 1, 2, \ldots. \tag{3}$$

In the subsequent analysis we will be concerned with two types of qualitative results: *local* stability properties of specific equilibrium points for system (3) and *global* stability properties of (3). Before proceeding to describe these results, it is necessary to clarify some of the stability terms. When using the term stability, we will have in mind the concept of Lyapunov stability of an equilibrium. For purposes of completeness, we provide here heuristic explanations for some of the concepts associated with the Lyapunov theory. The precise delta-epsilon (δ-ε) definitions of these notions can be found, for example, in [31, Chap. 5].

The neural network model (3) describes the process by which a system changes its state [e.g., how $x(k)$ is transformed to $x(k+1)$]. Let $\phi(k+\tau, \tau, u)$ denote the solution of (3) for all $k \geqslant 0,\ k = 0, 1, 2, \ldots, \tau \geqslant 0$, with $\phi(\tau, \tau, u) = u$. If $\phi(k+\tau, \tau, u^*) = u^*$ for all $k \geqslant 0$, then u^* is called an *equilibrium* for system (3).

The following characterizations pertain to an equilibrium u^* of system (3).

(a) If it is possible to force solutions $\phi(k+\tau, \tau, u)$ to remain as close as desired to the equilibrium u^* for all $k \geqslant 0$ by choosing u sufficiently close to u^*, then the equilibrium u^* is said to be *stable*. If u^* is not stable, then it is said to be *unstable*.

(b) If an equilibrium u^* is stable and if in addition the limit of $\phi(k+\tau, \tau, u)$ as k goes to infinity equals u^* whenever u belongs to $D(u^*)$, where $D(u^*)$ is an open subset of R^n containing u^*, then the equilibrium u^* is said to be *asymptotically stable*. Furthermore, if the norm of $\phi(k+\tau, \tau, u)$, denoted by $\|\phi(k+\tau, \tau, u)\|$, approaches u^* exponentially, then u^* is *exponentially stable*. The largest set $D(u^*)$ for which the foregoing property is true is called the *domain of attraction* or the *basin of attraction of* u^*. If $D(u^*) = R^n$, then u^* is said to be *asymptotically stable in large* or *globally asymptotically stable*.

Note, however, one should not confuse the term global stability used in the neural networks literature with the concept of global asymptotic stability introduced previously. A neural network [such as, e.g., system (3)] is called *globally stable* if every trajectory of the system (every solution of the system) converges to some equilibrium point.

In applications of neural networks to associative memories, equilibrium points of the networks are utilized to store the desired memories (library vectors). Recall that a vector $x^* \in R^n$ is an equilibrium of (3) if and only if

$$x^* = Ts(x^*) + I. \tag{4}$$

Stability results of an equilibrium in the sense of Lyapunov usually assume that the equilibrium under investigation is located at the origin. In the case of system (3) this can be assumed without loss of generality. If a given equilibrium, say x^*, is not located at the origin (i.e., $x^* \neq 0$), then we can always transform system (3) into an equivalent system (7) such that when p^* for (7) corresponds to x^* for (3), then $p^* = 0$. Specifically, let

$$p(k) = x(k) - x^*, \tag{5}$$

$$g\big(p(k)\big) = s\big(x(k)\big) - s(x^*), \tag{6}$$

where x^* satisfies Eq. (4), and $g(\cdot) = (g_1(\cdot), \ldots, g_n(\cdot))^T$ and $g_i(x(k)) = g_i(x_i(k)) = s_i(x_i(k)) - s_i(x_i^*)$. Then Eq. (3) becomes

$$p(k+1) = Tg\big(p(k)\big), \tag{7}$$

which has an equilibrium $p^* = 0$ corresponding to the equilibrium x^* for (3). In component form, system (7) can be rewritten as

$$p_i(k+1) = \sum_{j=1}^{n} T_{ij} g_j\big(p_j(k)\big), \qquad i = 1, \ldots, n, \ k = 0, 1, 2, \ldots. \tag{8}$$

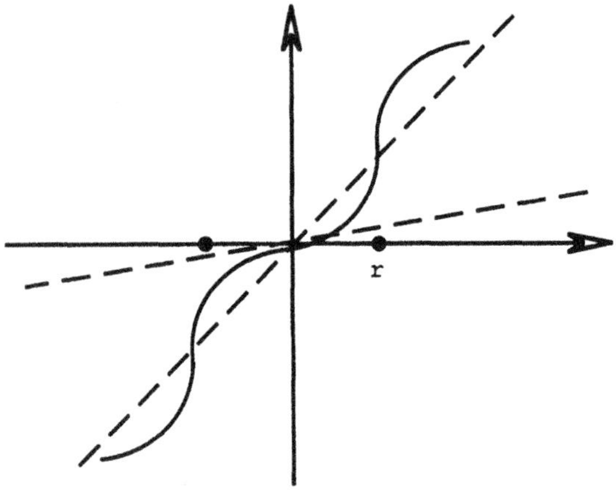

Figure 3 Illustration of the sector condition. Reprinted with permission from J. Si and A. N. Michel, *IEEE Trans. Neural Networks* 6:105–116, 1995 (©1995 IEEE).

Henceforth, whenever we study the local properties of a given equilibrium point of the neural networks considered herein, we will assume that the network is in the form given by (7).

The properties of the functions $s_i(\cdot)$ (in class A) ensure that the functions $g_i(\cdot)$ satisfy a *sector condition* which is phrased in terms of the following Assumption 1.

Assumption 1. There are two real constants $c_{i1} \geqslant 0$ and $c_{i2} \geqslant 0$ such that

$$c_{i1} p_i^2 \leqslant p_i g_i(p_i) \leqslant c_{i2} p_i^2 \quad \text{for } j = 1, \ldots, n,$$

for all $p_i \in B(r_i) = \{p_i \in R\colon |p_i| < r_i\}$ for some $r_i > 0$.

Note that $g_i(p_i) = 0$ if and only if $p_i = 0$ and that $g_i(\cdot)$ is monotonically increasing and bounded. A graphical explanation of Assumption 1 is given in Fig. 3.

C. Stability of an Equilibrium

Following the methodology advocated in [29], we now establish stability results of the equilibrium $p = 0$ of system (7). The proofs of these results, given in the Appendix, are in the spirit of the proofs of results given in [13]. We will require the following hypotheses.

Assumption 2. For system (3),

$$0 \leqslant \sigma_i \triangleq \left(|T_{ii}|c_{i2}\right) < 1,$$

where c_{i2} is defined in Assumption 1.

Remark 1. In Section III we will devise a design procedure which will enable us to store a desired set of library vectors $\{v^1, \ldots, v^r\}$ corresponding to a set of asymptotically stable equilibrium points for system (3), given by $\{x^1, \ldots, x^r\}$, that is,

$$v^i = \left(v_1^i, \ldots, v_n^i\right)^T, \qquad x^i = \left(x_1^i, \ldots, x_n^i\right)^T,$$

and

$$v_j^i = s_j\left(x_j^i\right), \qquad i = 1, \ldots, r, \; j = 1, \ldots, n.$$

In this design procedure things will be arranged in such a manner that the components of the desired library vectors will be integer-valued. In other words, the components of the desired library vectors will correspond to points p_i^*, located on the plateaus of the graph of $s_i(\cdot)$ given in Fig. 2.

Now recall that the purpose of the functions $s_i(\cdot)$ (belonging to class A) is to approximate quantization nonlinearities $\tilde{s}_i(\cdot)$ as closely as desired. At the points p_i^* (see Fig. 2), such approximations will result in arbitrarily small, positive, fixed constants m_i^* given in Eq. (2). This in turn implies that for such approximations, the sector conditions for the functions $g_i(\cdot)$ in Assumption 1 will hold for c_{i2} positive, fixed, and as small as desired. This shows that for a given T_{ii}, c_{i2} can be chosen sufficiently small to ensure that Assumption 2 is satisfied [by choosing a sufficiently good approximation $s(\cdot)$ for the quantization nonlinearity $\tilde{s}(\cdot)$].

Assumption 3. Given $\sigma_i = |T_{ii}|c_{i2}$ of Assumption 2, the successive principal minors of matrix $D = [D_{ij}]$ are all positive, with

$$D_{ij} = \begin{cases} -(\sigma_i - 1), & i = j, \\ -\sigma_{ij}, & i \neq j, \end{cases}$$

where $\sigma_{ij} = |T_{ij}|c_{j2}$ (c_{j2} is defined in Assumption 1).

The matrix D in Assumption 3 is an M matrix (see, e.g., [29]). For such matrices it can be shown that Assumptions 3 and 4 are equivalent.

Assumption 4. There exist constants $\lambda_j > 0$, $j = 1, \ldots, n$, such that

$$\sum_{j=1}^{n} \lambda_j D_{ij} > 0, \quad \text{for } i = 1, \ldots, n.$$

Remark 2. If the equilibrium $p = 0$ of system (7) corresponds to a library vector v with integer-valued components, then a discussion similar to that given in Remark 1 leads us to the conclusion that for sufficiently accurate approximations of the quantization nonlinearities, the constants c_{i2}, $i = 1, \ldots, n$, will be sufficiently small to ensure that Assumption 4 and, hence, Assumption 3 will be satisfied. Thus, the preceding two (equivalent) assumptions are realistic.

THEOREM 1. *If Assumptions 1, 2, and 3 (or 4) are true, then the equilibrium $p = 0$ of the neural network (7) is asymptotically stable.*

Using the methodology advanced in [29], we can also establish conditions for the exponential stability of the equilibrium $p = 0$ of system (7) by employing Assumption 5. We will not pursue this. Assumption 5 is motivated by Assumption 4; however, it is a stronger statement than Assumption 4.

Assumption 5. There exists a constant $\varepsilon > 0$ such that

$$1 - \sum_{j=1}^{n} |T_{ij}| c_{j2} \geqslant \varepsilon, \quad \text{for } i = 1, \ldots, n.$$

In the synthesis procedure for the neural networks considered herein, we will make use of Assumption 5 rather than Assumption 4.

D. Global Stability Results

The results of Section II.C are concerned with the local qualitative properties of equilibrium points of neural networks (3). Now we address global qualitative properties of system (3). We will show that under reasonable assumptions,

1. system (3) has finitely many equilibrium points, and
2. every solution of system (3) approaches an equilibrium point of system (3).

The output variables $v_i(k)$, $i = 1, \ldots, n$, of system (1) are related to the state variables $x_i(k)$, $i = 1, \ldots, n$, by functions $s_i(\cdot)$. Whereas each of these functions is invertible, system (1) may be expressed as

$$\begin{aligned} v_i(k+1) &= s_i\left(\sum_{j=1}^{n} T_{ij} v_j(k) + I_i\right) \\ &\triangleq f_i\big(v_1(k), \ldots, v_n(k), I_i\big), \qquad i = 1, \ldots, n, \ k = 0, 1, 2, \ldots. \end{aligned} \tag{9}$$

Equivalently, system (3) may be expressed as

$$\begin{aligned} v(k+1) &= s\big(Tv(k) + I\big) \\ &\triangleq f\big(v(k), I\big), \qquad k = 0, 1, 2, \ldots, \end{aligned} \tag{10}$$

where $f(\cdot)^T = (f_1(\cdot), \ldots, f_n(\cdot))$. System (9) [and, hence, system (10)] can be transformed back into system (1) by applying the functions $s_i^{-1}(\cdot)$ to both sides of Eq. (9). Note that if x^i, $i = 1, \ldots, s$, are equilibria for (3), then the corresponding vectors $v^i = s(x^i)$, $i = 1, \ldots, s$, are equilibria for (10).

Using the results given in [32], it can be shown that the functions $s_i(\cdot)$ (belonging to class A), constitute stability preserving mappings. This allows us to study qualitative properties of the class of neural networks considered herein (such as stability of an equilibrium and global stability) in terms of the variables $x_i(k)$, $i = 1, \ldots, n$ [using (3) as the neural network description], or, equivalently, in terms of the variables $v_i(k)$, $i = 1, \ldots, n$ [using (10) as the neural network description].

For system (10) we define an "energy function" of the form

$$\begin{aligned} E\big(v(k)\big) &= -\tfrac{1}{2}\sum_{i=1}^{n}\sum_{j=1}^{n} T_{ij} v_i(k) v_j(k) - \sum_{i=1}^{n} v_i(k) I_i + \sum_{i=1}^{n} \int_0^{v_i(k)} s_i^{-1}(\sigma)\, d\sigma \\ &= -\tfrac{1}{2} v^T(k) T v(k) - v^T(k) I + \sum_{i=1}^{n} \int_0^{v_i(k)} s_i^{-1}(\sigma)\, d\sigma \end{aligned} \tag{11}$$

under the following assumption:

Assumption 6. The interconnection matrix T for system (10) is symmetric and positive semidefinite, and the functions $s_i(\cdot)$, $i = 1, \ldots, n$, belong to class A.

In the development of the subsequent results we will employ first order and higher order derivatives $DE(\cdot,\cdot)$, $D^2E(\cdot,\cdot,\cdot)$, and $D^3E(\cdot,\cdot,\cdot,\cdot)$ of the energy function $E(\cdot)$. We define

$$(-d, d)^n = \{v \in R^n\colon -d < v_i < d,\ i = 1, \ldots, n\}.$$

The *first order derivative* of E, $DE\colon (-d, d)^n \to L(R^n; R)$, is given by

$$DE(v, y) = \nabla E(v)^T y,$$

where $\nabla E(\cdot)$ denotes the gradient of $E(\cdot)$, given by

$$\nabla E(v) = \left(\frac{\partial E}{\partial v_1}(v), \ldots, \frac{\partial E}{\partial v_n}(v)\right)^T = -Tv + s^{-1}(v) - I, \tag{12}$$

where $s^{-1}(\cdot) = (s_1^{-1}(\cdot), \ldots, s_n^{-1}(\cdot))^T$.

The *second order derivative* of E, $D^2E\colon (-d, d)^n \to L^2(R^n; R)$, is given by

$$D^2E(v, y, z) = y^T J_E(v) z,$$

where $J_E(v)$ denotes the Jacobian matrix of $E(\cdot)$ given by

$$J_E(v) = \left[\frac{\partial^2 E}{\partial v_i \partial v_j}(v)\right] = -T + \operatorname{diag}\big((s_1^{-1}(v_1))', \ldots, (s_n^{-1}(v_n))'\big). \tag{13}$$

The *third order derivative* of E, $D^3E\colon (-d,d)^n \to L^3(R^n; R)$, is given by

$$D^3E(v, y, z, u) = \sum_{i=1}^{n} \left(s_i^{-1''}(v_i)\right) y_i z_i u_i,$$

where $s_i^{-1''}(v_i) = (-d^2/dv_i^2)s_i^{-1}(v_i)$.

In the proof of the main result of the present section (Theorem 2) we will require some preliminary results (Lemmas 1 and 2) and some additional realistic assumptions (Assumptions 7 and 8).

LEMMA 1. *If system (10) satisfies Assumption 6 and the energy function E is defined as before, then for any $(-d,d)^n \supset \{v_m\}$, such that $v_m \to \partial(-d,d)^n$ as $m \to \infty$, we have $E(v_m) \to +\infty$ as $m \to \infty$ ($\partial(-d,d)^n$ denotes the boundary of $(-d,d)^n$).*

LEMMA 2. *If system (10) satisfies Assumption 6, then $v \in (-d,d)^n$ is an equilibrium of (10) if and only if $\nabla E(v) = 0$. Thus the set of critical points of E is identical to the set of equilibrium points of system (10).*

As mentioned earlier, we will require the following hypothesis.

Assumption 7. Given Assumption 6, we assume

(a) There is no $v \in (-d,d)^n$ satisfying simultaneously the conditions (i)–(iv):

(i) $\nabla E(v) = 0$,
(ii) $\det(J_E(v)) = 0$,
(iii) $J_E(v) \geqslant 0$,
(iv) $(s_1^{-1''}(v_1), \ldots, s_n^{-1''}(v_n))^T \perp N$, where $N = \{z = (y_1^3, \ldots, y_n^3)^T \in R^n\colon J_E(v)(y_1, \ldots, y_n)^T = 0\}$.

(b) The set of equilibrium points of (10) [and hence of (3)] is discrete [i.e., each equilibrium point of (10) is isolated].

Assumption 8. Given Assumption 6, assume that there is no $v \in (-d,d)^n$ satisfying simultaneously the two conditions

(i) $\nabla E(v) = 0$,
(ii) $\det(J_E(v)) = 0$.

Remark 3. Assumption 8 clearly implies the first part of Assumption 7. By the inverse function theorem [33], Assumption 8 implies that each zero of $\nabla E(v)$ is isolated, and thus, by Lemma 2, each equilibrium point of (3) is isolated. It follows that Assumption 8 implies Assumption 7. Note, however, that Assumption 8 may be easier to apply than Assumption 7.

Our next result states that for a given matrix T satisfying Assumption 6, Assumption 8 is true for almost all $I \in R^n$, where I is the bias term in system (3) or (10).

LEMMA 3. *If Assumption 6 is true for system (10) with fixed T, then Assumption 8 is true for almost all $I \in R^n$ (in the sense of Lebegue measure).*

We are now in a position to establish the main result of the present section.

THEOREM 2. *If system (10) satisfies Assumptions 6 and 7, then:*

1. *Along a nonequilibrium solution of (10), the energy function E given in (11) decreases monotonically, and thus no nonconstant periodic solutions exist.*
2. *Each nonequilibrium solution of (10) converges to an equilibrium of (10) as $k \to \infty$.*
3. *There are only finitely many equilibrium points for (10).*
4. *If $\tilde{v}$ is an equilibrium point of system (10), then $\tilde{v}$ is a local minimum of the energy function E if and only if $\tilde{v}$ is asymptotically stable.*

Remark 4. Theorem 2 and Lemma 3 tell us that, if Assumption 6 is true, then system (3) will be globally stable for almost all $I \in R^n$.

III. NEURAL SYSTEM SYNTHESIS FOR ASSOCIATIVE MEMORIES

Some of the first works to use pseudo-inverse techniques in the synthesis of neural networks are reported in [6, 7]. In these works a desired set of equilibrium points is guaranteed to be stored in the designed network; however, there are no guarantees that the equilibrium points will be asymptotically stable. The results in [6, 7] address discrete-time neural networks with symmetric interconnecting structure having neurons represented by sign functions. These networks are globally stable.

In the results given in [12], pseudo-inverse techniques are employed to design discrete-time neural networks with continuous sigmoidal functions which guarantee to store a desired set of asymptotically stable equilibrium points. These networks are not required to have a symmetric interconnecting structure. There are no guarantees that networks designed by the results given in [12] are globally stable.

In the present section we develop a synthesis procedure which guarantees to store a desired set of asymptotically stable equilibrium points into neural network (3). This network is globally stable and is endowed with multithreshold neurons. Accordingly, the present results constitute some improvements over the earlier results already discussed.

A. System Constraints

To establish the synthesis procedure for system (3) characterized previously, we will make use of three types of constraints: equilibrium constraints, local stability constraints, and global stability constraints.

1. Equilibrium Constraints

Let

$$\Delta = \{v^1, \dots, v^r\}$$

denote the set of desired library vectors which are to be stored in the neural network (3). The corresponding desired asymptotically stable equilibrium points for system (3) are given by x^i, $i = 1, \dots, r$, where

$$v^i = s(x^i), \qquad i = 1, \dots, r,$$

where $v^i = (v_1^i, \dots, v_n^i)^T$, $x^i = (x_1^i, \dots, x_n^i)^T$, and $s(x^i) = (s_1(x_1^i), \dots, s_n(x_n^i))$.

Assumption 9. Assume that the desired library vectors v^i, $i = 1, \dots, r$, belong to the set B^n, where

$$B^n = \{x = (x^1, \dots, x^n)^T \in R^n\colon x_i \in \{-d, -d+1, \dots, d-1, d\}$$

and $d \in Z$.

For v^i to correspond to an equilibrium x^i for system (3), the following condition must be satisfied [see Eq. (4)]:

$$x^i = Tv^i + I, \qquad i = 1, \dots, r. \tag{14}$$

To simplify our notation, let

$$V = [v^1, \dots, v^r], \tag{15}$$
$$X = [x^1, \dots, x^r]. \tag{16}$$

Then (14) can equivalently be expressed as

$$X = TV + \Pi, \tag{17}$$

where Π is an $n \times r$ matrix with each of its columns being I.

Our objective is to determine a set (T, I) so that the constraint (14) is satisfied when V and X are given. Let

$$U = [V^T, Q]$$

and let

$$W_j = [T_{j1}, T_{j2}, \ldots, T_{jn}, I_j],$$

where $Q = (1, \ldots, 1)^T \in R^r$. Solving (14) is equivalent to solving the equations

$$X_j^T = UW_j^T \quad \text{for } j = 1, \ldots, n, \tag{18}$$

where X_j denotes the jth row of X. A solution of Eq. (18) may not necessarily exist; however, the existence of an approximate solution to (18), in the least squares sense, is always ensured [25, 26], and is given by

$$W_j^T = PX_j^T = U^T(UU^T)^+X_j^T, \tag{19}$$

where $(UU^T)^+$ denotes the pseudo-inverse of (UU^T). When the set $\{v^1, \ldots, v^r\}$ is linearly independent, which is true for many applications, (18) has a solution of the form

$$W_j^T = PX_j^T = U^T(UU^T)^{-1}X_j^T. \tag{20}$$

When the library vectors are not linearly independent, the equilibrium constraint (14) can still be satisfied as indicated in Remark 5(b) (see Section III.B).

2. Asymptotic Stability Constraints

Constraint (14) allows us to design a neural network (3) which will store a desired set of library vectors v^i, $i = 1, \ldots, r$, corresponding to a set of equilibrium points x^i, $i = 1, \ldots, r$, which are not necessarily asymptotically stable. To ensure that these equilibrium points are asymptotically stable, we will agree to choose nonlinearities for neuron models which satisfy Assumption 5. We state this as a constraint

$$1 - \sum_{j=1}^{n} |T_{ij}|c_{j2} \geqslant \varepsilon, \quad \text{for } i = 1, \ldots, n. \tag{21}$$

Thus, when the nonlinearities for system (3) are chosen to satisfy the sector conditions in Assumption 1 and if for each desired equilibrium point x^i, $i = 1, \ldots, r$, the constraint (21) is satisfied, then in accordance with Theorem 1, the stored equilibria, x^i, $i = 1, \ldots, r$, will be asymptotically stable (in fact, exponentially stable).

3. Global Stability Constraints

From the results given in Section II.D, it is clear that when constraints (14) and (21) are satisfied, then all solutions of the neural network (3) will converge to one of the equilibrium points in the sense described in Section II.D, provided that the interconnection matrix T is positive semidefinite. We will state this condition as our third constraint:

$$T = T^T \geqslant 0. \tag{22}$$

B. Synthesis Procedure

We are now in a position to develop a method of designing neural networks which store a desired set of library vectors $\{v^1, \ldots, v^r\}$ (or equivalently, a corresponding set of asymptotically stable equilibrium points $\{x^1, \ldots, x^r\}$). To accomplish this, we establish a synthesis procedure for system (3) which satisfies constraints (14), (21), and (22).

To satisfy (22), we first require that the interconnection matrix T be symmetric. Our next result which makes use of the following assumption (Assumption 10), ensures this.

Assumption 10. For the desired set of library vectors $\{v^1, \ldots, v^r\}$ with corresponding equilibrium points for (3) given by the set $\{x^1, \ldots, x^r\}$, we have

$$v^i \triangleq s(x^i) = x^i, \qquad i = 1, \ldots, r. \tag{23}$$

PROPOSITION 1. *If Assumption 10 is satisfied, then constraint (18) yields a symmetric matrix T.*

Remark 5. (a) For the nonlinear function $s(\cdot)$ belonging to class A, Assumption 10 has already been hypothesized (see Section II.A).

(b) If Assumption 10 is satisfied, then the constraint Eq. (18) will have exact solutions which in general will not be unique. One of those solutions is given by Eq. (19). Thus, if Assumption 10 is satisfied, then the vectors x^i, $i = 1, \ldots, r$ (corresponding to the library vectors v^i, $i = 1, \ldots, r$) will be equilibrium points of (3), even if they are not linearly independent.

Our next result ensures that constraint (22) is satisfied.

PROPOSITION 2. *For the set of library vectors $\{v^1, \ldots, v^r\}$ and the corresponding equilibrium points $\{x^1, \ldots, x^r\}$, if Assumption 10 is satisfied and if the external vector I is zero, then the interconnection matrix T for system (3), given by*

$$T = VV^T(VV^T)^+, \tag{24}$$

is positive semidefinite [V is defined in Eq. (15)].

A neural network (3) which satisfies the constraints (14), (21), and (22) and which is endowed with neuron models belonging to class A will be globally stable in the sense described in Section II.D and will store the desired set of library vectors $\{v^1, \ldots, v^r\}$ which corresponds to a desired set of asymptotically stable equilibrium points $\{x^1, \ldots, x^r\}$. This suggests the following synthesis procedure:

Step 1. All nonlinearities $s_i(\cdot)$, $i = 1, \ldots, n$ are chosen to belong to *class A*.

Step 2. Given a set of desired library vectors v^i, $i = 1, \ldots, r$, the corresponding desired set of equilibrium points x^i, $i = 1, \ldots, r$, is determined by $v^i = s(x^i) = x^i$, $i = 1, \ldots, r$.

Step 3. With V and X specified, solve for T and I, using Eq. (20). The resulting neural network is not guaranteed to be globally stable, and the desired library vectors are equilibria of system (3) only when $\{v^1, \ldots, v^r\}$ are linearly independent.

Alternatively, set $I = 0$ and compute T by Eq. (24). In this case, the network (3) will be globally stable in the sense described in Section II.D, and the desired library vectors are guaranteed to be equilibria of system (3).

Step 4. In (21), set $c_{j2} = m_j^* + \delta$, $\delta > 0$ arbitrarily small, $j = 1, \ldots, n$ [m_j^* is defined in Eq. (2)]. Substitute the T_{ij} obtained in Step 3 into constraint (21). If for a desired (fixed) $\varepsilon > 0$, the constraint (21) is satisfied, then stop. Otherwise, modify the nonlinearities $s_j(\cdot)$ to decrease c_{j2} sufficiently to satisfy (21).

Remark 6. Step 4 ensures that the desired equilibrium points x^i, $i = 1, \ldots, r$, are asymptotically stable even if the system (3) is not globally stable (see Step 3).

IV. SIMULATIONS

In the present section we study the average performance of neural networks designed by the present method by means of simulations. A neural network with 13 units is used to obtain an indication of the storage capacity of system (3) and of the extent of the domains of attraction of the equilibrium points. The system is allowed to evolve from a given initial state to a final state. The final state is interpreted as the network's response to the given initial condition.

In the present example, each neuron may assume the integers $\{-2, -1, 0, 1, 2\}$ as threshold values. To keep our experiment tractable, we used as initial conditions only those vectors which differ from a given stored asymptotically stable equilibrium by at most one threshold value in each component (that is, $|v_j^i - y_j| \leqslant 1$ for all j and $\sum_{i=1}^{13} |v_j^i - y_j| < 13$, where v_j^i is the jth component of library vector i and y_j is the jth component of the initial condition).

In our experiment we wished to determine how the network is affected by the number of patterns to be stored. For each value of r between 1 and 13, 10 trials (simulations) were made (recall that r = number of desired patterns). Each trial consisted of choosing randomly a set of r output patterns of length $n = 13$.

For each set of r patterns, a network was designed and simulated. The outcomes of the 10 trials for each value of r were then averaged. The results are summarized in Fig. 4. In this figure, the number of patterns to be stored is the independent variable. The dependent variable is the fraction of permissible initial conditions that converge to the desired output (at a given Hamming distance from an equilibrium).

It is emphasized that all the desired library vectors are stored as asymptotically stable equilibrium points in system (3). As expected, the percentage of patterns converging from large Hamming distances drops off faster than the percentage from a smaller Hamming distance. The shape of Fig. 4 is similar to the "waterfall" graphs common in coding theory and signal processing. Waterfall graphs are used to display the degradation of the system performance as the input noise increases. Using this type of interpretation, Fig. 4 displays that the ability of the network to handle small signal to noise ratios (large Hamming distances) decreases as the number of patterns stored (r) increases.

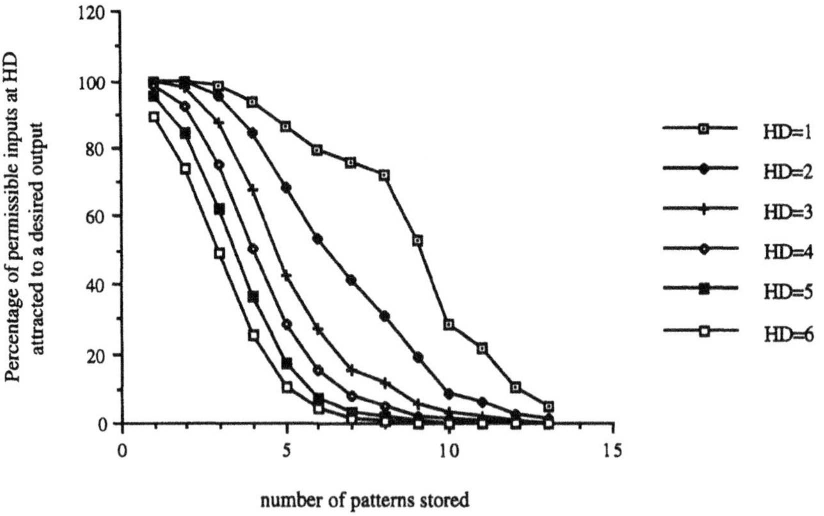

Figure 4 Convergence rate as a function of the number of patterns stored. The convergence rate is specified as the ratio of the number of initial conditions which converge to the desired equilibrium point to the number of all the possible initial conditions, from a given Hamming distance. Reprinted with permission from J. Si and A. N. Michel, *IEEE Trans. Neural Networks* 6:105–116, 1995 (©1995 IEEE).

V. CONCLUSIONS AND DISCUSSIONS

In this chapter, we have proposed a neural network model endowed with multilevel threshold functions as an effective means of realizing associative memories. We have conducted a qualitative analysis of these networks and we have devised a synthesis procedure for this class of neural networks. The synthesis procedure presented in Section III guarantees the global stability of the synthesized neural network. It also guarantees to store all the desired memories as asymptotically stable equilibrium points of system (3).

From the local stability analysis results obtained in Section II, a neural network with n neurons each of which has m states may have at least m^n asymptotically stable equilibria. On the other hand, confined by the result obtained in Theorem 2, part 3, the number of equilibrium points for (3) is finite. As noted in the beginning of the chapter, the local stability analysis of neural networks with neurons having binary states is a special case of the results obtained in the present chapter, that is, neural networks with binary state neurons may have at least 2^n asymptotically stable equilibria.

However, as demonstrated in Section IV, the domain of attraction of each desired equilibrium decreases as the number of desired memories increases. This implies that the number of spurious states in system (3) increases with the number of desired memories.

APPENDIX

Proof of Theorem 1. We choose a Lyapunov function for (7) of the form

$$v\big(p(k)\big) = \sum_{i=1}^{n} \lambda_i \big|p_i(k)\big|,$$

where $\lambda_i > 0$, for $i = 1, \ldots, n$, are constants. This function is clearly positive definite.

The first forward difference of v along the solutions of (7) is given by

$$\begin{aligned}\Delta v_{(\Sigma)}\big(p(k)\big) &= v(k+1) - v(k) = \sum_{i=1}^{n} \lambda_i \big\{\big|p_i(k+1)\big| - \big|p_i(k)\big|\big\} \\ &= \sum_{i=1}^{n} \lambda_i \left\{\left|\sum_{j=1}^{n} T_{ij} g_j\big(p_j(k)\big)\right| - \big|p_i(k)\big|\right\}\end{aligned}$$

$$\leqslant \sum_{i=1}^{n} \lambda_i \left\{ \sum_{j=1}^{n} |T_{ij}| \cdot |g_j(p_j(k))| - |p_i(k)| \right\}$$

$$\leqslant \sum_{i=1}^{n} \lambda_i \left\{ \sum_{j=1}^{n} |T_{ij}| c_{j2} |p_j(k)| - |p_i(k)| \right\}$$

$$= \sum_{i=1}^{n} \lambda_i (\sigma_i - 1) |p_i(k)| + \sum_{i=1}^{n} \lambda_i \sum_{\substack{j=1 \\ j \neq i}} \sigma_{ij} |p_j(k)|$$

$$= -\lambda^T Dq,$$

where $\lambda = (\lambda_1, \ldots, \lambda_n)^T$ and $q = (|p_1|, \ldots, |p_n|)^T$. Whereas D is an M matrix, there is a vector $y = (y_1, \ldots, y_n)^T$, with $y_i > 0,\ i = 1, \ldots, n$, such that [29]

$$-y^T q < 0, \quad \text{where } y^T = \lambda^T D$$

in some neighborhood $B(r) = \{p \in R^n \colon |p| < r\}$ for some $r > 0$. Therefore, $\Delta v_{(\Sigma)}$ is negative definite. Hence, the origin $p = 0$ of system (7) is asymptotically stable. ■

Proof of Lemma 1. Let $a = \sup\{|-\frac{1}{2}v^T T v - v^T I| \colon v \in (-d, d)^n\}$. We have $a \leqslant \frac{1}{2}|T| + |I| < \infty$, because $d < \infty$. Let $f_i(\xi) = \int_0^\xi s_i^{-1}(\sigma) d\sigma,\ \xi \in (-d, d)$. Whereas $s_i(\cdot)$ is in class A, we have for each $i,\ i = 1, \ldots, n,\ f_i(\xi) \geqslant 0$ and $\lim_{\xi \to \pm d} f_i(\xi) = +\infty$. Let $f(v) = \max_{1 \leqslant i \leqslant n}\{f_i(v_i)\}$. We obtain $E(v) \geqslant f(v) - a$. The lemma now follows, because $f(v_m) \to +\infty$ as $v_m \to \partial(-d, d)^n$. ■

Proof of Lemma 2. From Eq. (12), it follows that $\nabla E(v)$ is zero if and only if $-Tv - I + s^{-1}(v) = 0$. The result now follows from Eq. (4). ■

Proof of Lemma 3. For fixed T, we define the C^1 function $K \colon (-d, d)^n \to R^n$ by

$$K(v) = \nabla E(v) + I = -Tv + s^{-1}(v) = \big(k_1(v), \ldots, k_n(v)\big)^T$$

and let

$$DK(v) = \big(\nabla K_1(v)^T, \ldots, \nabla K_n(v)^T\big)^T.$$

By Sard's theorem [33], there exists $Q,\ R^n \supset Q$, with measure 0, such that if $K(v) \in R^n - Q$, then $\det(D(K(v))) \neq 0$. Thus when $I \in R^n - Q$, if $\nabla E(v) = 0$, then $K(v) = 0 + I = I \in R^n - Q$, and $\det(J_E(v)) = \det(D(K(v))) \neq 0$. ■

Proof of Theorem 2. (1) Let $\Delta v_i(k) = v_i(k+1) - v_i(k)$ and let

$$S_i\big(v_i(k)\big) = \int_0^{v_i(k)} s_i^{-1}(\sigma) d\sigma.$$

Then for the energy function given in (11), we have

$$\begin{aligned}
\Delta E_{(10)}\big(v(k)\big) &= E\big(v(k+1)\big) - E\big(v(k)\big) \\
&= -\sum_{i=1}^{n}\left(\sum_{j=1}^{n} T_{ij} v_j(k) + I_i\right)\Delta v_i(k) \\
&\quad - \frac{1}{2}\sum_{i=1}^{n}\Delta v_i(k)\sum_{j=1}^{n} T_{ij}\Delta v_j(k) \\
&\quad + \sum_{i=1}^{n}\big[S_i\big(v_i(k+1)\big) - S_i\big(v_i(k)\big)\big] \\
&= -\sum_{i=1}^{n}\left[x_i(k+1) - \frac{S_i(v_i(k+1)) - S_i(v_i(k))}{\Delta v_i(k)}\right]\Delta v_i(k) \\
&\quad - \frac{1}{2}\sum_{i=1}^{n}\Delta v_i(k)\sum_{j=1}^{n} T_{ij}\Delta v_j(k).
\end{aligned}$$

By the mean value theorem we obtain

$$\frac{S_i(v_i(k+1)) - S_i(v_i(k))}{\Delta v_i(k)} = S_i'(c) = s_i^{-1}(c),$$

where

$$c \in \big(v_i(k), v_i(k+1)\big), \quad \text{if } v_i(k+1) \geqslant v_i(k),$$

and

$$c \in \big(v_i(k+1), v_i(k)\big), \quad \text{if } v_i(k) \geqslant v_i(k+1).$$

Then

$$\begin{aligned}
\Delta E_{(10)}\big(v(k)\big) &= -\sum_{i=1}^{n}\big\{s_i^{-1}\big(v_i(k+1)\big) - s_i^{-1}(c)\big\}\Delta v_i(k) \\
&\quad - \tfrac{1}{2}\sum_{i=1}^{n}\Delta v_i(k)\sum_{j=1}^{n} T_{ij}\Delta v_j(k). \qquad (25)
\end{aligned}$$

Whereas the $s_i(\cdot)$ are strictly increasing, it follows that

$$-\big\{s_i^{-1}\big(v_i(k+1)\big) - s_i^{-1}(c)\big\}\Delta v_i(k) \leqslant 0, \qquad i = 1, \ldots, n. \qquad (26)$$

Also, whereas T is positive semidefinite, we have

$$-\tfrac{1}{2}\sum_{i=1}^{n}\Delta v_i(k)\sum_{j=1}^{n}T_{ij}\Delta v_j(k) \leqslant 0. \tag{27}$$

Thus $\Delta E(v(k)) = 0$ only when $\Delta v_i(k) = 0$, $i = 1, \ldots, n$. This proves part 1.

(2) By part 1 and Lemma 1, for any nonequilibrium solution $v(\cdot, \tilde{v})$: $Z^+ \to (-d, d)^n$ of (10), there exists a $\sigma > 0$ such that $C \supset v(Z^+) \triangleq \{v(k),\ k = 0, 1, 2, \ldots\}$, where $C = (-d + \sigma, d - \sigma)^n$. Let $\Omega(v) = \{y \in (-d, d)^n$: there exists $Z^+ \supset \{k_m\}$, $k_m \to +\infty$, such that $y = \lim_{k\to\infty} v(k_m)\}$. Each element in $\Omega(v)$ is said to be an *Ω-limit point* of v (see, e.g., [31]). We have $\Omega(v) \subset \bar{v}(Z^+) \subset \overline{C} \subset (-d, d)^n$. Whereas $\overline{C}$ is compact and $v(Z^+)$ contains infinitely many points, we know that $\Omega(v) \neq \emptyset$ (by the Bolzano–Weierstrass property). By an invariance theorem [31], $v(k)$ approaches $\Omega(v)$ (in the sense that for any $\varepsilon > 0$, there exists $\hat{k} > 0$, such that for any $k > \hat{k}$, there exists $v_k \in \Omega(v)$ such that $|v(k) - v_k| < \varepsilon$) and for every $v \in \Omega(v)$, $\Delta E_{(10)}(v(k)) = 0$. This implies $\Delta v(k) = 0$ [see Eqs. (26) and (27)]. Therefore, every Ω-limit point of v is an equilibrium of system (10). By Assumption 7, the set of equilibrium points of (10) is discrete. So is $\Omega(v)$. Whereas $\overline{C} \supset \Omega(v)$ and whereas $\overline{C}$ is compact, it follows that $\Omega(v)$ is finite. We claim that $\Omega(v)$ contains only one point. For if otherwise, without loss of generality, let $\hat{v}, \tilde{v} \in \Omega(v)$. Note, as previously discussed, $\hat{v}, \tilde{v}$ are also equilibrium points of (10). Then for any $\varepsilon > 0$, there exists a $\hat{k} > 0$, such that when $k > \hat{k}$, $|v(k) - \hat{v}| < \varepsilon/2$ and also $|v(k) - \tilde{v}| < \varepsilon/2$. Thus we have $|\hat{v} - \tilde{v}| \leqslant |v(k) - \hat{v}| + |v(k) - \tilde{v}| < \varepsilon$. This contradicts that $\hat{v}$ and $\tilde{v}$ are isolated. We have thus shown that each solution of system (10) converges to an Ω-limit set which is a singleton, containing an equilibrium of (10).

(3) Let $b = \sup\{|-Tv - I|\colon v \in (-d, d)^n\}$. We have $b \leqslant |T| + |I| < +\infty$. For each i, we have $s_i^{-1}(\sigma) \to \pm\infty$ as $\sigma \to \pm d$. Therefore $|\nabla E(v)| \geqslant |s^{-1}(v)| - b \to \infty$ as $v \to \partial(-d, d)^n$. Hence, there exists δ, $0 < \delta < d/2$, such that $\nabla E(v) \neq 0$, outside of $C = (-d+\delta, d-\delta)^n$. By Lemma 1, all equilibrium points of (10) are in $\overline{C}$ which is compact. By compactness of $\overline{C}$ and the assumption that all equilibrium points are isolated, the set of equilibrium points of (10) is finite.

(4) First, we show that if $\tilde{v}$ is an asymptotically stable equilibrium point of (10), then $\tilde{v}$ is a local minimum of the energy function E. For purposes of contradiction, assume that $\tilde{v}$ is not a local minimum of E. Then there exists a sequence $\{v_k\}$, $(-d, d)^n \supset \{v_k\}$, such that $0 < |v_k - \tilde{v}| < 1/k$ and $E(v_k) < E(\tilde{v})$. By Assumption 7, there exists an $\varepsilon > 0$ such that there are no equilibrium points in $B(\tilde{v}, \varepsilon) - \{\tilde{v}\}$. Then for any $\delta > 0$, $\varepsilon > \delta > 0$, choose k such that $1/k < \delta$. In this case we have $v_k \in B(\tilde{v}, \delta) - \{\tilde{v}\}$ and $B(\tilde{v}, \varepsilon) - \{\tilde{v}\} \supset B(\tilde{v}, \delta) - \{\tilde{v}\}$ and v_k is not an equilibrium. From part 2 of the present theorem, it follows that the solution $v(\cdot, v_k)$ converges to an equilibrium of (10), say, $\hat{v}$. By part 1 of the present theorem, $E(\hat{v}) < E(v_k) < E(\tilde{v})$, $\hat{v} \neq \tilde{v}$. Hence, $\hat{v}$ is not contained in $B(\tilde{v}, \varepsilon)$ and

$v(\cdot, v_k)$ will leave $B(\tilde{v}, \varepsilon)$ as $k \to \infty$. Therefore, $\tilde{v}$ is unstable. We have arrived at a contradiction. Hence, $\tilde{v}$ must be a local minimum of E.

Next, we show that if $\tilde{v}$ is a local minimum of the energy function E, then $\tilde{v}$ is an asymptotically stable equilibrium point of (10). To accomplish this, we show that (a) if $\tilde{v}$ is a local minimum of energy function E, then $J_E(\tilde{v}) > 0$, and (b) if $J_E(\tilde{v}) > 0$, then $\tilde{v}$ is asymptotically stable. ∎

For part (a) we distinguish between two cases.

Case 1. $J_E(\tilde{v})$ is not positive definite, but is positive semidefinite. By the first part of Assumption 7, there exists $y \in R^n$, $y \neq 0$ such that $J_E(\tilde{v})y = 0$, $D^3E(\tilde{v}, y, y, y) = (s_i^{-1''}(\tilde{v}_1), \ldots, s_n^{-1''}(\tilde{v}_n))(y_1^3, \ldots, y_n^3)^T \neq 0$. From the Taylor expansion of E at $\tilde{v}$ [33], we obtain

$$\begin{aligned} E(\tilde{v} + ty) &= E(\tilde{v}) + t\nabla E(\tilde{v})y + (t^2/2)y^T J_E(\tilde{v})y \\ &\quad + \left(t^3/6\right)D^3(\tilde{v}, y, y, y) + o(t^3), \qquad t \in [1, 1], \end{aligned}$$

where $\lim_{t\to 0} o(t^3)/t^3 = 0$. Whereas $\nabla E(\tilde{v}) = 0$ and $J_E(\tilde{v})y = 0$, we have

$$E(\tilde{v} + ty) = E(\tilde{v}) + (t^3/6)D^3(\tilde{v}, y, y, y) + o(t^3), \qquad t \in [-1, 1].$$

Whereas $D^3(\tilde{v}, y, y, y) \neq 0$, there exists $\delta > 0$ such that

$$\begin{aligned} E(\tilde{v} + ty) - E(\tilde{v}) &= (t^3/6)D^3(\tilde{v}, y, y, y) + o(t^3) < 0, \\ &\qquad t \in (-\delta, 0), \text{ if } D^3(\tilde{v}, y, y, y) > 0, \end{aligned}$$

and

$$\begin{aligned} E(\tilde{v} + ty) - E(\tilde{v}) &= (t^3/6)D^3(\tilde{v}, y, y, y) + o(t^3) < 0, \\ &\qquad t \in (0, \delta), \text{ if } D^3(\tilde{v}, y, y, y) < 0. \end{aligned}$$

Therefore, $\tilde{v}$ is not a local minimum of E.

Case 2. $J_E(\tilde{v})$ is not positive semidefinite. Then there exists $y \in R^n$ such that $y \neq 0$, $y^T J_E(\tilde{v})y < 0$. A Taylor expansion of E at $\tilde{v}$ yields

$$E(\tilde{v} + ty) = E(\tilde{v}) + t\nabla E(\tilde{v})y + (t^2/2)y^T J_E(\tilde{v})y + o(6), \qquad t \in [0, 1],$$

where $\lim_{t\to 0} o(t^2)/t^2 = 0$. Whereas $\nabla E = 0$, we have

$$E(\tilde{v} + ty) = E(\tilde{v}) + (t^2/2)y^T J_E(\tilde{v})y + o(6), \qquad t \in [0, 1].$$

Whereas $y^T J_E(\tilde{v})y < 0$, there exists a $\delta > 0$ such that

$$E(\tilde{v} + ty) - E(\tilde{v}) = (t^2/2)y^T J_E(\tilde{v})y + o(6) < 0, \qquad t \in (0, \delta).$$

Once more $\tilde{v}$ is not a local minimum of E. Therefore, if $\tilde{v}$ is a local minimum of E, then $J_E(\tilde{v}) > 0$.

We now prove part (b). If $J_E(\tilde{v}) > 0$, then there exists an open neighborhood U of $\tilde{v}$ such that on U, the function defined by $E_d(v) = E(v) - E(\tilde{v})$ is positive definite with respect to $\tilde{v}$ [i.e., $E_d(\tilde{v}) = 0$ and $E_d(v) > 0,\ v \neq \tilde{v}$] and

$$\begin{aligned} E_d\big(v(k+1)\big) - E_d\big(v(k)\big) &= \Delta E_d(v) \\ &= -\sum_{i=1}^{n} \big\{s_i^{-1}\big(v_i(k+1)\big) - s_i^{-1}(c)\big\} \\ &\quad \times \Delta v_i(k) - \tfrac{1}{2}\sum_{i=1}^{n} \nabla v_i(k) \sum_{j=1}^{n} T_{ij}\Delta v_j(k) < 0 \end{aligned}$$

for $v \neq \tilde{v}$ [see Eqs. (26) and (27)]. It follows from the principal results of the Lyapunov theory [32, Theorem 2.2.23] that $\tilde{v}$ is asymptotically stable. ■

Proof of Proposition 1. From Eq. (19) we have

$$[T_{i1}, T_{i2}, \ldots, T_{in}, I_i]^T = U^T(UU^T)^+\big[x_1^1, x_1^2, \ldots, x_1^r\big]^T. \tag{28}$$

The matrix $U' = (UU^T)^+$ is symmetric. Substituting $v_j^i = x_j^i$ ($i = 1, \ldots, r$ and $j = 1, \ldots, n$) into (28), we have

$$T_{ij} = \big[v_j^1, v_j^2, \ldots, v_j^r\big]U'\big[v_i^1, v_i^2, \ldots, v_i^r\big]^T$$

and

$$T_{ij} = \big[v_i^1, v_i^2, \ldots, v_i^r\big]U'\big[v_j^1, v_j^2, \ldots, v_j^r\big]^T$$

or

$$T_{ij} = T_{ji}, \qquad i, j = 1, \ldots, n.$$ ■

Proof of Proposition 2. If Assumption 10 is true, then $V = X$ [H is defined in (16)]. With $I = 0$, the solution of (14) assumes the form $T = VV^T(VV^T)^+$. Thus T is a projection operator (see [34]). As such, T is positive semidefinite. ■

REFERENCES

[1] M. Cohen and S. Grossberg. *IEEE Trans. Systems Man Cybernet.* SMC-13:815–826, 1983.
[2] S. Grossberg. *Neural Networks* 1:17–61, 1988.
[3] J. J. Hopfield. *Proc. Nat. Acad. Sci. U.S.A.* 81:3088–3092, 1984.
[4] J. J. Hopfield and D.W. Tank. *Biol. Cybernet.* 52:141–152, 1985.
[5] D. W. Tank and J. J. Hopfield. *IEEE Trans. Circuits Systems* CAS-33:533–541, 1986.
[6] L. Personnaz, I. Guyon, and G. Dreyfus. *J. Phys. Lett.* 46:L359–L365, 1985.
[7] L. Personnaz, I. Guyon, and G. Dreyfus. *Phys. Rev. A* 34:4217–4228, 1986.

[8] C. M. Marcus, F. R. Waugh, and R. M. Westervelt. *Phys. Rev. A* 41:3355–3364, 1990.
[9] C. M. Marcus and R. M. Westervelt. *Phys. Rev. A* 40:501–504, 1989.
[10] J. Li, A. N. Michel, and W. Porod. *IEEE Trans. Circuits Systems* 35:976–986, 1988.
[11] J. Li, A. N. Michel, and W. Porod. *IEEE Trans. Circuits Systems* 36:1405–1422, 1989.
[12] A. N. Michel, J. A. Farrell, and H. F. Sun. *IEEE Trans. Circuits Systems* 37:1356–1366, 1990.
[13] A. N. Michel, J. A. Farrell, and W. Porod. *IEEE Trans. Circuits Systems* 36:229–243, 1989.
[14] C. Jeffries. *Code Recognition and Set Selection with Neural Networks*. Birkhäuser, Boston, 1991.
[15] B. Kosko. *Neural Networks and Fuzzy Systems*. Prentice-Hall, Englewood Cliffs, NJ, 1992.
[16] J. Hertz, A. Krogh, and R. G. Palmer. *Introduction to the Theory of Neural Computation*. Addison-Wesley, Reading, MA, 1991.
[17] P. K. Simpson. *Artificial Neural Systems*. Pergamon Press, New York, 1990.
[18] S. Haykin. *Neural Networks: A Comprehensive Foundation*. Macmillan, New York, 1994.
[19] A. N. Michel and J. A. Farrell. *IEEE Control Syst. Mag.* 10:6–17, 1990.
[20] K. Sakurai and S. Takano. *Annual International Conference of the IEEE Engineering in Medicine and Biology Society, IEEE Eng. Med. Biol. Mag.* 12:1756–1757, 1990.
[21] B. Simic-Glavaski. In *Proceedings of the 1990 International Joint Conference on Neural Networks*, San Diego, 1990, pp. 809–812.
[22] W. Banzhaf. In *Proceedings of the IEEE First International Conference on Neural Nets*, San Diego, 1987, Vol. 2, pp. 223–230.
[23] M. Fleisher. In *Neural Information Processing Systems: AIP Conference Proceedings* (D. Anderson, Ed.), pp. 278–289. Am. Inst. of Phys., New York, 1987.
[24] A. Guez, V. Protopopsecu, and J. Barhen. *IEEE Trans. Systems Man, Cybernet.* 18:80–86, 1988.
[25] C. Meunier, D. Hansel, and A. Verga. *J. Statist. Phys.* 55:859–901, 1989.
[26] H. Rieger. In *Statistical Mechanics of Neural Networks* (L. Garrido, Ed.), pp. 33–47. Springer-Verlag, New York, 1990.
[27] S. Jankowski, A. Lozowski, and J. M. Zurada. *IEEE Trans. Neural Networks* 7:1491–1496, 1996.
[28] J. Yuh and R. W. Newcomb. *IEEE Trans. Neural Networks* 4:470–483, 1993.
[29] A. N. Michel and R. K. Miller. *Qualitative Analysis of Large Scale Dynamical System*. Academic Press, New York, 1977.
[30] A. N. Michel. *IEEE Trans. Automat. Control* AC-28:639–653, 1983.
[31] R. K. Miller and A. N. Michel. *Ordinary Differential Equations*. Academic Press, New York, 1972.
[32] A. N. Michel and R. K. Miller. *IEEE Trans. Circuits Systems* 30:671–680, 1983.
[33] A. Avez. *Differential Calculus*. Wiley, New York, 1986.
[34] A. Albert. *Regression and the Moore–Penrose Pseudo-Inverse*. Academic Press, New York, 1972.

Probabilistic Design

Sumio Watanabe
Advanced Information Processing Division
Precision and Intelligence Laboratory
Tokyo Institute of Technology
4259 Nagatuda, Midori-ku
Yokohama, 226 Japan

Kenji Fukumizu
Information and Communication
R&D Center
Ricoh Co., Ltd.
Kohoku-ku
Yokohama, 222 Japan

I. INTRODUCTION

Artificial neural networks are now used in many information processing systems. Although they play central roles in pattern recognition, time-sequence prediction, robotic control, and so on, it is often ambiguous what kinds of concepts they learn and how precise their answers are. For example, we often hear the following questions from engineers developing practical systems.

1. What do the outputs of neural networks mean?
2. Can neural networks answer even to unknown inputs?
3. How reliable are the answers of neural networks?
4. Do neural networks have abilities to explain what kinds of concepts they have learned?

In the early stage of neural network research, there seemed to be no answer to these questions because neural networks are nonlinear and complex black boxes. Even some researchers said that the design of neural networks is a kind of art. However, the statistical structure of neural network learning was clarified by recent studies [1, 2], so that we can answer the preceding questions. In this chapter,

Algorithms and Architectures

we summarize the theoretical foundation of learning machines upon which we can answer the foregoing questions, and we try to establish design methods for neural networks as a part of engineering.

This chapter consists of four parts. In Section II, we formulate a unified probabilistic framework of artificial neural networks. It is explained that neural networks are considered as statistical parametric models, whose inference is characterized by the conditional probability density, and whose learning process is interpreted to be the iterative maximum likelihood method.

In Section III, we propose three design methods to improve conventional neural networks. Using the first method, a neural network can answer how familiar it is with a given input, with the result that it obtains an ability to reject unknown inputs. The second method makes a neural network answer how reliable its own inference is. This is a kind of meta-inference, by which we can judge whether the neural network's outputs should be adopted or not. The last method concerns inverse inference. We devise a neural network that illustrates input patterns for a given category.

In Section IV, a typical neural network which has the foregoing abilities is introduced—a probability competition neural network. This is a kind of mixture models in statistics, which has some important properties in information processing. For example, it can tell familiarity of inputs, reliability of its own inference, and examples in a given category. It is shown how these abilities are used in practical systems by applications to character recognition and ultrasonic image understanding.

In Section V, we discuss two statistical techniques. The former is how to select the best model for the minimum prediction error in a given model family; the latter is how to optimize a network that can ask questions for the most efficient learning. Although these techniques are established for regular statistical models, some problems remain in applications to neural networks. We also discuss such problems for future study.

II. UNIFIED FRAMEWORK OF NEURAL NETWORKS

A. DEFINITION

In this section, we summarize a probabilistic framework upon which our discussion of neural network design methods is based. Our main goal is to establish a method to estimate the relation between an input and an output. Let X and Y be the input space and the output space, respectively. We assume that the input–output pair has the probability density function $q(\mathbf{x}, \mathbf{y})$ on the direct product space $X \times Y$. The function $q(\mathbf{x}, \mathbf{y})$ represents the true relation between the input and the output, but it is complex and unknown in general. The probability density on the input space is defined by

$$q(\mathbf{x}) = \int q(\mathbf{x}, \mathbf{y})\, d\mathbf{y},$$

and the probability density on the output space for a given input x is

$$q(\mathbf{y}|\mathbf{x}) = \frac{q(\mathbf{x}, \mathbf{y})}{q(\mathbf{x})}.$$

The functions $q(\mathbf{x})$ and $q(\mathbf{y}|\mathbf{x})$ are referred to as the true occurrence probability and the true inference probability, respectively. To estimate $q(\mathbf{x}, \mathbf{y})$, we employ a parametric probability density function $p(\mathbf{x}, \mathbf{y}; \mathbf{w})$ which is realized by some learning machine with a parameter $\mathbf{w}$. We choose the best parameter $\mathbf{w}$ of $p(\mathbf{x}, \mathbf{y}; \mathbf{w})$ to approximate the true relation $q(\mathbf{x}, \mathbf{y})$.

For simplicity, we denote the probability density function of the normal distribution on the L dimensional Euclidean space R^L by

$$g_L(\mathbf{x}; \mathbf{m}, \sigma) = \frac{1}{(2\pi\sigma^2)^{L/2}} \exp\left(-\frac{\|\mathbf{x} - \mathbf{m}\|^2}{2\sigma^2}\right), \tag{1}$$

where $\mathbf{m}$ is the average vector and σ is the standard deviation.

EXAMPLE 1 (Function approximation neural network). Let M and N be natural numbers. The direct product of the input space and the output space is given by $R^M \times R^N$. A function approximation neural network is defined by

$$p(\mathbf{x}, \mathbf{y}; \mathbf{w}, \sigma) = q(\mathbf{x}) g_N(\mathbf{y}; \boldsymbol{\varphi}(\mathbf{x}; \mathbf{w}), \sigma), \tag{2}$$

where $\mathbf{w}$ and σ are parameters to be optimized, $q(\mathbf{x})$ is the probability density function on the input space, and $\boldsymbol{\varphi}(\mathbf{x}; \mathbf{w})$ is a function realized by the multilayer perceptron (MLP), the radial basis functions, or another parametric function. Note that, in the function approximation neural network, $q(\mathbf{x})$ is left unestimated or unknown.

EXAMPLE 2 (Boltzmann machine). Suppose that the direct product of the input space and the output space is given by $\{0, 1\}^M \times \{0, 1\}^N$. Let $\mathbf{s}$ be the variable of the Boltzmann machine with H hidden units,

$$\mathbf{s} = \mathbf{x} \times \mathbf{h} \times \mathbf{y} \in \{0, 1\}^M \times \{0, 1\}^H \times \{0, 1\}^N.$$

The Boltzmann machine is defined by the probability density on $R^M \times R^N$,

$$p(\mathbf{x}, \mathbf{y}; \mathbf{w}) = \frac{1}{Z(\mathbf{w})} \sum_{\mathbf{h} \in \{0,1\}^H} \exp\left(-\sum_{(i,j)} w_{ij} s_i s_j\right), \tag{3}$$

where s_i is the ith unit of $\mathbf{s}$, $\mathbf{w} = \{w_{ij}\}$ $(w_{ij} = w_{ji})$ is the set of parameters, and $Z(\mathbf{w})$ is a normalizing constant,

$$Z(\mathbf{w}) = \sum_{\mathbf{xxhxy} \in \{0,1\}^{M+H+N}} \exp\left(-\sum_{(i,j)} w_{ij} s_i s_j\right). \tag{4}$$

This probability density is realized by the equilibrium state where neither inputs nor outputs are fixed.

Once the probability density function $p(\mathbf{x}, \mathbf{y}; \mathbf{w})$ is defined, the inference by the machine is formulated as follows. For a given input sample $\mathbf{x}$ and a given parameter $\mathbf{w}$, the probabilistic output of the machine is defined to be a random sample taken from the conditional probability density

$$p(\mathbf{y}|\mathbf{x}; \mathbf{w}) = \frac{p(\mathbf{x}, \mathbf{y}; \mathbf{w})}{p(\mathbf{x}; \mathbf{w})}, \tag{5}$$

where $p(\mathbf{x}; \mathbf{w})$ is a probability density on the input space defined by

$$p(\mathbf{x}; \mathbf{w}) = \int p(\mathbf{x}, \mathbf{y}; \mathbf{w})\, d\mathbf{y}. \tag{6}$$

The functions $p(\mathbf{x}; \mathbf{w})$ and $p(\mathbf{y}|\mathbf{x}; \mathbf{w})$ are referred to as the estimated occurrence probability and the estimated inference probability, respectively. The average output of the machine and its variance are also defined by

$$\mathbf{E}(\mathbf{x}; \mathbf{w}) = \int \mathbf{y} p(\mathbf{y}|\mathbf{x}; \mathbf{w})\, d\mathbf{y}, \tag{7}$$

$$V(\mathbf{x}; \mathbf{w}) = \int \|\mathbf{y} - \mathbf{E}(\mathbf{x}; \mathbf{w})\|^2 p(\mathbf{y}|\mathbf{x}; \mathbf{w})\, d\mathbf{y}. \tag{8}$$

Note that $V(\mathbf{x}; \mathbf{w})$ depends on a given input $\mathbf{x}$, in general.

EXAMPLE 3 (Inference by the function approximation neural networks). It is easy to show that the average output and its variance of the function approximation neural network in Example 1 are

$$\mathbf{E}(\mathbf{x}; \mathbf{w}) = \varphi(\mathbf{x}; \mathbf{w}), \tag{9}$$

$$V(\mathbf{x}; \mathbf{w}) = N\sigma^2, \tag{10}$$

where N is the dimension of the output space. Note that the function approximation neural network assumes that the variance of outputs does not depend on a given input $\mathbf{x}$.

EXAMPLE 4 (Inference by the Boltzmann machine). The Boltzmann machine's output can be understood as a probabilistic output. Its inference probability is given by

$$p(\mathbf{y}|\mathbf{x};\, \mathbf{w}) = \frac{1}{Z(\mathbf{x};\, \mathbf{w})} \sum_{\mathbf{h}\in\{0,1\}^H} \exp\left(-\sum_{(i,j)} w_{ij} s_i s_j\right), \tag{11}$$

where $Z(\mathbf{x};\, \mathbf{w})$ is a normalizing value for a fixed $\mathbf{x}$,

$$Z(\mathbf{x};\, \mathbf{w}) = \sum_{\mathbf{hxy}\in\{0,1\}^{H+N}} \exp\left(-\sum_{(i,j)} w_{ij} s_i s_j\right). \tag{12}$$

The preceding inference probability is realized by the equilibrium state with a fixed input $\mathbf{x}$. The occurrence probability is given by $p(\mathbf{x};\, \mathbf{w}) = Z(\mathbf{x};\, \mathbf{w})/Z(\mathbf{w})$.

B. Learning in Artificial Neural Networks

1. Learning Criterion

Let $\{(\mathbf{x}_i, \mathbf{y}_i)\}_{i=1}^n$ be a set of n input–output samples which are independently taken from the true probability density function $q(\mathbf{x}, \mathbf{y})$. These pairs are called training samples. We define three loss functions $L_k(\mathbf{w})$ $(k = 1, 2, 3)$ which represent different kinds of distances between $p(\mathbf{x}, \mathbf{y};\, \mathbf{w})$ and $q(\mathbf{x}, \mathbf{y})$ using the training samples

$$L_1(\mathbf{w}) = \frac{1}{n}\sum_{i=1}^{n} \|\mathbf{y}_i - E(\mathbf{x}_i;\, \mathbf{w})\|^2, \tag{13}$$

$$L_2(\mathbf{w}) = -\frac{1}{n}\sum_{i=1}^{n} \log p(\mathbf{y}_i|\mathbf{x}_i;\, \mathbf{w}), \tag{14}$$

$$L_3(\mathbf{w}) = -\frac{1}{n}\sum_{i=1}^{n} \log p(\mathbf{x}_i, \mathbf{y}_i;\, \mathbf{w}). \tag{15}$$

If the number of training samples is large enough, we can approximate these loss functions using the central limit theorem,

$$L_1(\mathbf{w}) \approx \int \|\mathbf{y} - \mathbf{E}(\mathbf{x};\, \mathbf{w})\|^2 q(\mathbf{x}, \mathbf{y})\, d\mathbf{x}\, d\mathbf{y}, \tag{16}$$

$$L_2(\mathbf{w}) \approx \int \log p(\mathbf{y}|\mathbf{x};\, \mathbf{w}) q(\mathbf{y}|\mathbf{x}) q(\mathbf{x})\, d\mathbf{x}\, d\mathbf{y}, \tag{17}$$

$$L_3(\mathbf{w}) \approx \int \log p(\mathbf{x}, \mathbf{y};\, \mathbf{w}) q(\mathbf{x}, \mathbf{y})\, d\mathbf{x}\, d\mathbf{y}. \tag{18}$$

The minima of the loss functions $L_k(\mathbf{w})$ $(k = 1, 2, 3)$ are attained if and only if

$$\mathbf{E}(\mathbf{x}; \mathbf{w}) = \mathbf{E}(\mathbf{x}), \qquad \text{a.e. } q(\mathbf{x}), \tag{19}$$

$$p(\mathbf{y}|\mathbf{x}; \mathbf{w}) = q(\mathbf{y}|\mathbf{x}), \qquad \text{a.e. } q(\mathbf{x}, \mathbf{y}), \tag{20}$$

$$p(\mathbf{x}, \mathbf{y}; \mathbf{w}) = q(\mathbf{x}, \mathbf{y}), \qquad \text{a.e. } q(\mathbf{x}, \mathbf{y}), \tag{21}$$

respectively. In the preceding equations, a.e. means that the equality holds with probability 1 for the corresponding probability density function, and $\mathbf{E}(\mathbf{x})$ is the true regression function defined by

$$\mathbf{E}(\mathbf{x}) = \int \mathbf{y} q(\mathbf{y}|\mathbf{x})\, d\mathbf{y}.$$

Note that

$$p(\mathbf{x}, \mathbf{y}; \mathbf{w}) = q(\mathbf{x}, \mathbf{y}) \quad \Rightarrow \quad p(\mathbf{y}|\mathbf{x}; \mathbf{w}) = q(\mathbf{y}|\mathbf{x}) \quad \text{and} \quad p(\mathbf{x}; \mathbf{w}) = q(\mathbf{x}) \tag{22}$$

and that

$$p(\mathbf{y}|\mathbf{x}; \mathbf{w}) = q(\mathbf{y}|\mathbf{x}) \quad \Rightarrow \quad \mathbf{E}(\mathbf{x}; \mathbf{w}) = \mathbf{E}(\mathbf{x}) \quad \text{and} \quad V(\mathbf{x}) = V(\mathbf{x}; \mathbf{w}), \tag{23}$$

where $V(\mathbf{x})$ is the true variance of the output for a given $\mathbf{x}$,

$$V(\mathbf{x}) = \int \|\mathbf{y} - \mathbf{E}(\mathbf{x})\|^2 q(\mathbf{y}|\mathbf{x})\, d\mathbf{y}.$$

If one uses the loss function $L_1(\mathbf{w})$, then $\mathbf{E}(\mathbf{x})$ is estimated but $V(\mathbf{x})$ is not. If one uses the loss function $L_2(\mathbf{w})$, both $\mathbf{E}(\mathbf{x})$ and $V(\mathbf{x})$ are estimated but the occurrence probability $q(\mathbf{x})$ is not. We should choose the appropriate loss function for the task which a neural network performs.

2. Learning Rules

After the loss function $L(\mathbf{w})$ is chosen, the parameter $\mathbf{w}$ is optimized by the stochastic dynamical system

$$\frac{d\mathbf{w}}{dt} = -\frac{\partial L(\mathbf{w})}{\partial \mathbf{w}} + T\mathbf{R}(t), \tag{24}$$

where $\mathbf{R}(t)$ shows a white Gaussian noise with average 0 and deviation 1, and T is a constant called temperature. If $T = 0$, then this equation is called the *steepest descent method*, which is approximated by the iterative learning algorithm.

$$\Delta\mathbf{w} = -\beta \frac{\partial L(\mathbf{w})}{\partial \mathbf{w}}, \tag{25}$$

where $\Delta\mathbf{w}$ means the added value of $\mathbf{w}$ in the updating process and $\beta > 0$ is a constant which determines the learning speed. After enough training cycles $t \to \infty$, the solution of the stochastic differential equation, Eq. (24), converges to the

Boltzmann distribution,

$$\rho(\mathbf{w}) = \frac{1}{Z}\exp\left(-\frac{1}{2T}L(\mathbf{w})\right). \tag{26}$$

If noises are controlled slowly enough to zero ($T \to 0$), then $\rho(\mathbf{w}) \to \delta(\mathbf{w} - \widehat{\mathbf{w}})$, where $\widehat{\mathbf{w}}$ is the parameter that minimizes the loss function $L(\mathbf{w})$. [For the loss functions $L_2(\mathbf{w})$ and $L_3(\mathbf{w})$, $\widehat{\mathbf{w}}$ is called the maximum likelihood estimator.] If no noises are introduced ($T = 0$), then the deterministic dynamical system Eq. (24) often leads the parameter to a local minimum.

EXAMPLE 5 (Error backpropagation). For the function approximation neural network, the training rule given by the steepest descent method for the loss function $L_1(\mathbf{w})$ is

$$\Delta\mathbf{w} = -\frac{\beta}{n}\sum_{i=1}^{n}\frac{\partial}{\partial\mathbf{w}}\|\mathbf{y}_i - \boldsymbol{\varphi}(\mathbf{x}_i;\mathbf{w})\|^2. \tag{27}$$

This method is called *the error backpropagation*. The training rules for the loss functions $L_2(\mathbf{w})$ and $L_3(\mathbf{w})$ result in the same form:

$$\Delta\mathbf{w} = -\frac{\beta}{n}\sum_{i=1}^{n}\frac{1}{2\sigma^2}\frac{\partial}{\partial\mathbf{w}}\left\|\mathbf{y}_i - \boldsymbol{\varphi}(\mathbf{x}_i;\mathbf{w})\right\|^2, \tag{28}$$

$$\Delta\sigma = \frac{\beta}{n}\sum_{i=1}^{n}\frac{1}{\sigma^3}\left\{\left\|\mathbf{y}_i - \boldsymbol{\varphi}(\mathbf{x}_i;\mathbf{w})\right\|^2 - N\sigma^2\right\}. \tag{29}$$

Note that Eq. (28) resembles Eq. (27).

EXAMPLE 6 (Boltzmann machine's learning rule). In the case of the Boltzmann machine, the steepest descent methods using $L_2(\mathbf{w})$ and $L_3(\mathbf{w})$, respectively, result in the different rules

$$\Delta w_{jk} = -\frac{\beta}{n}\sum_{i=1}^{n}\left\{E(s_j s_k|\mathbf{x}_i,\mathbf{y}_i;\mathbf{w}) - E(s_j s_k|\mathbf{x}_i;\mathbf{w})\right\}, \tag{30}$$

$$\Delta w_{jk} = -\frac{\beta}{n}\sum_{i=1}^{n}\left\{E(s_j s_k|\mathbf{x}_i,\mathbf{y}_i;\mathbf{w}) - E(s_j s_k;\mathbf{w})\right\}, \tag{31}$$

where $E(a|b; w)$ means the expectation value of a in the equilibrium state with the fixed b and the fixed parameter $\mathbf{w}$. For example, we have

$$E(a|\mathbf{x},\mathbf{y};\mathbf{w}) = \frac{\sum_h aZ(\mathbf{x},\mathbf{h},\mathbf{y};\mathbf{w})}{\sum_h Z(\mathbf{x},\mathbf{h},\mathbf{y};\mathbf{w})},$$

$$E(a|\mathbf{x};\mathbf{w}) = \frac{\sum_{h\times y} aZ(\mathbf{x},\mathbf{h},\mathbf{y};\mathbf{w})}{\sum_{h\times y} Z(\mathbf{x},\mathbf{h},\mathbf{y};\mathbf{w})},$$

where

$$Z(\mathbf{x}, \mathbf{h}, \mathbf{y}; \mathbf{w}) = \exp\left(-\sum_{(j,k)} w_{jk} s_j s_k\right).$$

The training rule, Eq. (30) can be derived as

$$\begin{aligned}
\frac{\partial L_2(\mathbf{w})}{\partial w_{jk}} &= -\frac{1}{n}\sum_{i=1}^{n} \frac{\partial}{\partial w_{jk}} \log p(\mathbf{y}_i|\mathbf{x}_i; \mathbf{w}) \\
&= -\frac{1}{n}\sum_{i=1}^{n} \frac{\partial}{\partial w_{jk}} \left\{\log \sum_{h} Z(\mathbf{x}_i, \mathbf{h}, \mathbf{y}_i; \mathbf{w}) - \log \sum_{h \times y} Z(\mathbf{x}_i, \mathbf{h}, \mathbf{y}; \mathbf{w})\right\} \\
&= \frac{1}{n}\sum_{i=1}^{n} \left\{\frac{\sum_h s_j s_k Z(\mathbf{x}_i, \mathbf{h}, \mathbf{y}_i; \mathbf{w})}{\sum_h Z(\mathbf{x}_i, \mathbf{h}, \mathbf{y}_i; \mathbf{w})} - \frac{\sum_{h\times y} s_j s_k Z(\mathbf{x}_i, \mathbf{h}, \mathbf{y}; \mathbf{w})}{\sum_{h\times y} Z(\mathbf{x}_i, \mathbf{h}, \mathbf{y}; \mathbf{w})}\right\} \\
&= \frac{1}{n}\sum_{i=1}^{n} \left\{E(s_k s_j|\mathbf{x}_i, \mathbf{y}_i; \mathbf{w}) - E(s_k s_j|\mathbf{x}_i; \mathbf{w})\right\}.
\end{aligned}$$

We can show the second rule Eq. (31) by similar calculation. Note that if one applies the first training rule, then only the conditional probability $q(\mathbf{y}|\mathbf{x})$ is estimated, and the occurrence probability $q(\mathbf{x})$ is not estimated, with the result that the inverse inference probability

$$q(\mathbf{x}|\mathbf{y}) = \frac{q(\mathbf{x})q(\mathbf{y}|\mathbf{x})}{q(\mathbf{y})}$$

is not estimated either.

Answer to the First Question

Based on the foregoing framework, we can answer the first question in the Introduction. In a pattern classification problem, input signals in R^M are classified into N categories. In other words, the input space is R^M and the output space is $[0, 1]^N$. If the probability density of signals contained in the ith category is given by $f_i(\mathbf{x})$, then the true probability density is

$$q(\mathbf{x}, \mathbf{y}) = \sum_{i=1}^{N} \mu_i f_i(\mathbf{x})\delta(\mathbf{y} - \mathbf{t}_i),$$

where μ_i is the *a priori* probability on the ith category which satisfies

$$\sum_{i=1}^{N} \mu_i = 1$$

and $\mathbf{t}_i = (0, 0, \ldots, 0, 1, 0, \ldots, 0)$ (only the ith element is 1). Then the ith element $E_i(\mathbf{x})$ of the regression function vector $\mathbf{E}(\mathbf{x})$ is given by

$$E_i(\mathbf{x}) = \frac{\int y_i q(\mathbf{x}, \mathbf{y})\, d\mathbf{y}}{\int q(\mathbf{x}, \mathbf{y})\, d\mathbf{y}} = \frac{\mu_i f_i(\mathbf{x})}{\sum_{j=1}^{N} \mu_j f_j(\mathbf{x})},$$

which is equal to the *a posteriori* probability of the ith category. If a neural network learns to approximate the true regression function, then its output represents the *a posteriori* probability.

III. PROBABILISTIC DESIGN OF LAYERED NEURAL NETWORKS

A. Neural Network That Finds Unknown Inputs

As we showed in the previous section, the inference in neural networks is based on the conditional probability. One can classify patterns into categories using the conditional probability, but cannot identify patterns. To identify the patterns or to judge whether an input signal is known or unknown, we need the occurrence probability. We consider a model

$$p(\mathbf{x}, \mathbf{y}; \mathbf{w}_1, \mathbf{w}_2) = p(\mathbf{x}; \mathbf{w}_1) p(\mathbf{y}|\mathbf{x}; \mathbf{w}_2), \tag{32}$$

which consists of two neural networks. The former neural network $p(\mathbf{x}; \mathbf{w}_1)$ estimates the occurrence probability $q(\mathbf{x})$, and the latter $p(\mathbf{y}|\mathbf{x}; \mathbf{w}_2)$ estimates the inference probability $q(\mathbf{y}|\mathbf{x})$. It should be emphasized that the conditional probability $p(\mathbf{y}|\mathbf{x}; \mathbf{w}_2)$ is ill defined when $p(\mathbf{x}; \mathbf{w}_1) \approx 0$. Therefore, the occurrence probability $p(\mathbf{x}_1; \mathbf{w})$ tells not only how familiar the neural network is with a given input $\mathbf{x}$, but also how well defined the inference probability is.

The training rules for $\mathbf{w}_1$ and $\mathbf{w}_2$ are given by

$$\Delta \mathbf{w}_1 = \beta \frac{\partial}{\partial \mathbf{w}_1} \sum_{i=1}^{n} \log p(\mathbf{x}_i; \mathbf{w}_1),$$

$$\Delta \mathbf{w}_2 = \beta \frac{\partial}{\partial \mathbf{w}_2} \sum_{i=1}^{n} \log p(\mathbf{y}_i|\mathbf{x}_i; \mathbf{w}_2),$$

which are derived from the steepest descent of the loss function $L_3(\mathbf{w})$ in Eq. (15). The latter training rule is the same as that of conventional neural network models.

We apply the preceding method to the design of a function approximation neural network with occurrence probability estimation. Suppose that the input and output space is $R^M \times R^N$. The simultaneous probability density function is given by

$$p(\mathbf{x}, \mathbf{y}; \mathbf{w}_1, \mathbf{w}_2, \sigma) = p(\mathbf{x}; \mathbf{w}_1) g_N(\mathbf{y}; \boldsymbol{\varphi}(\mathbf{x}; \mathbf{w}_2), \sigma). \tag{33}$$

In this model, the inference probability is realized by the ordinary function approximation model. A mixture model is applied for the occurrence probability. Let $r(\mathbf{x}; \boldsymbol{\xi}, \rho)$ be a probability density with a shift and a scaling transform of a fixed probability density $r(\mathbf{x})$ on R^M:

$$r(\mathbf{x}; \boldsymbol{\xi}, \rho) = \frac{1}{\rho^M} r\left(\frac{\mathbf{x} - \boldsymbol{\xi}}{\rho}\right).$$

The neural network for the occurrence probability can be designed as

$$p(\mathbf{x}; \mathbf{w}_1) = \frac{1}{Z(\boldsymbol{\theta})} \sum_{h=1}^{H} \exp(\theta_h) r(\mathbf{x}; \xi_h, \rho_h), \tag{34}$$

$$Z(\boldsymbol{\theta}) = \sum_{h=1}^{H} \exp(\theta_h), \tag{35}$$

where $\mathbf{w}_1 = \{\theta_h, \xi_h, \rho_h; h = 1, 2, \ldots, H\}$ is the set of parameters optimized during learning. Note that $p(\mathbf{x}; \mathbf{w}_1)$ can approximate any probability density function on the input space with respect to the L_p norm $(1 \leqslant p < +\infty)$ if $r(\mathbf{x})$ belongs to the corresponding function space.

Figure 1 shows a neural network given by Eq. (33). This network consists of a conventional function approximation neural network and a neural network for occurrence probability estimation. The former provides the average output, and the latter determines how often a given input occurs.

The learning rule for $\mathbf{w}_2$ is the same as that of the conventional function approximation neural networks. The learning rule for $\mathbf{w}_1$ can be derived from Eq. (33). When $r(\mathbf{x}) = g_M(\mathbf{x}; 0, 1)$, the learning rules for $\mathbf{w}_1 = \{\theta_h, \xi_h, \rho_h; h = 1, 2, \ldots, H\}$ have simple form

$$\Delta\theta_h = \beta c_h \sum_{i=1}^{n} \{d_{hi} - 1\},$$

$$\Delta\boldsymbol{\xi}_h = \beta c_h \sum_{i=1}^{n} d_{hi} \left\{\frac{\mathbf{x}_i - \boldsymbol{\xi}_h}{\rho_h^2}\right\},$$

$$\Delta\rho_h = \beta c_h \sum_{i=1}^{n} d_{hi} \left\{\frac{\|\mathbf{x}_i - \boldsymbol{\xi}_h\|^2 - M\rho_h^2}{\rho_h^3}\right\},$$

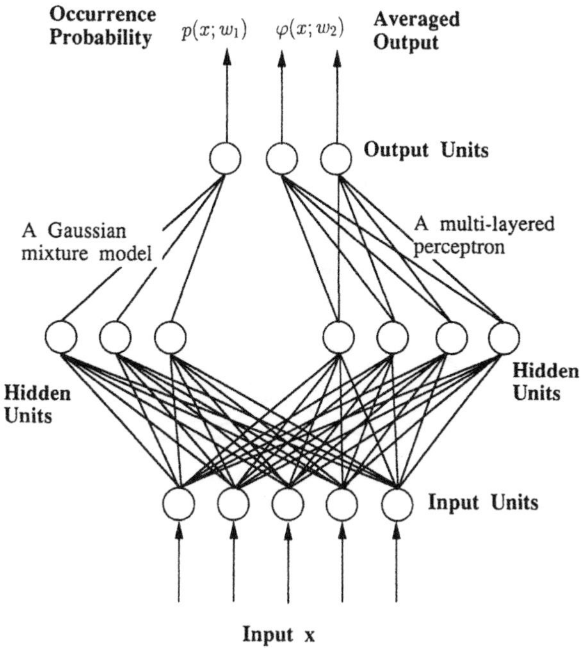

Figure 1 A function approximation neural network with estimated occurrence probability. The occurrence probability is estimated by using a Gaussian mixture model, and the expectation value of the inference probability is estimated by using the multilayered perceptron, for example.

where

$$c_h = \frac{\exp(\theta_h)}{Z(\boldsymbol{\theta})},$$
$$d_{hi} = \frac{r(\mathbf{x}_i; \xi_h, \rho_h)}{p(\mathbf{x}_i; \mathbf{w}_1)}.$$

Figure 2 shows the experimental result for the case $M = N = 1$. The true probability density is

$$q(x, y) = q(x) g_1(y; \varphi_0(x), 0.05),$$
$$q(x) = \tfrac{1}{2}\{g_1(x; 0.25, 0.05) + g_1(x; 0.67, 0.1)\},$$
$$\varphi_0(x) = 0.5 + 0.3\sin(2\pi x).$$

Four hundred training samples were taken from this probability density. The foregoing network $p(x; \mathbf{w}_1)$ with $H = 2$ was used for estimating $q(x)$, and a three-layer perceptron with 10 hidden units was used for $q(y|x)$. The estimated regres-

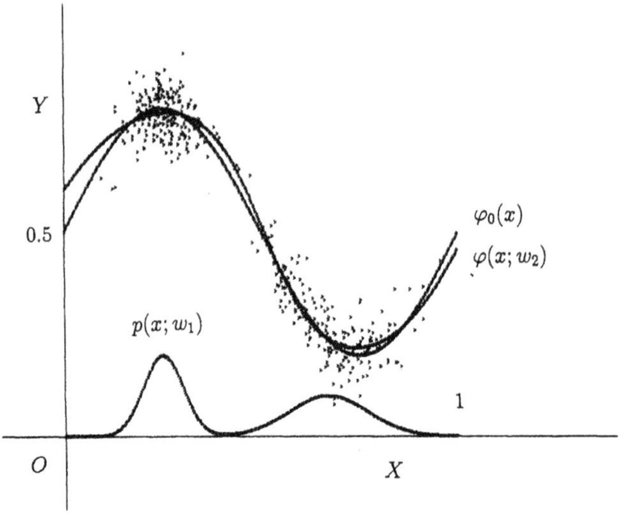

Figure 2 Experimental results for occurrence probability estimation. The estimated occurrence probability $p(\mathbf{x}; \mathbf{w}_1)$ shows not only familiarity of a given input, but also how well defined $\varphi(\mathbf{x}; \mathbf{w}_2)$ is.

sion function, which is equal to the output of the three-layer perceptron, is close to the true regression function $\varphi_0(x)$ for the input x whose probability density $q(x)$ is rather large, but is different from $\varphi_0(x)$ for the input x whose probability density $q(x)$ is smaller.

Answer to the Second Question

We can answer the second question in the Introduction. The conditional probability becomes ill defined for the input $\mathbf{x}$ with the small occurrence probability $p(\mathbf{x}; \mathbf{w}_1)$, which means that the neural network cannot answer anything for perfectly unknown input $[q(\mathbf{x}) = 0]$. Except these cases, we can add a new network which can tell whether the input is known or unknown, and can reject unknown signals.

B. Neural Network That Can Tell the Reliability of Its Own Inference

The second design method is an improved function approximation neural network with variance estimation. We consider the neural network

$$p(\mathbf{x}, \mathbf{y}; \mathbf{w}_2, \mathbf{w}_3) = q(\mathbf{x}) g_N(\mathbf{y}; \varphi(\mathbf{x}; \mathbf{w}_2), \sigma(\mathbf{x}; \mathbf{w}_3)) \tag{36}$$

on the input and output space $R^M \times R^N$. If this model is used, the standard deviation of the network's outputs is estimated. After training, the kth element y_k of the output $\mathbf{y}$ is ensured in the region

$$|y_k - \varphi_k(\mathbf{x}; \mathbf{w}_2)| \leqslant \sigma(\mathbf{x}; \mathbf{w}_3)L, \qquad k = 1, 2, 3, \ldots, N, \tag{37}$$

with the probability $\Pr(L)^N$, where

$$\Pr(L) = \int_{|x| \leqslant L} g_1(x; 0, 1)\, dx.$$

In the preceding equation, $\varphi_k(\mathbf{x}; \mathbf{w}_2)$ is the kth element of $\boldsymbol{\varphi}(\mathbf{x}; \mathbf{w}_2)$. The function $\boldsymbol{\varphi}(\mathbf{x}; \mathbf{w}_2)$ shows the average value of the output for a given input $\mathbf{x}$. The function $\sigma(\mathbf{x}; \mathbf{w}_3)$ shows how widely the output is distributed for $\mathbf{x}$ or it shows the reliability of the regression function $\varphi(\mathbf{x}; \mathbf{w}_2)$. The structure of this neural network is given by Fig. 3.

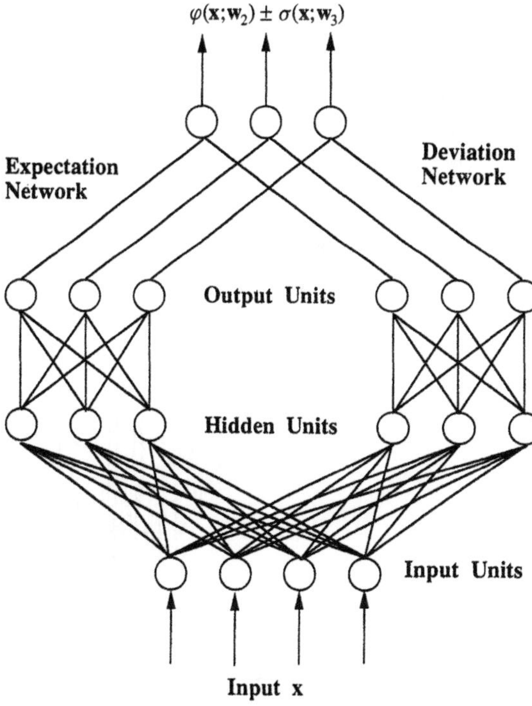

Figure 3 A function approximation neural network with estimated deviation. This network answers the expectation values and their reliability.

The learning rule for $\mathbf{w}_2$ and $\mathbf{w}_3$ are given by

$$\Delta \mathbf{w}_2 = -\frac{\beta}{n}\sum_{i=1}^{n} \frac{1}{2\sigma(\mathbf{x}_i;\mathbf{w}_3)^2}\frac{\partial}{\partial \mathbf{w}_2}\left\|\mathbf{y}_i - \boldsymbol{\varphi}(\mathbf{x}_i;\mathbf{w}_2)\right\|^2, \tag{38}$$

$$\Delta \mathbf{w}_3 = \frac{\beta}{n}\sum_{i=1}^{n}\left\{\frac{\|\mathbf{y}_i - \boldsymbol{\varphi}(\mathbf{x}_i;\mathbf{w}_2)\|^2}{\sigma(\mathbf{x}_i;\mathbf{w}_3)^2} - N\right\}\cdot\frac{1}{\sigma(\mathbf{x}_i;\mathbf{w}_3)}\frac{\partial\sigma(\mathbf{w}_3;\mathbf{x}_i)}{\partial \mathbf{w}_3}. \tag{39}$$

If the first training procedure for $\mathbf{w}_2$ is approximated by the ordinary error back-propagation, Eq. (27), it can be performed independently of $\mathbf{w}_3$. Then the second procedure for $\mathbf{w}_3$ can be added after the training process for $\mathbf{w}_2$ is finished.

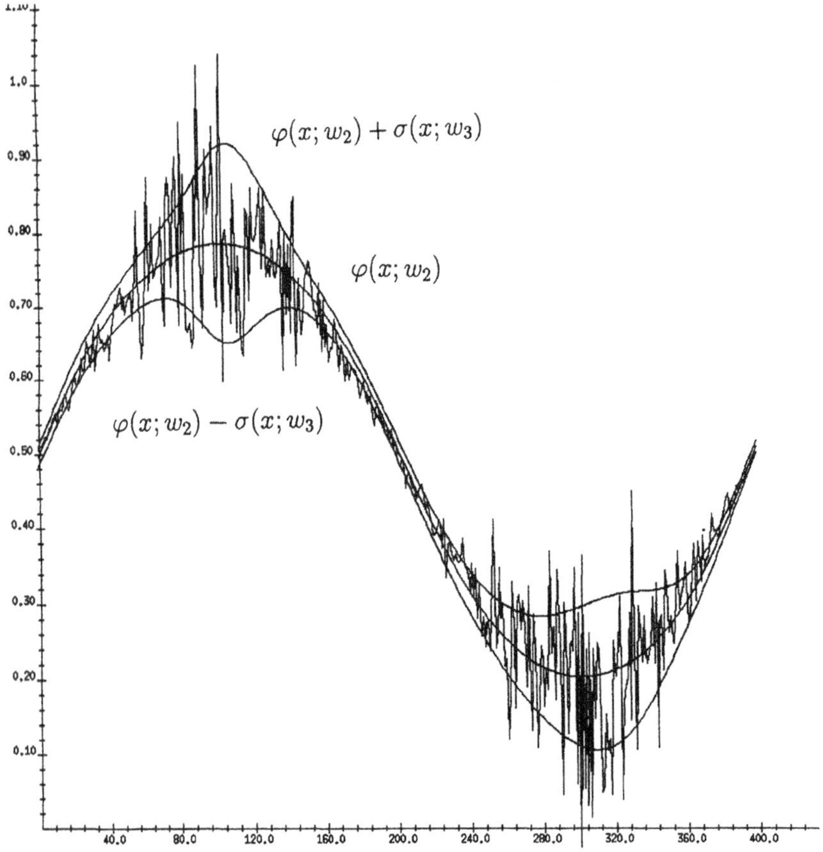

Figure 4 Experimental results for deviation estimation. The estimated deviation $\sigma(\mathbf{x}, \mathbf{w}_3)$ shows how widely outputs are distributed for a given input.

Figure 4 shows the simulation results. The input space is the interval [0, 1], and the output space is the set of real numbers. The true probability density function is

$$\begin{aligned} q(y|x) &= g_1(y; \varphi_0(x); \sigma_0(x)), \\ \varphi_0(x) &= 0.5 + 0.3\sin(2\pi x), \\ \sigma_0(x) &= 0.1 \cdot \left\{ \exp\left(-\frac{(x-0.25)^2}{2(0.1)^2} \right) + \exp\left(-\frac{(x-0.75)^2}{2(0.1)^2} \right) \right\}. \end{aligned}$$

The set of input samples was $\{i/400; i = 0, 1, 2, \ldots, 399\}$ and the output samples were independently taken from the foregoing conditional probability density function. To estimate $\varphi_0(x)$ and $\sigma_0(x)$, we used three-layered perceptrons with 10 and 20 hidden units. First, $\varphi_0(x)$ was approximated by the ordinary back propagation with 2000 training cycles, and then $\sigma_0(x)$ was approximated by Eq. (39) with 5000 training cycles. It is shown by Fig. 4 that the reliability of the estimated regression function is clearly estimated.

By combining the first design method with the second one, we integrate an improved neural network model,

$$p(\mathbf{x}, \mathbf{y}; \mathbf{w}_1, \mathbf{w}_2, \mathbf{w}_3) = p(\mathbf{x}; \mathbf{w}_1) g_N(\mathbf{y}; \boldsymbol{\varphi}(\mathbf{x}; \mathbf{w}_2), \sigma(\mathbf{x}; \mathbf{w}_3)). \tag{40}$$

Figure 5 shows the information processing realized by this model. If $p(\mathbf{x}; \mathbf{w}_1)$ is smaller than $\varepsilon > 0$, then $\mathbf{x}$ is rejected as an unknown signal. Otherwise, $\sigma(\mathbf{x}; \mathbf{w}_3)$

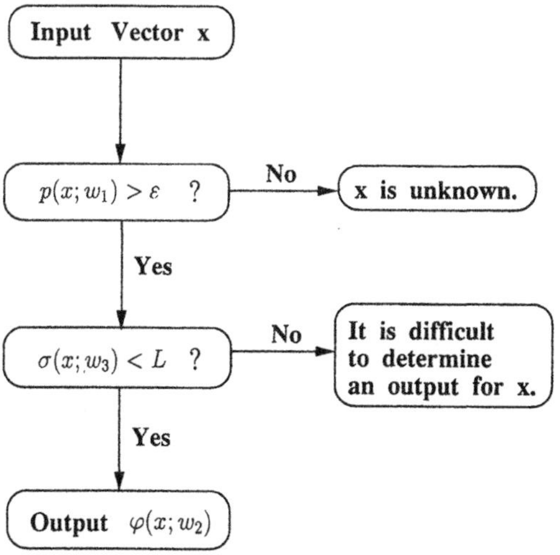

Figure 5 Neural information processing using $p(\mathbf{x}; \mathbf{w}_1)$, $\varphi(\mathbf{x}, \mathbf{w}_2)$, and $\sigma(\mathbf{x}; \mathbf{w}_3)$. When the occurrence probability and the inference probability are estimated, the neural network obtains new abilities.

is calculated. If $\sigma(\mathbf{x}; \mathbf{w}_3) > L$, $\mathbf{x}$ is also rejected by the reasoning that it is difficult to determine one output. If $\sigma(\mathbf{x}; \mathbf{w}_3) \leqslant L$, the output is given by the estimated regression function $\varphi(\mathbf{x}; \mathbf{w}_2)$.

Answer to the Third Question

The third question in the Introduction can be answered as follows. The conventional neural networks cannot answer how reliable their inferences are. However, we can add a new network which can tell the width the outputs are distributed.

C. Neural Network That Can Illustrate Input Patterns for a Given Category

In the preceding discussions, we implicitly assumed that a neural network approximated the true relation between inputs and outputs. However, in practical applications, it is not so easy to ascertain that a neural network has learned to closely approximate the true relation. In this section, for the purpose of analyzing what concepts a neural network has learned, we consider an interactive training method.

The ordinary training process for neural networks is the cycle of the training phase and the testing phase. We train a neural network by using input–output samples and examine it by the testing samples. If the answers to the testing samples are not so good, we repeat the training phase with added samples until the network has the desired performance. However, if a neural network can illustrate input patterns for a given output, we may have a dialogue with the network for learned concepts, with the result that we may find the reason why the network's inference is not so close to the true inference.

Suppose that a neural network $p(\mathbf{x}, \mathbf{y}; \mathbf{w})$ has already been trained. The inverse inference probability is defined by

$$p(\mathbf{x}|\mathbf{y}; \mathbf{w}) = \frac{p(\mathbf{x}, \mathbf{y}; \mathbf{w})}{p(\mathbf{y}; \mathbf{w})},$$

$$p(\mathbf{y}; \mathbf{w}) = \int p(\mathbf{x}, \mathbf{y}; \mathbf{w})\, d\mathbf{x}.$$

To generate $\mathbf{x}$ with the probability $p(\mathbf{x}|\mathbf{y}; \mathbf{w})$, we can employ the stochastic steepest descent,

$$\begin{aligned}\frac{d\mathbf{x}}{dt} &= \frac{\partial}{\partial \mathbf{x}} \log p(\mathbf{x}|\mathbf{y}; \mathbf{w}) + \mathbf{R}(t)\\ &= \frac{\partial}{\partial \mathbf{x}} \log p(\mathbf{x}, \mathbf{y}; \mathbf{w}) + \mathbf{R}(t),\end{aligned}$$

where $\mathbf{R}(t)$ is the white Gaussian noise with average 0 and variance 1. The probability distribution of $\mathbf{x}$ generated by the foregoing stochastic differential equation converges to the equilibrium state given by $p(\mathbf{x}|\mathbf{y}; \mathbf{w})$, when the time goes to infinity. For example, if we use the network in Eq. (32), it follows that

$$\frac{d\mathbf{x}}{dt} = \frac{\partial}{\partial \mathbf{x}} \log p(\mathbf{y}|\mathbf{x}; \mathbf{w}) + \frac{\partial}{\partial \mathbf{x}} \log p(\mathbf{x}; \mathbf{w}) + \mathbf{R}(t).$$

By this stochastic dynamics, the neural network can illustrate input signals from which a given output is inferred, in principle. However, it may not be so easy to realize the equilibrium state by this dynamics. In the following section, we introduce a probability competition neural network, which rather easily realizes the inverse inference.

Answer to the Last Question

The answer to the last question in the Introduction is that neural networks, in general, cannot answer what concepts they have learned during training. However, we can improve the neural networks to illustrate input patterns from which a given output category is inferred. This design method suggests that an interactive training method may be realized.

IV. PROBABILITY COMPETITION NEURAL NETWORKS

The previous two sections explained how the design method based on the probabilistic framework helps us to develop network models with various abilities, and showed a couple of new models as the answers to the questions in the Introduction. In this section, we further exemplify the usefulness of the method by construction of another probabilistic network model, called the *probability competition neural network* (PCNN) model [1]. The PCNN model is defined as a mixture of probabilities on the input–output space. In addition to the useful properties of the occurrence probability estimation and the inverse inference, the model can approximate any probability density function with arbitrary accuracy if it has a sufficiently large number of hidden units. In the last part of this section, we verify the practical usefulness of the PCNN model through application to a character recognition problem and an ultrasonic object recognition problem.

A. Probability Competition Neural Network Model and Its Properties

1. Definition of the Probability Competition Neural Network Model

a. *Probability Competition Neural Network as a Statistical Model*

Let $r(\mathbf{x})$ and $s(\mathbf{y})$ be probability density functions on X and Y, respectively. Although we need no condition on $r(\mathbf{x})$ and $s(\mathbf{y})$ in the general description of the model, unimodal functions like the Gaussian function are appropriate for them. We define parametric families of density functions by

$$r(\mathbf{x}; \boldsymbol{\xi}, \rho) = \frac{1}{\rho^M} r\left(\frac{\mathbf{x} - \boldsymbol{\xi}}{\rho}\right),$$

$$s(\mathbf{y}; \boldsymbol{\eta}, \tau) = \frac{1}{\tau^N} s\left(\frac{\mathbf{y} - \boldsymbol{\eta}}{\tau}\right), \tag{41}$$

where $\boldsymbol{\xi} \in R^M$, $\boldsymbol{\eta} \in R^N$, $\rho > 0$, and $\tau > 0$ are the parameters. The probability density function on $X \times Y$ to define the PCNN model is

$$p(\mathbf{x}, \mathbf{y}; \mathbf{w}) = \frac{1}{Z(\boldsymbol{\theta})} \sum_{h=1}^{H} \exp(\theta_h) r(\mathbf{x}; \boldsymbol{\xi}_h, \rho_h) s(\mathbf{y}; \boldsymbol{\eta}_h, \tau_h), \tag{42}$$

where

$$Z(\boldsymbol{\theta}) = \sum_{h=1}^{H} \exp(\theta_h). \tag{43}$$

The model has a parameter vector

$$\mathbf{w} = (\theta_1, \boldsymbol{\xi}_1, \boldsymbol{\eta}_1, \rho_1, \tau_1, \ldots, \theta_H, \boldsymbol{\xi}_H, \boldsymbol{\eta}_H, \rho_H, \tau_H)$$

to be optimized in learning.

One of the characteristics of the model is its symmetric structure about $\mathbf{x}$ and $\mathbf{y}$; the input and output are treated in the same manner in modeling the simultaneous distribution $q(\mathbf{x}, \mathbf{y})$. This enables us to utilize easily all the marginal distributions and the conditional distributions induced by $p(\mathbf{x}, \mathbf{y}; \mathbf{w})$. Especially, the estimate of the marginal probability $q(\mathbf{x})$ induces the occurrence probability estimation, and the estimate of the conditional probability $q(\mathbf{x}|\mathbf{y})$ induces the inverse inference ability.

The PCNN model is defined by a sum of the density functions of the form $r(\mathbf{x}; \boldsymbol{\xi}, \rho)s(\mathbf{y}; \boldsymbol{\eta}, \tau)$ which indicates the independence of $\mathbf{x}$ and $\mathbf{y}$. Thus, the model is a finite mixture of probability distributions each of which makes **x** and **y** independent. In practical applications, one appropriate choice of $r(\mathbf{x})$ and $s(\mathbf{y})$ is a normal distribution. In this case, the PCNN model as a statistical model is equal to the normal mixture on the input–output space.

The model resembles probabilistic neural networks (PNN [3]). However, the statistical basis for PNN is nonparametric estimation, which uses all the training data to obtain an output for a new input data. The approach of PNN is different from ours in that the framework for the PCNN model is parametric estimation, which uses only a fixed dimensional parameter to draw an inference.

b. Probabilistic Output of a Probability Competition Neural Network

The computation to obtain a probabilistic and average output of a PCNN is realized as a layered network. First, we explain how a probabilistic output is computed. The estimated inference probability of the network is

$$p(\mathbf{y}|\mathbf{x};\mathbf{w}) = \sum_{h=1}^{H} \alpha_h(\mathbf{x}) s(\mathbf{y};\eta_h,\tau_h), \tag{44}$$

where

$$\alpha_h(\mathbf{x}) = \frac{\exp(\theta_h) r(\mathbf{x};\xi_h,\rho_h)}{\sum_{h=1}^{H} \exp(\theta_h) r(\mathbf{x};\xi_h,\rho_h)}. \tag{45}$$

The computation is illustrated in Fig. 6. The network has two hidden layers with H units. The connection between hth unit in the first hidden layer and the mth input unit has a weight ξ_{hm}. The hth unit in the first hidden layer has the values ρ_h and θ_h, and calculates its output $o_h^{(1)}(\mathbf{x})$ according to

$$o_h^{(1)}(\mathbf{x}) = \exp(\theta_h) r(\mathbf{x};\xi_h,\rho_h). \tag{46}$$

The normalizing unit calculates the sum of these outputs:

$$o(\mathbf{x}) = \sum_{h=1}^{H} o_h^{(1)}(\mathbf{x}). \tag{47}$$

The input value into the hth unit in the second hidden layer, $\alpha_h(\mathbf{x})$, is normalized as

$$\alpha_h(\mathbf{x}) = \frac{o_h^{(1)}(\mathbf{x})}{o(\mathbf{x})}. \tag{48}$$

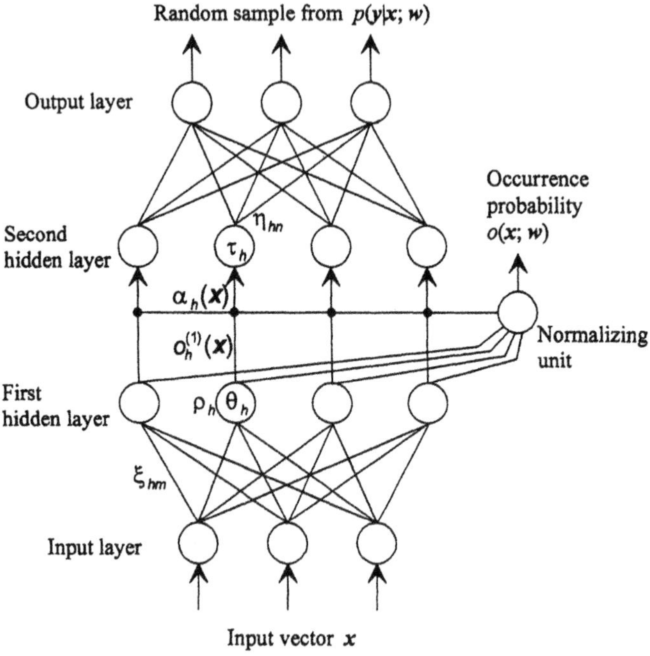

Figure 6 PCNN (probabilistic output).

Note that these values define a discrete distribution; that is,

$$\sum_{h=1}^{H} \alpha_h(\mathbf{x}) = 1, \qquad \alpha_h(\mathbf{x}) \geqslant 0, \qquad 1 \leqslant h \leqslant H. \tag{49}$$

Only one of the units in the second hidden layer is stochastically selected according to the discrete distribution. If the kth unit is chosen, the output of the second hidden layer is determined as

$$(0, \ldots, 0, \overset{k\text{th}}{\check{1}}, 0, \ldots, 0),$$

and the probabilistic output of a PCNN is a sample from the probability $s(\mathbf{y}; \eta_k, \tau_k)$. It is easy to obtain independent samples if we use a normal distribution for $s(\mathbf{y})$. We can apply a famous routine like the Box–Muller algorithm [4].

The computation in the second hidden layer is considered to be probabilistic competition. The units in the second hidden layer compete and only one of them survives. The decision is probabilistic, unlike the usual competitive or winner-take-all learning [5].

c. *Average Output*

The average output of a PCNN is obtained if we replace the probability competition process with the expectation process. Assume that the mean value of the density function $r(\mathbf{y})$ is 0 for simplicity. Then the average output of a PCNN is given by

$$\mathbf{E}(\mathbf{x};\mathbf{w}) = \sum_{h=1}^{H} \eta_h \alpha_h(\mathbf{x}). \tag{50}$$

The computation is realized by the network in Fig. 7, which has a similar structure to the network with a probabilistic output, but has different computation in the second hidden layer and the output layer. The output of the second hidden layer is $\alpha_h(\mathbf{x}) = o^{(1)}(\mathbf{x})/o(\mathbf{x})$. The output of a network is the weighted sum of $\alpha_h(\mathbf{x})$ with η_{hn}, the weight between the hth hidden unit and the nth output unit.

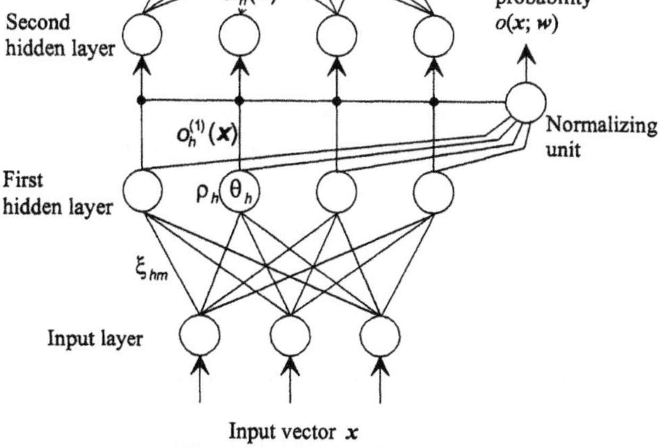

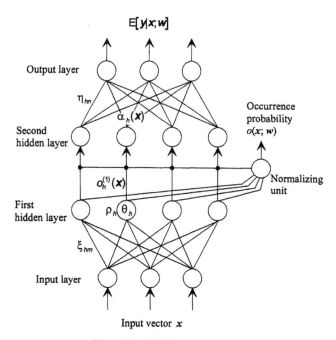

Figure 7 PCNN (average output).

2. Properties of the Probability Competition Neural Network Model

a. Occurrence Probability

The output of the normalizing unit $o(\mathbf{x})$ represents the occurrence probability $p(\mathbf{x}; \mathbf{w})$, because

$$p(\mathbf{x}; \mathbf{w}) = \int p(\mathbf{y}, \mathbf{x}; \mathbf{w})\, d\mathbf{y} = \frac{o(\mathbf{x})}{Z(\boldsymbol{\theta})}. \tag{51}$$

Thus, we can utilize the output value of the normalizing unit to secure the reliability at a given $\mathbf{x}$. We investigate the ability experimentally through a character recognition task in Section IV.C.

b. Inverse Inference

Whereas the PCNN model is symmetric on $\mathbf{x}$ and $\mathbf{y}$, it is straightforward to perform the inverse inference. The computation of the probability $p(\mathbf{x}|\mathbf{y}; \mathbf{w})$ is carried out in exactly the inverse way to that of the probability $p(\mathbf{y}|\mathbf{x}; \mathbf{w})$. We demonstrate the inverse inference ability through a character recognition problem in Section IV.C.

c. Approximation Ability

One of the advantages of using the PCNN model is its capability to approximate a density function. In fact, Theorem 1 shows that a PCNN is able to approximate any density function with arbitrary accuracy if it has a sufficiently large number of hidden units. In the theorem, P is a real number satisfying $1 \leqslant P < \infty$, and $\|\cdot\|_P$ is the L^P norm.

THEOREM 1. *Let $r(\mathbf{x})$ and $s(\mathbf{y})$ be probability density functions on R^M and R^N, respectively. Let $q(\mathbf{x}, \mathbf{y})$ be an arbitrary density function on R^{M+N}. Assume $p(\mathbf{x}, \mathbf{y}; \mathbf{w})$ is defined by Eq. (42). Then, for any positive real number ε, there exist a natural number H and a parameter $\mathbf{w}$ in the PCNN model with H hidden units such that*

$$\|p(\mathbf{x}, \mathbf{y}; \mathbf{w}) - q(\mathbf{x}, \mathbf{y})\|_P < \varepsilon. \tag{52}$$

(For the proof, see [1].)

This universal approximation ability is not realized by ordinary function approximation neural network models, which assume regression with a fixed noise level. They cannot approximate a multivalued function or regression with the deviation dependent on $\mathbf{x}$.

B. Learning Algorithms for a Probability Competition Neural Network

We use $L_3(\mathbf{w})$ for the loss function of a PCNN, because the loss function is symmetric about $\mathbf{x}$ and $\mathbf{y}$. If the training attains the minimum of the loss function, the obtained parameter is the maximum likelihood estimator. We can utilize several methods to teach a PCNN, although the steepest descent method is of course available as a general learning rule. Before we explain the three methods and compare their performance, we review the important problem of the likelihood of a mixture model.

1. Nonexistence of the Maximum Likelihood Estimator

It is well known that the maximum likelihood estimator *does not* exist for a finite mixture model like the PCNN model. Let $\{(\mathbf{x}_i, \mathbf{y}_i)\}_{i=1}^{n}$ be training samples and assume that the density functions $r(\mathbf{x})$ and $s(\mathbf{y})$ attain their maximum at 0 without loss of generality. Then, if we set $\boldsymbol{\xi}_1 := \mathbf{x}_1, \boldsymbol{\eta}_1 := \mathbf{y}_1$, and let the deviation parameters ρ_1, τ_1 go to 0, the value of the likelihood function approaches infinity (Fig. 8). Such parameters, however, do not represent a suitable probability to explain the training samples. We should not try to find the global maximum of the likelihood function in the learning of a PCNN, but try to find a good local maximum.

One solution of this problem is to restrict the values of ρ and τ so that the likelihood at one data point can be bounded. There is still the possibility that the parameters reach an undesirable global maximum at the boundary. Computer

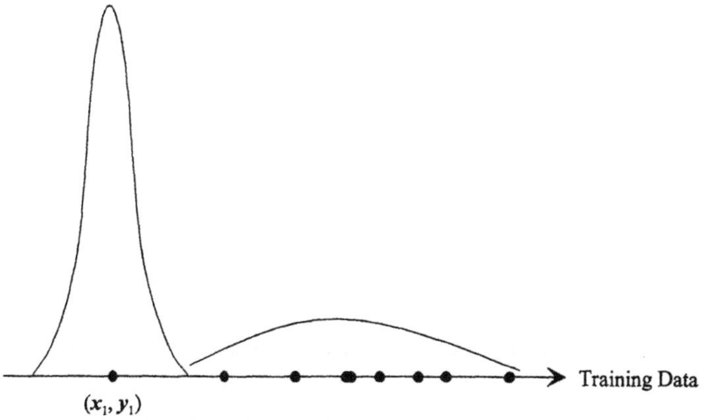

Figure 8 Likelihood function of the PCNN.

simulations show, however, that the steepest descent and other methods avoid the useless global maximum if we initialize ρ and τ appropriately, because the optimization of a nonlinear function tends to be trapped easily at a local maximum.

2. Steepest Descent Method

We show the steepest descent update rule of the PCNN model briefly. We use

$$
\begin{aligned}
c_h &= \frac{\exp(\theta_h)}{Z(\boldsymbol{\theta})}, \\
d_{hi} &= \frac{r(\mathbf{x}_i; \boldsymbol{\xi}_h, \rho_h) s(\mathbf{y}_i; \boldsymbol{\eta}_h, \tau_h)}{p(\mathbf{x}_i, \mathbf{y}_i; \mathbf{w})}
\end{aligned} \tag{53}
$$

for simplicity. Direct application of the general rule leads us to

$$
\begin{aligned}
\theta_h^{(t+1)} &= \theta_h^{(t)} + \beta\, c_h \sum_{i=1}^{n} \Big(d_{hi} - 1 \Big), \\
\boldsymbol{\xi}_h^{(t+1)} &= \boldsymbol{\xi}_h^{(t)} + \beta\, c_h \sum_{i=1}^{n} d_{hi} \left(\frac{\mathbf{x}_i - \boldsymbol{\xi}_h^{(t)}}{\rho_h^{(t)2}} \right), \\
\rho_h^{(t+1)} &= \rho_h^{(t)} + \beta\, c_h \sum_{i=1}^{n} d_{hi} \left(\frac{\|\mathbf{x}_i - \boldsymbol{\xi}_h^{(t)}\|^2 - M\rho_h^{(t)^2}}{\rho_h^{(t)3}} \right), \\
\boldsymbol{\eta}_h^{(t+1)} &= \boldsymbol{\eta}_h^{(t)} + \beta\, c_h \sum_{i=1}^{n} d_{hi} \left(\frac{\mathbf{y}_i - \boldsymbol{\eta}_h^{(t)}}{\tau_h^{(t)2}} \right), \\
\tau_h^{(t+1)} &= \tau_h^{(t)} + \beta\, c_h \sum_{i=1}^{n} d_{hi} \left(\frac{\|\mathbf{y}_i - \boldsymbol{\eta}_h^{(t)}\|^2 - N\tau_h^{(t)^2}}{\tau_h^{(t)3}} \right).
\end{aligned} \tag{54}
$$

The preceding is the rule for batch learning. For on-line learning, one must omit the $\sum_{i=1}^{n}$.

3. Expectation–Maximization Algorithm

The expectation–maximization (EM) algorithm is an iterative technique to maximize a likelihood function when there are some *invisible* variables which cannot be observed [6, 7]. Before going into the EM learning of a PCNN, we summarize the general idea of the EM algorithm. Let $\{p(\mathbf{v}, \mathbf{u}; \mathbf{w})\}$ be a parametric family of density functions on $(\mathbf{v}, \mathbf{u})$ with a parameter vector $\mathbf{w}$. The random vector $\mathbf{v}$ is *visible*, and we can observe its samples drawn from the true probability density $q(\mathbf{v}, \mathbf{u})$. The random vector $\mathbf{u}$, whose samples are not available in estimating the parameter $\mathbf{w}$, is *invisible*. Our purpose is to maximize the log likelihood function

$$\sum_{i=1}^{n} \log p(\mathbf{v}_i, \mathbf{u}_i; \mathbf{w}), \tag{55}$$

but this is unavailable because $\mathbf{u}_i$ is not observed. Instead, we maximize the expectation of the foregoing log likelihood function,

$$E_{\mathbf{u}_1,\ldots,\mathbf{u}_n|\mathbf{v}_1,\ldots,\mathbf{v}_n;\widehat{\mathbf{w}}^{(t)}}\left[\sum_{i=1}^{n} \log p(\mathbf{v}_i, \mathbf{u}_i; \mathbf{w})\right], \tag{56}$$

which is evaluated using the conditional probability at the current estimate of the parameter $\widehat{\mathbf{w}}^{(t)}$,

$$\begin{aligned} p(\mathbf{u}_1, \ldots, \mathbf{u}_n|\mathbf{v}_1, \ldots, \mathbf{v}_n; \widehat{\mathbf{w}}^{(t)}) &= \prod_{i=1}^{n} p(\mathbf{u}_i|\mathbf{v}_i; \widehat{\mathbf{w}}^{(t)}) \\ &= \prod_{i=1}^{n} \frac{p(\mathbf{v}_i, \mathbf{u}_i; \widehat{\mathbf{w}}^{(t)})}{\int p(\mathbf{v}_i, \mathbf{u}_i; \widehat{\mathbf{w}}^{(t)})\, d\mathbf{u}_i}. \end{aligned} \tag{57}$$

The calculation of the conditional probability is called the E-step, and the maximization of Eq. (56) is called the M-step in which we obtain the next estimator,

$$\widehat{\mathbf{w}}^{(t+1)} = \arg\max_{\mathbf{w}} E_{\mathbf{u}_1,\ldots,\mathbf{u}_n|\mathbf{v}_1,\ldots,\mathbf{v}_n;\widehat{\mathbf{w}}^{(t)}}\left[\sum_{i=1}^{n} \log p(\mathbf{v}_i, \mathbf{u}_i; \mathbf{w})\right]. \tag{58}$$

Gradient methods like the conjugate gradient and the Newton method are available for the maximization in general. The maximization is solved if the model is a mixture of exponential families. The E-step and M-step are carried out iteratively until the stopping criterion is satisfied.

Next, we apply the EM algorithm to the learning of a PCNN. We introduce an invisible random vector that indicates from which component a visible sample $(\mathbf{x}_i, \mathbf{y}_i)$ comes. Precisely, we use the statistical model

$$p(\mathbf{x}, \mathbf{y}, \mathbf{u}; \boldsymbol{\theta}, \boldsymbol{\xi}, \boldsymbol{\eta}, \rho, \tau) = \prod_{h=1}^{H} \left\{ \frac{1}{Z(\boldsymbol{\theta})} \exp(\theta_h) r(\mathbf{x}; \xi_h, \rho_h) s(\mathbf{y}; \eta_h, \tau_h) \right\}^{u_h}, \tag{59}$$

where the invisible random vector $\mathbf{u} = (u_1, \ldots, u_H)$ takes its value in $\{(1, 0, \ldots, 0), (0, 1, 0, \ldots, 0), \ldots, (0, \ldots, 0, 1)\}$. It is easy to see that the marginal distribution $p(\mathbf{x}, \mathbf{y}; \boldsymbol{\theta}, \boldsymbol{\xi}, \boldsymbol{\eta}, \rho, \tau)$ is exactly the same as the probability of the PCNN model [Eq. (42)].

Applying the general EM algorithm to this case, we obtain the EM learning rule for the PCNN model. We use the notation

$$\hat{\beta}_h^{(t)}(\mathbf{x}_i, \mathbf{y}_i) := \frac{\hat{c}_h^{(t)} r(\mathbf{x}_i; \widehat{\boldsymbol{\xi}}_h^{(t)}, \hat{\rho}_h^{(t)}) s(\mathbf{y}_i; \widehat{\boldsymbol{\eta}}_h^{(t)}, \hat{\tau}_h^{(t)})}{\sum_{h=1}^{H} \hat{c}_h^{(t)} r(\mathbf{x}_i; \widehat{\boldsymbol{\xi}}_h^{(t)}, \hat{\rho}_h^{(t)}) s(\mathbf{x}_i; \widehat{\boldsymbol{\eta}}_h^{(t)}, \hat{\tau}_h^{(t)})}. \tag{60}$$

Note that

$$\sum_{h=1}^{H} \hat{\beta}_h^{(t)}(\mathbf{x}_i, \mathbf{y}_i) = 1. \tag{61}$$

The value $\hat{\beta}_h^{(t)}(\mathbf{x}_i, \mathbf{y}_i)$ shows how much the hth component plays a part in generating $(\mathbf{x}_i, \mathbf{y}_i)$. The EM learning rule is described as follows;

EM Algorithm.

(1) Initialize $\widehat{\mathbf{w}}^{(0)}$ with random numbers.
(2) $t := 1$.
(3) **E(t) STEP**: Calculate $\hat{\beta}_h^{(t-1)}(\mathbf{x}_i, \mathbf{y}_i)$.
(4) **M(t) STEP**:

$$\begin{aligned}
\hat{c}_h^{(t)} &= \frac{1}{n} \sum_{i=1}^{n} \hat{\beta}_h^{(t-1)}(\mathbf{x}_i, \mathbf{y}_i), \\
(\widehat{\boldsymbol{\xi}}_h^{(t)}, \hat{\rho}_h^{(t)}) &= \arg \max_{(\boldsymbol{\xi}_h, \rho_h)} \sum_{i=1}^{S} \hat{\beta}_h^{(t-1)}(\mathbf{x}_i, \mathbf{y}_i) \log r(\mathbf{x}_i; \boldsymbol{\xi}_h, \rho_h), \\
(\widehat{\boldsymbol{\xi}}_h^{(t)}, \hat{\rho}_h^{(t)}) &= \arg \max_{(\eta_h, \tau_h)} \sum_{i=1}^{S} \hat{\beta}_h^{(t-1)}(\mathbf{x}_i, \mathbf{y}_i) \log s(\mathbf{x}_i; \boldsymbol{\eta}_h, \tau_h).
\end{aligned} \tag{62}$$

(5) $t := t + 1$, and go to (3).

If $r(\mathbf{x})$ and $s(\mathbf{y})$ are normal distributions, the maximizations in the M-step are solved. Then the M-step in the normal mixture PCNN is as follows.

M(t) Step (Normal mixture).

$$\begin{aligned}
\hat{c}_h^{(t)} &= \frac{1}{n} \sum_{i=1}^{n} \hat{\beta}_h^{(t-1)}(\mathbf{x}_i, \mathbf{y}_i), \\
\widehat{\boldsymbol{\xi}}_h^{(t)} &= \frac{\sum_{i=1}^{n} \hat{\beta}_h^{(t-1)}(\mathbf{x}_i, \mathbf{y}_i)\mathbf{x}_i}{\sum_{i=1}^{n} \hat{\beta}_h^{(t-1)}(\mathbf{x}_i, \mathbf{y}_i)}, \\
\widehat{\rho_h^2}^{(t)} &= \frac{\sum_{i=1}^{n} \hat{\beta}_h^{(t-1)}(\mathbf{x}_i, \mathbf{y}_i) \|\mathbf{x}_i - \widehat{\boldsymbol{\xi}}_h^{(t)}\|^2}{M \sum_{i=1}^{n} \hat{\beta}_h^{(t-1)}(\mathbf{x}_i, \mathbf{y}_i)},
\end{aligned}$$

$$\widehat{\boldsymbol{\eta}}_h^{(t)} = \frac{\sum_{i=1}^n \hat{\beta}_h^{(t-1)}(\mathbf{x}_i, \mathbf{y}_i)\mathbf{y}_i}{\sum_{i=1}^n \hat{\beta}_h^{(t-1)}(\mathbf{x}_i, \mathbf{y}_i)},$$

$$\widehat{\tau_h^2}^{(t)} = \frac{\sum_{i=1}^n \hat{\beta}_h^{(t-1)}(\mathbf{x}_i, \mathbf{y}_i)\|\mathbf{y}_i - \widehat{\boldsymbol{\eta}}_h^{(t)}\|^2}{N\sum_{i=1}^n \hat{\beta}_h^{(t-1)}(\mathbf{x}_i, \mathbf{y}_i)}. \quad (63)$$

4. *K*-Means Clustering

We can use the extended K-means clustering algorithm for the learning rule of a PCNN. First, we describe the extended K-means algorithm using the PCNN model.

Extended K-Means Algorithm.

(1) Initialize $\widehat{\mathbf{w}}^{(0)}$ using training data

$$\begin{aligned}
\hat{c}_h^{(0)} &= \frac{1}{H}, \\
\widehat{\boldsymbol{\xi}}_h^{(0)} &= \mathbf{x}_{I(h)}, \\
\widehat{\boldsymbol{\eta}}_h^{(0)} &= \mathbf{y}_{I(h)}, \\
\hat{\rho}_h^{2(t)} &= \sigma^2, \\
\hat{\tau}_h^{2(t)} &= \sigma^2,
\end{aligned} \quad (64)$$

where σ is a positive constant and the initial references $I(h)$ $(h = 1, \ldots, H)$ are determined with some method.

(2) $t := 1$.

(3) For each $(\mathbf{x}_i, \mathbf{y}_i)$, find $h \in \{1, 2, \ldots, H\}$ such that

$$\hat{c}_h^{(t-1)} r\big(\mathbf{x}_i; \widehat{\boldsymbol{\xi}}_h^{(t-1)}, \hat{\rho}_h^{(t-1)}\big) s\big(\mathbf{y}_i; \widehat{\boldsymbol{\eta}}_h^{(t-1)}, \hat{\tau}_h^{(t-1)}\big)$$

attains maximum, and set $h(i) := h$.

(4) For each h, update

$$\begin{aligned}
\hat{c}_h^{(t)} &= \frac{1}{n}\#\{i \mid h(i) = h\}, \\
(\widehat{\boldsymbol{\xi}}_h^{(t)}, \hat{\rho}_h^{(t)}) &= \arg\max_{(\boldsymbol{\xi}_h, \rho_h)} \sum_{\{i \mid h(i)=h\}} \log r(\mathbf{x}_i; \boldsymbol{\xi}_h, \rho_h), \\
(\widehat{\boldsymbol{\eta}}_h^{(t)}, \hat{\tau}_h^{(t)}) &= \arg\max_{(\boldsymbol{\eta}_h, \tau_h)} \sum_{\{i \mid h(i)=h\}} \log s(\mathbf{y}_i; \boldsymbol{\eta}_h, \tau_h).
\end{aligned} \quad (65)$$

(5) $t := t + 1$, and go to (3).

Especially, if $r(\mathbf{x})$ and $s(\mathbf{u})$ are normal distributions, the maximization in procedure (4) is solved, and the procedure is replaced as follows.

Normal Mixture.

(4) Set $S_h := \#\{i \mid h(i) = h\}$, and update

$$\begin{aligned}
\hat{c}_h^{(t)} &= \frac{S_h}{S}, \\
\widehat{\boldsymbol{\xi}}_h^{(t)} &= \frac{1}{S_h} \sum_{\{i|h(i)=h\}} \mathbf{x}_i, \\
\widehat{\rho_h^2}^{(t)} &= \frac{1}{MS_h} \sum_{\{i|h(i)=h\}} \|\mathbf{x}_i - \widehat{\boldsymbol{\xi}}_h^{(t)}\|^2, \\
\widehat{\boldsymbol{\eta}}_h^{(t)} &= \frac{1}{S_h} \sum_{\{i|h(i)=h\}} \mathbf{y}_i, \\
\widehat{\tau_h^2}^{(t)} &= \frac{1}{NS_h} \sum_{\{i|h(i)=h\}} \|\mathbf{y}_i - \widehat{\boldsymbol{\eta}}_h^{(t)}\|^2.
\end{aligned} \tag{66}$$

If ρ and τ are the equal constants that are not estimated, the foregoing procedure is exactly the same as the usual K-means clustering algorithm [8, Chap. 6].

The extended K-means algorithm applied to the PCNN model can be considered as an approximated EM algorithm. We explain it in the case of a normal mixture. In the EM learning rule, $\hat{\beta}_h^{(t)}(\mathbf{x}_i, \mathbf{y}_i)$ represents the probability that the sample $(\mathbf{x}_i, \mathbf{y}_i)$ comes from the hth component $c_h^{(t)} r(\mathbf{x}; \widehat{\boldsymbol{\xi}}_h^{(t)}, \hat{\rho}_h^{(t)}) s(\mathbf{y}; \widehat{\boldsymbol{\eta}}_h^{(t)}, \hat{\tau}_h^{(t)})$. Assume that $\hat{\beta}_h^{(t)}(\mathbf{x}_i, \mathbf{y}_i)$ is approximately 1 for only one h (say, h_i) and 0 for the others; that is,

$$\begin{aligned}
\hat{\beta}_{h_i}^{(t)}(\mathbf{x}_i, \mathbf{y}_i) &\approx 1, \\
\hat{\beta}_h^{(t)}(\mathbf{x}_i, \mathbf{y}_i) &\approx 0, \qquad h \neq h_i.
\end{aligned} \tag{67}$$

According to this approximation, h_i is equal to $h(i)$ in the extended K-means algorithm, and Eq. (63) is reduced to Eq. (66). In other words, the EM algorithm for a PCNN realizes soft clustering using a K-meanslike method.

5. Comparison of Learning Algorithms

We compare the preceding three learning algorithms through a simple estimation problem. We use on-line learning for the steepest descent method, and update the parameter for only one training datum at each iteration. We utilize the normal distribution as the components of the PCNN model. The input space is two dimensional and the output space is one dimensional. The number of hidden units is 4. The training data are independent samples from

$$\begin{aligned} p(\mathbf{x}, \mathbf{y}; \mathbf{w}_0) = {} & \tfrac{1}{4} g_2(\mathbf{x}; (0,0), 0.2) g_1(\mathbf{y}; 0, 0.2) \\ & + \tfrac{1}{4} g_2(\mathbf{x}; (0,1), 0.2) g_1(\mathbf{y}; 1, 0.2) \\ & + \tfrac{1}{4} g_2(\mathbf{x}; (1,0), 0.2) g_1(\mathbf{y}; 1, 0.2) \\ & + \tfrac{1}{4} g_2(\mathbf{x}; (1,1), 0.2) g_1(\mathbf{y}; 0, 0.2). \end{aligned} \tag{68}$$

We can call this relation the stochastic exclusive OR. Figure 9 shows the average output $\mathbf{E}(\mathbf{x}; \mathbf{w}_0)$ of the target probability.

We use 100 samples for each experiment, and perform 50 experiments by changing the training data set. For each experiment with the steepest descent algorithm, 100 data are presented 30,000 times and the parameters are updated each time. For the EM and K-means algorithms, there are 30 iterations. Table I

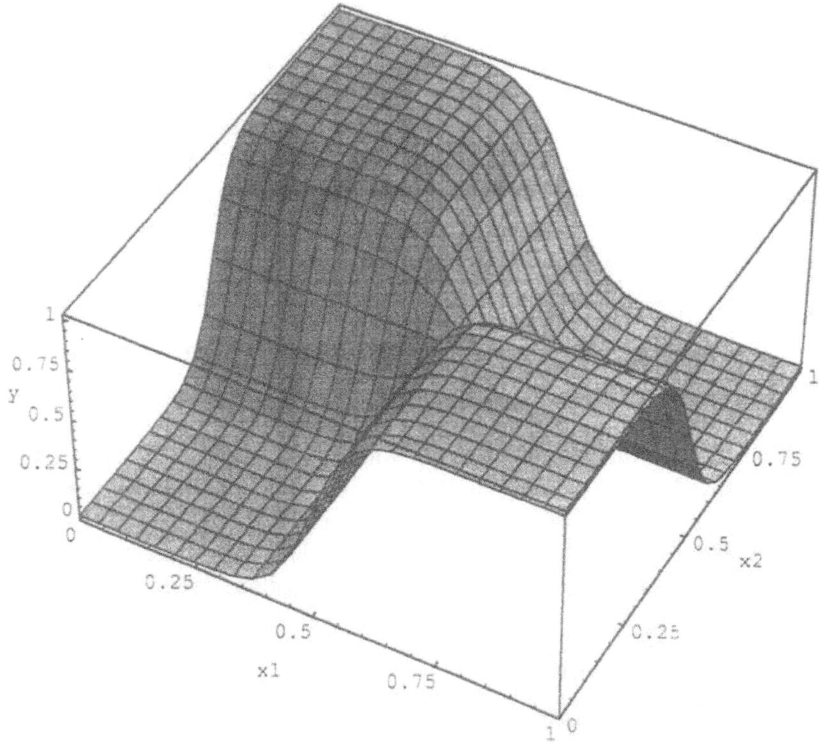

Figure 9 Target function of experiments.

Table I

Comparison of Learning Algorithms

Algorithm	Log likelihood	KL divergence	CPU time[a] (50 experiments)
Steepest descent	−69.3518	0.1379	8005 (s/30,000 itrs.)
EM	−69.4337	0.1388	5.5 (s/30 itrs.)
K-means	−70.8778	0.1409	4.1 (s/30 itrs.)

[a] The abbreviation "itrs." denotes iterations.

shows the average value of the log likelihood with respect to the training data, the Kullback–Leibler divergence between the target and the trained probability, and the CPU time (SparcStation 20). The Kullback–Leibler divergence of $p(\mathbf{z})$ for $q(\mathbf{z})$ is a well-known criterion to evaluate the difference of two probabilities. It is defined as

$$\mathrm{KL}(p : q) = \int q(\mathbf{z}) \log \frac{q(\mathbf{z})}{p(\mathbf{z})}\, d\mathbf{z}.$$

The result shows that the steepest descent algorithm is the best, both for likelihood with respect to the training data and for the Kullback–Leibler divergence, whereas the computation is by far slower than the other algorithms. Whereas the difference of the Kullback–Leibler divergence among these methods is very small, the EM algorithm and K-means algorithm are preferable when computation cost is important.

C. Applications of the Probability Competition Neural Network Model

We show two applications of the PCNN model, and compare the results with the conventional multilayer perceptron (MLP) model. One problem is a character recognition problem that demonstrates the properties of the PCNN model; the other is an ultrasonic object recognition problem, which is more practical than the former and is intended to be used for a factory automation system.

1. Character Recognition

We apply the PCNN model to a problem of classifying three kinds of handwritten characters to demonstrate the properties described in Section IV.A. The characters are ○ (circle), × (multiplication), and △ (triangle), which are written

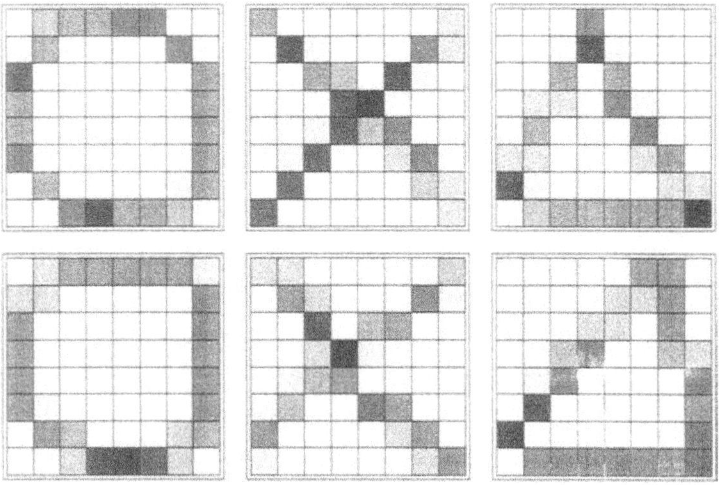

Figure 10 Feature vectors.

on a computer screen with a mouse. After normalizing an original image into a binary one with 32×32 pixels, we extract a 64 dimensional feature vector as an input by dividing the image into an 8×8 block and counting the ratio of black pixels in each block (4×4 pixels). The elements of an input vector range from 0 to 1, quantized by $1/16$. Figure 10 shows some of the extracted feature vectors used for our experiments.

We apply the normal mixture PCNN model to learn the input–output relation between the feature vectors and the corresponding character labels. The character ○, ×, and △ are labeled as $(1, 0, 0)$, $(0, 1, 0)$, and $(0, 0, 1)$, respectively. We use 600 training samples (200 samples for each category) written by 10 people.

We evaluate the performance of the average output of a trained PCNN by using a test data set of 600 samples written by another 10 people. The maximum of the three average output values is used to decide the classification. For the training of a PCNN, the K-means method is used for initial learning, followed by the steepest descent algorithm. In comparison, we trained a MLP network with the sigmoidal activation function using the same training data set, and evaluated its performance. The number of hidden units is varied from 3 to 57 for both models. Note that a PCNN with H hidden units has $70 \times H$ parameters, and a MLP network with H hidden units has $68 \times H + 3$ parameters. Figure 11 shows the experimental results. We see that the best recognition rate of the PCNN model is better than that of the MLP model, although we cannot say the former is much superior to the latter. This suggests that the approximation ability of the PCNN is sufficient for various problems for which the MLP model is used.

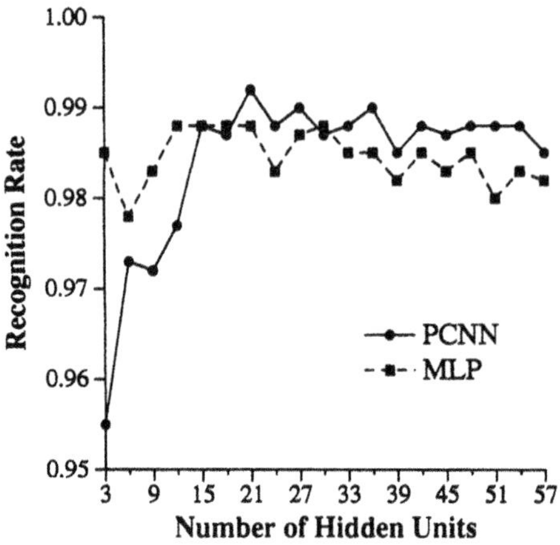

Figure 11 Character recognition rates of PCNN and MLP.

A more remarkable difference between these models is that a PCNN is able to estimate the occurrence probability. Figure 12 shows the presented input vectors and Table II shows the occurrence probability and the corresponding average output vectors. This result shows that the output of the normalization unit of a PCNN

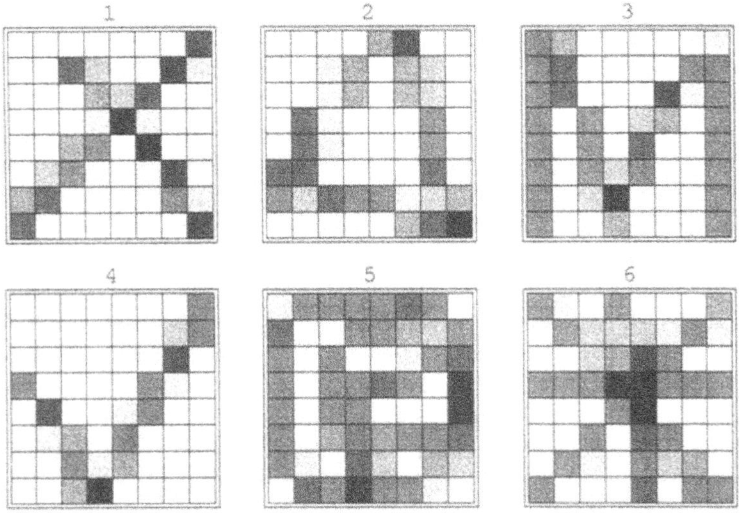

Figure 12 Input vectors for occurrence probability estimation.

Table II

Responses to Unknown Input Data

Input	PCNN Output			PCNN $o(\mathbf{x})$	MLP output		
1	0.00	1.00	0.00	0.0006836521	0.00	1.00	0.00
2	0.00	0.00	1.00	0.0002822327	0.00	0.00	1.00
3	0.49	0.06	0.45	0.0000000187	0.05	0.02	0.46
4	0.23	0.12	0.65	0.0000000706	0.43	0.00	0.07
5	1.00	0.00	0.00	0.0000000404	1.00	0.00	0.00
6	0.00	0.96	0.04	0.0000000154	0.00	1.00	0.00

distinguishes whether a given input vector is known or unknown. The values of $o(\mathbf{x})$ for inputs 3, 4, 5, and 6 are much smaller than those for 1 and 2. We can use $o(\mathbf{x})$ to reject unreliable outputs for unlearned input vectors if necessary. On the other hand, a MLP cannot distinguish unknown input vectors. The output of a MLP for a totally unknown input vector is sometimes equal to a desired output for some category, as we see in the output of 5 and 6. This shows the advantage of the PCNN model in that the occurrence probability is available.

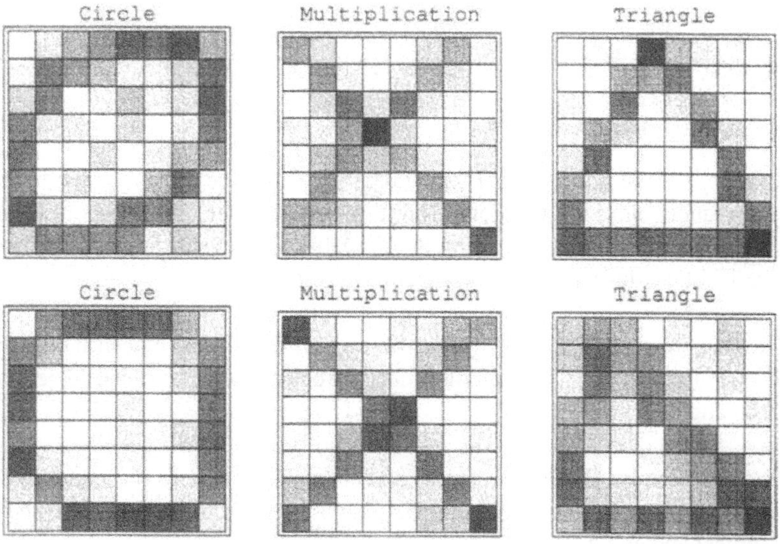

Figure 13 Examples of inverse inference.

Next we demonstrate the inverse inference ability of the PCNN model. We present the labels of the characters and get corresponding probabilistic input vectors. Figure 13 shows some of obtained input feature vectors, which are the samples drawn from $p(\mathbf{x}|\mathbf{y}; \widehat{\mathbf{w}})$ learned from the training data. As we see in these examples, the inverse inference ability enables us to check what is learned as a category.

2. Application to Ultrasonic Image Recognition

Ultrasonic imaging has been studied in the machine vision field because three dimensional (3-D) images of objects can be obtained directly even in dark or smoky environments. However, it has seldom been used in practical object recognition systems because of its low image resolution. To improve the ultrasonic imaging systems, intelligent resolution methods are needed [9, 10]. In this section, we introduce a 3-D object identification system that combines ultrasonic imaging with the probability competition neural network [11, 12]. Whereas this system is more useful than video cameras in the classification of metal or glass objects, it is applied to a factory automation system in a lens production line [13].

Figure 14 shows an ultrasonic 3-D visual sensor [14]. By using 40 kHz ultrasonic waves (wavelength = 8.5 mm), 3-D images such as Fig. 15 can be obtained for the spanner in Fig. 16. This image is obtained by the acoustical holography method. By Nyquist's sampling theorem, we obtain the shortest length of resolution. From the 3-D image $f(x, y, z)$, the calculated feature value is

$$s(r, z) = \int_{D(r)} f(x, y, z)\, dx\, dy,$$

where

$$D(r) = \{(x, y); r^2 \leqslant (x - x_g)^2 + (y - y_g)^2 < (r + a)^2\}$$

and (x_g, y_g) is the gravity center of $f(x, y, z)$. The value $s(r, z)$ is theoretically invariant under shift and rotation. From this feature value, 30 objects in Fig. 16 were identified and classified using the probability competition neural network. Figure 17 illustrates the block diagram of the system.

Training Sample Patterns Thirty objects in Fig. 16 were placed at the origin and rotated 0 and 45°. Ten sample images were collected for each object and rotation angle.

Testing Sample Patterns Thirty objects in Fig. 16 were placed at 20 mm from the origin and rotated 0, 5, 10, 15, ..., 45°. Ten samples were collected for each object and angle.

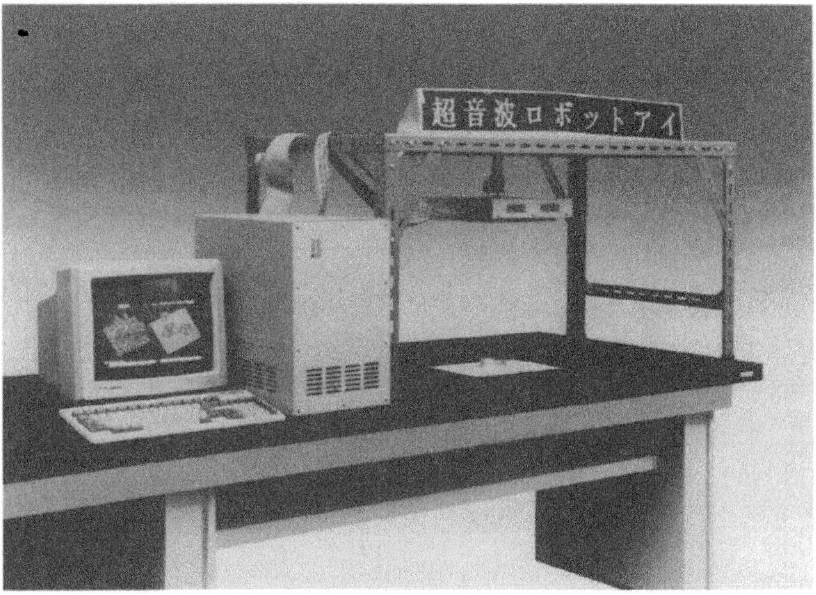

Figure 14 Ultrasonic 3-D visual sensor. Reproduced from [14] with permission of the publisher, Ellis Horwood.

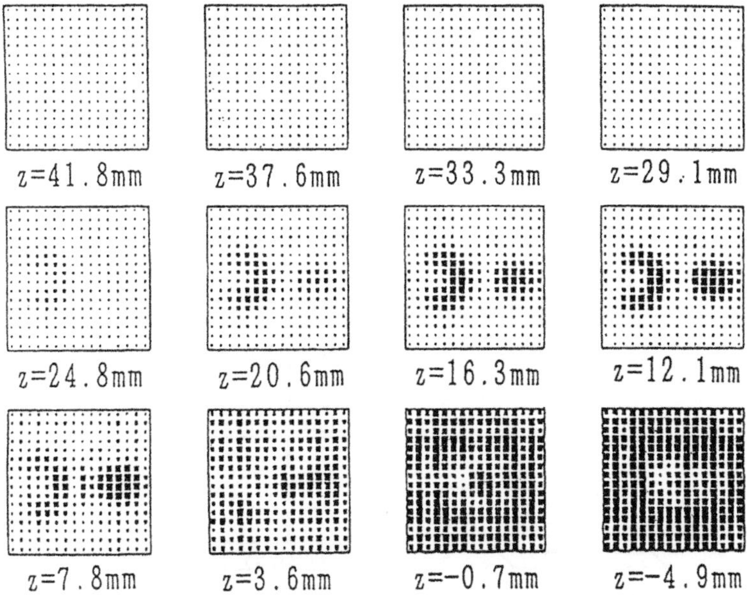

Figure 15 Three-dimensional image for the spanner.

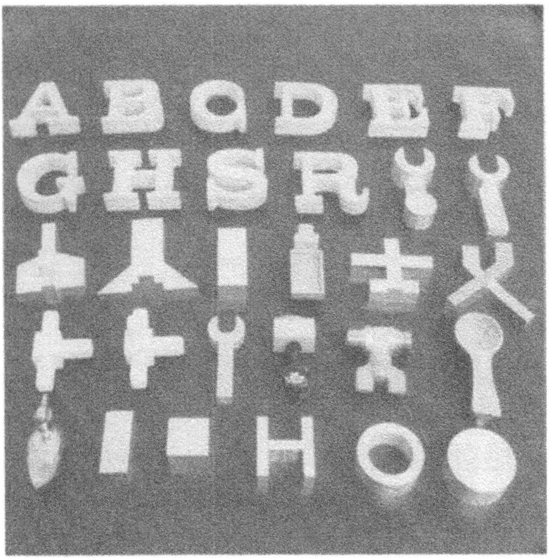

Figure 16 Thirty objects used for experiments.

We compared the recognition rates of the three-layer perceptron with that of a probability competition neural network using the testing samples. From Fig. 18, it is clear that both networks were classified at almost the same rates. The probability competition neural network needed more hidden units than the three-layer perceptron.

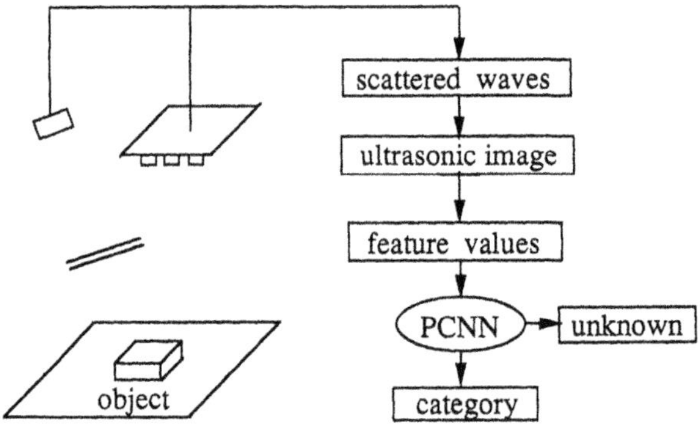

Figure 17 Block diagram of the system. Reproduced from [14] with permission of the publisher, Ellis Horwood.

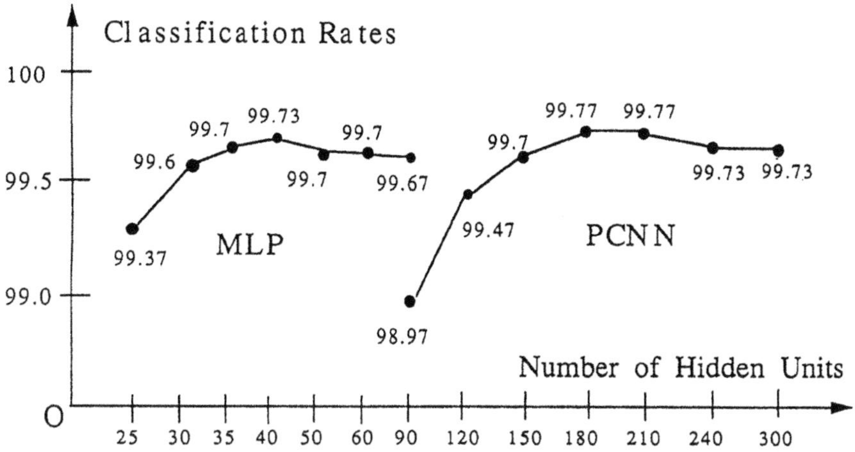

Figure 18 Recognition rates by MLP and PCNN. Reproduced from [14] with permission of the publisher, Ellis Horwood.

Table III shows the outputs of the normalizing unit of the probability competition neural network. When learned objects were inputted, its outputs were larger, and when unknown patterns were inputted, they were smaller. This shows that the probability competition neural network can reject unknown objects by setting an appropriate threshold. In the construction of an automatic production line, this should ensure that the system finds something unusual or accidental. The probability competition neural network is appropriate for such practical purposes.

Table III
Outputs of the Normalizing Units

	Objects	Familiarity = output of normalizing unit $\log P(w; x)$
Learned objects	Cube	−5.5
	Block	−12.3
	Spanner	−7.2
Unknown objects	Sphere	−72.1
	Pyramid	−136.3
	Cylinder	−56.5

V. STATISTICAL TECHNIQUES FOR NEURAL NETWORK DESIGN

In the previous section, we discussed what kinds of neural network models should be applied for given tasks. In this section, we consider how to select the optimal model and how to optimize the training samples under the condition that the set of models is already determined.

A. Information Criterion for the Steepest Descent

When we design a neural network, we should determine the appropriate size of a model. If a model smaller than necessary is applied, it cannot approximate the true probability density function; if a larger one is used, it learns noises in training samples. For the purpose of optimal model selection, some information criteria like Akaike's Information Criterion (AIC), Bayesian Information Criterion (BIC), and Minimum Description Length (MDL) are proposed in statistics and information theory. Unfortunately, these criteria need maximum likelihood estimators for all models in the model family. In this section, we consider a modified and softened information criterion, by which the optimal model and parameter can be found simultaneously in the steepest descent method.

Let $p(\mathbf{y}|\mathbf{x};\mathbf{w})$ be a conditional probability density function which is realized by a sufficiently large neural network, where $\mathbf{w} = (w_1, w_2, \ldots, w_{P_{\max}})$ is the parameter ($P_{\max}$ is the number of parameters). This neural network model is referred to as $S_{\max}$. From this model $S_{\max}$, $2^{P_{\max}}$ different models can be obtained by setting some parameters to be 0. These models are called *pruned models*, because the corresponding weight parameters are eliminated. Let S be the set of all pruned models. In this section, we consider a method to find the optimal pruned model.

When a neural network $p(\mathbf{y}|\mathbf{x},\mathbf{w})$ which belongs to S and training samples $\{(\mathbf{x}_i, \mathbf{y}_i); i = 1, 2, 3, \ldots, n\}$ are given, we use the empirical error $L_2(\mathbf{w})$ for n training samples. We use $L(\mathbf{w})$ instead of $L_2(\mathbf{w})$ for simplicity,

$$L(\mathbf{w}) = -\frac{1}{n}\sum_{i=1}^{n}\log p(\mathbf{y}_i|\mathbf{x}_i;\mathbf{w}), \tag{69}$$

and define the prediction error

$$L_{\mathrm{pred}}(\mathbf{w}) = -\int \log p(\mathbf{y}|\mathbf{x};\mathbf{w})q(\mathbf{x},\mathbf{y})\,d\mathbf{x}\,d\mathbf{y}. \tag{70}$$

As we have shown in Eq. (17), $L(\mathbf{w})$ converges to $L_{\mathrm{pred}}(\mathbf{w})$. However, the difference between them is the essential term for optimal model selection. The parameters are called the maximum likelihood estimator and the true parameter when they minimize $L(\mathbf{w})$ and $L_{\text{pred}}(\mathbf{w})$, respectively. If the set of true parameters

$$W_0 = \{\mathbf{w} \in W;\ p(\mathbf{y}|\mathbf{x}, \mathbf{w}) = q(\mathbf{y}|\mathbf{x}) \quad \text{a.e.} \quad q(\mathbf{x}, \mathbf{y})\}$$

consists of one point $\mathbf{w}_0$, and the *Fisher information matrix*,

$$I_{ij}(\mathbf{w}_0) = -\int \frac{\partial^2}{\partial w_i\, \partial w_j} \log p(\mathbf{y}|\mathbf{x}, \mathbf{w}_0) q(\mathbf{x}, \mathbf{y})\, d\mathbf{x}\, d\mathbf{y},$$

is positive definite, then the parametric model $p(\mathbf{y}|\mathbf{x}, \mathbf{w})$ is called *regular*. For the regular model, Akaike [15] showed that the relation

$$E_n\{L_{\text{pred}}(\widehat{\mathbf{w}})\} = E_n\{L(\widehat{\mathbf{w}})\} + \frac{P(S)}{n} + o\left(\frac{1}{n}\right),$$

holds, where $E_n\{\cdot\}$ denotes the average value over all sets of n training samples, $\widehat{\mathbf{w}}$ is the maximum likelihood estimator, and $P(S)$ is equal to the number of parameters in the model S. Based on this property, it follows that the model that minimizes the criterion (AIC),

$$\text{AIC}(S) = L(\widehat{\mathbf{w}}) + \frac{2P(S)}{2n}, \tag{71}$$

can be expected to be the best model for the minimum prediction error.

On the other hand, from the framework of Bayesian statistics, the model that maximizes the Bayesian factor Factor(S) should be selected. It is defined by the marginal likelihood for the model S,

$$\text{Factor}(S) = \int \exp(-nL(\mathbf{w}))\rho_0(\mathbf{w})\, d\mathbf{w}, \tag{72}$$

where $\rho_0(\mathbf{w})$ is the *a priori* probability density function on the parameter space in the model S. Schwarz [16] showed that it is asymptotically equal to

$$\frac{\log(\text{factor}(S))}{n} \approx -L(\widehat{\mathbf{w}}) - \frac{P(S)\log n}{2n} + o\left(\frac{1}{n}\right)$$

using the saddle point approximation. This equation shows that the model that minimizes the criterion (BIC),

$$\text{BIC}(S) = L(\widehat{\mathbf{w}}) + \frac{P(S)\log n}{2n}, \tag{73}$$

should be selected. From the viewpoint of information theory, Rissanen [17] showed that the best model for the minimum description length of both the data and the model can be found by BIC. It is reported that smaller models are important for generalized learning [18]. Using a framework in statistical physics, Levin *et al.* [19] showed that the Bayesian factor in Eq. (72) can be understood to be the partition function and that the generalization error by the Bayesian method, which is calculated by differentiation of the free energy, is minimized by the same criterion as AIC. If the true probability density is perfectly contained in the model family, BIC or MDL is more effective than AIC (when the number of samples goes to infinity, the true model can be found with probability 1). However, Shibata [20] showed that, if the true probability density is not contained in the model family, AIC is better than BIC or MDL, balancing the error of function approximation and that of statistical estimation.

Based on the foregoing properties, we define an information criterion $I(S)$ for the model $S \in \mathcal{S}$:

$$I(S) = L(\widehat{\mathbf{w}}) + \frac{AP(S)}{2n}. \tag{74}$$

If we choose $A = 2$, then $I(S)$ is equal to AIC, and if $A = \log n$, then it is BIC or MDL.

We modify the information criterion $I(S)$ so that it can be used during the steepest descent dynamics. The modified information criterion is defined by

$$I_\alpha(\mathbf{w}) = L(\mathbf{w}) + \frac{A}{2n}\sum_{j=1}^{P_{\max}} f_\alpha(w_j), \tag{75}$$

where $f_\alpha(\mathbf{x})$ is a function which satisfies the following conditions.

1. $f_0(x)$ is 0 if $x = 0$, and 1 otherwise.
2. When $\alpha \to 0$, $f_\alpha(x) \to f_0(x)$ (in a pointwise manner).
3. If $|x| \leqslant |y|$, then $0 \leqslant f_\alpha(x) \leqslant f_\alpha(y) \leqslant 1$.

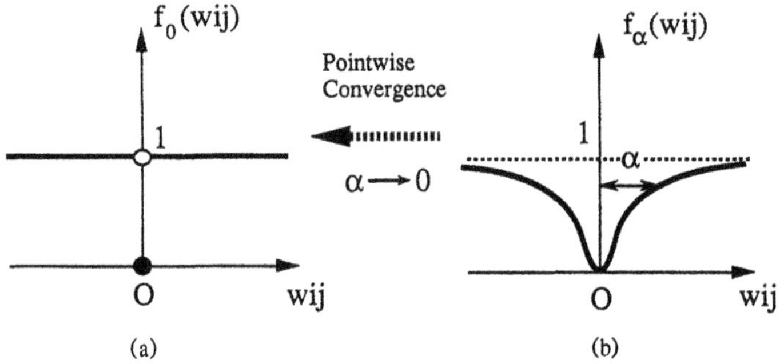

Figure 19 Control of the freedom of the model. (a) A function for the freedon of the parameter. (b) A softener function for the modified information criterion. The parameter α plays the same role as temperature in the simulated annealing. Reproduced from [14] with permission of the publisher, Ellis Horwood.

Figure 19 illustrates $f_\alpha(x)$. Then we can prove that

$$\min_{S \in \mathcal{S}} I(S) = \lim_{\alpha \to 0} \min_{w} I_\alpha(w). \tag{76}$$

This equality is not trivial because $f_\alpha(x) \to f_0(x)$ is not the uniform convergence. For the proof of Eq. (76), see [21]. From the engineering point of view, Eq. (76) shows that the optimal model and the parameter that minimizes $I(S)$ can be found by minimizing $I_\alpha(w)$ while controlling $\alpha \to 0$. The training rule for $I_\alpha(w)$ is given by

$$\Delta \mathbf{w} = -\beta \frac{\partial I_{\alpha(t)}}{\partial \mathbf{w}}, \tag{77}$$

$$\alpha(t) \to 0. \tag{78}$$

Note that $\alpha(t)$ plays a role similar to the inverse temperature in the simulated annealing. However, its optimal control method is not yet clarified.

To illustrate the effectiveness of the modified information criterion, we introduce some experimental results [21]. First, we consider a case when the true distribution is contained in the model family. Figure 20a shows the true model from which the training samples were taken. One thousand input samples were taken from the uniform probability on $[-0.5, 0.5]^3$. The output samples were calculated as the sum of the outputs from the true network and the random variable whose distribution is the normal distribution with average 0 and variance 3.33×10^{-3}. Ten thousand testing samples were taken from the same probability distribution. The three-layer perceptron with 10 hidden units in Fig. 20b was trained to learn the true relation in Fig. 20a. Figure 20c and d shows the obtained models and parameters. When $A = 5$, the true model was selected.

For a softener function, we used

$$f_\alpha(w) = 1 - \exp(-w^2/2\alpha^2),$$

and α was controlled as

$$\alpha(k) = \alpha_0\left(1 - \frac{k}{k_{\max}}\right) + \varepsilon,$$

where k is the number of training cycles, $k_{\max} = 50{,}000$ is the maximum number of training cycles, $\varepsilon = 0.01$, and α_0 is the initial value of α. The effect of the initial value α_0 is shown in Figs. 21 and 22. Two graphs in Fig. 21 show the empirical error and the prediction error for the initial value $\alpha_0 = 1.5$ and the corresponding A, respectively. Two graphs in Fig. 22 show, respectively, the empirical error and the prediction error for the initial value $\alpha_0 = 3.0$ and the corresponding A.

For the case in which the true distribution is not contained in the model, we used a function

$$y = \tfrac{1}{4}\big\{\sin\big(\pi(x_1 + x_2)\big) + \tanh(x_3) + 2\big\}.$$

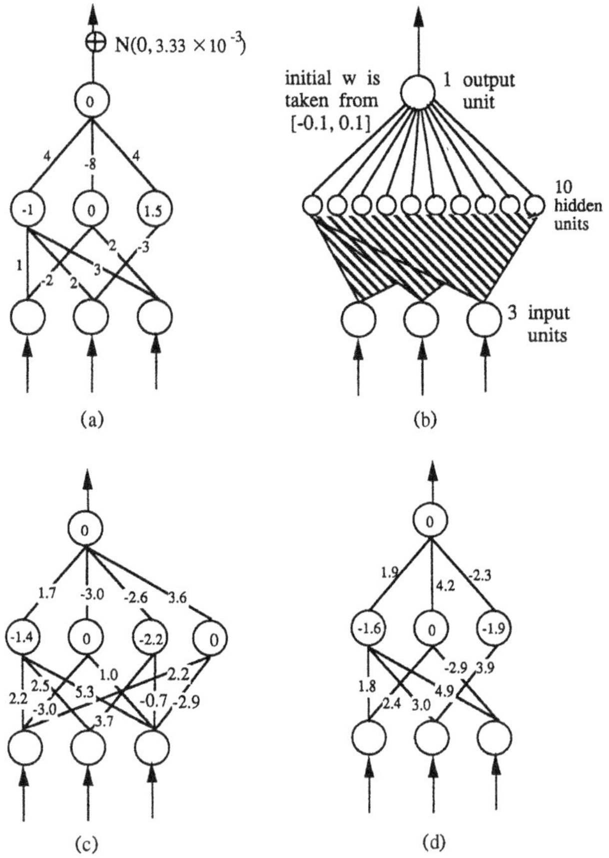

Figure 20 True and estimated models. (a) The true model. (b) The initial model for learning. (c) Model optimized by AIC ($A = 2$); $E_{emp}(\mathbf{w}^*) = 3.29 \times 10^{-3}$; $E(\mathbf{w}^*) = 3.39 \times 10^{-3}$. (d) Model optimized by $A = 5$; $E_{emp}(\mathbf{w}^*) = 3.31 \times 10^{-3}$; $E(\mathbf{w}^*) = 3.37 \times 10^{-3}$. The best value for A seems to be between AIC and MDL. Reproduced from [14] with permission of the publisher, Ellis Horwood.

The other conditions were same as the preceding case. Figure 23a and b show the true model and the model estimated by the AIC, respectively. Figure 23b shows that variables x_1 and x_2 were almost separated from x_3. The empirical errors and the prediction error using the other A are shown in Figs. 24 and 25. These results show that when the true probability was not contained in the model family, the optimal model with the minimum prediction error could be found by AIC.

It was clarified recently that the multilayer neural network is *not* a regular model in general [22, 23]. Strictly speaking, the ordinary information criterion

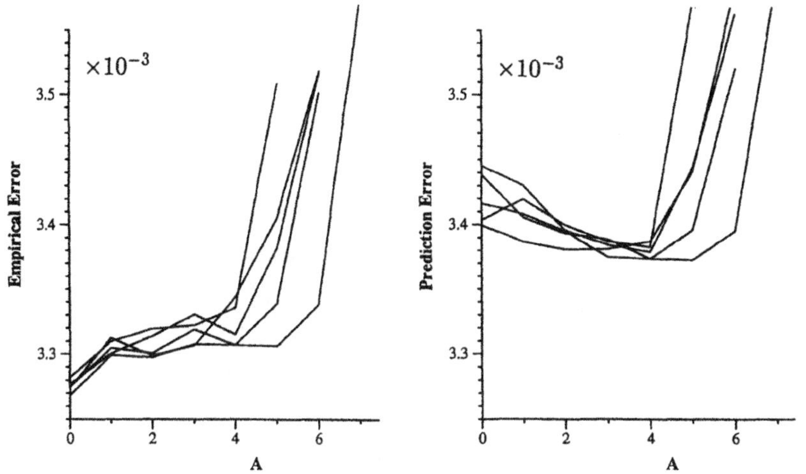

Figure 21 Empirical error and prediction error. The true distribution is contained in the model. $\alpha_0 = 1.5$.

based on the regularity condition cannot be applied to the neural network model selection problem. It is conjectured that the multilayer neural networks have larger generalization errors than the regular models if they are trained by the maximum likelihood method. It is also conjectured that they have smaller generalization

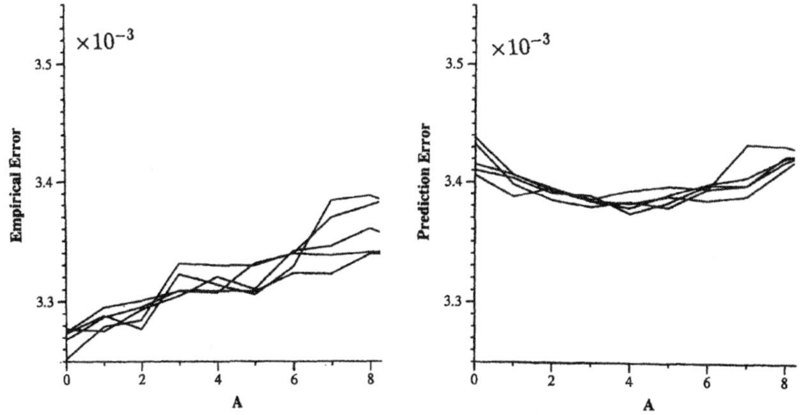

Figure 22 Empirical error and prediction error. The true distribution is contained in the model. $\alpha_0 = 3.0$.

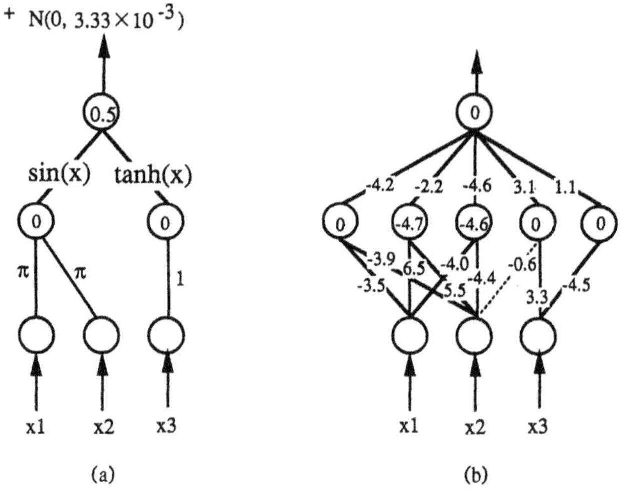

Figure 23 Unknown distribution and estimated model. (a) The true distribution. The true distribution in Eq. (32), which is represented as a network, is not contained in models. (b) A network optimized by AIC ($A = 2$). The empirical error is 3.31×10^{-3} and the prediction error is 3.41×10^{-3}. x_3 is almost separated from x_1 and x_2.

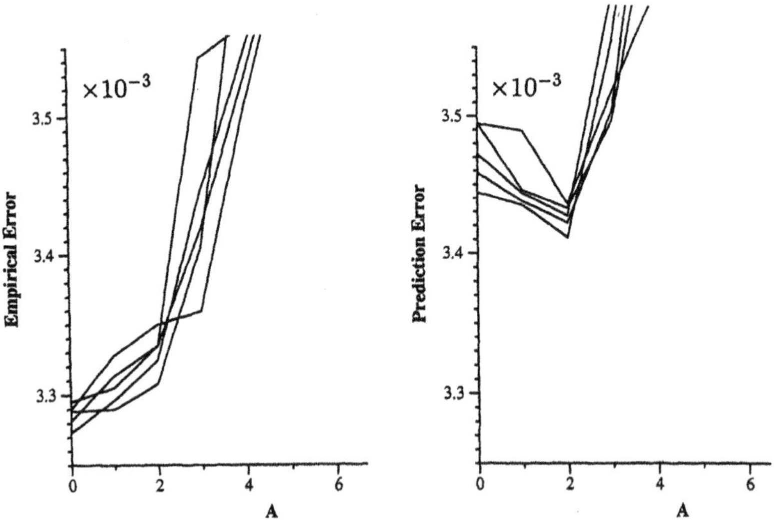

Figure 24 Empirical error and prediction error. The true distribution is not contained in the model. $\alpha_0 = 1.5$.

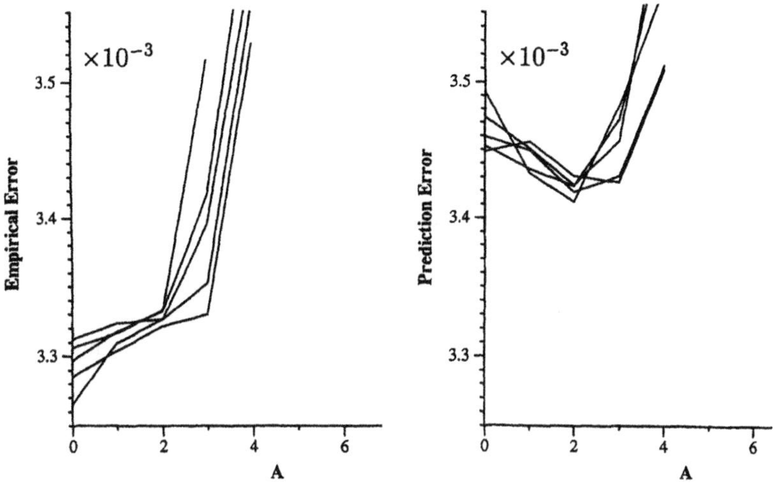

Figure 25 Empirical error and prediction error. The true distribution is not contained in the model. $\alpha_0 = 3.0$.

errors than the regular models if they are trained by the Bayesian method [24]. Although the model with the smaller prediction error can be selected by the conventional information criteria, more precise analysis is needed to establish the correct information criterion for artificial neural networks.

B. Active Learning

We introduce a statistical method of improving the estimation of the true inference probability $q(\mathbf{y}|\mathbf{x})$. In the previous sections, training samples were taken from the true probability $q(\mathbf{x}, \mathbf{y})$. When our purpose is to estimate the inference $q(\mathbf{y}|\mathbf{x})$ using function approximation neural networks, we do not have to use the true occurrence probability $q(\mathbf{x})$ to obtain the training samples. It is well known that the ability of the estimation can be improved by designing the input vectors of training samples. Such methods of selecting input vectors are called *active learning* and have been studied for regression problems in the name of experimental design [25] and response surface methodology [26] in statistics. Based on the statistical framework of neural networks described in Section II, we can apply the active learning methodology to function approximation neural networks.

We consider function approximation neural networks (Example 1, Section II), but we do not estimate the deviation parameter σ here. The three loss functions give the same learning criterion in this case. We assume that the true inference probability $q(\mathbf{y}|\mathbf{x})$ is realized by a network and is given by

$$q(\mathbf{y}|\mathbf{x}) = \frac{1}{(2\pi\sigma^2)^{N/2}} \exp\left\{-\frac{1}{2\sigma^2}\|\mathbf{y} - \varphi(\mathbf{x}; \mathbf{w}_0)\|^2\right\}, \tag{79}$$

where $\mathbf{w}_0$ is the unique true parameter.

We describe the general idea of a probabilistic active learning method [27] in which the input data of training samples are obtained as independent samples from a probability $r(\mathbf{x})$ called the *probability for training*. The point of the active learning method is that the density $r(\mathbf{x})$ can be different from the true occurrence probability $q(\mathbf{x})$, which generates input vectors in the true environment. If training samples are taken from the true probability $q(\mathbf{x}, \mathbf{y})$, such learning is called *passive*.

Our purpose is to minimize the prediction error (70)—the most natural criterion to evaluate the estimator—by optimizing the probability $r(\mathbf{x})$. It is easy to see that L_{pred} is given by

$$\frac{\sigma^2}{2} + \frac{1}{2}\int \|\varphi(\mathbf{x}; \widehat{\mathbf{w}}) - \varphi(\mathbf{x}; \mathbf{w}_0)\|^2 q(\mathbf{x})\, d\mathbf{x} + \frac{N}{2}\log(2\pi\sigma) - \int q(\mathbf{x}) \log q(\mathbf{x})\, d\mathbf{x}.$$

Whereas the accuracy of the estimator affects only the second term, we define the *generalization error* as the expectation of the mean square error between the estimated function and the true function:

$$E_{\text{gen}} = E_n\left\{\int \|\varphi(\mathbf{x}; \widehat{\mathbf{w}}) - \varphi(\mathbf{x}; \mathbf{w}_0)\|^2 q(\mathbf{x})\, d\mathbf{x}\right\}. \tag{80}$$

In the preceding equation, $E_n\{\cdot\}$ denotes the expectation with respect to training samples, which are independent samples from $q(\mathbf{y}|\mathbf{x})r(\mathbf{x})$.

A calculation similar to the derivation of AIC gives

$$E_{\text{gen}} \approx \frac{\sigma^2}{N} \operatorname{Tr}\left[I(\mathbf{w}_0) J^{-1}(\mathbf{w}_0)\right], \tag{81}$$

where matrixes I and J are the Fisher information matrixes evaluated by $q(\mathbf{x})$ and $r(\mathbf{x})$, respectively. In this case, we obtain

$$\begin{aligned} I_{ab}(\mathbf{x}; \mathbf{w}) &= \frac{\partial \varphi^T(\mathbf{x}; \mathbf{w})}{\partial w_a} \frac{\partial \varphi(\mathbf{x}; \mathbf{w})}{\partial w_b}, \\ I(\mathbf{w}) &= \int I(\mathbf{x}; \mathbf{w}) q(\mathbf{x})\, d\mathbf{x}, \\ J(\mathbf{w}) &= \int I(\mathbf{x}; \mathbf{w}) r(\mathbf{x})\, d\mathbf{x}. \end{aligned}$$

We should minimize $\operatorname{Tr}[IJ^{-1}]$ by optimizing the probability for training $r(\mathbf{x})$. The calculation of the trace, however, requires the true parameter $\mathbf{w}_0$. Thus, the practical method is an iterative one in which the estimation of **w** and the optimization of $r(\mathbf{x})$ are performed by turns [27].

The foregoing active learning method as well as many others requires the inverse of a Fisher information matrix J. As we described in Section V.A, the Fisher information of a neural network is not always invertible. Fukumizu [23] proved that the Fisher information matrix of a three-layer perceptron is singular if and only if the network has a hidden unit that makes no contributions to the output or it has a pair of hidden units that can be collapsible to a single unit. We can deduce that if the information matrix is singular, we can make it nonsingular by eliminating redundant hidden units without changing the input–output map. An active learning method with hidden unit reduction was proposed according to this principle [27]. In this method, redundant hidden units are removed during leaning, which enables us to use the active learning criterion $\mathrm{Tr}[IJ^{-1}]$.

We performed an experiment of active and passive learning of multilayer perceptrons. We used a multilayer perceptron with four input units, seven hidden units, and one output unit. The true function is

$$\varphi(\mathbf{x}) = \mathrm{erf}(x_1),$$

where $\mathrm{erf}(t)$ is the *error function*. Because this function is not realized by a multilayer perceptron, the theoretical assumption is not completely satisfied. We set $q(\mathbf{x}) = g_4(0, 5)$, train a network actively/passively based on 10 different data sets, and evaluated mean square errors of function values. Figure 26 shows the experimental result, which shows that the generalization error of active learning is smaller than that of passive learning.

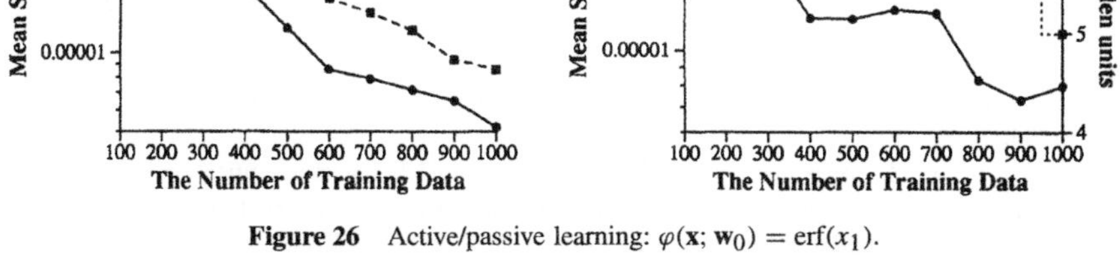

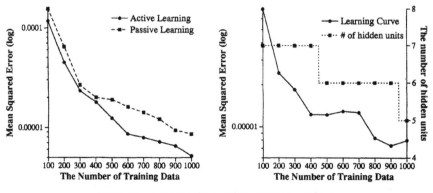

Figure 26 Active/passive learning: $\varphi(\mathbf{x}; \mathbf{w}_0) = \mathrm{erf}(x_1)$.

VI. CONCLUSION

We proposed probabilistic design techniques for artificial neural networks and introduced their applications. First, we showed that neural networks can be understood to be parametric models, and their training algorithm is an iterative search of the maximum likelihood estimator. Second, based on this framework, we designed three models which have new abilities to reject unknown inputs, to tell the reliability of their own inferences, and to illustrate input patterns for a given category. Third, we considered the probability competition neural network—a typical neural network that has such abilities—and experimentally compared its performance with three-layer perceptrons. Last, we studied statistical asymptotic techniques in neural networks. However, strictly speaking, the statistical properties of layered models are not yet clarified because artificial neural networks are not regular models. This is an important problem for the future.

We expect that advances in neural network research based on the probabilistic framework will build a bridge between biological information theory and practical engineering in the real world.

REFERENCES

[1] S. Watanabe and K. Fukumizu. Probabilistic design of layered neural networks based on their unified framework. *IEEE Trans. Neural Networks* 6:691–702, 1995.

[2] H. White. Learning in artificial neural networks: a statistical perspective. *Neural Comput.* 1:425–464, 1989.

[3] D. F. Specht. Probabilistic neural networks. *Neural Networks* 3:109–118, 1990.

[4] W. H. Press, S. A. Teukolsky, W. T. Vettering, and B. P. Flannery. *Numerical Recipes in C*, 2nd ed., pp. 287–290. Cambridge University Press, Cambridge, 1992.

[5] D. E. Rumelhart and D. Zipser. In *Parallel Distributed Processing* (D. E. Rumelhart, J. L. McClelland, and the PDP Research Group, Eds.), Vol. 1, pp. 151–193. MIT Press, Cambridge, MA, 1986.

[6] A. P. Dempster, N. M. Laird, and D. B. Rubin. Maximum likelihood from incomplete data via the EM algorithm. *J. Roy. Statist. Soc. Ser. B* 39:1–38, 1977.

[7] R. A. Render and H. F. Walker. Mixture densities, maximum likelihood and the EM algorithm. *SIAM Rev.* 26:195–239, 1984.

[8] R. O. Duda and P. E. Hart. *Pattern Classification and Scene Analysis.* Wiley, New York, 1973.

[9] S. Watanabe and M. Yoneyama. Ultrasonic robot eyes using neural networks. *IEEE Trans. Ultrasonics, Ferroelectrics, Frequency Control* 37:141–147, 1990.

[10] S. Watanabe and M. Yoneyama. An ultrasonic 3-D visual sensor using neural networks. *IEEE Trans. Robotics Automation* 6:240–249, 1992.

[11] S. Watanabe and M. Yoneyama. An ultrasonic 3-D object recognition method based on the unified neural network theory. In *Proceedings of the IEEE US Symposium*, Arizona, 1992, pp. 1191–1194.

[12] S. Watanabe, M. Yoneyama, and S. Ueha. An ultrasonic 3-D object identification system combining ultrasonic imaging with a probability competition neural network. In *Proceedings of the Ultrasonics International 93 Conference*, Vienna, 1993, pp. 767–770.

[13] S. Watanabe and M. Yoneyama. A 3-D object classification method combining acoustical imaging with probability competition neural networks. *Acoustical Imaging*, Vol. 20, pp. 65–72. Plenum Press, New York, 1993.

[14] S. Watanabe. An ultrasonic 3-D robot vision system based on the statistical properties of artificial neural networks. In *Neural Networks for Robotic Control: Theory and Applications* (A. M. S. Zalzala and A. S. Morris, Eds.), pp. 192–217. Ellis Horwood, London, 1996.

[15] H. Akaike. A new look at the statistical model identification. *IEEE Trans. Automat. Control* AC-19:716–723, 1974.

[16] G. Schwarz. Estimating the dimension of a model. *Ann. Statist.* 6:461–464, 1978.

[17] J. Rissanen. Universal coding, information, prediction, and estimation. *IEEE Trans. Inform. Theory* 30:629–636, 1984.

[18] Y. Le Cun, J. S. Denker, and S. A. Solla. Optimal brain damage. *Adv. in Neural Inform. Process. Syst.* 2:598–605, 1991.

[19] E. Levin, N. Tishby, and S. A. Solla. A statistical approach to learning and generalization in layered neural networks. *Proc. IEEE* 78:1568–1574, 1990.

[20] R. Shibata. Selection of the order of an autoregressive model by Akaike's information criterion. *Biometrika* 63:117–126, 1976.

[21] S. Watanabe. A modified information criterion for automatic model and parameter selection in neural network learning. *IEICE Trans.* E78-D:490–499, 1995.

[22] K. Hagiwara, N. Toda, and S. Usui. On the problem of applying AIC to determine the structure of a layered feed-forward neural network. In *Proceedings of the 1993 International Joint Conference on Neural Networks*, 1993, pp. 2263–2266.

[23] K. Fukumizu. A regularity condition of the information matrix of a multilayer perceptron network. *Neural Networks* 9:871–879, 1996.

[24] S. Watanabe. A generalized Bayesian framework for neural networks with singular Fisher information matrices. In *Proceedings of the International Symposium on Nonlinear Theory and Its Applications*, Las Vegas, 1995, pp. 207–210.

[25] V. V. Fedorov. *Theory of Optimal Experiments*. Academic Press, New York, 1972.

[26] R. H. Myers, A. I. Khuri, and W. H. Carter, Jr. Response surface Methodology: 1966–1988. *Technometrics* 31:137–157, 1989.

[27] K. Fukumizu. Active learning in multilayer perceptrons. In *Advances in Neural Information Processing Systems* (D. S. Touretzky, M. C. Mozer, and M. E. Hasselmo, Eds.), Vol. 8, pp. 295–301. MIT Press, Cambridge, MA, 1996.

Short Time Memory Problems*

M. Daniel Tom
GE Corporate Research and Development
General Electric Company
Niskayuna, New York 12309

Manoel Fernando Tenorio
Purdue University
Austin, Texas 78746

I. INTRODUCTION

Ever wondered why we remember? Or rather why we forget so quickly? We remember because we have long term memory. We forget quickly because recent events are stored in short term memory. Long term memory has yet to be constructed. Most computational neuron models do not address the issue of short term memory. Each artificial neuron is a memoryless device that translates input to output in a nonlinear fashion. A network of such neurons is therefore memoryless, unless memory devices external to the neurons are used in the network.

For example, the time-delayed neural network [2] uses shift registers to hold a time series in the input field. Elman's recurrent neural network [3, 4] uses a register to hold the hidden layer node values to be presented at the input in the next time step, akin to state automata. The registers in these devices constitute the "short term memory" of the network. The neurons are still memoryless devices. Long term memory is stored in the weights as the network is trained. If these models can achieve amazing results with a memory device external to the neural

*Based on [1]. © 1995 IEEE.

unit, we can expect even more when we implement short term memory characteristics at the neuron level. Specifically, we would like to produce a neural model that recognizes spatiotemporal patterns on its own merit, without the help of shift registers.

Where do we start? Too simple a model like the McCulloch–Pitts neuron would have no memory at all. Complex physiology-based neural models make it hard to isolate the salient features we need: nonlinear computation and short term memory. So we seek alternative models, and they need not be neurobiologically inspired. We ask the question: What simple things on earth have memory? Immediately, the magnet comes to mind.

Magnetic materials retain a residual magnetic field after being exposed to a strong magnetic field. Under oscillatory fields, magnetic materials show hysteresis: a nonlinear response that lags behind the induced field, creating a looped trace on an oscilloscope. The hysteresis loop looks like two displaced sigmoids. Now if the neuron has short term memory, should it not produce a hysteresislike response instead of a sigmoidal response?

To confirm our guess we return to square one to perform our own neural response measurements, taking care to preserve recordings indicating short term memory. We then construct a neuron model with magnetlike hysteresis behavior. We show how this hysteresis model can store and distinguish any bipolar sequence of finite length. We give an example of spatiotemporal pattern recognition using the hysteresis model. We also provide proofs of two theorems concerning the memory characteristics of the hysteresis model.

II. BACKGROUND

The cognitive science and intelligent systems engineering literature recognizes two types of memories: long term memory and short term memory. Long term memory is responsible for the adaptive change in animal behavior that lasts from hours to years. It usually involves either structural or physical modification of a medium. Short term memory, on the other hand, lasts from seconds to minutes. Short term memory is usually chemically or electrically based, and is thus more plastic and ephemeral in nature. In engineering, one of the most important problems in intelligent system design is the recognition of patterns in spatiotemporal signals, for which biological systems employ short term memory.

The task of performing spatiotemporal pattern recognition is difficult because of the temporal structure of the pattern. Neural network models created to solve this problem have been based on either the classical approach or on recursive feedback within the network. However, the latter makes learning algorithms numerically unstable. Classical approaches to this problem have also proven unsatisfactory. They range from "projecting out" the time axis to "memorizing" an entire sequence before a decision can be made. The latter approach can be particularly difficult if no *a priori* information about signal length is present, if the signal undergoes compression or expansion, if the entire pattern is immense, as in the case of time varying images. Some form of short term memory therefore seems necessary for spatiotemporal pattern processing. Particularly helpful would be the use of a processing element with intrinsic short term memory characteristics.

We approach the short term memory problem by studying the neuron from a computational point of view. The goal is to create model neurons which not only compute, but also have short term memory characteristics. Neurocomputation models are appropriately named in light of the inspirational use of biological computing techniques being reproduced in artificial devices. The modeling process helps us better understand biological systems and points out new directions in intelligent systems design. Here we use a deeper analysis and modeling of a biological neuron and propose an improved artificial neural computation model. The analysis and modeling also aid in the design of effective spatiotemporal pattern recognition systems which display a biologically plausible short term memory mechanism, but do not suffer from the limitations of current approaches.

Before we proceed to construct a neural model with memory, we need to understand why today's artificial neurons have sigmoidal nonlinearities and no memory characteristics.

III. MEASURING NEURAL RESPONSES

The graded neural response is measured by probing the neuron when it is exposed to certain stimuli under controlled conditions. However, this response includes measurement error and the effects of the particular experimental methodology. Whereas the environment surrounding the neuron cannot be easily controlled, there are always stray stimuli that affect the measured response. More importantly, the measurement methodology itself may be in question. The stimulus is usually not increased or decreased steadily. Rather, it is randomized to overcome the transient effects of the neural response. The response, an average firing frequency, is computed from the reciprocals of the interspike intervals. Whereas these experiments are designed to overcome the short term memory effects, it is therefore fair to say that the typical sigmoidal response curve obtained from these experiments does not account for memory characteristics. Complex, nonassociative learning or memory processes such as habituation, sensitization, and accommodation are known to occur within neurons [5–7]. If we now turn the question around, would we observe interesting memory characteristics if we steadily increase and decrease the stimulus strength?

Before we experimented with a real cell, we made the following hypothesis: If the natural input to a spiking projection neuron is steadily increased and decreased, accommodation can cause the neural response output to follow two displaced sigmoids, thus resembling a magnetic hysteresis loop [8]. The fact that magnetic materials retain a magnetic field after an imposed electric field is removed is the basis of all magnetic storage or memory devices [9–13]. We infer that a hysteresislike response is therefore an adequate characterization of the short term memory characteristics of the neuron. In fact, as we will show in later sections, this simple generalization of the sigmoidal model has important implications for neurocomputer engineering:

1. demonstrates sensitization and habituation phenomena;
2. presents other forms of nonassociative learning;
3. differentiates spatiotemporal patterns embedded in noise;
4. maps an arbitrary length sequence into a single response value;
5. models an adaptive delay that grows with pattern size.

We validated our hypothesis in the laboratory by testing for hysteresis memory behavior in real nerve cells [14]. We took intracellular recordings from representative intrinsic neurons, namely, the retinular cells in the eye of *Limulus polyphemus* (the horseshoe crab). The cell membrane was penetrated by a microelectrode filled with 3 M KCl solution. A reference electrode was placed in the bath of sea water which contains the eye of *Limulus*. Extrinsic current was injected into the cell through the microelectrode; artifacts were canceled by resistive and capacitative bridges. The amplitude of the current was controlled by a computer, so that a 1 Hz sawtoothlike current variation was created. Our results show that the intracellular potential in response to a current injection was indeed a hysteresislike loop and not just a simple sigmoidal response.

IV. HYSTERESIS MODEL

In this section we present our model neuron, called the hysteresis model, which is inspired by the memory characteristics of magnetic materials. The hysteresis model differs only slightly from the standard sigmoidal neural model with hyperbolic tangent nonlinearity. We hypothesize that neural responses resemble hysteresis loops. The upper and lower halves of the hysteresis loop are described by two sigmoids. Generalizing the two sigmoids to two families of curves accommodates loops of various sizes. The hysteresis model is capable of memorizing the entire history of its bipolar inputs in an adaptive fashion, with larger memory for longer sequences. We theorize and prove that the hysteresis model's response converges asymptotically to hysteresislike loops. In the next section, we will show a simple application to temporal pattern discrimination using the nonlinear short term memory characteristics of this hysteresis model.

The hysteresis unit uses two displaced hyperbolic tangent functions for the upper and lower branches of a hysteresis loop. We assume that the displacement of these functions along the x axis is H_c (modeled after the coercive magnetic field required to bring the magnetic field in magnetic materials to zero). Here, H_c is taken to be a magnitude and is thus a positive quantity. The largest magnitude of the response is B_s (modeled after the saturated magnetic flux in magnetic materials).

To accommodate any starting point in the x, y plane, the lower and upper branches of the hysteresis loop are actually described as two families of curves. When x is increasing, a rising curve is followed, causing the response y to rise with x. As soon as x starts decreasing, a falling curve is traced, causing the response y to decay with x. The set of rising curves that passes through all possible starting points forms the family of rising curves (Fig. 1). Each member, indexed by η, has the form

$$y = \eta + (1 - \eta)\tanh(x - H_c) \tag{1}$$

for some η satisfying

$$y_0 = \eta + (1 - \eta)\tanh(x_0 - H_c) \tag{2}$$

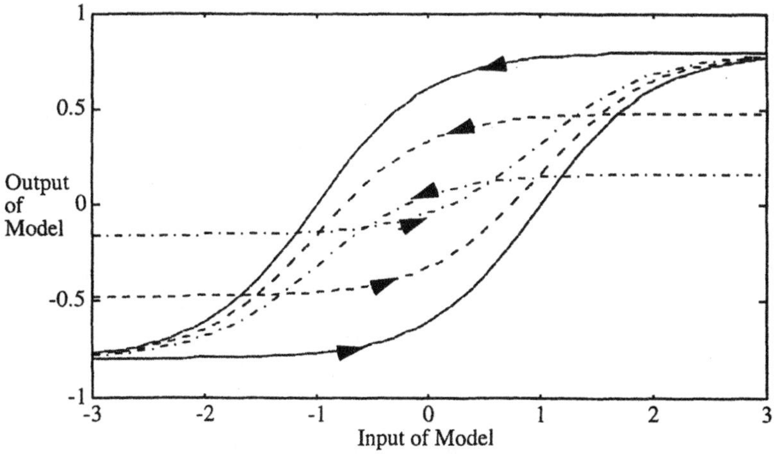

Figure 1 The hysteresis model of short term memory is described by two equations: one for the rising family and the other for the falling family of nonlinearities (indicated by arrows). Three members of each family are shown here. Loops are evident. Similar loops have been found in the retinular cells of *Limulus polyphemus* (horseshoe crab). Reprinted with permission from M. D. Tom and M. F. Tenorio, *Trans. Neural Networks* 6:387–397, 1995 (©1995 IEEE).

with (x_0, y_0) being a point on the curve, where $x_0 < x$. We can solve for η given (x_0, y_0):

$$\eta = \frac{y_0 - \tanh(x_0 - H_c)}{1 - \tanh(x_0 - H_c)}. \tag{3}$$

If (x_0, y_0) is the origin, then η is now specifically

$$\eta = \frac{\tanh H_c}{1 + \tanh H_c}. \tag{4}$$

The "magnetization curve" (a member of the family which passes through the origin) can be obtained by substituting η in Eq. (4) into Eq. (1):

$$y = \frac{\tanh(x - H_c) + \tanh H_c}{1 + \tanh H_c}. \tag{5}$$

For the case where $x_0 > x$, the family of falling curves is (see Fig. 1)

$$y_0 = -\eta + (1 - \eta)\tanh(x_0 + H_c), \tag{6}$$

$$\eta = \frac{y_0 - \tanh(x_0 + H_c)}{-1 - \tanh(x_0 + H_c)}. \tag{7}$$

Thus, the index η controls the vertical displacement as well as the compression of the hyperbolic tangent nonlinearity. This type of negative going response has been reported to be superior over its strictly positive counterpart. In fact, spiking projection neurons possess this type of bipolar, continuous behavior.

It is natural to test the memory properties of magnetic materials with sinusoidal inputs. So we drive the hysteresis model with an a.c. (alternate current) excitation and observe its response. Interestingly, we observe that the excitation/response trace converges to a hysteresislike loop, much like what Ewing recorded around the turn of the century with very slowly varying inputs [5].

Further testing of the hysteresis model reveals that the response still converges asymptotically to hysteresis loops even when the a.c. input is d.c. (direct current) biased. Also, convergence is independent of the starting point: the hysteresis model need not be initially at rest. These observations can be summarized by the following theorems about the properties of the hysteresis model. We provide rigorous proofs of these nonlinear behaviors in the Appendix.

THEOREM 1. *η_k converges to* $\sinh 2H_c/(\cosh 2a + \exp(2H_c))$, *where η_k denotes the successive indices of the members of the two families of curves followed under unbiased a.c. input of amplitude a.*

Note. When the input increases, the response of the hysteresis model follows one member of the family of rising curves. Similarly when the input decreases, the response of the hysteresis model follows one member of the family of falling curves. Therefore in one cycle of a.c. input from the negative peak to the positive peak and back to the negative peak, only one member of each family of curves is followed. It is thus only necessary to consider the convergence of the indices.

THEOREM 2. *Hysteresis is a steady state behavior of the hysteresis model under constant magnitude a.c. input.*

These theorems provide a major clue to the transformation of short term memory into long term memory. Most learning algorithms today are of the rote learning type, where excitation and desired response are repeatedly presented to adjust long term memory parameters. The hysteresis model of short term memory is significantly different in two ways. First, learning is nonassociative. There is no desired response, but repeated excitation will lead to convergence (much like mastering a skill). Second, there are no long term memory parameters to adjust. Rather, this short term memory model is an intermediate stage between excitations and long term memory. Under repetitive stimulus, the hysteresis model's response converges to a steady state of resonance. As Stephen Grossberg says, "Only resonant short term memory can cause learning in long term memory." This can also be deduced from the Hebb learning rule applied to the hysteresis model, where the presynaptic unit first resonates, followed by the postsynaptic unit. When the two resonate together, synapse formation is facilitated.

The proofs of these two theorems can be found in the Appendix. These proofs should be easy to follow. The lengths of the proofs are necessitated by the nonlinearities involved, but no advanced mathematics is required. In short, the proof of Theorem 1 shows that the sequence of indices is an asymptotically convergent oscillating sequence. The proof of Theorem 2 divides this oscillating sequence into nonoscillatory odd and even halves. There are two possible cases for each half: each converges to an asymptotic value either greater than or smaller than the indices.

V. PERFECT MEMORY

The hysteresis model for short term memory proposed in the preceding text has not been studied before. We therefore experiment with its memory capabilities, guided by the vast knowledge and practices in neurophysiology. Because neurons transmit information mostly via spikes (depolarizations of the membrane potential), we stimulate the hysteresis model with spike sequences. At a synapse, where the axon of the presynaptic neuron terminates, chemical channels open for the passage of ions through the terminal. At the postsynaptic end, two general types of neurotransmitters cause EPSPs and IPSPs (excitatory and inhibitory postsynaptic potentials). The postsynaptic neuron becomes less or more polarized,

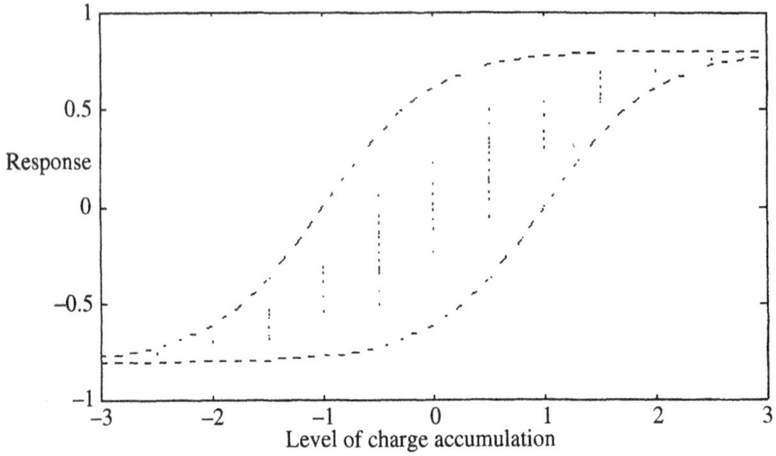

Figure 2 All different sequences of excitation resulting in accumulation of five or fewer charge quanta inside the membrane. (A single charge quantum would produce one-half unit of charge accumulation on this scale.) The responses of the hysteresis model are distinct for all different sequences of excitation (shown by the different dots). The entire history of excitation can be identified just from the response. Hence the perfect memory theorem. Reprinted with permission from M. D. Tom and M. F. Tenorio, *Trans. Neural Networks* 6:387–397, 1995 (©1995 IEEE).

respectively, due to these neurotransmitters. This study, as we will show below, has very interesting engineering implications.

We begin the experiment by applying the excitation starting from the rest state of the hysteresis model (i.e., zero initial input and output values). To represent ions that possess quantized charges, we use integral units of excitation. EPSPs and IPSPs can be easily represented by plus and minus signs. A simple integrating model for the postsynaptic neuron membrane is sufficient to account for its ion collecting function. To summarize, the excitation is quantized, bipolar, and integrated at the postsynaptic neuron (the full hysteresis model).

If we trace through all possible spike sequences of a given length and plot only the final response verses accumulated charge inside the membrane of the hysteresis model, we would observe a plot of final coordinates similar to that in Fig. 2. In this figure, the horizontal axis is the charge accumulation (up to five quanta) inside the membrane. The vertical axis is the response of the model, with parameters $B_s = 0.8$ and $H_c = 1.0$. Each dot is a final coordinate, and the dashed lines show the members of the families of rising and falling curves with the index $\eta = 1$ (the boundary).

Whereas the integral of charge quanta (total charge accumulated inside the membrane) can only assume discrete values, the final coordinates line up vertically at several locations on the horizontal axis. However, no two final coordinates are the same. Even the intermediate coordinates are different. More strikingly, when all these intermediate and final coordinates are projected onto the vertical axis (that is, looking at the response alone), they still remain distinct. This property distinguishes the hysteresis model of short term memory from its digital counterpart—registers. A digital register stores only a single bit, and thus the number of devices needed is proportional to the length of the bit sequence. A huge bandwidth is therefore required to store long sequences. In contrast, the analog hysteresis model represents the entire sequence in the response value of one single device. If higher accuracy is required, the parameters B_s and H_c can always be varied to accommodate additional response values produced by longer sequences. Otherwise, the longer sequences would produce responses that are closer together (which also illustrates the short term and graded nature of the memory).

From the foregoing observed characteristics, we offer the following theoretical statement: The final as well as the intermediate responses of the hysteresis model, excited under sequences of any length, are all distinct. Thus when a response of the hysteresis model is known, and given that it is initially at rest, a unique sequence of excitation must have existed to drive the hysteresis model to produce that particular response. The hysteresis model thus retains the full history of its input excitation. In other words, the hysteresis model maps the time history of its quantum excitations into a single, distinct, present value. Knowing the final response is sufficient to identify the entire excitation sequence.

These graded memory characteristics are often found in everyday experiences. For example, a person could likely remember a few telephone numbers, but not the entire telephone book. More often than likely, a person will recognize the name of an acquaintance when mentioned, but would not be able to name the acquaintance on demand. This differs significantly from digital computers, in which information can be stored and retrieved exactly. On the other hand, whereas humans excel in temporal pattern recognition, the performance of automated recognition algorithms has not been satisfactory. The usual method of pattern matching requires the storage of at least one pattern, and usually more, for each class. The incoming pattern to be identified needs to be stored also. Recognition performance cannot be achieved in real time. The following sections are the result of the first step toward solving the spatiotemporal pattern recognition problem. We first show the temporal differentiation property of the hysteresis model. We then apply this property in the construction of a simple spatiotemporal pattern classifier.

VI. TEMPORAL PRECEDENCE DIFFERENTIATION

Further study of the responses of the hysteresis model to different sequences provides deeper insight into its sequence differentiation property. In particular, the hysteresis model is found to distinguish similar sequences of stimulation based on the temporal order of the excitations. A memoryless device would have integrated the different sequences of excitations to the same value, giving a nonspectacular

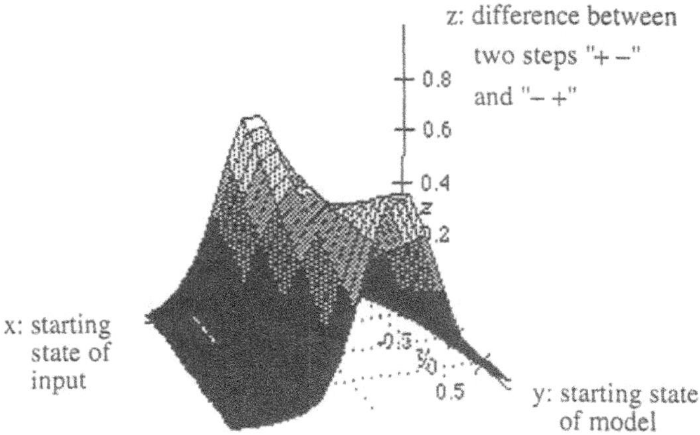

Figure 3 $z = y^{+}_{k+2} - y^{-}_{k+2}$ plotted over the x, y plane with x ranging from -3 to 3 and y ranging from -1 to 1. Within this region, z, the difference in response of the two steps "+ −" and "− +", is positive. Reprinted with permission from M. D. Tom and M. F. Tenorio, *Trans. Neural Networks* 6:387–397, 1995 (©1995 IEEE).

response. Subsequently, we will show this temporal differentiation property of the hysteresis model with mathematical analysis and figures.

From the responses of the hysteresis model to various input sequences, it is observed that an input sequence of four steps, "− − − −" always gives the smallest response, whereas "+ + + +" always gives the largest response. Sequences with a single "+" are ordered as "− − − +," "− − + −," "− + − −," and "+ − − −" from the smallest to the largest response value. Similarly, sequences with a single "−" are ordered as "− + + +," "+ − + +," "+ + − +," and "+ + + −" from the smallest to the largest.

The following analysis shows that this is the case for an input of arbitrary length; the key concept can be visualized in Fig. 3. Consider the preceding four sequences with a single "−." To show that the first sequence produces a smaller response than the second, all we have to consider are the leftmost subsequences of length 2, which are "− +" and "+ −." The remaining two inputs are identical, and because the family of rising curves is nonintersecting, the result holds for the rest of the input sequences. To show that the second sequence produces a smaller response than the third, only the middle subsequences of length 2 need be considered. They are also "− +" and "+ −." Using the foregoing property of the family of rising curves, this result holds for the rest for the sequence, and can be compounded with that for the first two sequences. In a similar manner, the fourth sequence can be iteratively included, producing the ordered response for the four input sequences.

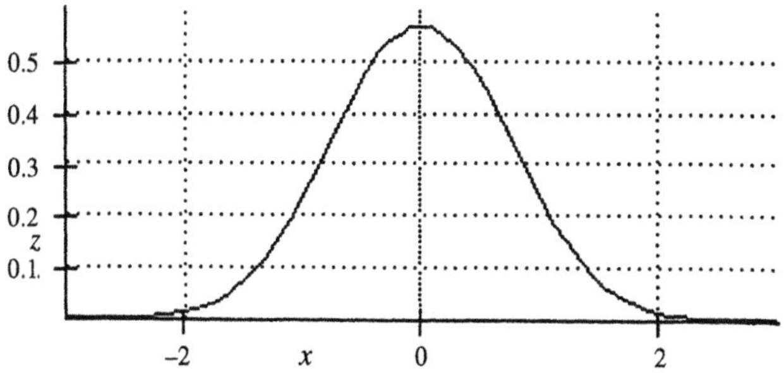

Figure 4 $z = y^+_{k+2} - y^-_{k+2}$ plotted along the curve through the origin (the "magnetization curve" of the hysteresis model). Reprinted with permission from M. D. Tom and M. F. Tenorio, *Trans. Neural Networks* 6:387–397, 1995 (©1995 IEEE).

Now let us consider the critical part, which is to show that the sequence "− +" always produces a smaller response than "+ −" when starting from the same point. Let the starting point be (x_k, y_k) and let the step size be a. Consider the first input sequence "− +." Then $x^-_{k+1} = x_k - a$ and $x^-_{k+2} = x_k$. Denote the response of the hysteresis model to this sequence by y^+_{k+2}. Similarly, for the second input sequence "+ −", $x^+_{k+1} = x_k + a$ and $x^+_{k+2} = x_k$. The response is denoted by y^-_{k+2}. The three-dimensional plot of (x_k, y_k, z) is shown in Fig. 3 and is positive in the x, y plane. Figure 4 shows that the cross section of the plot of $z = y^+_{k+2} - y^-_{k+2}$ is above zero along the "magnetization curve" of the hysteresis model (5). The significance of this sorting behavior is that, although excitations might be very similar, their order of arrival is very important to the hysteresis model. The ability to discriminate based on temporal precedence is one of the hysteresis model's short term memory characteristics which does not exist in memoryless models.

VII. STUDY IN SPATIOTEMPORAL PATTERN RECOGNITION

Because our study is prompted by the inadequacy of classical as well as neural network algorithms for spatiotemporal pattern recognition, here we would like to test the performance of the hysteresis model. We would like to see how the discovered properties, namely, perfect memory and temporal precedence sorting, would help in the spatiotemporal pattern recognition task. Here we report the ability and potential of the single neuron hysteresis model. We simplified the problem to a two-class problem.

The two-class problem is described as follows: There are two basic patterns, $A(t)$ and $B(t)$. In general, the spatial magnitude of A increases with time, whereas

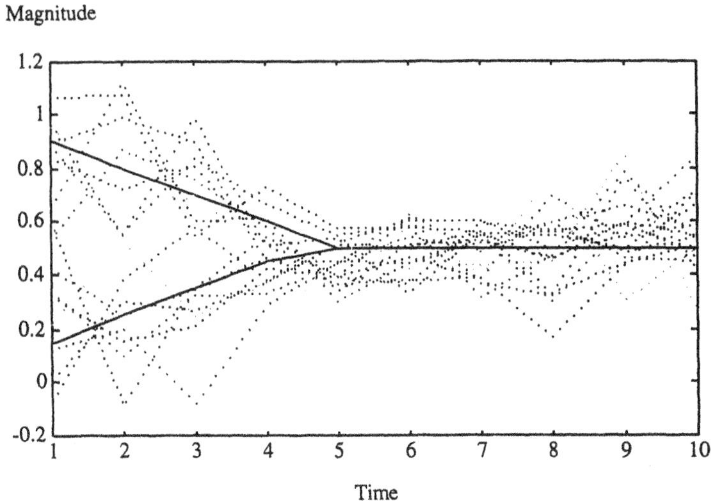

Figure 5 Noise superimposed patterns (dotted lines) and basic patterns (solid lines). The noise process is gaussian, white, and nonstationary, with a larger variance where the two basic patterns are more separated. Reprinted with permission from M. D. Tom and M. F. Tenorio, *Trans. Neural Networks* 6:387–397, 1995 (©1995 IEEE).

that of B decreases. At a certain point in time, their spatial magnitudes become identical and they become indistinguishable. Upon each basic pattern, nonstationary gaussian white noise is superimposed. The noise process has a larger variance where the two basic patterns are more separated. Thus the noisy patterns are less distinguishable than the same basic patterns superimposed with stationary noise. These noise embedded patterns (Fig. 5) become the unknown patterns that are used for testing.

An unknown spatiotemporal pattern is first preprocessed by two nearness estimators. Each estimator provides an instantaneous measure of the inverse distance between the input signal and the representative class. The two scores are passed on to the full hysteresis model. The operation of the full hysteresis model is described in the previous section.

The key results can be visualized in Figs. 6 and 7, and are typical of all 36 unknown patterns tested. Figure 6 shows the inverse distance measures provided by the two nearness estimators. Note that at the beginning the inverse distance score of the noisy test pattern is higher for one basic pattern than the other. This is because the two basic patterns are widely separated initially. When they converge, the difference of the two inverse distance scores become smaller.

As described in the previous section, the hysteresis model uses these two scores as excitation and produces a response trace as shown in Fig. 7 (solid line).

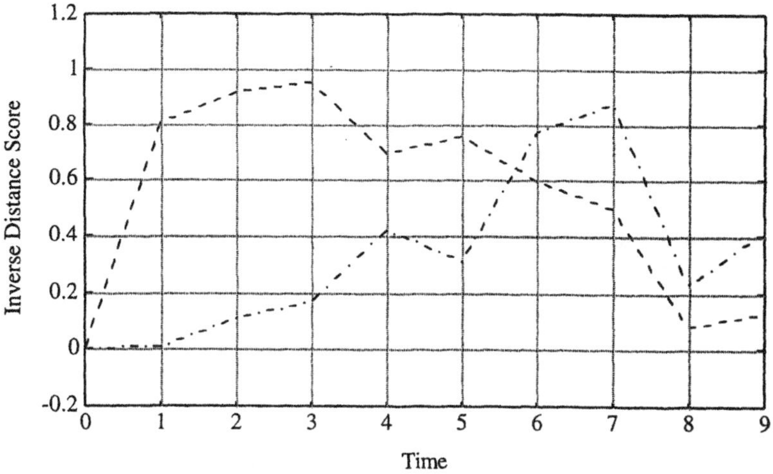

Figure 6 The inverse distance measures provided by the nearness estimators for an unknown pattern generated by superimposing nonstationary noise on either basic pattern *A* or *B*. Reprinted with permission from M. D. Tom and M. F. Tenorio, *Trans. Neural Networks* 6:387–397, 1995 (©1995 IEEE).

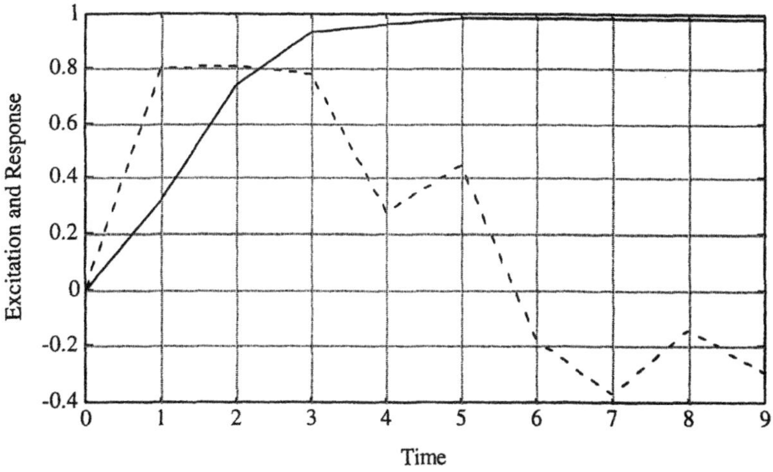

Figure 7 The difference of the two inverse distance measures (dashed) and the response of the hysteresis model (solid) using the two measures as excitation. Reprinted with permission from M. D. Tom and M. F. Tenorio, *Trans. Neural Networks* 6:387–397, 1995 (©1995 IEEE).

Whereas the inverse distance scores are highly separated initially, the hysteresis model builds up the correct response rapidly (toward one). Although the difference of the two scores is negative near the end, the response of the hysteresis model has not diminished, showing its memory capability. A memoryless system that takes the difference of the two instantaneous scores would give a response similar to the dotted lines in Fig. 7. As this response is negative, such a memoryless system has incorrectly classified the noisy test pattern.

We tested the performance of the hysteresis model on another pattern classification problem. Two basic patterns that diverge, $C(t)$ and $D(t)$, are created. Nonstationary gaussian white noise is superimposed on them to generate test patterns. The noise variance increases toward the end, and thus one noisy pattern may be closer to the other basic pattern instead. This is exactly the case shown in Figs. 8 and 9.

The two inverse distance measures are shown in Fig. 8. Initially the two basic patterns are close together and thus the noisy test pattern generates about the same score. When the basic patterns diverge, the difference of the two scores becomes larger.

The performance of the hysteresis model is shown by the solid line in Fig. 9. The dotted line shows the performance of a memoryless system that takes the instantaneous difference of the two scores. The memoryless system gives an incorrect identification at the end. The hysteresis model's memory prevents its response to decay, giving a correct final classification.

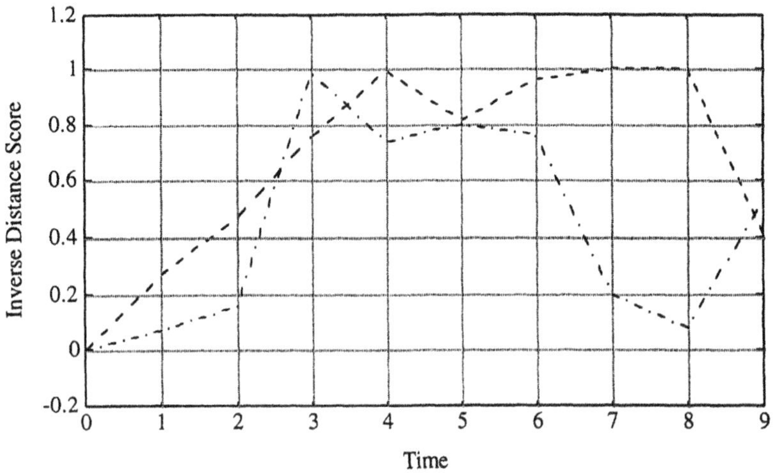

Figure 8 The inverse distance measures provided by the nearness estimators for an unknown pattern generated by superimposing nonstationary noise on either basic pattern A or B. Reprinted with permission from M. D. Tom and M. F. Tenorio, *Trans. Neural Networks* 6:387–397, 1995 (©1995 IEEE).

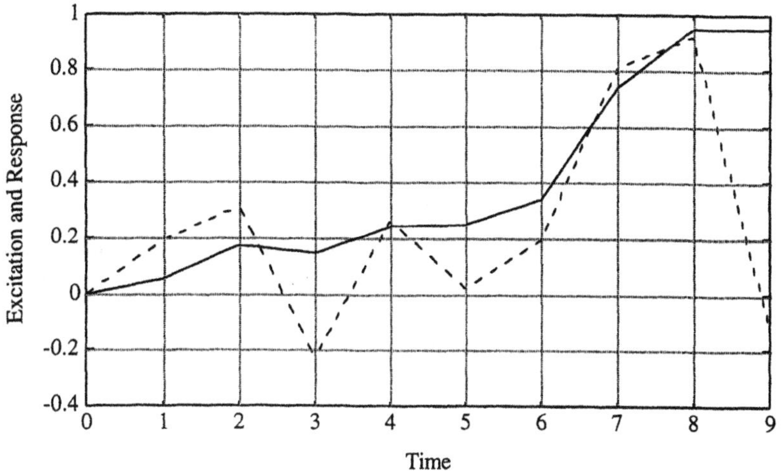

Figure 9 The difference of the two inverse distance measures (dashed) and the response of the hysteresis model (solid) using the two measures as excitation. Reprinted with permission from M. D. Tom and M. F. Tenorio, *Trans. Neural Networks* 6:387–397, 1995 (©1995 IEEE).

VIII. CONCLUSION

In this chapter, we introduced the hysteresis model of short term memory—a neuron architecture with built-in memory characteristics as well as a nonlinear response. These short term memory characteristics are present in the nerve cell, but have not yet been well addressed in the neural computation literature. We theorized that the hysteresis model's response converges under repetitive stimulus (see proofs in the Appendix), thereby facilitating the transformation of short term memory into long term synaptic memory. We conjectured that the hysteresis model retains a full history of its stimuli. We also showed how the hysteresis model discriminates between different temporal patterns based on temporal significance, even under the presence of large time varying noise (signal-to-noise ratio less than 0 dB). A preliminary study in spatiotemporal pattern recognition is reported.

The following are some research areas in expanding this hysteresis neuron model with respect to biological modeling and other applications:

- Neurons are known to respond differently to inputs of different frequencies. By replacing the accumulator with a leaky integrator, we introduced frequency dependency.
- An automatic reset mechanism in the temporal pattern recognition task would be desirable. We achieved this by injecting a small amount of noise

at the input. The noise amplitude regulates the reset time, thus the duration of memory.

- As mentioned in the Introduction, sensitization and habituation are two types of short term memory. The hysteresis unit models sensitization. By modifying a few parameters, we derive a whole new line of neuron architectures that address habituation as well as other interesting properties.
- Experiments with *Limulus polyphemus* using retinular cells and eccentric cells demonstrated the hysteresis mechanism which acts as an adaptive memory system.
- This model may have important applications for time-based computation such as control, signal processing, and spatiotemporal pattern recognition, especially if it can take advantage of existing hysteresis phenomena in semiconductor materials.

APPENDIX

Proof of Theorem 1. The proof will consist of three parts. The first part is to find the limit η to which η_k converges. The second part is to show that $\{\eta_k\}$ is a sequence that oscillates about η. The third part is to show that if $\eta_1 > \eta$, then $\eta_{2k+1} < \eta_{2k-1}$ and $\eta_{2k+2} > \eta_{2k}$.

Assume $\lim_{k\to\infty} \eta_k = \eta$. Then $\lim_{k\to\infty} \eta_{2k} = \eta$ and $\lim_{k\to\infty} \eta_{2k+1} = \eta$. Without loss of generality, assume

$$\eta_1 = \frac{y_0 - \tanh(x_0 - H_c)}{1 - \tanh(x_0 - H_c)}$$

and the a.c. input driving the hysteresis unit has a magnitude of a:

$$\begin{aligned} \eta_{2k+1} &= \frac{y_{2k} - \tanh(-a - H_c)}{1 - \tanh(-a - H_c)} \\ &= \frac{-\eta_{2k} + (1 - \eta_{2k}) \tanh(-a + H_c) + \tanh(a + H_c)}{1 + \tanh(a + H_c)}. \end{aligned} \tag{8}$$

Taking the limit as k approaches infinity on both sides,

$$\eta = \frac{-\eta + (1 - \eta) \tanh(-a + H_c) + \tanh(a + H_c)}{1 + \tanh(a + H_c)}, \tag{9}$$

$$\eta\big[1 + \tanh(a + H_c)\big] = -\eta + (1 - \eta) \tanh(-a + H_c) + \tanh(a + H_c), \tag{10}$$

$$\begin{aligned} &\eta\big[2 + \tanh(a + H_c) + \tanh(-a + H_c)\big] \\ &\quad = \tanh(a + H_c) + \tanh(-a + H_c), \end{aligned} \tag{11}$$

$$\eta\big[2+\tanh(a+H_c)-\tanh(a-H_c)\big]$$
$$=\tanh(a+H_c)-\tanh(a-H_c), \tag{12}$$

$$\eta=\frac{\tanh(a+H_c)-\tanh(a-H_c)}{2+\tanh(a+H_c)-\tanh(a-H_c)}. \tag{13}$$

As derived earlier,

$$\tanh(a+H_c)-\tanh(a-H_c)=\frac{2\sinh 2H_c}{\cosh 2a+\cosh 2H_c}. \tag{14}$$

Therefore,

$$\begin{aligned}\eta &= \frac{2\sinh 2H_c/(\cosh 2a+\cosh 2H_c)}{2+2\sinh 2H_c/(\cosh 2a+\cosh 2H_c)}\\ &= \frac{\sinh 2H_c}{\cosh 2a+\cosh 2H_c+\sinh 2H_c}\\ &= \frac{\sinh 2H_c}{\cosh 2a+\exp(2H_c)}.\end{aligned} \tag{15}$$

To show that $\{\eta_k\}$ is an oscillation sequence, consider (8):

$$\begin{aligned}\eta_{2k+1} &= \frac{-\eta_{2k}+(1-\eta_{2k})\tanh(-a+H_c)+\tanh(a+H_c)}{1+\tanh(a+H_c)}\\ &= \frac{\tanh(a+H_c)-\tanh(a-H_c)-[1-\tanh(a-H_c)]\eta_{2k}}{1+\tanh(a+H_c)}.\end{aligned}$$

Alternatively, from the definitions,

$$\begin{aligned}\eta_{2k} &= \frac{y_{2k-1}-\tanh(a+H_c)}{-1-\tanh(a+H_c)}\\ &= \frac{-y_{2k-1}+\tanh(a+H_c)}{1+\tanh a+H_c}\\ &= \frac{-\eta_{2k-1}-(1-\eta_{2k-1})\tanh(a-H_c)+\tanh(a+H_c)}{1+\tanh(a+H_c)}\\ &= \frac{\tanh(a+H_c)-\tanh(a-H_c)-[1-\tanh(a-H_c)]\eta_{2k-1}}{1+\tanh(a+H_c)}.\end{aligned} \tag{16}$$

Thus both η_{2k+1} and η_{2k} can be expressed in the common form

$$\eta_{k+1}=\frac{\tanh(a+H_c)-\tanh(a-H_c)-[1-\tanh(a-H_c)]\eta_k}{1+\tanh(a+H_c)}. \tag{17}$$

If $\eta_{k+1} < \eta$,

$$\eta > \frac{\tanh(a + H_c) - \tanh(a - H_c) - [1 - \tanh(a - H_c)]\eta_k}{1 + \tanh(a + H_c)},$$

$$\eta_k > \frac{\tanh(a + H_c) - \tanh(a - H_c) - [1 - \tanh(a - H_c)]\eta}{1 + \tanh(a + H_c)}. \tag{18}$$

Let $\gamma = \tanh(a + H_c) - \tanh(a - H_c)$. From (13),

$$\eta = \frac{\gamma}{2 + \gamma}, \tag{19}$$

$$2\eta + \gamma\eta = \gamma,$$

$$2\eta = \gamma(1 - \eta),$$

$$\gamma = \frac{2\eta}{1 - \eta}. \tag{20}$$

Also, whereas $\gamma = \tanh(a + H_c) - \tanh(a - H_c)$,

$$\begin{aligned} 1 - \tanh(a - H_c) &= 1 + \gamma - \tanh(a + H_c) \\ &= 1 + \frac{2\eta}{1 - \eta} - \tanh(a + H_c). \end{aligned} \tag{21}$$

Continuing, we have

$$\begin{aligned} \eta_k &> \frac{2\eta/(1 - \eta) - [1 + \tanh(a + H_c)]\eta}{1 + 2\eta/(1 - \eta) - \tanh(a + H_c)} \\ &= \frac{2\eta - \eta(1 - \eta)[1 + \tanh(a + H_c)]}{1 - \eta + 2\eta - (1 - \eta)\tanh(a + H_c)} \\ &= \frac{2\eta - \eta(1 - \eta)[1 + \tanh(a + H_c)]}{1 + \eta - (1 - \eta)\tanh(a + H_c)} \\ &= \frac{2\eta - \eta(1 - \eta)[1 + \tanh(a + H_c)]}{1 + \eta + (1 - \eta) - (1 - \eta)[1 + \tanh(a + H_c)]} \\ &= \frac{\eta\{2 - (1 - \eta)[1 + \tanh(a + H_c)]\}}{2 - (1 - \eta)[1 + \tanh(a + H_c)]} \\ &= \eta. \end{aligned} \tag{22}$$

Otherwise, if $\eta_{k+1} > \eta$, then $\eta_k < \eta$. Thus the sequence $\{\eta_k\}$ is oscillating about η.

The last part of the proof is to show that η_{2k} and η_{2k+1} are monotonically increasing and decreasing, or vice versa. From (17), increasing the index by 1,

$$\eta_{k+2} = \frac{\tanh(a + H_c) - \tanh(a - H_c) - [1 - \tanh(a - H_c)]\eta_{k+1}}{1 + \tanh(a + H_c)}. \tag{23}$$

Using the previous shorthand notation γ and letting $T = \tanh(a + H_c)$,

$$\begin{aligned}\eta_{k+2} &= \frac{1}{1+T}\big[\gamma - (1 - T + \gamma)\eta_{k+1}\big]\\ &= \frac{1}{1+T}\left\{\gamma - \frac{1-T+\gamma}{1+T}[\gamma - 1 - T + \gamma]\eta_k\right\}\\ &= \frac{1}{1+T}\left\{\gamma - \gamma\frac{1-T+\gamma}{1+T} + \frac{(1-T+\gamma)^2}{1+T}\eta_k\right\}\\ &= \frac{\gamma(1+T-1+T-\gamma) + (1-T+\gamma)^2\eta_k}{(1+T)^2},\end{aligned} \tag{24}$$

$$\begin{aligned}\eta_{k+2} - \eta_k &= \frac{\gamma(2T-\gamma) + [(1-T+\gamma)^2 - (1+T)^2]\eta_k}{(1+T)^2}\\ &= \frac{\gamma(2T-\gamma) + [\gamma^2 - 2\gamma - 2\gamma T - 4T]\eta_k}{(1+T)^2}\\ &= \frac{\gamma(2T-\gamma) + [\gamma(\gamma - 2T) + 2(\gamma - 2T)]\eta_k}{(1+T)^2}\\ &= \frac{(2T-\gamma)}{(1+T)^2}\big[\gamma - (\gamma+2)\eta_k\big].\end{aligned} \tag{25}$$

Because $T = \tanh(a + H_c) > -1$, so $(1 + T)^2 > 0$ and

$$\begin{aligned}2T - \gamma &= \tanh(a + H_c) + \tanh(a - H_c)\\ &= \frac{2\sinh 2a}{\cosh 2a + \cosh 2H_c}\\ &> 0 \quad \text{since } a > 0.\end{aligned} \tag{26}$$

If $\gamma - (\gamma + 2)\eta_k < 0$ or, equivalently, $\eta_k > \gamma/(2 + \gamma) = \eta$, then $\eta_{k+2} < \eta_k$ and the sequence is monotonically decreasing. Conversely, if $\eta_k < \eta$, then $\eta_{k+2} > \eta_k$ and the sequence is monotonically increasing. Following the assumption that

$$\eta_1 = \frac{y_0 - \tanh(x_0 - H_c)}{1 - \tanh(x_0 - H_c)} > 0,$$

the sequence $\{\eta_1, \eta_3, \eta_5, \ldots\}$ is monotonically decreasing with all terms greater than η and thus converges to η. Similarly, $\{\eta_2, \eta_4, \eta_6, \ldots\}$ is monotonically increasing with all terms less than η and therefore also converges to η (see Fig. 10). ■

Now Theorem 1 is proved independent of a, the magnitude of the a.c. input (Fig. 11), and (x_0, y_0), the starting point before applying the a.c. input. It is there-

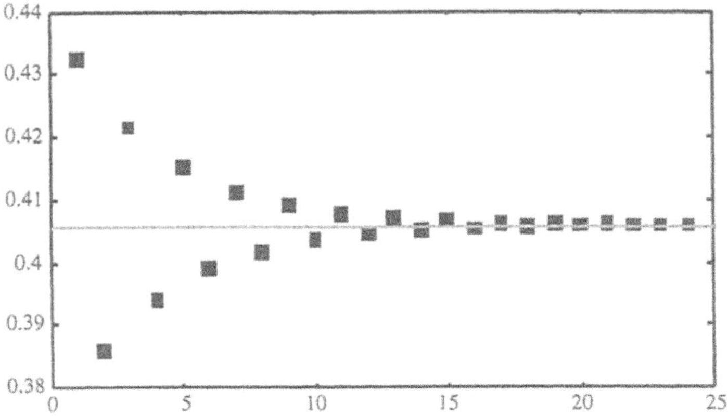

Figure 10 Convergence of the index into the family of curves under no bias. The a.c. magnitude is 0.5; $B_s = 1$; $H_c = 1$; starting from (0, 0). Reprinted with permission from M. D. Tom and M. F. Tenorio, *Trans. Neural Networks* 6:387–397, 1995 (©1995 IEEE).

fore possible to start at some point outside the realm of magnetic hysteresis loops (see Figs. 12–16).

Proof of Theorem 2. Theorem 2 is a generalization of Theorem 1, stating that a.c. input with d.c. bias can also make the hysteresis unit converge to steady state.

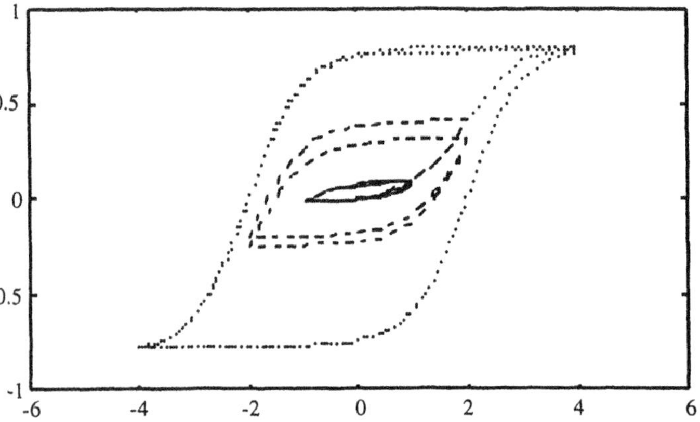

Figure 11 Convergence of the hysteresis model under various a.c. input magnitudes. The solid line, dashed line, and dotted line represent responses to a.c input of magnitudes 1, 2, and 4, respectively. $B_s = 0.8$; $H_c = 2$. Reprinted with permission from M. D. Tom and M. F. Tenorio, *Trans. Neural Networks* 6:387–397, 1995 (©1995 IEEE).

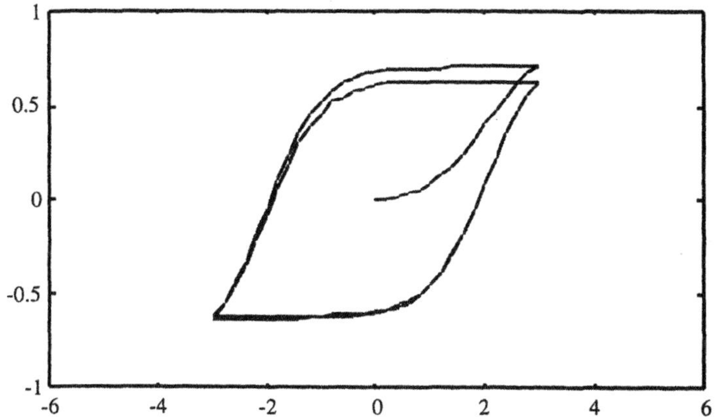

Figure 12 Convergence of the hysteresis model when driven from (0, 0). The amplitude of the a.c. input is 3; $B_s = 0.8$; $H_c = 2$. Reprinted with permission from M. D. Tom and M. F. Tenorio, *Trans. Neural Networks* 6:387–397, 1995 (©1995 IEEE).

The proof of Theorem 2 will be different from that of Theorem 1. This proof is divided into two parallel parts outlined as follows. The first half is to prove that the sequence $\{\eta_k^+\}$ converges to η^+. To prove this, first the limit η^+ to which $\{\eta_k^+\}$ converges is found. Then $\eta_k^+ > \eta^+$ for all k (or $\eta_k^+ < \eta^+$ for all k) is established.

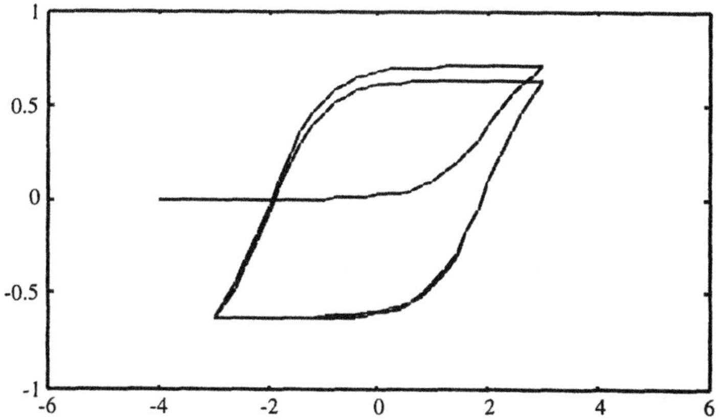

Figure 13 Convergence of the hysteresis model when driven from (−4, 0). The amplitude of the a.c. input is 3; $B_s = 0.8$; $H_c = 2$. Reprinted with permission from M. D. Tom and M. F. Tenorio, *Trans. Neural Networks* 6:387–397, 1995 (©1995 IEEE).

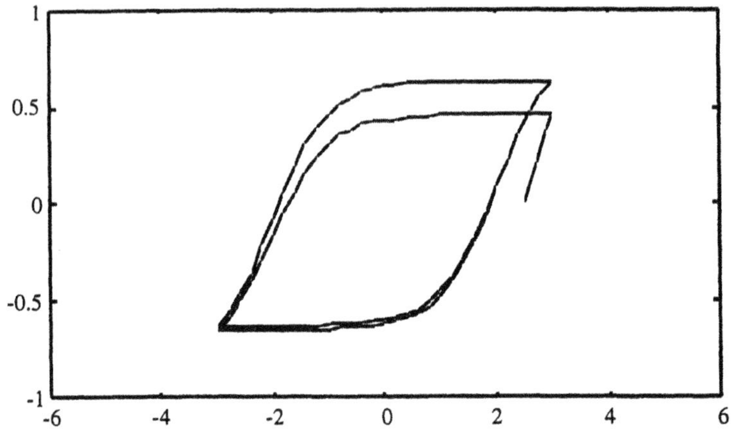

Figure 14 Convergence of the hysteresis model when driven from (2.5, 0). The amplitude of the a.c. input is 3; $B_s = 0.8$; $H_c = 2$. Reprinted with permission from M. D. Tom and M. F. Tenorio, *Trans. Neural Networks* 6:387–397, 1995 (©1995 IEEE).

Finally, the proof that η_k^+ is monotonically decreasing (or increasing) completes the proof of the first half of Theorem 2. The second half is to prove that the sequence $\{\eta_k^-\}$ converges to η^-, using a similar approach.

As previously mentioned, the set of equations for the families of rising and falling curves may be renamed more clearly as follows:

$$y_k^+ = \eta_k^+ + (1 - \eta_k^+)\tanh(x_k^+ - H_c),$$

where

$$\eta_k^+ = \frac{y_{k-1}^- - \tanh(x_{k-1}^- - H_c)}{1 - \tanh(x_{k-1}^- - H_c)}, \tag{27}$$

$$y_k^- = -\eta_k^- + (1 - \eta_k^-)\tanh(x_k^- + H_c),$$

where

$$\eta_k^- = \frac{y_k^+ - \tanh(x_k^+ + H_c)}{-1 - \tanh(x_k^+ + H_c)}. \tag{28}$$

Without loss of generality, let $x_k^+ = b + a$ and $x_k^- = b - a$. It will be convenient to use the shorthand notations

$$\begin{aligned} T_1 &= \tanh(b - a - H_c), \qquad S_1 = \sinh(b - a - H_c), \\ C_1 &= \cosh(b - a - H_c), \\ T_2 &= \tanh(b - a + H_c), \qquad S_2 = \sinh(b - a + H_c), \end{aligned}$$

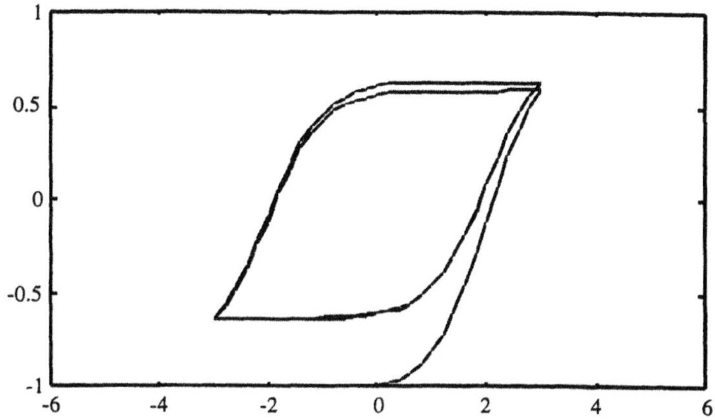

Figure 15 Convergence of the hysteresis model when driven from $(0, -1)$. The amplitude of the a.c. input is 3; $B_s = 0.8$; $H_c = 2$. Reprinted with permission from M. D. Tom and M. F. Tenorio, *Trans. Neural Networks* 6:387–397, 1995 (©1995 IEEE).

$$
\begin{aligned}
C_2 &= \cosh(b - a + H_c), \\
T_3 &= \tanh(b + a + H_c), \qquad S_3 = \sinh(b + a + H_c), \\
C_3 &= \cosh(b + a + H_c), \\
T_4 &= \tanh(b + a - H_c), \qquad S_4 = \sinh(b + a - H_c), \\
C_4 &= \cosh(b + a - H_c).
\end{aligned}
$$

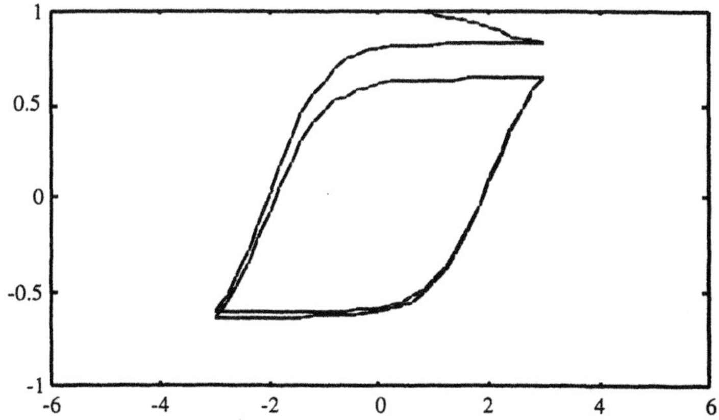

Figure 16 Convergence of the hysteresis unit when driven from $(0, 1)$. The amplitude of the a.c. input is 3; $B_s = 0.8$; $H_c = 2$. Reprinted with permission from M. D. Tom and M. F. Tenorio, *Trans. Neural Networks* 6:387–397, 1995 (©1995 IEEE).

Combining (27) and (28),

$$\begin{aligned}\eta_{k+1}^{+} &= \frac{1}{1-T_1}\left\{-T_1+T_2-\frac{1+T_2}{1+T_3}\left[T_3-T_4-(1-T_4)\eta_k^{+}\right]\right\}\\ &= \frac{T_2-T_1}{1-T_1}-\frac{1+T_2}{1+T_3}\frac{T_3-T_4}{1-T_1}+\frac{1+T_2}{1+T_3}\frac{1-T_4}{1-T_1}\eta_k^{+}. \qquad (29)\end{aligned}$$

Assume there exists η^{+} such that

$$\lim_{k\to\infty}\eta_{k+1}^{+}=\lim_{k\to\infty}\eta_k^{+}=\eta^{+}.$$

Then, by taking the limit on both sides of (29),

$$\eta^{+} = \frac{T_2-T_1}{1-T_1}-\frac{1+T_2}{1+T_3}\frac{T_3-T_4}{1-T_1}+\frac{1+T_2}{1+T_3}\frac{1-T_4}{1-T_1}\eta^{+}, \qquad (30)$$

$$\begin{aligned}\eta^{+} &= \frac{(1+T_3)(T_2-T_1)-(1+T_2)(T_3-T_4)}{(1+T_3)(1-T_1)-(1+T_2)(1-T_4)}\\ &= \frac{(1+S_3/C_3)(S_2/C_2-S_1/C_1)-(1+S_2/C_2)(S_3/C_3-S_4/C_4)}{(1+S_3/C_3)(1-S_1/C_1)-(1+S_2/C_2)(1-S_4/C_4)}\\ &= \frac{C_4(C_3+S_3)(C_1S_2-S_1C_2)-C_1(C_2+S_2)(C_4S_3-S_4C_3)}{C_2C_4(C_3+S_3)(C_1-S_1)-C_1C_3(C_2+S_2)(C_4-S_4)}. \qquad (31)\end{aligned}$$

The following identities will be useful:

$$\begin{aligned}\cosh x+\sinh x &= e^{x},\\ \cosh x-\sinh x &= e^{-x},\\ \cosh x\cosh y &= \tfrac{1}{2}\left[\cosh(x+y)+\cosh(x-y)\right],\\ \cosh x\sinh y-\sinh x\cosh y &= \sinh(y-x).\end{aligned}$$

Continuing, the numerator for η^{+} is

$$\begin{aligned}&C_4(C_3+S_3)(C_1S_2-S_1C_2)-C_1(C_2+S_2)(C_4S_3-S_4C_3)\\ &\quad=\cosh(b+a-H_c)e^{b+a-H_c}\sinh 2H_c\\ &\qquad-\cosh(b-a-H_c)e^{b-a-H_c}\sinh 2H_c\\ &\quad=\sinh 2H_c\left[\cosh(b+a-H_c)e^{b+a-H_c}-\cosh(b-a-H_c)e^{b-a-H_c}\right]\\ &\quad=\tfrac{1}{2}\sinh 2H_c\left[e^{2(b+a)}+e^{2H_c}-e^{2(b-a)}-e^{2H_c}\right]\\ &\quad=\tfrac{1}{2}\sinh 2H_c\left[e^{2(b+a)}-e^{2(b-a)}\right]\\ &\quad=\tfrac{1}{2}\sinh 2H_c\left[e^{2a}-e^{-2a}\right]e^{2b}. \qquad (32)\end{aligned}$$

The denominator in the expression for η^+ is

$$\begin{aligned}
&C_2C_4(C_3+S_3)(C_1-S_1) - C_1C_3(C_2+S_2)(C_4-S_4)\\
&\quad = \tfrac{1}{2}\big[\cosh 2b + \cosh 2(a-H_c)\big]e^{b+a+H_c}e^{-b+a+H_c}\\
&\qquad - \tfrac{1}{2}\big[\cosh 2b + \cosh 2(a+H_c)\big]e^{b-a+H_c}e^{-b-a+H_c}\\
&\quad = \tfrac{1}{2}\cosh 2b\big[e^{2(a+H_c)} - e^{2(-a+H_c)}\big]\\
&\qquad - \tfrac{1}{2}\big[\cosh 2(a-H_c)e^{2(a+H_c)} - \cosh 2(a+H_c)e^{2(-a+H_c)}\big]\\
&\quad = \cosh 2b \sinh 2a e^{2H_c} + \tfrac{1}{4}\big[e^{4H_c} + e^{4a} - e^{-4a} - e^{4H_c}\big]\\
&\quad = \cosh 2b \sinh 2a e^{2H_c} + \tfrac{1}{4}\big[e^{4a} - e^{-4a}\big].
\end{aligned} \tag{33}$$

Combining the numerator and denominator for η^+,

$$\begin{aligned}
\eta^+ &= \frac{\tfrac{1}{2}\sinh 2H_c[e^{2a}-e^{-2a}]e^{2b}}{\cosh 2b \sinh 2a e^{2H_c} + \tfrac{1}{4}[e^{2a}+e^{-2a}][e^{2a}-e^{-2a}]}\\
&= \frac{\sinh 2H_c \sinh 2a e^{2b}}{\cosh 2b \sinh 2a e^{2H_c} + \cosh 2a \sinh 2a}\\
&= \frac{\sinh 2H_c e^{2b}}{\cosh 2a + \cosh 2b e^{2H_c}}.
\end{aligned} \tag{34}$$

Note that if $b = 0$, then $\eta^+ = \eta = (\sinh 2H_c)/[\cosh 2a + \exp(2H_c)]$.

Next, it is shown subsequently that if $\eta_k^+ > \eta^+$, then $\eta_{k+1}^+ > \eta^+$ also holds. Taking (29) and letting $\eta_k^+ > \eta^+$,

$$\begin{aligned}
\eta_{k+1}^+ &= \frac{T_2-T_1}{1-T_1} - \frac{1+T_2}{1+T_3}\frac{T_3-T_4}{1-T_1} + \frac{1+T_2}{1+T_3}\frac{1-T_4}{1-T_1}\eta_k^+\\
&> \frac{T_2-T_1}{1-T_1} - \frac{1+T_2}{1+T_3}\frac{T_3-T_4}{1-T_1} + \frac{1+T_2}{1+T_3}\frac{1-T_4}{1-T_1}\eta^+,
\end{aligned} \tag{35}$$

$$\begin{aligned}
(1+T_3)(1-T_1)\eta_{k+1}^+ > {} & (1+T_3)(T_2-T_1) - (1-T_2)(T_3-T_4)\\
& + (1+T_2)(1-T_4)\eta^+.
\end{aligned} \tag{36}$$

Substituting in η^+ from (31) in the right side of the inequality, it becomes

$$\begin{aligned}
&(1+T_3)(T_2-T_1) - (1+T_2)(T_3-T_4)\\
&+(1+T_2)(1-T_4)\,\frac{(1+T_3)(T_2-T_1) - (1+T_2)(T_3-T_4)}{(1+T_3)(1-T_1) - (1+T_2)(1-T_4)}\\
&\quad = (1+T_3)(T_2-T_1) - (1+T_2)(T_3-T_4)\\
&\qquad + \frac{(1+T_2)(1-T_4)(1+T_3)(T_2-T_1) - (1+T_2)(1-T_4)(1+T_2)(T_3-T_4)}{(1+T_3)(1-T_1) - (1+T_2)(1-T_4)}\\
&\quad = \big\{(1+T_2)(1+T_4)(1+T_3)(T_2-T_1)
\end{aligned}$$

$$
\begin{aligned}
&- (1+T_2)(1-T_4)(1+T_2)(T_3-T_4) \\
&+ (1+T_3)(T_2-T_1)(1+T_3)(1-T_1) \\
&- (1+T_3)(T_2-T_1)(1+T_2)(1-T_4) \\
&- (1+T_2)(T_3-T_4)(1+T_3)(1-T_1) \\
&+ (1+T_2)(T_3-T_4)(1+T_2)(1-T_4)\big\}/ \\
&\big[(1+T_3)(1-T_1)-(1+T_2)(1-T_4)\big] \\
= {}&(1+T_3)(1-T_1)\frac{(1+T_3)(T_2-T_1)-(1+T_2)(T_3-T_4)}{(1+T_3)(1-T_1)-(1+T_2)(1-T_4)} \\
= {}&(1+T_3)(1-T_1)\eta^+. \qquad (37)
\end{aligned}
$$

Therefore $(1+T_3)(1-T_1)\eta^+_{k+1} > (1+T_3)(1-T_1)\eta^+$ or $\eta^+_{k+1} > \eta^+$ follows from $\eta^+_k > \eta^+$. On the contrary, $\eta^+_{k+1} < \eta^+$ if $\eta^+_k < \eta^+$ holds.

The following derivations show that if $\eta^+_k > \eta^+$, then $\eta^+_{k+1} < \eta^+_k$ and the sequence $\{\eta^+_k\}$ is monotonically decreasing. Conversely, if $\eta^+_k < \eta^+$, then the sequence $\{\eta^+_k\}$ is monotonically increasing:

$$
\begin{aligned}
\eta^+_{k+1} - \eta^+_k &= \frac{T_2-T_1}{1-T_1} - \frac{1+T_2}{1+T_3}\frac{T_3-T_4}{1-T_1} + \left(\frac{1-T_2}{1+T_3}\frac{1-T_4}{1-T_1} - 1\right)\eta^+_k \\
&= \big\{(1+T_3)(T_2-T_1)-(1-T_2)(T_3-T_4) \\
&\quad + \big[(1+T_2)(1-T_4)-(1+T_3)(1-T_1)\big]\big\} \\
&\quad \times \big[(1+T_3)(1-T_1)\big]^{-1}\eta^+_k. \qquad (38)
\end{aligned}
$$

Suppose $\eta^+_k > \eta^+$. Then the numerator

$$
\begin{aligned}
&(1+T_3)(T_2-T_1)-(1-T_2)(T_3-T_4) \\
&\quad -\big[(1+T_3)(1-T_1)-(1+T_2)(1-T_4)\big]\eta^+_k \\
&\quad < (1+T_3)(T_2-T_1)-(1-T_2)(T_3-T_4) \\
&\qquad -\big[(1+T_3)(1-T_1)-(1+T_2)(1-T_4)\big]\eta^+ \\
&\quad = (1+T_3)(T_2-T_1)-(1-T_2)(T_3-T_4) \\
&\qquad -\big[(1+T_3)(T_2-T_1)-(1-T_2)(T_3-T_4)\big] \\
&\quad = 0. \qquad (39)
\end{aligned}
$$

Thus, if $\eta^+_k > \eta^+$, then $\eta^k_{k+1} < \eta^+_k$ and the sequence $\{\eta^+_k\}$ is monotonically decreasing, converging to η^+. (See Fig. 17, odd time indices, upper half of the graph.) Conversely, if $\eta^+_k < \eta^+$, then $\eta^+_{k+1} > \eta^+_k$ and the sequence $\{\eta^+_k\}$ is monotonically increasing, converging to η^+. (See Fig. 18, odd time indices, upper half of the graph.)

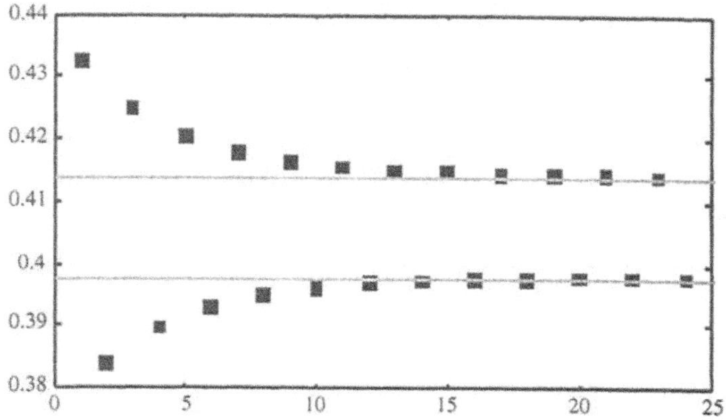

Figure 17 Convergence of the index into the family of curves under a bias of 0.01. The a.c. magnitude is 0.5; $B_s = 1$; $H_c = 1$; starting from (0, 0). Reprinted with permission from M. D. Tom and M. F. Tenorio, *Trans. Neural Networks* 6:387–397, 1995 (©1995 IEEE).

To complete the second half of the proof of Theorem 2, here is the counterpart of (29):

$$\begin{aligned}\eta_{k+1}^{-} &= \frac{1}{1+T_3}\left\{T_3 - T_4 - \frac{1-T_4}{1-T_1}\left[-T_1 + T_2 - (1+T_2)\eta_k^{-}\right]\right\}\\ &= \frac{T_3 - T_4}{1+T_3} - \frac{1-T_4}{1-T_1}\frac{T_2 - T_1}{1+T_3} + \frac{1-T_4}{1-T_1}\frac{1+T_2}{1+T_3}\eta_k.\end{aligned} \tag{40}$$

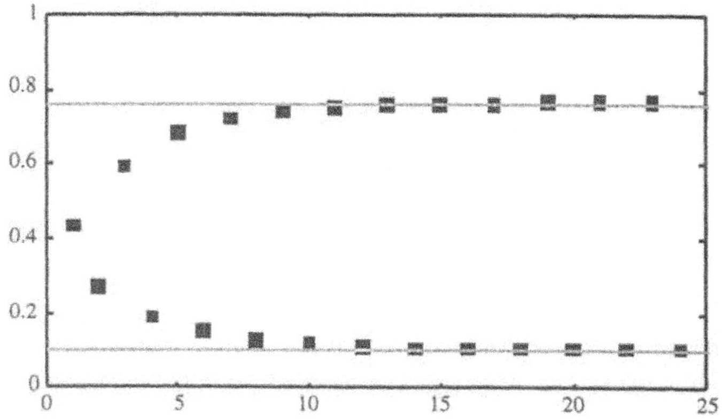

Figure 18 Convergence of the index into the family of curves under a bias of 0.5. The a.c. magnitude is 0.5; $B_s = 1$; $H_c = 1$; starting from (0, 0). Reprinted with permission from M. D. Tom and M. F. Tenorio, *Trans. Neural Networks* 6:387–397, 1995 (©1995 IEEE).

Let $\lim_{k\to\infty} \eta_{k+1}^- = \lim_{k\to\infty} \eta_k^- = \eta^-$. Then

$$\eta^- = \frac{(1-T_1)(T_3-T_4)-(1-T_4)(T_2-T_1)}{(1-T_1)(1+T_3)-(1-T_4)(1+T_2)}. \tag{41}$$

By going through a similar derivation or by observing $-b$ may be substituted for b in the solution for η^+,

$$\eta^- = \frac{\sinh 2H_c e^{-2b}}{\cosh 2a + \cosh 2b e^{2H_c}}. \tag{42}$$

If $\eta_k^- < \eta^-$, then

$$\eta_{k+1}^- < \frac{T_3-T_4}{1+T_3} - \frac{1-T_4}{1-T_1}\frac{T_2-T_1}{1+T_3} + \frac{1-T_4}{1-T_1}\frac{1+T_2}{1+T_3}\eta^-. \tag{43}$$

Following the foregoing derivations in a similar fashion,

$$\eta_{k+1}^- < \eta^-. \tag{44}$$

Alternatively, if $\eta_k^- > \eta^-$, then $\eta_{k+1}^- > \eta^-$. The difference of η_{k+1}^- and η^- is

$$\eta_{k+1}^-\eta^- < \frac{T_3-T_4}{1+T_3} - \frac{1-T_4}{1-T_1}\frac{T_2-T_1}{1+T_3} + \left(\frac{1-T_4}{1-T_1}\frac{1+T_2}{1+T_3} - 1\right)\eta^-.$$

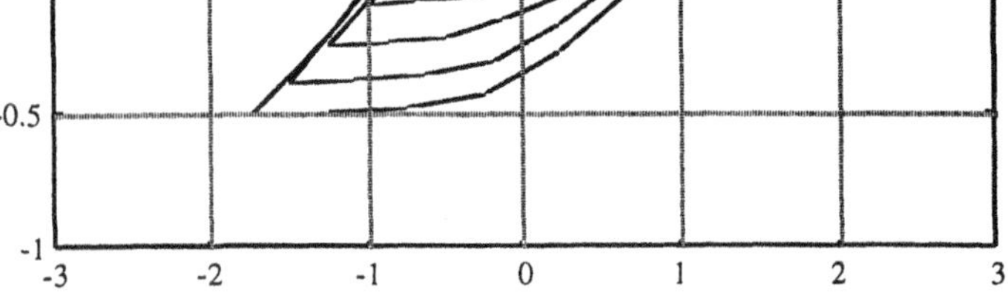

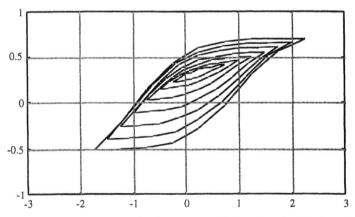

Figure 19 Several steady state loops of the hysteresis model when driven by biased a.c. The bias is 0.25; $B_s = 0.8$; $H_c = 1$. The inner through the outer loops are driven by a.c. of magnitudes 0.5, 0.75, 1, 1.25, 1.5, 1.75, and 2, respectively. Reprinted with permission from M. D. Tom and M. F. Tenorio, *Trans. Neural Networks* 6:387–397, 1995 (©1995 IEEE).

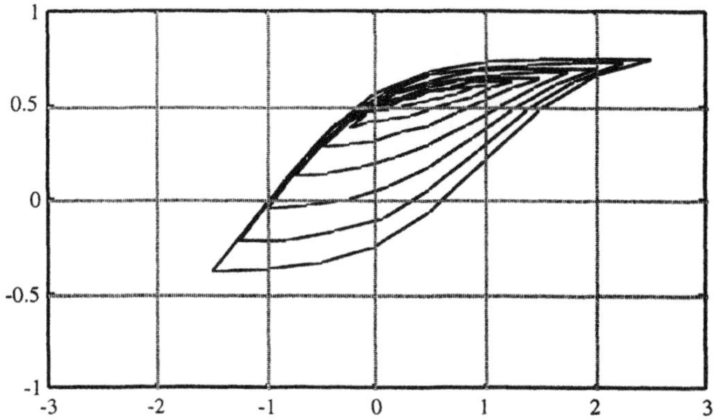

Figure 20 Several steady state loops of the hysteresis model when driven by biased a.c. The bias is 0.5; $B_s = 0.8$; $H_C = 1$. The inner through the outer loops are driven by a.c. of magnitudes 0.5, 0.75, 1, 1.25, 1.5, 1.75, and 2, respectively. Reprinted with permission from M. D. Tom and M. F. Tenorio, *Trans. Neural Networks* 6:387–397, 1995 (©1995 IEEE).

Again, following the foregoing derivations, $\eta_{k+1}^{-} > \eta_k^{-}$ if $\eta_k^{-} < \eta^{-}$, and the sequence $\{\eta_k^{-}\}$ is monotonically increasing, converging to η^{-}. (See Fig. 17, even time indices, lower half of the graph.) Conversely, if $\eta_k^{-} > \eta^{-}$, then $\eta_{k+1}^{-} < \eta_k^{-}$ and the sequence $\{\eta_k^{-}\}$ is monotonically decreasing, converging to η^{-}. (See

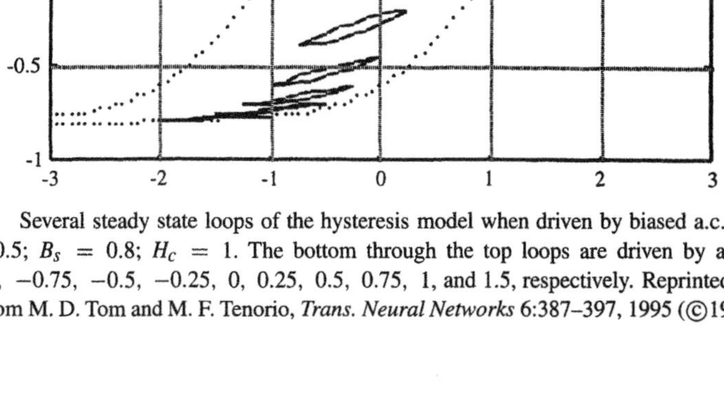

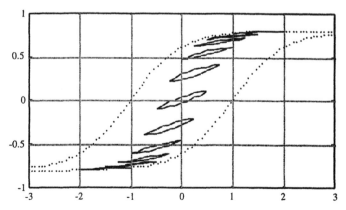

Figure 21 Several steady state loops of the hysteresis model when driven by biased a.c. The magnitude is 0.5; $B_s = 0.8$; $H_C = 1$. The bottom through the top loops are driven by a.c. of bias −1.5, −1, −0.75, −0.5, −0.25, 0, 0.25, 0.5, 0.75, 1, and 1.5, respectively. Reprinted with permission from M. D. Tom and M. F. Tenorio, *Trans. Neural Networks* 6:387–397, 1995 (©1995 IEEE).

Fig. 18, even time indices, lower half of the graph.) This completes the proof of Theorem 2. Similar to Theorem 1, the proof of Theorem 2 is independent of a, the magnitude of the a.c. input, and b, the d.c. bias. Figure 19 shows some loops with constant bias and various magnitudes. Figure 20 is generated with a bias larger than in Fig. 19. Figure 21 is generated with a fixed magnitude a.c. while the bias is varied. ■

REFERENCES

[1] M. D. Tom and M. F. Tenorio. A neural computation model with short-term memory. *Trans. Neural Networks* 6:387–397, 1995.

[2] J. B. Hampshire, II, and A. H. Waibel. A novel objective function for improved phoneme recognition using time-delay neural networks. *IEEE Trans. Neural Networks* 1:216–228, 1990.

[3] J. L. Elman. Finding structure in time. *Cognitive Sci.* 14:179–211, 1990.

[4] J. L. Elman. Distributed representations, simple recurrent neural networks, and grammatical structure. *Machine Learning* 7:195–225, 1991.

[5] P. M. Groves and G. V. Rebec. *Introduction to Biological Psychology, 3rd ed.* Brown, Dubuque, IA, 1988.

[6] D. Purves and J. W. Lichtman. *Principles of Neural Development.* Sinaver, Sunderland, 1985.

[7] G. M. Shepherd. *Neurobiology*, 2nd ed. Oxford University Press, London, 1988.

[8] L. T. Wang and G. S. Wasserman. Direct intracellular measurement of non-linear postreceptor transfer functions in dark and light adaptation in limulus. *Brain Res.* 328:41–50, 1985.

[9] R. M. Bozorth. *Ferromagnetism.* Van Nostrand, New York, 1951.

[10] F. Brailsford. *Magnetic Materials*, 3rd ed. Wiley, New York, 1960.

[11] C.-W. Chen. *Magnetism and Metallurgy of Soft Magnetic Materials.* North-Holland, Amsterdam, 1977.

[12] S. Chikazumi. *Physics of Magnetism.* Wiley, New York, 1964.

[13] D. J. Craik. *Structure and Properties of Magnetic Materials.* Pion, London, 1971.

[14] M. D. Tom and M. F. Tenorio. Emergent properties of a neurobiological model of memory. In *International Joint Conference on Neural Networks*, 1991.

Reliability Issue and Quantization Effects in Optical and Electronic Network Implementations of Hebbian-Type Associative Memories

Pau-Choo Chung
Department of Electrical Engineering
National Cheng-Kung University
Tainan 70101, Taiwan, Republic of China

Ching-Tsorng Tsai
Department of Computer and
Information Sciences
Tunghai University
Taichung 70407, Taiwan, Republic of China

I. INTRODUCTION

Hebbian-type associative memory (HAM) has been applied to various applications due to its simple architecture and well-defined time domain behavior [1, 2]. As such, many studies have focused on analyzing its dynamic behaviors and on estimating its memory storage capacity [3–9]. Amari [4], for example, proposed using statistical neurodynamics to analyze the dynamic behavior of an autocorrelation associative memory, from which the memory capacity is estimated. McEliece and Posner [7] showed that, asymptotically, the network can store only about $N/(2\log N)$ patterns, where N is the number of neurons in the network, if perfect recall is required. This limited memory storage capability has invoked considerable research. Venkatesh and Psaltis [10] proposed using spectral strategy to construct the memory matrix. With their approach, the memory capacity is improved from $O(N/\log N)$ to $O(N)$. Other researchers have proposed including higher-order association terms to increase the network's nonredundant parameters and hence increase the network storage capacity [11–15]. Analysis of the storage capacity of high-order memories can be found in the work of Personnaz *et al.* [12]. Furthermore, high-order terms also have been adopted in certain networks to enable them to have the capability to recognize transformed patterns [14].

With these advanced studies in HAM's dynamic behavior and in its improvement of network storage capability, the real promise for practical applications of HAM depends on our ability to develop it into a specialized hardware. Very large scale integration (VLSI) and opto-electronics are the two most prominent techniques being investigated for physical implementations. With today's integration densities, a large number of simple processors, together with the necessary interconnections, can be implemented inside a single chip to make a collective computing network. Several research groups have embarked on experiments with VLSI implementations and have demonstrated several functioning units [16–27]. A formidable problem with such large scale networks is to determine how the HAMs are affected by interconnection faults. It is claimed that neural networks have the capability of fault tolerance, but to what degree can the fault be tolerated? In addition, how can we estimate the results quantitatively in advance? To explore this issue, Chung *et al.* [28–30] used neurostatistics to investigate the effects of open- and short-circuited interconnection faults on the probability of one-step correct recall of HAMs. Their investigation also extended to cover the analysis of network reliability when the radius of attraction is taken into account. The radius of attraction (also referred to as basin of attraction) here indicates the number of input error bits that a network can tolerate and still give an acceptably high probability of correct recall. Analysis of the memory capacity of HAMs by taking the radius of attraction into account was conducted by Newman [5], Amit [3], and Wang *et al.* [6].

Another problem associated with the HAMs in VLSI implementations is the unexpectedly large synaptic area required as the number of stored patterns grows: a synaptic weight (or interconnection) computed according to Hebbian rules may take any integer value between $-M$ and $+M$ when M patterns are stored. Furthermore, as the network size N increases, the number of interconnections increases on the order of N^2, which also causes an increase in the chip area when implementing the network. The increase in the required chip area caused by the increase of the number of stored patterns, as well as the increase in network size, significantly obstructs the feasibility of the network, particularly when hardware implementation is considered. Therefore, a way to reduce the range of interconnection values or to quantize the interconnection values into a restricted number of levels is thus indispensable. In addressing this concern, Verleysen and Sirletti [31] presented a VLSI implementation technique for binary interconnected associative memories with only three interconnection values $(-1, 0, +1)$. Sompolinsky [32] and Amit [3], using the spin-glass concept, also indicated that a clipped HAM actually retains certain storage capability. A study on the effects of weight (or interconnection) quantization on multilayer neural networks was conducted by Dundar and Rose [33] using a statistical model. Their results indicated that the levels of quantization for the network to keep sufficient performance were around 10 bits. An analysis of interconnection quantization of HAMs was also conducted by Chung *et al.* [34]. In their analysis, the quantization strategy was extended by setting the interconnection values within $[-G, +G]$ to 0, whereas those values smaller than $-G$ were set to -1 and those larger than $+G$ were set to $+1$. Based on statistical neurodynamics, equations were developed to predict the probabilities that the network gives a correct pattern recall when various Gs are used. From these results, the value of G can be selected optimally, in the sense that the quantized network retains the highest probability of correct recall.

In this chapter, the two main issues of network reliability and quantization effects in VLSI implementations will be discussed. The discussion of reliability will include the open-circuit and short-circuit effects on linear- and quadratic-order associative memories. Comparison of the two types of network models with regard to their capacity, reliability, and tolerance capability for input errors will also be discussed. The analysis of quantization effects is conducted on linear-order associative memories. The quantization strategies discussed include when (a) interconnections of their values beyond the range $[-G, +G]$ are clipped to -1 or $+1$ according to the sign of their original values, whereas the interconnections of their values within the range $[-G, +G]$ are set to zero, and (b) interconnections between the range of $[-B, -G]$ or $[G, B]$ retain their original values: greater than B set to B; smaller than $-B$ set to $-B$; and between $[-G, G]$ set to zero.

Organization of this chapter is as follows. The linear and quadratic Hebbian-type associative memories are introduced in Section II. Review of properties of the networks with and without self-interconnections also will be addressed in this section. Section III presents the statistical model for estimating the probability of the network giving perfect recall. The analysis is based on the signal-to-noise ratio of the total input signal in a neuron. Then, the reliability of linear and quadratic networks that have open- and short-circuit interconnection faults is stated in Section IV, followed by the comparison of linear- and quadratic-order HAMs in Section V. The comparison is conducted from the viewpoint of reliability, storage capacity, and tolerance capability for input errors. The quantization effects of linear-order HAMs is discussed in Section VI. Finally, conclusions are drawn in Section VII.

II. HEBBIAN-TYPE ASSOCIATIVE MEMORIES

A. Linear-Order Associative Memories

The autoassociative memory model proposed by Hopfield has attracted much interest, both as a content addressable memory and as a method for solving complex combinatorial problems [1, 2, 35–37]. A Hopfield associative memory, also called a linear Hopfield associative memory or first-order associative memory, is constructed by interconnecting a large number of simple processing units. For a network consisting of N processing units, or neurons, each neuron i, $1 \leq i \leq N$, receives an input from neuron j, $1 \leq j \leq N$, through a connection, or weight, T_{ij}, as shown in Fig. 1. Assume that M binary-valued vectors denoted by $x^k = [x_1^k, x_2^k, \ldots, x_N^k]$, $1 \leq k \leq M$, with each $x_i^k = +1$ or 0, are stored in the network. The connection matrix $T = [T_{ij}]$ for nonzero autoconnections (NZA) and zero autoconnections (ZA) is obtained by

$$T_{ij} = \begin{cases} \sum_{k=1}^{M}(2x_i^k - 1)(2x_j^k - 1) & \text{(for NZA)} \\ \sum_{k=1}^{M}(2x_i^k - 1)(2x_j^k - 1) - M\delta_{ij} & \text{(for ZA)}, \end{cases} \tag{1}$$

where δ_{ij} is the Kronecker delta function. Note that the removal of the diagonal terms, $M\delta_{ij}$, in the ZA case means that no neuron has a synaptic connection back to itself. The recall process consists of a matrix multiplication followed by a hard-limiting function. Assume that at time step t, the probe vector appearing at the network input is $x^f(t)$. For a specific neuron i, after time step $t+1$, the network

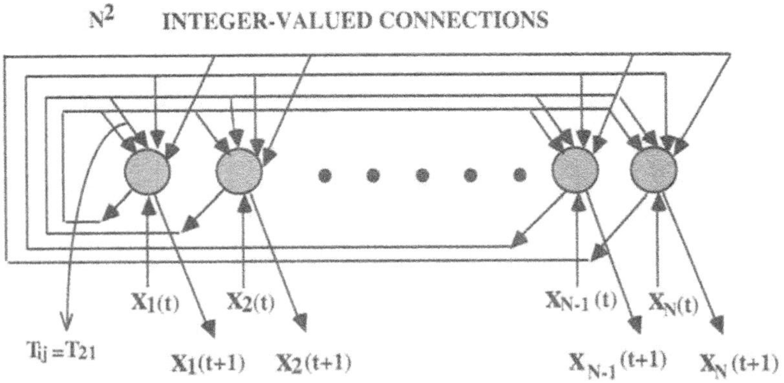

Figure 1 Network structure of Hopfield associative memories in the NZA case.

evolves as

$$x_i(t+1) = F_h\left(\sum_{j=1}^{N} T_{ij} x_j^f(t)\right), \tag{2}$$

where $F_h(\,)$ is the hard-limiting function defined as $F_h(x) = 1$ if $x \geq 0$ and 0 if $x < 0$.

A different network can be obtained by using a bipolar binary representation, $(-1, +1)$, of the state variables. In this case, the connection matrix is obtained as

$$T_{ij} = \begin{cases} \sum_{k=1}^{M} x_i^k x_j^k & \text{(for NZA)} \\ \sum_{k=1}^{M} x_i^k x_j^k - M\delta_{ij} & \text{(for ZA).} \end{cases} \tag{3}$$

Note that in constructing the interconnection matrix, the elements of the pattern vectors in the unipolar representation are converted from (0, 1) to $(-1, +1)$. The interconnection matrices obtained from the bipolar-valued representation are therefore identical to those obtained from the unipolar representation. During network recall, the linear summation of the network inputs is performed exactly the same way as in the unipolar representation. However, in the update rule, the hard-limiting function is replaced with a function that forces the output of a neuron to -1 or $+1$; that is, $F_h(\,)$ is defined as $F_h(x) = 1$ if $x \geq 0$ and -1 if $x < 0$ in the bipolar representation.

Given a network state $x = [x_1, x_2, \ldots, x_N]$, there is an energy function associated with all network types (ZA and NZA), defined as

$$E = -\tfrac{1}{2} x^T T x. \tag{4}$$

This energy function has a lower bound,

$$E = -\tfrac{1}{2} \sum_{i=1}^{N} \sum_{j=1}^{N} T_{ij} x_i x_j \geq -\tfrac{1}{2} \sum_{i=1}^{N} \sum_{j=1}^{N} |T_{ij}| \geq -\tfrac{1}{2} M N^2, \tag{5}$$

where M is the number of vectors stored in the network.

Networks can operate either in a synchronous or asynchronous mode. In the synchronous mode of operation, all neuron states are updated simultaneously in each iteration. On the other hand, only one of the N neurons is free to change state at a given time in asynchronous operation. By this definition, asynchronous operation does not necessarily imply randomness. The neurons, for example, could fire periodically one at a time in sequence.

It is shown in [37] that, with the bipolar representation and NZA interconnection matrix, both synchronous and asynchronous modes of operation result in an energy reduction (i.e., $\Delta E \leq 0$) after each iteration. However, with the bipolar representation and ZA interconnection matrix only the asynchronous mode of operation shows an energy reduction after every iteration. In synchronous operation, in some cases, the energy transition can be positive. This positive energy transition causes the oscillatory behavior occasionally exhibited in the ZA synchronous mode of operation. From [35], it was also shown that networks with nonzero diagonal elements perform better than networks with zero diagonal elements.

B. Quadratic-Order Associative Memories

Essentially, quadratic associative memories come from the extension of binary correlation in Hopfield associative memories to quadratic, or three-neuron, interactions. Let $x^\kappa = [x_1^\kappa, x_2^\kappa, \ldots, x_N^\kappa]$, $1 \le \kappa \le M$, be M binary vectors stored in a quadratic network consisting of N neurons, with each $x_i^\kappa = +1$ or -1. The interconnection matrix, also called a tensor, $T = [T_{ijk}]$, is obtained as

$$T_{ijk} = \sum_{\kappa=1}^{M} x_i^\kappa x_j^\kappa x_k^\kappa \tag{6}$$

for nonzero autoconnection (NZA) networks. In zero autoconnection (ZA) networks, the diagonal terms, T_{ijk} with $i = j$ or $i = k$ or $j = k$, are set to zero. Assume that, during network recall, a vector $x^f(t) = [x_1^f(t), x_2^f(t), \ldots, x_N^f(t)]$ is applied in the network input. A specific neuron i changes its state according to

$$x_i(t+1) = F_h\left(\sum_{j=1}^{N}\sum_{k=1}^{N} T_{ijk} x_j^f(t) x_k^f(t)\right). \tag{7}$$

As in linear-type associative memories, the updating of neurons can be done either synchronously or asynchronously. The asynchronized dynamic converges if the correlation tensor has diagonal term values of zero, that is, we have a ZA network [38]. With quadratic correlations, networks with diagonal terms, that is, NZA networks, have a worse performance than networks without diagonal terms, that is, ZA networks. This result can be illustrated either through simulations or numerical estimations. This is different from the linear case where NZA networks have a better performance than ZA networks. In the rest of this chapter, our analysis for quadratic associative memories will be based on networks with zero autoconnections.

III. NETWORK ANALYSIS USING A SIGNAL-TO-NOISE RATIO CONCEPT

A general associative memory is capable of retrieving an entire memory item on the basis of sufficient partial information. In the bipolar representation, when a vector $x = [x_1, x_2, \ldots, x_N]$, with each $x_i = +1$ or -1, is applied to a first-order

Hopfield-type associative memory (HAM), the input to neuron i is obtained as $\sum T_{ij}x_j$. This term can be separated into signal and noise terms, represented as S and $\mathcal{N}$. If $x_i^{q'}$ denotes the result we would like to obtain from neuron i, this neuron gives an incorrect recall if $S + \mathcal{N} > 0$ when $x_i^{q'} < 0$ and $S + \mathcal{N} < 0$ when $x_i^{q'} > 0$. The signal term is a term which pulls the network state toward the expected result; hence, it would be positive if $x_i^{q'} > 0$ and negative if $x_i^{q'} < 0$. Therefore, the signal term can be represented as $S = |S|x_i^{q'}$, where $|S|$ is the magnitude of the signal. Following this discussion, the probability of a neuron being in an incorrect state after updating is

$$\begin{aligned} P_{\text{inc}} &= P(S+\mathcal{N} > 0 \& x_i^{q'} < 0) + P(S+\mathcal{N} < 0 \& x_i^{q'} > 0) \\ &= P((|S|x_i^{q'} + \mathcal{N})x_i^{q'} < 0) \\ &= P\left(\left|\frac{S}{\mathcal{N}}\right| < -x_i^{q'} \& \mathcal{N} > 0\right) + P\left(\left|\frac{S}{\mathcal{N}}\right| < x_i^{q'} \& \mathcal{N} < 0\right) \\ &= P\left(0 < \left|\frac{S}{\mathcal{N}}\right| < 1 \& \mathcal{N} > 0 \middle| x_i^{q'} = -1\right) P\left(x_i^{q'} = -1\right) \\ &\quad + P\left(0 < \left|\frac{S}{\mathcal{N}}\right| < 1 \& \mathcal{N} < 0 \middle| x_i^{q'} = 1\right) P\left(x_i^{q'} = 1\right). \end{aligned} \tag{8}$$

In associative memories, noise originates from the interference of the input vector with stored vectors other than the target vector. Hence $\mathcal{N}$ and $x_i^{q'}$ are independent and P_{inc} can be written as

$$\begin{aligned} P_{\text{inc}} &= P\left(0 < \left|\frac{S}{\mathcal{N}}\right| < 1 \& \mathcal{N} > 0\right) P\left(x_i^{q'} = -1\right) \\ &\quad + P\left(0 < \left|\frac{S}{\mathcal{N}}\right| < 1 \& \mathcal{N} < 0\right) P\left(x_i^{q'} = 1\right). \end{aligned} \tag{9}$$

Consider that each bit in the stored vectors is sampled from a Bernoulli distribution with probability 0.5 of being either 1 or -1. The probability of incorrect recall can be further simplified as

$$\begin{aligned} P_{\text{inc}} &= \frac{1}{2}\left(P\left(0 < \left|\frac{S}{\mathcal{N}}\right| < 1 \& \mathcal{N} > 0\right) + P\left(0 < \left|\frac{S}{\mathcal{N}}\right| < 1 \& \mathcal{N} < 0\right)\right) \\ &= \frac{1}{2} P\left(0 < \left|\frac{S}{\mathcal{N}}\right| < 1\right). \end{aligned} \tag{10}$$

Note that we have assumed that the signal magnitude and noise are independent of the to-be-recalled pattern component $x_i^{q'}$. In some cases when either the signal magnitude, $|S|$, or the noise term, $\mathcal{N}$, is correlated with $x_i^{q'}$, Eq. (8), instead of (10), should be used for estimating the probability of incorrect recall. If the vectors stored in the network have nonsymmetric patterns, that is, $p(x_i^{q'} = 1) \neq p(x_i^{q'} = -1)$, Eq. (9) should be used even when both the signal magnitude and noise are independent of $x_i^{q'}$.

In the usual case where the noise, $\mathcal{N}$, is normally distributed with mean 0 and variance σ^2, we can use a transformation of variables to show that the probability distribution function (pdf) of $z = |S/\mathcal{N}|$ is given by

$$g(z) = \frac{2|S|}{\sqrt{2\pi}\, z^2 \sigma} \exp\left(-\frac{S^2}{2z^2\sigma^2}\right). \tag{11}$$

Using integration by parts and following some mathematical manipulations, it can be shown that

$$\begin{aligned} P(0 < z < 1) &= \int_0^1 \frac{2|S|}{\sqrt{2\pi}\, z^2 \sigma} \exp\left(-\frac{S^2}{2z^2\sigma^2}\right) dz \\ &= 2\phi\left(\left|\frac{S}{\sigma}\right|\right) \\ &= 2\phi(C), \end{aligned} \tag{12}$$

where $\phi(\,)$, the standard error function, is represented as

$$\phi(x) = \frac{1}{\sqrt{2\pi}} \int_x^\infty e^{-t^2/2}\, dt. \tag{13}$$

The ratio of signal to the standard deviation of noise, $C = |S/\sigma|$, was defined by Wang *et al.* for characterizing a Hopfield neural network [6]. A similar analysis concept can be applied to quadratic-order neural networks, except that correlation terms resulting from the high-order association have to be rearranged.

IV. RELIABILITY EFFECTS IN NETWORK IMPLEMENTATIONS

Optoelectronics and VLSI are two major techniques proposed for implementing a neural network. In optical implementations, a hologram or a spatial light modulator, with optical or electronic addressing of cells, is used to implement the interconnection weights (also called synaptic weights). For VLSI implementations, the network synaptic weights are implemented with either analog or digital circuits. In analog circuits, synapses consist of resistors or field effect transistors between neurons [22]. The analog circuits can realize compact high-speed network operations, but they cannot achieve high accuracy and large synaptic weight values. In digital circuits, registers are used to store the synaptic weights [23]. The registers offer greater flexibility and better accuracy than analog circuits, but they suffer spatial inefficiency.

Regardless of the technique used for implementation, the interconnections, which make up the majority of the circuit, tend to be laid out in a regular matrix form. The amount of interconnections in a practical network is huge. Defects in the interconnections are usually unavoidable; they may come from wafer contamination, incorrect process control, and the finite lifetimes of components. Therefore, evaluation of the reliability properties of a neural network relative to the interconnection faults during the design process is one of the essential issues in network implementations. Based on this concern, the Oregon Graduate Center developed a simulator to evaluate the effects of manufacturing faults [39]. This simulator compares the faulted network to an unfaulted network and design trade-offs can be studied.

The purpose of an interconnection is to connect an input signal to its receiving neuron. Damage to the interconnection could result in an open circuit, a short circuit, or drift of the interconnection from its original value. The effects of open- and short-circuit interconnections on linear- and quadratic-order HAMs will be discussed in the following subsections.

A. Open-Circuit Effects

1. Open-Circuited Linear-Order Associative Memories

Open-circuited interconnections block input signals from flowing into the receiving lead of the neurons. From a mathematical point of view, this is the same as having an interconnection value of zero. In the analysis it is assumed that p fractions of interconnections are disconnected and the disconnected interconnections are evenly distributed among the network. Let A contain the indexes of the failed interconnections to neuron i; that is, $A = \{j|T_{ij}$ is open-circuited$\}$. Assume that the network to be studied is a linear-order NZA network which holds M bipolar binary vectors $x^k = [x_1^k, x_2^k, \dots, x_N^k]$, $1 \le k \le M$, each with $x_i^k = +1$ or -1. When a probe vector $x^f(t)$ is applied to the network input, according to Eqs. (2) and (3), the state of neuron i evolves as

$$\begin{aligned} x_i(t+1) &= F_h\left(\sum_{\substack{j=1\\ j\notin A}}^{N}\sum_{k=1}^{M} x_i^k x_j^k x_j^f(t)\right) \\ &= F_h\left(x_i^{q'}\sum_{\substack{j=1\\ j\notin A}}^{N} x_j^{q'} x_j^f(t) + \sum_{\substack{j=1\\ j\notin A}}^{N}\sum_{\substack{k=1\\ k\neq q'}}^{M} x_i^k x_j^k x_j^f(t)\right). \end{aligned} \tag{14}$$

If the self-interconnection T_{ii} is not failed, that is, $i \notin A$, the second term of the equation can be further decomposed into two terms: one coming from $j = i$ and the other containing other subitems where $j \neq i$. In this situation, the evolution of neuron i can be written as

$$
\begin{aligned}
x_i(t+1) &= F_h\left(x_i^{q'} \sum_{\substack{j=1 \\ j \notin A}}^{N} x_j^{q'} x_j^f(t) + \sum_{\substack{k=1 \\ k \neq q'}}^{M} (x_i^k)^2 x_i^f(t) + \sum_{\substack{j=1 \\ j \notin A \cup \{i\}}}^{N} \sum_{\substack{k=1 \\ k \neq q'}}^{M} x_i^k x_j^k x_j^f(t)\right) \\
&= F_h\left(x_i^{q'} \sum_{\substack{j=1 \\ j \notin A}}^{N} x_j^{q'} x_j^f(t) + (M-1) x_i^f(t) + \sum_{\substack{j=1 \\ j \notin A \cup \{i\}}}^{N} \sum_{\substack{k=1 \\ k \neq q'}}^{M} x_i^k x_j^k x_j^f(t)\right).
\end{aligned}
\tag{15}
$$

Looking at Eq. (15), $x_i^{q'}$ is the result we would like to obtain from neuron i; hence, $x_i^{q'} \sum x_j^{q'} x_j^f(t)$ can be interpreted as a signal term which helps to retrieve the expected result from the network. On the other hand, the third term comes from the interferences of different patterns; hence, it is considered as "cross-talk noise." Given that each element of the stored patterns is randomly sampled from numbers $+1$ and -1, each x_i^k can be modeled as a Bernoulli distribution of probability equal to 0.5. This results in each item within the summation of the third term being independent and identically distributed. The central limit theorem states:

CENTRAL LIMIT THEOREM. *Let $\{Z_i, i = 1, \ldots, n\}$ be a sequence of mutually independent random variables having an identical distribution with mean equal to μ and variance equal to σ^2. Then their summation $Y = Z_1 + Z_2 + \cdots + Z_n$ approaches a Gaussian distribution, as n approaches infinity. This Gaussian distribution has mean μ and variance $n\sigma^2$.*

According to the central limit theorem, whereas the number of items in the summation is large, the third term within the bracket of Eq. (15) can be approximated as a zero-mean Gaussian distribution with variance equal to $(N - pN - 1)(M - 1)$.

Now, let us look at the first two terms. The $\sum x_j^{q'} x_j^f(t)$ in the first term, $x_i^{q'} \sum x_j^{q'} x_j^f(t)$, can be viewed as the inner product of the stored pattern $x^{q'}$ and the probe vector $x^f(t)$. Hence it has a constant value. Assume that the probe vector is exactly the stored vector and that the failed interconnections are evenly distributed. Then this constant value can be estimated as $N - pN$. Based on this assumption, we could also see that the second term contributes a signal $(M-1)x_i^{q'}$ to the network recall, causing the total signal value to equal $(N - pN + M - 1)x_i^{q'}$.

In the previous discussion, we assumed that the self-interconnection T_{ii} is not damaged, that is, $i \notin A$. On the other hand, if the self-interconnection T_{ii} is open-circuited, that is, $i \in A$, the second term in Eq. (15) would not exist. In this case the signal value becomes $(N - pN)x_i^{q'}$ and the variance becomes

$(N - pN)(M - 1)$. Previously, we assumed that each of the interconnections could be failed with the probability p. This also applies to T_{ii}. By summing the two conditions from a probability point of view, we have the averaged ratio of signal to the standard deviation of noise:

$$C = \frac{p(N - pN)}{\sqrt{(N - pN)(M - 1)}} + \frac{(1 - p)(N - pN + M - 1)}{\sqrt{(N - pN - 1)(M - 1)}}. \tag{16}$$

Then, from Eqs. (10) and (12) the probability that neuron i is incorrect is computed as $\phi(C)$. The activity of each neuron is considered to be independent of any other neurons. The probability of the network having correct pattern recall is therefore estimated as

$$P_{\text{dc}} = \left(1 - \phi(C)\right)^N. \tag{17}$$

2. Open-Circuited Quadratic-Order Associative Memories

As mentioned in Section III, the quadratic associative memory results from the extension of two-neuron to three-neuron association. Let $x^\kappa = [x_1^\kappa, x_2^\kappa, \ldots, x_N^\kappa]$, $1 \le \kappa \le M$, be M binary vectors stored in the network, each with $x_i^\kappa = +1$ or -1. When a probe vector $x^f(t) = [x_1^f(t), x_2^f(t), \ldots, x_N^f(t)]$ is applied to the input, the network evolves as in Eq. (7). Consider that part of the interconnections of the network are failed with open-circuit state. Let A contain the indexes of the open-circuited interconnections; that is, $A = \{(j, k) | T_{ijk}$ is open-circuited$\}$. Taking these failed interconnections into consideration, replacing T_{ijk} in Eq. (7) by Eq. (6), and separating the summation term inside the bracket in Eq. (7) into two terms (one related to the to-be-retrieved pattern and the other containing cross-talk between different patterns), evolution of neuron i can then be rewritten as

$$x_i(t+1) = F_h\left(x_i^{q'} \sum_{\substack{j \ne i \\ (j,k) \notin A}}^{N} \sum_{\substack{k \ne i \\ k \ne j}}^{N} x_j^{q'} x_k^{q'} x_j^f(t) x_k^f(t) + \sum_{\kappa \ne q'}^{M} \sum_{\substack{j \ne i \\ (j,k) \notin A}}^{N} \sum_{\substack{k \ne i \\ k \ne j}}^{N} x_i^\kappa x_j^\kappa x_k^\kappa x_j^f(t) x_k^f(t)\right). \tag{18}$$

Similar to the linear-order network in Eq. (15), the first term in this equation results from the correlation of the probe vector $x^f(t)$ and the to-be-retrieved vector $x^{q'}$. Assuming that the probe vector is exactly the to-be-retrieved vector, that is, $x^{q'} = x^f(t)$, we have the first term approximately equal to $x_i^{q'}(N - 1)(N - 2)(1 - p)$, which is considered to be a signal helping to pull the evolution result of neuron i to $x_i^{q'}$ (the result we would like to obtain from neuron i). On the other hand, the second term in Eq. (18) is the "cross-talk noise" generated from the correlation of various vectors other than $x^{q'}$. Because of the quadratic correlation, items within the noise term are not all independent. This can be observed as follows: switching indices j and k, we obtain the same value for $x_i^\kappa x_j^\kappa x_k^\kappa x_j^f(t) x_k^f(t)$. To rearrange the correlated items, the noise term is further divided into cases $(j,k) \notin A,\ (k,j) \notin A$ and $(j,k) \notin A,\ (k,j) \in A$. Combining the identical items, the noise term can be rewritten as

$$\mathcal{N} = 2\left\{ \sum_{\kappa \neq q'}^{M} \sum_{\substack{j \neq i \\ (j,k)\notin A \& (k,j)\notin A}}^{N} \sum_{\substack{k \neq i \\ k=j+1}}^{N} x_i^\kappa x_j^\kappa x_k^\kappa x_j^f(t) x_k^f(t) \right\}$$
$$+ \sum_{\kappa \neq q'}^{M} \sum_{\substack{j \neq i \\ (j,k)\notin A \& (k,j)\in A}}^{N} \sum_{\substack{k \neq i \\ k \neq j}}^{N} x_i^\kappa x_j^\kappa x_k^\kappa x_j^f(t) x_k^f(t). \tag{19}$$

After this rearrangement, items within the two summation terms are independent and identically distributed with mean 0 and variance 1. The probability of the occurrence of any given (j,k), such that $(j,k) \notin A$ and $(k,j) \notin A$, is $(1-p)^2$. The total number of pairs, (j,k), $1 \leq j \leq N$, $(j+1) \leq k \leq N$, $j \neq i$, $k \neq j$, $k \neq i$, is $(N-1)(N-2)/2$. As N gets large, the central limit theorem states that $\sum\sum\sum x_i^\kappa x_j^\kappa x_k^\kappa x_j^f(t) x_k^f(t)$ in the first term of Eq. (19) can be approximated as a Gaussian random variable with mean 0 and variance $(M-1)(N-1)(N-2)(1-p)^2/2$. Hence, the first term of Eq. (19), that is, $2\sum\sum\sum x_i^\kappa x_j^\kappa x_k^\kappa x_j^f(t) x_k^f(t)$, is approximately Gaussian distributed with mean 0 and variance $2(M-1)(N-1)(N-2)(1-p)^2$. Similarly, the second term can be approximated as a normal distribution with mean 0 and variance $(M-1)(N-1)(N-2)p(1-p)$. The first term and the second term of Eq. (19) are independent because they result from different index pairs (j,k). Furthermore, they possess the same mean value. Therefore, the resultant summation is approximated as a zero-mean Gaussian distribution with variance equal to

$$\begin{aligned} \sigma_q^2 &= 2(M-1)(N-1)(N-2)(1-p)^2 + (M-1)(N-1)(N-2)p(1-p) \\ &= (M-1)(N-1)(N-2)(2-3p+p^2). \end{aligned}$$

Thus, the ratio of signal to the standard deviation of noise for a quadratic autoassociative memory with disconnected failed interconnections is obtained as

$$C = \frac{(N-1)(N-2)(1-p)}{\sqrt{(M-1)(N-1)(N-2)(2-3p+p^2)}}. \tag{20}$$

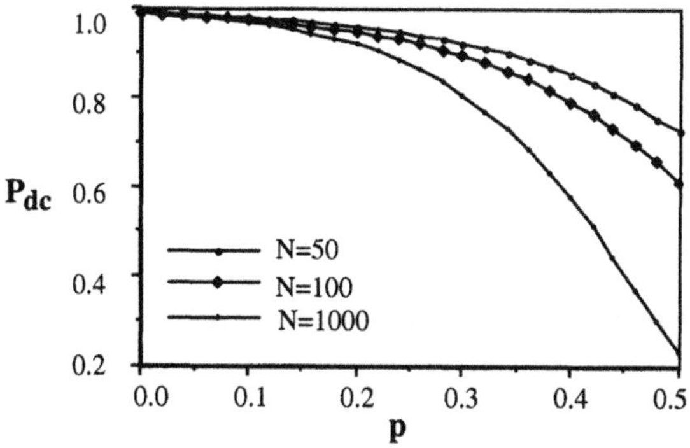

Figure 2 Network performances of liner-order HAMs when p fraction of interconnections are open-circuited. N here is the size of the network. Reprinted with permission from P. C. Chung and T. F. Krile, *IEEE Trans. Neural Networks* 3:969–980, 1992 (© 1992 IEEE).

Based on the results, the probability of correct recall of the network is computed as $(1 - \phi(C))^N$. Figures 2 and 3 show the network performances of linear- and quadratic-order associative memories, respectively, versus the fraction of failed interconnections p. From these two figures, it is also clear that when p is small, the effect of open-circuit interconnections on network performance is almost negligible. As a consequence, a neural network has been claimed to possess the ca-

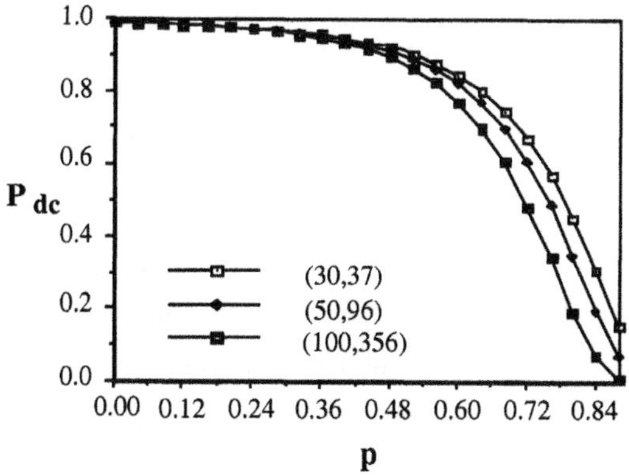

Figure 3 Network performances of quadratic-order HAMs when p fraction of interconnections are open-circuited. The numbers inside the parentheses represent the network size and the number of patterns stored. Reprinted with permission from P. C. Chung and T. F. Krile, *IEEE Trans. Neural Networks* 6:357–367, 1995 (© 1995 IEEE).

pability of fault tolerance. However, as the fraction of open-circuited interconnections increases, network performance decreases dramatically. Then reliability becomes an important issue to physical implementations.

B. SHORT-CIRCUIT EFFECTS

1. Short-Circuited Linear-Order Associative Memories

In circuit theory, a short circuit results in tremendously large signal even if its input signal is small. This phenomenon is similar to having a tremendously large interconnection weight in the network. To mimic this situation, the short-circuited interconnection weights are assumed to have a large magnitude value of G. Interconnections of networks can be classified as excitatory or inhibitory weights. The excitatory weights have positive values whereas inhibitory weights have negative values. An excitatory short-circuited interconnection results in a large signal added to its receiving neuron whereas an inhibitory short-circuited interconnection causes a signal to flow away from the neuron. To realize this phenomenon, the short-circuited interconnections are assumed to have the value of GS_{ij}, with $G > 0$ and $S_{ij} = \operatorname{sgn}(T_{ij})$, where sgn( ) is defined as $\operatorname{sgn}(x) = 1$ if $x > 0$, $\operatorname{sgn}(x) = 0$ if $x = 0$, and $\operatorname{sgn}(x) = -1$ if $x < 0$. Then the state of neuron i evolves as

$$x_i(t+1) = F_h\left(\sum_{\substack{j=1 \\ j \notin A}}^{N} \sum_{k=1}^{M} x_i^k x_j^k x_j^f(t) + \sum_{j \in A} GS_{ij} x_j^f(t)\right). \tag{21}$$

The first term of this equation is the same as the resultant total input of neuron i in the open-circuited network in Eq. (14), whereas the second term results from the short-circuited interconnections. By expanding T_{ij}, the S_{ij} here is obtained as $S_{ij} = \operatorname{sgn}(x_i^1 x_j^1 + x_i^2 x_j^2 + \cdots + x_j^{q'} + \cdots + x_i^M x_j^M)$. For $i \neq j$, each $x_i^k x_j^k$ is a random variable with $P(x_i^k x_j^k = 1) = 0.5$ and $P(x_i^k x_j^k = -1) = 0.5$. Consider the situation in which the probe vector is the same as the to-be-retrieved pattern; that is, $x^f(t) = x^{q'}$. Further assume that the self-interconnection weight is not failed, that is, $i \notin A$. By computing the conditional probability distribution of S_{ij} given the value of $x_j^{q'}$, and applying the Bayes rule, the probability distribution function of $S_{ij} x_j^f(t)$, which is also equal to $S_{ij} x_j^{q'}$ under this assumption, can be obtained. Let

$$\mu_s = \left(\tfrac{1}{2}\right)^{M-1} C_{[(M-1)/2]}^{M-1}. \tag{22}$$

The mean of this distribution is obtained as $\mu_s x_i^{q'}$ and the variance is $1-(\mu_s)^2$. For different j, all the $S_{ij} x_j^f(t)$s are independent and they all have identical distribu-

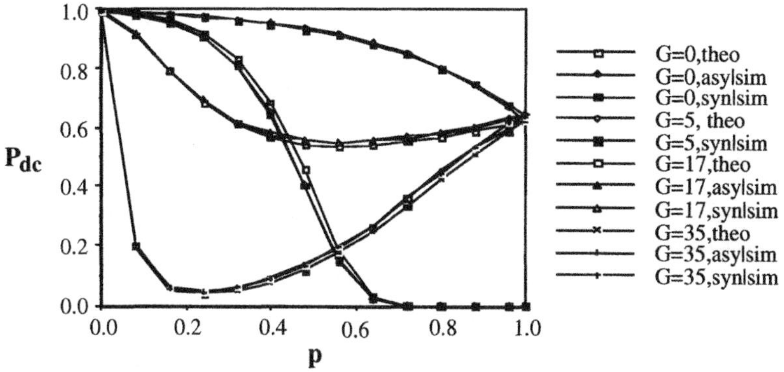

Figure 4 Performances of linear-order networks with short-circuited interconnections. Reprinted with permission from P. C. Chung and T. F. Krile, *IEEE Trans. Neural Networks* 3:969–980, 1992 (© 1992 IEEE).

tion. Hence their summation term can be approximated as a Gaussian distribution with mean equal to $x_i^{q'} \mu_s GNp$ and variance equal to $G^2 Np(1-(\mu_s)^2)$. From the analysis in the previous section, the first term is also approximated by a normal distribution. The items in the first summation term of Eq. (21) are independent of the items in the second summation term. Hence, neuron evolution of the network can be viewed as adding up the two independent normal distributions obtained in this section and the previous section, respectively. Figure 4 shows one typical result of network performances with $(N, M) = (500, 35)$ when various fractions of short-circuited interconnections are used.

2. Short-Circuited Quadratic-Order Associative Memories

For analysis of the short-circuit effect on quadratic associative memories, the failed interconnections are assumed to have a value of GS_{ijk}, with $G > 0$ and $S_{ijk} = \mathrm{sgn}(T_{ijk})$. Let A contain the index pairs of the failed interconnections to the input leads of neuron i; that is, $A = \{(j,k) | T_{ijk} \text{ is short-circuited}\}$. Then, evolution of neuron i of a quadratic associative memory of N neurons and M patterns stored is written as

$$x_i(t+1) = F_h\left\{ \sum_{\substack{j\neq i \\ (j,k)\notin A}}^{N} \sum_{\substack{k\neq i \\ k\neq j}}^{N} \sum_{\kappa=1}^{M} x_i^\kappa x_j^\kappa x_k^\kappa x_j^f(t) x_k^f(t) \right. \\ \left. + G \sum_{\substack{j\neq i \\ (j,k)\in A}}^{N} \sum_{\substack{k\neq i \\ k\neq j}}^{N} S_{ijk} x_j^f(t) x_k^f(t) \right\}. \tag{23}$$

As mentioned earlier, the importance of analyzing a quadratic associative memory is to rearrange items into independent terms. This decomposition can be analyzed as follows. For an index pair (j, k), switching j and k, $x_j^f(t)x_k^f(t)$ has the same value. These identical terms have to be combined. Cases for this combination can be classified as follows:

1. $(j, k) \notin A$, $(k, j) \notin A$; both interconnections T_{ijk} and T_{ikj} are failed.
2. $(j, k) \in A$, $(k, j) \notin A$; either T_{ijk} or T_{ikj} is failed.
3. $(j, k) \in A$, $(k, j) \in A$; both interconnections T_{ijk} and T_{ikj} are good.

Then, separating the first term of Eq. (23) into signal and cross-talk noise, and combining the identical items in the cross-talk noise based on the previous three cases, network evolution of neuron i can be written as

$$\begin{aligned} x_i(t+1) = F_h\Bigg\{ & x_i^{q'} \sum_{\substack{j\neq i \\ (j,k)\notin A}}^{N} \sum_{\substack{k\neq i \\ k\neq j}}^{N} x_j^{q'} x_k^{q'} x_j^f(t) x_k^f(t) \\ & + 2\sum_{\kappa\neq q'}^{M} \sum_{\substack{j\neq i \\ (j,k)\notin A \& (k,j)\notin A}}^{N} \sum_{\substack{k\neq i \\ k=j+1}}^{N} x_i^{\kappa} x_j^{\kappa} x_k^{\kappa} x_j^f(t) x_k^f(t) \\ & + 2G \sum_{\substack{j\neq i \\ (j,k)\in A \& (k,j)\in A}}^{N} \sum_{\substack{k\neq i \\ k=j+1}}^{N} S_{ijk} x_j^f(t) x_k^f(t) \\ & + \sum_{\substack{j\neq i \\ (j,k)\notin A \& (k,j)\in A}}^{N} \sum_{\substack{k\neq i \\ k\neq j}}^{N} \Bigg(\Bigg(\sum_{\kappa\neq q'}^{M} x_i^{\kappa} x_j^{\kappa} x_k^{\kappa}\Bigg) \\ & + G S_{ikj}\Bigg) x_j^f(t) x_k^f(t) \Bigg\}. \end{aligned} \tag{24}$$

After this rearrangement, each term of the preceding equation is independent of other terms. Furthermore, all the items within a summation term are independently and identically distributed (i.i.d.). If the numbers of items within the summation terms are significantly large, these summation terms can be approximated as independent Gaussian distributions. From the result, network probability of correct recall can be obtained.

In the foregoing analysis, it is assumed that the short-circuited interconnections are of value G. The value of G indicates the signal strength that a short-circuit interconnection causes to the network. The larger the value of G, the stronger the signal which damaged interconnections would convey to the network. Performances of the network where $(N, M) = (42, 69)$, when various values of G

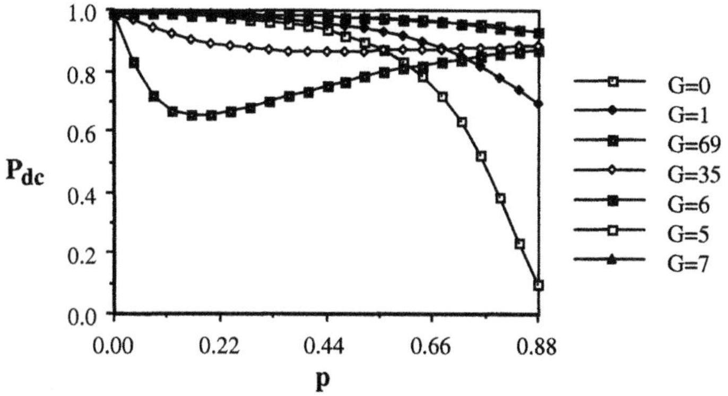

Figure 5 Network performance of quadratic networks when various Gs are used. Reprinted with permission from P. C. Chung and T. F. Krile, *IEEE Trans. Neural Networks* 6:357–367, 1995 (© 1995 IEEE).

are used, are illustrated in Fig. 5. From the curves, it is easy to see that some relatively large values of G affect network performance only mildly, leaving the network performance almost unchanged, disregarding the percentage of failed interconnections. This also implies that for each network there exist some G_{opt} which affect the network performance the least as the percentage of failed interconnections increases. Assigning the failed interconnection a value that has the same sign as the original interconnection is the same as changing it to the absolute value of its original interconnection. Therefore it is expected that the G_{opt} is equal to $E\{|T_{ijk}|\}$. From the curves, it is also observed that, actually, there exists a range of values of G which would give the network competitively high reliability. Table I shows such values of G compared to G_{opt} estimated according to

Table I

Comparison of the Best Values of G Obtained from Trial and Error with Values from the Expectation Operator[a]

	(N, M)			
G_{opt}	(30, 37)	(42, 69)	(50, 95)	(60, 135)
Trial and error	3–6	4–8	5–9	5–11
$E\{\vert T_{ijk}\vert\}$	4.48	6.65	7.80	9.28

[a] Reprinted with permission from P. C. Chung and T. F. Krile, *IEEE Trans. Neural Networks* 6:357–367, 1995 (© 1995 IEEE).

$E\{|T_{ijk}|\}$. It was found that the G_{opt}s do fall within the range of those optimal values obtained from trial and error simulations. From the results, it is also expected that if a test-and-replace mechanism, which will replace the failed interconnections by the value of G_{opt}, can be installed within the hardware realizations, the fault-tolerance capability of the network will be achieved.

V. COMPARISON OF LINEAR AND QUADRATIC NETWORKS

Higher-order associative memories are proposed to increase network storage capacity. To have a probability of correct recall approximately 0.99, a Hopfield linear-order associative memory, with $N = 42$, can store only 6 vectors, but a quadratic associative memory with the same number of neurons can store up to 69 vectors. The storage capacities of the quadratic-order and the first-order associative memories are discussed in [4, 15–17].

Despite the fact that a quadratic associative memory has a much higher storage capacity, its fault-tolerance capability is much worse than that of a linear network. The increase in the number of error bits in the probe vectors decreases the probability of network correct recall considerably. For $N = 42$, a quadratic associative memory can store 69 vectors and still have $P_{\text{dc}} = 0.99$. However, if there are three error bits in the applied input vectors, that is, the probe vectors, the probability of correct recall is only 0.7834. If there are six error bits in the probe vectors, the P_{dc} is only 0.1646. Hence, as mentioned in the results of Chung and Krile [29], to allow a certain range of attraction radius in a quadratic-order associative memory, we need to decrease the network storage to have the same P_{dc}; otherwise, the probability of correct recall will decrease dramatically.

In this chapter, one of our major concerns is the reliability issue, or the fault-tolerance capability with interconnection failures, of both types of networks. Let a parameter with superscript Q represent a parameter of quadratic networks and let superscript L represent a parameter of linear networks. The reliability of a quadratic associative memory can be compared with that of a linear associative memory from various aspects in the following ways:

1. Assume both networks have the same network size, that is, $N^Q = N^L$, and start from the same P_{dc}, that is, $P^Q_{\text{dc}} = P^L_{\text{dc}}$, when $p = 0$. A comparison of the quadratic and linear types of networks is shown in Fig. 6, based on these conditions. Results indicate that the quadratic networks have higher reliability under interconnection failure.
2. Assume both networks store the same number of vectors, that is, $M^Q = M^L$, and start from the same P_{dc}, that is, $P^Q_{\text{dc}} = P^L_{\text{dc}}$, when $p = 0$. A comparison of the quadratic and the linear types of networks, based on

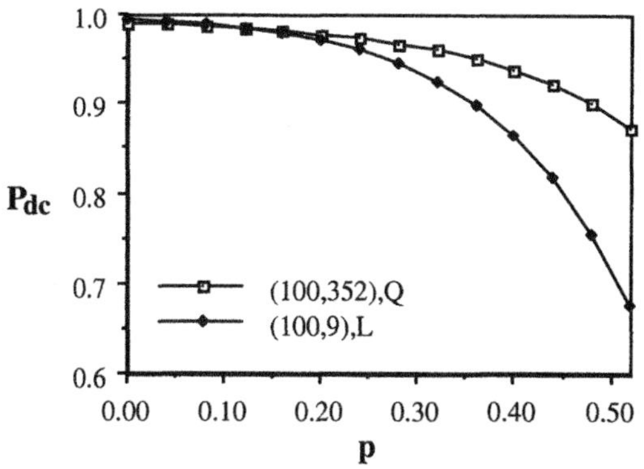

Figure 6 Comparison of linear and quadratic associative memories with the same number of neurons N. Reprinted with permission from P. C. Chung and T. F. Krile, *IEEE Trans. Neural Networks* 3:357–367, 1995 (© 1995 IEEE).

these conditions, is shown in Fig. 7. Results indicate that the quadratic networks have a higher reliability.

3. Assume both networks have the same number of interconnections, that is, $(N^Q)^3 = (N^L)^2$, and start from the same P_{dc}, that is, $P_{\mathrm{dc}}^Q = P_{\mathrm{dc}}^L$, when $p = 0$. A comparison of the quadratic and the linear types of networks, based on these conditions, is shown in Fig. 8. Results indicate that quadratic networks have a higher reliability.

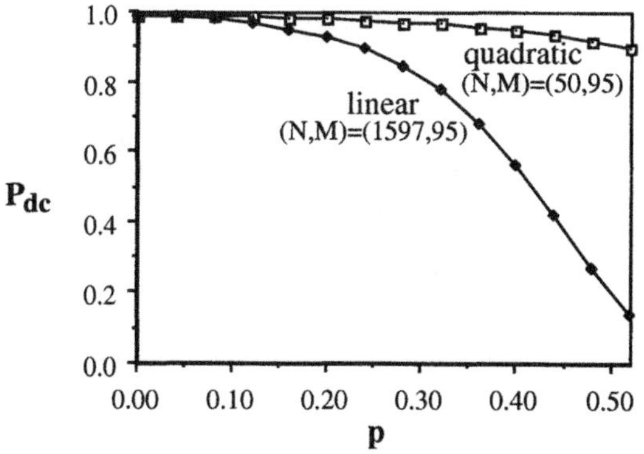

Figure 7 Comparison of linear and quadratic associative memories with the same number of stored vectors M. Reprinted with permission from P. C. Chung and T. F. Krile, *IEEE Trans. Neural Networks* 6:357–367, 1995 (© 1995 IEEE).

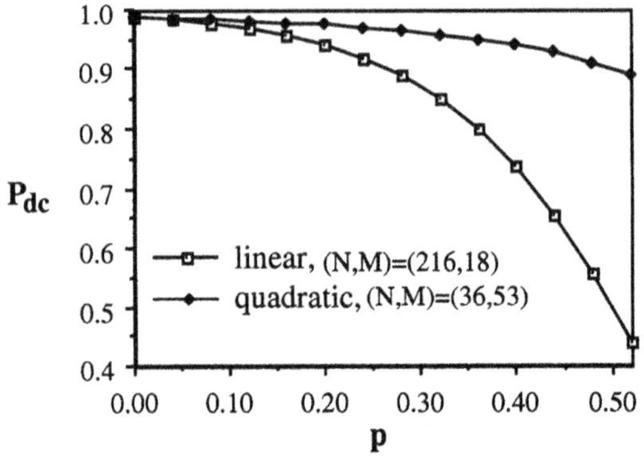

Figure 8 Comparison of linear and quadratic associative memories with the same number of interconnections. Reprinted with permission from P. C. Chung and T. F. Krile, *IEEE Trans. Neural Networks* 6:357–367, 1995 (© 1995 IEEE).

4. Assume both networks have the same information capacity, defined as the number of bits stored in a network, that is, $N^Q M^Q = N^L M^L$, and start from the same P_{dc}, that is, $P_{\text{dc}}^Q = P_{\text{dc}}^L$, when $p = 0$. Figure 9 shows that quadratic associative memories have higher reliability than linear associative memories.

Hence, we conclude that a quadratic associative memory not only has higher storage capacity, but also demonstrates higher robustness under interconnection

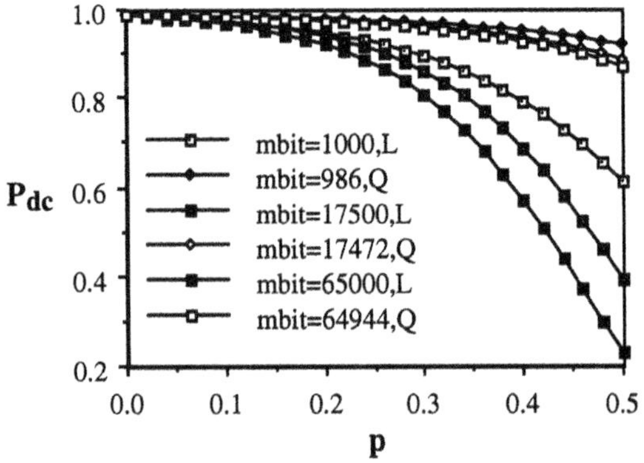

Figure 9 Comparison of linear and quadratic associative memories with the same capacity in terms of the number of bits. Reprinted with permission from P. C. Chung and T. F. Krile, *IEEE Trans. Neural Networks* 6:357–367, 1995 (© 1995 IEEE).

failure. However, the fault-tolerance capability in its input (or the capability of error correction or generalization of the input signal) is poorer than that of linear associative memory.

VI. QUANTIZATION OF SYNAPTIC INTERCONNECTIONS

Another possible problem in the VLSI implementation of Hebbian-type associative memories arises from the tremendous amount of interconnections. In associative memories, the number of interconnections increases with $O(N^2)$, where N is the size of the network. Furthermore, the range of possible interconnection values increases linearly as the number of stored patterns increases. In practical applications, both the size of the network and the number of stored patterns are very large. Implementation of the large amount of interconnections with a large range of interconnection values requires significantly large chip area. This drawback hinders the application of Hebbian-type associative memories in real situations. The problem associated with the increased amount of interconnections and the unlimited range of the interconnection values also occurs in other types of neural networks [39]. To resolve the problem, a quantization technique to reduce the number of interconnection levels and the number of interconnections in the implementation is required. Techniques of quantization also have been applied significantly in the digital implementations of an analog signal. The larger the number of quantization levels used, the higher the accuracy of the results. However, a large number of quantization levels also implies that a large chip area is required for representing a number, causing higher implementation complexity. Therefore a trade-off between network performance and complexity has to be carefully balanced.

From a network point of view, quantization can be achieved either by clipping the interconnections into the value of -1 or $+1$, or by reducing the number of quantization levels. In the following discusion, network performance—in terms of probability of direct convergence of correct recall—is analyzed when a quantization technique is used. The analysis of network performance includes two situations:

1. Interconnections beyond the range $[-G, +G]$ are clipped to -1 and $+1$ according to the sign of their original values, whereas interconnections of their values within the range $[-G, +G]$ are set to zero. A zero-valued interconnection does not have to be implemented, because it would not carry any signal to its receiving node. Thus, setting interconnections to zero has the same effect as removing these interconnections.

2. The interconnections between the range of $[-B, -G]$ or $[G, B]$ retain their original values: greater than B set to B; smaller than $-B$ set to $-B$; between $[-G, G]$ set to zero. The quantization in case 1, where the interconnections are clipped to a value of either -1 or $+1$, is refered to as three-level quantization.

A. Three-Level Quantization

For the three-level quantization, interconnections that have values within $(-G, +G)$ are removed, whereas others are changed to the value of $S_{ij} = \mathrm{sgn}(T_{ij})$, where sgn( ) is defined as $\mathrm{sgn}(x) = 1$ if $x > G$, $\mathrm{sgn}(x) = -1$ if $x < G$, and $\mathrm{sgn}(x) = 0$ otherwise. Then the evolution of neuron i is conducted as

$$x_i(t+1) = F_h\left\{\sum_{j=1}^{N} S_{ij} x_j^f(t)\right\} = F_h\left\{x_i^f(t) + \sum_{j\neq i} S_{ij} x_j^f(t)\right\}. \tag{25}$$

The S_{ij} can be rewritten as

$$S_{ij} = \mathrm{sgn}\left(x_i^1 x_j^1 + x_i^2 x_j^2 + \cdots + x_j^{q'} + \cdots + x_i^M x_j^M\right). \tag{26}$$

Each term of $x_i^k x_j^k$, $1 \le k \le M$, $k \neq q'$, is a random variable with $P(x_i^k x_j^k = 1) = 0.5$ and $P(x_i^k x_j^k = -1) = 0.5$. Given $x_j^{q'} = 1$, from Eq. (5) there must be at least $(M+G)/2$ terms of $x_i^k x_j^k$ equal to 1 for S_{ij} to be greater than 0. Define $\lceil x \rceil$ as the smallest integer that is greater than or equal to x. The conditional probabilities of S_{ij}, where $j \neq i$, are calculated as

$$\begin{aligned} P(S_{ij} = 1 | x_j^{q'} = 1) &= P(S_{ij} = -1 | x_j^{q'} = -1) \\ &= \left(\tfrac{1}{2}\right)^{M-1} \sum_{x=\lceil (M+G)/2 \rceil - 1}^{M-1} C_x^{M-1}, \end{aligned} \tag{27}$$

$$\begin{aligned} P(S_{ij} = -1 | x_j^{q'} = 1) &= P(S_{ij} = 1 | x_j^{q'} = -1) \\ &= \left(\tfrac{1}{2}\right)^{M-1} \sum_{x=\lceil (M+G)/2 \rceil}^{M-1} C_x^{M-1}, \end{aligned} \tag{28}$$

where $C_a^b = b!/(a!(b-a)!)$. Whereas S_{ij} is related to the stored patterns and $x_j^f(t)$ is one element of the probe vector, they are independent. From the results, the probability density distribution of $S_{ij} x_j^f(t)$ can be obtained based on the equation

$$\begin{aligned} P(\mathcal{S}_{ij}x_j^f = +1) = {} & P\big(\mathcal{S}_{ij} = +1 | x_j^{q'} = +1\big)P(x_j^{q'} = +1 \& x_j^f = +1) \\ & + P\big(\mathcal{S}_{ij} = +1 | x_j^{q'} = -1\big)P(x_j^{q'} = -1 \& x_j^f = +1) \\ & + P\big(\mathcal{S}_{ij} = -1 | x_j^{q'} = +1\big)P(x_j^{q'} = +1 \& x_j^f = -1) \\ & + P\big(\mathcal{S}_{ij} = -1 | x_j^{q'} = -1\big)P(x_j^{q'} = -1 \& x_j^f = -1). \end{aligned} \tag{29}$$

The second item in each term of the preceding equation measures the probabilities that the probe bit $x_j^f(t)$ does or does not match the to-be-recalled bit $x_j^{q'}$. Assume that we already know that there exist b incorrect bits in the probe vector. For a situation that neuron i is a correct bit, the second item in each term can be estimated as

$$P\big(x_j^{q'} = +1 \& x_j^f = +1\big) = P\big(x_j^{q'} = -1 \& x_j^f = -1\big) = \frac{N-1-b}{2(N-1)} \tag{30}$$

and

$$P\big(x_j^{q'} = +1 \& x_j^f = -1\big) = P\big(x_j^{q'} = -1 \& x_j^f = +1\big) = \frac{b}{2(N-1)}. \tag{31}$$

Then the probabilities of $\mathcal{S}_{ij}x_j^f(t)$ can be obtained as

$$\begin{aligned} & P\big(\mathcal{S}_{ij}x_j^f(t) = +1\big) \\ & \quad = \left(\tfrac{1}{2}\right)^{M-1}\left\{\sum_{x=\lceil (M+G)/2\rceil -1}^{M-1} C_x^{M-1} - \frac{b-1}{N-1} C_{\lceil (M+G)/2\rceil -1}^{M-1}\right\}, \end{aligned} \tag{32}$$

$$\begin{aligned} & P\big(\mathcal{S}_{ij}x_j^f(t) = -1\big) \\ & \quad = \left(\tfrac{1}{2}\right)^{M-1}\left\{\sum_{x=\lceil (M+G)/2\rceil}^{M-1} C_x^{M-1} + \frac{b-1}{N-1} C_{\lceil (M+G)/2\rceil -1}^{M-1}\right\}, \end{aligned} \tag{33}$$

and

$$\begin{aligned} & P\big(\mathcal{S}_{ij}x_j^f(t) = 0\big) \\ & \quad = 1 - \left(\tfrac{1}{2}\right)^{M-1}\left\{\sum_{x=\lceil (M+G)/2\rceil -1}^{M-1} C_x^{M-1} + \sum_{x=\lceil (M+G)/2\rceil}^{M-1} C_x^{M-1}\right\}. \end{aligned} \tag{34}$$

Based on these results, the mean and variance can be obtained as

$$\mu_c = E\{S_{ij}x_j^f(t)\} = \left\{1 - \frac{2b}{N-1}\right\}\left(\frac{1}{2}\right)^{M-1} C^{M-1}_{\lceil (M+G)/2\rceil - 1} \tag{35}$$

and

$$\sigma_c^2 = \left(\tfrac{1}{2}\right)^{M-1}\left\{2^* \sum_{x=\lceil (M+G)/2\rceil - 1}^{M-1} C_x^{M-1} + C^{M-1}_{\lceil (M+G)/2\rceil}\right\} - (\mu_c)^2, \tag{36}$$

respectively, if neuron i receives a correct input bit, that is, $x_i^f(t) = x_i^{q'}$, and

$$\mu_i = E\{S_{ij}x_j^f(t)\} = \left\{1 - \frac{2(b-1)}{N-1}\right\}\left(\frac{1}{2}\right)^{M-1} C^{M-1}_{\lceil (M+G)/2\rceil - 1} \tag{37}$$

and

$$\sigma_i^2 = \left(\tfrac{1}{2}\right)^{M-1}\left\{2^* \sum_{x=\lceil (M+G)/2\rceil - 1}^{M-1} C_x^{M-1} + C^{M-1}_{\lceil (M+G)/2\rceil}\right\} - (\mu_i)^2, \tag{38}$$

respectively, if neuron i receives an incorrect probe bit. According to neurostatistical analysis, the probability of direct convergence, denoted as P_{dc}, for the quantized network can be calculated as

$$P_{\text{dc}} = \left(1 - \phi(C_c)\right)^{N-b}\left(1 - \phi(C_i)\right)^{b}. \tag{39}$$

The C_c and C_i here denote the ratio of signal to the standard deviation of noise of correct and incorrect bits, respectively, and are calculated as

$$C_c = \frac{1 + (N-1)\mu_c}{\sqrt{(N-1)\sigma_c^2}} \tag{40}$$

and

$$C_i = \frac{-1 + (N-1)\mu_i}{\sqrt{(N-1)\sigma_i^2}}. \tag{41}$$

Figure 10 illustrates the results of network performance when various cutoff values G are used. When $G = 0$, which is the leftmost point in each curve, the quantization sets the positive interconnections to $+1$ and the negative interconnections to -1. Quantization under this special situation is referred to as binary quantization. On the other hand, for three-level quantization at a certain point of $G = x$, $x > 0$, interconnections which have their values between $[-x, x]$ will be removed, whereas those greater than G are set to $+1$ and those smaller

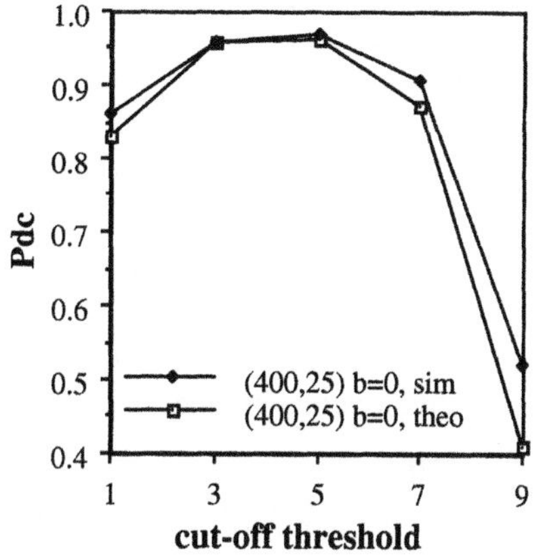

Figure 10 Probabilities of network convergence with three-level quantization. Reprinted with permission from P. C. Chung, C. T. Tsai, and Y. N. Sun, *IEEE Trans. Circuits Systems I Fund. Theory Appl.* 41, 1994 (© 1994 IEEE).

than $-G$ are set to -1. Results of Fig. 10 also reveal that three-level quantization, which removes interconnections of relatively small values, enhances the network performance relative to the binary quantization, which retains such interconnections. Furthermore, there exist certain cutoff values which, when used, only slightly reduce network performance. The optimal cutoff value G_{opt} is estimated by $E\{|T_{ij}|\}$. Table II gives the two values of G_{opt} obtained from simulations and from the expectation operator. It is obvious that as the network size and the number of stored patterns increase, the range of Gs which degrade the network performance only mildly increases. Thus, as the network gets larger, it becomes much easier to select G_{opt}. By removing these relatively small-valued intercon-

Table II

Comparison of the Optimal Cutoff Threshold G_{opt} Obtained from Simulation and the Value of $E\{|T_{ij}|\}$ When Various (N, M)s Are Used[a]

Optimal cutoff	(N, M)						
	(200, 21)	(500, 41)	(1100, 81)	(1700, 121)	(2700, 181)	(3100, 201)	(4100, 261)
$E\{\|T_{ij}\|\}$	3.7	5.1	7.2	8.8	10.7	11.3	12.9
G_{opt}	3	5	7	9	11	11	13

[a] Reprinted with permission from P. C. Chung, C. T. Tsai, and Y. N. Sun, *IEEE Trans. Circuits Systems I Fund. Theory Appl.* 41, 1994 (© 1994 IEEE).

nections within $[-G_{\text{opt}}, G_{\text{opt}}]$, network complexity is reduced. According to Eq. (3), T_{ij} is computed as the summation of independent and identical Bernoulli distributions. If we approximate it by the normal distribution of zero mean and variance M, the expectation of its absolute value is calculated as

$$E\{|T_{ij}|\} = \frac{2}{\sqrt{2\pi M}} \int_0^{\infty} |x| \exp\left(-\frac{x^2}{2M}\right) dx. \tag{42}$$

The equation is obtained as having the value of $\sqrt{2M/\pi}$. Thus the fraction of interconnections which have their values smaller than $E\{|T_{ij}|\}$ is

$$\frac{2}{\sqrt{2\pi M}} \int_0^{\sqrt{2M/\pi}} \exp\left(-\frac{x^2}{2M}\right) dx = \operatorname{erf}\left(\frac{1}{\sqrt{\pi}}\right). \tag{43}$$

Surprisingly, the result is independent of the value of M. Furthermore, the value obtained from Eq. (43) is 0.57 which implies that about 50% of interconnections will be removed in a large three-level quantized network. Furthermore the value of each remaining interconnection is coded as one bit for representing -1 or $+1$, compared to the original requirement that $\log_2(2M)$ bits are necessary for coding each interconnection. Hence the complexity of the network in terms of the total number of bits for implementing interconnections is reduced to only $0.5/(\log_2(2M))$.

For VLSI implementation, HAM weights are implemented with analog or digital circuits. In analog circuits, synapses are realized by resistors or field effect transistors between neurons [22, 31]. In digital circuits, registers are used to store the synaptic weights [23]. Interconnections quantized with binary memory points (bits), that is, the interconnections are restricted to values of $(+1, 0, -1)$, enable a HAM to be implemented more easily. For a dedicated analog circuit, the synapse between a neuron i and a neuron j can be either disconnected when T_{ij} is zero or connected when T_{ij} is nonzero. When the weight $T_{ij} = -1$ or $+1$, the synapse could be connected with (or without) using a sign-reversing switch to implement the weight values of -1 (or $+1$). For a digital circuit, as mentioned, each synaptic register needs only one bit to store weight values in a quantized network, whereas it requires $\log_2(2M)$ bits on the original unquantized network.

B. Three-Level Quantization with Conserved Interconnections

As pointed out in the work of Wang *et al.* [40], interconnections that have relatively small values are more important than those that have significantly small or large values. Thus the improvement of network performance becomes an issue if those more important interconnections are conserved. Network performance

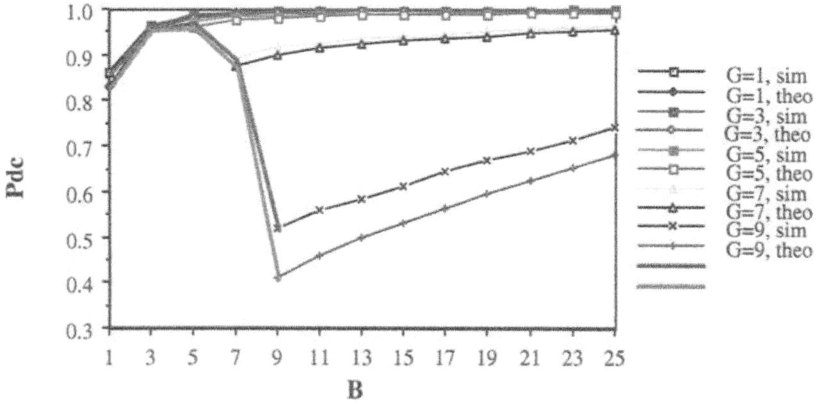

Figure 11 Performances of the network $(N, M) = (400, 25)$ with conserved interconnections under three-level quantization.

under such a quantization condition may be analyzed as such: let $0 < G < B$ and in modeling the quantization policy, set the interconnection values greater than B to B, those smaller than $-B$ to $-B$, and those within interval $[-G, G]$ to zero, whereas other values, which are located within either $[-B, -G]$ or $[G, B]$, remain unchanged. For easier analysis, also let the sets Y and Z be defined as $Y = \{j||T_{ij}| \geq B\}$ and $Z = \{j|G \leq |T_{ij}| < B\}$. Under this assumption, evolution of the network is written as

$$x_i(t+1) = F_h\left\{B^* x_i^f(t) + \sum_{j \neq i} S_{ij} x_j^f(t)\right\}, \tag{44}$$

where S_{ij} is defined as $S_{ij} = B^*\text{sgn}(T_{ij})$ if $j \in Y$, T_{ij} if $j \in Z$, and 0 otherwise. In this case, each $S_{ij}x_j^f(t)$ takes a value within the intervals $[G, B]$ or $[-B, -G]$, or takes a value of 0. Using an analysis method similar to that applied in the foregoing analysis of three-level quantization, equations can then be derived to estimate the network performances when various Bs and Gs are used. Figures 11 and 12 show some typical results of the system. In both of these figures, the left-most point where $G = B = 1$ in the $G = 1$ curve is the case when network interconnections are binary quantized in which the positive interconnections are set to $+1$ and the negative interconnections are set to -1. Following the $G = 1$ curve from $B = 1$ to the right is the same as moving the truncated point B from 1 to its maximal value M. Therefore, network performance improves. On the contrary, following the curve where G is the optimal value G_{opt}, which is equal to 3 or 5 in Figs. 11 and 12, the increase of B from G to M slightly improves network performance. The network approaches its highest level of performance when B

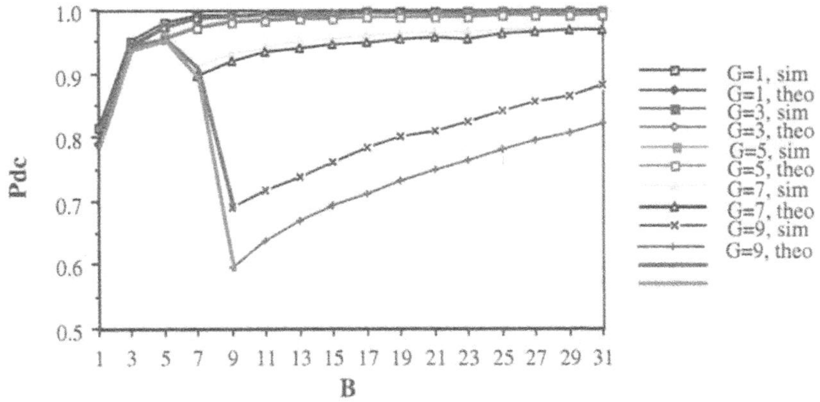

Figure 12 Performances of the network $(N, M) = (500, 31)$ with conserved interconnections under three-level quantization.

increases only slightly. This result also implies that the preserved interconnection range that is necessary to enable the network to return its original level of performance is small, particularly when G already has been chosen to be the optimal value G_{opt}. The bold lines in Figs. 11 and 12, where $G = B$, correspond to the three-level quantization results with various cutoff thresholds G. From the figures, network performances with various G and B combinations can be noticed easily.

VII. CONCLUSIONS

Neural networks are characterized by possessing a large number of simple processing units (neurons) together with a huge amount of necessary interconnections to perform a collective computation. In practical situations, it is commonplace to see large scale networks applied in physical applications. To take the advantage of parallel computation, the networks are realized through VLSI or optical implementation, with the tremendous amount of interconnections implemented on a large network chip or, optically, with a two-dimensional spatial light modulator mask. It was found that as networks grow larger, the required chip size grows significantly and the effects of failed interconnections become more severe. Hence, reducing the required chip area and the fraction of failed interconnections becomes very important in physical implementations of large networks.

Because of the high-order correlations between the neurons, high-order networks are regarded as possessing the potential for high storage capacity and invariance of affine transformation. With the high-order terms, the number of interconnections of the network would be even larger. As mentioned earlier, the high-order networks have similar characteristics to linear models concerning interconnection faults, but their tolerance capabilities are different. Various comparative analyses showed that networks with quadratic association have a higher storage capability and greater robustness to interconnection faults; however, the tolerance for input errors is much smaller. Hence trade-offs between these two networks should be judiciously investigated before implementation.

As the network size grows, the number of interconnections increases quadratically. To reduce the number of interconnections, and hence the complexity of the network, pruning techniques have been suggested in other networks [41]. One approach is to combine network performance and its complexity into a minimized cost function, thereby achieving balance between network performance and complexity. Another approach is to dynamically reduce some relatively unimportant interconnections during the learning procedures, thus reducing the network complexity while maintaining a minimum required level of performance. In this chapter, network complexity was reduced through the quantization technique by clipping the interconnections into -1, 0, and $+1$. With an optimal cutoff threshold G_{opt}, interconnections within $[-G_{\text{opt}}, G_{\text{opt}}]$ are changed to zero, whereas those greater than G_{opt} are set to $+1$ and those smaller than $-G_{\text{opt}}$ are set to -1. These changes actually have the same effect as removing some relatively less correlated and unimportant interconnections.

REFERENCES

[1] J. J. Hopfield and D. W. Tank. Neural computation of decisions in optimization problems. *Biol. Cybernet.* 52:141–152, 1985.

[2] D. W. Tank and J. J. Hopfield. Simple optimization networks: A/D converter and a linear programming circuit. *IEEE Trans. Circuits Systems* CAS-33:533–541, 1986.

[3] D. J. Amit. *Modeling Brain Function: The World of Attractor Neural Networks.* Cambridge Univ. Press, 1989.

[4] S. Amari. Statistical neurodynamics of associative memory. *Neural Networks* 1:63–73, 1988.

[5] C. M. Newman. Memory capacity in neural network models: rigorous lower bounds. *Neural Networks* 1:223–238, 1988.

[6] J. H. Wang, T. F. Krile, and J. F. Walkup. Determination of Hopfield associative memory characteristics using a single parameter. *Neural Networks* 3:319–331, 1990.

[7] R. J. McEliece and E. C. Posner. The capacity of the Hopfield associative memory. *IEEE Trans. Inform. Theory* 33:461–482, 1987.

[8] A. Kuh and B. W. Dickinson. Information capacity of associative memories. *IEEE Trans. Inform. Theory* 35:59–68, 1989.

[9] C. M. Newman. Memory capacity in neural network models: rigorous lower bounds. *Neural Networks* 1:223–238, 1988.

[10] S. S. Venkatesh and D. Psaltis. Linear and logarithmic capacities in associative neural networks. *IEEE Trans. Inform. Theory* 35:558–568, 1989.

[11] D. Psaltis, C. H. Park, and J. Hong. Higher order associative memories and their optical implementations. *Neural Networks* 1:149–163, 1988.

[12] L. Personnaz, I. Guyon, and G. Dreyfus. Higher-order neural networks: information storage without errors. *Europhys. Lett.* 4:863–867, 1987.

[13] F. J. Pineda. Generalization of backpropagation to recurrent and higher order neural networks. *Neural Information Processing Systems*. American Institute of Physics, New York, 1987.

[14] C. L. Giles and T. Maxwell. Learning, invariance, and generalization in high order neural networks. *Appl. Opt.* 26:4972–4978, 1987.

[15] H. H. Chen, Y. C. Lee, G. Z. Sun, and H. Y. Lee. *High Order Correlation Model for Associative Memory*, pp. 86–92. American Institute of Physics, New York, 1986.

[16] H. P. Graf, L. D. Jackel, and W. E. Hubbard. VLSI implementation of a neural network model. *IEEE Computer* 21:41–49, 1988.

[17] M. A. C. Maher and S. P. Deweerth. Implementing neural architectures using analog VLSI circuits. *IEEE Trans. Circuits Systems* 36:643–652, 1989.

[18] M. K. Habib and H. Akel. A digital neuron-type processor and its VLSI design. *IEEE Trans. Circuits Systems* 36:739–746, 1989.

[19] K. A. Boahen and P. O. Pouliquen. A heteroassociative memory using current-mode MOS analog VLSI circuits. *IEEE Trans. Circuits Systems* 36:747–755, 1989.

[20] D. W. Tank and J. J. Hopfield. Simple neural optimization networks: an A/D converter, signal decision circuit, and a linear programming circuit. *IEEE Trans. Circuits Systems* 36:533–541, 1989.

[21] C. Mead. Neuromorphic electronic systems. *IEEE Proc.* 78:1629–1636, 1990.

[22] R. E. Howard, D. B. Schwartz, J. S. Denker, R. W. Epworth, H. P. Graf, W. E. Hubbard, L. D. Jackel, B. L. Straughn, and D. M. Tennant. An associative memory based on an electronic neural network architecture. *IEEE Trans. Electron Devices* 34:1553–1556, 1987.

[23] D. E. Van Den Bout and T. H. Miller. A digital architecture employing stochasticism for the simulation of Hopfield neural nets. *IEEE Trans. Circuits Systems* 36:732–738, 1989.

[24] S. Shams and J. L. Gaudiot. Implementing regularly structured neural networks on the DREAM machine. *IEEE Trans. Neural Networks* 6:407–421, 1995.

[25] P. H. W. Leong and M. A. Jabri. A low-power VLSI arrhythmia classifier. *IEEE Trans. Neural Networks* 6:1435–1445, 1995.

[26] G. Erten and R. M. Goodman. Analog VLSI implementation for stereo correspondence between 2-D images. *IEEE Trans. Neural Networks* 7:266–277, 1996.

[27] S. Wolpert and E. Micheli-Tzanakou. A neuromime in VLSI. *IEEE Trans. Neural Networks* 7:300–306, 1996.

[28] P. C. Chung and T. F. Krile. Characteristics of Hebbian-type associative memories having faulty interconnections. *IEEE Trans. Neural Networks* 3:969–980, 1992.

[29] P. C. Chung and T. F. Krile. Reliability characteristics of quadratic Hebbian-type associative memories in optical and electronic network implementations. *IEEE Trans. Neural Networks* 6:357–367, 1995.

[30] P. C. Chung and T. F. Krile. Fault-tolerance of optical and electronic Hebbian-type associative memories. In *Associative Neural Memories: Theory and Implementation* (M. H. Hassoun, Ed.). Oxford Univ. Press, 1993.

[31] M. Verleysen and B. Sirletti. A high-storage capacity content-addressable memory and its learning algorithm. *IEEE Trans. Circuits Systems* 36:762–765, 1989.

[32] H. Sompolinsky. The theory of neural networks: the Hebb rule and beyond. In *Heidelberg Colloquium on Glassy Dynamics* (J. L. Van Hermmen and I. Morgenstern, Eds.). Springer-Verlag, New York, 1986.

[33] G. Dundar and K. Rose. The effects of quantization on multilayer neural networks. *IEEE Trans. Neural Networks* 6:1446–1451, 1995.

[34] P. C. Chung, C. T. Tsai, and Y. N. Sun. Characteristics of Hebbian-type associative memories with quantized interconnections. *IEEE Trans. Circuits Systems* I *Fund. Theory Appl.* 41, 1994.

[35] G. R. Gindi, A. F. Gmitro, and K. Parthasarathy. Hopfield model associative memory with nonzero-diagonal terms in memory matrix. *Appl. Opt.* 27:129–134, 1988.

[36] A. F. Gmitro and P. E. Keller. Statistical performance of outer-product associative memory models. *Appl. Opt.* 28:1940–1951, 1989.

[37] K. F. Cheung and L. E. Atlas. Synchronous vs asynchronous behavior of Hopfield's CAM neural net. *Appl. Opt.* 26:4808–4813, 1987.

[38] H. H. Chen, Y. C. Lee, G. Z. Sun, and H. Y. Lee. *High Order Correlation Model for Associative Memory*, pp. 86–92. American Institute of Physics, New York, 1986.

[39] N. May and D. Hammerstrom. Fault simulation of a wafer-scale integrated neural network. *Neural Networks* 1:393, suppl. 1, 1988.

[40] J. H. Wang, T. F. Krile, and J. Walkup. Reduction of interconnection weights in high order associative memory networks. *Proc. International Joint Conference on Neural Networks*, p. II-177, Seattle, 1991.

[41] M. Gottrell, B. Girard, Y. Girard, M. Mangeas, and C. Muller. Neural modeling for time series: a statistical stepwise method for weight elimination. *IEEE Trans. Neural Networks* 6:1355–1364, 1995.

Finite Constraint Satisfaction

Angelo Monfroglio
Omar Institute of Technology
28068 Romentino, Italy

I. CONSTRAINED HEURISTIC SEARCH AND NEURAL NETWORKS FOR FINITE CONSTRAINT SATISFACTION PROBLEMS

A. INTRODUCTION

Constraint satisfaction plays a crucial role in the real world and in the fields of artificial intelligence and automated reasoning. Discrete optimization, planning (scheduling, engineering, timetabling, robotics), operations research (project management, decision support systems, advisory systems), data-base management, pattern recognition, and multitasking problems can be reconstructed as finite constraint satisfaction problems [1–3]. An introduction to programming by constraints may be found in [4]. A recent survey and tutorial paper on constraint-based reasoning is [5]. A good introductory theory of discrete optimization is [6].

The *general constraint satisfaction problem* (CSP) can be formulated as follows [5]: Given a set of N variables, each with an associated domain and a set of constraining relations each involving a subset of k variables in the form of a set of admissible k-tuple values, find one or all possible N-tuples such that each

Algorithms and Architectures

N-tuple is an instantiation of the N variables satisfying all the relations, that is, included in the set of admissible k-tuples.

We consider here only finite domains, that is, variables that range over a finite number of values. These CSPs are named *finite constraint satisfaction problems* (FCSP). A given unary relation for each variable can specify its domain as a set of possible values. The required solution relation is then a subset of the Cartesian product of the variable domains.

Unfortunately, even the finite constraint satisfaction problem belongs to the NP class of hard problems for which polynomial time deterministic algorithms are not known; see [5, 7]. As an example of FCSP, consider the following:

> *Variables*: x_1, x_2, x_3, x_4;
> *Domains*: $\text{Dom}(x_1) = \{a, b, c, d\}, \text{Dom}(x_2) = \{b, d\}, \text{Dom}(x_3) = \{a, d\}$, $\text{Dom}(x_4) = \{a, b, c\}$;
> *Constraints*: $x_1 < x_2,\ x_3 > x_4$ in alphabetical order; x_1, x_2, x_3, x_4 must have each a different value.

An admissible instantiation is $x_1 = a,\ x_2 = b,\ x_3 = d,\ x_4 = c$.

It is useful to remember the following hierarchy: The logic programming language Prolog is based on Horn first order predicate calculus (HFOPC). HFOPC restricts first order predicate calculus (FOPC) by only allowing Horn clauses, a disjunction of literals with at most one positive literal.

Definite clause programs (DCP) have clauses with exactly one positive literal. DCPs without predicate completion restrict HFOPC by allowing only one negative clause which serves as the query. Datalog restricts DCP by eliminating function symbols. FCSPs restrict Datalog by disallowing rules. However, even FCSPs have NP-hard complexity. As we will see, FCSPs can be represented as constraint networks (CN). There are several further restrictions on FCSPs with corresponding gain in tractability, and these correspond to restrictions in constraint networks. For instance, there are directed constraint networks (DCNs). In a DCN, for each constraint, some subset of the variables can be considered as input variables to the constraint and the rest as output variables.

Any FCSP can be represented as binary CSP. The literature on constraint satisfaction and consistency techniques usually adopts the following nomenclature: Given a set of n variables, where each variable has a domain of m values, and a set of constraints acting between pairs of variables, find an assignment such that the constraints are satisfied. It is also possible to consider random FCSPs; for instance, we may consider p_1 constraints among the $n \cdot (n-1)/2$ possible constraints. We may then assume that p_2 is the fraction of m^2 value pairs in each constraint that is disallowed; see Prosser [8].

An important FCSP is timetabling, that is, to automatic construction of suitable timetables in school, academic, and industrial establishments. It is easy to show that both timetabling and graph coloring problems directly reduce to the conjunctive normal form (CNF) satisfaction problem, that is, a satisfiability problem (SAT) for a particular Boolean expression of propositional calculus (CNF-SAT). Mackworth [5] described *the crucial role that* CNF-SAT plays for FCSPs, for both proving theorems and finding models in propositional calculus. CNF-SAT through neural networks is the core of this chapter.

In a following section we will describe an important FCSP restriction that we call *shared resource allocation* (SRA). SRA is tractable, that is, it is in the P class of complexity. Then we will describe several neural network approaches to solving CNF-SAT problems.

1. Related Work

Fox [9] described an approach to scheduling through a "contention technique," which is analogous to our heuristic constraint satisfaction [10]. He proposed a model of decision making that provides structure by combining constraint satisfaction and heuristic search, and he introduced the concepts of *topology* and *texture* to characterize problem structure. Fox identified some fundamental problem textures among which the most important are *value contention*—the degree to which variables contend for the same value—and *value conflict*—the degree to which a variable's assigned value is in conflict with existing constraints. These textures are decisive for identifying bottlenecks in decision support.

In the next sections we will describe techniques that we first introduced [10] which use a slightly different terminology: We quantify value contention by using *shared resource index* and value conflict by using an *exclusion index*. However, a sequential implementation of this approach for solving CSPs continues to suffer from the "sequential malady," that is, only one constraint at a time is considered. Constraint satisfaction is an intrinsically *parallel problem*, and the same is true of the contention technique. Distributed and parallel computation are needed for the "contention computation."

We will use a successful heuristic technique and connectionist networks, and combine the best of both fields. For comparison, see [11].

B. Shared Resource Allocation Algorithm

Let us begin with the the shared resource allocation algorithm, which we first present informally. This presentation represents preliminary education for solution of the more important and difficult problem of conjunctive normal form satisfaction, which we will discuss in Section I.C.

We suppose that there are variables (or processes) and many shared resources. Each variable can obtain a resource among a choice of alternatives, but two or more variables cannot have the same resource. It is usual to represent a CSP by means of a *constraint graph*, that is, a graph where each node represents a variable and two node are connected by an edge if the variables are linked by a constraint (see [12]).

For the problem we are considering the constraint graph is a complete graph, because each variable is constrained by the others to not share a resource (alternative). So we cannot use the fundamental Freuder result [12]: A sufficient condition for a backtrack-free search is that the level of strong consistency is greater than the width of the constraint graph and a connected constraint graph has width 1 if and only if it is a tree. Our constraint graph is not a tree and the width is equal to the order of the graph minus 1.

As an example of our problem consider:

EXAMPLE 1.

$$v_1\colon\ E, C, B, \qquad v_2\colon\ A, E, B, \qquad v_3\colon\ C, A, B,$$
$$v_4\colon\ E, D, D, \qquad v_5\colon\ D, F, B, \qquad v_6\colon\ B, F, D,$$

where $v_1, v_2, \ldots$ are variables (or processes) and $E, C, \ldots$ are resources. Note that a literal may have double occurrences, because our examples are randomly generated. Figure 1 illustrates the constraint graph for this example.

Let us introduce our algorithm. Consider the trivial case for only three variables, where

$$v_1\colon\ B, \qquad v_2\colon\ E, \qquad v_3\colon\ A.$$

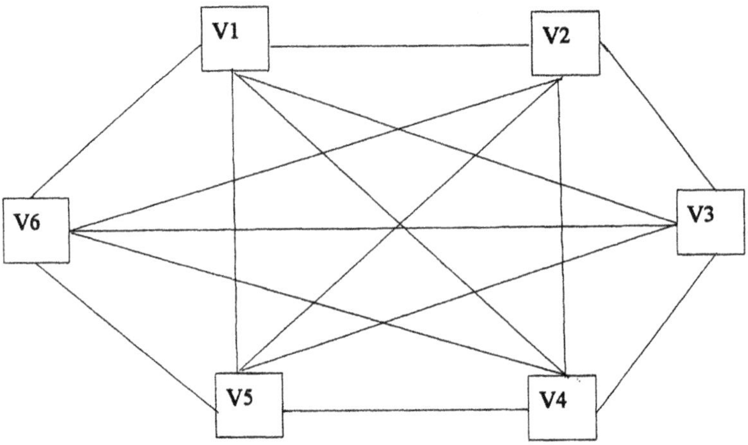

Figure 1 Traditional constraint graph for Example 1. Each edge represents an inequality constraint: the connected nodes (variables) cannot have the same value. Reprinted with permission from A. Monfroglio, *Neural Comput. Appl.* 3:78–100, 1995 (© 1995 Springer-Verlag).

Obviously the problem is solved: We say that each variable has a shared resource index equal to 0. Now let us slightly modify the situation:

$$v_1\colon A, B, \qquad v_2\colon E, \qquad v_3\colon A.$$

Now v_1 shares with v_3 the resource A, so we say that v_1 has a shared resource index greater than v_2. Moreover, the alternative A for v_1 has a shared resource index greater than B. Our algorithm is based on these simple observations and on the shared resource index. It computes four shared resource indices:

1. the first shared resource index for the alternatives
2. the first shared resource index for the variables
3. the total shared resource index for the alternatives
4. the total shared resource index for the variables.

Now we go back to our example with six variables $v_1, v_2, \ldots$ and describe all the steps of our algorithm. For v_1 E is shared with v_2 and v_4, C with v_3, B with v_2, v_3, v_4, and v_6. The algorithm builds the shared resource list for each alternative of each variable and then the length of each list that we name first shared resource index for the alternatives. We can easily verify that the first shared indices for the alternatives are

$$v_1\colon 2, 1, 4, \qquad v_2\colon 1, 2, 4, \qquad v_3\colon 1, 1, 4,$$
$$v_4\colon 2, 2, 2, \qquad v_5\colon 2, 1, 4, \qquad v_6\colon 4, 1, 2.$$

Then the algorithm builds the first shared resource index for each variable as the sum of all the first shared resource indices of its alternatives:

$$v_1\colon 7, \qquad v_2\colon 7, \qquad v_3\colon 6, \qquad v_4\colon 6, \qquad v_5\colon 7, \qquad v_6\colon 7.$$

Through the shared resource list for each alternative the system computes the total shared resource index as the sum of the first variable indices:

$$v_1\colon 13, 6, 27, \qquad v_2\colon 6, 13, 27, \qquad v_3\colon 7, 7, 28,$$
$$v_4\colon 14, 14, 14, \qquad v_5\colon 13, 7, 27, \qquad v_6\colon 27, 7, 13.$$

For instance, for v_1 we have the alternative E which is shared with v_2 (index 7) and v_4 (index 6) for a sum of 13.

Finally the algorithm determines the total shared resource index for each variable as the sum of its total shared resource indices for the alternatives:

$$v_1\colon 46, \qquad v_2\colon 46, \qquad v_3\colon 42, \qquad v_4\colon 42, \qquad v_5\colon 47, \qquad v_6\colon 47.$$

If at any time a variable has only one alternative, this is immediately assigned to that variable. Then it assigns for the variable with the lowest shared index the alternative with the lowest shared resource index: v_3 with C (also v_4 has the same shared resource index).

The system updates the problem by deleting the assigned variable with all its alternatives and the assigned alternative for each variable. Then the algorithm continues as a recursive call. In the example the assignments are

$$v_3\colon C, \quad v_1\colon E, \quad v_2\colon A, \quad v_4\colon D, \quad v_5\colon F, \quad v_6\colon B.$$

In case of equal minimal indices, the algorithm must compute additional indices by using a recursive procedure. For more details the reader may consult [10]. Appendix I gives a formal description of the algorithm.

1. Theoretical and Practical Complexity

Let suppose we have N variables each with at most N alternative values. To compute the preceding indices, the algorithm has to compare each alternative in the list of each variable with all the other alternatives. One can easily see that there are in the worst case $N * N * (N - 1) = N^2 * (N - 1)$ comparisons for the first assignment. Then $(N-1)*(N-1)*(N-2)$, $(N-2)*(N-2)*(N-3)$, etc., for the following assignments. The problem size is $p = N * N$ (the number of variables times the number of alternatives for each variable). The asymptotic cost is thus $O(p^2)$. The real complexity was about $O(p^{1.7})$ in the dimension p of the problem. As one can see in [9], Fox used a similar technique in a system called CORTES, which solves a scheduling problem using constraint heuristic search.

Fox reported his experience using conventional CSP techniques that do not perform well in finding either an optimized or feasible solution. He found that for a class of problems where each variable contends for the same value, that is, the same resource, it is beneficial to introduce another type of graph, which he called a contention graph. It is necessary to identify where the highest amount of contention is; then is clear where to make the next decision. The easy decisions are activities that do not contend for bottlenecked resources; the difficult decisions are activities that contend more. Fox's contention graph is quite similar to our techniques with shared resource indices.

Fox considered as an example the factory scheduling problem where many operations contend for a small set of machines. The allocation of these machines over time must be optimized. This problem is equivalent to having a set of variables, with small discrete domains, each competing for assignment of the same value but linked by a disequality constraint.

A *contention graph* replaces disequality constraints (for example, used in the conventional constraint graphs of Freuder [12]) by a node for each value under contention, and links these value nodes to the variables contending for it by a demand constraint. Figure 2 shows the contention graph for Example 1.

The constraint graph is a more general representation tool, whereas the contention graph is more specific, simpler, and at the same time more useful for contention detection. The constraint graph is analogous to a syntactic view of

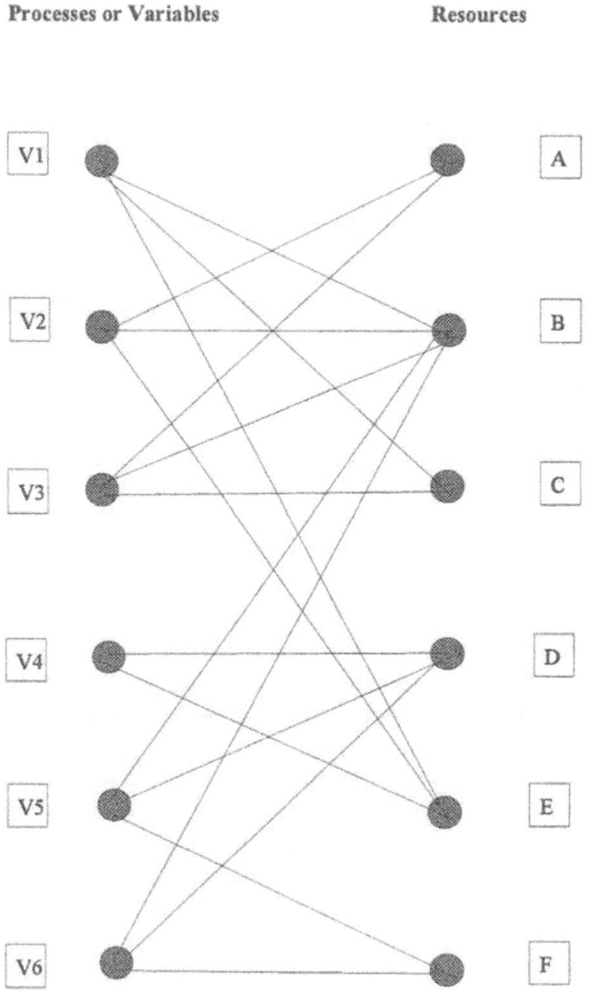

Figure 2 Contention graph for Example 1. Resource contention is easy to see considering the edges incident to resource nodes. Reprinted with permission from A. Monfroglio, *Neural Comput. Appl.* 3:78–100, 1995 (© 1995 Springer-Verlag).

the problem, whereas the contention graph is analogous to a semantic view. In data-base terminology, we may call the constraint graph a reticular model and the contention graph a relational model.

It is very natural to think at this point that connectionist networks are well suited to encode the contention graph or our shared resource indices. It is straightforward to look at links between variables that share a resource or links between resources that share a variable as connections from one processing element to another. It is immediate to think of hidden layers as tools for representing and storing the meaning of our higher level indices. The connectionist network for our problem is then the dynamical system which implements a "living" version of the contention graph of Fox.

As we will see in the following sections, our approach to FCSPs is to consider two fundamental type of constraints:

- *Choice constraints*: Choose only one alternative among those available.
- *Exclusion constraints*: Do not choose two incompatible values (alternatives).

Herein, this modelization technique is applied to resource allocation and conjunctive normal form satisfaction problems—two classes of theoretical problems that have very practical counterparts in real-life problems. These two classes of constraints are then represented by means of neural networks. Moreover, we will use a new representation technique for the variables that appear in the constraints. This problem representation is known as *complete relaxation*.

Complete relaxation means that a new variable (name) is introduced for each new occurrence of the same variable in a constraint. For instance, suppose we have three constraints c_1, c_2, c_3 with the variables A, B, C, D. Suppose also the variable A appears in the constraint c_1 and in the constraint c_3, the variable B appears in the constraints c_2 and c_3, etc. In a complete relaxation representation the variable A for the first constraint will appear as A_1, in the constraint c_3 as A_3, etc. Additional constraints are then added to ensure that A_1 and A_3 do not receive incompatible values (in fact, they are the same variable). This technique can be used for any finite constraint satisfaction problem.

In general, we can say that, in the corresponding neural network, choice constraints force excitation (with only one winner) and exclusion constraints force mutual inhibition. A well designed *training data base* will force the neural network to learn these two fundamental aspects of any FCSP.

C. Satisfaction of a Conjunctive Normal Form

Now let us consider a more difficult case: the classic problem of the satisfaction of a conjunctive normal form. This problem is considered a NP problem and is very important because all NP problems may be reduced in polynomial time to CNF satisfaction. In formal terms the problem is stated: Given a conjunctive normal form, find an assignment for all variables that satisfies the conjunction.

An example of CNF follows.

EXAMPLE 2.

$$(A + B) \cdot (C + D) \cdot ({\sim}B + {\sim}C) \cdot ({\sim}A + {\sim}D),$$

where $+$ means OR, $\cdot$ means AND, and $\sim$ means NOT. A possible assignment is $A =$ true, $B =$ false, $C =$ true, and $D =$ false. We call m the number of clauses and n the number of distinct literals. Sometimes it is useful to consider the number l of literals per clause. Thus we may have a 3-CNF-SAT for which each clause has exactly three literals. We will use the n-CNF-SAT notation for any CNF-SAT problem with n globally distinct literals. Our approach is not restricted to cases where each clause has the same number of literals. To simplify some cost considerations, we also consider $l = m = n$ without loss of generality.

We reconduct the problem to a shared resource allocation with additional constraints that render the problem much harder (in fact, it is NP-hard):

- We create a variable for each clause such as $(A + B)$, $(C + D)$, ...
- Each term must be satisfied: whereas this term is a logical OR, it is sufficient that A or B is true.
- We consider as alternative each literal A, B, ...
- We use uppercase letters for nonnegated alternatives and lowercase letters for negated alternatives.

So we achieve

$$v_1\colon\ A, B, \qquad v_2\colon\ C, D, \qquad v_3\colon\ b, c, \qquad v_4\colon\ a, d.$$

Of course, the choice of A for the variable 1 does not permit the choice of NOT A, that is, the alternative a, for the variable 4. If we find an allocation for the variables, we also find an assignment true/false for the CNF. For example,

$$v_1\colon\ A, \qquad v_2\colon\ C, \qquad v_3\colon\ b, \qquad v_4\colon\ d,$$

leads to $A =$ true, $C =$ true, $B =$ false, and $D =$ false.

There may be cases where the choices leave some letter undetermined. In this case more than one assignment is possible. Consider the following example:

EXAMPLE 3.

$$(A + B) \cdot ({\sim}A + {\sim}C + D) \cdot ({\sim}A + {\sim}B + C) \cdot ({\sim}D),$$

which is transformed to

$$v_1\colon\ A, B, \qquad v_2\colon\ a, c, D, \qquad v_3\colon\ a, b, C, \qquad v_4\colon\ d.$$

For example, the choice

$$v_1\colon\ B, \qquad v_2\colon\ a, \qquad v_3\colon\ a, \qquad v_4\colon\ d$$

leads to the assignment A = false, B = true, D = false, and C = undetermined (C = true or C = false). Each uppercase letter excludes the same lowercase letter and vice versa. A with A, b with b, c with c, B with B, etc., are not of course considered mutually exclusive.

We compute

1. the first alternative exclusion index, $i1$
2. the first variable exclusion index, $i2$
3. the total alternative exclusion index, $i3$
4. the total variable exclusion index, $i4$

In our example,

v_1: 2, 1,	v_2: 1, 1, 1,	v_3: 1, 1, 1,	v_4: 1,
v_1: 3,	v_2: 3,	v_3: 3,	v_4: 1,
v_1: 6, 3,	v_2: 3, 3, 1,	v_3: 3, 3, 3,	v_4: 3,
v_1: 9,	v_2: 9,	v_3: 7,	v_4: 3.

Now we assign the variable with the lowest exclusion index and the alternative for that variable, with the lowest exclusion index:

$$v_4\colon d, \quad \text{that is,} \quad D = \text{false}.$$

Note that this variable v_4 is immediately instantiated even if the index is not the lowest because it has only one alternative. Then we update the problem by deleting all the alternatives not permitted by this choice, that is, all the D alternatives.

In our case, we find

v_1: A, B,	v_2: a, b, C,	v_3: a, c,
v_1: 2, 1,	v_2: 1, 1, 1,	v_3: 1, 1,
v_1: 3,	v_2: 3,	v_3: 2;

v_3: a (A = false), v_2: a, v_1: B (B = true), C = undetermined.

If at any time a variable has only one choice it is immediately instantiated to that value.

Appendix II contains a formal description of the algorithm.

Now let us consider another example:

EXAMPLE 4.

			$i3$	$i4$
v_1: A, B	1, 1	2	3, 3	6
v_2: a, C	1, 2	3	2, 7	9
v_3: b, D	2, 1	3	5, 4	9
v_4: c, d	2, 2	4	6, 6	12
v_5: B, C	1, 2	3	3, 7	10
v_6: c, D	2, 1	3	6, 4	10

Here, the first variable to be assigned is v_1 (index $= 6$). v_1 has two alternatives with equal indices of 3. If we assign A to v_1, the problem has no solutions. If we assign B to v_1, the solution is

a (false),	B (true),	c (false),	D (true);
a solves v_2,	B solves v_1, v_5,	c solves v_4, v_6,	D solves v_3, v_6.

So our algorithm must be modified. We compute other indices,

5. the first alternative compatibility index, $i5$
6. the first variable compatibility index, $i6$
7. the total alternative compatibility index, $i7$
8. the total variable compatibility index, $i8$

which consider the fact that a chosen alternative solves more than one variable. In this case, the alternative will get preference.

As the difference between the corresponding indices, we calculate

9. the first alternative constraint index $= i1$–$i5$;
10. the first variable constraint index $= i2$–$i6$;
11. the total alternative constraint index $= i3$–$i7$;
12. the total variable constraint index $= i4$–$i8$.

In our example,

		$i7$	$i8$	$i3$–$i7$	$i4$–$i8$
v_1: 0, 1	1	0, 2	2	3, 1	4
v_2: 0, 1	1	0, 2	2	2, 5	7
v_3: 0, 1	1	0, 2	2	5, 2	7
v_4: 1, 0	1	2, 0	2	4, 6	10
v_5: 1, 1	2	1, 1	2	2, 6	8
v_6: 1, 1	2	1, 1	2	5, 3	8

So the choice for v_1 is the alternative B (index $= 1$) because the situation here is different with respect to that of the shared resource allocation algorithm. If an alternative has the same exclusion index but solves more variables, we must prefer that choice.

As another example, consider:

EXAMPLE 5.

v_1: $A, B,$	v_2: $a, H,$	v_3: $h, C, D,$
v_4: $c, G,$	v_5: $c, g,$	v_6: $d, G,$
v_7: $d, g,$	v_8: $f, G,$	v_9: $b, F,$
v_{10}: $F, g, I,$	v_{11}: $f, D, J.$	

The exclusion indices are (for brevity we report here only two indices)

v_1:	1, 1	2	2, 3	5,
v_2:	1, 1	2	2, 5	7,
v_3:	1, 2, 2	5	2, 8, 8	18,
v_4:	1, 3	4	2, 8	10,
v_5:	1, 3	4	2, 8	10,
v_6:	2, 3	5	6, 8	14,
v_7:	2, 3	5	6, 8	14,
v_8:	2, 3	5	6, 8	14,
v_9:	1, 2	3	2, 6	8,
v_{10}:	2, 3, 0	5	8, 8, 0	16,
v_{11}:	2, 2, 0	4	5, 9, 0	14.

The compatibility indices are

v_1:	0, 0	0	0, 0	0,
v_2:	0, 0	0	0, 0	0,
v_3:	0, 0, 1	1	0, 0, 2	2,
v_4:	1, 2	3	3, 6	9,
v_5:	1, 2	3	3, 6	9,
v_6:	1, 2	3	3, 6	9,
v_7:	1, 2	3	3, 6	9,
v_8:	1, 2	3	2, 6	8,
v_9:	0, 1	1	0, 3	3,
v_{10}:	1, 2, 0	3	1, 6, 0	7,
v_{11}:	1, 1, 0	2	3, 1, 0	4.

The final constraint indices are

v_1: 2, 3	5,	v_2: 2, 5	7,
v_3: 2, 8, 6	16,	v_4: −1, 2	1,
v_5: −1, 2	1,	v_6: 3, 2	5,
v_7: 3, 2	5,	v_8: 4, 2	6,
v_9: 2, 3	5,	v_{10}: 7, 2, 0	9,
v_{11}: 2, 8, 0	10.		

Here v_4 and v_5 have minimal indices. By choosing the first, we find $v_4 : c$ and $v_5 : c$. Updating the problem and repeating the procedure, we have $v_2 : a$ and $v_1 : B$. Again updating, we find

$$v_9\colon F, \quad v_{10}\colon F, \quad v_8\colon G, \quad v_6\colon G,$$
$$v_7\colon d, \quad v_3\colon h, \quad v_{11}\colon J.$$

More examples and details can be found in [10].

1. Theoretical and Experimental Complexity Estimates

From the formal description of Appendix II it is easy to see that the worst case complexity of this algorithm is the same as the SRA, that is, $O(p^2)$ in the size p of the problem (p = the number m of clauses times the number l of literals per clause if all clauses have the same number of literals). In fact, the time needed to construct the indices for CNF-SAT is the same as the time for constructing the indices for SRA (there are, however, 12 indices to compute; in the SRA there are 4 indices). The experimental cost of the algorithm in significant tests has been about $O(p^{1.9})$. In a following section we will describe the testing data base.

D. Connectionist Networks for Solving n-Conjunctive Normal Form Satisfiability Problems

In the next subsections we present classes of connectionist networks that learn to solve CNF-SAT problems. The role of the neural network is to replace the sequential algorithm which computes a resource index for a variable. Network learning is thus a model of the algorithm which calculates the "scores" used to obtain the assignments for the variables; see Fig. 3. We will show how some neural networks may be very useful for hard and high level symbolic computation problems such as CNF-SAT problems.

The input layer's neurons [processing elements (PEs)] encode the alternatives for each variable (the possible values, i.e., the constraints). A 1 value in the corresponding PE means that the alternative can be chosen for the corresponding

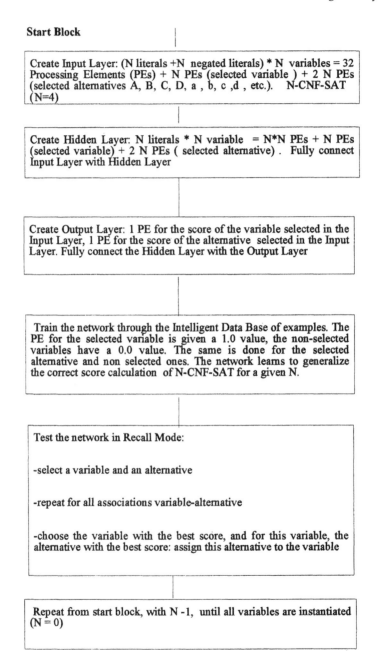

Start Block

Create Input Layer: (N literals +N negated literals) * N variables = 32 Processing Elements (PEs) + N PEs (selected variable) + 2 N PEs (selected alternatives A, B, C, D, a , b, c ,d , etc.). N-CNF-SAT (N=4)

Create Hidden Layer: N literals * N variable = N*N PEs + N PEs (selected variable) + 2 N PEs (selected alternative) . Fully connect Input Layer with Hidden Layer

Create Output Layer: 1 PE for the score of the variable selected in the Input Layer, 1 PE for the score of the alternative selected in the Input Layer. Fully connect the Hidden Layer with the Output Layer

Train the network through the Intelligent Data Base of examples. The PE for the selected variable is given a 1.0 value, the non-selected variables have a 0.0 value. The same is done for the selected alternative and non selected ones. The network learns to generalize the correct score calculation of N-CNF-SAT for a given N.

Test the network in Recall Mode:

-select a variable and an alternative

-repeat for all associations variable-alternative

-choose the variable with the best score, and for this variable, the alternative with the best score: assign this alternative to the variable

Repeat from start block, with N -1, until all variables are instantiated (N = 0)

Figure 3 Block diagram of data flow for the neural network algorithm. Reprinted with permission from A. Monfroglio, *Neural Comput. Appl.* 3:78–100, 1995 (© 1995 Springer-Verlag).

variable; a 0 means it cannnot. Moreover, in the first network we describe, additional input PEs encode the variable selected as the next candidate to satisfy, and the possible alternative: again, a 1 value means the corresponding variable (or alternative) is considered; all other values must be 0.

The output PEs give the scores for the variable and for the alternative which have been selected as candidates in the input layer. All the scores are obtained and then the variable and the alternative which gained the best score are chosen. Then the PEs for the variable and the alternative are deleted and a new network is trained with the remainder PEs. The neural network thus does not provide the complete solution in one step: the user should let the network run in the learning and recall modes N times for the N variables. In the next subsections, however, we will present other networks that are able to give all scores for all variables and alternatives at the same time, that is, the complete feasible solution.

The network is trained over the whole class of n-CNF-SAT problems for a given n, that is, it is not problem-specific, it is n-specific. The scores are, of course, based on value contention, that is, on the indices of Section I.C.

Let us begin with a simple case, the CNF-SAT with at most four alternatives per variable and at most four variables. The network is trained by means of our heuristic indices of previous sections, with supervised examples like

1. v_1: A, B, v_2: C, v_3: B, c, v_4: a, b;
2. v_1: A, B, v_2: a, C, v_3: b, v_4: b, C;

etc.,

with four variables (v_1, v_2, v_3, v_4) and literals A, B, C, a, b, c, etc.

The chosen representation encodes the examples in the network as

$$\text{A B C D a b c d} \qquad (4+4 \text{ alternatives}) = 8 \text{ neurons (PEs)}.$$

```
/*problem 1
/*section of the input that encodes the initial
constraints of the problem*/
/*variable v1*/
/*A      B                                          */
i   1.0   1.0   0.0   0.0   0.0   0.0   0.0   0.0
/*v2*/
/*              C                                   */
    0.0   0.0   1.0   0.0   0.0   0.0   0.0   0.0
/*v3*/
/*       B                               c          */
    0.0   1.0   0.0   0.0   0.0   0.0   1.0   0.0
/v4*/
/*                          a     b                 */
```

```
    0.0   0.0   0.0   0.0   1.0   1.0   0.0   0.0
/*in total there are 8*4=32 neurons, that is,
 processing elements (PEs)*/
/*section of the input that encodes the choices of the
 variable and the alternative*/
/*choice among the variables to satisfy*/
/*clause v1*/
    1.0   0.0   0.0   0.0
/*choice among the possible alternative assignments*/
/*A                                                   */
    1.0   0.0   0.0   0.0   0.0   0.0   0.0   0.0
/* in total there are 4+8=12 PEs */
/*output*/
/* score for the choice of the variable (in this case
v1)
    and the choice of the alternative (in this case A)
/*desired output: v1 has score 1, the alternative 1 has
score 1*/
d   1.0   1.0          /* 2 PEs */
/*remember that the first value is the score for the
 choice of the variable*/
/*the second value is the score for the choice of the
alternative
/*other choices*/
i    1.0   1.0   0.0   0.0   0.0   0.0   0.0   0.0
     0.0   0.0   1.0   0.0   0.0   0.0   0.0   0.0
     0.0   1.0   0.0   0.0   0.0   0.0   1.0   0.0
     0.0   0.0   0.0   0.0   1.0   1.0   0.0   0.0

/*v1                          */
     1.0   0.0   0.0   0.0
/*         B                                          */
     0.0   1.0   0.0   0.0   0.0   0.0   0.0   0.0
/*score*/
d  1.0  0.0
i  1.0  1.0  0.0  0.0  0.0  0.0  0.0  0.0
   0.0  0.0  1.0  0.0  0.0  0.0  0.0  0.0
   0.0  1.0  0.0  0.0  0.0  0.0  1.0  0.0
   0.0  0.0  0.0  0.0  1.0  1.0  0.0  0.0
   0.0  1.0  0.0  0.0                           /*v2*/
   0.0  0.0  1.0  0.0  0.0  0.0  0.0  0.0       /*choice C*/
d  1.0  1.0
```

```
etc.

/*problem 2
i   1.0  1.0  0.0  0.0  0.0   0.0  0.0   0.0
etc.
```

Remember that *i* means input and *d* means desired output.

For simplicity, the scores reported for the desired output are only the first indices, but the procedure indeed uses the total indices.

First we present a modified backpropagation network with the following layers:

Input layer: 44 processing elements. As can be seen in the preceding examples, we use a PE for each possible alternative (negative or positive literals) for each variable (i.e., 4 literals + 4 negated literals × 4 variables = 32). From left to right eight PEs correspond to the first variable, eight to the second, etc. In addition, on the right, four PEs encode the choice of the variable for which we obtain the score, and eight PEs encode an alternative among the eight possible (four negated and four nonnegated) literals.

Hidden layer: 28 PEs (4 variables ×4 alternatives for each variable +8 + 4 PEs as in the input layer). Note that only positive alternatives are counted. The PE connection weights (positive or negative) will encode whether an alternative is negated or not

Output layer: Two PEs (one element encodes the total index for the variable and one encodes for the alternative both chosen in the input layer).

1. Learning and Tests: Network Architecture

The bias element is fully connected to the hidden layers and the output layer using variable weights. Each layer except the first is fully connected to the prior layer using variable weights. The number of training cycles per test is 1000. Details on this first network can be found in [13]. However, we will report in the Section I.E.5 the most interesting experimental results and show how the performance of the algorithm improves (on unseen examples) with progressive training.

The network has been tested with previously unseen problems such as

1. v_1: $A, c,$ v_2: $a, C,$ v_3: $B, D,$ v_4: $B, D;$
2. v_1: $B, C,$ v_2: $a, c,$ v_3: $B, D,$ v_4: $b,$

   etc.

2. Intelligent Data Base for the Training Set

Mitchell *et al.* [14] and Franco and Paull [15] showed that certain classes of randomly generated formulas are very easy, that is, for some of them one can simply return "unsatisfiable," whereas for the others almost any assignment will work. To demonstrate the usefulness of our algorithm we have used tests on formulas outside of the easy classes, as we will discuss in the following sections.

To train the network, we have identified additional techniques necessary to achieve good overall performance. A training set based on random examples was not sufficient to bring the network to an advanced level of performance: Intelligent data-base design was necessary. This data base contains, for example, classes of problems that are quite *symmetrical* with respect to the resource contention (about 30%) and classes of problems with nonsymmetrical resource contention (about 70%). Moreover, the intelligent data base must be tailored to teach the network the major aspects of the problem, that is, the fundamental FCSP constraints:

1. x and negated x literals inhibition (about 60% of the examples)
2. Choose only literals at disposition
3. Choose exactly one literal per clause (Constraints 2 and 3 together are about 40% of the examples).

To obtain this result, we had to include in the example data base many special cases such as

$$v_1\colon a, \qquad v_2\colon B, \qquad v_3\colon d, \quad \text{etc.,}$$

where the alternative is unique and the solution is immediate.

It is very important to accurately design the routine that automatically constructs the training data base, so as to include the preceding cases and only those that are needed. This is a very important point because the data base becomes very large without a well designed construction technique.

Moreover, note that we have used a training set of about $2*n^2-n$ problems for $2 < n < 50$, and an equal sized testing set (of course not included in the training set) for performance judgment. This shows the fundamental role of generalization that the network plays through learning.

The performance results are that this network always provided 100% correct assignments for the problems which were used to train the network. For unseen problems, the network provided the correct assignments in more than 90% of the tests.

3. Network Size

The general size of this first networks is (for $m = n$) $2n^2+3n$ input processing elements and n^2+3n hidden processing elements for the version with one hidden layer and two output processing elements.

E. Other Connectionist Paradigms

The following subsections survey different paradigms we have implemented and tested for the CNF-SAT problem. We chose these networks because they are the most promising and appropriate. For each network we give the motivations for its use.

We used the tools provided by a neural network simulator (see [16]) to construct the prototypes easily. Then we used the generated C language routines and modified them until we reached the configurations shown. We found this procedure very useful for our research purposes.

For each class of networks we give a brief introduction with references and some figures to describe topologies and test results.

Finally, a comprehensive summary of the network performance in solving the CNF-SAT problems is reported. The summary shows how well each network met our expectations.

All the networks learn to solve n-CNF-SAT after training through the intelligent data base. As we have seen, this data base uses the indices of Section I.C to train the network. The intermediate indices are represented in the hidden layer, whereas the final indices are in the output layer. Ultimately, the network layers represent all the problem constraints.

Notice that for the functional-link fast backpropagation (FL-F-BKP), delta-bar-delta (DBD), extended delta-bar-delta (EDBD), digital backpropagation (DIGI-B and DIGI-I), directed random search (DRS), and radial basis function (RBFN) networks, we have implemented the following architecture to solve n-CNF-SAT:

- Input layer: $2 * n^2$ PEs (processing elements)
- One hidden layer: $2 * n^2$ PEs
- Output layer: $2 * n^2$ PEs

In this architecture n-CNF-SAT means n clauses and at most n literals per clause. More details can be found in [17].

For brevity and clarity, we will give examples for 2-CNF-SAT problems; however, the actual tests were with $2 < n \leq 100$. For instance, for a simple 2-CNF-SAT case such as

$$v_1\colon A, b, \qquad v_2\colon a,$$

we have input layer, 8 PEs; hidden layer, 8 PEs; output layer; 8 PEs:

	v_1				v_2			
	A	B	a	b	A	B	a	b
Input:	1.0	0.0	0.0	1.0	0.0	0.0	1.0	0.0
Output:	0.0	0.0	0.0	1.0	0.0	0.0	1.0	0.0

In brief, this is the final solution.

As one can observe, the architecture is slightly different from that of Section I.D.3. This is due to a more compact representation for the supervised learning: all the scores for all the choices are presented in the same instance of the training example. In the network of Section I.D.3, a training example contained only one choice and one score for each clause and for an assignment. We have found this representation to be more efficient. So the output PEs become $2 * n^2$. All the networks are hetero-associative.

Remember that this knowledge representation corresponds to the complete relaxation we introduced previously. In fact, a new neuron is used for each occurrence of the same variable (i.e., alternative) in a clause (i.e., in a constraint). The training set size and the testing set size are about $2 * n^2 - N$ for $2 < n \leq 100$. For learning vector quantization (LVQ) networks and probabilistic neural networks (PNN), we have adopted the configuration

Input layer: $2 * n^2 + n$ PEs,
Hidden layer: $2 * n^2$ for LVQ PEs,
Hidden layer: # of PEs = the number of training examples for PNN,
Output layer: $2 * n$ PEs,

because the categorization nature of these networks dictates that in the output only one category is the winner (value of 1.0). Single instances should code each possible winner, and the representation is less compact, that is, in the foregoing example we will use the following data:

Instance 1	A	B	a	b	A	B	a	b	v_1	v_2
Input:	1.0	0.0	0.0	1.0	0.0	0.0	1.0	0.0 |	1.0	0.0
Output:	0.0	0.0	0.0	1.0						

Instance 2	A	B	a	b	A	B	a	b	v_1	v_2
Input:	1.0	0.0	0.0	1.0	0.0	0.0	1.0	0.0 |	0.0	1.0
Output:					0.0	0.0	1.0	0.0.		

For the cascade-correlation (CASC) and Boltzmann machine (BOL) network architectures, see the corresponding subsections.

1. Functional-Link Fast Backpropagation Network

The functional-link network is a feedforward network that uses backpropagation algorithms to adjust weights. The network has additional nodes at the input layer that serve to improve the learning capabilities. The reader can consult [18] for reference.

In the outer product (or tensor) model that we used, each component of the input pattern multiplies the entire input pattern vector. This means an additional set of nodes where the combination of input items is taken two at time. The number of additional nodes is $n * (n - 1)/2$. For example, in the 2-CNF-SAT with eight inputs the number of additional nodes is $8 * 7/2 = 28$. In addition, here we have adopted the fast model variation of the backpropagation algorithm suggested by Samad [19]. This variation improves the convergence too.

As one can easily argue, functional links are appropriate for our problem because the input configuration is not as easy to learn as, for instance, a pattern in image understanding. Here the pattern recognition task is a very 'intelligent' one, as we said in the previous section on intelligent example data base. In addition, the learning speed is very important for networks which have to learn so much. Thus all attempts are made in the following paradigms to gain speed.

2. Delta-Bar-Delta Network

The delta-bar-delta model of Jacobs [20] attempts to speed up convergence through general heuristics: past values of the gradient are used to calculate the curvature of the local error surface. For a constrained heuristic search problem such as ours it is probably useful to incorporate such general heuristics.

3. Extended Delta-Bar-Delta Network

A technique named momentum adds a term proportional to the previous weight change, with the aim of reinforcing general trends and reducing oscillations. This enhancement of the DBD network is owing to Minia and Williams [21].

4. Digital Backpropagation Neural Networks

The network that we used is a software implementation of a novel model of network architecture developed at Neural Semiconductor, Inc. for a very large scale integration (VLSI) digital network through hardware implementation; see Tomlinson *et al.* [22]. We experimented with two variants: the first uses standard backpropagation (DIGI-B); the second uses the norm-cumulative-delta learning rule (DIGI-I).

5. Directed Random Search Network

All previous learning paradigms used delta rule variations, that is, methods based on calculus. The DRS adopts a very different technique: random steps are taken in the search space and then attempts are made to pursue previously successful directions. The approach is based on an improved random optimization method of Matyas [23]. Over a compact set, the method converges to global minimum with a probability $\rightarrow 1$; see [24, 25].

We tested this paradigm too, for completeness purposes. As can be seen in our performance summary, the convergence was slow as is expected for a network using random search.

6. Boltzmann Machine

The Boltzmann machine (BOL) differs from the classical Hopfield machine in that it incorporates a version of the simulating annealing procedure to search the state space for a global minimum and a local learning rule through the difference between the probabilistic states of the network in free running mode and when it is clamped by the environment. Ackley, Hinton and Sejnowski [26] developed the Boltzmann learning rule in 1985; also see [27]. The concept of "consensus" is used as a desirability measure of the individual states of the units. It is a global measure of how the network has reached a consensus about its individual states subject to the desirabilities expressed by the individual connection strength. Thus Boltzmann machines can be used to solve combinatorial optimization problems by choosing the right connection pattern and appropriate connection strengths. Maximizing the consensus is equivalent to finding the optimal solutions of the corresponding optimization problem. This approach can be viewed as a parallel implementation to simulated annealing. We used the asynchronous (simulated) parallelism.

If the optimization problem is formulated as a 0–1 programming problem (see, for example, this formulation in [28]) and the consensus function is feasible and order-preserving (for these definitions, see [1]), then the consensus is maximal for configurations corresponding to an optimal and feasible solution of the optimization problem.

7. Cascade-Correlation Network with One Hidden Layer

In the cascade-correlation network model, new hidden nodes are added incrementally, one at a time, to predict the remaining output error. A new hidden node uses input PEs and previously trained hidden PEs. The paradigm was suggested by Fahlman and Lebiere of Carnegie Mellon University [16]. Its advantages are that the network incrementally improves its performance following the course of learning and errors, and one hidden node at a time is trained.

Why did we use this paradigm? Our networks for solving n-CNF-SAT grow quadratically in dimension N, so each attempt to reduce the number of neurons by incrementally adding only those that are necessary is welcome. We fixed a convergence value (prespecified sum squared error) and the network added only the neurons necessary to reach that convergence.

It is very important to note that our tests showed that the number of hidden nodes added was about equal to the size N of the problem, that is, hidden layer grows linearly in the dimension of the n-CNF-SAT problem. This is a great gain over the quadratic growth of the hidden layer in the first five networks.

8. Radial Basis Function Network

This network paradigm is described and evaluated in [29, 30]. A RBFN has an internal representation of hidden processing elements (pattern units) that is radially symmetric. We used a three layer architecture: input layer, hidden layer (pattern units), and output layer. For details on the architecture, the reader can consult [16].

We have chose to try this network because it often yields the following advantages:

- It trains faster than a backpropagation network.
- It leads to better decision boundaries when used in decision problems (the CNF-SAT is a decision problem too).
- The internal representation embodied in the hidden layer of pattern units has a more natural interpretation than the hidden layer of simple backpropagation networks.

Possible disadvantages are that backpropagation can give more compact representations and the initial learning phase may lose some important discriminatory information.

9. Self-Organizing Maps and Backpropagation

The network of self-organizing maps (SOMs) creates a two-dimensional feature map of the input data in such a mode that the order is preserved, so SOMs visualize topologies and hierarchical structures of higher-dimensional input spaces. SOMs can be used in hybrid networks as a front end to backpropagation (BKP) networks. We have implemented this hybrid neural network (SOM + BKP). The reader may consult [31, 32].

The reason we decided to test this network is that we need a network with strong capabilities to analyze input configurations, as we said in previous sections.

10. Learning Vector Quantization Networks

Learning vector quantization (LVQ) is a classification network that was suggested by Kohonen [31]. It assigns input vectors to classes. In the training phase, the distance of any training vector from the state vector of each PE is computed and the nearest PE is the winner. If the winning PE is in the class of the input vector, it is moved toward the training vector; if not, it is moved away (repulsion). In the classification mode, the nearest PE is declared the winner. The input vector is then assigned to the class of that PE. Because the basic LVQ suffers shortcomings, variants have been developed. For instance, some PEs tend to win too often, so a "conscience" mechanism was suggested by DeSieno [33]: A PE that wins too often is penalized. The version of LVQ we used adopts a mix of LVQ variants.

This network was chosen for reasons similar to those in the previous section. One can ask whether all classification networks are well suited for our problem. The answer is of course no. Consider, for example, a Hamming network. Like a neural network it implements a minimum error classifier for binary vectors. However, the error is defined using Hamming distance. This distance does not make sense for our problem. Two CNF-SAT problems may have a great Hamming distance and have the same solution, that is, they are in the same class. So, it is very important to accurately examine a paradigm before trying it, because the testing requires significant time and effort. Some paradigms are well suited for the n-CNF-SAT problem; others are not.

11. Probabilistic Neural Networks

Following this paradigm, an input vector called a feature vector is used to determine a category. The PNN uses the training data to develop distribution functions which serve to estimate the likelihood of a feature vector being within the given categories.

The PNN is a connectionist implementation of the statistical method called Bayesian classifier. Parzen estimators are used to construct the probability density functions required by the Bayes theory. Bayesian classifiers, in general, provide an optimum approach to pattern classification and Parzen estimators asymptotically reach the true class density functions as the number of training cases increases. For details the reader can consult [20, 34–36].

We tested this paradigm too for the categorization capabilities of the network: the network performed very well, probably owing to the excellent classification capabilities of this kind of network.

The network architecture is shown in Table I. The pattern layer has a number of processing elements (neurons) that equals the number of training examples.

Table I

Layer	Connection mode	Weight type	Learning rule
Input buffer	Corresponding to the inputs	Fixed	None
Normalizing	Full	Variable	None
Pattern	Special	Variable	Kohonen
Summation	Equal to the # of categories	Fixed	PNN
Classifying	Equal to the # of categories	—	None

F. Network Performance Summary

In Table II we briefly summarize the relative performances of the various implementations. Remember that all networks gave an accuracy of 100% on the problems used to train the network. Thus, the reported accuracy is relative to the CNF-SAT problems of the testing set. The accuracy is in percent of correct results with respect to the total number of testing problems. For n-CNF-SAT with $2 < N \leq 100$, 10,000 test were performed (about 100 for each n). All reported results are the average for the n-CNF-SAT problems with $2 < N \leq 100$.

For the first network, Fig. 4 shows the root-mean-square (rms) error converging to zero, four confusion matrices, and the weight histograms. The rms error graph shows the root-mean-square error of the output layer. As learning progresses, this graph converges to an error near 0. When the error equals the predetermined convergence threshold value (we have used 0.001), training ceases.

The *confusion matrix* provides an advanced way to measure network performance during the learning and recall phase. The confusion matrices allow the correlation of the actual results of the network with the desired results in a visual display. Optimal learning means only the bins on the diagonal from the lower left to the upper right are nonempty. For example, if the desired output for an instance of the problem is 0.8 and the network, in fact, produced 0.8, the bin that is the intersection of 0.8 on the x axis and 0.8 on the y axis would have its count updated. This bin appears on the diagonal. If the network, in fact, produced 0.2, the bin is off the diagonal (in the lower right), which visually indicates that the network is predicting low when it should be predicting high. Moreover, a *global*

Table II

Network	# of learning cycles needed for convergence	% Accuracy [(# correct results /total tests)∗100]
FL-F-BKP	< 400	> 90
DBD	< 2,000	> 90
EDBD	< 1,000	> 75
DIGI-B	< 4,000	> 50
DIGI-I	< 1,000	> 50
CASC	< 400	> 90
DRS	< 20,000	> 75
BOL	< 20,000	> 60
CASC	< 400	> 90
RBFN	< 2,700	> 90
SOM + BKP	< 5,600	> 75
LVQ	< 600	> 75
PNN	< 60	> 90

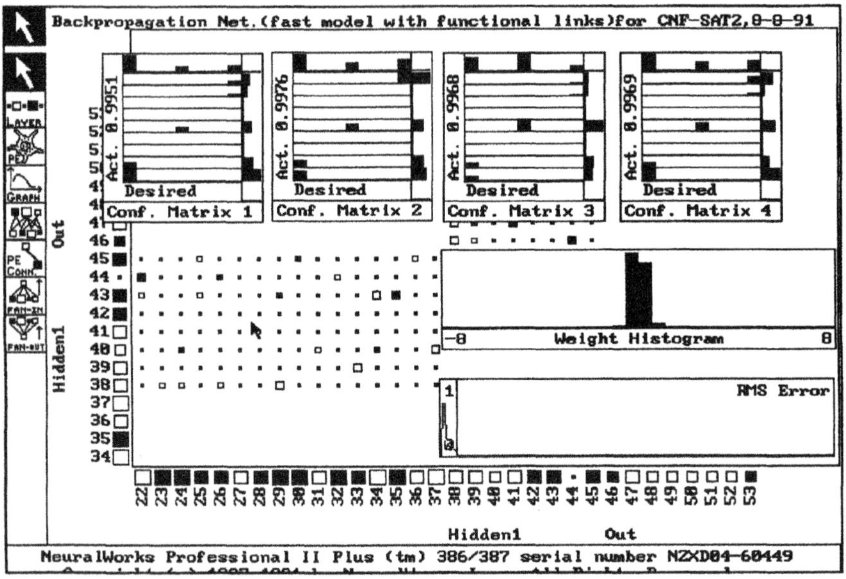

Figure 4 Backpropagation network (FL-F-BKP) with rms error converging to 0, four confusion matrices, the weight histogram, and a partial Hinton diagram. Reprinted with permission from A. Monfroglio, *Neural Comput. Appl.* 3:78–100, 1995 (© 1995 Springer-Verlag).

index (correlation) is reported that lies between 0 and 1. The optimal index is 1 (or 0.999...), that is, the actual result equals the desired result.

The *weight histogram* provides a normalized histogram that shows the raw weight values for the input leading into the output layer. As the weights are changed during the learning phase, the histogram will show the distribution of weights in the output layer. Initially, the weights start out close to 0 (central position) owing to the randomization ranges. As the network is trained, some weights move away from their near 0 starting points. For more detail, see [36]. It is interesting to note that the weight histograms for all networks but cascade correlation are very similar. CASC has a very different weight histogram.

The *Hinton diagram* (Fig. 5) is a graphically displayed interconnection matrix. All of the processing elements in the network are displayed along the x axis as well as the y axis. Connections are made by assuming that the outputs of the PEs are along the x axis. These connections are multiplied by weights shown graphically as filled or unfilled squares to produce the input for the PEs in the y axis. The connecting weights for a particular PE can be seen by looking at the row of squares to the right of the PE displayed on the y axis. The input to each weight is the output from the PE immediately below along the x axis.

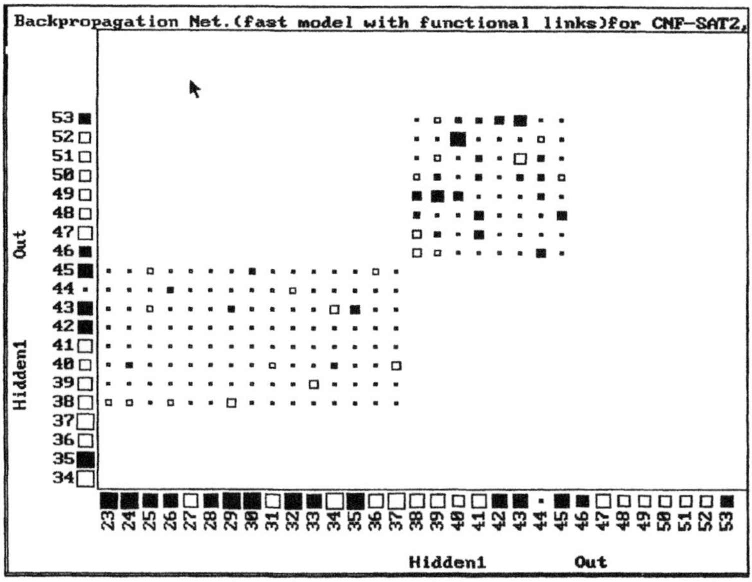

Figure 5 A significant part of the Hinton diagram. Reprinted with permission from A. Monfroglio, *Neural Comput. Appl.* 3:78–100, 1995 (© 1995 Springer-Verlag).

The *network diagram* (Fig. 6) is arranged by layers. The layer lowest on the figure is the input layer, whereas the highest up is the output layer. Connections between PEs are shown as solid or broken lines.

Figures 7 and 8 show how the performance of the proposed algorithm (FL-F-BKP and CASC networks) improves on unseen examples with progressive train-

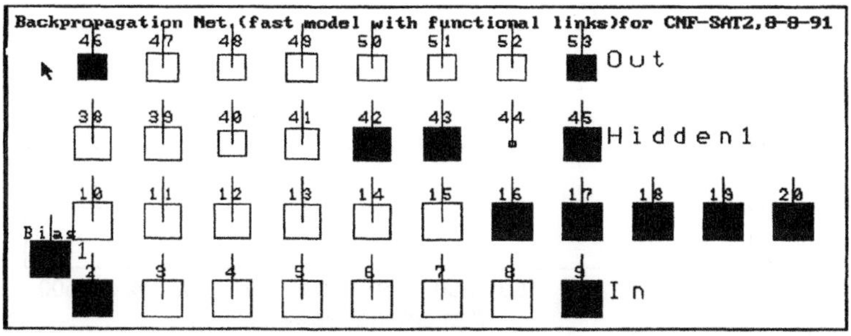

Figure 6 The FL-F-BKP network topology. Reprinted with permission from A. Monfroglio, *Neural Comput. Appl.* 3:78–100, 1995 (© 1995 Springer-Verlag).

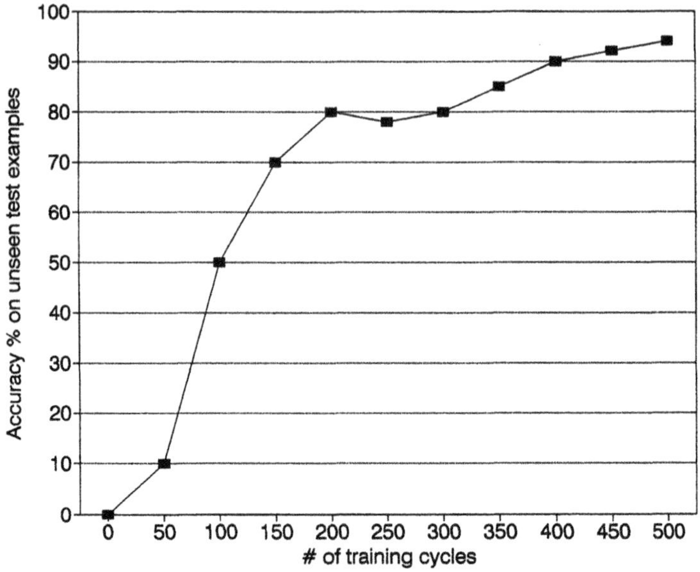

Figure 7 FL-F-BKP performance improvement with training. Reprinted with permission from A. Monfroglio, *Neural Comput. Appl.* 3:78–100, 1995 (© 1995 Springer-Verlag).

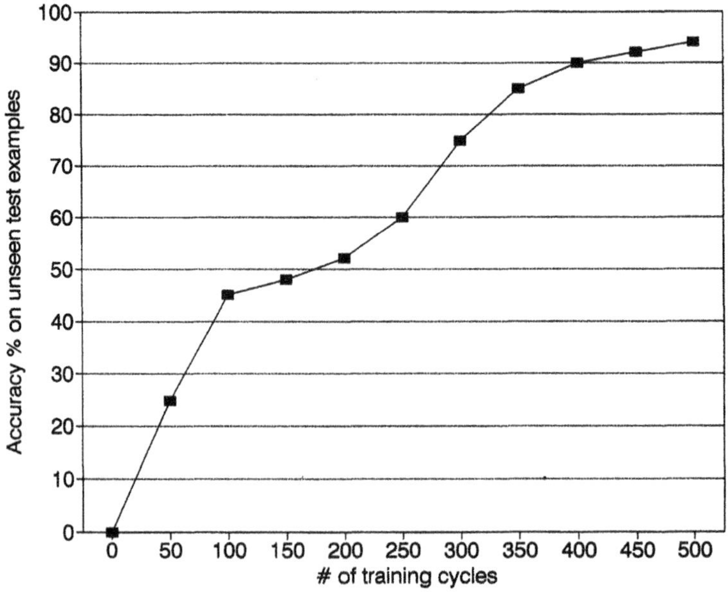

Figure 8 FL-F-BKP average correlation improvement. Reprinted with permission from A. Monfroglio, *Neural Comput. Appl.* 3:78–100, 1995 (© 1995 Springer-Verlag).

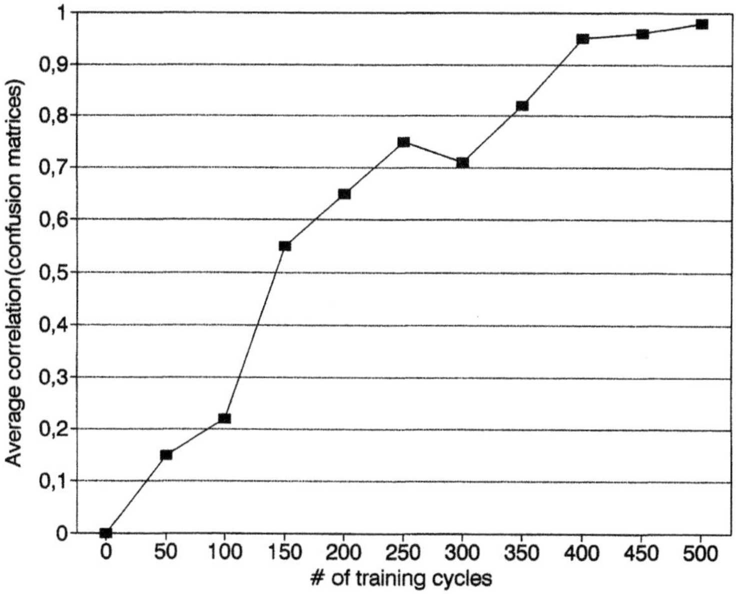

Figure 9 CASC performance improvement with training. Reprinted with permission from A. Monfroglio, *Neural Comput. Appl.* 3:78–100, 1995 (© 1995 Springer-Verlag).

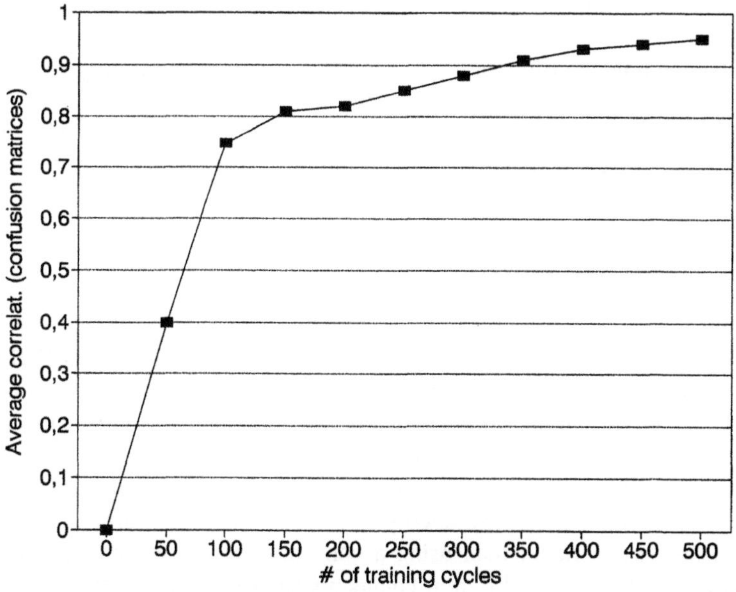

Figure 10 CASC average correlation improvement. Reprinted with permission from A. Monfroglio, *Neural Comput. Appl.* 3:78–100, 1995 (© 1995 Springer-Verlag).

ing. Figures 9 and 10 report how the average correlation of the confusion matrices improves with training on the examples of the training set. As one can see, FL-F-BKP and CASC exhibit very good performance. For the other networks the reader can consult [37].

Figures 7 and 9 also show the typical "plateau" behavior of the FL-F-BKP (a backpropagation network): an interval of the training phase where the network is in a local minimum.

1. Analysis of Networks' Performances

A further analysis of the networks' performances is important to show the characteristics of our algorithm. By analyzing the reasons why FL-F-BKP and CASC have good performance and DRS has worse, we can say that our algorithm seems to rely strongly on backpropagation and on the additional work done by the functional links in FL-F-BKP. Moreover, CASC has the benefit of attempting to minimize the number of hidden nodes. This is very important because our model has considerable complexity in problem size. Our algorithm is based on heuristic constrained search in a very large state space.

The good performance of FL-F-BKP for our algorithm is not surprising. It is well known that additional functional-link nodes in the input layer may dramatically improve the learning rate. This is very important for the CNF-SAT problem and the particular algorithm we are using. The learning task is very hard and our algorithm is based on the relation between an input value and each other value. Thus the combination of input items taken two at a time seems very well suited. The additional complexity is rewarded by learning speed improvement.

As one can see in our performance summary, PNN trains very quickly due to excellent classification capabilities of this kind of network. Random steps in the weight space, as done in DRS, and impetus to pursue previously successful search seem unsuitable for good convergence speed and accuracy. A partially successful search means a partially successful instantiation for our original CNF-SAT problem. A partially successful instantiation may often take us away from the global solution.

EDBD versus DBD shows better convergence but worse accuracy. EDBD uses a technique that reinforces general trends and reduces oscillations. This is only partially suited for our algorithm, which is based on a global heuristic evaluation of the configuration and not on general trends.

Our approach can be important and useful because it is very natural and more efficient to implement a constrained search technique as a neural network with parallel processing rather than using a conventional and sequential algorithm. In addition, we compare different connectionist paradigms for the same problem (CNF-SAT) through significant tests. In particular, we have shown that some paradigms not usually chosen for typical search and combinatorial problems such as FCSPs can, in fact, be used with success as we will see further in the conclusions.

We implemented the preceding algorithms during seven years of research on logic constraint solving and discrete combinatorial optimization that aimed to reduce or eliminate backtracking; see [17, 28, 38–41].

II. LINEAR PROGRAMMING AND NEURAL NETWORKS

First, we introduce a novel transformation from clausal form CNF-SAT to an integer linear programming model. The resulting matrix has a regular structure and is no longer problem-specific. It depends only on the number of clauses and the number of variables, but not on the structure of the clauses. Because of the structure of the integer program we can solve it by means of standard linear programming (LP) techniques. More detail can be found in [42].

Next, we describe a connectionist network to solve the CNF-SAT problem. This neural network (NN) is effective in choosing the best pivot selection for the Simplex LP procedure. A genetic algorithm optimizes the parameters of the NN algorithm. The NN improves the LP performance and Simplex guarantees always to find a solution.

Linear programming has sparked great interest among scientists due to its practical and theoretical importance. LP plays a special role in optimization theory: In one sense, it is a continuous optimization problem (the first optimization problem) because the decision variables are real numbers. However, it also may be considered the combinatorial optimization problem to identify an optimal basis containing certain columns from the constraint matrix (the second optimization problem). Herein we will use *an artificial neural network* to solve the second optimization problem in linear programs for the satisfaction of a conjunctive normal form (CNF-SAT). As shown by significant tests, this neural network is effective in solving this problem.

Modern optimization began with Dantzig's development of the Simplex algorithm (1947). However, the worst case complexity of the Simplex algorithm is exponential, even if the Simplex typically requires a low-order polynomial number of steps to compute an optimal solution. The recently introduced Khachian ellipsoid algorithm [43] and Karmarkar projective scaling algorithm [44], are provable polynomial. Theoretically, *any polynomial time algorithm can detect an optimal basis in polynomial time*. However, as pointed out by Ye [45], keeping all columns active during the entire iterative process especially degrades the practical performance. Ye gave a pricing rule under which a column can be identified early as an optimal nonbasic column and be eliminated from further computation.

We will describe an alternative approach based on neural networks. This approach compares favorably and can be implemented easily on parallel machines. We will first describe a novel transformation from clausal form conjunctive normal form satisfaction (CNF-SAT) to an integer linear programming model. The resulting matrix is larger than that for the well known default transformation method, but it has a regular structure and is no longer problem-specific. It depends only on the number of clauses and the number of variables, but not on the structure of the clauses.

Our representation incorporates all problem-specific data of a particular n-CNF-SAT problem in the objective function, and the constraint matrix is general, given m and n. The structure of the integer program allows solution by means of standard linear programming techniques.

A. Conjunctive Normal Form Satisfaction and Linear Programming

We will use boldface letters for matrices and vectors to render the text more readable.

As is well known, every linear program can be rearranged into matrix form (called primal):

$$\min \mathbf{c}_1\mathbf{x}_1 + \mathbf{c}_2\mathbf{x}_2,$$

$$\mathbf{A}_{11}\mathbf{x}_1 + \mathbf{A}_{12}\mathbf{x}_2 \geq \mathbf{b}_1,$$

$$\mathbf{A}_{21}\mathbf{x}_1 + \mathbf{A}_{22}\mathbf{x}_2 = \mathbf{b}_2,$$

with $\mathbf{x}_1 \geq 0$, $\mathbf{x}_2$ unrestricted. By adding nonnegative slack or surplus variables to convert any inequalities to equalities, replacing any unrestricted variables by differences of nonnegative variables, deleting any redundant rows, and taking the negative of a maximize objective function (if any), a linear program can be written in the famous Simplex standard form $\min \mathbf{cx}$, $\mathbf{Ax} = \mathbf{b}$, $\mathbf{x} \geq 0$. An integer problem in Simplex standard linear programming has the form $\min \mathbf{cx}$, $\mathbf{Ax} = \mathbf{b}$, $\mathbf{x} \geq 0$, $\mathbf{x}$ integer.

The integrity constraint renders the problem more difficult and in fact, 0–1 integer solvability is, in general, an NP-hard problem, whereas linear programming is in the class of P complexity. Remember that 0–1 integer solvability may be formulated as follows: Given an integer matrix $\mathbf{A}$ and an integer vector $\mathbf{b}$, does there exist a 0–1 vector $\mathbf{x}$ such that $\mathbf{Ax} = \mathbf{b}$?

1. Transformation of a Conjunctive Normal Form Satisfiability Problem in an Integer Linear Programming Problem

We show here how we can transform a generic CNF-SAT problem in an integer LP problem of the form

$$\min \mathbf{cx}, \qquad \mathbf{Ax} = \mathbf{b}, \qquad \mathbf{x} \geq 0, \qquad \mathbf{x} \text{ integer},$$

with $\mathbf{A}$ an integer matrix and $\mathbf{b}$, $\mathbf{c}$ integer vectors. Moreover, all elements of $\mathbf{A}, \mathbf{b}, \mathbf{c}$ are 0 or 1. The solutions of the integer LP problem include a valid solution of the CNF-SAT problem.

We have the CNF-SAT problem in the form

$$\begin{aligned} &v_1\colon a_{11}, a_{12}, \ldots, a_{1p1}, \\ &v_2\colon a_{21}, a_{22}, \ldots, a_{2p2}, \\ &\vdots \\ &v_m\colon a_{m1}, a_{m2}, \ldots, a_{mpm}, \end{aligned}$$

with m variables, n distinct nonnegated alternatives, and n negated alternatives, that is, $2n$ distinct alternatives.

In Karp [46] taxonomy, the following problem is classified as NP (CNF-SAT): Given an integer matrix $\mathbf{A}$ and an integer vector $\mathbf{b}$, does there exist a 0–1 vector $\mathbf{x}$ such that $\mathbf{Ax} = \mathbf{b}$ where $a_{ij} = 1$ if x_j is a literal in clause c_i, -1 if negated x_j is a literal in clause c_i, and 0 otherwise? With this representation, the problem is NP because the matrix $\mathbf{A}$ is specific to the particular instance of the CNF-SAT problem. Therefore, to say that the n-dimensional CNF-SAT problem with a particular dimension n is solvable through LP, we must test all instances of that dimension. These instances grow exponentially with the dimension of the problem.

2. Formal Description

The idea is to devise a transformation from n-CNF-SAT to integer programming in which the resulting matrix $\mathbf{A}$ and the right-hand side $\mathbf{b}$ are dependent only on the numbers of variables and clauses in the instance, but not on their identity. The identity of a specific n-CNF-SAT problem is encoded into the weight vector $\mathbf{c}$. To obtain this result, we use a different representation than that of Karp. Our representation gives a matrix $\mathbf{A}$ that is *general and valid* for any n-dimensional instance of the problem. We represent the problem in general terms as

$$\begin{array}{lccccccc} & A & B & C & \cdots a & b & c\cdots & \\ v_1 & x_{11} & x_{12} & x_{13} & \cdots x_1 & \cdots x_1 & \cdots x_{1\,2n} & \\ \vdots & & & & & & & \\ v_m & x_{m1} & x_{m2} & x_{m3} & \cdots x_m & \cdots x_{m\,2n} & & \text{with } m, n > 0, \end{array} \tag{1}$$

where x_{11}, x_{12}, etc. are assignable 0–1 values: 0 means the respective alternative is not chosen; 1 means it is chosen. Then we rearrange the matrix of x_{ij} in a column vector $\mathbf{x}$:

$$\begin{array}{cc} x_{11} & x_1 \\ \vdots & \vdots \\ x_{m\,2n} & x_{2mn} \end{array}$$

of $m * 2 * n$ values.

At this point, we construct our constraint matrix $\mathbf{A}$ using the following constraints:

(c) *Multiple choice constraints* which ensure that exactly one and only one of several 0–1 x_{ij} in each row must equal 1, that is, for each variable v_i and for each j of x_{ij} in Eq. (1) a 1 value must be present in the matrix $\mathbf{A}$;

(e) *Constraints* which ensure that each pair literal such as A and a, B and b, etc. (i.e., nonnegated and negated forms) are mutually exclusive, that is, at most one of two is 1. For each couple of such a values, the respective positions in the matrix $\mathbf{A}$ must hold a 1 value.

3. Some Examples

Let us illustrate our formal algorithm through some examples. For instance, if $m = 2$, $n = 2$, we have

$$\begin{array}{lcccc} & A & B & a & b \\ v_1: & x_{11} & x_{12} & x_{13} & x_{14} \\ v_2: & x_{21} & x_{22} & x_{23} & x_{24}. \end{array}$$

If $x_1 = x_{11}$, $x_2 = x_{12}$, $x_3 = x_{13}$, $x_4 = x_{14}$, $x_5 = x_{21}$, $x_6 = x_{22}$, $x_7 = x_{23}$, $x_8 = x_{24}$, let $\mathbf{x} = [x_1\ x_2\ x_3\ x_4\ x_5\ x_6\ x_7\ x_8]^{\mathrm{T}}$ be the column vector of eight elements (plus four slack variables), and $\mathbf{b} = [1\ 1\ 1\ 1\ 1\ 1]^{\mathrm{T}}$. The matrix $\mathbf{A}$ results:

$$\begin{array}{cccccccc|cccc l}
1 & 1 & 1 & 1 & 0 & 0 & 0 & 0 & 0 & 0 & 0 & 0 & \text{c-type constraints} \\
0 & 0 & 0 & 0 & 1 & 1 & 1 & 1 & 0 & 0 & 0 & 0 & \text{c-type constraints} \\
1 & 0 & 0 & 0 & 0 & 0 & 1 & 0 & 1 & 0 & 0 & 0 & \text{e-type constraints} \\
0 & 1 & 0 & 0 & 0 & 0 & 0 & 1 & 0 & 1 & 0 & 0 & \text{e-type constraints} \\
0 & 0 & 1 & 0 & 1 & 0 & 0 & 0 & 0 & 0 & 1 & 0 & \text{e-type constraints} \\
0 & 0 & 0 & 1 & 0 & 1 & 0 & 0 & 0 & 0 & 0 & 1 & \text{e-type constraints.}
\end{array}$$

The first row assures $x_{11} + x_{12} + x_{13} + x_{14} = 1$, that is, exactly one of the 0–1 x_{1i} must equal 1; that is, one and only one alternative is chosen for the variable v_1. The second row is analogous. The third and the following rows ensure compatibility among the choices. For example, the third row ensures that $x_{11} + x_{23} \leq 1$, that is, either A or a, in exclusive manner, is chosen. The $\leq$ is necessary here because there may be cases where neither A nor a is chosen. As usual for the Simplex, we add a slack variable to gain equality. It is easy to see that the number of e-type constraints is two times n times m times $(m-1)/2$, that is, $2n * m(m-1)/2$. The $\mathbf{b}$ column vector does contain $m + 2n * m(m-1)/2$ elements all equal 1.

The $\mathbf{c}$ vector of the integer linear program is constructed for each particular problem and serves to maximize the assignments for all variables. It does contain $m * 2 * n$ elements plus $2 * n * m * (m-1)/2$ (slack) elements. For example, if we have the problem

$$v_1\colon A, b, \qquad v_2\colon a,$$

$$A \quad B \quad a \quad b \quad A \quad B \quad a \quad b \ \text{slacks,}$$

the $\mathbf{c}$ row vector is

$$1 \quad 0 \quad 0 \quad 1 \quad 0 \quad 0 \quad 1 \quad 0 \quad 0 \quad 0 \quad 0 \quad 0$$

(one for each alternative in the problem), which is then transformed in

$$-1 \quad 0 \quad 0 \quad -1 \quad 0 \quad 0 \quad -1 \quad 0 \quad 0 \quad 0 \quad 0 \quad 0$$

to obtain a minimization problem from the original maximization, as required.

Applying the usual Simplex procedure, we find the following outcome for the preceding example. For the nonbasis variables, the usual zero values:

$$x_2 = 0 \geq x_{12} = 0 \quad \text{(in the original matrix),}$$

$$x_3 = 0 \geq x_{13} = 0, \qquad x_5 = 0 \geq x_{21} = 0, \qquad x_6 = 0 \geq x_{22} = 0,$$

$$x_9 = 0 \geq x_{01} = 0 \quad \text{(slack variable in the original constraints),}$$

$$x_{12} = 0 \geq x_{04} = 0 \quad \text{(slack variable).}$$

For the six basic variables:

$$\begin{aligned} x_1 &= b_1 = 0 \geq x_{11} = 0, \\ x_4 &= b_8 = 1 \geq x_{14} = 1, \\ x_7 &= b_3 = 1 \geq x_{23} = 1, \\ x_8 &= b_2 = 0 \geq x_{24} = 0, \\ x_{10} &= b_4 = 1 \geq x_{02} = 1 \quad \text{(slack variable)}, \\ x_{11} &= b_5 = 1 \geq x_{03} = 1 \quad \text{(slack variable)}. \end{aligned}$$

The meaning is $x_{14} = 1 \geq v_1$ is assigned to b, $x_{23} = 1 \geq v_2$ is assigned to a, $x_{02} = 1$, $x_{03} = 1$ slack variables equal 1 (because A is not chosen for v_1, etc.).

The objective function is minimized for -2, that is, it is maximized for a value of 2; that is, the two variables to which a value is assigned. Note that because one and only one alternative is chosen for each variable, the only way to maximize the objective function is to give an assignment to all variables and the choice must be one where the corresponding alternative is present. Thus the original problem is solved. The matrix **A** is general and valid for any two-variables problem and the **c** vector is specific.

Appendix III gives an example with $n = 3$. Appendix IV gives an outline of the proof. In brief, the reason why linear programming is sufficient to obtain an integer solution is that the constraint characterization we used has the following fundamental properties:

- There is always at least one integer solution for the LP problem.
- There is always at least one optimal integer solution for the LP problem.
- The optimal solution for the LP problem has the same value of the objective function as the associated integer programming optimal solution. This value is equal to the number m of clauses of the original CNF-SAT problem.
- The optimal value of the LP problem is the value that the objective function has after the tableau has been put into canonical form.
- To put the LP problem in canonical form, m pivot operations, one for each of the first m rows, are required.

Thus, by using a special rule for choosing the row positions of the pivot operations, the LP program does guarantee integer solutions.

4. Cost of the Algorithm

The matrix **A** is larger than that for the well known default transformation method, but it has a regular structure and is no longer problem-specific. The worst case cost in the dimensions $[m * n]$ of our original CNF-SAT problem is

number of columns:	$m * 2n + 2n * m * (m - 1)/2,$
number of rows:	$m + 2n * m * (m - 1)/2.$

If we consider the case where $m = n$, we have

$$c = n^3 + n^2, \qquad r = n^3 - n^2 + n,$$

which gives a cubic worst case cost.

However, we have considered the complete case, that is, the case where for each variable each alternative is present. This is not the case of course: if all alternatives are present, the problem is not yet solved. Thus the number of constraints that are necessary is always lower and so is the algorithm's cost.

B. Connectionist Networks That Learn to Choose the Position of Pivot Operations

The following text surveys several different paradigms we implemented and tested for pivot selection in the n-CNF-SAT problem. Notice that to solve n-CNF-SAT for the first three networks we chose the following architecture:

Input layer: $2 * n^2$ PEs (processing elements),
One hidden layer: $2 * n^2$ PEs,
Output layer: $2 * n^2$ PEs,

where n-CNF-SAT means n clauses and at most n literals per clause. For instance, for a simple 2-CNF-SAT case such as

$$v1\text{: } A, b, \qquad v2\text{: } a,$$

we have input layer, 8 PEs; hidden layer, 8 PEs; output layer, 8 PEs:

	v_1				v_2			
	A	B	a	b	A	B	a	b
Input:	1.0	0.0	0.0	1.0	0.0	0.0	1.0	0.0
Output:	0.0	0.0	0.0	1.0	0.0	0.0	1.0	0.0

The 1.0 output values correspond to the positions of all the Simplex pivot operations in the matrix **A** of Section II.A.1, that is, the column positions because the row positions are chosen with the procedure of that section. So the output PEs become $2 * n^2$. The output layer encodes all the choices, that is, for all the variables to instantiate.

Because of the categorization nature of the LVQ and PNN networks (only one category as winner), we have adopted the configuration

> Input layer: $2 * n^2 + n$ PEs (n PEs are added to code the choice of the variable to instantiate),
> Hidden layer for LVQ: $2 * n$ PEs,
> Hidden layer for PNN: PEs = the number of training examples,
> Output layer: $2 * n$ PEs,

because in each output only one category is the winner (value of 1.0). Single instances should code the successive winners (successive pivot operations), and the representation is less compact. Each output encodes a single choice, that is, a single variable to instantiate, that is, a single pivot position. Here, the single 1.0 value corresponds to the next pivot operation.

For the preceding example, we have

	A	B	a	b	A	B	a	b	v_1	v_2
Input:	1.0	0.0	0.0	1.0	0.0	0.0	1.0	0.0 |	1.0	0.0
Output:	0.0	0.0	0.0	1.0						

	A	B	a	b	A	B	a	b	v_1	v_2
Input:	1.0	0.0	0.0	1.0	0.0	0.0	1.0	0.0 |	0.0	1.0
Output:					0.0	0.0	1.0	0.0		

1. Performance Summary

A brief summary of the relative performances of our implementations is given in Table III. Remember that all networks give an accuracy of 100% on the problems used to train the network. Thus, the reported accuracy is relative to the CNF-SAT problems of the testing set, which is not included in the training set. The accuracy is in percent of correct choices with respect to the total number of testing problems. These choices are, of course, the positions of the pivot operations.

Note that we have adopted a training set of 15% of the total cases for learning and a testing set (of course not included in the training set) of 10% of the possible

Table III

Network	# of learning cycles needed for convergence	% Accuracy [(# correct results /total tests)*100]
FL-F-BKP	< 300	> 90
DBD	< 1500	> 90
EDBD	< 1000	> 75
LVQ	< 500	> 75
PNN	< 60	> 90

cases for performance judgment. This shows the fundamental role of generalization that the network plays through learning.

The testing environment was C language routines generated by the network simulator and then modified by the author. The hardware was UNIX and MS-DOS workstations. For n-CNF-SAT with $2 < N < 30$, 10,000 were performed.

As one can see, FLFBKP and PNN have a very good performance. More details and other neural network implementations can be found in [47, 48].

III. NEURAL NETWORKS AND GENETIC ALGORITHMS

The following section describes another NN approach for the n-CNF-SAT problem. The approach is similar to that used by Takefuji [49] for other NP-hard optimization problems.

CNF-SAT is represented as a linear program and as a neural network. The neural network (whose parameters are optimized by means of a genetic algorithm) runs for a specified maximum number of iterations. If the obtained solution is optimal, then the algorithm ends. If not, the partial solution found by the neural network is given to the linear programming procedure (Simplex), which will find the final (optimal) solution. For a more complete treatment, the reader can consult [50].

Notice that we have chosen the following neural network architecture: A $[m \times 2n]$ neural array for a n-CNF-SAT problem, where n-CNF-SAT means m clauses and a number n of global variables. There are m rows, one for each clause, and $2n$ columns, that is, one for each nonnegated and negated version of a variable (called literals in any clause).

For instance, in the previous 3-CNF-SAT example,

$$v_1\colon\ A, B, C, \qquad v_2\colon\ A, b, \qquad v_3\colon\ a,$$

we have three clauses, three global variables, six literals, three rows, and six columns; thus we have a 3×6 neural array.

Takefuji [49] described unsupervised learning NNs for solving many NP-hard optimization problems (such as K-colorability) by means of first order simultaneous differential equations. In fact, he adopted a discretization of the equations, which are implemented by Pascal or C routines. A very attractive characteristic of his algorithms is that they scale up linearly with problem size.

Takefuji's [49] approach is different from the classical Hopfield net in that he proved that the use of a decay term in the energy function of the Hopfield neural network is harmful and shoul be avoided. Takefuji's NN provides a parallel gradient descent method to minimize the constructed energy function. He gives convergence theorems and proofs for some of the neuron models including McCulloch–Pitts and McCulloch–Pitts hysteresis binary models. We will use these artificial neurons.

In this model, the derivative with respect to the time of the input U_i (of neuron i) is equal to the partial derivative of the energy function (a function of all outputs V_i, $i = 1, \ldots, n$) with respect to the output V_i, with minus sign. More detail can be found in [49].

The goal of the NN for solving the optimization problem is to minimize a defined energy function which incorporates the problem constraints and optimization goals. The energy function not only determines how many neurons should be used in the system, but also the strength of the synaptic links between the neurons. The system is constructed by considering the necessary and sufficient constraints and the cost function (the objective function) to optimize in the original problem. The algorithm ends only when the exact optimum value has been found.

In general Takefuji obtained very good average performance and algorithms which have an average execution time that scales up linearly with the dimension of the problem. He does not present a NN for CNF-SAT or for SAT problems in general. We will introduce a similar technique for CNF-SAT.

A. Neural Network

The neuron model we have chosen is the McCulloch–Pitts. The McCulloch–Pitts neuron model without hysteresis has the input–output function

$$\text{output} = 1 \text{ if input} > 0;\ 0 \text{ otherwise.}$$

In the hysteresis model the input–output function is

output = 1 if input > UTP (upper trip point, i.e., the upper threshold),
output = 0 if input < LTP (lower trip point, i.e., the lower threshold),
output unchanged otherwise.

Hysteresis has the effect of suppressing (or at least of limiting) oscillatory behavior. Outputs are initially assigned to randomly chosen 0 or 1 values.

We have experimented with two different energy functions. The first included three terms:

1. The first term ensures that exactly one neuron per row is active, that is, one alternative is chosen for each clause. If the row_sum is not 1, the energy function does not have the minimum value.
2. The second term ensures that no incompatible values are chosen. If there are two incompatible active neurons, the energy function does not have the minimum value.

3. The last term ensures that only available alternatives are chosen; for instance, if the first clause is $(A + b + D)$, we cannot choose the alternative C or the alternative d.

For the ijth neuron we have

$$\begin{aligned} dU_{ij}/dt &= -E1 * \left(\left(\sum_k V_{ik},\ k = 1, \ldots, n\right) - 1\right) - E2 \\ &\quad * (E_{pq} \not\subset [i, k, p, q],\ p = i + 1, \ldots, m,\ q = 1, \ldots, n) \\ &\quad + E3 * \left(\sum_k D[i, k] * V[i, k],\ k = 1, \ldots, n\right), \end{aligned} \quad (2)$$

where $D[i, j]$ is an input data array, which specifies the literals in each clause. The procedure ends when the energy function reaches the minimum value.

Of course, these three terms correspond to the choice constraint and the exclusion constraints, and the objective function to maximize (minimize) in the LP. In the energy function these three terms are weighted by three coefficients (parameters): $E1$, $E2$, and $E3$. $E1$ and $E2$ are added with a minus sign; $E3$ is added with a plus sign. The values of these parameters greatly influence the network performance. We will describe in Section III.B a genetic algorithm (GA) for optimizing these parameters. Moreover, in the McCulloch–Pitts neuron model with hysteresis, there are two other parameters that may be optimized by means of GA, that is, the two hysteresis thresholds UTP (upper trip point) and LTP (lower trip point). A general method to choose the best values for the two thresholds is not known. The second energy function we tested includes only two terms:

1. The first term ensures that one and only one neuron per row is active, that is, one alternative is chosen for each clause. If the row_sum is not 1, the energy function is not minimized. Note that this does not mean that there is only one variable which satisfies each clause. Recall that we use a different variable for each occurrence of a global variable in a different clause.
2. The second term ensures that no incompatible values are chosen. If there are two incompatible active neurons, the energy function is not minimized.

Moreover, a modified McCulloch–Pitts model with hysteresis neuron activation also ensures that only available alternatives are chosen. See the example in Section III.B. The average performances of the two approaches are quite similar, even when the second energy function is simpler.

Consider the CNF-SAT problem $(A+B+C)\cdot(A+\sim B)\cdot(\sim A)$. In our notation,

$$v_1\colon A, B, C, \qquad v_2\colon A, b, \qquad v_3\colon a.$$

We have $m = 3$ clauses and $n = 6$ global literals A, B, C, a, b, c. The neuron network array is thus of $3 * 6$ elements. The input array $U[1 \cdots 3, 1 \cdots 6]$,

$$\begin{array}{ccccccc} & A & B & C & a & b & c \\ 1 & r & r & r & r & r & r \\ 2 & r & r & r & r & r & r \\ 3 & r & r & r & r & r & r \end{array}$$

initially contains a random value r chosen between 0 and 1 at each position. The output array $V[1 \cdots 3, 1 \cdots 6]$ is

$$\begin{array}{ccccccc} & A & B & C & a & b & c \\ 1 & x & x & x & x & x & x \\ 2 & x & x & x & x & x & x \\ 3 & x & x & x & x & x & x \end{array}$$

The solution is $A =$ false, $B =$ false, and $C =$ true, or

$$v_1 := C, \qquad v_2 := b, \qquad v_3 := a.$$

The input data array $D[1 \cdots 3, 1 \cdots 6]$ is

$$\begin{array}{c|cccccc} & A & B & C & a & b & c \\ 1 & 1 & 1 & 1 & 0 & 0 & 0 \\ 2 & 1 & 0 & 0 & 0 & 1 & 0 \\ 3 & 0 & 0 & 0 & 1 & 0 & 0 \end{array}$$

Thus,

$$\begin{array}{lll} D[1,1] := 1, & D[1,2] := 1, & D[1,3] := 1, \\ D[2,1] := 1, & D[2,5] := 1, & D[3,4] := 1. \end{array}$$

The final neuron activation array is

$$\begin{array}{c|cccccc} & A & B & C & a & b & c \\ 1 & 0 & 0 & 1 & 0 & 0 & 0 \\ 2 & 0 & 0 & 0 & 0 & 1 & 0 \\ 3 & 0 & 0 & 0 & 1 & 0 & 0 \end{array}$$

The exclusion constraints (valid for any $3 * 6$ problem instance) are

$$\begin{array}{lll} E[1,1,2,4] := 1; & E[1,1,3,4] := 1; & E[1,2,2,5] := 1; \\ E[1,2,3,5] := 1; & E[1,3,2,6] := 1; & E[1,3,3,6] := 1; \\ E[1,4,2,1] := 1; & E[1,4,3,1] := 1; & E[1,5,2,2] := 1; \\ E[1,5,3,2] := 1; & E[1,6,2,3] := 1; & E[1,6,3,3] := 1; \end{array}$$

$$E[2,1,3,4] := 1; \qquad E[2,2,3,5] := 1; \qquad E[2,3,3,6] := 1;$$

$$E[2,4,3,1] := 1; \qquad E[2,5,3,2] := 1; \qquad E[2,6,3,3] := 1;$$

The meaning of $E[1,1,2,4] := 1$ is that the activation (output $V_{11} = 1$) of the neuron $1, 1$ (v_1: A) excludes the activation (output $V_{24} = 1$) of the neuron $2, 4$ (v_2: a). In general, $E[i, j, p, q]$ means that the activation of the neuron i, j excludes the contemporary activation of the neuron p, q. However, only the exclusion constraints related to available alternatives are activated. In the foregoing example only the following exclusion constraints are activated:

$$E[1,1,3,4] := 1 \quad \text{(i.e., } v_1\text{: } A \text{ and } v_3\text{: } a\text{)},$$

$$E[1,2,2,5] := 1 \quad \text{(i.e., } v_1\text{: } B \text{ and } v_2\text{: } b\text{)},$$

$$E[2,1,3,4] := 1 \quad \text{(i.e., } v_2\text{: } A \text{ and } v_3\text{: } a\text{)}.$$

For each row an available alternative (i.e., for which $D[i, j] = 1$) has to be chosen.

The Pascallike code for the first energy function is

$$\text{for } k := 1 \text{ to } n \text{ do satisfy} := \text{satisfy} + D[i,k] * V[i,k].$$

If satisfy $= 0$, then the third term h in the energy function is > 0; if(satisfy $=$ 0), then $h := h + 1$. A term excl calculates the number of violated exclusion constraints for each row:

```
for k := 1 to n do
    for p := 1 to m do
        for q := 1 to n do
            excl := excl + V[i, j] * E[i, j, p, q].
```

The discretized version of Eq. (2) becomes

$$U[i,j] := U[i,j] - E1 * (\text{sum\_row} - 1) - E2 * \text{excl} + E3 * h.$$

In the second energy function only two terms are present:

$$U[i,j] := U[i,j] - E1 * (\text{sum\_row} - 1) - E2 * \text{excl}$$

and a modified neuron activation model is used:

$$\text{if } \big((U[i,j] > \text{UTP}) \text{ and } (D[i,j] = 1)\big), \text{ then } V[i,j] := 1.$$

B. Genetic Algorithm for Optimizing the Neural Network

Genetic algorithms (GAs), a computer technique inspired by natural evolution and proposed by Holland [51], are good candidates for this achievement and also have been used successfully for similar tasks. As well known, GAs are search procedures based on natural selection and genetics. As pointed out by Goldberg [52], GAs are very attractive for a number of reasons:

- GAs can solve hard problems reliably.
- Gas can be straightforwardly interfaced to existing simulations and models.
- GAs are extensible.
- GAs are easy to hybridize.

See also Davis [53].

We have chosen, in particular to hybridize the GA with our previous algorithm, or more precisely, to incorporate the previous algorithm into a GA. A simple GA may consist of a population generator and selector; a fitness (objective function) estimator; two genetic operators—the mutation operator and the crossover operator.

The first part generates a random population of individuals each of which has a single "chromosome," that is, a string of "genes." Here, genes are binary codes, that is, bit strings, for the parameters to optimize. Here the fitness, that is, the objective function, of each individual is the average number of iteration steps used by the neural network to reach the optimum. The mutation operator simply inverts a randomly chosen bit with a certain probability, usually low, but often not constant as evolution proceeds.

The crossover operator is more complex and important. Two individuals (the "parents") are chosen based on some fitness evaluation (a greater fitness gives more probability of being chosen). Parts of the chromosomes of two individuals are combined to generate two new offspring whose fitness hopefully will be better than that of their parents. Ultimately, they will replace low fitness individuals in the population. Such events will continue for a certain number of "generations." Time constraints forced us to severely limit the number of generations: about 50 were used. A plethora of variations exist in the possible encoding (binary, real number, order based representations, etc.), in the selection and reproduction strategy, and in the crossover implementations. We have used a modified version of the well known GENESIS system written in C language by Grefenstette [54], and widely available.

The population size is 50 randomly generated chromosomes each with 5 genes encoding in a binary representation:

	Range	Bits
E1	$1 \leq \text{E1} \leq 255$	8
E2	$1 \leq \text{E2} \leq 255$	8
E3	$1 \leq \text{E3} \leq 255$	8
UTP	$1 \leq \text{UTP} \leq 15$	4
LTP	$1 \leq \text{LTP} \leq 15$	4

One point crossover is chosen, the reproduction strategy is elitism (the new offspring are recorded only if their fitness is better than that of their parents), and the parent selection technique is the well known roulette wheel. The initial crossover and mutation rates are 0.65 and 0.002, respectively.

The GA procedure found the following optimal values for the parameters:

$$E1 = 15, \qquad E2 = 6, \qquad E3 = 12,$$

$$\text{UTP} = 2, \qquad \text{LTP} = 2.$$

We found similar results using the second energy function with only two terms.

With these values for the five parameters the NN required an average of 1000 solution steps. This number was almost constant for almost all the clauses in the CNF-SAT between 3 and 100 in the CNF-SAT original problem. However, the average appears to be of very little use because a tremendous variability was observed in the distribution of steps versus problem instances of the same size N. For instance, for CNF-SAT with 10 clauses, some problem instances were solved through less than 20 steps, whereas a hard instance required more than 2000 steps. Out of all the problems, only a small fraction are really hard ones. Thus, most of the instances required a very small number of iterations. A similar result was described by Gent and Walsh [55].

We decided to impose a limit on the number of iterations: if the NN does not converge in 2500 steps, the hybrid algorithm stops the NN procedure and passes the current (approximate) solution to the LP procedure which is capable of obtaining the final (exact) complete solution. More details and figures can be found in [50].

C. Comparison with Conventional Linear Programming Algorithms and Standard Constraint Propagation and Search Techniques

We will compare our hybrid technique based on neural networks with the standard Simplex rule and with a more recent technique. We will also do a comparison to standard constraint propagation and search algorithms. A standard reference for any new approach to SAT problems is [56]. Other fundamental references are [57, 58].

As quoted by Jeroslow and Wang [57], the famous Davis and Putnam algorithm in the Loveland form (DPL) is, in fact, an algorithm framework. DPL is applied to a proposition in CNF that consists of three subroutines: clausal chaining (CC), monotone variable fixing (MON), and splitting (SPL). In addition, the unit propagation step (UP) was used, that is, recursive elimination of one-literal clauses. For a fair comparisons, the same unit propagation was added to the proposed algorithm as preprocessing. Note that a similar unit propagation also was used in the heuristic procedure described in the following sections.

CC removes clauses containing both some letter and its negation (the clause is always true). MON, as long as there are monotone letters, set these to truth valuations. A letter Li is monotone in a CNF if either Li does not occur as a literal, or li (the negated form of Li) does not occur. SPL is a more complex procedure. It operates in the following way: Choose a letter Li in the list of distinct literals for the CNF-SAT problem. Then the clauses can be divided into three groups:

I. Li OR $R_1, \dots,$ Li OR R_j—clauses containing Li positively.
II. ~li OR $S_1, \dots,$ ~li OR S_k—clauses containing Li negatively.
III. $T_1, \dots, T_q$—clauses not containing Li.

Then the clause list is split into two lists of clauses:

$R_1, \dots, R_k,\ T_1, \dots, T_q$, and Li is set to false.
$S_1, \dots, S_l,\ T_1, \dots, T_q$, and Li is set to true.

These sublists are added to the set of clauses. The procedure operates then recursively.

As one can see, DPL implementation depends on the strategy for choosing the letter Li in the subroutine SPL [analogous to the branching variable in any branch-and-bound (BB) algorithm], and the strategy for selecting which list is processing next (analogous to heuristic rules).

The so-called standard representation (SR) of a disjunctive clause via integer programming represents a clause Ci by a single linear constraint. For instance, the clause $A + {\sim}B + {\sim}E + G$ is represented by

$$z(A)+\big(1-z(B)\big)+\big(1-z(E)\big)+z(G) \geq 1, \quad z(A),\ z(B),\ z(E),\ z(G) \text{ in } \{0, 1\}.$$

In Jeroslow's opinion the BB method applied to SR is quite similar to DPL, if both are equipped with the same variable choice rules and subproblem selection rules. However, DPL has monotone variable fixing, whereas BB does not. Moreover, BB has an "incumbent finding" capability, whereas DPL does not. Incumbent finding consists of the fact that linear relaxation (LR) at a node of the BB search tree may give an integer solution (an "incumbent"). For example, in the CNF $(\sim A + B) \cdot (\sim A + B)$ CC takes no action, whereas LR gives $z(A) = z(B) = 0$, which derives from a basic feasible solution to the LR.

A possible disadvantage of BB (and of our approach) is its need to carry and manipulate the large data structures such as matrices and vectors of linear and integer programming.

Jeroslow and Wang [57] described a new algorithm (DPLH) that is based on DPL with the addition of a heuristic part, which plays two roles: splitting rule and incumbent finder. A comparison to our approach is now easy. Our algorithm is based on integer programming as is BB. However, the problem representation and structure give the possibility of solving it by a modification of standard Simplex for linear programming or by a modification of Karmarkar's LP routine. A part of DPL procedure has been incorporated into our algorithm as described in the following section.

It is useful to note that our representation of CNF-SAT as an integer programming problem is quite different from SR and usual BB. We may call our representation a "total relaxation": each new literal in a clause is given a different 0–1 variable name. As we said, this gives a LP matrix of larger size but not problem-instance-specific. A recent very efficient algorithm for SAT is described in [58].

To compare our algorithm with another recent linear programming technique to improve Simplex and Karmarkar procedures, we tested the Ye [45] approach too. Ye proposed a "build-down" scheme for Karmarkar's algorithm and the Simplex method. It starts with an optimal basis "candidate" set S including all columns of the constraint matrix, and then constructs a dual ellipsoid containing all optimal dual solutions. A pricing rule is developed for checking whether or not a dual hyperplane corresponding to a column intersects the containing ellipsoid. If the dual hyperplane has no intersections with the ellipsoid, its corresponding column will not appear in any of the optimal bases and can be eliminated from set S.

In the summary in Table IV the column labeled KP reports results obtained through our implementation of Ye's technique. GNN means our hybrid algorithm (LP plus neural networks plus a genetic algorithm). DPLH is our implementation of the Davis and Putnam [56] algorithm and SAT is our implementation of the algorithm of Selman *et al.* [58].

In the linear program, R is the number of constraints and C is the number of variables. The average time for solving the 100 test problems of 3-CNF-SAT is used as base (about 0.5 s on a PC486-66). All other average times for solving n-CNF-SAT test cases are normalized to 3-CNF-SAT.

The GNN results compare favorably with those that we achieved by means of Ye's [45] procedure. As expected, efficient algorithms (i.e., GSAT) recently implemented and based on constraint propagation and heuristic search are quite competitive with our proposal for small (mid-sized) instances.

Table IV

			C Average Time Normalized for				
n	*R*	C average time	Standard Simplex	KP	GNN	DPLH	SAT
3	21	36	1	0.81	0.81	1.05	0.52
4	52	80	4	3.21	3.22	4.19	2.46
⋮							
10	910	1100	47	37.57	37.27	49.35	30.05
⋮							
50	122,550	127,500	1453	1189.31	1142.56	1579.43	1352.66
⋮							
100	990,100	1,010,000	5942	4989.55	4329.55	6338.51	4329.92

D. Testing Data Base

Most randomly generated CNF-SAT problems are too easy: almost any assignment is a solution. Thus these problems cannot be significant tests. Rutgers University Center for Discrete Mathematics and Theoretical Computer Science maintains a data base of very hard SAT problems and problem generators that can serve as benchmarks (they are available through anonymous ftp from dimacs.rutgers.edu/pub/).

It is known that very hard, challenging instances can be obtained by choosing three literals for each clause (3-CNF-SAT) and a number m of clauses that is r times the number of globally distinct literals (i.e., $n = 3,\ m = r * n$). Ratios r are different for different n. For instance, if $n = 50,\ r$ is between 4 and 5. Hogg *et al.* [59] reported several useful ratios for very hard problems. Thus, we have used these parameters. In addition, a new test generation procedure has been used.

Note that the so-called K-SAT problems have been used, that is, fixed clause length CNFs produced by randomly generating p clauses of length 3, where each clause has three distinct variables randomly chosen from the set of n available and negating each with probability 0.5. There is another model, called random P-SAT (constant-density model), with less hard problems, which we did not consider in our tests.

A recent survey on hard and easy FCSPs is [59]. However, there is no general agreement on this subject. For instance, in the opinion of Hooker [60, 61] most benchmarks for satisfiability tests are inadequate: they are just constructed to show the effectiveness of the algorithms that they are supposed to test. Moreover, the same author reports that a fair comparison of algorithms is often impossible because one algorithm's performance is greatly influenced by the use of clever data structures and optimizations. The question is still open.

We also used a second test generation procedure:

1. We start from a solution, for instance,

$$v_1\colon d, \qquad v_2\colon A, \qquad \ldots, \qquad v_n\colon c.$$

2. We add a given number of alternatives to each variable v_i. For instance,

$$v_1\colon d, E, \qquad v_2\colon A, b, \qquad \ldots, \qquad v_n\colon c, D, \quad \text{etc.}$$

3. We submit the generated problem instance to a "too-easy" filter (see the following explanation for this filter). If this problem instance is judged too easy, discard it; else record it in the testing data base.
4. Repeat until the desired number of testing cases has been achieved.

The too-easy filter acts in the following manner:

1. A given number r of randomly generated assignments are constructed for the problem instance to judge.
2. These assignments are checked to determine how many of them do satisfy the CNF-SAT instance.
3. If a percentage greater than a given threshold is found, then the problem instance is judged too easy (random assignment will almost always satisfy the CNF).

IV. RELATED WORK, LIMITATIONS, FURTHER WORK, AND CONCLUSIONS

The algorithms by Spears [62–64] are among the first neural networks and genetic algorithms for satisfiability problems. Spears obtained good results on very hard satisfiability problems. His thesis [62] considered both the neural network and genetic algorithm approaches. He applied a Hopfield net. An annealing scheduled Hopfield net is compared with GSAT [58] in [63] and a simulated annealing algorithm is considered in [64]. Spears' algorithms are for solving arbitrary satisfiability problems, whereas GSAT assumes as we did that the Boolean expressions are in conjunctive normal form.

We have described a different approach based on hybrid algorithms. We have developed the hybrid approach to satisfiability problems in a seven year long research on logic constraint solving and discrete combinatorial optimization; see [10, 13, 17, 28, 38, 40–42, 48]. The main contributions of our proposal are the following:

- The comparison of different NN paradigms not usallly adopted for constraint satisfaction problems
- The hybridization of neural networks, genetic algorithms, and linear programming to solve n-CNF-SAT: LP will guarantee to obtain the solution, and neural networks and genetic algorithms help to obtain it in the lowest number of steps
- The comparison of this hybrid approach with the most promising recent technique based on linear programming procedures.
- A novel problem representation that models any FCSP with only two types of constraints—choice constraints and exclusion constraints—in a very natural way.

Note that Schaller [65] showed that for any FCSP with binary variables the preceding two constraints types are sufficient to efficiently model the problem. He used a slightly different terminology: he called these constraints "between-k-and-l-out-of-n constraints." If $k = l$ a k-out-of-n constraint results, which corresponds to our choice constraint; if $k < l$ the constraint corresponds to our exclusion constraint.

Also note that the traditional constraint representation as constraint graphs and evaluation as constraint propagation usually consider only exclusion constraints. A great amount of work has been published on consistency and propagation techniques for treating these exclusion constraints; see, for instance, [5].

Some limitations are present in our approach: even if CNF-SAT is a very crucial problem, it would be of great use to have a general procedure for every constraint satisfaction problem. To follow this objective we are considering the use of modelization technique analogous to the travelling salesperson problem. Further work is now in progress, and our initial results are promising. Consult [42, 50].

APPENDIX I. FORMAL DESCRIPTION OF THE SHARED RESOURCE ALLOCATION ALGORITHM

The shared resource allocation algorithm (SRAA) solves problems with a finite number of variables, each variable having a finite number of choices. In formal terms we have

$$\begin{aligned}
&v_1\colon\ a_{11}, a_{12}, \ldots, a_{1j}, \ldots, a_{1M},\\
&v_2\colon\ a_{21}, a_{22}, \ldots, a_{2j}, \ldots, a_{2M},\\
&\vdots\\
&v_i\colon\ a_{i1}, a_{i2}, \ldots, a_{ij}, \ldots, a_{iM},\\
&v_n\colon\ a_{n1}, a_{n2}, \ldots, a_{nj}, \ldots, a_{nM},
\end{aligned}$$

with $M, n > 0$ and finite and, lexicographically ordered, a finite number $P \geq n$ of distinct alternatives. Each variable must have an assignment among a set of alternatives, and two or more variables cannot have incompatible assignments. (Here, incompatibility means equal values. In CNF-SAT problems, two assigned values are incompatible if they are the negated and unnegated versions of the same literal, for example, A and NOT a, C and NOT c, etc.) We have to find the assignments

$$v_1\colon a_{1k}, \qquad v_2\colon a_{2l}, \qquad \ldots, \qquad v_n\colon a_{nz},$$

with a_{1k} not equal to a_{2l}, etc.

The main structure of the algorithm is the recursive call:

Step 1.

```
function v
   begin
        if (list_of_variables empty) then return
        else
          begin
          constraints;
          assign1;
          v;
          end
   end
```

The call holds while the list of variables to be assigned is not empty.

Step 2. The call *constraints* does the following: If the list of alternatives for a variable has length one, that is, has only one alternative, then this alternative is immediately assigned to that variable and then the procedure *update* is called.

Step 3. The *update* procedure deletes the assigned alternative in the set of currently available alternatives for each variable, and deletes the just instantiated variable in the list of variables to instantiate.

Step 4. The procedure *constraints* then performs the following constructions:

Step 4.1. Construct for each variable X, and for each alternative Y for X, a relation if that alternative is shared with another variable and the same relation has not been created yet. For example, if

$$v_1\colon B, C, E, \qquad \ldots, \qquad v_3\colon A, B,$$

the relation $c(1, B, 3)$ is created (if the same relation has not been created yet) and registered.

Step 4.2. Construct the four shared resource indices: FASRI, FVSRI, TASRI, TVSRI, as in Steps 4.2.1, 4.2.2, 4.2.3, and 4.2.4.

Step 4.2.1. Compute the first alternative shared resource index (FASRI) for the alternatives:

```
Initialize FASRI to zero;
for each variable X
        for each alternative Y in the set associated
        with the variable
          if there exists a relation c(X, Y, Z)
                  then increment the FASRI(X, Y)
```

Step 4.2.2. For each variable X, compute the sum first variable shared resource index FVSRI(X) of all the FASRI(X, Y).

Step 4.2.3.

```
Initialize TASRI (total alternative shared resource
 index) to zero;
    for each variable X
         for each alternative Y
              if there exists a relation c(X, Y, Z)
               then add the FVSRI(Z) to the
               current TASRI(X, Y).
```

Step 4.2.4. For each variable X, compute the sum total variable shared resource index TVSRI(X) of all the TASRI(X, Y).

Step 5. The procedure *assign1* finds the variable with Min TVSRI(X) and for that variable, the alternative with Min TASRI(X, Y). Then, this alternative is assigned to the corresponding variable. Finally the procedure *update* is called. If there are two or more equal indices for a variable, then additional indices are computed in the same manner, using the total indices currently computed as first indices to break ties. For details on this additional index, the reader can consult [13].

Outline of proof for the SRAA. First it is obvious that the solutions provided by our SRAA algorithm, if any, are correct. Indeed, each time a variable receives an assignment, the incompatible alternatives for all the variables are deleted through Step 3, so the algorithm cannot assign incompatible values.

We must ensure that the algorithm is complete too. We suppose we have the following solution for a problem with four variables:

$$v_1\text{: } B, \qquad v_2\text{: } A, \qquad v_3\text{: } D, \qquad v_4\text{: } C.$$

This solution was found, of course, through a choice among several alternatives for each variable:

$$v_1\colon \ldots, B, \ldots, \qquad v_2\colon \ldots, A, \ldots,$$

$$v_3\colon \ldots, D, \ldots, \qquad v_4\colon \ldots, C, \ldots.$$

Nevertheless we may suppose that this is the solution for a different problem, a problem that has only one alternative for each variable:

$$v_1\colon B, \qquad v_2\colon A, \qquad v_3\colon D, \qquad v_4\colon C.$$

Now this is the problem and the solution too. All the FASRI, FVSRI, TASRI, and TVSRI of Steps 4.2.1–4.2.4 are null because no alternatives are present.

Let us now slightly complicate our problem by adding an alternative for a variable. We have to consider the following cases:

1. The alternative is equal to the alternative that was assigned to that variable. This is a trivial case, for instance, $v_1\colon B, B$.

2. The alternative is different from all the present alternatives, for example, $v_1\colon B, E$. In this case the number of global distinct alternatives becomes larger and we have two different solutions, but the case is still trivial, because we do not have incompatible alternatives and our indices remain null.

3. The alternative is incompatible with some other, alternative, for example,

$$v_1\colon B, A, \qquad v_2\colon A, \qquad v_3\colon D, \qquad v_4\colon C,$$

where A in v_1 and A in v_2 are incompatible. This is equivalent to the problem

$$v_1\colon A, B, \qquad v_2\colon A, \qquad v_3\colon D, \qquad v_4\colon C,$$

where the alternatives are ordered in alphabetical order. Now the indices are different: A for v_1 has an index higher than B; v_1 and v_2 have higher indices than v_3 and v_4. The problem has only one solution from among the possible choices. The solution is, of course,

$$v_1\colon B, \qquad v_2\colon A, \qquad v_3\colon D, \qquad v_4\colon C,$$

which has all indices in accord with those of our algorithms. The choice

$$v_1\colon A, \qquad v_2\colon A, \qquad v_3\colon D, \qquad v_4\colon C,$$

which is not a solution (A and A are incompatible) does not respect the indices.

Now we complicate our example by adding two (or more) alternatives. We may find two cases:

3.1. The problem is *not symmetric* in respect to the indices of our algorithms, for instance,

$$\begin{array}{ll} v_1\colon A, B, & v_1\colon 1, 0, \\ v_2\colon A, C, & v_2\colon 1, 1, \\ v_3\colon D, & v_3\colon 1, \\ v_4\colon C, D, & v_4\colon 1, 1. \end{array}$$

The solution remains

$$v_1\colon B, \qquad v_2\colon A, \qquad v_3\colon D, \qquad v_4\colon C,$$

in accord with our algorithm.

3.2. The problem is *symmetric*:

$$\begin{array}{ll} & \text{Indices:} \\ v_1\colon B, A, & v_1\colon 1, 1, \\ v_2\colon A, C, & v_2\colon 1, 1, \\ v_3\colon D, B & v_3\colon 1, 1, \\ v_4\colon C, D & v_4\colon 1, 1. \end{array}$$

In this case all the indices are equal but our primitive solution remains the solution that is in accord with our algorithm.

In conclusion, there is no way to add new alternatives that do not fall in one of the cases 1, 2, 3.1, or 3.2.

We have illustrated the outline of the proof for a case of four variables. A general case with a finite number N of variables cannot contain different cases, because all the arguments of cases 1, 2, and 3 are not dependent on the number of variables.

In fact, in cases 1 we checked if the added alternative was equal to that yet assigned for that variable; in cases 2 we tested if the alternative was different from all the present alternatives; in cases 3 the alternative is incompatible with *some* other (it does not matter how many); in cases 3.1 and 3.2 the matter is symmetry. Indeed, if we start with a desired solution and complicate the problem by adding more and more alternatives, that solution remains in accord with our minimal indices and the algorithm finds it. More details are in [10].

APPENDIX II. FORMAL DESCRIPTION OF THE CONJUNCTIVE NORMAL FORM SATISFIABILITY ALGORITHM

Formally, the description of this algorithm is the same as the SRAA, apart from the following modifications:

1. The relation c (variable1, alternative, variable2), introduced in Step 4.1 in Appendix I is created if in the set of alternatives for the variable 1 there is a literal L, and in the set for the variable 2, there is the same literal in negated form or vice versa (i.e., L and $\sim L$). We used the notation A and a, that is, lower- and uppercase letters for the nonnegated and negated forms of a literal. The FAEI (First Alternative Exclusion Index), FVEI (First Variable Exclusion Index), TAEI (Total Alternative Exclusion Index), and TVEI (Total Variable Exclusion Index) indices are then computed in the same manner as the FASRI, FVSRI, TASRI, TVSRI indices.

2. The procedure *update* now has two parts:

Substep a. This substep deletes in the set of each variable the negated form of the literal currently assigned (in fact, the uppercase version if the currently assigned alternative is a lowercase letter, and vice versa).

Substep b. This substep does a search in the set of each variable for the same literal currently assigned. If another variable has the same alternative, this alternative is immediately assigned to that variable, and the variable is deleted in the list of variables to instantiate. So in this case a single call of the procedure *assign1* may assign more than one variable in the same substep.

3. The procedure that computes the minimum for TAEI checks if there are two or more identical values. If this is the case, four other indices are computed as discussed in the previously presented examples, that is, the FACI (First Alternative Constraint Index), FVCI (First Variable Constraint Index), TACI (Total Alternative Constraint Index), and TVCI (Total Variable Constraint Index) indices. Finally, the last four indices are computed and the assignment procedure is the same as in the algorithm in Appendix I.

Outline of Proof. We may find here the following cases:

Case I. Problems with solutions without multiple occurrences, for instance,

$$v_1\colon A, \qquad v_2\colon B, \qquad v_3\colon C, \qquad v_4\colon D.$$

We may find:

1. $v_1\colon A, A$ or $v_1\colon A, a$
2. $v_1\colon A, E$ (all trivial)
3. $v_1\colon A, B$
4. $v_1\colon A, b$.

Case II. Problems with solutions with multiple occurrences of the same alternative, for example,

$$v_1\colon A, \qquad v_2\colon B, \qquad v_3\colon B, \qquad v_4\colon C.$$

We may find the cases:

1. v_1: A, A or v_1: A, a
2. v_1: A, D, which are trivial.
3. v_1: A, C. We find here, for the alternative C, the same exclusion index (with greater compatibility index). If the variable 1 is selected for instantiation, the alternative C is chosen in preference (it also satisfies the variable 4).
4. v_1: A, c. Here we have a greater exclusion index for the choice c. Of course our algorithm must prefer the alternative A.
5. v_1: A, b. Greater exclusion index and for more variables if we choose the alternative b. This case is analogous to the previous case 4.
6. v_2: B, D. The same exclusion index for D and, if we assign D to v_2, less compatibility index (D solves only v_2 and does not solve v_3). As in case 3, our algorithm assigns B if the variable 2 currently requires instantiation.

A. Discussion

One suspects that the combination of cases II.3–II.6 may lead to a situation where, to find a solution, we must violate the principle of minimal indices. In particular, we may argue that starting with a variable or an alternative with worse exclusion index, we may find a solution, and the problem has only that solution, which cannot be found with our algorithm. Randomly generated tests never have exhibited such a case, but there may be hand constructed tests which fail. The technique thus can be considered a good heuristic which may fail in special cases, but is very useful in most practical instances.

Completeness may be lost because, in this case, there are, in fact, two heuristics: the compatibility index and the exclusion index. The interaction between the indices may loose completeness, whereas the computational efficiency in almost all tests remains very high, because the probability that the interaction violates the principle of minimal index is very low, because it requires a problem with only one feasible solution and with all exclusion indices equal to compatibility indices.

APPENDIX III. A 3-CNF-SAT EXAMPLE

Consider the 3-CNF-SAT case with $m = n = 3$. If we reorder the alternatives, we find

	A	a	B	b	C	c
v_1	x_{11}	x_{12}	x_{13}	x_{14}	x_{15}	x_{16}
v_2	x_{21}	x_{22}	x_{23}	x_{24}	x_{25}	x_{26}
v_3	x_{31}	x_{32}	x_{33}	x_{34}	x_{35}	x_{36}

The matrix **A** results:

$$
\begin{array}{cccccccccccccccccc|cccccccccccccccccc}
1&1&1&1&1&1 \\
&&&&&&1&1&1&1&1&1 \\
&&&&&&&&&&&&1&1&1&1&1&1 \\
1&&&&&&&1&&&&&&&&&&&1 \\
&1&&&&&1&&&&&&&&&&&&&1 \\
&&1&&&&&&&1&&&&&&&&&&&1 \\
&&&1&&&&&1&&&&&&&&&&&&&1 \\
&&&&1&&&&&&&1&&&&&&&&&&&1 \\
&&&&&1&&&&&1&&&&&&&&&&&&&1 \\
1&&&&&&&&&&&&&1&&&&&&&&&&&1 \\
&1&&&&&&&&&&&1&&&&&&&&&&&&&1 \\
&&1&&&&&&&&&&&&&1&&&&&&&&&&&1 \\
&&&1&&&&&&&&&&&1&&&&&&&&&&&&&1 \\
&&&&1&&&&&&&&&&&&&1&&&&&&&&&&&1 \\
&&&&&1&&&&&&&&&&&1&&&&&&&&&&&&&1 \\
&&&&&&1&&&&&&&1&&&&&&&&&&&&&&&&&1 \\
&&&&&&&1&&&&&1&&&&&&&&&&&&&&&&&&&1 \\
&&&&&&&&1&&&&&&&1&&&&&&&&&&&&&&&&&1 \\
&&&&&&&&&1&&&&&1&&&&&&&&&&&&&&&&&&&1 \\
&&&&&&&&&&1&&&&&&&1&&&&&&&&&&&&&&&&&1 \\
&&&&&&&&&&&1&&&&&1&&&&&&&&&&&&&&&&&&&1
\end{array}
$$

where for simplicity only the 1 values are reported.

Consider the example

$$v_1\colon A, B, C, \qquad v_2\colon A, b, \qquad v_3\colon a.$$

The **c** row vector is

$$1 \quad 0\,1\,0\,1\,0\,1\,0\,0\,1\,0\,0\,0\,1\,0\,0\,0\,0\;000000000000000000$$

transformed in

$$-1\,0 \quad -1\,0 \quad -1\,0 \quad -1\,0\,0 \quad -1\,0\,0\,0 \quad -1\,0\,0\,0\,0\;000000000000000000.$$

After a suitable Simplex procedure (with pivot operation for suitable elements in the first three rows of matrix **A**, we obtain for the nonbasis variables the 0 values, and for the 21 basis variables

$$x_5 = 1,\ x_{10} = 1,\ x_{14} = 1 \text{ (nonslack)} \geq v_1\colon C,$$
$$v_2\colon b,\ v_3\colon a \geq \mathrm{A} = \mathrm{B} = \mathrm{FALSE},\ \mathrm{C} = \mathrm{TRUE}.$$

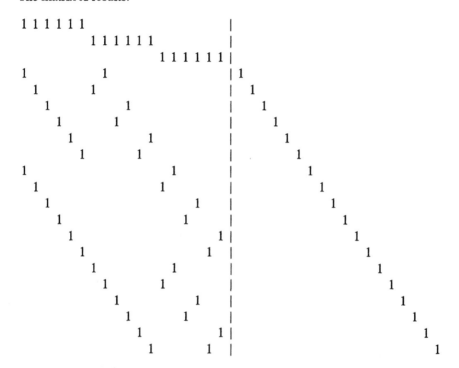

APPENDIX IV. OUTLINE OF PROOF FOR THE LINEAR PROGRAMMING ALGORITHM

In general the matrix **A** can be constructed with modules of the matrices for the problems with lower dimensions and has an even repetition schema for any dimension of the original problem; that is, by means of a recursive use of modules from constructions for smaller values of the parameters of our problem. More details on this construction can be found in [28].

A. Preliminary Considerations

There is a very compact and easy way to outline the algorithm's proof: it is based on the theoretical relationship between the separation problem and optimization. If we can efficiently do the former, then we can do the latter also. The separation problem can be formulated in the following way: Given an assignment of the **x** vector, determine whether it is an admissible solution. If not, show a violated constraint.

We need a concise linear programming description of the set of discrete solutions of the problem and a polynomial separation scheme for either showing that every inequality of the linear system is satisfied, or exhibiting a violated one; see [6]. It is easy to see that this problem can be efficiently solved in our formulation. Given an **x** vector, it is sufficient to substitute the values in the constraints: if all constraints are satisfied, it is an admissible solution and CNF-SAT is solved; else we find at least one violated constraint. Notice that all constraints are explicitly stated and grow polynomially with the number of clauses in the CNF-SAT problem. For instance, in the 3-CNF-SAT example of the previous section, consider the **x** vector with

$$x_{15} = 1, \qquad x_{24} = 1, \qquad x_{32} = 1,$$

and all other values equal to 0. Then substitute it in the constraints and easily find that all the constraints are satisfied.

For the assignment

$$x_{11} = 1, \qquad x_{21} = 1, \qquad x_{32} = 1,$$

and all other values 0, we can verify in polynomial time that the constraint

$$x_{11} + x_{32} \leq 1$$

is violated. Moreover, the constraint characterization we have used has the following fundamental properties:

- There is always at least one integer solution for the LP problem.
- There is always at least one optimal integer solution for the LP problem.

- The optimal solution for the LP problem has the same value of the objective function as the associated integer programming optimal solution. This value is equal to the number m of clauses of the original CNF-SAT problem.
- The optimal value of the LP problem is the value that the objective function has after the tableau has been put in canonical form.
- To put the LP problem in canonical form, m pivot operations, one for each of the first m rows, are required.

Consider 0–1 polytopes, a class of very interesting polytopes for combinatorial optimization; see Ziegler [66]. An useful generalization of a simplex (a 0–1 polytope where each vertex has only a 1 entry in its vector) is the hypersimplex. An hypersimplex $H(m)$ has vertices each having exactly m 1 entry in the related vector. The solution of the LP problem is a vertex of the associated hypersimplex. Several computer programs are available for analyzing polytopes and polyhedra. We have used PORTA, a collection of routines available by anonymous ftp (elib.zib-berlin.de). PORTA includes a function for finding all integral points contained in a polyhedron. We used PORTA to give further experimental evidence of the correctness of our algorithms and this was successful.

PORTA enumerates all the valid integral points contained in a polyhedron which is given by a system of linear equations and inequalities or by a convex hull of finite points. Moreover, the program also produces the vertex-facet incidence matrix from which one can derive the complete combinatorial structure of the polytope. As an example, we report here the 2-CNF-SAT and 3-CNF-SAT polytopes. Remember that PORTA can translate from a convex hull representation to equations–inequalities (i.e., intersection of finitely many closed half-spaces) representation and vice versa.

First, consider the 2-CNF-SAT polytope representation as a convex hull of the following points (i.e., possible solutions for 2-CNF-SAT cases):

$A \quad a \quad B \quad b \qquad A \quad a \quad B \quad b$

```
/*Input ******************************************/
1   0 0  0   1  0  0  0
1  0  0  0   0  0  1  0
1   0 0  0   0  0  0  1
0   1 0  0   0  1  0  0
0   1 0  0   0  0  1  0
0   1 0  0   0  0  0  1
0   0 1  0   1  0  0  0
0  0  1  0   0  1  0  0
0  0  1  0   0  0  1  0
0  0  0  1   1  0  0  0
```

```
0  0  0  1   0  1  0  0
0  0  0  1   0  0  0  1
/***************************************************/
/*For instance, 0  0  0  1  0  1  0  0 means (B = false,
A = false)*/
```

PORTA produced the set of equalities and inequalities.

```
/* 2-CNF-SAT ****************************************/
DIM = 8
TOTAL VALID INTEGRAL POINTS = 12
INEQUALITIES_SECTION

( 1) +x1+x2+x3+x4-x5-x6-x7-x8 == 0
( 2)                +x5+x6+x7+x8 == 1
( 1) -x2                     <= 0
( 2)    -x3                  <= 0
( 3)       -x4               <= 0
( 4)          -x6            <= 0
( 5)             -x7         <= 0
( 6)                -x8      <= 0
( 7) -x2-x3-x4+x6            <= 0
( 8) +x2        -x6-x7-x8    <= 0
( 9)       +x4   +x7         <= 1
(10)    +x3         +x8      <= 1
(11)          +x6+x7+x8      <= 1
(12) +x2+x3+x4               <= 1
END
```

Please, note that the first two equations are equivalent to our riginal formulation of choice constraints. The first six inequalities are nonnegative constraints and the other are equivalent to the exclusion constraints.

PORTA also produced:

```
/*Strong validity table :****************************/
 \ P         |                |
  \ O        |                |
I  \ I       |                |
 N  \ N      | 1    6    11   | #
  E  \ T     |                |
   Q  \ S    |                |
     S  \    |                |
         \   |                |
----------------------------------
```

```
 1          | ***.. .**** **: 9
 2          | ***** *...* **: 9
 3          | ***** ****. ..: 9
 4          | ***.* **.** .*: 9
 5          | *.**. ***.* **: 9
 6          | **.** .**** *.: 9
 7          | ****. ..*.. *.: 6
 8          | *..** **..* ..: 6
 9          | .*..* ...** **: 6
10          | ..*.. ****. .*: 6
11          | .**** *.**. **: 9
12          | ...** ***** **: 9
            .................
#           | 88888 88888 88
```

As one can see, each vertex is exactly on eight facets. Whereas dimension $d = 8$, this means that the polytope is a *simple polytope*. For a simple polytope (i.e., a polytope of dimension d where each vertex is on d facets) the following theorem holds:

THEOREM 1. *There exists a combinatorially equivalent polytope with integral vertices. Of course, these integral vertices give the required solutions for our FCSPs.*

For 3-CNF-SAT there are 126 possible solutions, that is, 72 without duplications and 54 with duplications such as $A\ A\ B$, $B\ c\ B$, etc. Experimental results show that exactly 126 valid integral points have been found. Here we give as input the second representation, that is, as a linear system.

```
/* 3-CNF-SAT ***************************************/

Input:

DIM = 18

LOWER_BOUNDS

0 0 0 0 0 0 0 0 0 0 0 0 0 0 0 0 0 0

UPPER_BOUNDS

1 1 1 1 1 1 1 1 1 1 1 1 1 1 1 1 1 1
```

```
INEQUALITIES_SECTION

( 1) +x1 + x2 + x3 + x4 + x5 + x6   == 1
( 2) +x7  +x8 +x9 +x10 +x11 +x12    == 1
( 3) +x13 +x14 +x15 +x16 +x17 +x18 == 1
( 4) +x1  +x8  <= 1
( 5) +x2  +x7  <= 1
( 6) +x3  +x10 <= 1
( 7) +x4  +x9  <= 1
( 8) +x5  +x12 <= 1
( 9) +x6  +x11 <= 1
(10) +x1  +x14 <= 1
(11) +x2  +x13 <= 1
(12) +x3  +x16 <= 1
(13) +x4  +x15 <= 1
(14) +x5  +x18 <= 1
(15) +x6  +x17 <= 1
(16) +x7  +x14 <= 1
(17) +x8  +x13 <= 1
(18) +x9  +x16 <= 1
(19) +x10 +x15 <= 1
(20) +x11 +x18 <= 1
(21) +x12 +x17 <= 1
END
/**************************************************/
```

PORTA produced as output:

```
TOTAL VALID INTEGRAL POINTS = 126
/**************************************************/
```

THEOREM 2. *The matrix* **A** *is integer solvable in the n-CNF-SAT for* $n \geq 3$.

Note that the proof is not the same for the 2 case. In fact, the 2 case is a special case because every column has only two 1 values and the LP of matrix **A** is said to be a generalized-network problem.

We know in fact that the 2-CNF-SAT problem is well solved. With $n > 2$, every column has $q > 2$ 1 values, and the proof should be totally different: we cannot say that if the 2 case has a totally unimodular matrix, the n case as a totally unimodular matrix too.

Our general procedure for solving the integer problem is the following:

1. Consider the linear program in the general form
2. Consider the obtained Simplex tableau
3. For some negative values in the first row of such a tableau, that is, in the row of vector **c**, operate a pivot operation in the corresponding column and in a suitable row of the first m rows of the matrix **A**, that is, in the rows $2, \ldots, (m+1)$ of the tableau, until the tableau is in the canonical form.

Note that these pivot operations may be chosen in $m!$ different ways and in general may require $m!$ steps. However, we will introduce a novel technique based on neurocomputing, that gives us good choices of the pivot positions. If the instance of the SAT problem (encoded in the vector **c**) does not have a solution, we cannot obtain such a canonical form and the tableau gives a $b_i < 0$ with all $a_{ij} = 0$ $(j = 1, \ldots)$.

The pivot operation is performed (as usual) as follows:

1. Choose a $c_j < 0$ in the first row of the tableau with an $a_{ij} > 0$ in column j (note that there always exists such a term $a_{ij} > 0$ because the matrix **A** has all 0–1 values).
2. Add the row i to the first row in the tableau.
3. If in column j there are terms $a_{kj} > 0$, then consider row k and subtract row i from row k.
4. Repeat step 3 for all $a_{kj} > 0$.

Remember that the matrix **A** has all terms 0 or 1. After the steps 1–4, the matrix **A** contain 0, 1, and -1 values. The solution is always integer.

We say that a linear program is in canonical form if:

- Given $S = \{s_1, s_2, \ldots, s_p\}$ with p integer values (p is the number of rows in the matrix **A**, i.e., the number of equations).
- $C_s = |C_{s_1}, C_{s_2}, \ldots, C_{s_p}|$ column vector of dimension p obtained from the **c** vector of the original problem.
- $A_s =$ identity matrix I_p of dimension p ($p =$ the number of rows in matrix **A**)
- $C_s = 0$
- $b \geq 0$.

For our matrix **A**, there are $m * 2 * n + 2 * n * m * (m-1)/2$ columns and $m + 2 * n * m * (m-1)/2$ rows. We must provide an identity matrix of dimension $p = m + 2n * m * (m-1)/2$. We achieve this result by performing m pivot operations. After these m pivot operations in the $2, \ldots, (m+1)$ rows of the tableau, it is easy to see that the **c** vector (that is the first row of the tableau) has all values ≥ 0. The

$2, \ldots, (m+1)$ rows in fact have the structure

$$\begin{array}{cccccccc} 1 & 1 & \cdots & 1 & & & & \\ & & & & 1 & 1 & \cdots & 1, \end{array}$$

etc. Thus, after adding these rows to the first row (the **c** vector of the original LP problem), the first row becomes ≥ 0, because all -1 values are reduced to 0 values.

In a LP problem in canonical form, there always exists an admissible solution, called the basic solution:

$$\begin{aligned} X_{s_i} &= b_i, \qquad i \text{ in } \{1, 2, \ldots, p), \\ X_j &= 0. \end{aligned}$$

The fundamental theorem of the Simplex algorithm ensures that the basic solution is optimal because our **c** has all values ≥ 0, and the special form of the matrix **A** ensures that the solution is integer too. So the key result is to have our LP in canonical form.

In general, without considering any particular instance of the n-CNF-SAT problem, if it admits a solution, it is always possible to perform m pivot operation and to preserve the solvability of the LP, that is, to avoid cases of $b_i < 0$ with all $a_{ij} = 0$.

It is very important to keep in mind for our proof that *we perform exactly one pivot operation for each* $2, \ldots, (m+1)$ *rows of the tableau* in the block (i.e., first module):

$$\begin{array}{lll} 111 \cdots & & \\ & 111 \cdots & \\ & & 111 \cdots, \end{array}$$

etc. The row determines the chosen clause and the column determines the chosen alternative that satisfies this clause. We will use neural networks to choose this position. The output of the network will give us this choice.

None of these operations gives values > 1 in modulo. Then the solution of our LP has in the basis all the slack variables plus the variables obtained through these $2, \ldots, (m+1)$ pivot operations. Of course all these variables cannot receive a noninteger value.

If we randomly choose the pivot operation in a row in $2, \ldots, (m+1)$ positions, we may not be able to find the canonical form and we will have to use the Balinski and Gomory method to obtain it.

As we said, we will use connectionist networks that learn to choose the positions of the pivot operations so as to improve Simplex performance. The Simplex algorithm will, however, guarantee in any case to achieve a solution. Thus, this hybrid approach to optimization combines the best of both algorithms.

As pointed out by Karloff [67], it is an open question whether there is any pivoting rule that guarantees termination after a polynomial number of pivots. Exponential-time instances of Simplex are well known.

B. Interior Point Methods

A polynomial algorithm such as Karmarkar's is of course able to find all the solutions found by the standard Simplex algorithm for each problem. The Karmarkar algorithm is an interior point method and it does not directly provide the polytope vertices and thus the required integer solutions. We have done experimental work that has shown that the required integer values are simply the rounded values of the noninteger solutions provided by the Karmarkar algorithm (considering the maximum for each variable).

As is well known, Karmarkar's algorithm needs a feasible initial solution to start. This solution is always available for our general problem as one can easily see. As an example, consider the following problem:

```
/*CNF-TEST, 2 May, 1996 */
/* Problem
/*v1: A, B                */
/*v2: a                   */


  6  12
 1.0  1.0  1.0  1.0 0.0 0.0  0.0  0.0  0.0 0.0 0.0 0.0
 0.0  0.0  0.0  0.0 1.0 1.0  1.0  1.0  0.0 0.0 0.0 0.0
 1.0  0.0  0.0  0.0 0.0 0.0  1.0  0.0  1.0 0.0 0.0 0.0
 0.0  1.0  0.0  0.0 0.0 0.0  0.0  1.0  0.0 1.0 0.0 0.0
 0.0  0.0  1.0  0.0 1.0 0.0  0.0  0.0  0.0 0.0 1.0 0.0
 0.0  0.0  0.0  1.0 0.0 1.0  0.0  0.0  0.0 0.0 0.0 1.0
-1.0-1.0   0.0 0.0 0.0 0.0 -1.0   0.0 0.0 0.0 0.0 0.0
```

where 6 is the number of rows, 12 is the number of variables, and the following values are the matrix **A** and the **c** vector.

Karmarkar's algorithm requires an additional parameter m_u (0.010) and a feasible (interior) point (of course, not necessarily optimal):

0.9 0.01 0.01 0.01 0.9 0.01 0.01 0.01 0.01
0.9 0.01 0.9 0.010

Several versions of Karmarkar's algorithm are available. Consult, for instance, Sierksma [68]. Our modification of the included procedure has produced as output

```
*************************************************
/*Solution found from the initial interior point:*/
/*v1: A, v2: A (feasible but not optimal)
 /*mu is the initial interior path parameter*/
```

$m_u = 0.0100000$

$$x = 0.0217343\ 0.8828189\ 0.0120335\ 0.0134134\ 0.0142310\ 0.0219188$$
$$0.0814918\ 0.0123583\ 0.0167739\ 0.0248228\ 0.8937355\ 0.0846678$$
$$w = 0.3084937\ 0.0114386\ 0.7371058\ 0.7371487\ 0.4400535\ 0.4400964$$
$$0.0114415\ 0.7143864\ 0.5826605\ 0.2856054\ 0.0112726\ 0.0113155$$

```
primal obj = 1.66
/*Solution = v1: B, v2: a (optimal) */.
```

C. Correctness and Completeness

In summary our approach is the following:

1. The CNF-SAT problem is reduced to a 0–1 linear programming problem with the **c** vector customized by the clause format.
2. Pivots are performed to find a canonical form.
3. The solution is then read off of the pivoted **A** matrix.

We must then prove that the solution of the integer program derived from the original CNF-SAT problem is a solution for the latter and that if the CNF-SAT problem has a solution the integer programming problem has a solution too.

The integer program solution provides exactly one alternative for each variable among the set of available choices; thus each variable is assigned a value. The e-type constraints assure no incompatible values can be chosen, so the solution is admissible. In conclusion, the solution of the integer programming is always a solution for the CNF-SAT problem, although one can wonder whether there may be cases where the integer programming has no finite solution for an original CNF-SAT problem which is solvable.

The Simplex convergence theory assures that a LP, in canonical form, after a finite number of steps, shows either an optimal solution or that the objective function is not limited. Suppose that a CNF-SAT has a solution. Then the associated LP problem has a solution every time, because all variables have an assignment and thus all rows have exactly one element = 1, all (e) constraints are satisfied, and the objective function is maximized.

In conclusion, the Simplex algorithm must find such a solution in a finite (maybe exponential) number of steps. Moreover, the special form of the matrix **A** ensures that there is at least one integer solution.

ACKNOWLEDGMENTS

I thank Professor Cornelius T. Leondes, editor of this volume, for the invitation to contribute and for precious suggestions. I also thank the publisher, Academic Press, for this valuable work.

Part of the material in this chapter is quoted, adapted, or reprinted from the following sources: *Connection Science* 5:169–187, 1993, with kind permission from CARFAX Publishing Company, P.O. Box 25, Abingdon, Oxfordshire OX14 3UE, UK; *Neurocomputing* 6:51–78, 1994, with kind permission from Elsevier Science-NL, Sara Burgerhartstraat 25, 1055 KV Amsterdam, The Netherlands; *Neural Computing and Applications* 3:78–100, 1995, with kind permission from Springer-Verlag.

I am grateful to Thomas Christof, Universitaet Heidelberg, and Andreas Loebel, Konrad-Zuse-Zentrum fuer Informationtechnik (ZIB), Berlin, for PORTA routines for analyzing polytopes, and to Gerhard Reinelt for TSPLIB (TSP benchmark problems). I thank very much William M. Spears (a great pioneer in the use of neural networks and genetic algorithms for satisfiability problems), Naval Research Laboratory, Washington, DC, who gave me very useful technical reports and suggestions. I also thank the Center for Discrete Mathematics and Theoretical Computer Science (Dimacs) of Rutgers University for the benchmark problems.

REFERENCES

[1] E. Rich. *Artificial Intelligence.* McGraw-Hill, New York, 1983.

[2] L. Daniel. Planning and operation research. In *Artificial Intelligence.* Harper & Row, New York, 1983.

[3] T. Grant. Lessons for O.R. from A.I.: A scheduling case study. *J. Oper. Res.* 37, 1986.

[4] G. J. Sussman and G. L. Steele, Jr. Constraints: A language for expressing almost-hierarchical descriptions. *Artificial Intelligence* 14, 1980.

[5] A. K. Mackworth and E. C. Freuder, Eds. Special volume: Constraint-based reasoning. *Artificial Intelligence* 58, 1992.

[6] R. G. Parker and R. L. Rardin. *Discrete Optimization.* Academic Press, San Diego, 1988.

[7] M. R. Garey and D. S. Johnson. *Computer and Intractability.* Freeman, San Francisco, 1979.

[8] P. Prosser. An empirical study of phase transitions in binary constraint satisfaction problems. In *Artificial Intelligence. Special Volume on Frontiers in Problem Solving: Phase Transitions and Complexity* (T. Hogg, B. A. Huberman, and C. P. Williams, Eds.), Vol. 81. Elsevier, Amsterdam, 1996.

[9] M. Fox. Why is scheduling difficult? A CSP perspective. Invited talk, *Proceedings of the European Conference on Artificial Intelligence,* Stockholm, 1990.

[10] A. Monfroglio. General heuristics for logic constraint satisfaction. In *Proceedings of the First AIIA Conference*, Trento, Italy, 1989.

[11] G. Gallo and G. Urbani. Algorithms for testing the satisfiability of propositional formulae. *J. Logic Programming* 6, 1989.

[12] E. C. Freuder. A sufficient condition of backtrack-free search. *J. Assoc. Comput. Mach.* 29, 1, 1982.

[13] A. Monfroglio. Connectionist networks for constraint satisfaction. *Neurocomputing* 3, 1991.

[14] D. Mitchell, B. Selman, and H. Levesque. Hard and easy distributions for SAT problems. In *Procceedings of the Tenth National Conference on Artificial Intelligence*, 1992, pp. 459–465.

[15] J. Franco and M. Paull. Probabilistic analysis of the Davis–Putman procedure for solving the satisfiability problem. *Discrete Appl. Math.* 5, 1983.

[16] S. E. Fahlman and C. Lebiere. The cascade correlation learning architecture. Report CMU-CS-90-100, School of Computer Science, Carnegie Mellon Univ., Pittsburgh, 1990.

[17] A. Monfroglio. Logic decisions under constraints. *Decision Support Syst.* 11, 1993.
[18] Y. H. Pao. *Adaptive Pattern Recognition and Neural Networks.* Addison-Wesley, Reading, MA, 1989.
[19] T. Samad. Back-propagation extensions. Technical Report, Honeywell SSDC, 1989.
[20] R. A. Jacobs. Increased rates of convergence through learning rate adaptation. *Neural Networks* 1:295–307, 1988.
[21] A. A. Minia and R. D. Williams. Acceleration of back-propagation through learning rate and momentum adaptation. *International Joint Conference on Neural Networks*, 1990, Vol. 1, pp. 676–679.
[22] M. S. Tomlinson, D. J. Walker, and M. A. Sivilotti. A digital neural network architecture for VLSI. *International Joint Conference on Neural Networks*, 1990, Vol. II.
[23] J. Matyas. Random optimization. *Automat. Remote Control* 26:246–253, 1965.
[24] N. Baba. A new approach for finding the global minimum of error function of neural networks. *Neural Networks* 2:367–373, 1989.
[25] F. J. Solis and R. J. Wets. Minimization by random search techniques. *Math. Oper. Res.* 6:19–30, 1981.
[26] D. H. Ackley, G. H. Hinton, and T. J. Sejnowski. A learning algorithm for Boltzmann machines. *Cognitive Sci.* 9:147–169, 1985.
[27] E. Aarts and J. Korst. *Simulated Annealing and Boltzmann Machines.* Wiley, New York, 1989.
[28] A. Monfroglio. Integer programs for logic constraint satisfaction. *Theoret. Comput. Sci.* 97:105–130, 1992.
[29] J. A. Leonard, M. A. Kramer, and L. H. Ungar. Using radial basis functions to approximate a function and its error bounds. *IEEEE Trans. Neural Networks* 3:624–627, 1992.
[30] J. Moody and C. J. Darken. Fast learning in networks of locally tuned processing units. *Neural Comput.* 1:281–294, 1989.
[31] T. Kohonen. *Self-Organization and Associative Memory.* Springer-Verlag, New York, 1988.
[32] D. J. Willshaw and C. Von der Malsburg. How patterned neural connections can be set up by self-organization. *Proc. Roy. Soc. London Ser. A* 194, 1976.
[33] D. DeSieno. Adding a conscience to competitive learning. In *Proceedings of the Second Annual IEEE International Conference on Neural Networks*, 1988, Vol. I.
[34] B. G. Batchelor. *Practical Approach to Pattern Recognition.* Plenum, New York, 1974.
[35] D. F. Specht. Probabilistic neural networks. *Neural Networks*, 3, 1990.
[36] C. C. Klimasauskas. *Neural Computing* (a manual for NeuralWorks R). NeuralWare, Inc., Pittsburgh, PA, 1991 (version 5, 1993).
[37] A. Monfroglio. Neural networks for finite constraint satisfaction. *Neural Comput. Appl.* 3:78–100, 1995.
[38] A. Monfroglio. General heuristics for logic constraint satisfaction. In *Proceedings of the First Artificial Intelligence Italian Association Conference*, Trento, Italy, 1989, pp. 306–315.
[39] A. Monfroglio. Connectionist networks for constraint satisfaction. *Neurocomputing* 3:29–50, 1991.
[40] A. Monfroglio. Neural logic constraint solving. *J. Parallel Distributed Comput.* 20:92–98, 1994.
[41] A. Monfroglio. Neural networks for constraint satisfaction. In *Third Congress of Advances in Artificial Intelligence* (P. Torasso, Ed.). *Lecture Notes in Artificial Intelligence*, Vol. 728, pp. 102–107. Springer-Verlag, Berlin, 1993.
[42] H. J. Zimmermann and A. Monfroglio. Linear programs for constraint satisfaction problems. *European J. Oper. Res.* 97(1), 1997.
[43] L. G. Khachian. A polynomial algorithm for linear programming. *Sov. Math. Dokl.* 244, 1979.
[44] N. Karmarkar. A new polynomial time algorithm for linear programming. In *Proceedings of the Sixteenth Annual ACM Symposium on Theory of Computing*, 1984, pp. 1093–1096.

[45] Y. Ye. A "Build-down" scheme for linear programming. *Math. Program.* 46:61–72, 1990.

[46] R. M. Karp. Reducibility among combinatorial problems. In *Complexity of Computer Computations* (R. E. Miller and J. W. Thatcher, Eds.). Plenum, New York, 1972.

[47] A. Monfroglio. Backpropagation networks for logic constraint solving. *Neurocomputing* 6:67–98, 1994.

[48] A. Monfroglio. Connectionist networks for pivot selection in linear programming. *Neurocomputing* 8:51–78, 1995.

[49] Y. Takefuji. *Neural Network Parallel Computing*. Kluwer, Dordrecht, 1992.

[50] A. Monfroglio. Neural networks for satisfiability problems. *Constraints J.* 1, 1996.

[51] J. H. Holland. *Adaptation in Natural and Artificial Systems*. Univ. of Michigan Press, Ann Arbor, 1975.

[52] D. E. Goldberg. *Genetic Algorithms in Search, Optimization, and Machine Learning*. Addison-Wesley, Reading, MA, 1989.

[53] L. Davis, Ed. *Handbook of Genetic Algorithms*. Van Nostrand–Reinhold, New York, 1991.

[54] J. J. Grefenstette, L. Davis, and D. Cerys. GENESIS and OOGA: Two genetic algorithm systems, TSP, Melrose, MA, 1991.

[55] I. P. Gent and T. Walsh. Easy problems are sometimes hard. *Artificial Intelligence* 70:335–346, 1994.

[56] M. Davis and H. Putnam. A computing procedure for quantification theory. *J. Assoc. Comput. Mach.* 8:201–215, 1960.

[57] R. G. Jeroslow and J. Wang. Solving propositional satisfiability problems. *Ann. Math. Artificial Intelligence* 1, 1990.

[58] B. Selman, H. Levesque, and M. Mitchell. GSAT: A new method for solving hard satisfiability problems. In *Proceedings of the Tenth National Conference on Artificial Intelligence*, 1992, pp. 440–446.

[59] T. Hogg, B. A. Huberman, and C. P. Williams, Eds. Special volume on frontiers in problem solving: Phase transitions and complexity. *Artificial Intelligence* 81, 1996.

[60] J. N. Hooker. Testing heuristics: We have it all wrong. *J. Heuristics* 1:33–42, 1995.

[61] D. Mitchell, B. Selman, and H. Levesque. Hard and easy distributions for SAT problems. In *Proceedings of the Tenth National Conference on Artificial Intelligence*, 1992, pp. 459–465.

[62] W. M. Spears. Using neural networks and genetic algorithms as heuristics for NP-complete problems. Masters Thesis, George Mason University, Fairfax, VA, 1989.

[63] W. M. Spears. A NN algorithm for hard satisfiability problems. NCARAI Technical Report AIC-93-014, Naval Research Laboratory, Washington, DC, 1993.

[64] W. M. Spears. Simulated annealing for hard satisfiability problems. NCARAI Technical Report AIC-93-015, Naval Research Laboratory, Washington, DC, 1993.

[65] H. N. Schaller. Design of neurocomputer architectures for large-scale constraint satisfaction problems. *Neurocomputing* 8, 1995.

[66] G. M. Ziegler. *Lectures on Polytopes*. Springer-Verlag, Berlin, 1995.

[67] H. Karloff. *Linear Programming*. Birkhauser, Boston, 1991.

[68] G. Sierksma. *Linear and Integer Programming*. Dekker, New York, 1996.

[69] H. Simonis and M. Dincbas. Propositional calculus problems in CHIP. In *Algebraic and Logic Programming. Second International Conference* (H. Kirchner and W. Wechler, Eds.). *Lecture Notes in Computer Science*, pp.189–203. Springer-Verlag, Berlin, 1990.

Parallel, Self-Organizing, Hierarchical Neural Network Systems

O. K. Ersoy
School of Electrical and Computer Engineering
Purdue University
West Lafayette, Indiana 47907

Parallel, self-organizing, hierarchical neural networks (PSHNNs) involve a number of stages with error detection at the end of each stage and possibly also at the beginning of each stage. The input vectors to each stage are obtained by nonlinear transformations of some or all of the input vectors of the previous stage. In PSHNNs used in classification applications, only those input vectors which are rejected by an error-detection scheme due to errors at the output are fed into the next stage after a nonlinear transformation. In parallel, consensual neural networks (PCNNs), the error-detection schemes are replaced by consensus between the outputs of the stages. In PSHNNs with continuous inputs and outputs, which are typically used in applications such as regression, system identification, and prediction, all the input vectors of one stage are nonlinearly transformed and fed in to the next stage. The stages operate in parallel during testing. PSHNNs are highly fault-tolerant and robust against errors in the weight values due to the adjustment of the error-detection bounds to compensate errors in the weight values. They also result in highly competitive results in various applications when compared to other techniques.

Algorithms and Architectures

I. INTRODUCTION

Parallel, self-organizing, hierarchical neural networks (PSHNNs) were introduced in [1] and [2]. The original PSHNN involves a self-organizing number of stages, similar to a multilayer network. Each stage can be a particular neural network, to be referred to as the stage neural network (SNN). Unlike a multilayer network, each SNN is essentially independent of the other SNNs in the sense that each SNN does not receive its input directly from the previous SNN. At the output of each SNN, there is an error-detection scheme. If an input vector is rejected, it goes through a nonlinear transformation before being inputted to the next SNN. These are probably the most original properties of the PSHNN, as distinct from other artificial neural networks. The general comparison of the PSHNN architecture and a cascaded multistage network such as a backpropagation network [4] is shown in Fig. 1.

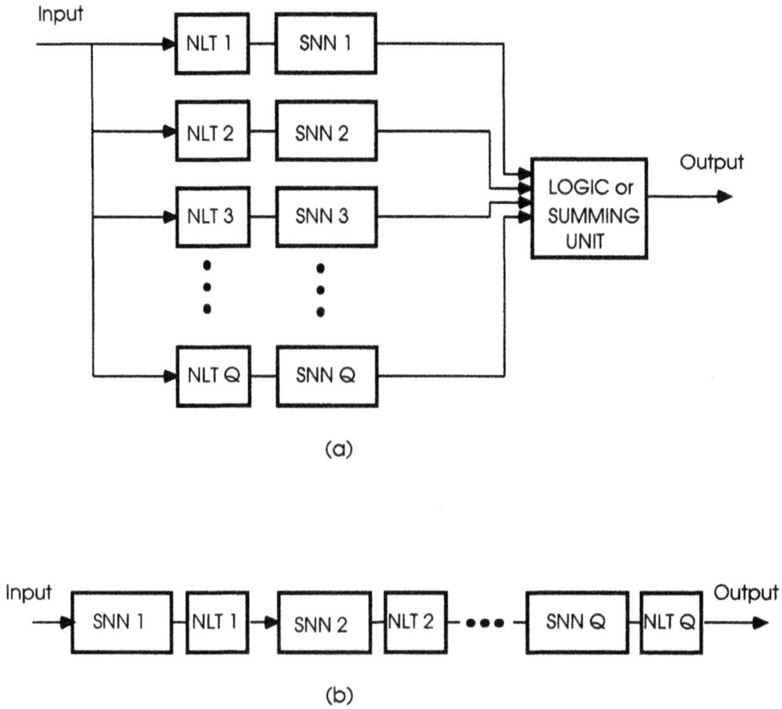

Figure 1 Block diagram for (a) the PSHNN and (b) a cascaded multistage network such as the backpropagation network. SNN i and NLT i refer to the ith stage network and the ith stage output nonlinearity, respectively.

The motivation for this architecture evolved from the consideration that most errors occur due to input signals to be classified that are linearly nonseparable or that are close to boundaries between classes. At the output of each stage, such signals are detected by a scheme and rejected. Then the rejected signals are passed through a nonlinear transformation so that they are converted into other vectors which are classified more easily by the succeeding stage.

Learning with the PSHNN is similar to learning with a multilayer network except that error detection is carried out at the output of each SNN and the procedure is stopped without further propagation into the succeeding SNNs if no errors are detected. Testing (recall) with the PSHNN can be done in parallel with all the SNNs simultaneously rather than each SNN waiting for data from the previous SNN, as seen in Fig. 1a.

Experimental studies with the original PSHNN in applications such as classification with satellite remote-sensing data [1–3] indicated that it can perform as well or better than multistage networks with backpropagation learning [4]. The PSHNN was found to be about 25 times faster in training than the backpropagation network, in addition to parallel implementation of stages during testing. This conclusion is believed to be valid no matter what technique is used for the computation of each stage. For example, if the conjugate-gradient algorithm is used for the computation of the backpropagation network weights [5], the same can be done for the computation of each stage of the PSHNN.

The PSHNN has been developed further in several major directions as follows:

- New approaches to error detection schemes [6, 7]
- New input and output representations [8, 9]
- Consensual neural networks [9, 10]
- PSHNNs with continuous inputs and outputs [11, 12]

This chapter highlights the major findings in these studies, and consists of 11 sections. Section II describes methods used for nonlinearly transforming input data vectors. The algorithms for training, testing, and generating error-detection bounds are the topic of Section III. The error-detection bounds are interpreted in Section IV. A comparison between the PSHNN, the backpropagation network, and the maximum likelihood method is given in Section V. *PNS* modules involving a prerejector unit before the neural network unit and a statistical unit after the neural network unit for statistically generating the error-detection bounds are the topic of Section VI. Parallel consensual neural networks, which replace error detection by consensus between the outputs of the SNNs, are described in Section VII. PSHNNs can also be generated with SNNs based on competitive learning, as discussed in Section VIII. For applications such as regression, system identification, and prediction, PSHNNs with continuous inputs and outputs are typically used, as discussed in Section IX. Some recent applications, including fuzzy input representation and image compression, are described in Section X. Section XI is conclusions.

II. NONLINEAR TRANSFORMATIONS OF INPUT VECTORS

A variety of schemes can be used to nonlinearly transform input data vectors. Two major categories of data to consider are binary data and analog data. The techniques used with both types of data are described next.

A. BINARY INPUT DATA

The first method for the desired transformation was achieved by using a fast transform followed by the bipolar thresholding (sign) function given by [1]:

$$S(n) = \begin{cases} 1, & S(n) \geq 0, \\ -1, & \text{otherwise}. \end{cases} \tag{1}$$

There are a number of fast transforms such as the real discrete Fourier transform (RDFT) [13] which can be utilized.

The nonlinear transformation using the RDFT is very sensitive to the Hamming distance between the binary vectors. The difference between two binary vectors is changed from one bit to many bits after using the nonlinear transformation.

Even though the nonlinear technique discussed in the preceding text works well, its implementation is not trivial. The implementation can be made easier by utilizing simple fast transforms such as the discrete Fourier preprocessing transforms (DFPTs) obtained by replacing the basis function $\cos(2\pi nk/N+\theta(n))$ with a very simple function [14]. There are manv DFPTs. The simplest one is class-2, type-5 DFPT [15]. Similarly, other simple transforms such as the Hadamard transform or the Haar transform can be used.

The simplest approach is to complement the input vector if it is represented in a binary code. Another simple approach which can be used together with complementing is to scramble the binary components of the input vector.

The binary input vectors can also be represented by a Gray code [1]. One simple possibility for input nonlinear transformation that worked well in practice is to use this scheme successively for succeeding stages. This is done by using the Gray-coded input of the previous SNN and then determining the Gray code of the Gray code.

B. ANALOG INPUT DATA

A general approach used for the transformation of analog input data was based on the wavelet packet transform (WPT) followed by the backpropagation algorithm [10]. The wavelet packet transform provides transformation of a signal from the time domain to the frequency domain and is a generalized version of the wavelet transform [16]. The WPT is computed on several levels with different time–frequency resolutions.

The full WPT for a time domain signal can be calculated by successive application of low-pass and high-pass decimation operations [16]. By proceeding down through the levels of the WPT, the tradeoff between time resolution and frequency resolution is obtained. The computational complexity of the WPT is $O(N \log N)$, where N is the number of data points.

C. Other Transformations

There are many other ways to conceive nonlinear transformations of input data vectors. For example, the revised backpropagation algorithm discussed in Section IX.A and fuzzy input signal representation discussed in Section X.A are two effective approaches.

III. TRAINING, TESTING, AND ERROR-DETECTION BOUNDS

In the following text, we summarize the training and testing procedures with the original PSHNN algorithm. In both cases, error detection is crucial. How this is done is discussed in Section III.C.

A. Training

To speed up learning, the upper limit of the number of iterations in each SNN during learning is restricted to an integer k. Let us assume that the ith SNN is denoted by SNN(i). Its training procedure is described as follows:

Assume that the number of iterations is upper bounded by k for each SNN.
Initialize: $i = 1$

1. *Train SNN* (i) *by a chosen learning algorithm in at most k iterations.*
2. *Check the output for each input vector.*

   (1) *If no error, stop the training.*
   (2) *If errors, get the error-detection bounds and go to step* 3.

3. *Select the input data which are detected to give output errors.*
   (1) *If all the chosen data are in one class, then assign the final class number (FCV) as indicating that class. Stop the training.*
   (2) *If not, go to step* 4.
4. *Compute the nonlinear transform (NLT) of the chosen data set. Increase i by* 1. *Go to step* 1.

B. Testing

Testing (recall) with the PSHNN is similar to testing with a multilayer network except that error detection is carried out at the output of each SNN and the procedure is stopped without further propagation into the succeeding SNNs if no errors are detected. The following describes the testing procedure:

Initialize: $i = 1$

1. *Input the test vector to SNN* (i).
2. *Check whether the output indicates an error-causing input data vector. If so, then,*
   (a) *if it is the last SNN, then classify with the FCV;*
   (b) *if it is not, nonlinearly transform the input test vector and go to step* 1, *else classify the output vector.*

An interesting observation is that the testing with the PSHNN can be done in parallel with all the SNNs simultaneously rather than each SNN waiting for data from the previous SNN [1].

C. Detection of Potential Errors

How do we reject and accept input vectors at each SNN? The output neurons yield 1, 0 (or -1) as their final value. The decision of which binary value to choose involves thresholding. It is possible to come up with a number of decision strategies. Subsequently we will describe a particular algorithm.

The value x obtained after the weighted summation at the ith output neuron is first passed through the sigmoid function defined by

$$y(i) = f(x) = \text{sigmoid}(x) = (1 + e^{-x})^{-1}. \tag{2}$$

to give a value $y(i)$ between 0 and 1. The value x actually equals the weighted summation plus a threshold term θ which is trained by using an extra input neuron whose input is 1. The final output value z is obtained by the hard limiter

$$z(i) = \begin{cases} 1, & \text{if } y(i) \geq 0.5, \\ 0, & \text{if } y(i) \leq 0.5. \end{cases} \quad (3)$$

In this process, it is assumed that the desired output of the system is represented by a binary number. It is observed that there are three vectors involved: the input vector X, the vector Y with elements y, and the output vector Z with elements $z(i)$. We can also show time dependence by using superscript i in the form X^i, Y^i, Z^i.

After training the SNN by a maximum of k iterations, we compare the output vector Z with the desired output vector. If they are different from each other, the input vector is counted as an "error-causing" vector of the SNN. The set of error-causing vectors is the input to the next SNN after being processed by one of the nonlinear transformation techniques discussed in Section II.

Now we need an algorithm to detect potential errors during testing. For this, we define error bounds and no-error bounds. The following is the original algorithm for estimating the error bounds:

Error Bounds

Assume: number of data vectors $= I$
length of input vectors $= n$
$y_j^i = j$*th component of the ith vector* Y^i.
Initialize the error bounds as

$$\begin{cases} y_j^0(\textit{upper}) = 0.5 \\ y_j^0(\textit{lower}) = 0.5 \end{cases} \quad \textit{where } j = 1, 2, \ldots, n$$

Initialize: $i = 1$.

1. *Check whether the* i*th data vector is an error-causing vector. If so,*

   (1) *If* $y_j^i \geq 0.5$, *then*

   $$y_j^i(\textit{upper}) = \max\left[y_j^{i-1}(\textit{upper}), y_j^i\right]$$

   (2) *If* $y_j^i < 0.5$, *then*

   $$y_j^i(\textit{lower}) = \min\left[y_j^{i-1}(\textit{lower}), y_j^i\right]$$

2. *If* $i = I$, *the final error bounds are*

$$r_j(\textit{upper}) = y_j^i(\textit{upper})$$
$$r_j(\textit{lower}) = y_j^i(\textit{lower})$$

else $i = i + 1$ *and go to step* 1
End

The output classes can be denoted by binary vectors. For example, the desired output of each class can be represented as

$$\begin{aligned} \text{class } 1 &\rightarrow (1, 0, 0, \ldots, 0), \\ \text{class } 2 &\rightarrow (0, 1, 0, \ldots, 0), \\ &\vdots \\ \text{class } n &\rightarrow (0, \ldots, 0, 1). \end{aligned}$$

Then an input vector is classified as an error-causing vector if the correct "1" bit at the output is 0 and vice versa.

The simplest rejection procedure during testing is to check whether or not any of the components y^i of the vector Y is within the error bounds. If it is, the corresponding input data vector is rejected. During testing, some misclassified data may not be rejected because no y^i is within the error bounds. Simultaneously some correctly classified data also may be rejected because some y^is are within the error bounds. These sources of error can be further reduced by simultaneously utilizing no-error bounds. The following is the current procedure for estimating the no-error bounds.

No-Error Bounds

Initialize the no-error bounds as

$$\begin{cases} y_j^0(upper) = 0.5 \\ y_j^0(lower) = 0.5 \end{cases} \quad \text{where } j = 1, 2, \ldots, n$$

Initialize $i = 1$.

1. *Check whether the* i*th data vector is not an error-causing vector.*
   If so, then $i = i + 1$, *and go to step* 1,
   else go to step 2.
2. *Update the no-error bounds* r_j^i *for* $j = 1, 2, \ldots, n$ *as follows:*

   (1) *If* $y_j^i \geq 0.5$, *then*

   $$y_j^i(upper) = \min\left[y_j^{i-1}(upper), y_j^i\right]$$

   (2) *If* $y_j^i < 0.5$, *then*

   $$y_j^i(lower) = \max\left[y_j^{i-1}(lower), y_j^i\right]$$

(3) *If* $i = I$, *then final no-error bounds are*

$$s_j(upper) = y^i_j(upper)$$
$$s_j(lower) = y^i_j(lower)$$

else $i = i + 1$ *and go to step* 1
end

With the no-error bounds, the rejection procedure can be to check whether the vector Y is not in the correct region determined by the no-error bounds. If it is not, then the corresponding input data vector is rejected.

A procedure which gave the best results experimentally is to utilize both the error and no-error bounds [1]. For this purpose, three intervals $I_1(j)$, $I_2(j)$, $I_E(j)$, $j = 1, 2, \ldots, n$, are defined as

$$\begin{aligned} I_1(j) &= [r_j(\text{lower}), r_j(\text{upper})], \\ I_2(j) &= [s_j(\text{lower}), s_j(\text{upper})], \\ I_E(j) &= I_1(j) \cap I_2(j). \end{aligned} \tag{4}$$

Then an input vector is classified as an error-causing vector if any y_j belongs to $I_E(j)$. With this procedure, better accuracy is achieved because correctly classified data vectors are not rejected even if some y_js are within the error bounds. However, some error-causing data vectors can still be among those not rejected because no y_j belongs to $I_E(j)$.

IV. INTERPRETATION OF THE ERROR-DETECTION BOUNDS

The error and no-error bounds in the preceding text can be statistically interpreted as threshold values for making reliable decisions. With the output representation discussed previously, the output y at an output neuron and $(1 - y)$ approximate the conditional probabilities $P(1|\mathbf{x})$, and $P(0|\mathbf{x})$, respectively [3]. By generating error and no-error bounds, we allow only those vectors with high enough $P(1|\mathbf{x})$ or $P(0|\mathbf{x})$ to be accepted, and the others are rejected.

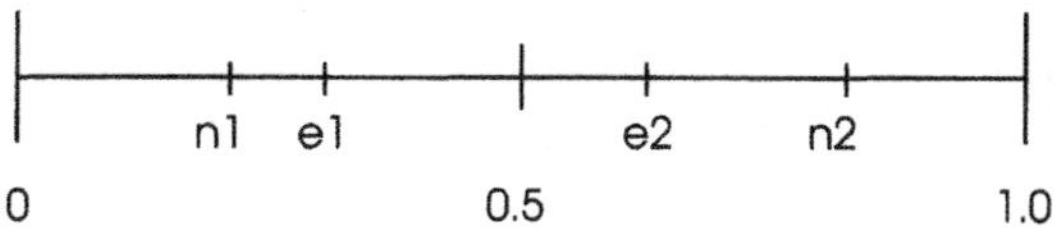

Figure 2 The threshold values of Case 1.

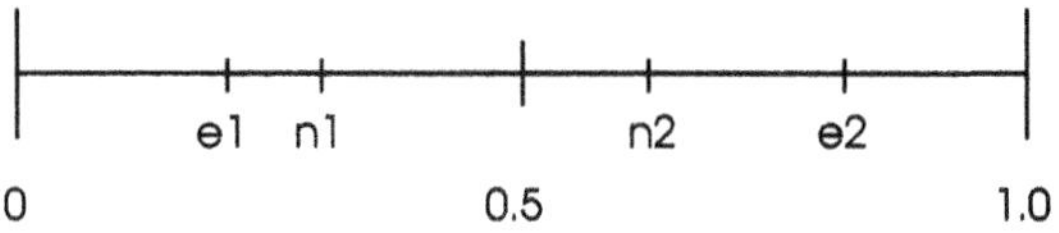

Figure 3 The threshold values of Case 2.

In Figs. 2–5, the lower and upper error bounds are denoted by e_1 and e_2, and the lower and upper no-error bounds are denoted by n_1 and n_2, respectively.

There are four possible combinations of error and no-error bounds as follows [in all cases y and $(1 - y)$ are written as $P(1|\mathbf{x})$ and $P(0|\mathbf{x})$, respectively]:

Case 1. Figure 2 shows the threshold values of Case 1.
Accept:

$$\text{if } P(1|\mathbf{x}) > e_2 \geq 0.5 \rightarrow \text{class 1,}$$
$$\text{if } P(0|\mathbf{x}) > 1 - e_1 \geq 0.5 \rightarrow \text{class 2;}$$

Reject:

$$\text{if } 0.5 < P(1|\mathbf{x}) \leq e_2 \rightarrow \text{reject,}$$
$$\text{if } 0.5 < P(0|\mathbf{x}) > 1 - e_1 \rightarrow \text{reject.}$$

Case 2. Figure 3 shows the threshold values of Case 2.
Accept:

$$\text{if } P(1|\mathbf{x}) > n_2 \geq 0.5 \rightarrow \text{class 1,}$$
$$\text{if } P(0|\mathbf{x}) > 1 - n_1 \geq 0.5 \rightarrow \text{class 2;}$$

Reject:

$$\text{if } 0.5 < P(1|\mathbf{x}) \leq n_2 \rightarrow \text{reject,}$$
$$\text{if } 0.5 < P(0|\mathbf{x}) > 1 - n_1 \rightarrow \text{reject.}$$

Case 3. Figure 4 shows the threshold values of Case 3.

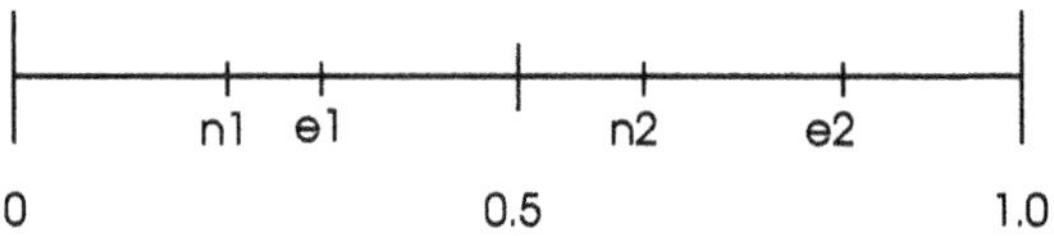

Figure 4 The threshold values of Case 3.

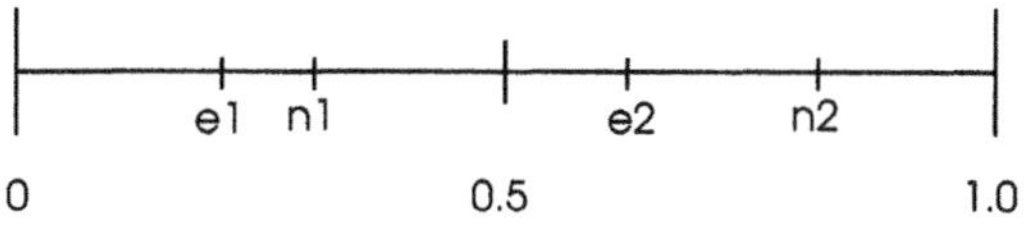

Figure 5 The threshold values of Case 4.

Accept:

$$\text{if } P(1|\mathbf{x}) > n_2 \geq 0.5 \rightarrow \text{class 1},$$
$$\text{if } P(0|\mathbf{x}) > 1 - e_1 \geq 0.5 \rightarrow \text{class 2};$$

Reject:

$$\text{if } 0.5 < P(1|\mathbf{x}) \leq n_2 \rightarrow \text{reject},$$
$$\text{if } 0.5 < P(0|\mathbf{x}) > 1 - e_1 \rightarrow \text{reject}.$$

Case 4. Figure 5 shows the threshold values of Case 4.
Accept:

$$\text{if } P(1|\mathbf{x}) > e_2 \geq 0.5 \rightarrow \text{class 1},$$
$$\text{if } P(0|\mathbf{x}) > 1 - n_1 \geq 0.5 \rightarrow \text{class 2};$$

Reject:

$$\text{if } 0.5 < P(1|\mathbf{x}) \leq e_2 \rightarrow \text{reject},$$
$$\text{if } 0.5 < P(0|\mathbf{x}) > 1 - n_1 \rightarrow \text{reject}.$$

In all cases discussed in the preceding text, the error and no-error bounds lead to decisions which have high probability of being correct. Classification is not attempted if the probability of being true is not high.

V. COMPARISON BETWEEN THE PARALLEL, SELF-ORGANIZING, HIERARCHICAL NEURAL NETWORK, THE BACKPROPAGATION NETWORK, AND THE MAXIMUM LIKELIHOOD METHOD

Three recognition techniques, the maximum likelihood (ML) method [17], the backpropagation network [4], and the PSHNN in which each SNN is a single delta rule network with output nonlinearity will be compared with some simple examples that have continuous inputs. In addition to this comparison, a major goal in this section is to illustrate how vectors are rejected at each stage of the PSHNN. In Section V.A, we compare the performances of the methods with a three-class problem in which the classes are normally distributed. In Section V.B, the same procedure is applied to three classes which are uniformly distributed. In the experiments, the four-layer backpropagation network (4NN) was found to give better results than the three-layer network. In the results discussed in the following text, the number of hidden nodes was optimized by trial and error.

A. Normally Distributed Data

Three two-dimensional, normally distributed classes were generated as in Fig. 6. The mean vectors of classes 1, 2, and 3 were chosen as $(-10, -10)$, $(0, 0)$, and $(10, 10)$, respectively. The standard deviation was 5 for each class. Two sets of data were generated. The number of the training samples and the testing samples in each class was 300 in the first set and 500 in the second set.

Figure 7 shows the classification error vectors of the ML method with the second set of data. Figure 8 shows the corresponding classification error vectors of the backpropagation network (4NN) with four layers. The length of the input vector of the 4NN is 2, the length of the output vector is 3, and the length of the

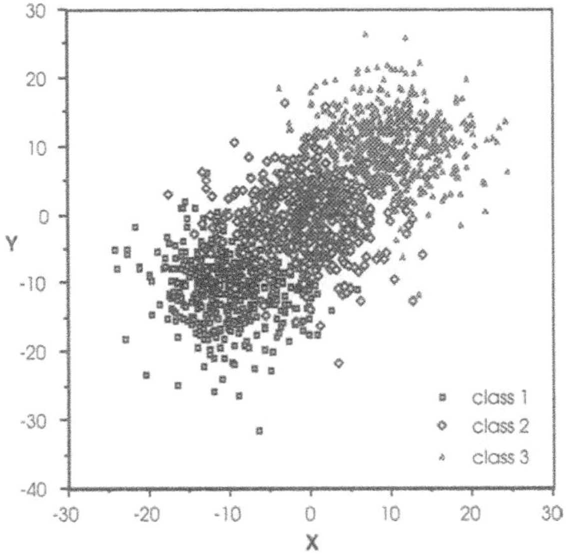

Figure 6 Distribution of three classes (Gaussian distribution). The number of samples of each class is 500.

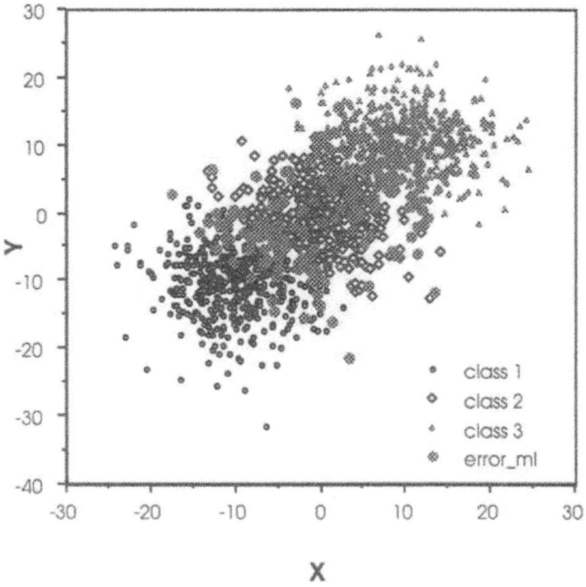

Figure 7 Error of the ML method of the three-class problem (Gaussian distribution). The number of samples of each class is 500.

hidden units is 6. The learning rate was 0.00001. The initial weight values were randomly chosen in the range [−0.01, 0.01].

Figure 9 shows the classification error of the PSHNN. The length of the input vector of the PSHNN is 2 and the length of the output vector is 3. The matching method and the error and no-error bounds were used as the rejection scheme [1]. The number of stages was 3. Because we do not use binary number representation at the input and the vector size is small, input nonlinear transformations were not utilized in this experiment. The learning rate was 0.00001 and the initial weights were randomly chosen in the range [−0.01, 0.01].

Figures 10 and 11 show which vectors are rejected in the first and second stages of the PSHNN. Figure 10 shows that the network attempts to separate classes 2 and 3 while totally rejecting class 1. The other rejected vectors in this stage also occur close to the boundary between classes 2 and 3. In stage 2, most vectors belong to classes 1 and 2, and thus the rejected vectors are close to the boundary between these two classes, as seen in Fig. 11.

Table I shows the classification accuracy of each case. The number of errors of PSHNN is similar to that of the ML method. The number of errors of the 4NN was larger than those of the ML and PSHNN methods.

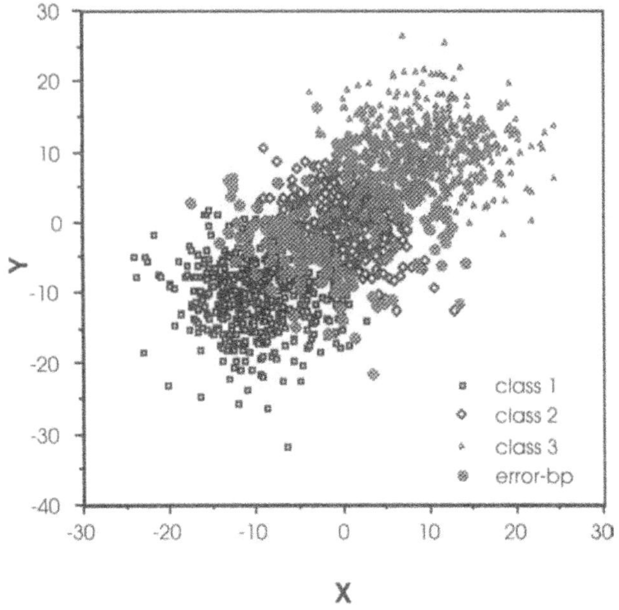

Figure 8 Error of the 4NN of the three-class problem (Gaussian distribution). The number of samples of each class is 500.

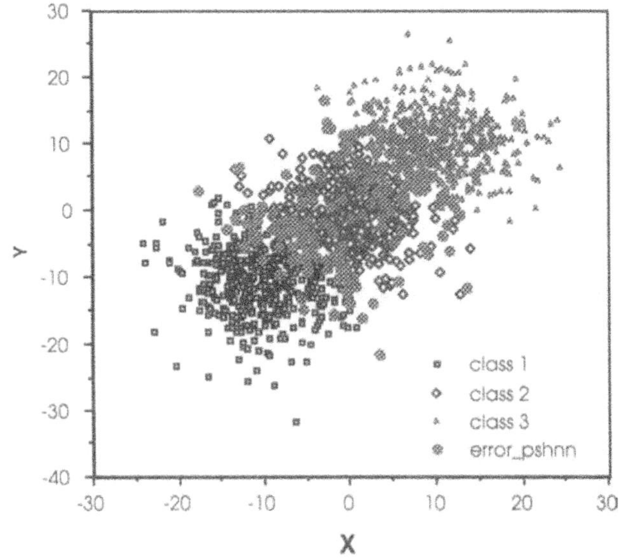

Figure 9 Error of the PSHNN of the three-class problem (Gaussian distribution). The number of samples of each class is 500.

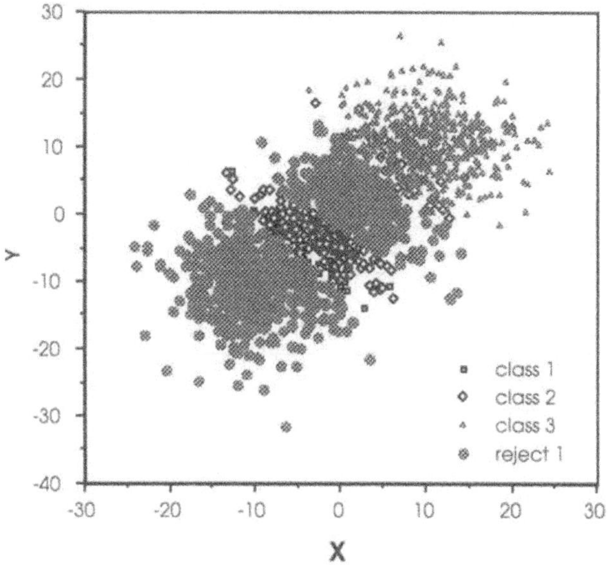

Figure 10 Rejection region of the first SNN of the PSHNN of the three-class problem (Gaussian distribution). The number of samples of each class is 500.

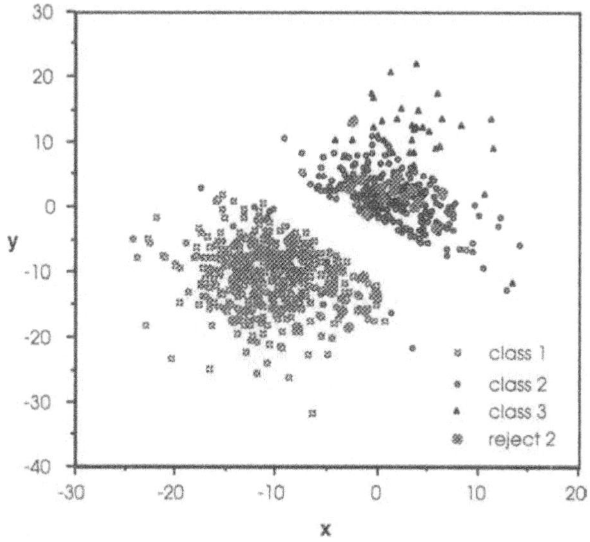

Figure 11 Rejection region of the second SNN of the PSHNN of the three-class problem (Gaussian distribution).

Table I

The Number of Error Samples of Each Method in the Three-Class Problem (Two-Dimensional Gaussian Distribution)

No. of samples per class	Number of error vectors		
	PSHNN	ML	BP
Train 300	115	110	125
Test 300	100	98	117
Train 500	164	158	213
Test 500	163	161	202

Another experiment was performed with three 16-dimensional, normally distributed classes. The mean vectors of classes 1, 2, and 3 were $(-10, -10, \ldots, -10)$, $(0, 0, \ldots, 0)$, and $(10, 10, \ldots, 10)$, respectively. The standard deviation was 5 for each class. Two sets of data were generated. The number of the training samples and the testing samples in each class were 300 in the first set and 500 in the second set.

Three stages are used in the PSHNN. Table II shows the classification accuracy of each case. The number of errors of PSHNN is similar to that of the ML method. The number of errors of the 4NN is larger than those of the ML and PSHNN methods.

Table II

The Number of Error Samples of Each Method in the Three-Class Problem (16-Dimensional Gaussian Distribution)

No. of samples per class	Number of error vectors		
	PSHNN	ML	BP
Train 300	16	19	18
Test 300	18	15	22
Train 500	35	34	35
Test 500	37	35	38

Table III

The Number of Error Samples of Each Method in the Three-Class Problem (Two-Dimensional Uniform Distribution)

No. of samples per class	Number of error vectors		
	PSHNN	ML	BP
Train 300	46	47	53
Test 300	55	55	57
Train 500	75	79	83
Test 500	81	83	86

B. Uniformly Distributed Data

Three two-dimensional, uniformly distributed classes were generated. The mean vectors of classes 1, 2, and 3 were chosen as $(-10, -10)$, $(0, 0)$, and $(10, 10)$, respectively. The data were uniformly distributed in the range $[m - 7, m + 7]$, with m being the mean value of the class. Two sets of data were generated. The number of the training samples and the testing samples in each class were 300 in the first set and 500 in the second set. The architecture and the parameters of the PSHNN were chosen as in Section V.A.

Table III shows the classification accuracy of each case. The number of errors of PSHNN was actually a little better than that of the ML method. This is believed to be due to the fact that data are assumed to be Gaussian in the ML method. The number of errors of the 4NN was larger than those of the ML and PSHNN methods.

VI. *PNS* MODULES

The *PNS* module was developed as an alternative building block for the synthesis of PSHNNs [7]. The *PNS* module contains three submodules (units), the first two of which are created as simple neural network constructs and the last of which is a statistical unit. The first two units are fractile in nature, meaning that each such unit may itself consist of a number of parallel *PNS* modules in a fractile fashion. Through a mechanism of statistical acceptance or rejection of input vectors for classification, the sample space is divided into a number of regions. The input vectors belonging to each region are classified by a dedicated set of *PNS* modules. This strategy resulted in considerably higher accuracy of classification and better generalization as compared to previous neural network models in applications investigated. If the delta rule network is used to generate the first two units, each region approximates a linearly separable region. In this sense, the total system becomes similar to a piecewise linear model. The various regions are determined nonlinearly by the first and third units of the *PNS* modules.

The concept of the *PNS* module has evolved as a result of analyzing the major reasons for errors in classification problems, some of which are given in the following list:

1. Patterns which are very close to the class boundaries are usually difficult to differentiate.
2. The classification problem may be extremely nonlinear.
3. A particular class may be undersampled such that the number of training samples for that class are too few, as compared to the other classes.

Initially, the total network consists of a single N unit. It has as many input neurons as the length of an input pattern and as many output neurons as the number of classes. The number of input and output neurons also may be chosen differently, depending on how the input patterns and the classes are represented. The N unit is trained by using the present training set. After the N unit converges, the S unit is created. The S unit is a parallel statistical classifier which performs bit-level three-class Bayesian analysis on the output bits of the N unit. One result of this analysis is the generation of the probabilities P_k, $k = 1, 2, M$, M being the number of classes. P_k signifies the probability of detecting an input pattern belonging to class k correctly. If this probability is equal to or smaller than a small threshold δ, the input vectors belonging to that class are rejected before they are inputed to the N unit.

The rejection of such classes before they are fed to the N unit is achieved by creation of the P unit. It is a two-class classifier trained to reject the input patterns belonging to the classes initially determined by the S unit. In this way, the P unit divides the sample space into two regions, allowing the N unit to be trained with patterns belonging to the classes which are easier to classify.

If a P unit is created, the N unit is retrained with the remaining classes accepted by the P unit. Afterward, the foregoing process is repeated. The S unit is also regenerated. It may again reject some classes. Then another P unit is created to reject these classes. This results in a recursive procedure. If there are no more classes rejected by the S unit, a *PNS* module is generated. The input patterns rejected by it are fed to the next *PNS* module.

The complicating factor in the foregoing discussion is that more than one P unit may be generated. Each P unit is a two-class classifier. Depending on the difficulty of the two-class classification problem, the P unit may itself consist of a number of *PNS* modules.

In addition to deciding which classes should be rejected, the S unit also generates certain other thresholds for acceptance or rejection of an input pattern. Thus, the input pattern may be rejected by the *P* unit or the *S* unit. The rejected vectors become input to the next stage of *PNS* modules. This process of creating stages continues until all (or a desired percentage of) the training vectors are correctly classified. In brief, the total network begins as a single *PNS* module and grows during training in a way similar to fractal growth. *P* and *NS* units may themselves create *PNS* modules.

The statistical analysis technique for the creation of the *S* unit involves bitwise rejection performed by bitwise classifiers. Each such classifier is a three-class maximum *a posteriori* (MAP) detector [17]. For the output bit *k* with the output value *z* of the in-unit, three hypotheses are possible:

$H0 =$ bit k should be classified as 0.
$H1 =$ bit k should be classified as 1.
$HR =$ bit k should be rejected.

The decision rule involves three tests to be performed between $H0$ and $H1$, $H0$ and HR, and HR and $H1$. The resulting decision rule corresponds to determining certain decision thresholds which divide the interval [0, 1] into several regions. The decision rule also can be interpreted as a voting strategy among the three tests [7]. The statistical procedure involves the estimation of conditional and *a priori* probabilities.

PSHNN networks generated with *PNS* modules were tested in a number of applications such as the 10-class Colorado remote sensing problem, exclusive-OR, (XOR), and classification with synthetically generated data. The results were compared to those obtained with backpropagation networks and previous versions of PSHNN. The classification accuracy obtained with the *PNS* modules was higher in all these application as compared to the other techniques [7].

VII. PARALLEL CONSENSUAL NEURAL NETWORKS

The parallel consensual neural network (PCNN) was developed as another type of PSHNN. It is mainly applied in classification of multisource remote-sensing and geographic data [9, 10]. The latest version of PCNN architecture involves statistical consensus theory [18, 19]. The input data transformed several times as input to SNNs are used as if they were independent inputs. The independent inputs are first classified using the stage neural networks. The output responses from the stage networks are then weighted and combined to make a consensual decision.

Two approaches used to compute the data transforms for the PCNN were the Gray code of Gray code method for binary data and the WPT technique for analog data. The experimental results obtained with the proposed approach show that the

PCNN outperforms both a conjugate-gradient backpropagation neural network and conventional statistical methods in terms of overall classification accuracy of test data [8].

In multisource classification, different types of information from several data sources are used for classification to improve the classification accuracy as compared to the accuracy achieved by single-source classification. Conventional statistical pattern recognition methods are not appropriate in classification of multisource data because such data cannot, in most cases, be modeled by a convenient multivariate statistical model. In [8], it was shown that neural networks performed well in classification of multisource remote-sensing and geographic data. The neural network models were superior to the statistical methods in terms of overall classification accuracy of training data. However, statistical approaches based on consensus from several data sources outperformed the neural networks in terms of overall classification accuracy of test data. The PCNN gets over this disadvantage and actually performs better than the statistical approaches.

The PCNN does not directly use prior statistical information, but is somewhat analogous to the statistical consensus theory approaches. In the PCNN, several transformed input data are fed into SNNs. The final output is based on the consensus among SNNs trained on the same original data with different representations.

A. Consensus Theory

Consensus theory [18, 19] is a well-established research field involving procedures with the goal of combining single probability distributions to summarize estimates from multiple experts (data sources) with the assumption that the experts make decisions based on Bayesian decision theory. In most consensus theoretic methods each data source is at first considered separately. For a given source an appropriate training procedure can be used to model the data by a number of source-specific densities that will characterize that source. The data types are assumed to be very general. The source-specific classes or clusters are therefore referred to as data classes, because they are defined from relationships in a particular data space. In general, there may not be a simple one-to-one relation between the user-desired information classes and the set of data classes available because the information classes are not necessarily a property of the data. In consensus theory, the information from the data sources is aggregated by a global membership function, and the data are classified according to the usual maximum selection rule into the information classes. The combination formula obtained is called a consensus rule. Consensus theory can be justified by the fact that a group decision is better in terms of mean square error than a decision from a single expert (data source).

Probably the most commonly used consensus rule is the linear opinion pool which has the (group probability) form

$$C_j(Z) = \sum_{i=1}^{n} \lambda_i p(w_j|z_i), \tag{5}$$

for the information class w_j if n data sources are used, where $p(w_j|z_i)$ is a source-specific posterior probability and λ_i's ($i = 1, 2 \ldots, n$) are source-specific weights which control the relative influence of the data sources. The weights are associated with the sources in the global membership function to express quantitatively the goodness of each source.

The linear opinion pool has a number of appealing properties. For example, it is simple, yields a probability distribution, and the weight λ_i reflects in some way the relative expertise of the ith expert. If the data sources have absolutely continuous probability distributions, the linear opinion pool gives an absolutely continuous distribution. In using the linear opinion pool, it is assumed that all of the experts observe the input vector Z. Therefore, (5) is simply a weighted average of the probability distributions from all the experts, and the result is a combined probability distribution.

The linear opinion pool also has several weaknesses; for example, it shows dictatorship when Bayes' theorem is applied, that is, only one data source will dominate in making a decision. It is also not externally Bayesian (does not obey Bayes' rule) because the linear opinion pool is not derived from the joint probabilities using Bayes' rule. Another consensus rule, the logarithmic opinion pool, has been proposed to overcome some of the problems with the linear opinion pool. The logarithmic opinion pool differs from the linear opinion pool in that it is unimodal and less dispersed.

B. Implementation

Implementing consensus theory in PSNN involves using a collection of SNNs (see Fig. 12). When the training of all the stages has finished, the consensus for the SNNs is computed. The consensus is obtained by taking class-specific weighted averages of the output responses of the SNNs. Thus, the PCNN attempts to improve its classification accuracy by weighted averaging of the SNN responses from several different input representations. By doing this, the PCNN attempts to give highest weighting to the SNN trained on the "best" representation of input data.

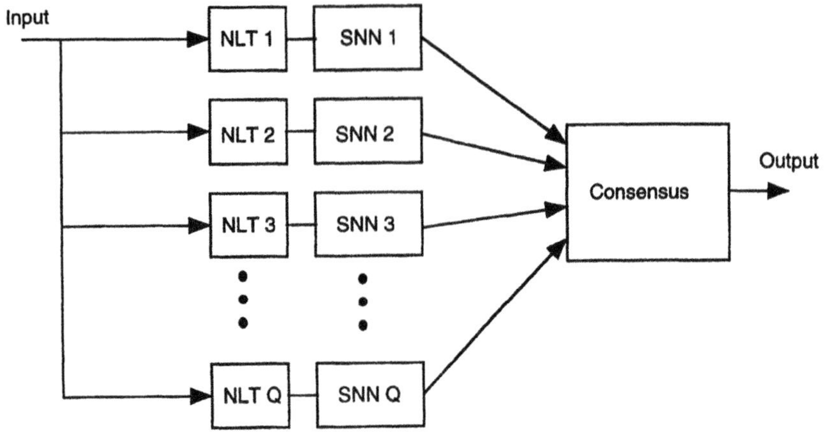

Figure 12 Block diagram of PSHNN with consensus at the output.

C. Optimal Weights

The weight selection schemes in the PCNN should reflect the goodness of the separate input data, that is, relatively high weights should be given to input data that contribute to high accuracy. There are at least two potential weight selection schemes. The first scheme is to select the weights such that they weight the individual stages but not the classes within the stages. In this scheme one possibility is to use equal weights for all the outputs of the SNNs, X_i, $i = 1, 2, \dots, n$, and effectively take the average of the outputs from the SNNs, that is,

$$Y = \frac{1}{n}\sum_{i=1}^{n} X_i, \tag{6}$$

where Y is the combined output response. Another possibility in this scheme is to use reliability measures which rank the SNNs according to their goodness. These reliability measures might be, for example, stage-specific classification accuracy of training data, overall separability, or equivocation [18].

The second scheme, called optimal weighting, is to choose the weights such that they not only weight the individual stages but also the classes within the stages. In this case, the combined output response, Y, can be written in matrix form as

$$Y = AX, \tag{7}$$

where X is a matrix containing the output of all the SNNs, and A contains all the weights. Assuming that X has full column rank, the preceding equation can be solved for A using the pseudo-inverse of X or a simple delta rule.

D. Experimental Results

Two experiments were conducted with the PCNN on multisource remote-sensing and geographic data. The WPT was used for input data transformations followed by the backpropagation (BP) network with conjugate gradient training. Each level of the full WPT consists of data for the different stage networks. Therefore, the stages will have the same original input data with different time–frequency resolutions. Thus, the PCNN attempts to find the consensus for these different representations of the input data, and the optimal weighting method consequently gives the best representation the highest weighting.

The experimental results obtained showed that the PCNN performed very well in the experiments in terms of overall classification accuracy [10]. In fact, the PCNN with the optimal weights outperformed both conjugate-gradient backpropagation and the best statistical methods in classification of multisource remote-sensing and geographic data in terms of overall classification accuracy of test data. Based on these results, the PCNN with optimal weights should be considered a desirable alternative to other methods in classification problems where the data are difficult to model, which was the case for the data used in the experiments. The PCNN is distinct from other existing neural network architectures in the sense that it uses a collection of neural networks to form a weighted consensual decision. In situations involving several different types of input representations in difficult classification problems, the PCNN should be more accurate than both single neural network classifiers and conventional statistical classification methods.

VIII. PARALLEL, SELF-ORGANIZING, HIERARCHICAL NEURAL NETWORKS WITH COMPETITIVE LEARNING AND SAFE REJECTION SCHEMES

The PSHNN needs long learning times when supervised learning algorithms such as the delta rule and the backpropagation algorithm are used in each SNN. In addition, the classification performance of the PSHNN is strongly dependent on its rejection scheme. Thus, it is possible that we can improve the classification accuracy by developing better error-detection and rejection schemes.

Multiple safe rejection schemes and competitive learning can be used as the learning algorithm of the PSHNN to get around the disadvantages of both supervised learning and competitive learning algorithms [6]. In this approach, we first compute the reference vectors in parallel for all the classes using competitive learning. Then, safe rejection boundaries are constructed in the training procedure so that there are no misclassified training vectors. The experimental results show that the proposed neural network has more speed and accuracy than the multilayer neural network trained by backpropagation and the PSHNN trained by the delta rule.

Kohonen developed several versions of competitive learning algorithms [20]. The main difference between our system and Kohonen's algorithms is safe rejection schemes and the resulting SNNs. Reference vectors are used for classification by the nearest neighbor principle in Kohonen's methods. In the proposed system, the decision surface of classification is determined by the rejection schemes in addition to the reference vectors.

Carpenter and Grossberg [21] developed a number of neural network architectures based on adaptive resonance theory (ART). For example, ART1 also uses competitive learning to choose the winning prototype (output unit) for each input vector. When an input vector is sufficiently similar to the winning prototype, the prototype represents the input correctly. Once a stored prototype is found that matches the input vector within a specific tolerance (the vigilance), that prototype is adjusted to make it still more like the input vector. If an input is not sufficiently similar to any existing prototype, a new classification category is formed by storing a prototype that is like the input vector. If the vigilance factor r, with $0 < r < 1$, is large, many finely divided categories are formed. On the other hand, a small r produces coarse categorization.

The current system is different from ART1 in that:

1. All of the available output processing elements are used, whereas in ART1, the value of the vigilance factor determines how many output processing elements are used.
2. The number of classes is predefined and each input vector is tagged with its correct class whereas in ART1 the vigilance factor determines the number of classes.
3. An input vector is tested for similarity to the reference vectors by an elaborate rejection scheme; if the input vector is rejected, it is fed in to the next SNN. In ART1, the vigilance factor determines acceptance or rejection and a classification category is created in case of rejection. In other words, the proposed system creates a new SNN whereas ART1 expands the dimension of its output layer for processing of the rejected training vectors.
4. The proposed system transforms nonlinearly the input vectors rejected by the previous SNN, etc.

One typical competitive learning algorithm can be described as

$$W_k(t+1) = \begin{cases} W_k(t) + C(t)\big[X(t) - W_k(t)\big], & \text{if } k \text{ wins,} \\ W_k(t), & \text{if } k \text{ loses,} \end{cases} \tag{8}$$

where $W_k(t+1)$ represents the value of the kth reference vector after adjustment, $W_k(t)$ is the value of the kth reference vector before adjustment, $X(t)$ is the training vector at time t, and $C(t)$ is the learning rate coefficient. Usually slowly decreasing scalar time functions are used as the learning rates. At each instant of time, the winning reference vector is the one which has the minimum Euclidean distance between the reference vector and $X(t)$.

If neural networks are trained using only competitive learning algorithms, the reference vectors are used for classification by the nearest neighbor principle, namely, by the comparison of the testing vector X with the reference vector W in the nearest neighbor sense. The classification accuracy relies on how correctly the reference vectors are computed. However, it is difficult to compute the reference vectors which produce globally minimum errors because reference vectors depends on initial reference vectors, learning rate, the order of training samples, and so on.

To overcome the limitations of competitive learning algorithms, our system incorporates the rejection schemes. The purpose of the rejection scheme is to reject the *hard* vectors, which are difficult to classify, and to accept the correctly classified vectors as much as possible. We train the next SNN with only those training vectors that are rejected in the previous SNN. During the training procedure, the correct classes are known, and we can check which ones are misclassified. However, this is not possible during the testing procedure. Thus, we need some criteria to reject error-causing vectors during both the training procedure and the testing procedure. For this purpose, we construct rejection boundaries for the reference vectors during the training procedure and use them during both the training procedure and the testing procedure.

A. Safe Rejection Schemes

The classification performance of the proposed system depends strongly on how well the rejection boundaries are constructed because the decision surface of classification is to a large degree determined by the rejection boundaries. One promising way for the construction of rejection boundaries is to use safe rejection schemes. Two possible definitions for safe rejection schemes are as follows:

Definition 1. A rejection scheme is said to be *safe* if every training vector is classified correctly and rejected otherwise by each SNN so that there are no misclassified training vectors if enough SNNs are utilized.

Definition 2. A rejection scheme is said to be *unsafe* if there exists a misclassified training vector at the output of the total network.

Two safe rejection schemes to construct the safe rejection boundaries for the reference vectors belonging to the jth class were developed. The procedure for the first scheme called RADPN is described next.

RADPN (RADP and RADN):

Initialize. $k = 1$ $\text{RADP}_{ni} = w_{ni}$ and $\text{RADN}_{ni} = w_{ni}$ for $n = 1, 2, \ldots, I$ and $i = 1, 2, \ldots, L$. The variable w_{ni} is the nth element of a reference vector W_i; I is the dimension of the training vectors, and L is the number of reference vectors that belong to the jth class.

Step 1. For a training vector $X_j(k)$ belonging to the jth class, find the nearest reference vector W_i using Euclidean distance measure.

Step 2. Compare $x_{nj}(k)$, the nth element of $X_j(k)$, with w_{ni}.

(1) If $x_{nj}(k)$ is bigger than w_{ni}, check whether $x_{nj}(k)$ is outside the previous rejection boundary RADP_{ni}.

(a) If $x_{nj}(k) > \text{RADP}_{ni}$, RADP_{ni} *is modified to* $\text{RADP}_{ni} = x_{nj}(k)$.
(b) If $x_{nj}(k) < \text{RADP}_{ni}$, RADP_{ni} is not changed.

(2) If $x_{nj}(k)$ is smaller than w_{ni}, check whether $x_{nj}(k)$ is outside the previous rejection boundary RADN_{ni}.

(a) If $x_{nj}(k) < \text{RADN}_{ni}$, RADN_{ni} *is modified to* $\text{RADN}_{ni} = x_{nj}(k)$.
(b) If $x_{nj}(k) \geq \text{RADN}_{ni}$, RADN_{ni} is not changed.

Step 3. Check whether $X_j(k)$ is the last training vector belonging to the jth class.

(1) If $k = M_j$, where M_j is the number of training vectors belonging to the jth class, stop the procedure and save the current RADP_{ni} and RADN_{ni}.
(2) If $k < M_j$, $k = k + 1$ and go to step 1.

The preceding procedure can be executed in parallel for all classes ($j = 1, 2, C$, where C is the number of possible classes) or can be executed serially.

Each reference vector generates the interconnection weights between the input nodes and a particular output node identified with the reference vector. The output of an output node is set to 1 when a training vector is inside or on its rejection boundary. It has output 0 when a training vector is outside its rejection boundary. For RADPN, a training vector $X(k)$ is judged to be inside or on the rejection boundary if it satisfies, for every $n = 1, 2, \ldots, I$, the condition

$$\text{RADN}_n \leq x_n(k) \leq \text{RADP}_n. \tag{9}$$

RADN_n and RADP_n represent the nth elements of RADN and RADP of the reference vector identified with the output node, respectively. The variable $x_n(k)$ is the nth element of $X(k)$. If at least one element of $X(k)$ does not satisfy (9), $X(k)$ is said to be outside the rejection boundary.

If one or more reference vectors belonging to a class has output 1, the class output is set to 1. If none of the reference vectors belonging to a class has output 1, the class output is set to 0. A training vector is rejected by the rejection scheme if more than one class has output 1. A training vector is not rejected if only one class has output 1.

B. TRAINING

Assume that a training set of vectors with known classification is utilized. Each sample in the training set represents an observed case of an input–output relationship and can be interpreted as consisting of attribute values of an object with a known class. The training procedure is described as follows:

Initialize: $m = 1$.

Step 1. For SNN_m (the mth stage neural network), compute the reference vectors using a competitive learning method.
Step 2. With the training vectors belonging to each class, construct safe rejection boundaries for reference vectors belonging to each class, as discussed in Section VIII.A.
Step 3. Determine the input vectors rejected by all safe rejection schemes. If there is no rejected training vector or the predetermined maximum number of SNNs is exceeded, stop the training procedure. Otherwise, go to step 4.
Step 4 (optional). Transform nonlinearly the rejected data set.
Step 5. $m = m + 1$. Go to step 1.

Assume a predetermined number of processing elements, each one provided with a reference vector W_k. Their number may be a multiple L (say, 10 times) of the number of classes considered. The variable L is determined by the total number of output processing elements and the number of classes:

$$L = \frac{\text{the total number of elements}}{\text{the number of classes}}. \qquad (10)$$

In step 1 of the training procedure, we investigated two possible methods for the computation of the reference vectors. In method I, all the reference vectors are computed together using the whole training data set. This is the way the reference vectors are computed in conventional competitive learning characterized by (8). In method II, competitive learning is performed in parallel for all the classes as follows: For the jth class,

$$W_j^i(t+1) = \begin{cases} W_j^i(t) + C^j(t)[X^j(t) - W_j^i(t)], & \text{if } i \text{ wins}, \\ W_j^i(t), & i \text{ loses}, \end{cases} \tag{11}$$

where $W_j^i(t+1)$ represents the value of the ith reference vector of class j after adjustment, $W_j^i(t)$ is the value of the ith reference vector before adjustment, $X^j(t)$ is the training vector belonging to the jth class used for updating the reference vectors at time t, and $C^j(t)$ is the learning rate coefficient for the computation of the reference vectors of the jth class.

When the reference vectors are computed separately for each class and in parallel for all the classes, the learning speed is improved by a factor approximately equal to the number of classes, in comparison to conventional competitive learning. Method I is obviously more optimal when traditional competitive learning algorithms are used without rejection schemes. Interestingly, method II gives better performance in terms of classification accuracy when rejection schemes are used [6].

C. Testing

The output of an output node is set to 1 when the testing vector is inside or on its rejection boundary. It has output 0 when the testing vector is outside its rejection boundary. For RADPN, the testing vector $X(k)$ is judged to be inside or on the rejection boundary if it satisfies (9) for every $n = 1, 2, \ldots, I$. Otherwise, $X(k)$ is said to be outside the rejection boundary.

If one or more output nodes belonging to a class has output 1, the class output is set to 1. If none of the output nodes belonging to a class has output 1, the class output is set to 0. A testing vector is not rejected by the rejection scheme if only one class has output 1. A testing vector is rejected if more than one class has output 1 or no class has output 1.

Every training vector exists inside or on at least one rejection boundary. However, this is not necessarily true for the testing vectors. It is logical to class such vectors to reduce the burden of the next SNN instead of just rejecting them. One promising way for this purpose is as follows: among the rejection boundaries of the rejection scheme by which no class has output 1, we find N nearest rejection boundaries. Then we check whether they all belong to one class. If they do, we classify the testing vector to that class. Otherwise, the vector is rejected. Usually, $1 \leq N \leq L$, where L is the number of reference vectors of each class. The greater N is, the harder it is for the testing vector to be classified to a class. If all the testing vectors are required to be classified, the last SNN involves classifying the rejected testing vector to the class of the nearest reference vector.

The following procedure describes the complete testing procedure:

Initialize: $m = 1$.

Step 1. Input the testing vector to SNN.
Step 2. Check whether the testing vector is rejected by every rejection scheme.

(1) If it is rejected by all rejections schemes, find N nearest reference boundaries and perform the steps (a) and (b) below for every rejection scheme by which all class outputs are 0s.

(a) If N nearest reference boundaries belong to one class, classify the input as belonging to that class.
(b) If N nearest reference boundaries come from more than one class, do not classify.
(c) If (a) and (b) are done for all rejection schemes, go to step 3.

(2) If it is rejected by all rejection schemes and there is no rejection scheme by which all class outputs are 0s, go to step 4.
(3) If it is not rejected by at least one rejection scheme, classify the input as belonging to the class whose output is 1. Stop the testing procedure.

Step 3. Count the number of classes to which the input is classified.

(1) If there is only one such class, assign the testing vector to that class. Stop the testing procedure.
(2) If more than one class is chosen, do not classify the testing vector. Go to step 4.

Step 4. Check whether or not the current SNN is the last.

(1) If it is the last SNN, then classify the testing vector to the class of the nearest reference vector, stop the testing procedure.
(2) If it is not, go to step 5.

Step 5 (optional). Take the nonlinear transform of the input vector.
Step 6. $m = m + 1$. Go to step 1.

Step 2 in the testing procedure can be executed in parallel or serially for all safe rejection schemes because every rejection scheme works independently.

Two or more rejection schemes can be used in parallel rather than serially. In the case of serial use of X and Y, X can be used after Y or vice versa. During the training step, the ordering of X *and* Y is immaterial because there are no misclassified training vectors. However, during testing, the actual ordering of X *and* Y may affect the classification performance. In the case of parallel use of more than one rejection scheme, all the rejection schemes are used simultaneously, and each rejection scheme decides which input vectors to reject. During testing, if an input vector accepted by some rejection schemes is classified to different classes by more than two rejection schemes, it is rejected.

D. Experimental Results

Two particular sets of remote-sensing data were used in the experiments. The classification performance of the new algorithms was compared with those of backpropagation and PSHNN trained by the delta rule.

The PSHNN with competitive learning and safe rejection schemes produced higher classification accuracy than the backpropagation network and the PSHNN with the delta rule [6]. In the case of simple competitive learning without rejection schemes characterized by (8), the training and testing accuracies were considerably lower than the present method.

The learning speed of the proposed system is improved by a factor approximately equal to 57 ($= 7.15 \times 8$) in comparison to the PSHNN with the delta rule when the reference vectors are computed in parallel for each class. Ersoy and Hong [1] estimated the learning speed of PSHNN and backpropagation networks. The 4NN requires about 25 times longer training time than the PSHNN. Thus, the training time for the PSHNN with competitive learning and safe rejection schemes is about 1425 ($= 57 \times 25$) times shorter than the time for the backpropagation network.

In learning reference vectors, the classification accuracies of methods I and II were compared. In method I, all reference vectors are computed together using the whole training data set. In method II, the reference vectors of each class are computed with the training samples belonging to that class, independently of the reference vectors of the other classes. Method II produced higher classification accuracy and needed a smaller number of SNNs than those of Method I. One reason for this is that method II constructs a smaller common area bounded by the rejection boundaries, and thus the number of rejected input vectors is less than that of method I [6].

IX. PARALLEL, SELF-ORGANIZING, HIERARCHICAL NEURAL NETWORKS WITH CONTINUOUS INPUTS AND OUTPUTS

PSHNNs discussed in the preceding text assume quantized, say, binary outputs. PSHNNs with continuous inputs and outputs (see Fig. 13) were discussed in [11, 12]. The resulting architecture is similar to neural networks with projection pursuit learning [22, 23]. The performance of the resulting networks was tested in

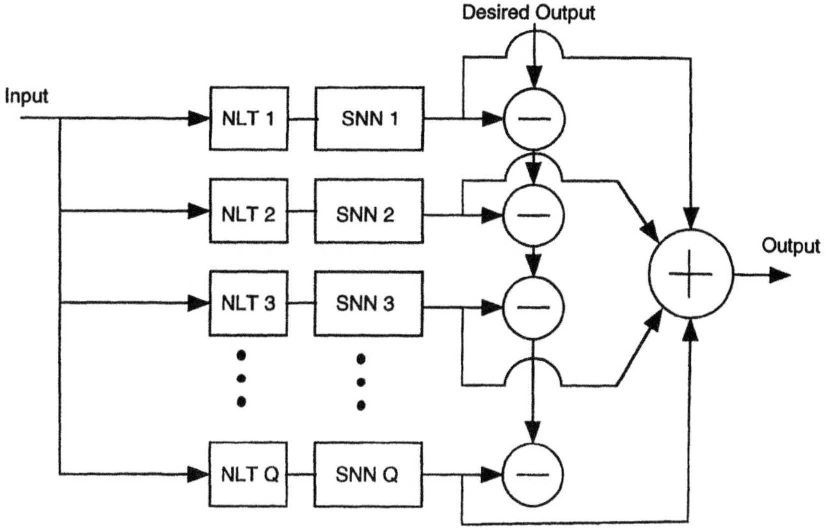

Figure 13 Block diagram of PSHNN with continuous inputs and outputs.

the problem of predicting speech signal samples from past samples. Three types of networks in which the stages are learned by the delta rule, sequential least squares, and the backpropagation (BP) algorithm, respectively, were investigated. In all cases, the new networks achieve better performance than linear prediction.

A revised BP algorithm also was developed for learning input nonlinearities. When the BP algorithm is to be used, better performance is achieved when a single BP network is replaced by a PSHNN of equal complexity in which each stage is a BP network of smaller complexity than the single BP network. This algorithm is further discussed subsequently.

A. Learning of Input Nonlinearities by Revised Backpropagation

In the preceding sections, it became clear that how to choose the input nonlinearities for optimal performance is an important issue. The revised backpropagation (RBP) algorithm can be used for this purpose. It consists of linear input and output units and nonlinear hidden units. One hidden layer is often sufficient. The hidden layers represent the nonlinear transformation of the input vector.

The RBP algorithm consists of two training steps, denoted as step I and step II, respectively. During step I, the RBP is the same as the usual BP algorithm [4]. During, step II, we fix the weights between the input layer and the hidden layers, but retrain the *weights* between the last hidden and the output layers.

Each stage of the PSHNN now consists of a RBP network, except possibly the first stage with NLT1 equal to the identity operator. In this way, the first stage can be considered as the linear part of the system.

There are a number of reasons why the two-step training may be preferable over the usual training with the BP algorithm. The first reason is that it is possible to use the PSHNN with RBP stages together with the SLS algorithm or the delta rule. For this purpose, we assume that the signal is reasonably stationary for N data points. Thus, the weights between the input and hidden layers of the RBP stages can be kept constant during such a time window. Only the last stage of the RBP network is then made adaptive by the SLS algorithm or the delta rule, which is much faster in learning speed than the BP algorithm requiring many sweeps over a data block. While the block of N data points is being processed with the SLS algorithm or the delta rule, the first $M \ll N$ data points of the block can be used to train the stages of the PSHNN by the BP algorithm. At the start of the next time window of N data points, the RBP stages are renewed with the new weights between the input and hidden layers. This process is repeated periodically every N data points. In this way, nonstationary signals which can be assumed to be stationary over short time intervals can be effectively processed.

The second reason is that the two-step algorithm allows faster learning. During the first step, the gain factor is chosen rather large for fast learning. During the second step, the gain factor is reduced for fine training. The end result is considerably faster learning than with the regular BP algorithm. It can be argued that the final error vector may not be as optimal as the error vector with the regular BP algorithm. We believe that this is not a problem because successive RBP stages compensate for the error. As a matter of fact, considerably larger errors, for example, due to imperfect implementation of the interconnection weights and nonlinearities, can be tolerated due to error compensation [3].

B. Forward–Backward Training

A forward–backward training algorithm was developed for learning of SNNs [11]. Using linear algebra, it was shown that the forward–backward training of an n-stage PSHNN until convergence is equivalent to the pseudo-inverse solution for a single, total network designed in the least-squares sense with the total input vector consisting of the actual input vector and its additional nonlinear transformations [11]. These results are also valid when a single long input vector is partitioned into smaller length vectors. A number of advantages achieved are small modules for easy and fast learning, parallel implementation of small modules during testing, faster convergence rate, better numerical error reduction, and suitability for learning input nonlinear transformations by other neural networks, such as the RBP algorithm discussed previously.

The most obvious advantage is that each stage is much easier to implement as a module to be trained than the whole network. In addition, all stages can be processed in parallel during testing. If the complexity of implementation without parallel stages is denoted by $f(N)$, where N is the length of input vectors, the parallel complexity of the forward–backward training algorithm during testing is $f(K)$, where K equals N/M with M equal to the number of stages.

The results obtained are actually valid for all linear least-squares problems if we consider the input vector and vectors generated from it by nonlinear transformations as the decomposition of a single, long vector. In this sense, the techniques discussed represent the decomposition of a large problem into smaller problems which are related through errors and forward–backward training. Generation of additional nodes at the input is common to a number of techniques such as generalized discriminant functions, higher order networks, and function-link networks. After this is done, a single total network can be trained by the delta rule. In contrast, the forward–backward training of small modules allows practical implementation, say, in VLSI, possible. At convergence, the forward–backward training solution is approximately the same as the pseudo-inverse solution, disregarding any possible numerical problems.

X. RECENT APPLICATIONS

Recently PSHNNs have been further developed and applied to new applications. Two examples follow. The first one involves embedding of fuzzy input signal representation in PSHNN with competitive learning and safe rejection schemes, both for improving classification accuracy and for being able to classify objects whose attribute values are in linguistic form. The second one is on low bit-rate image coding by using the PSHNN with continuous inputs and outputs.

A. Fuzzy Input Signal Representation

The fuzzy input signal representation scheme was developed as a preprocessing module [24]. It transforms imprecise input in linguistic form as well as precisely stated numerical input into multidimensional numerical values. The transformed multidimensional input is further processed in the PSHNN.

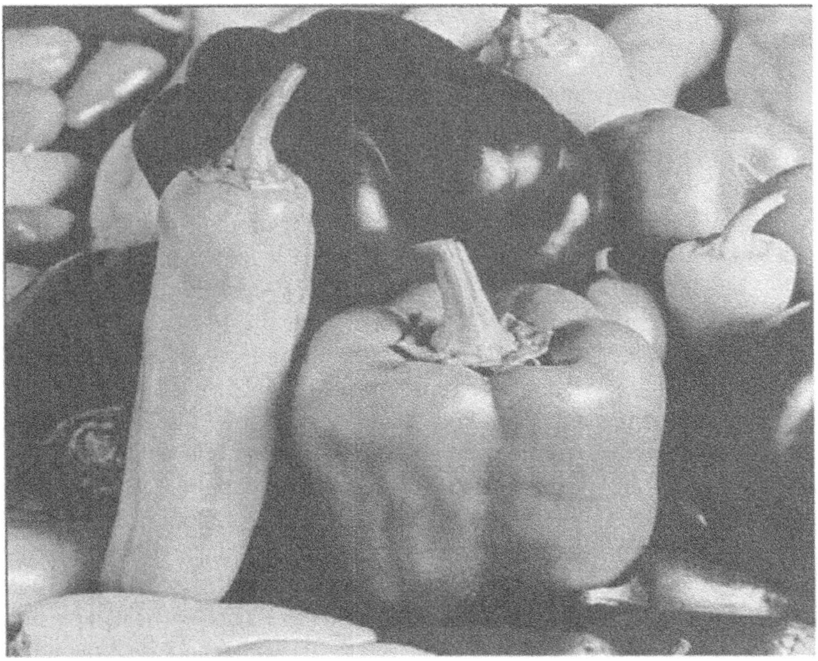

Figure 14 The 512 × 512 test image pepper.

The procedure for the fuzzy input signal representation of the training vectors is as follows:

Step 1. Derive the membership functions for the fuzzy sets from the training data set.

Step 2. Divide each fuzzy set into two new fuzzy sets to avoid ambiguity of representation.

Step 3. Select K fuzzy sets based on the class separability of the fuzzy sets. This step is included to avoid too many fuzzy sets.

Step 4. Convert the training vectors into the degree of match vectors using the computational scheme of the degree of match [25] and the fuzzy sets selected in Step 3.

Two particular sets of remote-sensing data, FLC1 data and Colorado data, were used in the experiments. The fuzzy competitive supervised neural network was compared with the competitive supervised neural network and the backpropagation network in terms of classification performance. The experimental results showed that the classification performance can be improved with the fuzzy input signal representation scheme, as compared to other representations [24].

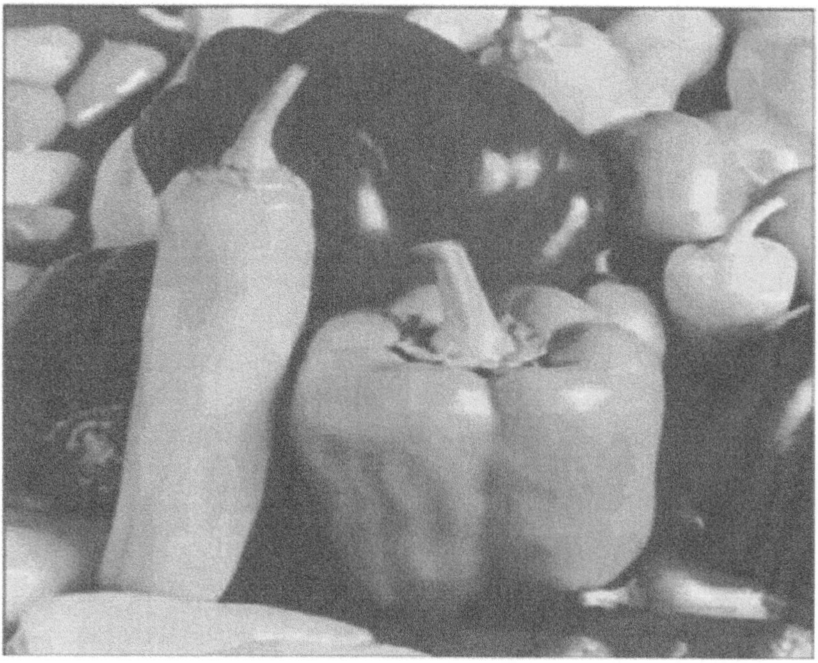

Figure 15 The encoded test image pepper with PSNR-based quadtree segmentation.

B. Multiresolution Image Compression

The PSHNN with continuous inputs and outputs (which can also be considered as neural network with projection pursuit learning) has recently been applied to low bit-rate image coding [26, 27]. In this approach, the image is first partitioned by quadtree segmentation of the image into blocks of different sizes based on the variance or the peak signal-to-noise ratio (PSNR) of each block. Then, a distinct code is constructed for each block by using PSHNN.

The peak signal-to-noise ratio for a b-bit image can be defined by

$$\mathrm{PSNR} = 10\log\left\{\frac{(2^b-1)^2}{(1/N^2)\sum_{i=1}^{N}\sum_{j=1}^{N}[f(i,j)-\hat{f}(i,j)]^2}\right\}, \tag{12}$$

where $N \times N$ is the size of the image; $f(i, j)$ is the pixel value at coordinates (i, j); $\hat{f}(i, j)$ is the pixel value modeled by the PSHNN. The two inputs of the neural network are chosen as the coordinates (i, j) of a block, and the single desired output is $f(i, j)$.

Figure 16 The JPEG encoded test image pepper at a bit rate of 0.14 and PSNR of 21.62.

It was shown that PSHNN can adaptively construct a good approximation for each block until the desired peak signal-to-noise ratio (PSNR) or bit rate is achieved. The experimental values for the PSNR objective measure of performance as well as the subjective quality of the encoded images were superior to the JPEG (joint photographic experts group) encoded images based on the discrete cosine transform coding, especially when the PSNR-based quadtree image segmentation was used.

The original test image pepper used in the experiments is shown in Fig. 14. The reconstructed test image pepper with PSNR-based quadtree segmentation at a bit rate of 0.14 bpp is shown in Fig. 15. The PSNR of the encode image is 30.22 dB. The JPEG encoded image at a bit rate of 0.14 bpp is shown in Fig. 16. The PSNR of the JPEG decoded image is 21.62. The reconstructed images with the proposed algorithm are superior to JPEG decoded images both in terms of PSNR and the subjective quality. The blockiness artifacts of JPEG decoded images are very obvious.

XI. CONCLUSIONS

The PSHNN systems have many attractive properties, such as fast learning time, parallel operation of SNNs during testing, and high performance in applications. Real time adaptation to nonoptimal connection weights by adjusting the error-detection bounds and thereby achieving very high fault-tolerance and robustness is also possible with these systems [3].

The number of stages (SNNs) needed with the PSHNN depends on the application. In most applications, two or three stages were sufficient, and further increases of the number of stages may actually lead to worse testing performance. In very difficult classification problems, the number of stages increases, and the training time increases. However, the successive stages use less training time, due to the decrease in the number of training patterns.

REFERENCES

[1] O. K. Ersoy and D. Hong. Parallel, self-organizing, hierarchical neural networks. *IEEE Trans. Neural Networks* 1:167–178, 1990.

[2] O. K. Ersoy and D. Hong. Neural network learning paradigms involving nonlinear spectral processing. In *Proceedings of the IEEE 1989 International Conference on Acoustics, Speech, and Signal Processing*, Glasgow, Scotland, 1989, pp. 1775–1778.

[3] O. K. Ersoy and D. Hong. Parallel, self-organizing, hierarchical neural networks II. *IEEE Trans. Industrial Electron.* 40:218–227, 1993.

[4] D. E. Rumelhart, J. L. McClelland, and PDP Research Group. *Parallel Distributed Processing*, MIT Press, Cambridge, MA, 1988.

[5] E. Barnard and R. A. Cole. A neural net training program based on conjugate gradient optimization. Technical Report CSE 89-104, Department of Electrical and Computer Engineering, Carnegie-Mellon University, 1989.

[6] S. Cho and O. K. Ersoy. Parallel self-organizing, hierarchical neural networks with competitive learning and safe rejection schemes. *IEEE Trans. Circuits Systems* 40:556–567, 1993.

[7] F. Valafar and O. K. Ersoy. PNS modules for the synthesis of parallel, self-organizing, hierarchical neural networks. *J. Circuits, Systems, Signal Processing* 15, 1996.

[8] J. A. Benediktsson, P. H. Swain, and O. K. Ersoy. Neural network approaches versus statistical methods in classification of multisource remote sensing-data. *IEEE Trans. Geosci. Remote Sensing* 28:540–552, 1990.

[9] H. Valafar and O. K. Ersoy. Parallel, self-organizing, consensual neural networks. Report TR-EE 90-56, Purdue University, 1990.

[10] J. A. Benediktsson, P. H. Swain, and O. K. Ersoy. Consensual neural networks. *IEEE Trans. Neural Networks* 8:54–64, 1997.

[11] S-W. Deng and O. K. Ersoy. Parallel, self-organizing, hierarchical neural networks with forward–backward training. *J. Circuits, Systems Signal Processing* 12:223–246, 1993.

[12] O. K. Ersoy and S-W. Deng. Parallel, self-organizing, hierarchical neural networks with continuous inputs and outputs. *IEEE Trans. Neural Networks* 6:1037–1044, 1995.

[13] O. K. Ersoy. Real discrete fourier transform. *IEEE Trans. Acoustics, Speech, Signal Processing* ASSP-33:880–882, 1985.

[14] O. K. Ersoy. A two-stage representation of DFT and its applications. *IEEE Trans. Acoustics, Speech, Signal Processing* ASSP-35:825–831, 1987.
[15] O. K. Ersoy and N-C Hu. Fast algorithms for the discrete Fourier preprocessing transforms. *IEEE Trans. Signal Processing* 40:744–757, 1992.
[16] I. Daubechies. *Ten Lectures on Wavelets. CBMS-NFS Regional Conference Series in Applied Mathematics*, Vol. 61. SIAM, Philadelphia, 1992.
[17] K. Fukunaga. *Introduction to Statistical Pattern Recognition.* Academic Press, New York, 1972.
[18] J. A. Benediktsson and P. H. Swain. Consensus theoretic classification methods. *IEEE Trans. Systems, Man Cybernetics* 22:688–704, 1992.
[19] C. Berenstein, L.N. Kanal, and D. Lavine. Consensus rules. In *Uncertainty in Artificial Intelligence* (L. N. Kanal and J. F. Lemmer, Eds.). North-Holland, New York, 1986.
[20] T. Kohonen. *Self-Organization and Associative Memory*, 2nd ed. Springer-Verlag, Berlin, 1989.
[21] G. A. Carpenter and S. Grossberg. The ART of adaptive pattern recognition by a self-organizing neural network. *Computer* 77–88, Mar. 1988.
[22] J. N. Hwang, S. R. Lay, M. Macchler, D. Martin, and J. Schimert. Regression modeling in back-propagation and projection pursuit learning. *IEEE Trans. Neural Networks* 5:342–353, 1994.
[23] J. N. Hwang, S-S You, S-R Lay, and I-C Jou. The cascade correlation learning: A projection pursuit learning perspective. *IEEE Trans. Neural Networks* 7:278–289, 1996.
[24] S. Cho and O. K. Ersoy. Parallel, self-organizing, hierarchical neural networks with fuzzy input signal representation, competitive learning and safe rejection schemes. Technical Report TR-EE-92-24, School of Electrical and Computer Engineering, Purdue University, 1992.
[25] S. Cho, O. K. Ersoy, and M. Lehto. An algorithm to compute the degree of match in fuzzy systems. *Fuzzy Sets and Systems* 49:285–300, 1992.
[26] M. T. Fardanesh, S. R. Safavian, H. R. Rabiee, and O. K. Ersoy. Multiresolution image compression by variance-based quadtree segmentation, neural networks, and projection pursuit. Unpublished.
[27] M. T. Fardanesh and O. K. Ersoy. Image compression and signal classification by neural networks, and projection pursuits. Technical Report TR-ECE-96-15, School of Electrical and Computer Engineering, Purdue University, 1996.

Dynamics of Networks of Biological Neurons: Simulation and Experimental Tools

M. Bove
Bioelectronics Laboratory and
Bioelectronic Technologies Laboratory
Department of Biophysical
and Electronic Engineering
University of Genoa
Genoa, Italy

M. Giugliano
Bioelectronics Laboratory and
Bioelectronic Technologies Laboratory
Department of Biophysical
and Electronic Engineering
University of Genoa
Genoa, Italy

M. Grattarola
Bioelectronics Laboratory and
Bioelectronic Technologies Laboratory
Department of Biophysical
and Electronic Engineering
University of Genoa
Genoa, Italy

S. Martinoia
Bioelectronics Laboratory and
Bioelectronic Technologies Laboratory
Department of Biophysical
and Electronic Engineering
University of Genoa
Genoa, Italy

G. Massobrio
Bioelectronics Laboratory and
Bioelectronic Technologies Laboratory
Department of Biophysical
and Electronic Engineering
University of Genoa
Genoa, Italy

Algorithms and Architectures

I. INTRODUCTION

The study of the dynamics of networks of neurons is a central issue in neuroscience research. An increasing amount of data have been recently collected concerning the behavior of invertebrate and vertebrate neuronal networks, toward the goal of characterizing the autoorganization properties of neuronal populations and to explain the cellular basis of behavior, such as the generation of rhythmic activity patterns for the control of movements and simple forms of learning [1].

The formal aspects of this study have contributed to the definition of an area of research identified as computational neuroscience. Its aim is to recognize the information content of biological signals by modeling and simulating the nervous system at different levels: biophysical, circuit, and system level.

The extremely rich and complex behavior exhibited by real neurons makes it very hard to build detailed descriptions of neuronal dynamics. Many models have been developed and a broad class of them shares the same qualitative features. There are basically two approaches to neural modeling: models that account for accurate ionic flow phenomena and models that provide input–output relationship descriptions.

With reference to the first approach, most of the models retain the general format originally proposed by Hodgkin and Huxley [2, 3], which is characterized by a common repertoire of oscillatory/excitable processes and by a nonlinear voltage dependence of proteic channels permeability. This approach includes models that examine spatially distributed properties of the neuronal membrane and others that utilize the space-clamp hypothesis (i.e., they assume the same voltage across the membrane for the entire cell). The former are usually referred to as multicompartment models,[1] and the latter as single-compartment or point neuron models.

A quite different approach to model the nervous system is to ignore much of the biological complications and to state a precise input–output mapping for elementary units, defining *a priori* what inputs and outputs will be [4, 5]. This seems to be the only way to gain some insights on collective emergent properties of wide-scale networks, and it is indeed the only analytically and computationally tractable description. On the other hand, even if this modeling approach had a strong impact in development of the theory of formal neural computation and the statistical theory of learning, it seems nowadays more interesting to investigate the dynamical properties of an ensemble of more realistic model neurons [6, 7].

Of course there are a number of intermediate description levels between the extremes of the two approaches. If the aim of the model to be developed is to obtain a better understanding of how the nervous system processes information, then the choice of level strongly depends on the availability of experimental neurobiological data. The modeling level which will be discussed in the following

[1] Multicompartment modeling generally leads to the *cable equation*, which describes temporal and spatial propagation of action potentials (APs).

text was motivated by the increasing amount of electrophysiological data made available by the use of new nonconventional electrophysiological recording techniques. A substantial experimental contribution to computational neuroscience is expected to be provided by new techniques for the culture of dissociated neurons *in vitro*. Dissociated neurons can survive for weeks in culture and reorganize into two-dimensional networks [8, 9]. Especially in the case of populations obtained from vertebrate embryos, these networks cannot be regarded as faithful reproductions of *in vivo* situations, but rather as new rudimentary neurobiological systems whose activity can change over time spontaneously or as a consequence of chemical/physical stimuli [10].

A nonconventional electrophysiological technique has been developed recently to deal with this new experimental situation. Standard techniques for studying the electrophysiological properties of single neurons are based on intracellular and patch-clamp recordings. These electrophysiological techniques are invasive and require that a thin glass capillary be brought near a cell membrane. Intracellular recording involves a localized rupture of the cell membrane. Patch-clamp methods can imply the rupture and (possible) isolation of a small membrane patch or, as in the case of the so-called whole-cell–loose-patch configuration [11], a seal between the microelectrode tip and the membrane surface. The new technique, appropriate for recording the electrical activity of networks of cultured neurons, is based on the use of substrate transducers, that is, arrays of planar microtransducers that form the adhesion surface for the reorganizing network. This nonconventional electrophysiological method has several advantages over standard intracellular recording that are related to the possibility of monitoring/stimulating noninvasively the electrochemical activities of several cells, independently and simultaneously for a long time [10, 12–14]. On the basis of this, the predictions of models that describe networks of synaptically connected biological neurons now can be compared with the results of *ad hoc* designed long-term experiments where patterns of coordinated activity are expected to emerge and develop in time. These models, which need to be at a somewhat intermediate level between Hodgkin–Huxley models and input–output models, will be discussed in detail in the following text and finally compared with experiments.

II. MODELING TOOLS

A. Conductance-Based Single-Compartment Differential Model Neurons

Focusing our attention on biophysical and circuit levels, we introduce classic modeling for a biological membrane, under the *space-clamp* assumption. Referring to an excitable membrane, we use the equation of conservation of charge through the phospholipidic double layer, assuming almost perfect dielectric properties:

$$\frac{dQ}{dt} = I_{\text{tot}}. \tag{1}$$

We indicate with Q the net charge flowing across the membrane and with I_{tot} the total current through it. If we expand the first term of Eq. (1), considering the capacitive properties, we obtain the general equation for the membrane potential:

$$C\frac{dV}{dt} = -F(V) + I_{\text{ext}} + I_{\text{pump}}. \tag{2}$$

We denote with $F(V)$ the voltage-dependent ionic currents, and with I_{ext} an applied external current. The current I_{pump} takes into account ionic currents related to *ATP-dependent* transport mechanisms. In consideration of the fact that usually its contribution is small [15], it will be omitted in the following descriptions.

Ionic currents can be expressed as [2]

$$F(V) = \sum_i G_i(t)\cdot(E_i - V), \qquad E_i = \frac{KT}{q}\cdot\ln\left(\frac{[C]_{\text{in}}}{[C]_{\text{out}}}\right). \tag{3}$$

E_i is the equilibrium potential corresponding to the ion producing the ith current, according to the Nernst equation, in which $[C]_{\text{in}}$ and $[C]_{\text{out}}$ are intracellular and extracellular ith ionic concentrations, respectively. It is possible to represent the evolution of the ionic conductances, interpreting $G_i(t)$ as the instantaneous number of open ionic channels per unity of area (see Fig. 1). Hodgkin and Huxley [2] described this fraction as a nonlinear function of the free energy of the system (proportional, in first approximation, to the membrane potential):

$$\begin{aligned} &F(V) = \sum_i^N \bar{g}_i\cdot m_i^{p_i}\cdot h_i^{q_i}\cdot(E_i - V),\\ &m_i, h_i \in [0;1],\ p_i, q_i \in \{0,1,2,3,\ldots\},\ i = 1,\ldots,N. \end{aligned} \tag{4}$$

In Eq. (4), m_i and h_i evolve according to a first order kinetic scheme, where the equilibrium constant of the kinetic reactions is a sigmoidal function of the potential V:

$$k \longleftrightarrow (1-k) \quad \Leftrightarrow \quad \frac{dk}{dt} = \lambda_k(V)\cdot[K_\infty(V) - k], \qquad k = m_i, h_i. \tag{5}$$

More complex differential models start basically from Eqs. (4) and (5) and give more detailed descriptions for ionic flow changes or let some constant parameter be a slowly varying dynamic variable.

In view of the goal of describing networks of biological neurons connected by biologically plausible synapses, we first consider the model proposed by Mor-

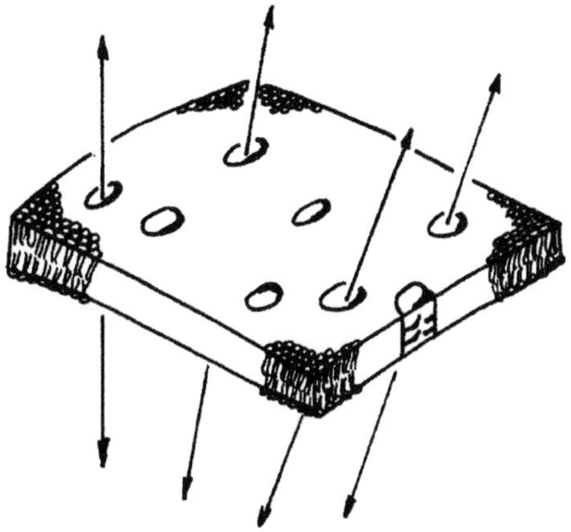

Figure 1 Sketch of a membrane patch. In the fluid mosaic model second-messenger-gated or voltage-gated proteic channels can diffuse, moving laterally and modifying their structure by changing intrinsic permeability of the membrane to specific ions.

ris and Lecar, which provides a reduction in complexity in comparison with the Hodgkin–Huxley model. It is characterized by a system of two activating variables of single gate ion channels. Although this description was conceived for the barnacle giant muscle fiber [3], it proves to be well suited for elementary modeling of excitatory properties of other systems, such as some pyramidal neurons in the cortex and pancreatic cells [3] (see Fig. 2).

The model is based on a system of three nonlinear differential equations that can be written as

$$C\frac{dV}{dt} = \overline{g}_{\text{leak}} \cdot (E_{\text{leak}} - V) + \overline{g}_{\text{Ca}} \cdot m \cdot (E_{\text{Ca}} - V) + \overline{g}_K \cdot n \cdot (E_K - V) + I_{\text{ext}}, \tag{6}$$

$$\frac{dm}{dt} = \lambda_M(V) \cdot (M_\infty(V) - m), \qquad \tau_M(V) = \frac{1}{\lambda_M(V)}, \tag{7}$$

$$\frac{dn}{dt} = \lambda_N(V) \cdot \big(N_\infty(V) - n\big), \qquad \tau_N(V) = \frac{1}{\lambda_N(V)}. \tag{8}$$

We note that Eq. (6) has the same form as Eq. (4) with parameters

$$N = 3,$$
$$\overline{g}_1 = \overline{g}_{\text{Ca}}, \qquad \overline{g}_2 = \overline{g}_K, \qquad \overline{g}_3 = \overline{g}_{\text{leak}},$$
$$p_1 = 1, \qquad p_2 = 1, \qquad p_3 = 0,$$

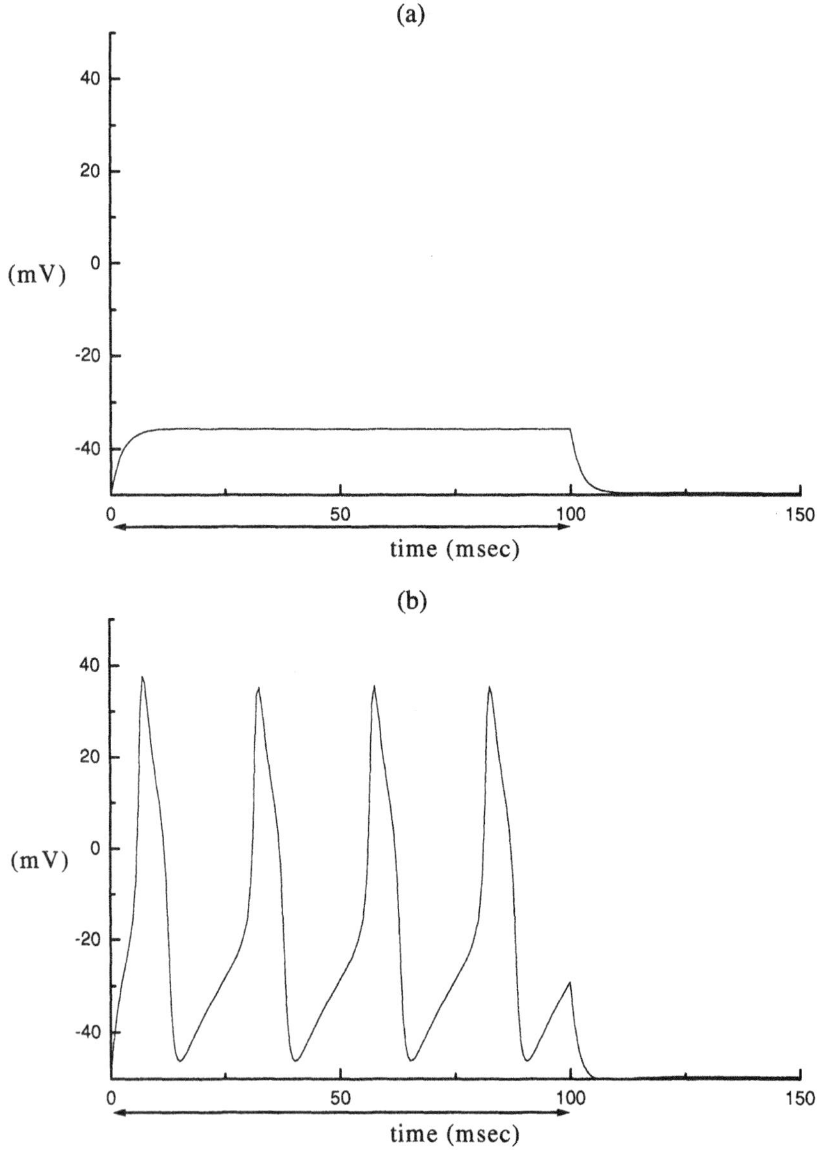

Figure 2 Basic behavior of excitable biological membranes. Simulations of the Morris–Lecar [Eqs. (6)–(8)] model lead to passive resistance–capacitance response (a) when the intensity of external constant current is not sufficient to produce oscillations ($I_{\text{ext}} = 6\ \mu\text{A/cm}^2$). (b) For $I_{\text{ext}} = 13\ \mu\text{A/cm}^2$ typical permanent periodic oscillations arise. These simulations were performed using $\bar{g}_{\text{Ca}} = 1\ \text{mS/cm}^2$ and $\bar{g}_K = 3\ \text{mS/cm}^2$. The arrows indicate the time interval of current stimulation.

$$
\begin{aligned}
q_1 &= 0, \qquad q_2 = 0, \qquad q_3 = 0, \\
E_1 &= E_{\mathrm{Ca}}, \qquad E_2 = E_K, \qquad E_3 = E_{\mathrm{leak}}, \\
\lambda_{m_1}(V) &= \cosh\left(\frac{V - V_1}{2 \cdot V_2}\right), \qquad \lambda_{m_2}(V) = \frac{1}{15} \cdot \cosh\left(\frac{V - V_3}{2 \cdot V_4}\right), \\
M_{1\infty} &= \frac{1}{2}\left[1 + \tanh\left(\frac{V - V_1}{V_2}\right)\right], \qquad M_{2\infty} = \frac{1}{2}\left[1 + \tanh\left(\frac{V - V_3}{V_4}\right)\right], \\
V_1 &= -1\,\mathrm{mV}, \qquad V_2 = 15\,\mathrm{mV}, \qquad V_3 = 10\,\mathrm{mV}, \qquad V_4 = 14.5\,\mathrm{mV}.
\end{aligned}
$$

For the simulations reported in this section, we considered the values[2]

$$
\begin{aligned}
C &= 1\,\mu\mathrm{F/cm}^2, \\
\bar{g}_{\mathrm{leak}} &= 0.5\,\mathrm{mS/cm}^2, \\
E_{\mathrm{leak}} &= -50\,\mathrm{mV}, \\
E_{\mathrm{Ca}} &= 100\,\mathrm{mV}, \\
E_K &= -70\,\mathrm{mV}, \\
V(0) &= -50\,\mathrm{mV}, \\
n(0) &= \frac{1}{2} \cdot \left(1 + \tanh\left(\frac{V(0) - 10}{14.5}\right)\right).
\end{aligned}
$$

It can be shown that $(\tau_M(V))/(\tau_N(V)) \ll 1$ for every value of the potential V. This allows us to reduce the dimensionality of the differential system, Eqs. (6)–(8). We can actually assume the dynamics associated with the m variable as instantaneous. This means to assume m instantaneously equal to its regime value [3], and then to neglect Eq. (7) and to replace Eq. (6) with

$$
\begin{aligned}
C\frac{dV}{dt} &= f(V, m, n, I_{\mathrm{ext}}) \approx f(V, M_\infty, n, I_{\mathrm{ext}}) \\
&= \bar{g}_{\mathrm{leak}} \cdot (E_{\mathrm{leak}} - V) + \bar{g}_{\mathrm{Ca}} \cdot M_\infty \cdot (E_{\mathrm{Ca}} - V) \\
&\quad + \bar{g}_K \cdot n \cdot (E_K - V) + I_{\mathrm{ext}}. \qquad (9)
\end{aligned}
$$

We analyzed this reduced model in detail. There is a nonlinear relationship between oscillation frequency and current stimulus amplitude: this can be viewed as a *Hopf bifurcation* in the phase plane [3]. There is actually a lower value for the stimulus I_{ext} where oscillations begin to arise, and there is a higher value, corresponding to permanent depolarization, where no oscillations occur. The most important quantities, which basically control all the dynamics, are the maximal conductances which affect existence, shape, and frequency of the periodic solution for $V(t)$, as reported in Fig. 3a and b.

[2] $E_{\mathrm{Ca}} = (KT/q) \cdot \ln([\mathrm{Ca}]_{\mathrm{in}}/[\mathrm{Ca}]_{\mathrm{out}})$ and $E_K = (KT/q) \cdot \ln([K]_{\mathrm{in}}/[K]_{\mathrm{out}})$.

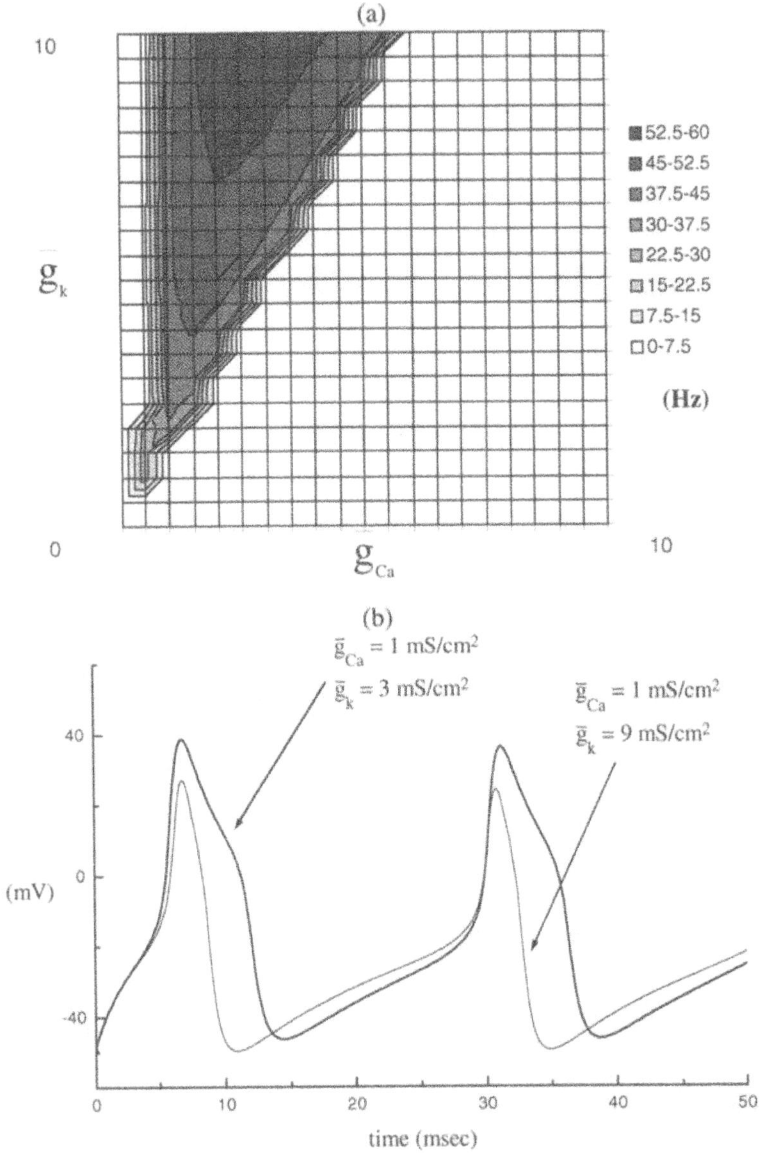

Figure 3 (a) The "peninsula" of permanent oscillation for the membrane potential. The mean frequency of the permanent oscillatory regime is plotted in the plane of positive maximal conductances, under a fixed stimulus $I_{ext} = 13\ \mu A/cm^2$. The lower right region is characterized by passive response to current stimulation, whereas the upper left is characterized by saturated permanent depolarization of the membrane potential. (b) Different sets for maximal conductance values may correspond to changes in the shape of action potentials, not only in their frequency.

B. Integrate-and-Fire Model Neurons

The model described in the foregoing text is still too complex for the purposes indicated in the Introduction. On the other hand, any further reduction of the differential model, Eqs. (8) and (9), corresponds essentially to ignoring one of the two equations [6]. We chose to keep integrative–capacitive properties [Eq. (9)] of nervous cells and to neglect refractoriness and generation of action potentials (AP) [Eq. (8)], because the amplitude and duration of refractory period of the APs are almost invariant to external current stimulations (synaptic currents too) and they probably do not play a significant role in specifying computational properties of a single unit in a network of synaptically connected neurons.Thus the dynamics of the biological network can be studied with considerable reduction of computation time.

Assuming the dynamics of n to be instantaneous, we can rewrite Eq. (9) as

$$C\frac{dV}{dt} \approx \bar{g}_{\text{leak}} \cdot (E_{\text{leak}} - V) + \bar{g}_{\text{Ca}} \cdot \left[\frac{1}{2} \cdot \left(1 + \tanh\left(\frac{V+1}{15}\right)\right)\right] \cdot (E_{\text{Ca}} - V) + \bar{g}_K \cdot \left[\frac{1}{2} \cdot \left(1 + \tanh\left(\frac{V-10}{14.5}\right)\right)\right] \cdot (E_K - V) + I_{\text{ext}}. \tag{10}$$

The second term of Eq. (10) is very close to 0 if $V \cong V_{\text{rest}}$, for $I_{\text{ext}} = 0\ \text{mA/cm}^2$, and it is possible to linearize the differential equation near that point (see Fig. 4a). For $\bar{g}_{\text{Ca}} = 0.75\ \text{mS/cm}^2$ and $\bar{g}_K = 1.49\ \text{mS/cm}^2$ we find

$$\begin{aligned} C\frac{dV}{dt} &\cong \tilde{f}(V_0, 0) + (V - V_0) \cdot \left.\frac{\partial \tilde{f}}{\partial V}\right|_{V=V_0, I_{\text{ext}}=0} + (I_{\text{ext}} - 0) \cdot \left.\frac{\partial \tilde{f}}{\partial I_{\text{ext}}}\right|_{V=V_0, I_{\text{ext}}=0} \\ &= \bar{g} \cdot (V_0 - V) + I_{\text{ext}} \end{aligned} \tag{11}$$

with $\bar{g} = 0.4799\ \text{mS/cm}^2$ and $V_0 = -49.67\ \text{mV}$.

Considering an AP as a highly stereotyped behavior, we can decide to neglect its precise modeling and artificially choose a threshold value for V. For the values reported previously, we choose $V_{\text{th}} = -22.586\ \text{mV}$ to mimic the same oscillation frequency of the complete model in the presence of the same stimulus. Crossing this threshold causes the potential to be set down to V_0. This approach is the main feature of the class of integrate-and-fire model neurons, which can be extended further by implementing the refractory period too (see Fig. 4b):

$$\begin{aligned} &C\frac{dV}{dt} = \bar{g} \cdot (V_0 - V) + I_{\text{ext}}, \quad \text{for } V(t) < V_{\text{th}}, \\ &V(\xi) = V_0, \qquad \xi \in \left[t_0^+; t_0^+ + \tau_{\text{ref}}\right], \quad \text{if } V(t_0^-) = V_{\text{th}}, \end{aligned} \tag{12}$$

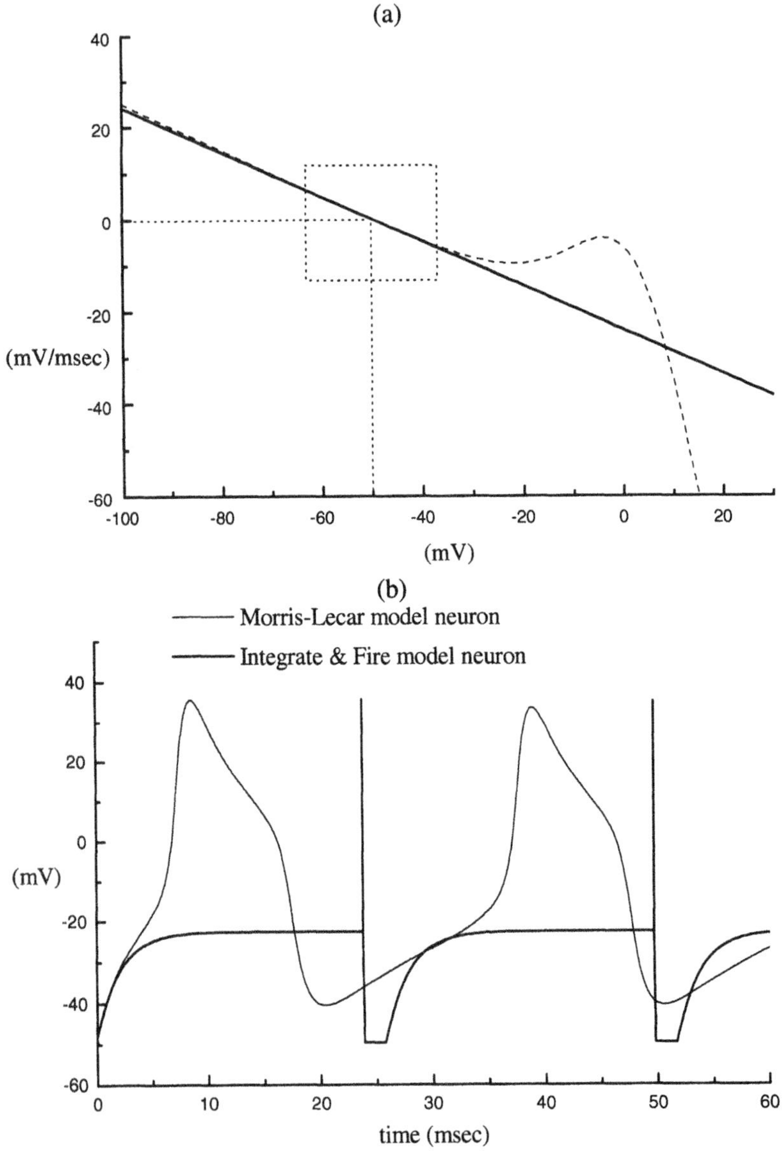

Figure 4 (a) Plot of the linear approximation of differential equation (10) near the resting value V_{rest}. The closer V is to its resting value and still remains under the excitability threshold, the more accurate is the approximation. (b) Behavior of the membrane potential in the integrate-and-fire model neuron including refractory period $\tau_{ref} = 2$ ms. Integrate-and-fire response is compared to the complex evolution of the action potential, as described by Eqs. (6)–(8), under the same stimulation and initial values in both models ($I_{ext} = 13\ \mu A/cm^2$, $V(0) = V_{rest}$).

where

$$V_0 = -49.67\,\text{mV}, \qquad V_{\text{th}} = -22.586\,\text{mV}, \qquad I_{\text{ext}} = 13\,\mu\text{A/cm}^2,$$
$$V(0) = V_0, \qquad C = 1\,\mu\text{F/cm}^2, \qquad \bar{g} = 0.4799\,\text{mS/cm}^2, \qquad \tau_{\text{ref}} = 2\,\text{ms}.$$

The last two hypotheses introduce a nonlinearity that could rescue some of the realism of the previous models. This kind of model is referred to as *leaky integrate-and-fire with refractoriness* [7].

The dependency of the membrane potential on I_{ext}, V_{th}, V_0, C, g, and τ_{ref} can be calculated by solving the first order differential Eq. (12) in closed form (see Fig. 5):

$$v = \begin{cases} (T + \tau_{\text{ref}})^{-1} = \left[\dfrac{C}{g} \cdot \ln\left(\dfrac{I_{\text{ext}}}{I_{\text{ext}} - g \cdot (V_{\text{th}} - V_0)}\right) + \tau_{\text{ref}}\right]^{-1}, \\ \qquad \text{iff } I_{\text{ext}} > \bar{g} \cdot (V_{\text{th}} - V_0), \\ 0, \quad \text{else } I_{\text{ext}} \leq \bar{g} \cdot (V_{\text{th}} - V_0). \end{cases} \tag{13}$$

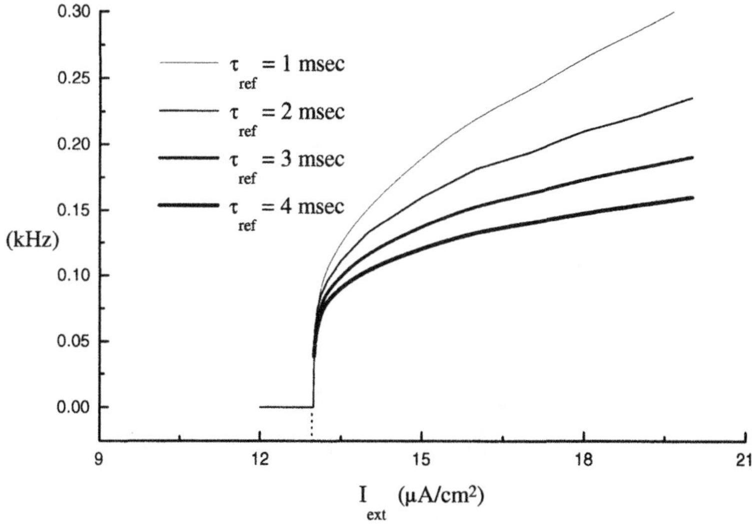

Figure 5 Mean frequency of oscillation of the membrane potential vs intensity of external constant current stimulus, for the integrate-and-fire model neuron. Different values for τ_{ref} leave the curve unaffected except for high frequency regimes. The introduction of a refractory period actually sets a bound on the maximal frequency of oscillations, as seen in Eq. (13).

Except for the absence of any saturation mechanism for higher frequencies, the integrate-and-fire model reproduces quite well the general characteristic frequency versus I_{ext} of Eqs. (6)–(9).

C. Synaptic Modeling

Exploring collective properties of large assemblies of model neurons is a challenging problem. Because of the very hard task of simulating large sets of nonlinear differential equations using traditional computer architectures, the general approach tends to reduce and simplify processes to obtain networks in which many elementary units can be densely interconnected and, during the simulations, to obtain reduced computation times.

We consider here the temporal evolution of the mutual electrical activities of coupled differential model neurons and how their basic general properties are retained by the integrate-and-fire model (see Fig. 6). The dynamics of state variables is analyzed by using both the complete model [Eqs. (6)–(8)] and the integrate-and-fire model [Eq. (12)], in the presence of a nonzero external constant current, so that each single neuron can be assumed to act as a generalized relaxation oscillator. In both cases, the frequency of oscillation for the membrane voltage is a function of the current amplitude, so that the natural frequencies of oscillation can be changed simply by choosing different I_{ext1} and I_{ext2}.

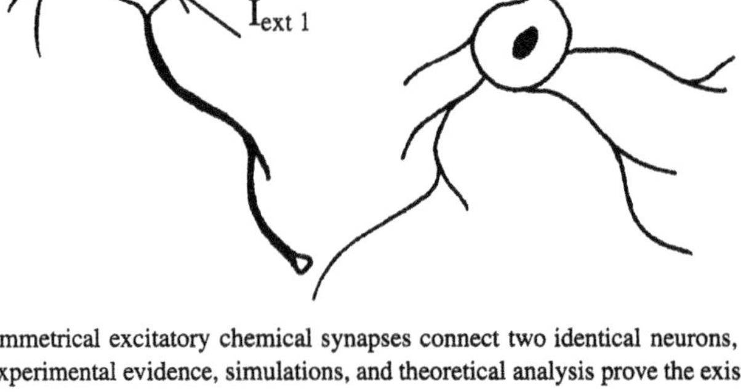

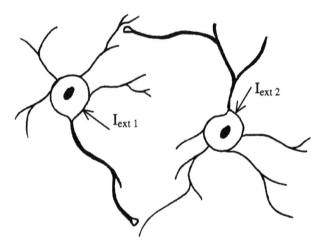

Figure 6 Symmetrical excitatory chemical synapses connect two identical neurons, under external stimulation. Experimental evidence, simulations, and theoretical analysis prove the existence of phase-locked behavior.

In simulations reported here,[3] symmetrical excitatory synapses were considered. In particular, chemical and electrical synapses were modeled by coupling the equations via the introduction of a synaptic contribution to the total membrane current.

We subsequently report the complete first order differential system, which represents the temporal evolution of the membrane voltages coupled by the synaptic contributions I_{syn1} and I_{syn2}:

$$\begin{aligned}
C\frac{dV_1}{dt} &= \bar{g}_{\text{leak}} \cdot (E_{\text{leak}} - V_1) + \bar{g}_{\text{Ca}} \cdot \left[\frac{1}{2} \cdot \left(1 + \tanh\left(\frac{V_1 + 1}{15}\right)\right)\right] \cdot (E_{\text{Ca}} - V_1) \\
&\quad + \bar{g}_K \cdot n_1 \cdot (E_K - V_1) + I_{\text{ext1}} + I_{\text{syn2}}, \\
\frac{dn_1}{dt} &= \frac{1}{15} \cdot \cosh\left(\frac{V_1 - 10}{29}\right) \cdot \left[\frac{1}{2} \cdot \left(1 + \tanh\left(\frac{V_1 - 10}{14.5}\right)\right) - n_1\right], \\
C\frac{dV_2}{dt} &= \bar{g}_{\text{leak}} \cdot (E_{\text{leak}} - V_2) + \bar{g}_{\text{Ca}} \cdot \left[\frac{1}{2} \cdot \left(1 + \tanh\left(\frac{V_2 + 1}{15}\right)\right)\right] \cdot (E_{\text{Ca}} - V_2) \\
&\quad + \bar{g}_K \cdot n_2 \cdot (E_K - V_2) + I_{\text{ext2}} + I_{\text{syn1}}, \\
\frac{dn_2}{dt} &= \frac{1}{15} \cdot \cosh\left(\frac{V_2 - 10}{29}\right) \cdot \left[\frac{1}{2} \cdot \left(1 + \tanh\left(\frac{V_2 - 10}{14.5}\right)\right) - n_1\right].
\end{aligned} \tag{14}$$

In the case of electrical synapses, or gap junctions, synaptic currents are easily derived by Kirchhoff laws and take the form

$$I_{\text{syn2}} = \bar{g}_{\text{gap}} \cdot (V_2 - V_1), \tag{15}$$

$$I_{\text{syn1}} = \bar{g}_{\text{gap}} \cdot (V_1 - V_2). \tag{16}$$

In the Morris–Lecar equations, synchronization of oscillations occurs for every positive value of the maximal synaptic conductances in a finite time: for $I_{\text{ext1}} = I_{\text{ext2}}$, once synchronization has been reached, it is retained even if couplings are broken (see also Fig. 10). For different intrinsic frequencies (i.e., $I_{\text{ext1}} \neq I_{\text{ext2}}$) electrical activities synchronize to the highest frequency, and if the connections are broken each neuron goes back to its natural oscillation frequency (see also Fig. 11b).

For chemical synapses (see Fig. 7), coupling currents were modeled according to the kinetic scheme of neurotransmitter–postsynaptic receptor binding [16], as a more realistic alternative to the classic alpha function [17]. The simple first order kinetic process $R + T \underset{\beta}{\overset{\alpha}{\rightleftarrows}} TR^*$ together with the hypothesis that neurotransmitter signaling in the synaptic cleft occurs as a pulse, lead to a simple closed form for the temporal evolution of the fraction of bound membrane receptor [Eq. (17)] [16].

[3]Because in the integrate-and-fire model neuron, only the subthreshold behavior of the membrane potential is described, electric synapses are not feasible and comparisons refer only to the chemical coupling.

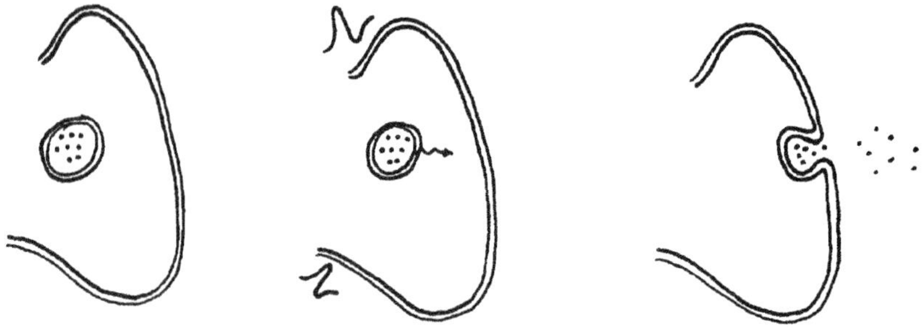

Figure 7 The mechanism of synaptic transmission. Neurotransmitter release is modeled as a sudden increase and decrease of the concentration $[T]$ of the neurotransmitter in the synaptic cleft.

Let $[R] + [TR^*] = a$ and $r = [TR^*]/a$. Then we can write $dr/dt = \alpha \cdot [T] \cdot (1 - r) - \beta \cdot r$, where α and β are the forward and backward reaction binding rates as stated in the kinetic scheme, expressed as per micromolar per millisecond and per millisecond, respectively (see Fig. 8):

$$r(t) = \begin{cases} [r(t_0) - r_\infty] \cdot e^{(t-t_0)/\tau_r} + r_\infty, & t_0 < t < t_1, \\ r(t_1) \cdot e^{-\beta[(t-t_0)-\tau]}, & t > t_1, \end{cases}$$

$$r_\infty = \frac{\alpha \cdot T_{\max}}{\alpha \cdot T_{\max} + \beta}, \qquad \tau_r = \frac{1}{\alpha \cdot T_{\max} + \beta}. \tag{17}$$

The chemical synaptic currents can be modeled after the standard ionic channels form [16]

$$I_{\text{syn2}} = \overline{g}_{\text{syn}} \cdot r_2(t) \cdot (E_{\text{syn}} - V_1), \qquad r_2 = r_2[V_2(t)], \tag{18}$$

$$I_{\text{syn1}} = \overline{g}_{\text{syn}} \cdot r_1(t) \cdot (E_{\text{syn}} - V_2), \qquad r_1 = r_1[V_1(t)]. \tag{19}$$

For both Morris–Lecar and integrate-and-fire models, computer simulations show the same evolution for synchronization of membrane potentials, under equal and unequal stimuli, exactly as described for electrical synapses, for every positive value of the maximal synaptic conductances (see Figs. 9–11).

An outstanding feature of the integrate-and-fire model has to be underlined: this kind of models allows chemical coupling, without forcing the use of unrealistic multiplicative weights, which represents synaptic efficacies in the classic theory of formal neural networks [4]. Moreover, using integrate-and-fire equations with an appropriate coupling scheme, it can be mathematically proved that the *phase* (i.e., instantaneous difference in synchronization of electrical activities) of two equally stimulated identical model neurons converges to zero in a finite time, for every coupling strength [18]. It is worth mentioning that a consistent reduction procedure, as the one we followed for model neurons, can be considered

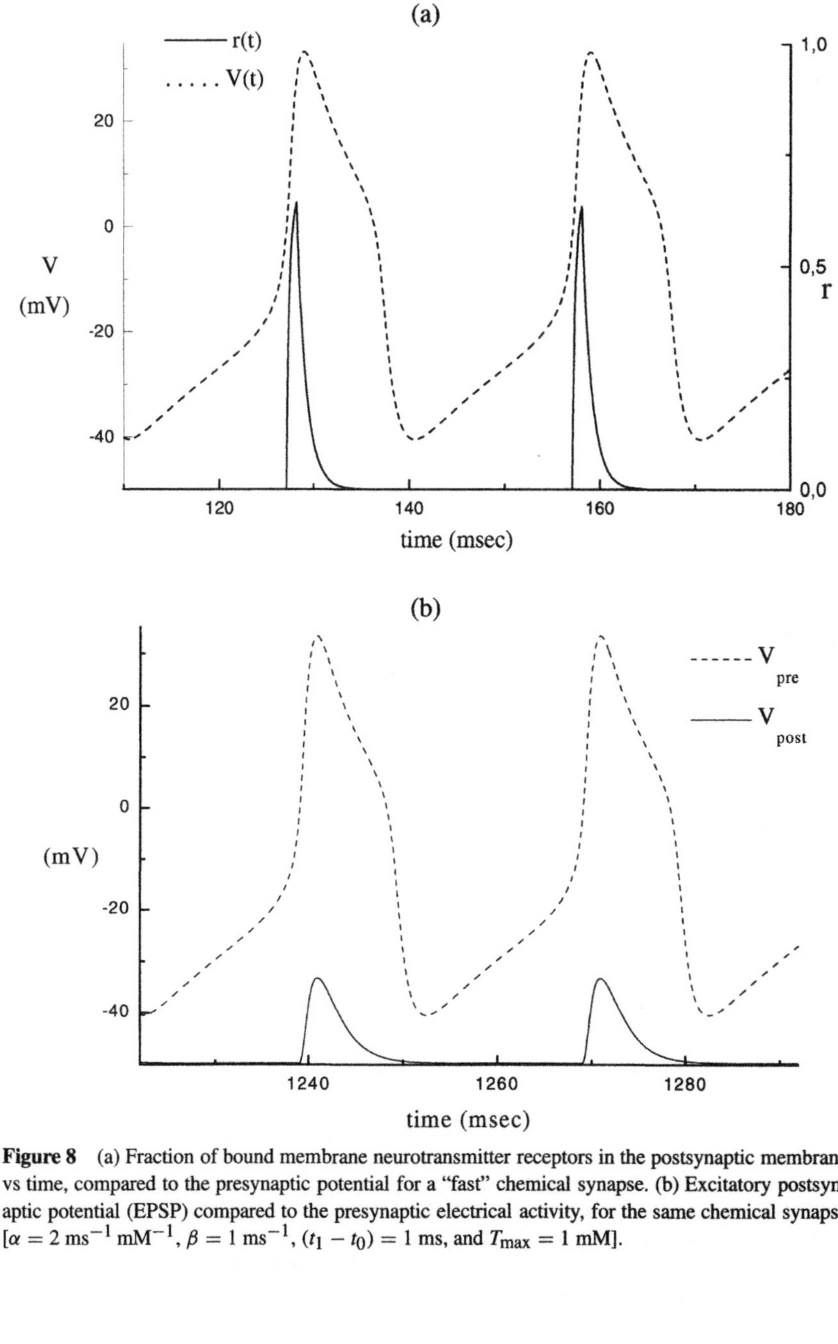

Figure 8 (a) Fraction of bound membrane neurotransmitter receptors in the postsynaptic membrane vs time, compared to the presynaptic potential for a "fast" chemical synapse. (b) Excitatory postsynaptic potential (EPSP) compared to the presynaptic electrical activity, for the same chemical synapse [$\alpha = 2$ ms^{-1} mM^{-1}, $\beta = 1$ ms^{-1}, $(t_1 - t_0) = 1$ ms, and $T_{max} = 1$ mM].

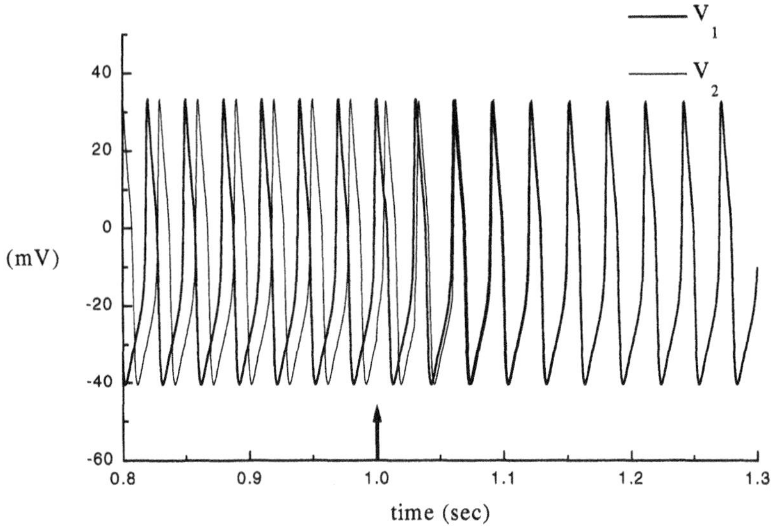

Figure 9 Synchronization of electric activities of two model neurons, under the same external current. Potentials are described by (14), using a symmetric excitatory "fast" chemical coupling [Eqs. (18) and (19)], with $\bar{g}_{syn} = 0.3\ mS/cm^2$. The arrow indicates the beginning of the coupling (i.e., $\bar{g}_{syn} = 0$, for $t < 1$ s).

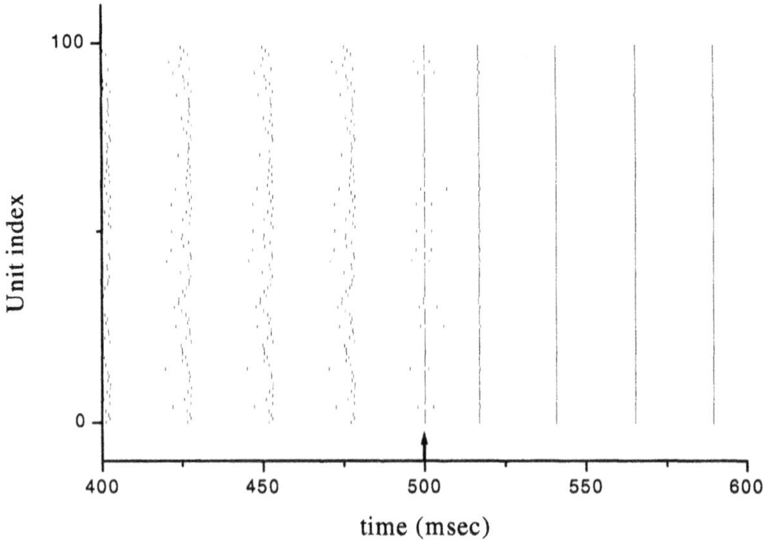

Figure 10 Raster scan of 100 integrate-and-fire model neurons. Each potential was initialized using a uniform random distribution between V_0 and V_{th}, and each unit was stimulated by the same external constant current $I_{ext} = 13\ \mu A/cm^2$. The arrow represents the beginning of all-to-all coupling via a fast chemical synapse, as described in the text, and each mark corresponds to an action potential. After a few milliseconds synchronization occurs.

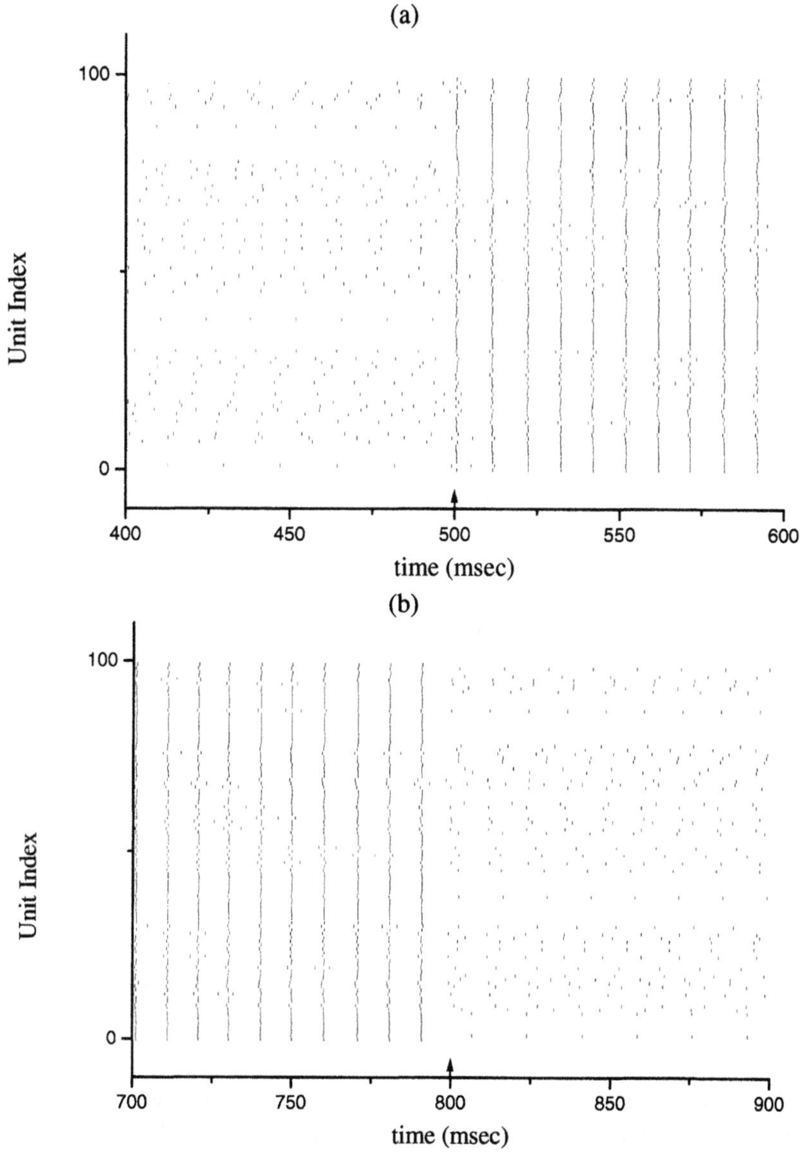

Figure 11 Raster scan of 100 integrate-and-fire model neurons stimulated with different current. Each unit is stimulated by an external constant current I_{ext}, uniformly and randomly distributed between 12.9 and 13.1 $\mu A/cm^2$. Note that some units are silent, due to an insufficient current stimulation, but (a) full network synchronization occurs at the highest frequency. Once coupling has been broken, (b) synchronization is quickly lost. The coupling scheme is as in Fig. 10, and arrows represent coupling and decoupling time.

to model synapses modeling, and important features of synaptic transmission can be retained through successive steps of simplification [19].

Other advantages of the study of this kind of simplified biophysical models (i.e., integrate-and-fire) of an excitable membrane come from the precise role that can be attributed to each unit of a network: integrator or coincidence detector, depending on the ratio of the membrane time constant and of synaptic propagation times [20].

In closing this section, let us summarize the main features of the chosen level of modelization:

- The reduction of the Morris–Lecar model [Eq. (6)–(8)] into an integrate-and-fire model neuron [Eq. (12)] makes the model unable to describe the action potential phenomenon, but computer simulations demonstrated that the model still retains the integrative properties that are responsible for the temporal summation of synaptic current contributions.
- Compared to other simplified models [5, 7], the proposed integrate-and-fire neuron can be assembled in a network by using a biophysically feasible synaptic connection [16], the same used in the complete neuron model. As a result, synchronization effects, as shown by simulated networks of Morris–Lecar neurons, also can be observed in networks of simplified integrate-and-fire neurons.
- The aim of the present work, based on the definition of a simplified model, is to obtain a reasonable balance between reduction in computation time and maintenance of significant neurobiological features for each unit of the network.

These features make the model appropriate for interpreting experiments dealing with simultaneous recording of the electrophysiological activity of networks of *in vitro* cultured neurons. Details on such experiments are given in the next section to enable a full appreciation of the appropriateness of the proposed model in interpreting experimental data.

III. ARRAYS OF PLANAR MICROTRANSDUCERS FOR ELECTRICAL ACTIVITY RECORDING OF CULTURED NEURONAL POPULATIONS

The effects on the synchronization among the neurons of a network as a function of their synaptic connectivity were investigated theoretically in the previous section. As already anticipated, a new technique for studying such effects experimentally is now available by utilizing arrays of planar microtransducers. As indicated in the Introduction, this nonconventional electrophysiological method has several advantages over standard electrophysiological recording that are related to the possibility of noninvasively monitoring/stimulating the electrochemical activities of several cells, independently and simultaneously for a long time.

Peculiar to this technique are at least two features:

- Several (i.e., hundreds) neurons are brought into simultaneous contact with several underlying microtransducers, with a neuron-to-microtransducer correspondence which can be supported by mechanical and/or chemical means [13, 21]. Simultaneous multisite recording from units at well localized positions is a unique feature of this technique, although an exact one-to-one coupling between neurons and electrodes is not always feasible.
- Recording/stimulation can be protracted for days [12]. During this period, which is very long compared with the typical time intervals allowed by intracellular techniques, the neuronal population in culture continuously develops and synaptic contacts change in the presence of different physiological conditions, thus producing changes in the network functions and dynamics.

A. Neuronal Cell Cultures Growing on Substrate Planar Microtransducers

For the sake of simplicity, we can divide the kinds of neuronal cultures utilized, to be connected to substrate planar microtransducers, into two broad categories:

(a) Neurons from ganglia of adult invertebrates.
(b) Neurons from nervous tissue of vertebrate embryos.

Cultures from the first category are characterized by the use of a small (e.g., 10^2) number of large (e.g., 50 μm in diameter) identified neurons. Most of the results described in the literature refer to the leech and the snail and are concerned with basic biophysical questions such as electrophysiological signal propagation on a single, arborized neuron [22, 23]. Attempts at chemically guiding the arborizations of a single neuron on patterned substrata also have been reported [24].

Cultures from vertebrate embryos are characterized by a large (e.g., 10^6) number of small (e.g., 10 μm in diameter) "similar" neurons. These cultures are considered mostly as random networks of (supposedly) identical units which form a dense, highly connected layer on the tops of the microelectrodes. Attempts to mechanically [13] or chemically [25] position the network over the array have been described in the literature. Most of these cell cultures are based on neurons obtained from chick or rat embryos. In both cases the networks of neurons developing *in vitro* cannot be regarded as faithful reproductions of *in vivo* situations, but rather as new rudimentary networks whose activity can change over time spontaneously or as a consequence of chemical/physical stimuli [10, 13, 26]. As already anticipated, the systematic study of these networks can therefore become a new powerful tool for addressing questions concerning the coherent behavior and the computational properties of neurobiological networks. It should be stressed that a key feature of the substrate microelectrode technique, as compared for example with the use of potentiometric fluorescent dyes [27], is the capability of stimulating, in a virtually noninvasive way, a selected subset of the neuronal population, thus allowing the experimenter to simulate a kind of rudimentary learning process.

B. Example of a Multisite Electrical Signal Recording from Neuronal Cultures by Using Planar Microtransducer Arrays and Its Simulations

In our lab, experiments on primary culture neurons from the dorsal root ganglia (DRG) of 8–10 day old chick embryos were performed [28]. The cultures were established according to the standard procedures described in the literature [29]. Neurons were transferred and plated on arrays of microelectrodes, previously coated with an adhesive natural protein (laminin) to promote cell adhesion and with the specific neuritic promoting factor nerve growth factor (NGF).

Signals collected from the microelectrode array had typical amplitudes in the range 20–600 μV and were embedded in biological and thermal noise ranging between 10 and 20 μV from peak to peak. High impedance amplification (with a gain of 190) and filtering (with a bandwidth ranging from 400 Hz to 8 kHz) custom stages were introduced before signal digitization. Each experiment was performed in a Faraday cage to avoid electromagnetic interference.

For long-term acquisition, a digital tape recorder (Bio-Logic DTR-1802) with 8 channels and 14 bits of sampling resolution, which was completely controlled by a general parallel interface bus (GPIB), was utilized.

An example of a phase of an experimental recording session referring to six simultaneously recorded signals from synaptically connected DRG neurons cultured *in vitro* is shown in Fig. 12.

In this experimental phase [28], the ionic medium was characterized by a nominally Mg^{++} - free and high Ca^{++} solution (Ca^{++} concentration: 2 mM). In such conditions most of the excitatory synapses connecting the neurons of the network were activated [30]. As a result, the neuronal dynamics shifted by a state of spontaneous and asynchronous firing to a periodic synchronized action potential bursting. Interestingly enough, comparable results very recently were obtained by utilizing the same technique for the study of networks of mammalian cortical neurons [31]. This synchronized behavior was then reproduced by appropriately choosing the excitatory synaptic strength of the model network described in Section II.B (see Fig. 10).

A variety of other network behaviors can be predicted by the model, thus providing valuable indications for further experimentation on networks of neurons constituted *in vitro*. Just to give an example, the model suggests the disappearance

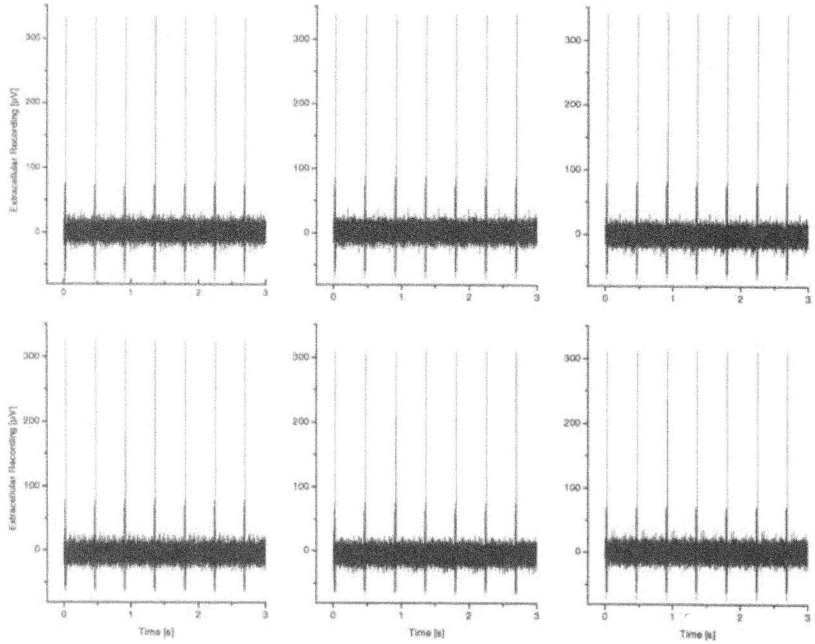

Figure 12 Six simultaneously recorded signals of synaptically connected DRG neurons in a nominally Mg^{++}-free and high Ca^{++} solution (Ca^{++} concentration: 2 mM).

of the pattern of synchronized burst as a consequence of a decrease of the synaptic strength (see Fig. 11b). This was experimentally obtained [28] by increasing the concentration of Mg^{++}, which is known to inhibit excitatory synapses [30].

IV. CONCLUDING REMARKS

In this work, through a well-defined and mathematically consistent approach, we simplified the complete Morris–Lecar model to obtain a reduced description suitable for extensive network simulation and theoretical studies. We showed that it is possible, to some extent, to keep biological feasibility and equivalence to more complex models.

The aim of this approach was to obtain a model appropriate for a detailed description of simple networks developing *in vitro* under controlled experimental conditions. This aim was motivated by the availability of new experimental tools which allow the experimenter to track the electrophysiological behavior of such a network with an accuracy never reached before. We believe that the "mixed" approach defined in this paper, based on the use of both modeling and experimental tools, will become of great relevance in explaining complex collective behaviors emerging from networks of neurons, thus providing new analysis tools to the field of computational neuroscience.

ACKNOWLEDGMENTS

The authors are very grateful to Dr. A. Kawana (Material Science Research Laboratory of NTT Basic Research Laboratories, Atsugi, Japan) and to Dr. G. T. A. Kovacs (Center for Integrated Systems, Stanford University) for kindly supplying the microelectrode arrays. This work was supported by the Italian Ministry of University and Scientific Research and by the National Research Council.

REFERENCES

[1] J. E. Dowling. *Neurons and Networks. An Introduction to Neuroscience.* Harvard University Press, Cambridge, MA, 1992.
[2] A. L. Hodgkin and A. F. Huxley. *J. Physiol. (London)* 117:500–544, 1952.
[3] C. Morris and H. Lecar. *Biophys. J.* 35:193–213, 1981.
[4] J. J. Hopfield. *Proc. Natl. Acad. Sci. U.S.A.* 79:2554–2558, 1982.
[5] J. J. Hopfield. *Proc. Natl. Acad. Sci. U.S.A.* 81:3088–3092, 1984.
[6] L. F. Abbott and T. B. Kepler. In *Statistical Mechanics of Neural Networks* (L. Garrido, Ed.), pp. 5–18. Springer-Verlag, Barcelona, 1990.
[7] J. J. Hopfield and A. V. M. Herz. *Proc. Natl. Acad. Sci. U.S.A.* 92:6655–6662, 1995.
[8] M. Barinaga. *Science* 250:206–207, 1990.
[9] A. G. M. Bulloch and N. I. Syed. *Trends Neurosci.* 15:422–427, 1992.
[10] G. W. Gross, B. K. Rhoades, and R. J. Jordan. *Sensor and Actuators* B6:1–8, 1992.
[11] W. Stühmer, W. M. Roberts, and W. Almers. In *Single-Channel Recording* (B. Sackmann and E. Neher, Eds.), pp. 123–132. Plenum, New York, 1983.
[12] Y. Jimbo and A. Kawana. *Bioelectrochem. Bioenerg.* 29:193–204, 1992.
[13] Y. Jimbo, H. P. C. Robinson, and A. Kawana. *IEEE Trans. Biomed. Eng.* 40:804–810, 1993.
[14] G. W. Gross and J. M. Kowalsky. In *Neural Networks Concepts, Applications and Implementations* (P. Antognetti and V. Milutinovic, Eds.), Vol. IV, pp. 47–110. Prentice-Hall, Englewood Cliffs, NJ, 1991.
[15] J. G. Nicholls, A. R. Martin, and B. C. Wallace. In *From Neuron to Brain.* Sinauser Associates, Sunderland, MA, 1992.
[16] A. Destexhe, Z. F. Mainen, and T. J. Sejnowski. *Neural Comput.* 6:14–18, 1994.
[17] W. Rall. *J. Neurophysiol.* 30:1138–1168, 1967.
[18] R. E. Mirollo and S. H. Strogatz. *SIAM J. Appl. Math.* 50:1645–1662, 1990.
[19] F. Chapeau-Blondeau and N. Chambet. *Neural Comput.* 7:713–734, 1995.
[20] P. Konig, A. K. Engel, and W. Singer. *Trends Neurosci.* 19:130–137, 1996.
[21] A. S. G. Curtis, L. Breckenridge, L. Connolly, J. A. T. Dow, C. D. W. Wilkinson, and R. Wilson. *Med. Biol. Eng. Comput.* CE33–C36, 1992.
[22] R. J. A. Wilson, L. Breckenridge, S. E. Blackshow, P. Connolly, J. A. T. Dow, A. S. G. Curtis, and C. D. W. Wilkinson. *J. Neurosci. Methods* 53:101–110, 1994.
[23] W. G. Regehr, J. Pine, C. S. Cohan, M. D. Mischke, and D. W. Tank. *J. Neurosci. Methods* 30:91–106, 1989.

[24] P. Fromhertz and H. Schaden. *J. Neurosci.* 6:1500–1504, 1994.
[25] P. Clark, P. Connolly, and G. R. Moores. *J. Cell. Sci.* 103:287–292, 1990.
[26] G. W. Gross, B. K. Rhoades, D. L. Reust, and F. U. Schwalm. *J. Neurosci. Methods* 50:131–143, 1993.
[27] P. Fromhertz and T. Vetter. *Proc. Natl. Acad. Sci. U.S.A.* 89:2041–2045, 1992.
[28] M. Bove, M. Grattarola, and G. Verreschi. *IEEE Trans. Biomed. Eng.*, in press.
[29] Y. A. Barde, D. Edgar, and H. Thoenen. *Proc. Natl. Acad. Sci. U.S.A.* 77:1199–1203, 1980.
[30] H. P. C. Robinson, M. Kawahara, Y. Jimbo, K. Torimitsu, Y. Kuroda, and A. Kawana. *J. Neurophys.* 70:1606–1616, 1993.
[31] E. Maeda, H. P. C. Robinson, and A. Kawana, *J. Neurosci.* 15:6834–6845, 1995.
[32] D. Amit and N. Brunel. *Cerebral Cortex* 7, 1996.
[33] M. Bove, M. Grattarola, S. Martinoia, and G. Verreschi. *Bioelectrochem. Bioenerg.* 38:255–265, 1995.
[34] D. A. Israel, W. H. Barry, D. Edell, and R. G. Mark. *Am. J. Physiol.* 247:669–674, 1984.
[35] M. Matsugu and A. L. Yuille. *Neural Networks* 7:419–439, 1994.
[36] J. Rinzel and G. B. Ermentrout. In *Methods in Neuronal Modeling: From Synapses to Networks* (C. Koch and I. Segev, Eds.), pp. 135–169. MIT Press, Cambridge, MA, 1989.

Estimating the Dimensions of Manifolds Using Delaunay Diagrams

Yun-Chung Chu
Department of Mechanical and Automation Engineering
The Chinese University of Hong Kong
Shatin, New Territories
Hong Kong, China

I. DELAUNAY DIAGRAMS OF MANIFOLDS

Given the Euclidean space $\mathbb{R}^n$ and a set of distinct points $\{w_1, w_2, \ldots, w_K\} \subset \mathbb{R}^n$, there is a natural partition of the Euclidean space into K regions $B_1, B_2, \ldots, B_K$:

$$B_i := \{x \in \mathbb{R}^n \mid \|x - w_i\| \leqslant \|x - w_j\| \text{ for all } w_j,\ j = 1, 2, \ldots, K\}, \quad (1)$$

that is, the partition is formed by each w_i grasping those points in $\mathbb{R}^n$ which are close to it. B_i is called the Voronoi region corresponding to w_i and w_i is called the center of the Voronoi region B_i. Clearly the union of all Voronoi regions is the whole $\mathbb{R}^n$ and the intersection of any two Voronoi regions is at most an $(n-1)$-dimensional face. Hence almost every point in $\mathbb{R}^n$ belongs to one and only one Voronoi region. We say that two Voronoi regions are neighbors of each other if their intersection is exactly an $(n-1)$-dimensional face.

Remark 1. Some people prefer the looser definition of saying that two Voronoi regions are neighbors of each other if they have nonempty intersection. If both definitions result in the same set of neighbors for each Voronoi region, the case is said to be nondegenerate.

The neighborhood relationship induces a graph structure which we shall call a Delaunay diagram. The Delaunay diagram has K nodes $q_1, q_2, \ldots, q_K$ representing the centers $w_1, w_2, \ldots, w_K$, respectively, and a link exists between any two nodes q_i and q_j if and only if the corresponding Voronoi regions B_i and B_j are neighbors.

The concepts of Voronoi region and Delaunay diagram are so natural that they have a long history and applications to many different areas. As mentioned in the book by Okabe, Boots, and Sugihara [1], they are "two of a few truly interdisciplinary concepts with relevant material to be found in, but not limited to, anthropology, archaeology, astronomy, biology, cartography, geology, marketing, metallography, meteorology, operations research, physics, physiology, statistics and urban and regional planning." In fact, the concepts have been independently discovered and rediscovered many times by many different people in many different areas and given many different names. We refer the reader to [1] for various facts about Voronoi region and Delaunay diagram.

Although, as will be seen subsequently, the concept of partitioning the Euclidean space into Voronoi regions can be generalized easily to partitioning a manifold, it has received much less attention in the literature. One reason is probably that practically the computation of Voronoi regions for a manifold is not so easy. For the Euclidean space it is known that each face of a Voronoi region is part of a hyperplane which bisects the centers of two Voronoi regions, but for a manifold the situation is more complicated.

However, Voronoi partitioning of manifolds recently has become a more active topic in the neural network community [2, 3] for two reasons: One is that in the context of artificial neural networks, the model of the manifold is quite often given by a sufficiently large amount of sampling points of the manifold instead of an analytical description, and this provides an easy way to compute the Delaunay diagram. The other reason is that the Voronoi partitioning of manifolds can help to precisely define the concept "preserving the topological order" which is well known in the neural network community.

The concept preserving the topological order may be explained as follows. Let (Q, N) be a graph where $Q = \{q_1, q_2, \ldots, q_K\}$ is the set of nodes and N is a map $Q \to \mathcal{P}(Q)$ (the power set of Q) which satisfies the conditions

[N1] $\forall q_i \in Q, q_i \in N(q_i)$,
[N2] $\forall q_i, q_j \in Q, q_i \in N(q_j)$ if and only if $q_j \in N(q_i)$,

that is, (Q, N) is a fully looped symmetrical graph. We call $N(q_i)$ the 1-neighborhood of q_i. One interpretation is that each q_i is a "neuron" and there exists an "interconnection" between two neurons q_i and q_j if and only if they are in the 1-neighborhood of each other. It is only a matter of convention that we define every neuron to be in the 1-neighborhood of itself.

Now let X be a closed subset of $\mathbb{R}^n$. X may be interpreted as the "input space," that is, the set of all possible input patterns. Consider a map w: $Q \to X$ which "places" all the neurons into the input space. Then preserving the topological or-

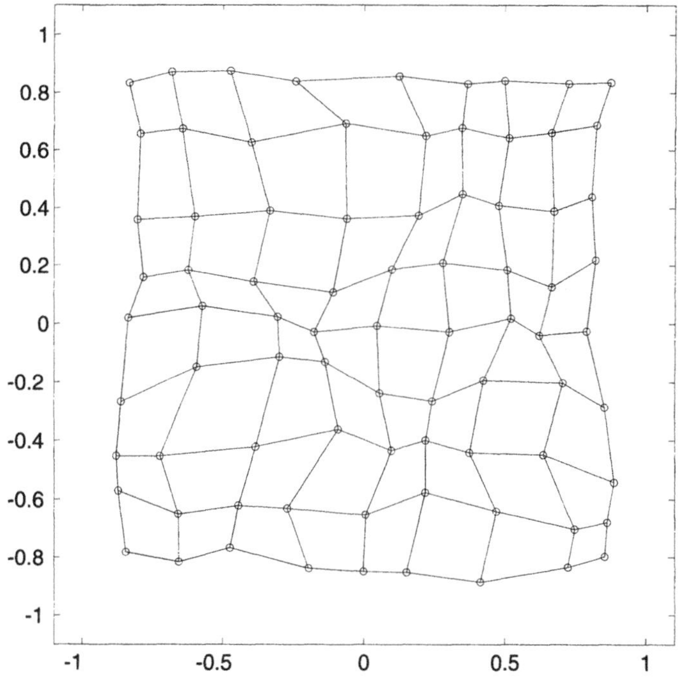

Figure 1 The topological order is preserved.

der is basically a question of how to make w and N consistent. For example, look at Figs. 1 and 2, where the input space $X = [-1, 1]^2 = [-1, 1] \times [-1, 1] \in \mathbb{R}^2$, the small circles are $w(q_i)$, $i = 1, 2, \ldots, 81$, and each straight line between two small circles means that there exists an interconnection between the corresponding two neurons. It is typically thought that in Fig. 1 the topological order is preserved whereas in Fig. 2 it is not.

Traditionally, N is fixed beforehand whereas w is to be chosen. To preserve the topological order in this case, the well-known Kohonen algorithm has been widely used. However, if w is fixed beforehand and N is to be chosen, then how should N be chosen so as to make w and N consistent? Subsequently, we will see that the Delaunay diagram can give a solution to this problem. This is how the Voronoi partitioning of the input space X and the concept preserving the topological order are connected. However, note that the Delaunay diagram is unique for each w, whereas many people's idea of preserving the topological order seems to be less rigid. For example, the graph shown in Fig. 1 is by no means the Delaunay diagram although most people think that in that case the topological order is preserved.

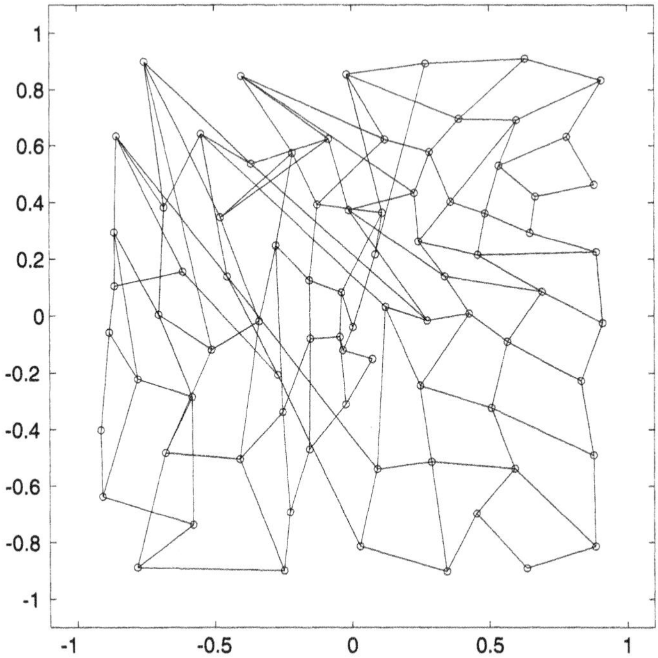

Figure 2 The topological order is not preserved.

There are two ways to generalize the Voronoi partitioning of the Euclidean space to the Voronoi partitioning of X. Both methods result in the same practical solution, but theoretically they are slightly different. Martinetz and Schulten [3] used the idea of masked Voronoi regions. The whole $\mathbb{R}^n$ is partitioned into K Voronoi regions first and then each masked Voronoi region is the intersection of each Voronoi region with the input space X. Then clearly these K masked Voronoi regions partition the input space X. However, we prefer another formulation which follows [2].

Note that theoretically it is not difficult to generalize the idea of the Voronoi regions to a general metric space X,

$$B_i := \{x \in X \mid \check{d}(x, w_i) \leqslant \check{d}(x, w_j) \text{ for all } w_j,\ j = 1, 2, \ldots, K\}, \tag{2}$$

where $\check{d}$ is the metric on X. Now if X is a closed path-connected subset of $\mathbb{R}^n$, we may simply let $\check{d}(x, x')$ be the length of the shortest path along X that connects x and x'. It easily is seen that even if X is not path-connected, it still can be partitioned into K regions by this means provided that every component of X has at least one w_i in it.

Remark 2. The shortest path may not be unique, but its length is unique.

Defining the Voronoi regions for X in this way has the advantage that certain important properties of the Voronoi regions for $\mathbb{R}^n$ are preserved. In particular, B_i is path-connected. This is in general not true for masked Voronoi regions. However, if K is sufficiently large and $w_1, w_2, \ldots, w_K$ are well distributed over X, the masked Voronoi regions can be made path-connected in practice. On the other hand, our formulation makes use of the length of the shortest path along X between two points which is, in general, difficult to measure. It also relies on K sufficiently large to make the length of the shortest path along X between two points sufficiently close to their Euclidean distance so as to practically construct the Voronoi regions. In fact, in [2] and [3] the practical constructions of the Delaunay diagram for X turned out to be the same.

The theoretical construction of the Delaunay diagram for X is a little bit complicated, however, because it is not so easy to define the neighbors of a Voronoi region for a manifold. Recall that for $\mathbb{R}^n$, we require that two Voronoi regions be said to be neighbors only when they share an $(n-1)$-dimensional face, not just a point. This is because we want to keep the number of neighbors of a Voronoi region as small as possible. Note that a lot of points in $\{w_1, w_2, \ldots, w_K\}$ are irrelevant in constructing the Voronoi region B_i. B_i is only determined by w_i and the centers of its neighbors. So conversely, the set of neighboring centers of w_i should be the *minimal* subset of $\{w_1, w_2, \ldots, w_K\}$ that is needed to reconstruct the Voronoi region B_i.

We define the Delaunay diagram (Q, N_I) as follows, assuming for convenience that X is path-connected. Let $\mathcal{N}$ be the class of maps $N\colon\ Q \to \mathcal{P}(Q)$ which satisfy

[N1] $\forall q_i \in Q, q_i \in N(q_i)$,
[N2] $\forall q_i, q_j \in Q, q_i \in N(q_j)$ if and only if $q_j \in N(q_i)$.

Define a partial order in $\mathcal{N}$ such that for any $N_1, N_2 \in \mathcal{N}$, we say that $N_1 \leqslant N_2$ if and only if

[$\leqslant$ 1] $\forall q_i \in Q, N_1(q_i) \subset N_2(q_i)$,
[$\leqslant$ 2] $\forall q_i \in Q, B_i(N_1(q_i)) = B_i(N_2(q_i))$, where for a set $O \subset Q$, $B_i(O)$ is defined as

$$B_i(O) := \left\{x \in X \middle| \breve{d}(x, w_i) \leqslant \breve{d}(x, w_j) \text{ for all } w_j \text{ such that } q_j \in O\right\}. \quad (3)$$

[$\leqslant$ 2] simply means that shrinking the set from $N_2(q_i)$ to $N_1(q_i)$ does not alter the Voronoi region it constructs for w_i. Of course what we want to do is to shrink the whole set Q to a minimal element. Let $N_Q \in \mathcal{N}$ denote the trivial map

$$N_Q(q_i) = Q \quad \text{for all } q_i \in Q. \quad (4)$$

Then N_I is defined as the union of all minimal elements under the partial order $\leqslant$ which are $\leqslant N_Q$, and the Delaunay diagram is defined as (Q, N_I). (The union is to take care of the possible nonuniqueness of the minimal elements.)

For more motivations for the preceding definition of the Delaunay diagram and also for the theoretical justification of the relation between this definition and the practical procedure subsequently presented, we refer the reader to [2]. The justification given in [2, Chap. 4] is quite technical and therefore is not included here.

Practically the Delaunay diagram may be approximated as follows. Two distinct neurons q_i and q_j are linked together if and only if there exists a point $x \in X$ such that w_i and w_j are the two closest centers to it among $w_1, w_2, \ldots, w_K$. If a large amount of samples of X are given and they are well distributed over X, then the procedure may be set up as follows. At the beginning there are only self-connections but no interconnection between any two neurons. All the samples are then presented sequentially, and for each sample the closest center and the second closest center to it are found and an interconnection is set up between them. After all the samples have been presented, the resulting graph reasonably approximates the Delaunay diagram. Note that if there are sufficiently many centers (i.e., K is large) and they are well distributed over X, then it does not matter whether the "closeness" is measured by the length of the shortest path along X or simply by the Euclidean distance. In other words, the Euclidean distances between the sample and the centers may be simply used to identify the closest and the second closest centers.

Before an example can be presented, it remains to mention how to place the neurons into the input space X; in other words, how to choose the map $w\colon\ Q \to X$. Of course the definition and the procedure mentioned in the foregoing paragraphs do not depend on how w is chosen. Given any w the Delaunay diagram is defined. However, as will be shown, one purpose of obtaining the Delaunay diagram is to obtain a "skeleton" of the input space X, so that by studying the Delaunay diagram (a graph) some information about the input space X (a topological space) can be obtained. For this purpose a reasonable distribution of the neurons over the input space X is essential. The method used here is a simple method which we call competitive learning. Let $\tilde{x}_1, \tilde{x}_2, \ldots, \tilde{x}_M$ be M samples of the input space X, $M \gg K$. At the beginning, $w(q_1), w(q_2), \ldots, w(q_K)$ are randomly distributed over X. For example they may simply be set to the first K samples $\tilde{x}_1, \tilde{x}_2, \ldots, \tilde{x}_K$ of X. Then all the samples are presented sequentially and for each sample $\tilde{x}_l$, the closest center to it is identified,

$$q_i \text{ such that } \quad \|\tilde{x}_l - w(q_i)\| \leqslant \|\tilde{x}_l - w(q_j)\| \quad \text{for all } q_j \in Q,$$

and $w(q_i)$ is modified according to

$$w^+(q_i) = w(q_i) + \eta[\tilde{x}_l - w(q_i)]. \tag{5}$$

Note that only the closest center to the sample is modified; hence, the name competitive learning. A reasonable w should be obtained after all the samples have been presented. For the simple examples included in this chapter the learning rate η is set to 0.1.

w hence obtained may not always put all the neurons into the input space X, so strictly speaking w is only a map $Q \to \mathbb{R}^n$. However, $w(q_1), w(q_2), \ldots, w(q_K)$ should be very close to X if K is sufficiently large. It is known that if the samples $\tilde{x}_1, \tilde{x}_2, \ldots, \tilde{x}_M$ are drawn from X according to a certain probability distribution, then the resulting $w(q_1), w(q_2), \ldots, w(q_K)$ will also reflect this probability distribution. More precisely, the Voronoi region corresponding to each center will tend to contain the same number of samples. It is also known that the resulting Voronoi regions are roughly isotropic.

Note that we have separated the stage of finding a reasonable w and the stage of constructing the Delaunay diagram. This treatment is meant to emphasize that the construction of the Delaunay diagram is independent of the map w. However, it is, in fact, possible to combine the two stages. Martinetz and Schulten [4, 3] developed a neural-gas algorithm which combines these two stages. This neural-gas algorithm has an interesting interpretation which is related to a Hebblike rule. The reader is referred to [4, 3] for details.

Now an example is presented. The input space $X = [-1, 1]^2$ and 10,000 samples are uniformly drawn from X. Then 81 neurons are placed into X using competitive learning and the Delaunay diagram is computed according to the above-mentioned practical procedure. The result is as shown in Fig. 3. Two interesting points should be noted here. One is that the Delaunay diagram in Fig. 3 consists mostly of triangles. In fact, in the so-called nondegenerate case, all of the shapes should be triangles. The nondegenerate case is typical. The degenerate case occurs only if the neurons are deliberately placed into the input space in a structured way. For example, if the 81 neurons are put into $[-1, 1]^2$ as a 9×9 square lattice as in Fig. 4, then the Delaunay diagram will consist only of squares and no triangles. If instead the competitive learning or the neural-gas algorithm is used to place the neurons based on a set of random samples of the input space X, then it is almost certain that the resulting case is nondegenerate. In the study of the so-called spatial tessellations, nondegeneracy is sometimes a necessary assumption so as to derive certain results. Here we do not want to introduce the nondegeneracy assumption into any part of our results and therefore we have avoided using terms like "Delaunay triangulation." We are trying to convince the reader that the results presented herein still hold even when the Delaunay diagram is degenerate.

The other point about Fig. 3 that should be noted is that whereas the competitive learning almost certainly produces a nondegenerate Delaunay diagram, why does the Delaunay diagram shown in Fig. 3 consist of something other than triangles? For example, look at the pentagon in the middle left of Fig. 3. If it is examined carefully, the reader should be convinced that there should be more links

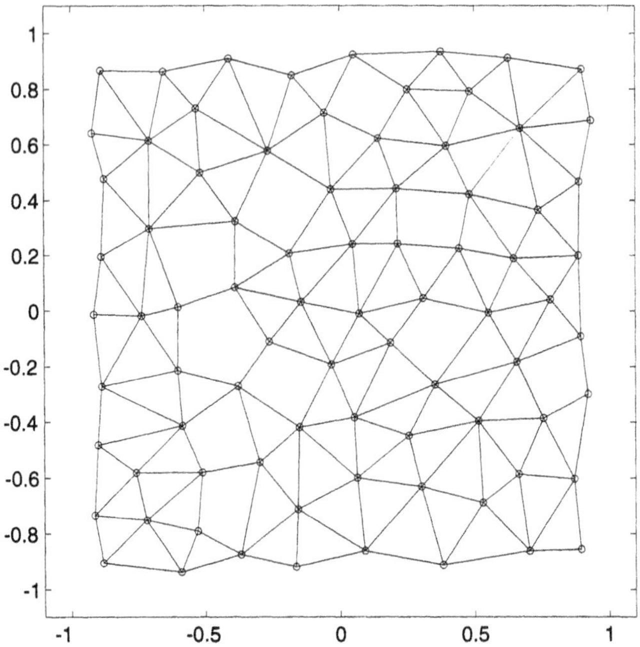

Figure 3 The Delaunay diagram $(Q, \tilde{N}_I)$ for $X = [-1, 1]^2$ with 81 neurons.

inside the pentagon, but for some reason they have disappeared. The reason can be only that there are not enough samples of X inside that pentagon to establish the links. Note that this Delaunay diagram is constructed only by the samples of the input space. Although there are already 10,000 samples, "defects" of the Delaunay diagram still occur. So we should emphasize that this is not the real Delaunay diagram, but only an approximant of it, and we shall denote it by $(Q, \tilde{N}_I)$ instead of (Q, N_I). The effect of insufficient samples to induce the links between neurons for the Delaunay diagram will be discussed further later.

Recall that to preserve the topological order is to make w and N consistent. The Delaunay diagram says that given any w, such an N can always be found. Of course this N need not be close to any prescribed graph structure. On the other hand, given a desirable graph structure N, finding a w such that w and N are consistent is a much more difficult problem. In fact, it can be seen easily that such a w does not necessarily exist. If the prescribed N is chosen cautiously, Kohonen algorithm may attempt to find a w, but how can this N be chosen cautiously? If too little is known about the input space X, for example, if only a large amount of samples of the input space are given, it is often insufficient to give an idea of how such a prescribed N should be. Just by looking at the set of samples it is difficult

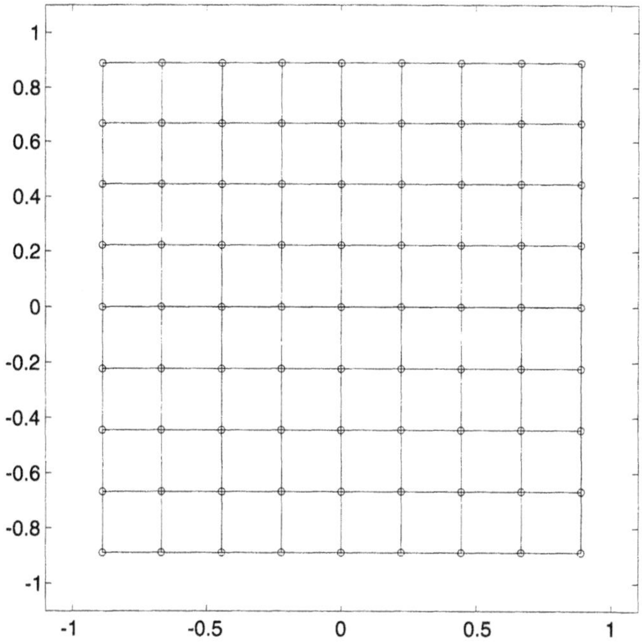

Figure 4 The Delaunay diagram (Q, N_I) for $X = [-1, 1]^2$ when the Voronoi centers are distributed as a square lattice.

to tell whether X is a linear or a nonlinear subset of $\mathbb{R}^n$, what its dimension is, whether it is simply connected, etc. So we see that the Delaunay diagram and Kohonen algorithm have limitations of their own which determine their different applications to the preservation of the topological order. They may sometimes complement each other, however.

Due to the connection between the Delaunay diagram and preserving the topological order, there have been attempts [2, 5, 6] to precisely define the concept preserving the topological order by means of the Delaunay diagram. However, as mentioned before, the Delaunay diagram is a rigorous mathematical object and it is unique for each w, whereas people's idea of preserving the topological order is rather vague. Therefore there is an intrinsic difficulty in arriving at a unique natural definition of the latter based on the former. However, such attempts have resulted in various measures or indicators which are helpful in determining whether the topological order is preserved in cases where "judgment by human inspection" is not possible, for example, when the input space X is a complicated four- or higher-dimensional object.

This section is closed with a further look at the meaning and properties of the Delaunay diagram. Recall that $N_I(q_i)$ is the (almost) minimal set of neurons which are sufficient to reconstruct the Voronoi region B_i. The Voronoi region is originally a "global" object. It is the set of $x \in X$ such that $\breve{d}(x, w(q_i))$ is the minimum among *all* $\breve{d}(x, w(q_1)), \breve{d}(x, w(q_2)), \ldots, \breve{d}(x, w(q_K))$. If the center $w(q_i)$ wants to determine whether a point $x \in X$ belongs to its own Voronoi region B_i, it should need to find out whether this x is closer to itself than to all other centers. However, with the Delaunay diagram, it now only needs to find out whether this x is closer to itself than to its own neighbors. In other words, the Delaunay diagram has reduced the global task to a local one, and moreover as local as possible by its minimality. This was in fact the original motivation of the work in [2]. In particular, suppose that X is convex so that every center can easily measure its distance to any point in X. [The length of the shortest path between x and $w(q_i)$ along X is now simply the Euclidean distance between x and $w(q_i)$.] Then if $w(q_i)$ wants to determine whether a point $x \in X$ is closest to it, it simply measures its own Euclidean distance to x and compares the result with those obtained by its neighbors to see whether its own result is the smallest, instead of comparing the result with all Voronoi centers. This fact was observed by Morasso and Sanguineti [7]. Its implication in the artificial neural networks is significant. In an artificial neural network all neurons can compute their own distances to the input pattern in parallel. To find out whether itself is the closest neuron to the input pattern, a neuron needs to exchange its measurement with other neurons through interconnection. Of course exchanging the information with all other neurons and exchanging the information with its direct neighbors only makes a huge difference in efficiency.

When the input space X is not convex, $w(q_i)$ cannot directly measure its distance along the input space to any point $x \in X$. In fact, as mentioned previously, measuring distances along X is, in general, a difficult problem. Here the Delaunay diagram can help to find the solution. The basic idea is as follows. Note that partitioning the input space into Voronoi regions is actually a vector quantization, which is analogous to the scalar quantization of the real line. Any two points $x, x' \in X$ may be "truncated" to the centers of the Voronoi regions they belong to, and all possible paths connecting them are then "quantized" to a finite number of paths joining the two centers through the Delaunay diagram. If the Voronoi centers are sufficiently dense in X, that is, the Voronoi regions are sufficiently small, so that the "quantization error" is small and the distance between any two neighboring centers along the input space can be approximated by their Euclidean distance, then the length of the shortest path between x and x' can be estimated. Moreover an approximant of the shortest path can be obtained. As stated in [3], this can be applied to certain path-planning problems where X is the whole Euclidean space minus some obstacles and the shortest path by-passing these obstacles from a given point to another is to be found.

II. ESTIMATING THE DIMENSIONS OF MANIFOLDS

Provided that the Voronoi centers are well distributed over the input space X, the Delaunay diagram is a description of the structure of the input space, so undoubtedly it has many applications. One application is to estimate the dimension of the input space X. Although every input pattern $x \in X \subset \mathbb{R}^n$ has n attributes, they need not be independent, and consequently X may have a dimension less than n. Therefore, how to determine the real dimension of X has been studied widely, but it is also difficult because X need not be a linear or affine subspace of $\mathbb{R}^n$.

Recently some researchers proposed to count the average number of neighbors of a Voronoi region to estimate the dimension of X. In fact, this approach is rather primitive and therefore has been used for a long time for low-dimensional Euclidean spaces. Given that the Voronoi centers are distributed over the Euclidean space under certain spatial stochastic point processes, various statistics including the average number of faces of a Voronoi region for different low-dimensional Euclidean spaces have been measured and recorded by many different researchers. (For example, see [1] for various results.) Møller's book [8] also provides a rigorous mathematical treatment of the topic. Naturally the number of neighbors of a Voronoi region increases with dimension. Whereas counting the number of neighbors is only a local activity, generalizing this approach from the Euclidean space to the general input space X is justified if X is locally Euclidean.

Define

$$\overline{\operatorname{card}(N_I)} := \frac{1}{K}\sum_{i=1}^{K} \operatorname{card}\big(N_I(q_i)\big), \tag{6}$$

where $\operatorname{card}(N_I(q_i))$ denotes the cardinality of the set $N_I(q_i) \subset Q$. [Note that our convention is that each neuron belongs to its own neighborhood, so $\overline{\operatorname{card}(N_I)}$ is 1 larger than the average number of neighbors in the traditional sense.] Now competitive learning is used to place 1000 neurons into the input space $X = [-1, 1]^n$ from which 50,000 samples have been drawn randomly under the uniform distribution. The statistics in Table I are then obtained. Note that we write $\tilde{N}_I$ instead of N_I in the table to emphasize that it is the approximate Delaunay diagram. Also $\overline{\operatorname{card}(\tilde{N}_I)} = 2.9980$ instead of 3 for $n = 1$ because there are two "end points" in the Delaunay diagram, which is called the boundary effect and will be discussed later.

If the data in Table I are plotted, then Fig. 5 is obtained, which seems to be close to a straight line. The frequency plots (i.e., the number of neurons whose 1-neighborhoods have a certain cardinality) for different dimensions n are shown

Table I

n	1	2	3	4	5	6	7	8
$\overline{\text{card}(\tilde{N}_I)}$	2.9980	6.2640	10.3860	14.5560	18.5940	22.4980	26.4520	29.1240

in Fig. 6, from which we see that as n becomes larger, the Voronoi regions consist of more different types of n-dimensional polytopes.

From Fig. 5 one may think that counting the average number of neighbors to estimate the dimension of the input space X is a workable idea, but in fact there are two disadvantages. The first is that those statistics clearly depend on the spatial process. In this case that means our foregoing statistics are not necessarily valid if the neurons are placed into the input space X by a means other than competitive learning. Figures 7–9 show six cases where $X = \mathbb{R}^2$ is partitioned into structured

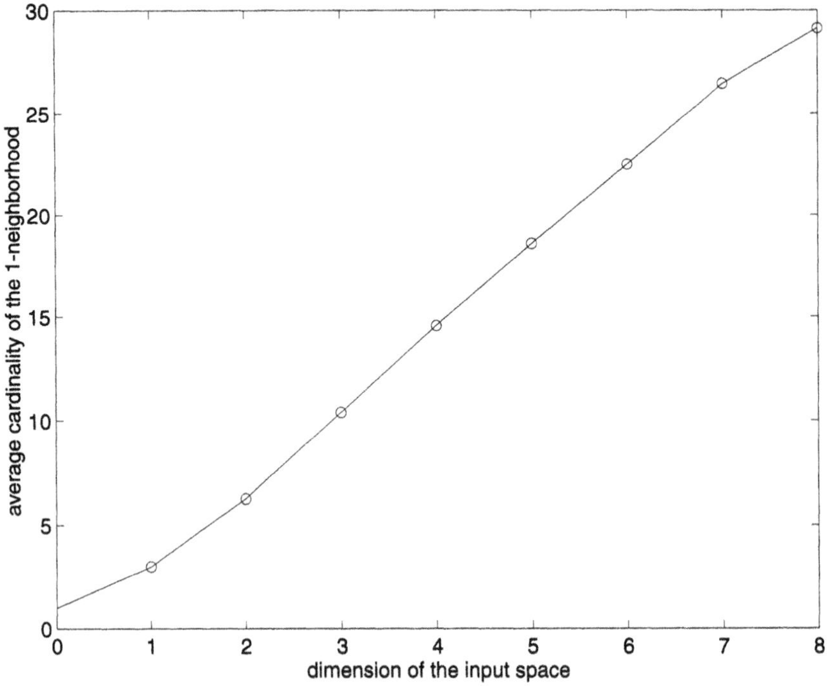

Figure 5 The average cardinality of a 1-neighborhood for different dimensions n.

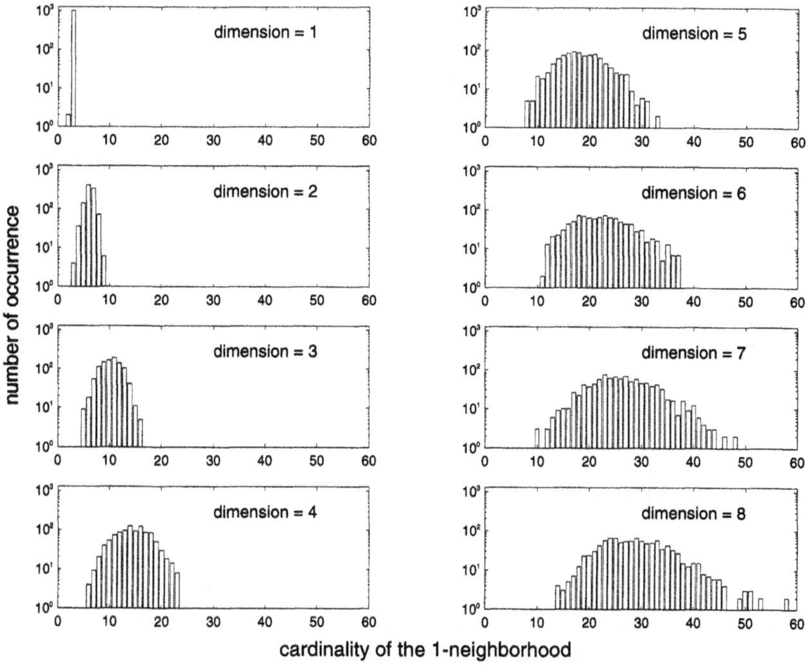

Figure 6 The frequency plots of the cardinality of the 1-neighborhood for $n = 1, 2, \ldots, 8$.

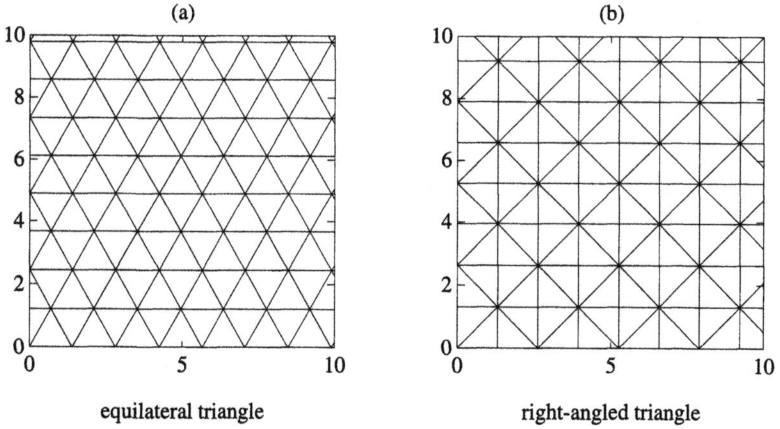

Figure 7 Voronoi partitioning of $\mathbb{R}^2$ into triangles. Reprinted with permission from Y.-C. Chu, Master's Thesis, The Chinese University of Hong Kong, 1992.

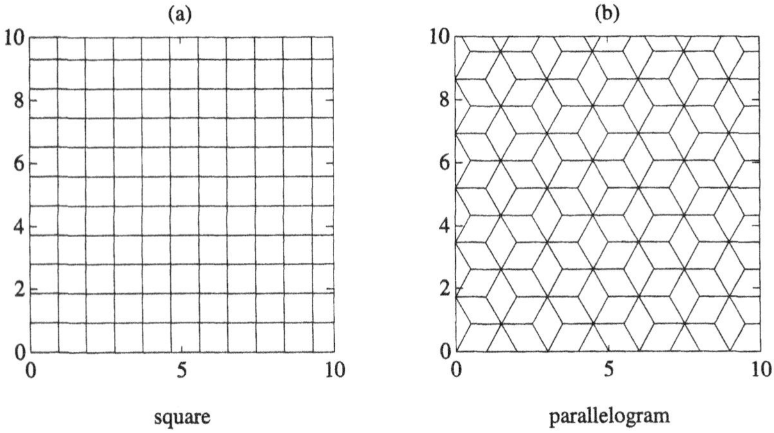

Figure 8 Voronoi partitioning of $\mathbb{R}^2$ into quadrilaterals. Reprinted with permission from Y.-C. Chu, Master's Thesis, The Chinese University of Hong Kong, 1992.

Voronoi regions; some cases are degenerate and some are not. Clearly in these six cases the average number of neighbors of a Voronoi region is quite different from 6.2640. The second disadvantage of the method is that although in theory the statistics should be quite independent of both K and M (the number of Voronoi centers and the number of samples of the input space X), there are in fact practical

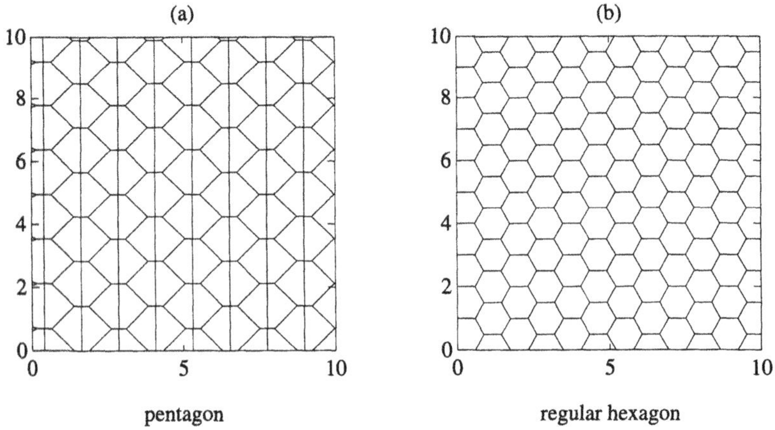

Figure 9 Voronoi partitioning of $\mathbb{R}^2$ into pentagons and hexagons. Reprinted with permission from Y.-C. Chu, Master's Thesis, The Chinese University of Hong Kong, 1992.

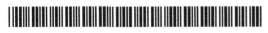

Table II

K	100	200	300	400	500	600	700	800	900	1000
$\overline{\text{card}(\tilde{N}_I)}$	6.0600	6.3700	6.3800	6.3900	6.3560	6.3767	6.3514	6.3675	6.3244	6.2640

problems. To illustrate this point, the dimension n is now fixed to 2. K is varied first from 100 to 1000 while M is still fixed to 50,000. The results are shown in Table II. Next M is varied from 5000 to 50,000 while K is fixed to the original value 1000. The results are shown in Table III.

We see that the statistics are basically unchanged when K varies until it becomes very small, $K = 100$. This is again due to the boundary effect. The Voronoi regions near the boundary of the input space have fewer neighbors. When the total number of Voronoi regions K is small, the boundary effect becomes more significant, but overall, the effect is only moderate because the change in the statistics is not large unless K is really small. On the other hand, decreasing M has a much more obvious impact on the statistics. We also plot the histograms of the cardinality of the 1-neighborhood for the cases $M = 5000$, 10,000, 25,000, and 50,000 in Fig. 10, where we see that the whole histogram shifts left as M decreases. The reason is related to how the approximate Delaunay diagram $(Q, \tilde{N}_I)$ is generated practically. The links in the graph are induced by the samples, and as shown in Fig. 3, defects of the Delaunay diagram may occur for regions of the input space where samples are insufficient. To support this claim the generated Delaunay diagram for $M = 5000$ is plotted in Fig. 11 together with samples of the input space X as small dots. Note that a link is missing wherever there are insufficient dots. Clearly the amount of such defects increases as the total number of samples M decreases. The missing links lead the Voronoi region to recognize fewer neighbors than it actually has, and as a result the average number of neighbors reported by the generated Delaunay diagram drops as M decreases. Moreover M need not be very small for the effect to become significant. Of course one may argue that the method of counting neighbors is not to be blamed here; rather it is the method used to generate the Delaunay diagram that should be blamed. However,

Table III

M	5000	10,000	15,000	20,000	25,000	30,000	35,000	40,000	45,000	50,000
$\overline{\text{card}(\tilde{N}_I)}$	4.3260	5.2060	5.5640	5.8140	5.9420	6.0440	6.1200	6.2240	6.2560	6.2640

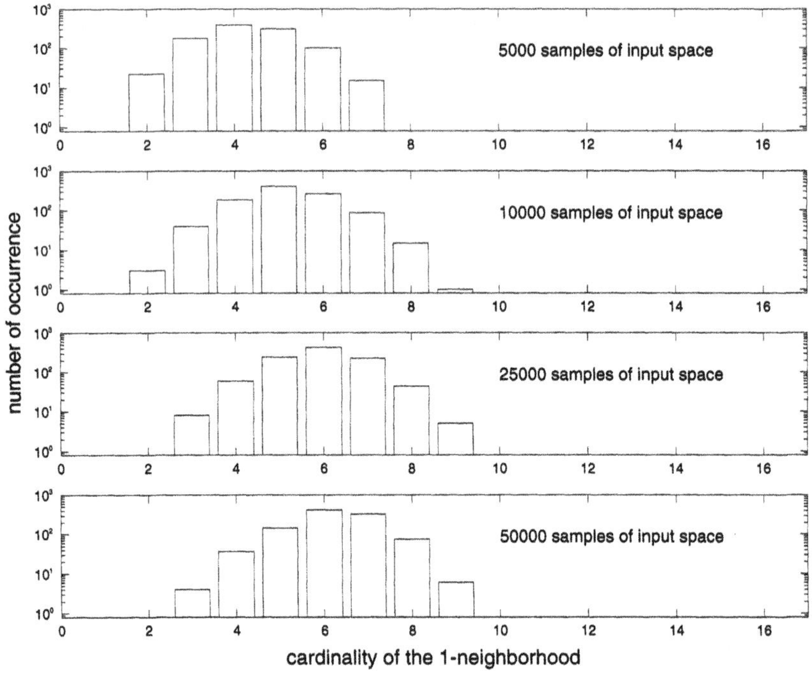

Figure 10 The frequency plots of the cardinality of the 1-neighborhood for $M = 5000, 10{,}000, 25{,}000$, and $50{,}000$ ($n = 2$).

we are going to propose a method for estimation of the dimension which is much less sensitive to such defects of the Delaunay diagram. This method, moreover, is meant to be more independent of w, that is, independent of how the Voronoi centers are distributed, and independent of whether the case is degenerate or not.

Remark 3. $K = 1000$ and $M = 50{,}000$ are in fact very insufficient for high dimensions such as $n = 6, 7, 8$. In view of the effects of K and M on $\overline{\text{card}(\tilde{N}_I)}$, it is reasonable to believe that the data given in Table I for $n = 6, 7, 8$ seriously underestimate the real values, and consequently Fig. 5 should not have shown a straight line. This explains why the curve in Fig. 5 looks more convex for small n, but more concave for large n.

In summary, counting the average number of neighbors of a Voronoi region to estimate the dimension of the input space X requires a lot of factors to be fixed such as the number of samples drawn from the input space and how to distribute the Voronoi centers over X. As a natural step toward a method which is more independent of the spatial distribution of the Voronoi centers, the growth

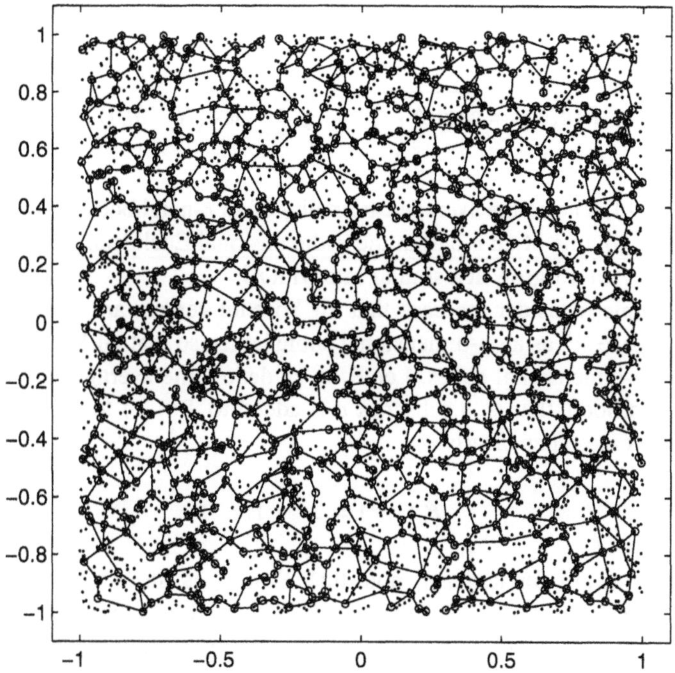

Figure 11 The Delaunay diagram $(Q, \widetilde{N}_I)$ for $X = [-1, 1]^2$ when $M = 5000$, with the samples of X shown as dots.

rate of the number of neighbors instead of the number of neighbors itself may be counted. This statement may be explained as follows. Recall that the volume of an n-dimensional ball in the Euclidean space $\mathbb{R}^n$ grows as r^n as the radius r increases. In a graph we may define an object analogous to a ball.

DEFINITION 1. Given a graph (Q, N). The r-neighborhood, where r is a nonnegative integer, of a neuron $q_i \in Q$ is a subset of Q which is defined recursively by

[Nr1] 0-neighborhood of $q_i := \{q_i\}$,
[Nr2] r-neighborhood of $q_i :=$ the union of all $N(q_j)$ such that $q_j \in (r-1)$-neighborhood of q_i.

The r-neighborhood of q_i will be denoted by $N^{(r)}(q_i)$ and r is called the radius of the neighborhood.

Note that this definition is consistent with calling $N(q_i)$ the 1-neighborhood of q_i. Our interest is not in a general graph, but in the Delaunay diagram (Q, N_I).

Given a Voronoi partition of $\mathbb{R}^n$, let

$$P(n,r) := \overline{\mathrm{card}(N_I^{(r)})} := \frac{1}{K}\sum_{i=1}^{K}\mathrm{card}\big(N_I^{(r)}(q_i)\big), \tag{7}$$

that is, $P(n,r)$ denotes the average cardinality of an r-neighborhood in (Q, N_I). Whereas the volume of an r-ball in the n-dimensional Euclidean space grows as r^n, then will $P(n,r)$ grow at a similar rate with r?

For example, consider the case that all Voronoi centers are placed into the Euclidean space $\mathbb{R}^n$ as an n-dimensional cubic lattice so that all Voronoi regions are simply n-dimensional cubes. Let $P_c(n,r)$ denote the average cardinality of an r-neighborhood, that is, a subscript c is added to $P(n,r)$ to distinguish this cubic-lattice case. Then clearly

$$P_c(1,r) = 2r + 1.$$

To deduce $P_c(n,r)$ for larger n, note that $P_c(n,r)$ is, in fact, the number of integral n-tuples $(\xi_1, \xi_2, \ldots, \xi_n)$ that satisfy $\sum_{l=1}^{n}|\xi_l| \leqslant r$, which can be broken down into the number of integral $(n-1)$-tuples $(\xi_1, \xi_2, \ldots, \xi_{n-1})$ satisfying $\sum_{l=1}^{n-1}|\xi_l| \leqslant m$ times the number of integral 1-tuples (ξ_n) satisfying $|\xi_n| = r - m$ and then summing over $m = 0, 1, \ldots, r$. The first term is simply $P_c(n-1, m)$ and the second term is 2 when $m < r$ or 1 when $m = r$. Hence the following proposition is obtained.

PROPOSITION 1. *$P_c(n,r)$ is given by the recursive formula*

$$P_c(n,r) = 2\sum_{m=0}^{r-1} P_c(n-1,m) + P_c(n-1,r) \tag{8}$$

with the initial condition $P_c(1,r) = 2r + 1$.

Alternatively the initial condition may be set to $P_c(0,r) = 1$. Applying Proposition 1 we get

$$\begin{aligned}
P_c(1,r) &= 2r + 1,\\
P_c(2,r) &= 2r^2 + 2r + 1,\\
P_c(3,r) &= \tfrac{4}{3}r^3 + 2r^2 + \tfrac{8}{3}r + 1,\\
P_c(4,r) &= \tfrac{2}{3}r^4 + \tfrac{4}{3}r^3 + \tfrac{10}{3}r^2 + \tfrac{8}{3}r + 1,
\end{aligned}$$

$$
\begin{aligned}
P_c(5,r) &= \tfrac{4}{15}r^5 + \tfrac{2}{3}r^4 + \tfrac{8}{3}r^3 + \tfrac{10}{3}r^2 + \tfrac{46}{15}r + 1, \\
P_c(6,r) &= \tfrac{4}{45}r^6 + \tfrac{4}{15}r^5 + \tfrac{14}{9}r^4 + \tfrac{8}{3}r^3 + \tfrac{196}{45}r^2 + \tfrac{46}{14}r + 1, \\
&\ \ \vdots\ .
\end{aligned} \tag{9}
$$

Hence we see that $P_c(n, r)$, the average size of an r-neighborhood when the Delaunay diagram is an n-dimensional cubic lattice, does not grow as r^n, but instead as a polynomial in r of degree n. Certainly it roughly grows as r^n when r is very large, but r indeed needs to be very large. Note that the coefficient of the r^n term in the polynomial decreases rapidly as the dimension n increases. The ratio of the coefficient of the r^n term to the coefficient of the r^{n-1} term is $2/n$ and therefore r must be at least much larger than $n/2$ if the r^n term is to dominate the other terms. When the value of r is moderate, all terms in the polynomial have nonnegligible contributions.

If the Voronoi centers are not distributed over $\mathbb{R}^n$ as an n-dimensional cubic lattice, the average cardinality of an r-neighborhood changes accordingly. We conjecture that this number $P(n, r)$ still can be described by a polynomial in r of degree n, but it is not known how the coefficients of the polynomial change with the distribution of the Voronoi centers except that the constant term must be 1. This is bad because having n unknown coefficients in the polynomial implies that $n + 1$ data $P(n, 1), P(n, 2), \ldots, P(n, n + 1)$ are needed to determine the dimension n. More precisely, if the dimension of the Euclidean space is unknown but the Delaunay diagram is given, then one may measure

$$
\overline{\mathrm{card}(N_I^{(1)})}, \overline{\mathrm{card}(N_I^{(2)})}, \overline{\mathrm{card}(N_I^{(3)})}, \ldots,
$$

and if any $n + 1$ data fit into a polynomial of degree n only, then it is known that the dimension of the Euclidean space is n. However this method is impractical because identifying the r-neighbors of a Voronoi region is computationally expensive when r is large. Also the larger the neighborhood, the greater the probability that it will suffer from the boundary effect. In addition, because we are going to apply the method to determine the dimension of the input space X which is only locally Euclidean, it is recommended that the Voronoi regions not require remote information. We aim at a method which requires local information only, so that it is computationally inexpensive, less sensitive to the boundary effect, and applicable to general manifolds which are only locally Euclidean.

Let us view the problem from another angle. A polynomial of degree n with the constant term fixed to 1 has n undetermined coefficients, so it can be identified with a point in an n-dimensional parameter space Θ^n. Hence every Voronoi partition of $\mathbb{R}^n$ such that $P(n, r)$ can be described by such a polynomial can be represented by a point in Θ^n. It has been conjectured that almost all Voronoi partitions of $\mathbb{R}^n$ can be represented by such a point, but do all these points occupy the whole Θ^n? Is it possible that all these points only occupy a subset of Θ^n which may even have a lower dimension than n? Recall that $n+1$ data $P(n,1), P(n,2), \ldots, P(n,n+1)$ are needed to determine the dimension of the Euclidean space because Θ^n is n-dimensional. If a lower-dimensional parameter subspace (not necessarily linear) can be found, then fewer data will be needed to determine the dimension of the Euclidean space. In particular if a one-dimensional parameter subspace can be found, only $P(n,1)$, $P(n,2)$ will be needed to determine the dimension of the Euclidean space, which satisfies our hope that only local information will be used. For this reason, even if those parameter points are not exactly distributed in a one-dimensional subspace, we still look for a characteristic one-dimensional subspace which can represent sufficiently many different Voronoi partitions of $\mathbb{R}^n$ of interest. So the problem becomes a one-dimensional approximation to the n-dimensional parameter space Θ^n. It may sound strange at first that a good one-dimensional approximation to an n-dimensional space is possible, but we are indeed going to propose such an approximation, which turns out to be excellent in estimating the dimension of the Euclidean space.

Of course such an approximation can hardly be obtained by pure guess. For example, we only know that $P(n,r)$ is a polynomial in r of degree n with the constant term equal to 1. So a blind guess may be $(\kappa r+1)^n$ for some parameter κ, but it can be checked easily that even $P_c(n,r)$ does not fit into this form.

Thus we proceed as follows. At first $P(n,r)$ is not expressed as a polynomial but as a linear combination of $P_c(n,r), P_c(n-1,r), \ldots, P_c(0,r)$, that is, the basis is changed. It will soon be seen that in the new coordinates an approximation can be found more easily. Let $\theta_0, \theta_1, \ldots, \theta_n$ be the coefficients of the linear combination

$$P(n,r)=\sum_{l=0}^{n}\theta_l P_c(n-l,r).$$

Whereas $P(n,0)=1$, $\theta_0=1-\sum_{l=1}^{n}\theta_l$. Hence $P(n,r)$ may be identified with a point $(\theta_1,\theta_2,\ldots,\theta_n)$ in the n-dimensional parameter space Θ_n. Suppose that $(\theta_1,\theta_2,\ldots,\theta_n)$ is restricted to a certain subspace Y of Θ^n. Then $(\theta_1,\theta_2,\ldots,\theta_n,0)$ falls in the subspace $Y\times\{0\}$ of Θ^{n+1}. Clearly both Y and $Y\times\{0\}$ have the same dimension, so this is actually a way, and in fact quite a trivial way, to pass a fixed-dimensional subspace from a lower-dimensional parameter space to a higher-dimensional parameter space. Nothing is special up to this point, but we are going to show that if Y is representative in Θ^n, then $Y\times\{0\}$ is also representative in Θ^{n+1} to a certain extent, and hence try to justify such a way of passing the subspace from Θ^n to Θ^{n+1}.

Suppose that for some Voronoi partition of $\mathbb{R}^n$, $P(n, r)$ can be expressed as a linear combination of $P_c(n, r)$, $P_c(n-1, r), \ldots, P_c(0, r)$:

$$P(n, r) = \sum_{l=0}^{n} \theta_l P_c(n-l, r). \tag{10}$$

Let B_i, $i = 1, 2, \ldots, K$, denote the Voronoi regions. Let

$$\{C_j \,|\, j = 1, 2, \ldots, L\}$$

be any partition of the real line $\mathbb{R}$. Then clearly

$$\{B_i \times C_j \,|\, i = 1, 2, \ldots, K;\ j = 1, 2, \ldots, L\}$$

is a Voronoi partition of $\mathbb{R}^{n+1}$. The corresponding $P(n+1, r)$ easily can be shown to satisfy

$$P(n+1, r) = 2\sum_{m=0}^{r-1} P(n, m) + P(n, r) \tag{11}$$

using an argument similar to the one used to obtain Eq. (8). Now substituting Eq. (10) into Eq. (11) we get

$$P(n+1, r) = \sum_{l=0}^{n} \theta_l P_c(n+1-l, r),$$

that is, $P(n+1, r)$ can be expressed as the same linear combination of $P_c(n+1, r)$, $P_c(n, r), \ldots, P_c(1, r)$. Note that there is no $P_c(0, r)$ term.

So for any Voronoi partition of $\mathbb{R}^n$ that falls in $Y \subset \Theta^n$, there exists at least one Voronoi partition of $\mathbb{R}^{n+1}$ that falls in $Y \times \{0\} \subset \Theta^{n+1}$. We are going to start with a good approximation to Θ^2 and then propagate it up to Θ^n, and the preceding result justifies a means of propagation which also preserves the dimension of the approximant. However, the statement is in fact rather weak. It does not imply that $Y \times \{0\}$ has to be one of the best approximations to Θ^{n+1} even if Y is exactly Θ^n.

The one-dimensional approximation to Θ^2 we propose is motivated by the following observations. Recall the Voronoi partitions of $\mathbb{R}^2$ shown in Figs. 7–9. For them, it is observed that

$$P(2, r) = \frac{\kappa_2}{4}[2r^2 + 2r] + 1, \tag{12}$$

where κ_2 is the number of sides of each Voronoi region. Now the following question is asked: Given any Voronoi partition of $\mathbb{R}^2$, can a real number κ always be found such that the approximation

$$P(2, r) \approx \kappa[2r^2 + 2r] + 1 \tag{13}$$

holds? This is certainly not true for all Voronoi partitions of $\mathbb{R}^2$. A trivial counterexample is that all Voronoi centers just line up into a straight line in $\mathbb{R}^2$, but many people would agree that this is not a "reasonable" way to distribute the Voronoi centers over a two-dimensional space. So it is still possibly true that such a κ can be found for all "reasonable" Voronoi partitions of $\mathbb{R}^2$.

Rewrite Eq. (13) as

$$P(2,r) \approx \kappa P_c(2,r) + [1-\kappa] P_c(0,r). \tag{14}$$

This is obviously a one-dimensional subspace of Θ^2 because it depends only on a single parameter κ. From the foregoing observations we are convinced that it is a good one-dimensional approximation to Θ^2, in the sense that most Voronoi partitions of $\mathbb{R}^2$ are represented by a parameter point in this one-dimensional subspace. By propagating this one-dimensional subspace up to Θ^n, the following approximation is obtained: For any $n \geqslant 2$ and any "reasonable" Voronoi partition of $\mathbb{R}^n$, there exists a real number κ such that

$$P(n,r) \approx \kappa\big[P_c(n,r) - P_c(n-2,r)\big] + P_c(n-2,r). \tag{15}$$

It is hard to check whether this is a good approximation to $P(n,r)$ in general, but as far as the estimation of the dimension of the Euclidean space is concerned, this approximation provides an excellent estimate of the dimension as will be shown in the simulation results later.

Remark 4. Equation (15) implies that if $P(n,r)$ is expressed as a linear combination of $P_c(n,r)$, $P_c(n-1,r)$, ..., $P_c(0,r)$, then the coefficient of $P_c(n-1,r)$ is 0. Whereas $P_c(n-2,r)$ is a polynomial of degree $n-2$ only, the coefficient of $P_c(n-1,r) = 0$ implies that $P(n,r)$ as a polynomial would have the coefficient of its r^n term always equal to $(2/n)$ times the coefficient of its r^{n-1} term for all "reasonable" Voronoi partitions of $\mathbb{R}^n$.

It was mentioned that if a one-dimensional approximation to Θ^n is found, measuring $P(n,1)$ and $P(n,2)$ from the Delaunay diagram is sufficient to estimate the dimension of the Euclidean space. It seems now that this can be done by putting $r=1$ and $r=2$ into Eq. (15) and then eliminating κ to solve for n. In doing so, however, $P_c(n,1)$, $P_c(n-2,1)$, $P_c(n,2)$, and $P_c(n-2,2)$ need to be known. It has been mentioned only that $P_c(n,r)$ can be computed by the recursive formula Eq. (8). This is not directly applicable. Now, substitute r by $r-1$ into Eq. (8) to get

$$P_c(n,r-1) = 2\sum_{m=0}^{r-2} P_c(n-1,m) + P_c(n-1,r-1) \tag{16}$$

and then subtract Eq. (16) from Eq. (8) to get

$$P_c(n,r) - P_c(n,r-1) = 2P_c(n-1,r-1) + P_c(n-1,r) - P_c(n-1,r-1)$$

or equivalently

$$P_c(n,r) = P_c(n-1,r) + P_c(n,r-1) + P_c(n-1,r-1). \tag{17}$$

Equation (17) can be used to prove the following proposition.

PROPOSITION 2. $P_c(n,r) = P_c(r,n)$.

Proof. We prove the proposition by induction. Suppose that the following three equalities are true:

$$\begin{aligned} P_c(n-1,r) &= P_c(r,n-1), \\ P_c(n,r-1) &= P_c(r-1,n), \\ P_c(n-1,r-1) &= P_c(r-1,n-1). \end{aligned}$$

Then

$$\begin{aligned} P_c(n,r) &= P_c(n-1,r) + P_c(n,r-1) + P_c(n-1,r-1) \\ &= P_c(r,n-1) + P_c(r-1,n) + P_c(r-1,n-1) \\ &= P_c(r,n). \end{aligned}$$

The initial condition $P_c(1,r) = 2r+1 = P_c(r,1)$ is trivial. ■

Proposition 2 is an indispensable tool in studying the local behavior of $P_c(n,r)$. To know $P_c(n,r)$ for small r, it suffices to know $P_c(n,r)$ for small n. In other words, if how the r-neighborhoods grow in low dimensions is known, how the r-neighborhoods locally grow in all dimensions is also known. So to compute $P_c(n,1)$, $P_c(n-2,1)$, $P_c(n,2)$, and $P_c(n-2,2)$, we need not use the recursive formula Eq. (8) which is inconvenient when n is large, but only compute $P_c(1,r)$, $P_c(1,r-2)$, $P_c(2,r)$, and $P_c(2,r-2)$ and then apply Proposition 2. Indeed we already know from Eq. (9) that

$$\begin{aligned} P_c(1,r) &= 2r+1, \\ P_c(2,r) &= 2r^2+2r+1. \end{aligned}$$

Hence

$$\begin{aligned} P(n,1) &= 2n+1, \\ P(n-2,1) &= 2n-3, \\ P(n,2) &= 2n^2+2n+1, \\ P(n-2,2) &= 2n^2-6n+5. \end{aligned}$$

Substituting all these and $r = 1, 2$ into Eq. (15) and eliminating κ we get a simple quadratic equation in n:

$$2n^2 + [-2P(n, 1) - 2]n + [P(n, 1) + P(n, 2) - 2] \approx 0. \tag{18}$$

This quadratic equation can be solved easily. It seems from the simulation results that the smaller root of this quadratic equation should be chosen as the estimate of the dimension n.

In summary, if a Euclidean space of an unknown dimension is given, first the Delaunay diagram $(Q, \widetilde{N}_I)$ is obtained, next $\overline{\mathrm{card}(\widetilde{N}_I^{(1)})}$ and $\overline{\mathrm{card}(\widetilde{N}_I^{(2)})}$ are measured, and at last

$$n \approx \frac{1 + \overline{\mathrm{card}(\widetilde{N}_I^{(1)})} - \sqrt{5 + \overline{\mathrm{card}(\widetilde{N}_I^{(1)})}^{2} - 2\overline{\mathrm{card}(\widetilde{N}_I^{(2)})}}}{2}. \tag{19}$$

Whereas only local information ($r \leqslant 2$) has been used, this method also applies to an input space which is only locally Euclidean but has a consistent dimension throughout. If X consists of regions of different dimensions, an average estimate of the dimensions should be expected because $\overline{\mathrm{card}(\widetilde{N}_I^{(1)})}$ and $\overline{\mathrm{card}(\widetilde{N}_I^{(2)})}$ are average values.

Now recall the experiment where 1000 neurons were placed into the input space $X = [-1, 1]^n$, $n = 1, 2, \ldots, 8$, using competitive learning and 50,000 samples of the input space. The Delaunay diagram was computed and $\overline{\mathrm{card}(\widetilde{N}_I^{(1)})}$ was measured in each case and the data were recorded in Table I. Now $\overline{\mathrm{card}(\widetilde{N}_I^{(2)})}$ is measured as well and the dimension is estimated by the new method. The results are recorded in Table IV, where $\tilde{n}$ denotes the estimate given by Eq. (19). The data are also plotted in Fig. 12. Again $\tilde{n} = 0.9990$ instead of 1 for $n = 1$ because of the boundary effect. Although the number of neurons K and the number of samples M are very insufficient for high dimensions $n = 6, 7, 8$, the estimate $\tilde{n}$ is still rather close to the real value.

When K varies as in Table II, the new method performs as shown in Table V. The trend is not much different from Table II, but the new method shows the superiority when M varies, as shown in Table VI.

Table IV

n	1	2	3	4	5	6	7	8
$\tilde{n}$	0.9990	2.0347	2.9874	3.9893	4.9537	5.7935	6.5909	7.2479

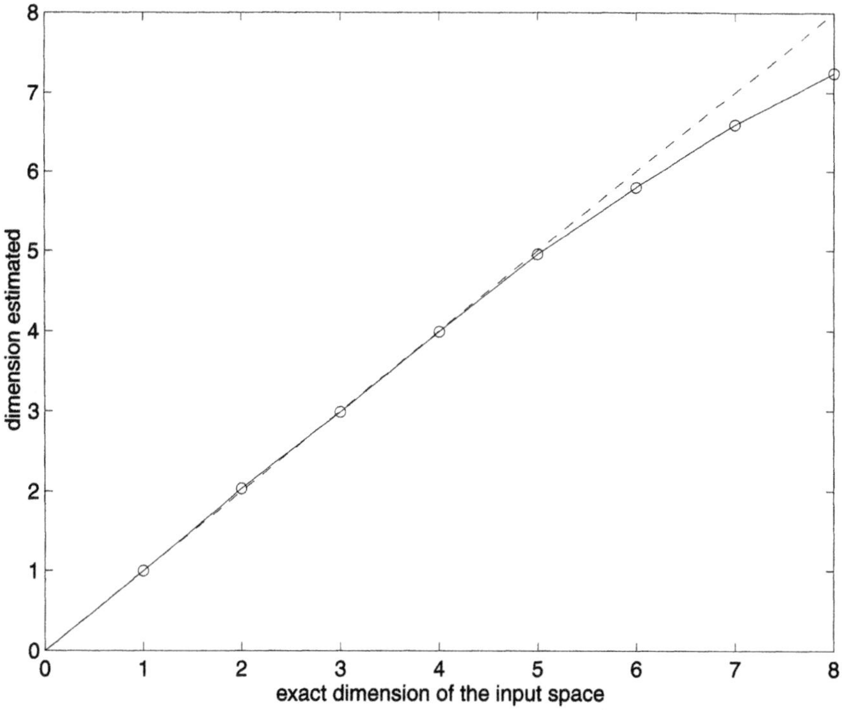

Figure 12 $(n, \tilde{n})$ plotted as small circles to see whether they fit into the straight line $\tilde{n} = n$.

Whereas Tables III and VI contain different types of data, to make a comparison both sets of data are normalized with respect to $M = 50{,}000$ and then plotted in Fig. 13. The solid line represents the data in Table VI and the dashed line represents the data in Table III. It is clear that $\tilde{n}$ is much less sensitive to M than $\overline{\text{card}(\widetilde{N}_I)}$. As mentioned before, when M decreases, there are more and more missing links in the Delaunay diagram $(Q, \widetilde{N}_I)$ and the estimate $\tilde{n}$ seems to be very robust to such defects of the Delaunay diagram.

Table V

K	100	200	300	400	500	600	700	800	900	1000
$\tilde{n}$	1.8504	1.9118	1.9533	1.9686	1.9905	1.9956	2.0107	2.0115	2.0229	2.0347

Table VI

M	5000	10,000	15,000	20,000	25,000	30,000	35,000	40,000	45,000	50,000
$\tilde{n}$	1.8350	2.0683	2.0818	2.0756	2.0586	2.0477	2.0515	2.0399	2.0426	2.0347

We give several more examples, some of which appeared in [2, Chap. 6] using a different set of random samples of the input space.

EXAMPLE 1. In the foregoing simulations, the samples of the input space were drawn under the uniform distribution. Intuitively, if they are not distributed over X uniformly, it does not matter much, because competitive learning will try to maintain the same number of samples per Voronoi region, and hence the basic graph structure of the Delaunay diagram remains unchanged. This example

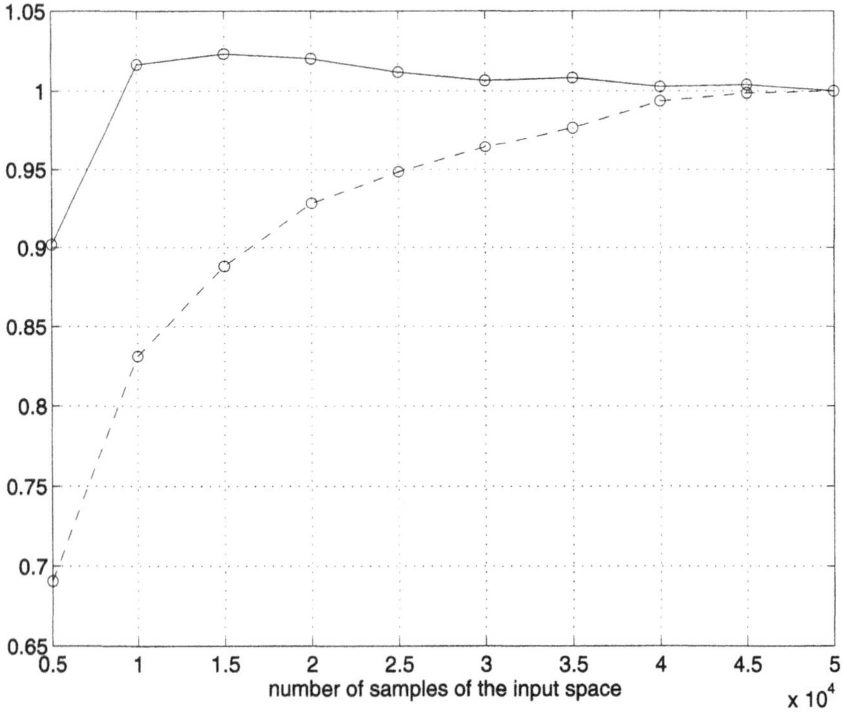

Figure 13 Normalized $\tilde{n}$ (solid line) and normalized $\mathrm{card}(\overline{\tilde{N}_I})$ (dashed line) when M varies.

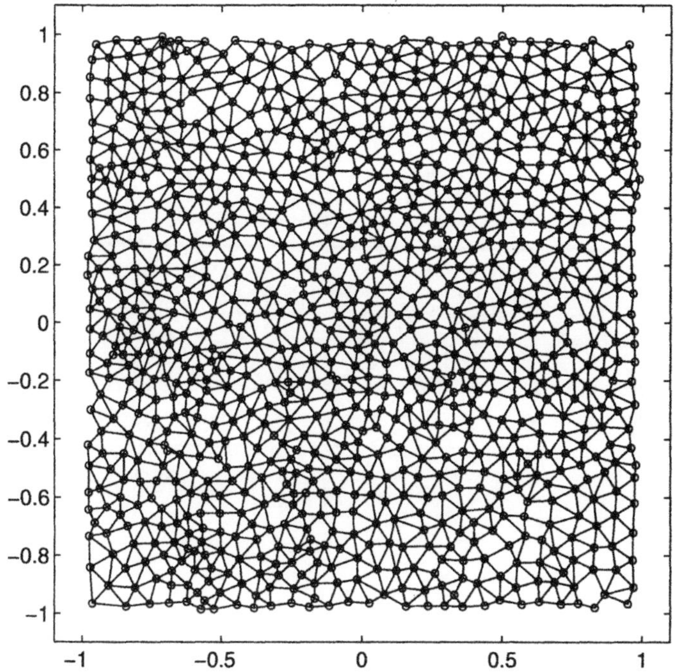

Figure 14 The Delaunay diagram $(Q, \widetilde{N}_I)$ for $X = [-1, 1]^2$ when the samples of X are uniformly distributed.

attempts to verify this intuition. Let $X = [-1, 1]^2$. The Delaunay diagram corresponding to $n = 2$ in Table I or IV is shown in Fig. 14. Now suppose that each sample $\tilde{x}_l$ of the input space is transformed componentwise into a new sample $\tilde{x}_l^+$ by $\tilde{x}_l^+ = \tilde{x}_l^3$. Then the new samples of X will greatly concentrate near the coordinate axes. If the competitive learning is based on this new set of samples, the Delaunay diagram will look like in Fig. 15. The estimate of the dimension $\tilde{n}$ will become 2.1062, which is not much different.

EXAMPLE 2. This example attempts to point out that the boundary effect is not necessarily undesirable, because the boundary may be regarded as part of the structure of the input space. For example, consider a rectangle in $\mathbb{R}^2$. If one pair of edges become longer and longer and the other pair of edges become shorter and shorter, it is then arguable whether the rectangle is being deformed from a two-dimensional object to an one-dimensional object. Anyway the fact is that more and more Voronoi regions suffer from the boundary effect, that is, have fewer neighbors than a normal two-dimensional Voronoi region should have, which may then be interpreted as "experiencing" a dimension lower than 2. For another ex-

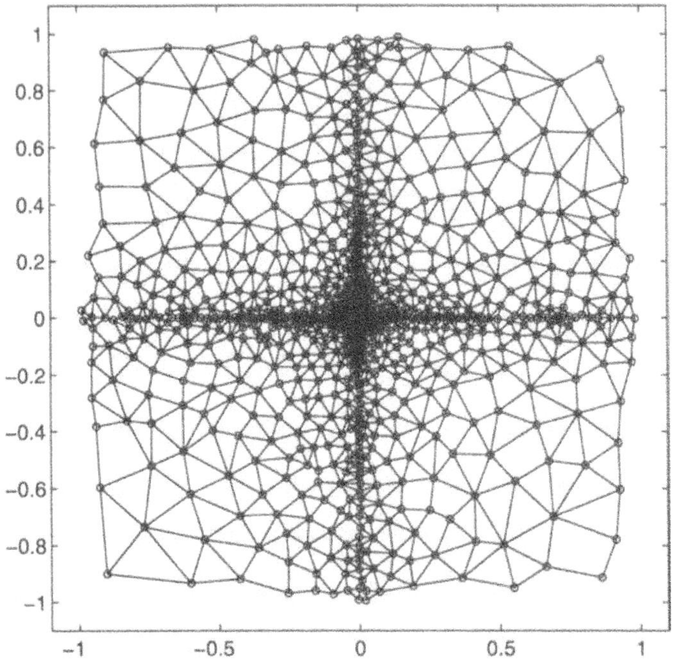

Figure 15 The Delaunay diagram $(Q, \widetilde{N}_I)$ for $X = [-1, 1]^2$ when the samples of X are not uniformly distributed.

ample, consider a ring in $\mathbb{R}^2$:

$$X = \{x \in \mathbb{R}^2 | 0.5 \leqslant \|x\| \leqslant 1\}$$
$$= \{(\rho \cos\phi, \rho \sin\phi) | \rho \in [0.5, 1]; \phi \in [-\pi, \pi)\}.$$

Ten thousand samples of X are drawn with ρ uniformly distributed on [0.5, 1) and ϕ uniformly distributed on $[-\pi, \pi)$, and therefore the samples are not uniformly distributed on the ring. The competitive learning is used to place 81 neurons into X. Figure 16 shows the Delaunay diagram. Some people might say that X is closer to a two-dimensional object whereas others might say that it is closer to a one-dimensional object. The estimate of the dimension $\tilde{n}$ turns out to be 1.6693.

EXAMPLE 3. In this example two nonlinear input spaces are considered. One is

$$X = \mathbf{S}^1 = \{(\cos\phi, \sin\phi) | \phi \in [-\pi, \pi)\},$$

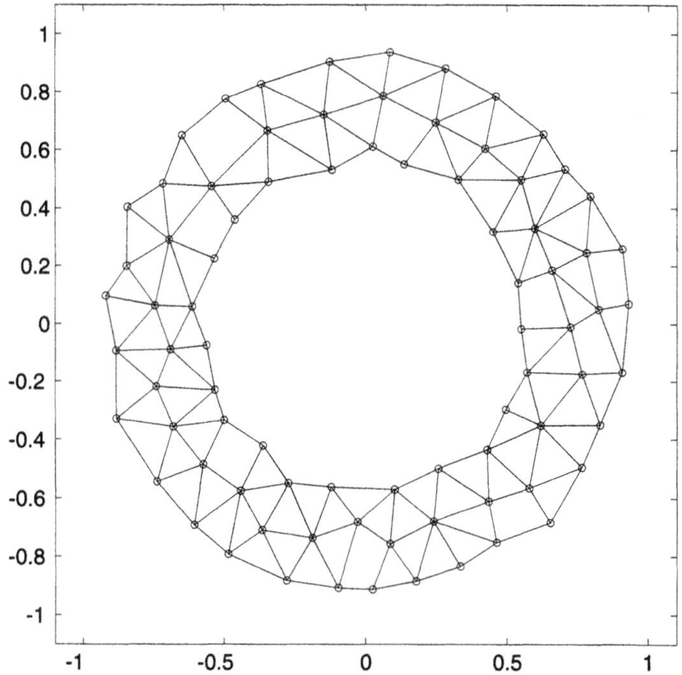

Figure 16 The Delaunay diagram $(Q, \widetilde{N}_I)$ for the ring in Example 2.

that is, a circle in $\mathbb{R}^2$, which is basically one-dimensional with no boundary, and the other is

$$\begin{aligned} X &= \mathbf{S}^1 \times \mathbf{S}^1 \\ &= \left\{([3 + 2\cos\phi_1]\cos\phi_2, [3 + 2\cos\phi_1]\sin\phi_2, 2\sin\phi_1) \middle| \phi_1, \phi_2 \in [-\pi, \pi)\right\}, \end{aligned}$$

that is, a torus in $\mathbb{R}^3$, which is basically two-dimensional with no boundary. The samples of the circle are drawn with ϕ uniformly distributed on $[-\pi, \pi)$ and therefore uniformly distributed on the circle. The samples of the torus are drawn with (ϕ_1, ϕ_2) uniformly distributed on $[-\pi, \pi) \times [-\pi, \pi)$ and therefore not uniformly distributed on the torus. Fifty thousand samples are drawn in each case and competitive learning is used to place 1000 neurons into the input space. The obtained results are shown in Table VII. Whereas $\mathbf{S}^1$ and $\mathbf{S}^1 \times \mathbf{S}^1$ are, respectively, a one-dimensional and a two-dimensional objects with no boundary, it may be interesting to compare the frequency plots of the cardinality of their 1-neighborhoods with the cases $X = [-1, 1]$ and $X = [-1, 1]^2$ which are, respectively, a one- and a two-dimensional objects with a boundary. The histograms are shown in Fig. 17.

Table VII

X	$\overline{\text{card}(\tilde{N}_I)}$	$\tilde{n}$
$\mathbf{S}^1$	3.0000	1.0000
$\mathbf{S}^1 \times \mathbf{S}^1$	6.4640	2.0983

The boundary effect can be observed easily: When the input space has a boundary, the histogram extends more into the low-end region.

EXAMPLE 4. In this last example, a nonlinear input space of higher dimension is considered. Let

$$X = \{([t_3^2 + t_4^2 + 1]\cos t_1, [t_3^2 + t_4^2 + 1]\sin t_1, [t_3^2 + t_4^2 + 1]\cos t_2, \\ [t_3^2 + t_4^2 + 1]\sin t_2, t_3, t_4) | t_1, t_2 \in [-\pi, \pi); t_3, t_4 \in [-1, 1]\}.$$

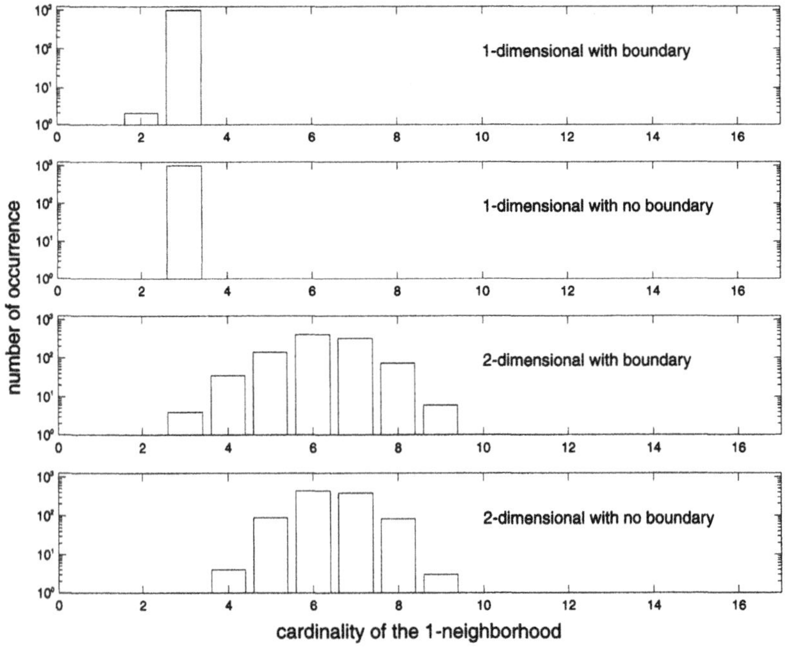

Figure 17 The frequency plots of the cardinality of the 1-neighborhood for $X = [-1, 1]$, $\mathbf{S}^1$, $[-1, 1]^2$, and $\mathbf{S}^1 \times \mathbf{S}^1$.

Then $X \subset \mathbb{R}^6$, but is in fact a four-dimensional object. The samples of X are drawn with (t_1, t_2) uniformly distributed on $[-\pi, \pi) \times [-\pi, \pi)$ and (t_3, t_4) uniformly distributed on $[-1, 1) \times [-1, 1)$. Again 50,000 samples are drawn and competitive learning is used to place 1000 neurons into X. At last $\overline{\text{card}(\tilde{N}_I)}$ and $\tilde{n}$ are found to be 15.2460 and 4.2057, respectively.

The preceding examples are all artificial. For a more practical use of this new method to estimate dimension, two applications were presented in [2, Chap. 6]. One estimated the dimension of the attractor of a chaotic time series and the other estimated the dimension of speech space. Whereas the data used at that time now may be obsolete, these two applications are not included here.

III. CONCLUSIONS

In this last section the content of this chapter is summarized.

Suppose that a closed subset X of $\mathbb{R}^n$, called here the input space, is the object of study. It is described by a large set of samples which are well distributed over the whole X. This description, however, is not suitable for revealing the structure of the input space X. Therefore another description of X is sought. This chapter suggested a new description which is based on the Voronoi regions and Delaunay diagram, and also gave a method to obtain this new description.

First, K points called Voronoi centers are chosen from X. For the new description to be useful, K must be sufficiently large and these K Voronoi centers must be distributed over X adequately. Then the whole X is cut into K small pieces, called Voronoi regions, according to Eq. (2). This partitioning may be regarded as a vector quantization of X and therefore the requirements that K be large and the K Voronoi centers be well distributed over X are in fact to guarantee that the "quantization error" is small. Certainly it is not sufficient just to quantize the input space X or just to cut X into small pieces. How these small pieces should be pasted together to get back the original X must be known, and this is told by the Delaunay diagram.

In general, it is difficult to compute the Voronoi regions and the Delaunay diagram for an arbitrary subset X of $\mathbb{R}^n$. However if a representative set of samples of X already exists, the Delaunay diagram, or strictly speaking a close approximation to the Delaunay diagram, can be computed easily. This "if" part is usually assumed to hold in the context of artificial neural networks. Note that if this set of samples of X does not already exist, obtaining it is generally a difficult problem, and therefore the claim that "in general, it is difficult to compute the Delaunay diagram for an arbitrary subset X of $\mathbb{R}^n$" is not contradicted. In particular the number of samples of X and the number of Voronoi centers both may need to grow exponentially with the dimension of X to obtain an representative Delaunay diagram.

With the new description of the input space X based on the Voronoi centers and the Delaunay diagram, more information about the structure of X becomes extractable. One example is the dimension of X. Suppose that an arbitrary closed subset X of $\mathbb{R}^n$ is the object of study. Its dimension is unknown, but it is known to be locally Euclidean. Assume that a representative set of samples of X is given. A Voronoi partition and the corresponding Delaunay diagram for X first are obtained. The method proposed in this chapter can then estimate the dimension of X based on the Delaunay diagram. This method requires that each Voronoi region count the number of its neighbors and the number of its neighbors' neighbors. Only local information is used because each Voronoi region need not know what is happening far away. Hence the method is computationally cheap.

In this chapter another more primitive method of estimating the dimension also has been described. It requires that each Voronoi region count the number of its direct neighbors only. It is basically a method of comparing statistics. Although the information it requires is even more local, and hence computationally is even cheaper, we have shown that the estimate based on it is more sensitive to the conditions under which the statistics are obtained such as the distribution of the Voronoi centers and the number of samples of the input space. Although the proposed new method requires a little bit more information, it turns out to be more reliable and therefore is recommended.

REFERENCES

[1] A. Okabe, B. Boots, and K. Sugihara. *Spatial Tessellations: Concepts and Applications of Voronoi Diagrams. Wiley Series in Probability and Mathematical Statistics.* Wiley, Chichester, 1992.

[2] Y. C. Chu. The induced topology of local minima with applications to artificial neural networks. Master's Thesis, The Chinese University of Hong Kong, 1992.

[3] T. Martinetz and K. Schulten. Topology representing networks. *Neural Networks* 7:507–522, 1994.

[4] T. Martinetz and K. Schulten. A "neural-gas" network learns topologies. In *Proceedings of International Conference on Artificial Neural Networks,* 1991, pp. 397–402.

[5] T. Villmann, R. Der, and T. Martinetz. A novel approach to measure the topology preservation of feature maps. In *Proceedings of International Conference on Artificial Neural Networks*, Sorrento, 1994, pp. 298–301.

[6] T. Villmann, R. Der, and T. Martinetz. A new quantitative measure of topology preservation in Kohonen's feature maps. In *Proceedings of IEEE International Conference on Neural Networks*, 1994, pp. 645–648.

[7] P. Morasso and V. Sanguineti. How the brain can discover the existence of external egocentric space. *Neurocomputing* 12:289–310, 1996.

[8] J. Møller. *Lectures on Random Voronoi Tessellations. Lecture Notes in Statistics*, Vol. 87. Springer-Verlag, New York, 1994.

Index

F

G

H

I

K

L

M

N